AMERICAN WRITERS

Selected Authors

LEONARD UNGER
A. WALTON LITZ

EDITORS IN CHIEF

VOLUME 1

CHARLES SCRIBNER'S SONS
Macmillan Library Reference USA
New York

An Imprint of Simon & Schuster Macmillan
1633 Broadway
New York, NY 10019-6785

PRINTED IN THE UNITED STATES OF AMERICA

LIBRARY OF CONGRESS CATALOGING-IN-PUBLICATION DATA

American writers: selected authors / Leonard Unger, A. Walton Litz.
    p.   cm.
    Includes bibliographical references and indexes.
    ISBN 0-684-80604-5 (set: alk. paper). — ISBN 0-684-80603-7 (v.1
: alk. paper). — ISBN 0-684-80602-9 (v. 2 : alk paper). — ISBN
0-684-80601-0 (v. 3 : alk. paper)
    1. American literature—History and criticism. 2. American
literature—Bio-biography. 3. Authors, American—Biography.
I. Unger, Leonard. II. Litz, A. Walton.
PS129.A58   1998
810.9—dc21
    [B]   98-36810
                                                              CIP

Contents

VOLUME 3

Publisher's Note

American Writers: Selected Authors comprises sixty-four unabridged essays chosen by the publisher from Scribners' thirteen-volume *American Writers*. The articles drawn from the four base volumes were originally published in a pamphlet series by the University of Minnesota Press. The articles drawn from the four two-volume supplements and the single-volume retrospective supplement were specially commissioned by Scribners. Volumes 1-4 and Supplement I were edited by Leonard Unger; Supplements II-IV and Retrospective Supplement I were edited by A. Walton Litz.

The need to make an affordable set has limited the selections, but we hope that readers wishing to explore American literature more fully will seek out the 238 articles in the parent set. A complete listing of subjects in the parent set appears in Volume 3.

Edward Albee

1928-

Abandoned soon after his birth on March 12, 1928, Edward Albee was adopted when he was two weeks old. His foster parents, Reed and Frances Albee, were, respectively, the millionaire owner of a chain of theaters and a former mannequin who was twenty-three years younger than her husband. They brought Edward up in the lap of luxuries he appreciated only sparely. He was a problem child at various expensive boarding schools, where he early began to write fiction and poetry. Years of disaccord with his foster parents were truncated by his departure from home at the age of twenty. For almost a decade afterwards he led a hand-to-mouth existence in Greenwich Village, working fitfully as office boy, salesman, and Western Union messenger. Continuing to write, he sought the advice of two authors—W. H. Auden, who suggested that he turn to pornographic verse, and Thornton Wilder, who suggested that he turn to plays. Albee wrote his first play, *The Zoo Story,* "as a sort of thirtieth birthday present to myself." The play was rejected by American producers but was performed at the Schiller-Theater Werkstatt in West Berlin; Albee attended, though he understood no German. Five years later, *Who's Afraid of Virginia Woolf?* catapulted Albee from avant-garde attention to public notoriety.

When *The Zoo Story* was first produced in America in January 1960, it shared the stage of Greenwich Village's Provincetown Playhouse with *Krapp's Last Tape* by Samuel Beckett, and since that time Albee has been intermittently linked with European dramatists of the Absurd. He himself has admitted: "My exposure to Beckett and to late O'Neill was probably important right at the time I gave up poetry and the novel." In a widely reprinted essay, "Which Theatre Is the Absurd One?" (1962), Albee himself distinguishes between Realistic theater and that of the Absurd: "The Theatre of the Absurd . . . facing as it does man's condition as it is, is the Realistic theatre of our time; and . . . the supposed Realistic theatre . . . pander[ing] to the public need for self-congratulation and reassurance and present[ing] a false picture of ourselves to ourselves, is . . . really and truly The Theatre of the Absurd."

Like European Absurdists, Albee has tried to dramatize the reality of man's condition, but whereas Beckett, Genet, Ionesco, and Pinter present that reality in all its alogical absurdity, Albee has been preoccupied with illusions that screen man from reality. For the Europeans, absurdity or non-sense *is* metaphysical reality; for Albee, the world "makes no sense because the moral, religious, political

1

and social structures man has erected to 'illusion' himself have collapsed." In Albee's drama, however, illusion is still present, and the action often dramatizes the process of collapse, so that we, the audience, arrive at a recognition of the reality behind illusion. Often, death helps dispel illusion, and often, obliquity helps reveal reality.

The Zoo Story already announces the suggestive indirection of subsequent works. Significantly, the method of indirection is explained by an Outsider who has suffered at the hands of the Establishment. Early in *The Zoo Story,* Jerry, the near-tramp informs Peter, the conformist: "I took the subway down to the Village so I could walk all the way up Fifth Avenue to the zoo. It's one of those things a person has to do; sometimes a person has to go a very long distance out of his way to come back a short distance correctly." The only purpose of Jerry's long walk is to accommodate his methodology. Jerry could have gone to New York City's Central Park Zoo by the cross-town bus, but, deliberately indirect, he chose the circuitous route. On Fifth Avenue, a street of many sights, Jerry apparently noticed nothing, though he has remarkable powers of observation. That luxury-laden avenue is simply the "distance out of his way to come back a short distance correctly" to the zoo. Through Jerry's explanation, indirection and animality enter Albee's play. Jerry couples these two themes to introduce his dog story, the verbal climax of the play: "THE STORY OF JERRY AND THE DOG! . . . What I am going to tell you has something to do with how sometimes it's necessary to go a long distance out of the way in order to come back a short distance correctly." By the time we hear the dog story, we are familiar with Jerry's "out of the way" dialogue, and we should be ready to see in the dog story an analogue for the zoo story.

In *The Zoo Story* non-conformist confronts conformist on a park bench; in the dog story man confronts animal in a dark hallway. Peter replaces the dog, friend-enemy to Jerry. Jerry views Peter as he does the dog—with sadness and suspicion; Jerry forces Peter to defend his premises as the dog defends *his* premises; Jerry hopes for understanding from the dog ("I hoped that the dog would . . . understand") and from Peter ("I don't know what I was thinking about; of course you don't understand"); as the dog bit Jerry, Peter stabs Jerry.

However, the dog's hostility to Jerry *begins* the dog story whereas Peter's hostility to Jerry *ends* the zoo story. The dog's hostility is at the surface of his animality, but Peter's hostility is calculatedly aroused by Jerry after he tells the dog story. Jerry went to the zoo to study "the way people exist with animals, and the way animals exist with each other, and with people too." But after he meets Peter, Jerry changes from student to teacher: "I have learned that neither kindness nor cruelty by themselves, independent of each other, creates any effect beyond themselves; and I have learned that the two combined, together, at the same time, are the teaching emotion." Jerry proceeds to combine the two in his education of Peter, with cruelty more apparent.

So vicious is Jerry's verbal attack that Peter screams when Jerry opens his knife: "YOU'RE GOING TO KILL ME!" But Jerry's intention is more subtle; combining cruelty with some of the previously announced kindness, "Jerry tosses the knife at Peter's feet"; he urges Peter to pick it up, and then punch-baits him into using the knife. Since Peter is a defensive animal only, not an attacker, Jerry "impales *himself* on the knife" (my italics). Though Jerry cries like a "fatally wounded animal," he dies like a man—talking. In dying, Jerry comes to partial self-recognition through his stream of associations: "Could I have planned all this? No . . . no, I couldn't have. But I think I did."

His final broken phrases imitate the disjunctive quality of his behavior.

Jerry's fragmented life and speech contrast with Peter's coherence and order. Peter's effort to light his pipe triggers Jerry's first pedagogic taunt: "Well, boy; *you're* not going to get lung cancer, are you?" With this thrust, Jerry exposes Peter's caution and upon this thrust death floats into the lazy Sunday air. It hovers over Jerry's account of his parents and aunt, over the dog story, and it culminates in Jerry's impalement. Only in dying does Jerry shift from cruel to kinder words, reassuring Peter: "You're not really a vegetable; it's all right, you're an animal. You're an animal, too." The "too" is significant; there are seals, birds, and lions at the zoo; there are parakeets and cats in Peter's apartment. In his dog story Jerry says he mixed *rat* poison with the hamburger bought as "a bite for . . . pussy-*cat*" (my italics) so as to kill the landlady's *dog*. Since animals are ubiquitous and virtually interchangeable, Albee's *Zoo Story* generalizes that men are animals; beneath the illusion of civilization, they may use words and knives instead of fangs and claws, but they still can kill.

Beyond this, however, *The Zoo Story* suggests another meaning in man's search for God. Albee himself has pointed out the influence upon *The Zoo Story* of *Suddenly Last Summer* by Tennessee Williams, Albee's play, like that of Williams, contains a search for God climaxed by violence. Like the Old Testament Jeremiah, whose cruel prophecies were a warning kindness to his people, Jerry may have educated Peter in his relation to God. Like his namesake, Jerry lapses into prophetic language: "And it came to pass that . . . ." "So be it!" Before the dog story, Jerry exclaims, "For God's sake." After poisoning the dog, Jerry promises its owner that he will pray for it though he does not "understand how to pray." At the end of the dog story, Jerry re-cites a list of those with whom he sought communication—a list that begins with animals and ends with God, anagram of dog. In his cruel-kind deviling of Peter, Jerry calls on Jesus, and Peter replies with a "God damn" and a "Great God," almost in the same breath.

This undercurrent of divine suggestion is climaxed by the final words of the play. Toward the beginning Peter reacted to Jerry's unconventional life story with "Oh, my; oh, my." And Jerry sneered, "Oh, your what?" Only after the impalement is Jerry's question answered—by Peter's whispered repetitions: "Oh my God, oh my God, oh my God," and these are the only words Peter speaks while Jerry dies, thanking Peter in biblical phrases: "I came unto you . . . and you have comforted me." After Jerry's revelation of Peter's animal nature, and Peter's subsequent departure according to Jerry's instructions, "OH MY GOD!" is heard offstage as a *howl*—the final proof of Peter's animality, but also of his humanity, since he howls to his God. Jerry, who tells animal stories, closes the play by echoing Peter's "Oh my God" in the difficult combination demanded by Albee's stage direction, "scornful mimicry and supplication." That tonal combination is Jerry's last lesson in the pedagogy of cruel kindness; much of his scornful wit has been mimetic, and yet the wit itself is an inverted plea for love and understanding; the very word *undesrtand* echoes through the play.

Because life is lonely and death inevitable, Jerry seeks to master them in a single deed of ambiguous suicide-murder; he stages his own death, and by that staging, he punctures Peter's illusion of civilization, converting Peter into his apostle who will carry the message of man's caged animality—the zoo story. Jerry's death brings us to dramatic definition of humanity—bounded by animal drives but reaching toward the divine. Though this definition is at least as old as Pascal, Albee invests it with contemporary significance through his highly contemporary idiom—an idiom manipulated in tense theatrical rhythms.

So forceful is the indirection in Albee's first drama that even amateurs compel attention in performance. In *The American Dream,* on the other hand, the caricature of contemporary America often depends, in production, on elaborate set and props. In *The American Dream* Mommy and Daddy spout the clichés of middle-class America, and the implication is that such clichés lead to a kind of death for Grandma, who represents the vigorous old frontier spirit. Grandma resembles Jerry in her independence, but age has made her crafty, and she has learned to roll with the punches. In both *The American Dream* and *The Sandbox* it is Mommy who delivers the punches, and yet she does not literally kill Grandma.

Of the relationship between these two plays, Albee has written: "For *The Sandbox,* I extracted several of the characters from *The American Dream* and placed them in a situation different than, but related to, their predicament in the longer play." *The Sandbox* is named for the grave of Grandma, the first-generation American, and *The American Dream* is named for the third-generation American, a grave in himself; in both plays, murderous intention is lodged in the middle generation, especially Mommy. In *The Sandbox* Mommy and Daddy deposit Grandma in a child's sandbox. Half-buried, Grandma finds that she can no longer move, and she accepts her summons by the handsome Young Man, an Angel of Death.

In *The American Dream* Ionesco is a strong influence on Albee. Like *The Bald Soprano,* *The American Dream* thrives on social inanities. Like Ionesco, Albee reduces events to stage entrances and exits. As in *The Bald Soprano,* a recognition scene is based on circum-stantial evidence; such proof reunites a husband and wife in the Ionesco play; in the Albee play such proof reunites Mrs. Barker with the American family for whom she barked. Albee also uses such Ionesco techniques as proliferation of objects (Grandma's boxes), pointless anecdotes (mainly Mommy's), meaningless nuances (beige, wheat, and cream), cliché refrains (I don't mind if I do; How fascinating, enthralling, spellbinding, gripping, or engrossing).

Within this stuffy apartment of Ionesco motifs, Albee places a family in the American grain, with its areas for senior citizens, and its focus on money. When Mommy was eight years old, she told Grandma that she was "going to mahwy a wich old man." Sterile, Mommy and Daddy have purchased a baby from the Bye-Bye Adoption Service, which puns on Buy-Buy. In *The Sandbox* Mommy and Daddy carry Grandma to *death,* but in *The American Dream* Mommy makes Grandma's *life* impossible. She informs a feebly protesting Daddy that he wants to put Grandma in a nursing home, and she threatens Grandma with a man in a van who will cart her away. Mommy treats Grandma like a naughty child; she discusses Grandma's toilet habits, warns her that she will take away her TV set, worries about her vocabulary: "I don't know where she gets the words; on the television, maybe."

And Grandma, who is treated like a child, tells the story of the family child to Mrs. Barker. Since "the bumble of joy" had eyes only for Daddy, Mommy gouged its eyes out; since it called Mommy a dirty name, they cut its tongue out. And because "it began to develop an interest in its-you-know-what," they castrated it and cut its hands off at the wrists. Our acquaintance with Mommy has prepared us for Grandma's account of Bringing Up Bumble. But more painful than the physical mutilations are the verbal ailments, containing

Mommy's cruel American platitudes: "it didn't have a head on its shoulders, it had no guts, it was spineless, its feet were made of clay." This is Mommy's more insidious castration, nagging the child into a diminutive Daddy, who is "all ears," but who has no guts since he has "tubes now, where he used to have tracts." In *The American Dream* "Like father, like son." Daddy "just want[s] to get everything over with," and his bumble-son does "get everything over with" by dying before Mommy can complete her murder of him.

In *The American Dream* it is an offstage bumble that predicts Grandma's death, as an offstage rumble announces Grandma's death in *The Sandbox*. Like the bumble, Grandma escapes Mommy's murderous malice by a kind of suicide. As Jerry turns Peter's reluctant threat into the reality of his own death, Grandma turns Mommy's repeated threats into the reality of her disappearance from the family.

When a handsome Young Man arrives, Grandma is alone onstage, and she recognizes in him the American Dream shaped by Mommy. He shares only appearance and initials with the Angel of Death in *The Sandbox*, but he has the same meaning. The American Dream is an Angel of Death who is linked both to the mutilated bumble and to Grandma. In a confessional monologue the Young Man tells Grandma of a twin "torn apart" from him, so that it seemed his heart was "wrenched from [his] body," draining him of feeling. As his twin brother was mutilated physically, the American Dream is mutilated emotionally.

When Mrs. Barker intrudes upon this confrontation of the numb young modern man with the vigorous old frontier spirit, Grandma introduces him as the man in the van, Mommy's bogeyman. Asking him to carry her boxes, Grandma follows the Young Man out. Boxes and sandbox are coffin and grave; the American Dream leads but to the grave, and

Grandma, accepting her fate, goes out in style—escorted by a handsome swain whose gallantry substitutes for feeling.

Though minatory Mommy later admits that "There is no van man. We . . . we made him up," she readily accepts the American Dream as a replacement for Grandma. Thus, the "comedy" ends happily, though Grandma is dead to Mommy: "Five glasses? Why five? There are only four of us." In spite of Mommy's malice—expressed in the clichés of contemporary America—Grandma and bumble manage to die their own kind of death. As in *The Zoo Story*, murderous invective leads indirectly to death, each victim staging his own stylized death.

The slackness of *The American Dream* contrasts with the tightness of *The Zoo Story*. In the earlier play indirection is both theme and technique, exploding into the death that reveals man's attachments to the animal and the divine. In *The American Dream* Albee borrows from Ionesco the techniques of proliferation and disjunction, using them as middle-class modes. Unlike Ionesco, however, Albee stops short of the savage anarchy of farce, and he dilutes his satire with a sympathetic Grandma and an ambiguous American Dream. In spite of her pithy frontier comments and her asides on "old people," Grandma does not oppose Mommy openly. And since the Young Man is first caricatured, then sentimentalized, the play sags when he speaks and preens. He will "do almost anything for money," and he tries to sell us the sad story of his life. Apparently ignorant of the mutilations to his twin brother, he describes his parallel loss of sensation that has resulted in his inability to love. His abstract statement of losses is much duller than Grandma's pungent summary of the mutilation of his twin. In spite of the Young Man's warning that his tale "may not be true," the mutual sympathy of Grandma and the American Dream is incongruously maudlin in this play that Grandma herself labels a "comedy." The Young Man claims to accept the syntax around him, but he is remarkably deaf to the tone of a satiric comedy that borders on farce. Albee makes an effort to restore that tone by bringing back Mommy and Daddy with their mindless clichés, and the play ends with Grandma's aside: "Everybody's got what he wants . . . or everybody's got what he thinks he wants." The American family accepts its illusion of sex and success.

In *The Death of Bessie Smith* Albee avoids sentimentality by keeping the sympathetic titular protagonist offstage. The play is based on a newspaper account of the death of the Negro blues singer; its documentary origin is unique in Albee's works. But his Bessie Smith is a presence rather than a character. The most sustained character, in contrast, is a voluble young Nurse who lashes out against her invalid Father, her Intern suitor, and her Negro Orderly. Lacking Jerry's self-proclaimed kindness and Mommy's hypocritical conformity, the dialogue of the Nurse is unrelievedly vicious, and yet she is not responsible for the death of Bessie Smith.

In the eight scenes of the play Albee attempts to counterpoint two story threads—the trip north of blues-singer Bessie Smith and the Nurse's sadistic control of a southern hospital. However, the Nurse story overshadows that of Bessie Smith, who is known only through the dialogue of her chauffeur-companion, Jack. The sympathetic Negroes have names—Jack, Bernie, Bessie Smith—whereas the white world is typecast—Nurse, Father, Intern, light-skinned Orderly, Second Nurse. The Nurse is the only coherent character in the play, and she coheres through her verbalization of scorn and conformity.

About halway through the play Jack's car, with Bessie Smith as passenger, crashes off-stage, while onstage the Nurse carries on a bored telephone conversation with a Second Nurse at another hospital. It is this Second Nurse who is indirectly responsible for the death of Bessie Smith, but we do not learn that until the end of the play.

In the two longest of the eight scenes (sixth and last) the cynical, reactionary Nurse and her liberal Intern suitor engage in a thrust-and-parry dialogue. At his rare dialectical best, the Intern is able to be as cruel as the Nurse. Though ideologically opposed to her, he desires her—a desire inflamed by her taunts. When his sneer about her chastity evokes her threat to "fix" him, he stares at her admiringly: "You impress me. No matter what else, I've got to admit that." But she also arouses his sadism: "I just had a lovely thought . . . that maybe sometime when you are sitting there at your desk opening mail with that stiletto you use for a letter opener, you might slip and tear open your arm . . . then you could come running into the emergency . . . and I could be there when you came running in, blood coming out of you like water out of a faucet . . . and I could take ahold of your arm . . . and just hold it . . . just hold it . . . and watch it flow . . . just hold on to you and watch your blood flow. . . ."

The death of Bessie Smith occurs between the last two scenes of the play. In the brief seventh scene the Second Nurse refuses hospital admission to Bessie Smith, injured in the automobile accident: "I DON'T CARE WHO YOU GOT OUT THERE, NIGGER. YOU COOL YOUR HEELS!" Similarly, when Jack brings Bessie Smith to the central hospital, the First Nurse refuses admission to the singer. As the Intern and Orderly go out to examine Bessie Smith in the car, Jack tells the Nurse about the accident, and she recalls the Intern's wish that he might watch while her blood came out "like water from a faucet." But it is Jack who had watched the ebb of the lifeblood of Bessie Smith. When the Intern and Orderly re-enter, "their uniforms are bloodied." They report the death of Bessie Smith.

In *The Death of Bessie Smith* nurses do not tend the sick; they sit at hospital admissions desks, refusing care to the injured. The First Nurse says she is sick of things, and Albee implies that Bessie Smith dies of such sickness. The Nurse speaks of her letter opener in the Intern's ribs, of a noose around his neck, but it is Bessie Smith who dies. The Nurse likes Negro blues, but she will not lift a finger to save a Negro blues singer; rather she mocks dead Bessie Smith, singing until the Intern slaps her. Albee indicts the whole South for the murder of Bessie Smith; nevertheless, the singer's story remains fragmentary, and we are left with a more vivid impression of the verbal duel of Nurse and Intern—gratuitous skirmishing in this loosely constructed morally earnest play.

The Intern exhibits more spirit than Peter in *The Zoo Story* or Daddy in *The American Dream*. In his thrust-and-parry exchange with the Nurse we can almost hear George and Martha of *Who's Afraid of Virgina Woolf?* In that play, as in Albee's shorter plays, murderous dialogue leads obliquely to murder. As the shadow of death lay over the sun-drenched afternoon of *The Zoo Story*, death lies like a sediment in Martha's gin, Nick's bourbon, Honey's brandy, and mainly George's "bergin." Though George claims that "musical beds is the faculty sport" in New Carthage, the sport that commands our attention is verbal fencing in the most adroit dialogue ever heard on the American stage.

Popular taste has often cloaked unpopular themes, and Albee has used the popular taste for punch lines to expose an anatomy of love. Although there are four characters, the play's three acts focus on the relationship of George

and Martha, who express their love in a lyricism of witty malice. Act I, "Fun and Games," rises toward a dissonant duet: Martha chants about George's failures as he tries to drown her voice in the party refrain, "Who's afraid of Virginia Woolf?" Toward the end of the Act III "exorcism" George and Martha reach "a hint of communion." Two of the three acts thus close on views of the togetherness of George and Martha, and during the three acts each is visibly tormented by the extended absence of the other. However malicious they sound, they *need* one another—a need that may be called love.

George and Martha have cemented their marriage with the fiction of their child. Outwardly conformist, they privately nourish their love upon this lie. Yet George's play-long preoccupation with death hints that such lies must be killed before they kill. George and Martha's distinctive love-duet is played against a background of death. In Act I George tells Martha "murderously" how much he is looking forward to their guests. Once Nick and Honey are on the scene, George shoots Martha with a toy gun, and then remarks that he might really kill her some day. In Act II Nick and George exchange unprovoked confessions; Nick reveals intimacies about his wife and her father, but George's anecodotes play upon death. He tells of a fifteen-year-old boy who accidentally shot his mother; then, when the boy was being taught to drive by his father, he swerved to avoid a porcupine; he crashed into a tree and killed his father. Later in Act II Martha summarizes George's novel about a boy who accidentally kills both his parents. Martha's father had forbidden George to publish the novel, and George had protested, "No, Sir, this isn't a novel at all . . . this is the truth . . . this really happened . . . to ME!" George reacts to Martha's narration with a threat to kill her, and he grabs her by the throat. Athletic Nick, who resembles the American Dream both in physique and in lack of feeling, tears George from Martha, and she accuses her husband softly, "Murderer. Mur . . . der . . . er." But George's murder kills only illusion.

While Nick and Martha disappear upstairs, drunken Honey voices her fear of having children, and George needles her: "How you do it? Hunh? How do you make your secret little murders stud-boy doesn't know about, hunh?" With Honey's unknowing help, George proceeds to plan the "secret little murder" of his child of fantasy. George and Martha declare "total war," and George vows "to play this one to the death." But death takes only their fantasy son, who, by George's account, swerves his car to avoid a porcupine, and crashes into a tree. George's imaginary child and his perhaps imaginary father die in precisely the same way.

Though George tries to throttle Martha, and she leaps at him when he kills their child, the only stage murder is verbal. Such murder is oblique, and George leads up to it obliquely, with his "flagellation." The idiom that has nurtured their love serves also to kill the illusion at its heart.

Their interdependence has been fed on a rhetoric of taunts. At the play's opening Martha evokes Bette Davis, the film star of acid wit. George acknowledges that Martha is a "devil with language," and she calls him "Phrasemaker." Though Martha may have downed George with boxing gloves, he outpoints her in linguistic tennis. And (to force the image) their imaginary child is the ball in this private game that keeps their love limber, preventing it from softening into academic mediocrity.

The sado-masochistic marriage of George and Martha is sustained through their verbal dexterity and their imaginary child. Far from

a *deus ex machina*, the child is mentioned before the arrival of Nick and Honey; George warns Martha not to "start in on the bit about the kid." By that time they have been sparring in their recurrent pattern, Martha beating George with his lack of professional success and George cutting at Martha's age, drinking, and promiscuity.

Guests heighten the pitch of the George-Martha exchange, as the couple moves into gamesmanship. Though George has cautioned Martha not to mention their child, he is tantalizingly evasive when Nick asks whether they have any children. While Martha "is changing," George learns that she has told Honey about their son, and that is the change that sets this evening off from similar evenings in the life of George and Martha. Once revealed, their son must die.

But George perceives this only slowly, and Martha never does. When Martha returns, changed, the verbal match continues with Nick as goad. And again it is Honey who introduces the subject of the son. After trying to retreat, Martha uses the child in Strindbergian fashion—as a weapon against her husband, taunting him with not being the father of the child. Unlike Strindberg's males, however, George is not vulnerable to this thrust about their "bean bag."

Act II, "Walpurgisnacht," introduces some variation in the verbal fencing: George and Nick toward the beginning, Martha and Nick in the middle, and George and Honey at the end; but the bedrock remains George versus Martha. They have a momentary fling in French, and like the tramps in *Waiting for Godot* George invents insults: "Book dropper! Child mentioner!" The insults point to the two lies of George's own life—the fictional murder which is the expression of the end of childhood, and the fictional murder to come, which may be the expression of the end of marriage.

George charges Martha with "slashing away at everything in sight, scarring up half the world." Each insists that the other is sick. In the prelude to their declaration of "total war," each assaults the other's dominant fantasy:

MARTHA: . . . before I'm through with you you'll wish you'd died in that automobile, you bastard.
GEORGE: *(Emphasizing with his forefinger)* And you'll wish you'd never mentioned our son!

Each predicts the other's wish to renounce lies, to embrace truth, but predictions are only obliquely fulfilled.

In the destruction of illusion, which may lead to truth, "snap" becomes a stage metaphor—sound, word, and gesture. Martha snaps her fingers at George and plays variations on the theme of snapping; she rhymes snap with crap, then uses snap as a synonym for the cipher she claims George has become. In Act III when George announces the death of their son, he pays her in kind. Entering from the garden with a bunch of snapdragons, George begins the game he calls "Bringing Up Baby": "Flores; flores para los muertos. Flores." Soon he throws snapdragons—*his* flowers for the dead—at Martha, one at a time, stem first, spear-like, phallic, as he echoes her "snaps" at him. St. George slew the dragon; Albee's George slays with snapdragons.

Before throwing snapdragons, however, George starts a story about a Mediterranean trip, a graduation present from his parents. "Was this after you killed them?" asks Nick. *"George and Martha swing around and look at him."* Then George replies ambiguously, "Truth or illusion. Who knows the difference, eh, toots?" And Martha charges, "You were never in the Mediterranean . . . truth or illusion . . . either way." It is when Martha tells George that he cannot distinguish between truth and illusion that he pelts her with snapdragons. Then Martha repeats the dichotomy: "Truth or illusion, George. Doesn't it matter to you . . . at all?" This time George doesn't bother to throw anything as he answers her, "SNAP!" And with relish, he sets the scene for the snapping of their common illusion from which truth *may* arise.

In his triumphant enactment of the murder, George snaps his fingers for Nick to join the final game, and he snaps his fingers for Honey to support his outrageous claim that he ate the death telegram. Death rites are played against this background of snaps, choreographed as a dance of death. The death scene and its aftermath contain the most perfectly cadenced dialogue of the drama. George's attack on Martha's illusion is so theatrically punitive that his redemptive intention is questionable.

George and Martha fire a salvo of mutual sexual accusation. Before breaking the news of the son's death, George joins Martha in a discordant duet, as at the end of Act I. Martha recites another litany of George's failures while George recites the Requiem Mass. As Martha slowly wilts like the scattered snapdragons, George repeats the best-known phrases: "Requiescat in pace . . . Requiem aeternam dona eis, Domine." Suddenly, Nick reveals his illumination about their child, asking, "You couldn't have . . . any?" And George replies, *"We* couldn't"—a sentence that Martha echoes with Albee's scenic direction: *"A hint of communion in this."* It is the broadest hint we have. After the departure of Nick and Honey, the dialogue narrows down to monosyllables until George hums the title refrain, and Martha admits that *she* is afraid of Virginia Woolf—a woman afflicted with a madness that drove her to suicide.

Martha's fear is understandable. Whatever will they do, now that their bean bag is dead, their illusion exorcised? Since Albee once planned to give the Act III title, "The Exorcism," to the entire play, we know the importance he attaches to it. To exorcise is to drive out evil spirits, and in New Carthage the evil spirits are the illusion of progeny—Honey's "hot air" pregnancy and Martha's imaginary son. These are comparable illusions, but they differ in causes and effects. Honey seems to have forced Nick into a marriage which "cured" her of the illusion of pregnancy. During marriage her "delicacy" is the apparent reason that they have no children. Without truth or illusion, they live in a vacuum of surface amenities, a mishmash of syrupy Honey and trivial Nicks. But when Martha indulges in an idealized biography of her son (before George kills him), Honey announces abruptly, "I want a child." She repeats this wish just before Martha shifts from the son as ideal biography to the son as weapon against George. Though Honey's conversion is sudden (and scarcely credible), it seems to be sustained.

For George and Martha, the exorcism is less certain, less complete, and more involving. The marriage of Nick and Honey kills their illusion, but the illusion of George and Martha is born in wedlock, perhaps because they could have no real children, and Martha "had wanted a child." Martha's recitation indicates that the conception of the child—intellectual rather than biological—may have originated as a game, but the lying game expressed their need. Since we never see George and Martha alone at their game, we do not know whether it is played soft or hard, though it probably varies between Martha's penchant for sentimentality and George's probing thrusts. Until this *Walpurgisnacht* when magic runs rampant, the couple seems to have kept private both tender and taunting use of the son.

Uninteresting in themselves, Nick and Honey function as foils and parallels of George and Martha: the syllabic similarity of the names, the parallel fantasies of the women, the opposing professions of the men, and the cross-couples advancing the plot. Without Nick, Martha's adultery would not have driven George to murder their son; without Honey, George could not have accomplished the murder.

Albee's repetitions of "True or False" and "Truth versus Illusion" emphasize truth, but it is problematical whether truth will succeed, and Albee deliberately leaves it problematical, refusing Martha the easy conversion of Honey. Unless the Act III title, "The Exorcism," is ironic, however, George and Martha rebuild their marriage on the base of truth, though their gifts seem more destructive than constructive. The lasting impression of the play is not of exorcising but of exercising the wits of George and Martha.

In *Who's Afraid of Virginia Woolf?* Albee reaches a pinnacle of mastery of American colloquial idiom. Since colloquialism is usually associated with realism, the play has been viewed as realistic psychology. But credible motivation drives psychological drama, and Albee's motivation is designedly flimsy: Why does George stay up to entertain Martha's guests? Why, for that matter, does she invite them? And why do Honey and Nick allow themselves to be "gotten"? The play coheres magnetically only if we accept the *Walpurgisnacht* as a *donnée;* these four people are together to dramatize more than themselves.

George describes his novel: "Well, it's an allegory, really—probably—but it can be read as straight, cozy prose. . . ." No one has called Albee's prose "cozy," but it too has been read and heard as "straight" realism, sometimes of "crooked" sexuality. Like George's novel, however, Albee's drama is "an allegory, really—probably."

Albee sets *"Who's Afraid of Virginia Woolf?* in a fictional New Carthage. Carthage, which means "New City," was founded in the ninth century B.C. by a semilegendary, deceitful Dido, and it was razed to the ground by real Romans in 146 A.D. By the fifth century it had again become a power, which St. Augustine in his *Confessions* called "a cauldron of unholy loves." Albee uses the historical conjunction of sex and power as spice for the American stew he simmers in this cauldron. He himself suggested: "George and Martha may represent the Washingtons and the play may be all about the decline of the West."

Albee's unholy lovers are George and Martha, whose names evoke America's first and childless White House couple. As the legendary George Washington could not tell a lie, Albee's George murders in the name of Truth. George describes his fictional son as "Our own little all-American something-or-other." Albee suggests that illusion is an American weakness, and American drama has been much concerned with illusion. But Albee's America is representative of contemporary Western civilization.

An early stage direction indicates Albee's inclusive intent: George *"With a handsweep tak[es] in not only the room, the house, but the whole countryside."* He characterizes the region as "Illyria . . . Penguin Island . . . Gomorrah. . . ." Realm of fantasy, realm of social satire, realm of sin—George's condemnatory geography seems to be that of Albee as well, with an academic foursome representing the decline of the fabulous, sinful West. Within the West, a humanistic George opposes a mechanized Nick; George can see the handwriting on the wall, and it is the penmanship of Oswald Spengler, whose book George flings at the chimes that become a death knell. On one broad level, then, *Who's Afraid of Virginia Woolf?* is in the American dramatic tradition of Attack-the-Illusion: O'Neill's *The Iceman Cometh,* Williams' *The Glass Menagerie,* and Miller's *Death of a Salesman.*

Albee also reaches out beyond America into a metaphysical examination of the nature of love, which may be a metaphor for Western civilization. Concealing eschatology beneath surface psychology, however, Albee's play is limited by its camouflage. George's vitriolic idiom overshadows his anemic humanist yearnings; his views of history are simplistic—the construct-a-civilization speech; his views of biology are simple-minded—the mechanical Nick-maker. George wants to defend Western civilization against its sex-oriented, success-oriented assailants ("I will not give up Berlin") but his defense of life and love is too closely centered in his scrotum. Better at attack than defense, George is more effective *against* illusory dragons than *for* bastions of civilization.

Since that civilization is classico-Christian in tradition, Albee unobtrusively sprinkles the play with classical and Christian resonances: Martha's opening expletive is "Jesus," and both men swear Christian oaths; the imaginary child is associated with the sun and golden fleece; the offstage fathers of Martha and Honey are seen as god-figures. But these hints remain peripheral in *Who's Afraid of Virginia Woolf?* The focus on human love leaves little room for the divine.

Tiny Alice, in contrast, interweaves human and divine love (and hatred) so that the strands are virtually inseparable. In an interview Albee claimed that *Tiny Alice* is a mystery play in two senses of the word: "That is, it's both a metaphysical mystery and, at the same time, a conventional 'Dial M for Murder'-type mystery." But the one murder in *Tiny Alice*—the Lawyer's shooting of Julian—takes place before our eyes, bereft of detective-story mystery. Instead, the mystery of what is happening onstage dissolves into the larger mystery of what happens in the realm of ultimate reality. Governing both is a conception of mystery as that which is hidden from human understanding. With *Tiny Alice* Albee's ambition grows as large as that of O'Neill, who claimed to be "interested only in the relation between man and God."

Albee's protagonist is Brother Julian, who claims to be "dedicated to the reality of things, rather than the appearance," but who has to be violently shocked—mortally wounded—before he recognizes reality, and even then he tries to rearrange it into familiar appearance. Using the disjunctive technique of Absurdism and the terminology of Christianity, Albee drapes a veil of unknowing over a mystery of wide relevance. Thus, the play is nowhere in place and time, though the flavor is vaguely contemporary and American. The three stage settings are fantastic, and Miss Alice's millions are counted in no currency. Time moves with the imprecision of a dream, and yet it is, as the Lawyer claims, "the great revealer." Except for pointed references to Julian's "six blank years," Albee obscures the *passing* of time; the Lawyer says that Miss Alice's grant is a hundred million a year for twenty years, and after Julian is shot, the Lawyer offers the Cardinal "two billion, kid, twenty years of grace for no work at all." The play may thus have lasted twenty years between the twelve "tick's" in the Lawyer's opening gibberish and Julian's dying question, "IS IT NIGHT . . . OR DAY? . . . Or does it matter?"

Of the five characters, two have names, two are named by their function, and one—Butler—bears the name of his function. Albee has denied the suggestion that Alice stands for Truth and Julian for Apostasy, but he cannot expunge such associations for us. Named or unnamed, however, all characters are locked into their functions: Brother Julian into serv-ice to his God, the Cardinal into service to his church, and the castle trio into service to their deity, knowable only as the mouse in the model. Servants of Tiny Alice, they appear to master the rest of the world. Like the trio in Sartre's *No Exit,* they are bound in an eternal love-hate triangle, but *their* mission is to deliver victims to Tiny Alice, at once a reduced truth and a small obscene aperture into an aspect of being. (Tiny Alice is homosexual slang for a tight anus.)

Julian, a lay brother, is Albee's Christian hero in this modern mystery play. John Gielgud, creator of the role, commented, "The wonderful relief that I had about this part was that I was *supposed* to keep wondering what it was all about." So pervasive is Julian's bewilderment that some critics have suggested the entire play takes place in Julian's mind. But Albee is working on a larger stage. As in medieval mystery plays, we are involved in the conflict within a tempted soul, but we are aware too of our world in which that conflict resonates. Rather than Virtue versus Vice, Albee's Julian is torn between Truth and Illusion, between a desire for the real and his irrepressible imagination.

Though Julian is at the center of the play, Albee delays introducing him. Instead, he begins the drama with personifications of power, à la Jean Genet: Cardinal and Lawyer, sacred and profane, church and state, buddies and enemies, with a long past behind them. We first see Julian at the castle, in conversation with the Butler, whose symbolic function is central—a stewardship based on his serving of wine, Christian metaphor for blood. The Butler also offers Julian water, tea, coffee, before port and champagne—sweet and effervescent forms of wine—and, appropriately, the Butler tries to sweeten the ineluctable claims of Tiny Alice upon Julian. The Butler guides Julian through the wine cellar of the castle, and he pours champagne at Julian's wedding, which is his last supper.

Albee mocks his own dialogue in *Tiny Alice*: Julian comments on the Butler's name, Butler, "You would be in for some rather tiresome exchanges," and the Butler retorts, "None more than this." The Butler describes the Lawyer's imagery, "This is an endless metaphor." Though Albee continues to build his dialogue with monologue and insulting exchange, he uses them somewhat differently in *Tiny Alice*: the verbal skirmishing often ends in a draw, and the monologues sound painfully explicit but are buried in the central mystery, which is unknowable.

As in earlier Albee plays, thrust-and-parry dialogue leads obliquely to murder. The master verbal fencer of *Tiny Alice,* the Lawyer, shoots Julian, but Miss Alice is the principal agent of his undoing, and she, as the Lawyer remarks, was "never one with words." Rather, she acts through surprises: the old hag turns into a lovely woman; unprompted, she confesses to Julian her carnal relations with the Butler and the Lawyer; abruptly, she inquires into Julian's sex life; before marrying and abandoning Julian, she alternates a mysterious prayer with an address to "someone in the model." She cradles the wounded Julian, making *"something of a Pietà."* At the end she is cruel and kind; her last words are "Oh, my poor Julian." Yet she leaves him.

Miss Alice's seduction of Julian is accomplished through deeds rather than words, but Julian himself translates the erotic into a highly verbal mysticism. He defends his loquacity to Miss Alice, "Articulate men often carry set paragraphs." In each of the play's three acts Julian indulges in a rhapsodic monologue that does not sound like a set paragraph, since the rhythms are jagged. The cumulative effect is apocalyptic, but Julian's apocalypse is sexually rooted, *lay* brother that he is (Albee's

pun). In Act I Julian describes a perhaps hallucinatory sexual experience with a woman who occasionally hallucinated as the Blessed Virgin. Not only does Julian speak of ejaculation; he speaks *in* ejaculations. Julian's mistress with an illusory pregnancy recalls the illusion-ridden women of *Virginia Woolf;* as the imaginary child of that play is an evil spirit to be exorcised, the imaginary pregnancy of the hallucinating woman of *Tiny Alice* proves to be a fatal cancer. And even as Julian confesses to Miss Alice what he believes to be his struggle for the real, she tempts him with her own desirability—very beautiful and very rich.

In Julian's Act II monologue about martyrdom he shifts his identity—a child, both lion and gladiator, then saint and the hallucinating self of the Act I monologue. While Julian describes this eroto-mystical, multi-personal martyrdom. Miss Alice shifts her attitude, first urging Julian to marry her, then spurring him to sacrifice himself to Alice, whom she invokes in the third person.

In Act III Julian, who left the asylum because he was persuaded that hallucination was inevitable and even desirable, embarks on his final hallucination which ends in his real death. Abandoned and dying, Julian recollects (or imagines) a wound of his childhood, as Miss Alice in her prayer recollected (or imagined) being hurt in *her* childhood. Alternately a child and the hallucinating woman who called for help, Julian is forced to face himself in death—the prototypical existential confrontation. With phrases of the Thirteenth Psalm, Julian very slowly and desperately dissolves Miss Alice into Tiny Alice into the Christian God. Unable to accept "the ceremony of Alice," Julian recoils from the hermetic, dust-free vacuum of Tiny Alice, from the unblinking eyes of the phrenological head ("Ah God! Is that the humor? THE ABSTRACT? . . . REAL?

THE REST? . . . FALSE?"). Unable to laugh at such absurd humor, Julian reverts to Christian illusion, to ready-made images that protect him from the reality of abstraction, which is death. Though buried in mystery, death is omnipresent in *Tiny Alice*.

Julian calls on deity in the words of Christ on the cross: "ALICE? MY GOD, WHY HAST THOU FORSAKEN ME?" As a "great presence" engulfs him, panting and stamping, Julian takes the crucifixion position, injecting his God into Alice, "God, Alice . . . I accept thy will." Albee's play opens on Genet's *Balcony*, and it closes on the blackness of Ionesco's dying king; both Julian and Bérenger go down fighting against predatory death, but they both go down—into the void. On a throne, or crucified, or whimpering in bed, Everyman is food for Tiny Alice, who devours in mystery.

Julian's three experiences pivot on his confusion between illusion and reality; the sexual experience may have been a hallucination; the experience of martyrdom has haunted Julian's imagination, and he dies in an evocation of Christ the martyr, who may be his last illusion. Rhythms of ecstatic agony and the image of blood link the three experiences, or the three descriptions of experience, which may become experience *through* description.

Between his three monologues as within them, Julian's speech is fragmentary, interrogative, recapitulatory. In contrast to the sinewy syntax of the Lawyer, Julian's sentence fragments are heavy with gerunds, adjectives, efforts at definition through synonyms. As Jerry's indirection mirrored the theme of *The Zoo Story,* Julian's phrasal fragmentation— skillfully arresting in the theater—mirrors the theme of *Tiny Alice,* and that fragmentation functions partly as synecdoche.

"In my Father's house are many mansions," said Christ (John 14:2), and in the mansion of Tiny Alice are many rooms; true to his heredity and calling, Brother Julian praises library, chapel, and wine cellar—all with religious associations. Alone in the library after his wedding, he recalls the childhood loneliness of an attic closet. But all rooms belong to Tiny Alice, and space does not contain them. When the fire in the model announces a fire in the chapel, Julian asks Miss Alice, "Why, why did it happen that way—in both dimensions?" After his wedding, Julian likens the disappearance of people to "an hour elaps[ing] or a . . . dimension." And shortly before shooting Julian, the Lawyer remarks to his buddy-enemy, the Cardinal: "We have come quite a . . . dimension, have we not?" In *Tiny Alice* dimensions are deliberately diffused and confused; one does not move, as in the Great Chain of Being, from an animal dimension, to a human, to angelic, to divine. Rather, all dimensions are interactive, and point to the whole metaphysical mystery in its private parts.

Those parts are sexual, but Albee also suggests them through insistence on birds and children—vulnerable both. Bird imagery embraces everyone: the play opens with a nonsense address to birds; the Cardinal has cardinals in his stone and iron garden; the Butler speaks of swallows "screeping"; the Lawyer's poem has the grace of a walking crow; Miss Alice is first visible in a *wing* chair, and she later envelops Julian in the "great wing" of her robe; Julian is variously a "bird of pray," a drab fledgling," and a "little bird, pecking away in the library," summarizing his piety, innocence, and sexual vulnerability. At times, too, the characters act like children, or they summon recollections of childhood. Julian is often and explicitly called "little," and in his dying soliloquy he becomes a little boy calling for his cookie. All these lines suggest the helplessness of birds and children in the world of Tiny Alice, who is mouselike, monstrous, and feline.

Like imagery and fragmentation, Albee's language in *Tiny Alice* is highly complex. Familiar is the stinging salaciousness of the opening scene between Cardinal and Lawyer. This functions symbolically since the Cardinal-church is the son of a whore, and the Lawyer-state eats offal and carrion. The titillation of these disclosures is counterpointed against the formality of the syntax—first-person plurals, avoidance of contractions, emphasis on prepositional nuance, and self-conscious wordplay (the eye of an odor). Only rarely does the Lawyer slip into a vigorous Americanism: "Oh, come on, Your Eminence." "You'll grovel, Buddy. . . . As automatically and naturally as people slobber on that ring of yours." "Everyone diddled everyone else." "We picked up our skirts and lunged for it! ɪɪɪɪɪ! Me! Me! Gimme!"

The Lawyer, who evokes Satan for the Cardinal, is the chief instrument of Albee's mutilating dialogue. Not only does he thrust at the Cardinal; he sneers endearments to the Butler, and he woos Miss Alice as "clinically" as he fondles her. At his first meeting with Julian he belittles the Cardinal and humiliates Julian. After shooting Julian, the Lawyer directs the death scene, with no pity for the dying martyr. The Butler characterizes the Lawyer: "You're a cruel person, straight through; it's not cover; you're hard and cold, saved by dedication; just that." And yet, both the Cardinal and the Butler call the Lawyer "good," for he *is* good in his dedication to Tiny Alice, and his virulent wit sparks through the play's dark mystery.

In *Virginia Woolf* George's wit lashes out to "Get the Guests," but his cruelties zero in on Martha, whose illusion he murders. Despite the four characters in that play, the sustained duel is between George and Martha. In *Tiny Alice* the Lawyer lashes out indiscriminately, though he claims never to have shot anyone

before Julian. The deed of murder is his, but the responsibility is shared by the other three; murder is "an accident"—"What does it matter . . . one man . . . in the face of so much"—for the dedicated agents of Tiny Alice.

On Julian's wedding day, which becomes his death day, the Lawyer sneeringly dubs him Frank Fearnought. Frightened that he may be married to Tiny Alice, Frank Fearnought threatens to return to his asylum; it is then that the Lawyer shoots Julian. The surrogates are evidently charged with wedding Julian to the castle in which Tiny Alice dwells, the castle which *is* Tiny Alice. Married by the Lawyer's shot rather than the Cardinal's ceremony, Julian slowly proceeds to pattern his passion on that of Christ.

Earlier, Julian used clichés of ecstasy for a business deal: "That God has seen fit to let me be His instrument in this undertaking." Dying, Julian flings the same word at the Lawyer, as a last insult: "Instrument." Albee's play has developed the Lawyer as the instrument of Absurd reality, which is Tiny Alice. Julian, on the other hand, is first and last the instrument of his own imagination. He is both Everyman and the victim of the "awful humor" of Tiny Alice, precisely because he claims to reject illusion for reality. *That* is his illusion, with which he commits himself to an asylum. And rather than accept the reality of Tiny Alice, he is ready to commit himself again but is prevented by the Lawyer's fatal shot. The cynical lucid Lawyer has already foretold the pattern of Julian's final behavior, mixing the formal and the colloquial in the same speech: "face the inevitable and call it what you have always wanted. How to come out on top, going under."

Because he bends his imagination to embrace the inevitable, Julian achieves the difficult martyrdom he seeks. Onstage the long dying scene borders on the ridiculous, as Julian's initial resistance to the inevitable is ridiculous. But, "going under," he summons the herioc illusion of his culture; not a "Gingerbread God with the raisin eyes," but a human god crucified for man. Julian dies in imitation of Christ, deaf to Tiny monstrous Alice, who comes thumping and panting to devour him. The curtain falls on blackness, Alice, truth, reality, after Julian has been crucified in his illusion. Our lasting impression is that of a hero—vulnerable, loquacious, willfully blind, but nevertheless heroic in the intensity of his imagination.

Even puzzled audiences have been involved in Julian's plight, which the Butler describes: "Is walking on the edge of an abyss, but is balancing." Albee's next play, *A Delicate Balance,* is named for that perilous equilibrium. Like *Virginia Woolf*, the play presents a realistic surface; as in *Virginia Woolf*, a love relationship in one couple is explored through the impact of another couple. There is enough talking and drinking to convey the impression of a muted, diluted *Virginia Woolf*. And yet *A Delicate Balance*, like *Tiny Alice*, is death-obsessed symbolism.

Each of the six characters of *A Delicate Balance* "is walking on the edge of an abyss, but is balancing"; a middle-aged marriage is balancing too, until a makeshift home in a "well-appointed suburban house" is threatened by both family and friends. In Friday night Act I, terror-driven friends seek refuge in the family home; in Saturday night Act II, the master of the house, Tobias, assures his friends of their welcome, but his daughter Julia reacts hysterically to their presence. In Sunday morning Act III, the friends know that they are not welcome, know that they would not have welcomed, and they leave. The delicate balance of the home is preserved.

The play begins and ends, however, on a different delicate balance—that of the mind of Agnes, mistress of the house, wife of Tobias, mother of Julia, sister of Claire. In convoluted Jamesian sentences she opens and closes the play with doubts about her sanity; at the beginning she also extends these doubts to an indefinite "you"—"that each of you wonders if each of *you* might not . . ." As we meet the other members of the family, we can understand the wonder: Claire the chronic drunk, Julia the chronic divorcée, and Tobias who heads the house. Though Agnes starts and finishes the play on her doubts about sanity, each of the acts dramatizes the precarious stability of the other members of the family: first Claire, then Julia, and finally Tobias. In each case the balance is preserved, a little more delicate, perhaps, for being threatened.

Each member of the family contributes to the atmosphere of emptiness, but no one exists in a vacuum; they are bound by love. In Claire's words to Tobias, "You love Agnes and Agnes loves Julia and Julia loves me and I love you . . . Yes, to the depths of our self-pity and our greed. What else but love?" Claire's definition may be brushed by modern psychology, but Albee's plays are never reducible to psychology. If Agnes is responsible for Claire's continuous drinking and Julia's four marriages, she is also concerned "to keep in shape." Blaming the others for their faults, she describes such blame as the "souring side of love" in this drama about the limits of love.

Agnes early characterizes the family to Tobias: "your steady wife, your alcoholic sister-in-law and occasional visits . . . from our melancholy Julia." But her description is only a first approximation; her own steadiness is severely strained, Claire insists that she is not "a alcoholic," and Julia is more hysterical than melancholy. By Act III a harassed Tobias, having suffered his Passion, offers a contrasting description of the same family: "And you'll all sit down and watch me carefully; smoke your pipes and stir the cauldron; watch." He thus groups wife, daughter, sister-in-law as three witches, or the three Fates "who make all the decisions, really rule the game . . ." and who preside over the term of life, until death cuts it off.

As in other Albee plays, death lurks in the dialogue of *A Delicate Balance*, but death is not actualized in this drama; violence is confined to a single slap, a glass of orange juice poured on the rug, and an ineffectual threat with a gun. In words, however, Claire urges Tobias to shoot them all, first Agnes, then Julia, and herself last. Agnes suggests that Claire kill herself, and Claire in turn asks Agnes, "Why don't you die?" It is this sisterly exchange between Claire and Agnes that inspires Tobias to his digressive monologue, his cat story. Because his cat inexplicably stopped liking him, Tobias first slapped her and then had her killed. Out of the depths of his self-pity and greed, he had her killed.

Like Jerry's dog story, Tobias' cat story (suggested by director Alan Schneider) is an analogue for the whole play of which it is part. As Tobias kills the cat, he will effectively kill his friends, Harry and Edna, when he denies them a home. As Claire and Agnes approve his conduct toward the cat, Claire and Julia will approve his conduct toward Harry and Edna. The death of the cat maintains Tobias' delicate emotional balance in spite of his bad conscience, and the departure of Harry and Edna will maintain Tobias' delicate family balance in spite of his bad conscience.

The threat of death is almost personified by Harry and Edna. Julia tries to aim her father's gun at the visitors, and Agnes calls their terror a plague. In demanding that Tobias make a decision with respect to Harry and Edna, Agnes reminds him of the intimate details of their sexual life after the death of their son, Teddy. By the end of the play, Harry and

Edna, conscious of their own mortality, decide to leave, taking their plague with them.

A Delicate Balance is itself in most delicate balance between the cruel kindness of its surface and dark depths below, between a dead child and a new dawn, between ways of living and ways of loving. Albee has posed his equilibrium discreetly without the symbolic histrionics of *Tiny Alice,* without the coruscating dialogue of *Virginia Woolf.* At the most general level, the arrival of Harry and Edna raises the question of the limits of love; Tobias to Harry: "I find my liking you has limits . . . BUT THOSE ARE MY LIMITS! NOT YOURS!" And Edna to the other women: "the only skin you've ever known . . . is your own." Harry and Edna reveal the terror beneath bland surfaces. Before their arrival, Agnes thanks Tobias for a life without mountains or chasms, "a rolling, pleasant land." But the plague can arrive in rolling, pleasant lands, and it is carried by one's best friends.

In Harry and Edna, Albee creates prismatic symbols, for they are at once Tobias and Agnes and their friend-enemies. Described in the players' list as "very much like Agnes and Tobias," Edna and Harry live in the same suburb and belong to the same club. They are godparents to Julia, as Agnes and Tobias are her parents. When Harry serves drinks, Agnes remarks that he is "being Tobias." When Edna scolds Julia, Albee's scenic direction indicates that she "become[s] Agnes." Just before leaving, Edna speaks in the convoluted formal sentences of Agnes.

Otherwise, however, Harry and Edna do not sound like Tobias and Agnes, and they did not look like them in the original production supervised by Albee. Edna weeps whereas Agnes rarely cries; Edna shows desire whereas Agnes conceals it. As clearsighted Claire (Albee's pun) points out to Tobias, all he shares with Harry is the memory of a summer infidelity with the same girl (who may be Claire). Tobias denies being frightened, while fright ambushes Harry and Edna. Harry admits honestly what Tobias conceals clumsily: "I wouldn't take them in." At the last, when her best friends leave, Agnes lapses into a rare cliché: "Don't be strangers," and Edna replies, "Oh, good Lord, how could we be? Our lives are . . . the same." Rather than being *like* Agnes and Tobias, Edna and Harry are *the same as* Agnes and Tobias—minus a family.

Terror drives Harry and Edna from their house because a couple is inadequate bulwark against emptiness; they are free of the blood ties which protect one from the loneliness of self and the encroachment of living death. Harry and Edna come onstage after a family conversation about the bonds of love; their terror has no cause: "WE WERE FRIGHTENED . . . AND THERE WAS NOTHING." They were frightened *because* there was nothing.

In dramatizing the failure of love, Albee is ascetically sparing of his dazzling dialogue and subtle imagery. Though he does not quite indulge in the fallacy of imitative form, he implies that a drama with emptiness at its center must echo in hollowness. Each time two characters start a verbal thrust-and-parry, the spark is damped. Each of the characters apologizes at least once, snuffing out verbal fireworks. Damped, too, are the few threads of imagery—the household, childhood, helping, and sinking.

Sparing his imagery, Albee plays upon the verb *want* to sustain the delicate balance. Its double meaning, wish and lack, were already suggested in *Tiny Alice*, and Albee exploits this ambiguity in *A Delicate Balance*. Claire wishes Agnes to die but doesn't know whether she want it. Hysterical, Julia shifts from "they [Harry and Edna] want" to "I WANT . . . WHAT IS MINE!!" Agnes asks Harry and Edna pointedly, "What do you *really* . . . *want*? And some

minutes later, Edna replies, playing on the same verb: "if all at once we . . . NEED . . . we come where we are wanted, where we know we are expected, not only where we want." Harry insistently questions Tobias: "Do you *want* us here?" And in Tobias' final aria, he shifts from: "I WANT YOU HERE!" to "I DON'T WANT YOU HERE! I DON'T LOVE YOU! BUT BY GOD . . . YOU STAY!!" Love is lack and love is wish in *A Delicate Balance*, and Albee suggests that the human condition is to be bounded by want—lack and wish.

Each of the sisters uses her own rhythm to state the play's theme:

AGNES: There *is* a balance to be maintained, after all, though the rest of you teeter, uncaring, *assuming* you're on level ground . . . by divine right, I gather, though that is hardly so. . . .

CLAIRE: We can't have changes—throws the balance off.

The death of their son, Teddy, has thrown off the balance in the home of Tobias and Agnes, who teetered in a household that gradually took on the new balance of a home. Rather than upset the balance, Claire and Harry both lie to Agnes about the infidelity of Tobias. Rather than upset the balance, the family members play out their identity patterns, with only momentary shifts: Agnes poses as Julia's father, Tobias imitates Julia's hysteria, Claire plays a Tobias who explains to a judge the murder of his family, Julia spouts the opinions of her most recent husband, and Claire may be the nameless upended girl whom Tobias and Harry seduced one "dry and oh, so wet July." Edna speaks of and for them all when she summarizes her recognition of the delicacy of all balance, which is life: "It's sad to come to the end of it, isn't it, nearly the end; so much more of it gone by . . . than left, and still not know—still not have learned

. . . the boundaries, what we may not do . . . not ask, for fear of looking in a mirror."

In generalizing the predicament of his characters into the human condition, Albee relies on biblical associations of "house," as on associations of the names of the two couples, and of the three days between Good Friday and Easter Sunday, when Christ suffered his Passion. Harry, whom clear-sighted Claire calls "old Harry," is a nickname of the devil, whereas Agnes is the lamb of God. The two couples, who are identical, range from angelic expressions of love to diabolic noncommitment. The other two names, Tobias and Edna, figure in the Book of Tobit; by angelic intervention Tobias was able to marry Sara, though her first seven bridegrooms died before possessing her; the mother of Sara was Edna. Albee's parallels with the Book of Tobit are obscure; nevertheless, the Book of Tobit is concerned, like *A Delicate Balance*, with ties of blood and with the burial of the dead. Albee's Tobias is occasionally called Toby or Tobe, and like his biblical eponym, he is faced with the problem of Being, assaulted by death.

In Albee's "two inter-related plays," *Box* and *Quotations from Chairman Mao Tse-tung*, he again explores being threatened by death. Like Proust, Albee finds that art alone conserves traces of being, and he conveys this by a unique dramatic form. Nothing happens onstage. The plays deny passing time, and the set abstracts specific place.

Box presents us with the titular box that takes up *"almost all of a small stage opening."* While we look at the box, in a constant bright light, we hear the disembodied voice of a woman, which *"should seem to be coming from nearby the spectator."* In the second of the two inter-related plays, *Quotations from Mao Tse-tung* (about eight times the length of *Box*), an ocean liner appears within the outline of the box. Aboard are four visible characters—Mao Tse-tung and an Old Woman who addresses the audience directly, a Long-Winded Lady in a deck chair who *"uses as a sounding board"* a silent clergyman in his deck chair. The three monologues are soon punctuated by phrases from the disembodied voice of *Box*. In a final *Reprise* about half the *Box* monologue is heard while we watch the four silhouettes of *Mao*—now silent. Throughout both plays we see a box, that three-dimensional building-block in space. The four characters, as Liliane Kerjan suggests, sail upon a sea of infinite time: the past of the Old Woman, the present of the Long-Winded Lady, the future of Chairman Mao, and the eternity of the silent clergyman.

Though the voice of *Box* does not emanate from the stage box, it uses that figure as a springboard. Albee has already used boxes in *The Sandbox* and *The American Dream*, where they were associated with Grandma, who is close to death. And coffin associations spring readily to mind in *Box*. But the voice of *Box* moves quickly beyond the visible, to the possibility of a rocking chair in the box, to generalizations about crafts, and on to art. Through a lyric threnody of loss, the voice suggests that art is powerless to prevent catastrophe— "seven hundred million babies dead"—and that the very practice of art is a kind of corruption in times of disaster. But only art can give us "the memory of what we have not known," can introduce us to experiences we cannot otherwise know, as sea sounds can frighten the landlocked. In a world where "nothing belongs" art strives for order.

Mao opens the second of the inter-related plays with a fable from Chapter XXI of the Red Book, which glorifies the Chinese masses. Mao then moves on to Communist theory and tactics, growing more and more aggressive in language, though *"his tone is always reasonable"* and his purpose always pedagogic. Many of his quotations are drawn from Chapter VI of the "little red book," "Imperialism and All Reactionaries are Paper Tigers." In that chapter the arch-imperialist is the United States, so Mao's final words damn America: "People of the world, unite and defeat the U.S. aggressors and all their running dogs." Mao's patiently positive attitude culminates in an injunction to widespread killing.

The Old Woman "*might nod in agreement with Mao now and again*," perhaps because she is poor, perhaps because she feels oppressed. We cannot know the reason, since her words, like those of Mao, are restricted to quotation—from Will Carleton's "Over the Hill to the Poor-House." The persona of that poem whines her way through rejection by each of her six children, and she closes on an accusation disguised as prayer: "And God'll judge between us; but I will al'ays pray/That you shall never suffer the half I do today."

Mao has delivered a formulaic diatribe, the Old Woman a formulaic lament, but the Long-Winded Lady is wholly personal. She starts with an onomatopoeic splash, imagining the reaction of "theoretical . . . onwatchers." Associationally, she continues to a childhood memory of breaking her thumb, then a more recent recollection of a taxi going wild. As she enters with a plate of crullers on the last bloody scene, the Long-Winded Lady comments on the utter inadequacy of any response to disaster. More and more, the theme of death begins to link her disparate associations: uncle, sister, and husband speak of death in her monologue, and her husband was aware of the perpetual process of dying before he was attacked by the cancer that killed him. Though his dying is now over, "his *death* stays." And it is with that death that the Long-Winded Lady lives, having no communion with her daughter, and no relationship with anyone else.

Finally, toward the end of the play, the Long-Winded Lady describes the opening splash in detail. It is *her* splash, but she describes it without a single "I." She fell off an ocean liner (like the one on which we see her) *splash* into the ocean. Ironically and improbably, however, she did not sink but was rescued. After congratulations came questions: Could anyone have pushed her? Did she throw herself off? Try to kill herself? The Long-Winded Lady closes her monologue and the *Mao* part of Albee's play with a half-laughing denial: "Good heavens, no; *I* have nothing to die for." It is a brilliant twist of the cliché: "I have nothing to live for." We live—most of us—by natural momentum, but voluntary death demands a dedication beyond the power of the Long-Winded Lady—or of most of us in the long wind of our lives.

As the disembodied woman's voice opens the "inter-related plays," so it closes them in a "reprise." But between *Box* and *Reprise*, Albee expunges catastrophe from the Voice's monologue, having suggested disaster in each of the three separate monologues of *Mao*. *Reprise* retains the *Box* images of music, birds, order, and an art that hurts. Though the Voice is matter-of-fact, even "*schoolmarmish*," it is lyrical in the hint that emotion alone invests events with meaning, and yet the emotion evoked by art cannot act upon events. Pain can merely be contained by the order of art— "Box."

From Chekhov on, we have been familiar with characters who talk past each other, rather than engaging one another in dialogue. But in *Mao* each of the characters is unaffected by the other's speech; we cannot even tell whether they hear it. And the speeches are linked not by plot but by the theme of death. Stylistically, they differ, but they all use repetition. Mao emphasizes single words or ideas by reiteration.

The Old Woman does not recite Carleton's poem straight through, but chooses certain lines or stanzas to linger over and dwell upon. Occasional phrases of the Long-Winded Lady recur—above all, "dying." After the initial performance of *Box*, all the words of the disembodied voice are repetitions, and the final *Reprise* is what it means—a repetition. The *Reprise* joins end to beginning of Albee's play in a kind of musical parallel for a box, but since music moves in time, repetition becomes thematic through the strains of the dialogue.

Because the Long-Winded Lady alone has a personal, a *dramatic* monologue, she is at the center of Albee's play. Seeking the counsel of a silent clergyman, she is implicitly threatened by the two other figures on this ship of fools within the box of art—the ruthless system of Mao and the maudlin poverty of the Old Woman. Long-winded, unrooted, the Lady is a middle-aged, middle-class Miss America, that dying outpost of Western civilization. But unlike George, Julian, or Tobias, who also represent the Western tradition in Albee's plays, the Long-Winded Lady utters no words of optimism or heroism. Harrowed by death, she offers the stuff of her life through the words of Albee's art. In these "inter-related plays" Albee has used the symbol of a box as both coffin and work of art. Living experience is coffined by the artifact of art, but, paradoxically, such coffining is the only way to preserve the experience. *Box-Mao-Box* is Albee's Cubist play, not only in form but in content. Like Cubist collage, *Box-Mao-Box* is *about* the art it is.

All Over returns to more traditional imitation of an action. As in *The Intruder* by Maeterlinck (who is mentioned in Albee's play) or *Waiting for Godot* by Beckett, the action is waiting. A family waits at the deathbed of its head. Seven people wait for a man to die.

"Waiting for death" might summarize these plays, as it might summarize the human condition. In *All Over* Albee moves death to the dead center of his drama. As the play's Nurse phrases it: "Death, yes; well, it gets us where we live, doesn't it?"

In the sequence of Albee's work, *All Over* seems to follow *A Delicate Balance* after the interlude of *Box-Mao-Box*. Both *A Delicate Balance* and *All Over* focus on a family at a point of crisis—Husband, Wife, Sister, Daughter in *A Delicate Balance;* Wife, Son, Daughter, and, almost family, Best Friend and Mistress in *All Over*. Both plays are set in a single large tastefully furnished room which seems to mute loud or vulgar sounds. The very language is muted in both plays, where short exchanges are punctuated by digressive monologues of recollection. Though *All Over* accommodates several monologues, the density of recollection is thin. One has the impression that the characters of *All Over* have spent their lives waiting for life, as they are now waiting for death. And that impression is reinforced by the paucity of physical action onstage. Behind a hospital screen backstage, a man is invisibly dying, but onstage the few exits and entrances become events: The Daughter slams out of the room three times, The Son leaves twice, and The Best Friend once. Doctor and Nurse occasionally disappear behind the screen of the dying man. Just before the Act I curtain The Daughter allows two Photographers and a Reporter to enter the stage room, but The Wife and Mistress drive them out.

The action of the play is rhythmed by a few signs of tension: near the beginning of the play The Wife and The Daughter exchange slaps. Toward the middle The Doctor announces that the dying man has skipped three heartbeats. Near the end The Nurse emerges from behind the hospital screen with bloody uniform (a vivid scarlet and white that recalls the death of Bessie Smith in Albee's second play). Physically, the action of *All Over* is nearly all over, lying in individual and collective reactions to the process of dying.

All the family is onstage almost all the time. Their type names darken the emphasis upon the central situation, and their type names darken the fact that the characters depend on the dying man for their definition of identity. In waiting for death, the seven characters connive at a kind of murder, as we all do when we outlive those we love.

Unusual in the family grouping is the inclusion of The Mistress, who says explicitly that she is always the Outsider at time of ritual. In this group, however, only The Daughter registers hostility toward her, whereas The Wife accepts her with something like friendship. Albee suggests the repetitive nature of the Wife-Mistress sharing of the life of a man. The Newspaper people· "have their families . . . their wives, their mistresses." The Nurse was long ago The Mistress in another triangle, where the dying man bears the only name we hear in the play—Dr. Dey, which puns on day, a metaphor for man's life. During that brief period a man lives both privately and publicly; he lives through a series of particular intimacies and a sequence of recognized rituals, and he is faithful in his fashion to both aspects of living. Onstage The Wife and The Mistress are aware of the intermittent primacy of the other. Only in a brief scene before the end does The Wife accuse The Mistress while the two are alone onstage.

Albee's use of type names and static situation caused reviewers to condemn *All Over* as "abstract," but Albee is experientially concrete in his depiction of reactions to dying. In the face of death, one becomes one's relationship to the dying person, and yet, in the last hours of what is ambiguously still called life, one registers that relationship through trivia, tensions, or an occasional sick joke—"Is it flame or worm?" Dutifully, one may try to summon memories, to discard stray thought, but the wayward mind will not be reined. A point of grammar may loom large; not "Is he dead?" but "Has he . . . *died*?"

Practical problems may recall us to the immediacy of death, as, in *All Over*, distaste for hospitals pits The Wife and The Mistress against The Daughter and The Nurse. Disposal of the body leads to brief battle between The Wife, who wants traditional burial, and The Mistress, who wants cremation. Though both try to re-create the man they both love, each can lean only on a pair of memories. The Wife recalls his traveling halfway round the world to his son's sickbed. When the children were grown, however, he asked incredulously whether he had really made them. The Mistress recalls that he didn't know about the affair between The Wife and The Best Friend because she ensured that he didn't. And she recalls that he missed his family at Christmas. The Son, The Daughter, and The Best Friend voice no memories, but The Son breaks down upon seeing the dying man's toilet articles—in their usual place in the bathroom. Here too, Albee is true to experience, for things often dominate a death-scene. Like the unnamed characters, unseen things reach out to generalize their meaning.

Generalization is not the abstraction for which Albee has been faulted. His characters are no more abstract than those of *Pilgrim's Progress*, who go through a comparable Valley of the Shadow of Death. Muffled hostility individualizes them: The Wife vs. The Daughter, The Wife vs. The Son, The Best Friend vs. The Son, and at the last The Wife vs. The Mistress. For us the characters take on varying density to the degree that they reveal an individual past. That of the family members is paper thin, but The Mistress has had three other loves in her life, and The Best Friend has had an insane wife whose emotional hold on him is still stronger than that of The Wife, with whom he has had an affair.

Because The Mistress and The Best Friend can recall a past, they can imagine a future of adjustment to the absence of the dying man. But the three members of the family will go their separate ways into a kind of dissolution. The Daughter's slamming of the door, The Son's sobbing, and The Wife's finally incantatory repetitions of "Because I'm unhappy" achieve emotional summits for this family that has lived in its shadow of death. For them, as for the new corpse, it will soon be "all over."

The play's title is heard in its last line—The Doctor's announcement of the death for which they have all been waiting. The two colorless words are a pun. Throughout the play the dying man has been "all over" in two senses—ubiquitous and dead. In spite of their poverty of recollection, the characters have lived largely through their relationship to the invisible man behind the screen. He has been "all over" them, and at the end it is "all over" for them.

A few minutes before the play ends, The Wife realizes: "All we've done . . . is think about ourselves." That is all most of us do in the face of death, and it is what we have heard this family do in the face of its particular death. We have heard it through Albee's deliberately stiff and stylized language, which Harold Clurman has aptly called "frozen fire."

Several reviewers have compared Albee's language to that of Henry James or Ivy Compton-Burnett, and such comparison is apposite for the bravura speeches of The Wife, The Mistress, or The Best Friend. But like the dog story in *The Zoo Story* or the cat story in *A Delicate Balance*, such pieces are rare, and the bulk of the dialogue consists of brief cool phrases, meaning more than they seem to say. The title is the most obvious example of this, but the opening quibble about grammar poses the problem of human nothingness: non-being should not use the verb "to be."

Deliberately muted, Albee's language can characterize or comment with extreme economy. In Act II of *All Over*, under the cover of extreme fatigue, characters repeat words of Act I, but with cumulative meaning. The Daughter's repetitions of "Stop it" contrast with The Mistress's repetitions of "Ah well!" The Daughter is the only character who never says "I'm sorry" (though she wants to waken her mother to tell her that), and she alone is empty of the grief that the others feel to different degrees. That The Wife repeats "I'm sorry" most often implies that her grief is deepest, though she manages her stiff upper lip until almost the end.

In a comparably telling way, Albee deploys the phrase "All right." The Daughter uses it to cut short her mother's account of all that is *wrong* in her life. Sporadically, several characters ask whether one or the other is "all right." It is used absently when a character has not been paying attention. At a climactic moment, when The Nurse enters from behind the screen, she quiets the group with: "It's all right," though the evidence of wrongness—a hemorrhage—is splotched on her uniform.

In their reflective monologues the characters sound similar, but this is Albee's way of underlining the similarity of human reaction to death—morassed in selfishness. In spite of such self-centeredness—almost too explicitly recognized in the play itself—there has been cross-talk, and words have communicated briefly, sharing an experience of death. And who but Albee could have written these lines about a dying man in our scientific age: "A city seen from the air? The rail lines and the roads? Or, an octopus: the body of the beast, the tentacles, electrical controls, recorders, modulators, breath and heart and brain waves, and the tubes?, in either arm and in the nostrils. Where had he gone? In all that . . . equipment. I thought for a moment *he* was keeping *it* . . . functioning. Tubes and wires."

Happy endings are not for Albee; nor does he strain, like Eugene O'Neill and Arthur Miller, for tragedy. Rather, Albee shares with Absurdist writers, in his words, "an absorption-in-art of certain existentialist and post-existentialist philosophical concepts having to do, in the main, with man's attempts to make sense for himself out of his senseless position in a world which makes no sense—which makes no sense because the moral, religious, political and social structures man has erected to 'illusion' himself have collapsed." In successive plays Albee has dramatized man's several attempts to make sense *of* himself and *for* himself.

Albee has been moving away from political and social structures toward moral and religious illusion. Thus, the greedy, conformist American family of *The American Dream* differs markedly from the greedy, love-bound family of *A Delicate Balance*, as apocalyptic Jerry of *The Zoo Story* differs markedly from apocalyptic Julian of *Tiny Alice*. Common to several of Albee's plays is the existentialist view of an Outsider who suffers at the hands of the Establishment—social, moral, or religious—which announces itself in "peachy-keen" clichés that indict those who mouth them— Peter, Mommy, the Nurse, Nick. Albee has moved from this American anti-American idiom into the metaphysical suggestiveness of *Tiny Alice, A Delicate Balance, Box,* and *All Over*. His language accommodates both colloquialism and convolution, both excruciating specificity and relentless generality.

The shadow of death darkens all Albee's plays, but witty dialogue sparks through his first few plays. Transitional, *Virginia Woolf* touches on the fear in human love without illusion. *Tiny Alice* probes the heroism of human illusion about the divine. *A Delicate Balance* returns to a shrunken earth; the house appointed for all living is shaken by the living dead, but accident and brinkmanship salvage the equilibrium. *Box* theatricalizes art and the inadequacy of art in the face of death. *All Over* presents a waiting for death, omnipresent and ineluctable.

Like the Absurdists whom he defends, Albee is anguished because men die and they cannot make themselves happy with illusion. He absorbs this condition into art by counterpointing interrogation and repetition, familiar phrase and diversified resonance, repartee and monologue, minute gesture and cosmic sweep, comic wit and a sense of tragedy. The Albeegory is that distinctive allegorical drama in which ideas are so skillfully blended into people that we do not know how to divorce them or how to care about one without the other.

Selected Bibliography

WORKS OF EDWARD ALBEE

PLAYS
The Zoo Story. New York: Coward-McCann, 1959.
The Death of Bessie Smith. New York: Coward-McCann, 1959.
The Sandbox. New York: Coward-McCann, 1959.
Fam and Yam. New York: Coward-McCann, 1960.
The American Dream. New York: Coward-McCann, 1960.
Bartleby. 1961. (Unpublished libretto adaptation of Herman Melville's short story.)

Who's Afraid of Virginia Woolf? New York: Atheneum, 1963.

The Ballad of the Sad Café. New York: Atheneum, 1963. (Adaptation of Carson McCullers' novel.)

Tiny Alice. New York: Atheneum, 1965.

Malcolm. New York: Atheneum, 1965. (Adaptation of James Purdy's novel.)

A Delicate Balance. New York: Atheneum, 1966.

Everything in the Garden. New York: Atheneum, 1967. (Adaptation of Giles Cooper's play.)

Box and *Quotations from Chairman Mao Tsetung.* New York: Atheneum, 1969.

All Over. New York: Atheneum, 1971.

ESSAYS

"Which Theatre Is the Absurd One?" *New York Times Magazine,* February 25, 1962, pp. 30-31. (Reprinted in *American Playwrights on Drama,* edited by Horst Frenz. New York: Hill and Wang, 1965. Pp. 168-74).

"Introduction" to *Three Plays,* by Noel Coward. New York: Doubleday, 1965.

"Apartheid in the Theater," *New York Times,* July 30, 1967, II, pp. 1, 6.

"Albee Says 'No, Thanks'—to John Simon," *New York Times,* September 10, 1967, II, pp. 1, 8.

"The Future Belongs to Youth," *New York Times,* November 26, 1967, II, pp. 1, 7.

CRITICAL STUDIES

Ballew, Leighton M. "Who's Afraid of *Tiny Alice?*" *Georgia Review,* 20:292-99 (Fall 1966).

Baxandall, Lee. "The Theatre of Edward Albee," *Tulane Drama Review,* 9:19-40 (Summer 1965).

Bigsby, C. W. E. "Edward Albee," in *Confrontation and Commitment.* London: MacGibbon and Kee, 1967. Pp. 71-92.

Brustein, Robert. *Seasons of Discontent.* New York: Simon and Schuster, 1965. Pp. 26-29, 46-49, 145-48, 155-58.

Chester, Alfred. "Edward Albee: Red Herrings and White Whales," *Commentary,* 35:296-301 (April 1963).

Coleman, D. C. "Fun and Games: Two Pictures of Heartbreak House," *Drama Survey,* 5:223-36 (Winter 1966-67).

Debusscher, Gilbert. *Edward Albee: Tradition and Renewal.* Brussels: American Studies Center, 1967.

Downer, Alan S., ed. "An Interview with Edward Albee," in *The American Theater.* Washington: USIS, 1967. Pp. 123-36.

Dukore, Bernard F. "A Warp in Albee's *Woolf,*" *Southern Speech Journal,* 30:261-68 (Spring 1965).

———. "Tiny Albee," *Drama Survey,* 5:60-66 (Spring 1966).

Esslin, Martin. *The Theatre of the Absurd.* New York: Doubleday, 1961. Pp. 225-26.

Flanagan, William. "Edward Albee," in *Writers at Work.* New York: Viking, 1967. Pp. 321-46.

Flasch, Mrs. Harold A. "Games People Play in *Who's Afraid of Virginia Woolf?*" *Modern Drama,* 10:280-88 (December 1967).

Goodman, Henry. "The New Dramatists: Edward Albee," *Drama Survey,* 2:72-79 (June 1962).

Gould, Jean. "Edward Albee and the Current Scene," in *Modern American Playwrights.* New York: Apollo Editions, 1966. Pp. 273-86.

Gussow, Mel. "Albee: Odd Man In on Broadway," *Newsweek,* 61:49-52 (February 4, 1963).

Hamilton, Kenneth. "Mr. Albee's Dream," *Queen's Quarterly,* 70:393-99 (Autumn 1963).

Hankiss, Elemér. "Who's Afraid of Edward Albee?" *New Hungarian Quarterly,* 5:168-74 (Autumn, 1964).

Harris, Wendell V. "Morality, Absurdity, and Albee," *Southwest Review,* 49:249-56 (Summer 1964).

Hilfer, Anthony Channell. "George and Martha: Sad, Sad, Sad," in *Seven Contemporary Authors,* edited by T. B. Whitbread. Austin: University of Texas Press, 1966. Pp. 119-40.

Knepler, Henry. "Conflict of Traditions in Edward Albee," *Modern Drama,* 10:274-79 (December 1967).

Kostelanetz, Richard. "Edward Albee," in *On Contemporary Literature.* New York: Avon Books, 1964. Pp. 225-31.

Lewis, Allan. "The Fun and Games of Edward Albee," in *American Plays and Playwrights of the Contemporary Theatre.* New York: Crown, 1965. Pp. 81-98.

Lyons, Charles R. "Two Projections of the Isolation of the Human Soul: Brecht's *Im Dickicht der Staedte* and Albee's *The Zoo Story*," *Drama Survey,* 4:121-38 (Summer 1965).

McDonald, Daniel. "Truth and Illusion in *Who's Afraid of Virginia Woolf?*" *Renascence,* 17:63-69 (Winter 1964).

Markus, Thomas B. *"Tiny Alice* and Tragic Catharsis," *Educational Theatre Journal,* 17:225-33 (October 1965).

Miller, Jordan Y. "Myth and the American Dream: O'Neill to Albee," *Modern Drama,* 7:190-98 (September 1964).

Nelson, Gerald. "Edward Albee and His Well-Made Plays," *Tri-Quarterly,* 5:182-88 (n.d.).

Oberg, Arthur K. "Edward Albee: His Language and Imagination," *Prairie Schooner,* 40:139-46 (Summer 1966).

Phillips, Elizabeth C. "Albee and the Theatre of the Absurd," *Tennessee Studies in Literature,* 10:73-80 (1965).

Plotinsky, Melvin L. "The Transformations of Understanding: Edward Albee in the Theatre of the Irresolute," *Drama Survey,* 4:220-32 (Winter 1965).

Roy, Emil. *"Who's Afraid of Virginia Woolf?* and the Tradition," *Bucknell Review,* 13:27-36 (March 1965).

Rule, Margaret W. "An Edward Albee Bibliography," *Twentieth Century Literature,* 14:35-44 (April 1968).

Samuels, Charles Thomas. "The Theatre of Edward Albee," *Massachusetts Review,* 6:187-201 (Autumn-Winter 1964-65).

Schechner, Richard. "Who's Afraid of Edward Albee?" *Tulane Drama Review,* 7:7-10 (Spring 1963).

Schneider, Alan. "Why So Afraid?" *Tulane Drama Review,* 7:10-13 (Spring 1963).

Valgemae, Mardi. "Albee's Great God Alice," *Modern Drama,* 10:267-73 (December 1967).

Way, Brian. "Albee and the Absurd," in *American Theatre.* London: Edward Arnold, 1966. Pp. 188-207.

Witherington, Paul. "Language of Movement in Albee's *The Death of Bessie Smith,*" *Twentieth Century Literature,* 13:84-88 (July 1967).

Wolfe, Peter. "The Social Theatre of Edward Albee," *Prairie Schooner,* 39:248-62 (Fall 1965).

Zimbardo, Rose A. "Symbolism and Naturalism in Edward Albee's *The Zoo Story,*" *Twentieth Century Literature,* 8:10-17 (April 1962).

—*RUBY COHN*

Sherwood Anderson

1876-1941

*L*IFE, not death, is the great adventure." So reads the inscription engraved on Sherwood Anderson's tombstone in southwestern Virginia in accordance with a request he made not long before his death at sixty-four in 1941. At first glance, the buoyancy of the epitaph seems strangely at variance with the facts of his career. For a few triumphant years after the publication of *Winesburg, Ohio* (1919), Anderson was acclaimed a major figure of modern literature. He was regarded with Theodore Dreiser as a liberator of American letters from the debilitating effects of the genteel tradition. Then, in the mid-1920's, repudiated by critics, abandoned by his early discoverers, parodied by his protégés, he slipped from the foreground, even though his writing continued to influence diverse writers such as Ernest Hemingway, Hart Crane, Erskine Caldwell, Katherine Anne Porter, Henry Miller, William Faulkner, Nathanael West, and James T. Farrell.

Anderson thought humbly of himself at the end as merely a minor artist who had contributed only a minor classic—*Winesburg, Ohio* —to American culture. Still, it was his dedication as an artist that enabled him to sustain his faith in the adventure of life—and fully examined, his career truly justifies his epitaph. It was with grace and justice that Faulkner,

responding to an inquiry from a *Paris Review* interviewer in 1956, declared of Anderson's stature: "He was the father of my generation of American writers and the tradition of American writing which our successors will carry on. He has never received his proper evaluation."

The major theme of Anderson's writing is the tradegy of death in life: modern man, lacking personal identity and with his senses anesthetized, has become a spiritless husk unfitted for love of man and community. This perennial theme is common enough in our time, though it was relatively dormant in the late 1910's when Anderson first enunciated it. It became his leitmotiv when, in 1912, at the age of thirty-six, he suffered a nervous breakdown and rejected his past. Thereafter he viewed this event as a symbolic rebirth which had purified him of false values and freed him from the confines of deadening institutions.

The pattern is classic in Western culture. It has recurred often in American life since Puritan times, with special frequency in the nineteenth century after the rise of transcendentalism. But in the 1920's it was somewhat anachronistic for a man to present himself dramatically, not only as artist but also as human being, in the messianic role of someone who had achieved a second birth and now had come forth to utter prophetic truths. Nor did Anderson's lower-class origins in Ohio, his vaunted and obvious lack of education, his emphasis upon the American and the common, his bohemian dress and manners, his concern with lust and love, and his charismatic religious overtones make him more palatable either to the intellectual or to the average man.

The reasons for suspicion are understandable. It followed upon a perversion of the idealism and romanticism of Emerson, Thoreau, and Whitman by nineteenth-century disciples who, regardless of their original motives, too often degenerated into cultists and opportunists. Emerson and Whitman are not responsible for followers who took advantage of the masters' paradoxical universality and founded quasi-religious movements such as New Thought, which misused idealistic concepts to justify materialism. Nor should the masters be blamed for the phenomenon of an Elbert Hubbard, who had publicized his idealistic escape from business in the 1890's in order to pursue a life of pure art, plain living, and high thinking, then proceeded to befoul American culture with a shamelessly commercial literature, handicraft, art, and thought until he sank with the *Lusitania* in 1915. Yet many had been fooled by the Emersonian-Whitmanian pose of Hubbard, with the result that Anderson—who, like Hubbard, came from the Midwest, sported an arty costume, and had also worked in business and advertising—was regarded with some wariness even while his writing was being praised.

In private life, letters, and autobiographical publications, Anderson tenaciously mixed art and life until he became a fictional character for himself and his times. Many supposedly objective details in *A Story Teller's Story* (1924), *Tar* (1926), and the posthumous *Memoirs* (1942) were products of "fancy," a term he used interchangeably with "imagina-

tion." He preferred these imaginative constructions to "facts" which he believed concealed "the essence of things." The angry corrections of relatives and friends did not alter his belief that a man's vision of himself and his world contained more meaningful truth than did a birth certificate or an identification card. There was no real ground for embarrassment. In the opening pages of his autobiographical works, readers were forewarned at once about Anderson's method. There is something playful and ingenuous in such typical fictions as his Italian grandmother and his southern father; they happened to be profoundly true in revealing the surprise and shock of a passionate "Ohio Pagan" who couldn't otherwise explain the incongruity of having been spawned in an American Midwest dominated by what he regarded as the chilly values of its "Puritan" New England settlers.

Sherwood Anderson was born on September 13, 1876, in Camden, Ohio. He was the third child of Irwin M. Anderson, who made and sold leather harness, and Emma Smith Anderson. The Anderson family had moved about from town to town in Ohio before Sherwood's birth. A few years after that event, Irwin Anderson's small business failed and the Anderson family resumed its travels. Not until 1884 was a permanent home established, this time in Clyde, a small farm town.

The strain of economic difficulties and wandering seems to have affected the father, who began to drink heavily and was so often unemployed that the family's needs frequently were satisfied only by the children's earnings and the strenuous efforts of their mother. Irwin Anderson as father and fictional character was to be an obsessive and ambivalently treated concern of Sherwood's thought and art. He and the other children would feel that Emma Anderson's death in 1895 might have been caused by her husband's neglect and frivolity. But Irwin was nevertheless lovable, in many respects admirable. His misfortunes had not soured his temper, and he joyfully gave rein to his aptitudes for music, theater, and literature. If a parade or vaudeville performance had to be arranged, Irwin Anderson was the man for the job; he acted; he blew the cornet in a local band; he entranced his friends and children with skillfully told tales. Such a role could excite admiration and respect; there were penalties too—family hardships and the probability that town and family alike would consider one a quixotic clown and fool. It was not until Sherwood Anderson was in his mid-forties that he highly valued what he had earlier feared, namely, his similarity to his father.

Young Sherwood's willingness to take on odd jobs earned him money and the nickname of "Jobby." He worked as a farmhand in the surrounding country; in Clyde as grocery delivery boy, laborer in a newly established bicycle factory, and newsboy, and in various menial capacities in a livery stable and a racehorse stable, where he mingled happily with drivers, jockeys, grooms, and trainers. Though an average student, his various jobs and interests made it difficult for him to attend school regularly; he finally quit high school before graduation.

Anderson's life in Clyde ended when he left in 1896 for Chicago, where his brother Karl had gone earlier. For the next two years, Anderson was a manual laborer in a cold-storage warehouse. With the outbreak of the Spanish-American War, he volunteered for army service in Cuba. His regiment arrived there in January 1899, almost four months after hostilities had ceased. Though he never underwent the combat experience which other American novelists such as Hemingway, John Dos Passos, Thomas Boyd, and Faulkner were to in-

corporate into their fiction, Anderson had an opportunity to become aware of the problems faced by the individual in a mass society requiring conformity to a single mode of conduct. That Anderson knew how to adjust himself may be gauged from his attainment of a corporal's rank. It was probably this slight success which encouraged a belief—embodied most fully in an early novel, *Marching Men* (1917)—that a man as individual was ineffectual until, absorbed into a faceless mass led by a charismatic leader, he contributed his will and body to an invincible social entity.

At loose ends in 1900 after his army service, Sherwood again followed his brother, this time to Springfield, Ohio, where the latter was employed as an artist by the Crowell Publishing Company, which issued mass-circulation magazines. Aware of his need for more education, Anderson in September enrolled at Wittenberg Academy, a preparatory school, where he earned eleven grades of A and three of B for his proficiency in Latin, German, geometry, English, and physics. He was twenty-four years old at the time, but he did not feel it demeaning to pay for his food and lodging by working as a "chore boy" in the boardinghouse where he, Karl, and various editors, artists, advertising men, and teachers resided.

These men and women were the most culturally advanced Anderson had met as yet. Their interests in art and literature, as well as business, uncovered new, if limited, worlds of action and thought for him. But as it happens it was in the field of business that the Springfield group ultimately did most for him. Through the intercession of the advertising manager of Crowell, Anderson was appointed to the Chicago advertising office of the firm as a copywriter. He was among the first and not the last of modern American writers whose imagination and expression have been affected by such experience.

Anderson initially took to advertising with gusto and a belief in the efficacy of the products he touted and the means used to sell them. Businessmen whom he met in his later role as advertising salesman liked him because of his "charm, interest, and sympathy," his physical attractiveness and lively spirit. His mental alertness and sensitivity to the language of the average mind made him an irresistible copywriter. One of his associates related that Anderson "bragged to the office girls that he could get them good husbands by mail-order letters."

The most revealing expression of his attitudes is to be found in the inspirational articles and sketches he contributed to *Agricultural Advertising*, his firm's house organ, during 1903 and 1904. Written in a clumsy, banal style, these pieces on the whole echo the platitudes of popular American business philosophy, uncritically expounding the virtues of industry, acquisition, aggressive competition, optimism, success, and service, while chiding those who prated reform morality and ignored the ethical values and practices of the businessman. Though Anderson in later years would denounce success and extol failure, he never became an enthusiast of social reform except sporadically during the 1930's. He regarded social liberals and revolutionists as opportunists who concealed their search for power under showers of misleading "talk." During the 1930's, when most of those who had championed his work were involved in leftist activities, his unwillingness to commit himself fully to radical programs led to sharp criticism or neglect of his last writings.

Whatever confidence and success advertising brought Anderson—and it also enabled him in 1904 to marry Cornelia Lane, the daughter of a wealthy Ohio wholesaler of footwear—the afflatus of sales promotion did not continue to satisfy him. His rising sense of frustration was fanned by the genteel achievements of his wife, who had been graduated from Western Reserve University, possessed the traditional knowledge of literature and the arts which he lacked, and had even studied in Europe. In a conversation of the mid-1900's with a Chicago advertising associate before departing on a business trip, Anderson said that he had decided to choose between becoming "a millionaire or an artist." He explained that, "if only a man will put the making of money above all other things in life," wealth could be attained. The role of an artist was more difficult, "but if it is in a fellow, he can do it. I don't know what I shall do—paint, sculpt, maybe write. But I think I will come back determined on an artistic career."

The transition from copy writing to literature as art, which Anderson was to make, seemed easy and natural to him because in both language is manipulated to give an illusion of meaningful reality. His view was implicit in an advertising man's comment on a verbally gifted railroad man in one of Anderson's *Agricultural Advertising* sketches: "He knows how to use words and that's why I think he'd make an advertising man. How to use words, and say, Mr. Cowman, that's what advertising is, just using words; just picking them out like that fellow picked out his swear words and then dropping them down in just the right place so they seem to mean something. I don't want you to be making fun of that brakeman. . . . He's a word man, that brakeman is, and words are the greatest things ever invented."

Anderson's reverent attitude toward language was a wholesome sign of his promise as a writer. In the 1900's, it was useful to him because of his limited vocabulary and his unfamiliarity with the range of rhetorical devices to be found in literature. But his emphasis upon "words" as self-sufficient entities, and his lack of concern with their meaning, foreshadowed his later obsessive preoccupation with them. As he struggled unsuccessfully with the expression of ideas and emotional nuances in his first two novels, he came to believe that his failure resulted from the faulty character of his words rather than from the absence of that profound imaginative experience which willy-nilly finds vivid expression even in a limited language. "There is a story.—I cannot tell it.—I have no words," he would write in 1921.

This was to an extent only an element of the guileless and natural literary personality Anderson fashioned as a self-portrait. It came properly indeed from one whose advertising experience had shown him that words could be used without responsible interest in their human meaning and was determined not to repeat his errors. On the one hand then, Anderson's love and fear of the word stimulated great stylistic purity; on the other hand, this ambivalence also led on occasion to a "basic mistrust of language itself" and to the artistically destructive belief that "reality remains ultimately inexpressible" to which Anderson alluded in the epigraph of *A New Testament* (1927): "They talked and their lips said audible words but the voices of their inner selves went on uninterrupted."

Anderson continued to nourish hopes of an artistic career while adjusting himself to the responsibilities of a bourgeois husband who had fathered three children. Leaving Chicago in 1906, he returned to northern Ohio. During the next six years, he managed a mail-order business in Cleveland and later two paint manufacturing firms. In dress, country club membership, church attendance, and all other externals, Anderson conformed to the standards of respectable convention. But first secretly, in the night-time privacy of an attic at home, and later openly, in his office and elsewhere, Anderson began to write with such industry and devotion that friends and business acquain-

tances could not help becoming aware of his double existence. He centered more and more energy in his writing as an estrangement from his wife deepened in intensity and as financial difficulties made it likely that his business was going to fail.

On November 27, 1912, Anderson left his office in Elyria, Ohio, suddenly and was not heard from again until he turned up in Cleveland on December 1, disheveled and in a state of shock. In the Cleveland hospital to which he was taken, examining physicians diagnosed his condition as a mental collapse. Although he recovered quickly, the event was a turning point. He severed connections with his manufacturing business and, in order to support himself and his family, returned to his old Chicago advertising job in February 1913, bringing with him the manuscripts of *Windy McPherson's Son, Marching Men,* and other works.

Anderson's version of his departure from Elyria, presented in an article entitled "When I Left Business for Literature" (*Century,* August 1924) and incorporated in *A Story Teller's Story,* became a classic anecdote in the 1920's and 1930's. For Anderson and some younger writers, it symbolized the heroism of rebellion against the materialistic values of a business-dominated culture. Predictably, however, not all of his version was accurate. As he viewed the event in 1924 and later in the *Memoirs,* he ignored his psychic breakdown and slighted his precarious financial state, thus giving the impression that his flight had resulted from a wholly conscious decision to repudiate wealth and embrace art. To this extent, his story was misleading. But he also stated the essential truth and it was unimpeachable: after much struggle, he had committed himself to a disinterested life of art and thereafter had flaunted his disbelief in the moral integrity and social value of the advertising copy he continued to write so brilliantly until 1922.

Anderson's first two novels are apprentice efforts. He was never proud of these books, even when they were published. Later, in the *Memoirs*, he called them imitative and "immature." It is regrettable that Anderson permitted them to be published without extensive improvement, for in 1915, before their appearance, he was already writing the first brilliant tales of *Winesburg, Ohio* and undoubtedly was aware of the weaknesses of the novels. At this time, as later in his career, Anderson made the mistake of publishing work which did not reflect his achieved talent and thus gave rise to mistaken impressions of his progress and promise.

Although Anderson later said that he had tricked the reader with a happy ending, *Windy McPherson's Son* (1916) has a tragic or at least an ambivalent ending. Sam McPherson's search for meaning in life concludes in a chaos of emptiness and negation. The dominant tone is one of darkness and frustration, steadily increasing in intensity. Young Sam—eager to acquire wealth—flees to Chicago from his Iowa village and becomes a robber baron. He is diverted from his unsatisfying material quest after meeting a perfect woman who convinces him that he will achieve fulfillment by creating perfect children with her. This eugenic goal is abandoned after she proves incapable of giving birth. Sam returns to business and finance, attaining vast power but no more satisfaction than before. He rules faceless men and cannot discover his own face. The social reform faddishly taken up by his frustrated wife does not attract him. In all action, idealistic or selfish, theories are discarded and the urge for power nakedly revealed as motive force. Sam flees Chicago in desperation.

Dressed in the costume of a Whitmanian rough, Sam McPherson wanders about as vagabond and workman "to seek Truth, to seek God" among the common people. He finds labor confused and its leaders power-hungry. Love is missing. Dissipation and vice have destroyed the moral character of the people. Sam cannot find God in man or society, thus repeating a boyhood experience when he had read the Bible and discovered that "Christ's simple message" of love and community had been rejected by the Iowa villagers. Wearied by "thinking" and searching, Sam loses faith in hope.

The resurgent theme of fertility rouses Sam briefly. He brings three neglected children home to his lonely wife, who has found solace, ironically, in the writing of Emersonian "articles about life and conduct." Upon Sam's return, she derides them as "pettiness." Both hope that, with the aid of the children, they may be able to realize their earlier unifying aim of nurturing perfect beings for the future. But the concluding paragraph of the novel is far from hopeful. The last lines are unmistakably despairing: "A shudder ran through his body and he had the impulse to run away into the darkness, to begin again, seeking, seeking. Instead he turned and going through the door, walked across the lighted room to sit again with Sue at his own table and to try to force himself back into the ranks of life." Nothing in the novel promises that Sam will be able to remain in the light.

Anderson's later weakness as a novelist is evident in his inability to make Sam McPherson see, feel, and evaluate his experience with concrete details and expanding complexity. Sam yearns to break loose from the sterilizing confines of existence but his spirit is subdued by a numbing sameness that renders him unfit for observation and participation. Had Anderson created suspense by involving Sam in a more detailed inner drama of conflicting emotion and idea or a more detailed outer drama of disturbing social interaction, the tragic conclusion would have embodied a persuasive force. As it is, Sam's impotent isolation ultimately tends to become more pathetic than deeply tragic.

The limited dimension of Sam is paralleled in most of the other characters, who remain undeveloped sentimental stereotypes. Some of these recur with haunting regularity in Anderson's later work: the kind, maternal schoolteacher who talks about books and art; the loved and hated braggart father; the exhausted, sacrificial mother who dies too soon; the wife who doesn't understand her husband or give herself to love; the promiscuous woman who cheapens physical passion.

The strengths of *Windy McPherson's Son* reside primarily in the first eight chapters dealing with Sam's village life before his quest for money and power in Chicago. This section of the book might almost be a discarded draft of *Winesburg, Ohio*. Many sentences are packed with the hum of feeling and have a Biblical cadence; "tears" express a specific emotional reaction and are not just plashed for dubious sentimental effect; imagery and diction generally are free from cliché and stereotype. Three characters anticipate the figures of *Winesburg, Ohio* in their expressiveness, the depth of their passion and insight, and the incongruity between their powers and their limited achievement.

John Telfer is an articulate and vivid man whose failure as painter has led him to a richer role: artist of living. His talk of Whitman, love, purpose, and ideals almost sways Sam from devotion to money; it is Telfer who emphasizes the difference between corn as a symbol of materialism and corn as a symbol of the *élan vital*: "I see the long corn rows with the men and the horses half hidden, hot and breathless, and I think of a vast river of life. I catch a breath of the flame that was in the mind of the

man who said, 'The land is flowing with milk and honey.'" But Telfer cannot affect Sam's future any more than Sam's emotionally profound father, Windy McPherson, or the "savage and primitive" Mike McCarthy. The latter delights in fertilizing village wives whose miserly husbands have forsworn "carnal love," and the children it produces, in favor of saving money. Like Telfer, both have virtues worth emulating. Yet each is ultimately defeated, Windy by his hollow pretensions and Mike by the uncontrollable passion which leads to his murdering a resentful cuckold.

Anderson's second published novel, *Marching Men* (1917), although structurally flawed, is noteworthy for its stylistic fluency and its fusion of ideas and dramatic action. This is not surprising, for Anderson was by no means a literary *naïf* in the mid-1910's as he and others have suggested. In Chicago after 1912 he had come to know such literary figures as Floyd Dell, Carl Sandburg, Margaret Anderson, and Ben Hecht; Anderson also contributed to the *Little Review*, along with *Poetry* the most important American "little magazine" of the 1910's. There are references to Poe, Browning, Carlyle, Keats, Balzac, Whitman, and Mark Twain in *Windy McPherson's Son*, as well as allusions to unspecified French, Russian, and other European writers; in a 1923 letter, Anderson asserted that he had read Turgenev about 1911 and Tolstoi and Dostoevski afterward. Shakespeare and Dante are mentioned in *Marching Men*. According to Anderson's *Memoirs*, he was already familiar with the novels of Bennett, Wells, Hardy, and Moore. His brother Karl had introduced him to Gertrude Stein's experimental *Tender Buttons* (1914) soon after its appearance; he had read her *Three Lives* (1909) earlier.

Marching Men is a social novel. In it Anderson examined the destructive impact of industrialism in a Pennsylvania coal-mining town upon a sensitive boy and traced the harmful effect of his warped personality upon society. Ironically nicknamed "Beaut" because of his gawkiness and physical ugliness, Norman McGregor's lyrical response to nature and his affectionate spirit are brutally crushed. Beaut McGregor grows to hate man and society. In Chicago he finds opportunity, as lawyer and charismatic leader, to obtain revenge for his youthful sufferings. Viewing urban, industrial man as a dehumanized shell, he accelerates the dehumanization by organizing the masses into battalions which, subjected to strict discipline, march in military fashion. His intelligence and emotional mystique bring him the devotion of many men who are glad to surrender the last remnants of individuality. McGregor thus becomes the master of a terrifying collective force whose power can be exerted against society. The collective mass, rejecting the false premises of a democracy that is disorderly, will create a new order, a new mind. "When you have marched until you are one giant body then will happen a miracle," McGregor tells his followers. "A brain will grow in the giant you have made."

Had Anderson been able to stop the novel at that point, he would have written a meaningful indictment of American life and a warning of its self-destructiveness. Supporting the indictment are many valid social criticisms, some in the form of Anderson's authorial comments and others in passages of description and narration. His ideas on the shoddy ugliness of goods, homes, cities, and living patterns, on the inequitable character of law, on the avid quest for sensation, and on other problems of the day were pertinent for the early twentieth century and are still relevant in many respects. Anderson was echoing earlier protests by Melville, Thoreau, and Whitman; he was in tune with such perceptive contemporaries as Thorstein Veblen, Frank Lloyd Wright, and William James.

But though Anderson could objectively summon up the root causes for McGregor's Nietzschean nihilism, clearly portrayed as a negative philosophy, he paradoxically shared McGregor's faith in blind action. The novel struggles unsuccessfully to maintain equilibrium between Anderson's constructive critical temper and his unabashed impulse for collective physical violence and social destruction. As if to mark his inability to resolve the novel's chaotic lack of focus, Anderson dropped McGregor from his narrative before its close. The final chapter completes the book's disintegration. A foreshadowing of *Many Marriages* (1923), the conclusion whips up a mélange of sex and philosophy in portraying the success of a Chicago industrialist's effort to persuade his daughter that he is more desirable than McGregor, whom she has loved but to whom she has been afraid to give herself.

The idea and form of *Marching Men* were confused. But Anderson's style had progressed beyond the clumsy rawness of most of his earlier novel, had moved closer to the prose poetry of *Winesburg, Ohio*. His growing mastery of imaginative detail is visible in young McGregor's shocked perception that the coaltown minister is laughing callously at a cruel story about the boy: "The Reverend Minot Weeks also laughed. He thrust four fingers of each hand into the pockets of his trousers, letting the extended thumbs lie along the swelling waist line. From the front the thumbs looked like two tiny boats on the horizon of a troubled sea. They bobbed and jumped about on the rolling shaking paunch, appearing and disappearing as laughter shook him."

The urban scene evokes cold, sharp disgust: "The people of Chicago go home from their work at evening—drifting they go in droves, hurrying along. It is a startling thing to look closely at them. The people have bad mouths. Their mouths are slack and the jaws do not hang right. The mouths are like the shoes they wear. The shoes have become run down at the corners from too much pounding on the hard pavements and the mouths have become crooked from too much weariness of soul. . . . It is evening and the people of Chicago go home from work. Clatter, clatter, clatter, go the heels on the hard pavements, jaws wag, the wind blows and dirt drifts and sifts through the masses of the people. Every one has dirty ears. The stench in the street cars is horrible. The antiquated bridges over the rivers are packed with people. The suburban trains going away south and west are cheaply constructed and dangerous. A people calling itself great and living in a city also called great go to their houses a mere disorderly mass of humans cheaply equipped. Everything is cheap. When the people get home to their houses they sit on cheap chairs before cheap tables and eat cheap food. They have given their lives for cheap things."

In opposition to that nightmare horror, Anderson chanted the promise of nature in prophetic Biblical cadences: "And back of Chicago lie the long corn fields that are not disorderly. There is hope in the corn. Spring comes and the corn is green. It shoots up out of the black land and stands up in orderly rows. The corn grows and thinks of nothing but growth. Fruition comes to the corn and it is cut down and disappears. Barns are filled to bursting with the yellow fruit of the corn. And Chicago has forgotten the lesson of the corn. All men have forgotten. It has never been told to the young men who come out of the corn fields to live in the city."

The invigorating effect of Gertrude Stein's experimentation with language in *Tender Buttons* is evident in *Marching Men*. Her theory is virtually summed up by Anderson in the novel: "It is a terrible thing to speculate on how man has been defeated by his ability to say words. The brown bear in the forest has no such power and the lack of it has enabled

him to retain a kind of nobility of bearing sadly lacking in us. On and on through life we go, socialists, dreamers, makers of laws, sellers of goods and believers in suffrage for women and we continuously say words, worn-out words, crooked words, words without power or pregnancy in them."

For Anderson, Miss Stein always remained a "writer's writer," a literary pioneer, not a writer for the general reader. He recognized that her abandonment of conventional syntax, punctuation, and spelling was therapeutic for the American writer because it made him conscious of the deadness of conventional language and rhythm, of a literature based on literary custom rather than on objects, associations, functions, and speech freshly articulated. In 1914 such a revivification of style was needed. Gertrude Stein was a pioneer in the undertaking, soon to be joined by Anderson, Pound, Eliot, Joyce, the Dadaists, Cummings, Hemingway, and Faulkner. The poetic repetition and variation of words and phrases, the uncluttered images of objects, the varying musical beat and swing of sentences and paragraphs, noticeable in the passages quoted above from *Marching Men*, were stylistic techniques Anderson learned from her and passed along to Hemingway and Faulkner.

In the late fall of 1915, Anderson began to write the tales that make up *Winesburg, Ohio*. The majority were executed before the middle of 1916. A controlling plan apparently guided him, for the tales were composed in almost the sequence they occupy in the book. (An exception must be made for the four-part "Godliness," which Anderson salvaged from an unfinished novel of 1917.) The tales' unusual quality was recognized almost at once by "little magazine" editors in rebellion against the values dominating American letters and culture. Floyd Dell, Anderson's Chicago friend who helped arrange publication of *Windy McPherson's Son* and was an editor of *Masses*, printed three tales in 1916 beginning with "The Book of the Grotesque." Waldo Frank, editor with James Oppenheim and Van Wyck Brooks of *Seven Arts,* published four tales in 1916 and 1917. Two tales appeared in 1916 and 1918 respectively in the *Little Review.* Anderson had gained an audience that was small but appreciative of his lyrical prose.

William Phillips' study of the Winesburg manuscripts shows that Anderson wrote his first drafts with spontaneity and speed, and then polished with considerable care. The manuscript of "Hands," the second tale written, bears "almost two hundred instances in which earlier words and phrases are deleted, changed, or added to, to provide the readings of the final published version of the story." The revisions, ninety per cent of which were made after the initial writing, added to the size of the draft; they amplified the tale's subtlety by increasing its suggestive elements and symbolic content. The style was molded into greater informality by the addition of colloquial words and repetitive rhythms, and by the deletion of words that were "overworked or awkwardly used."

Much in the tales had prior existence in Clyde, Ohio, and Anderson's earlier life, thus justifying the subtitle: "A Group of Tales of Ohio Small Town Life." But the book, written in retrospect in Chicago, also reflects and illuminates urban American life. Winesburg as a microcosm is ultimately more than a national phenomenon; its proportions are universal, like the whale ship in Melville's *Moby Dick* and Faulkner's mythical Yoknapatawpha County.

The structure of *Winesburg, Ohio* was suggested by Edgar Lee Masters' *Spoon River Anthology,* an elegiac series of character sketches in poetry. The influence of Turgenev's *A Sportsman's Sketches*, in which a sympathetic but unsentimental narrator permits Russian character types to reveal themselves, is also evident. There are as well precedents for the book in nineteenth-century American literature, most notably the local-color collection of tales centered in a single geographical place, the obsessed monomaniacs of Hawthorne's fiction, and the mordant temper of E. W. Howe's *The Story of a Country Town.* The uniqueness of Anderson's book consists of the unusual quality of the precise, ironic voice offering delicate accounts of grotesque human creatures.

A partial key to the elegiac form and tone of the tales is embodied in the book's theory of the grotesque. At some distant time in the past, man had created and believed many satisfying, contradictory truths, "each truth . . . a composite of a great many vague thoughts." Then the healthy wholeness of a multiplicity of truths was lost; man picked out one particular truth, based his life upon it, and became a grotesque, his exclusive truth "a falsehood." The theory, like Hawthorne's statement in *The House of the Seven Gables* that in "an odd and incomprehensible world . . . a man's bewilderment is the measure of his wisdom," epitomizes the philosophy of uncertainty that dominated Anderson's thought and art: the "meaning of life" could not be defined by an absolute truth which limited man's possibilities, for the universe was open rather than closed. "Seeds," a tale first published in 1918, rounds out Anderson's theory by asserting that a confused woman who has mistaken selfish lust for selfless love "is a grotesque, but then all the people in the world are grotesques. We all need to be loved. What would cure her would cure the rest of us also. The disease she had is, you see, universal. We all want to be loved and the world has no plan for creating our lovers."

Everything in *Winesburg, Ohio* sets forth Anderson's vision of the grotesquerie of modern life, though in surrealistic rather than realistic fashion. The characters are deluded and solipsistic; they misunderstand themselves and others; they speak jerkily, explosively, mumblingly, or are inarticulate; their bodies are deformed or subject to muscular twitches, sometimes remain rigid while parts such as hands or feet move about independently. Frustrated, distorted, violent or passive, aggressive or self-destructive, the citizens of Winesburg are the living dead, victims of limited, life-denying truths and guilty for having chosen them.

The grotesques strive to tell their life stories to George Willard, young newspaper reporter. Their recitals are disjointed; their encounters with Willard episodic and inconclusive; his understanding of them incomplete. The tales are static episodes, empty of discovery and change. George Willard is on the whole a passive participant, himself a victim like the others, incapable of distinguishing between love and lust until the conclusion of the book, at which time he leaves Winesburg for a future that is dubious.

Anderson's subtle literary voice enriched the static nightmare of grotesquerie by infusing it with the dynamism of irony. The self-depreciating narrator struggles to be free of the limitations imposed upon him as a Winesburg grotesque. "And yet that is but crudely stated," he confesses humbly and typically in "Hands." "It needs the poet there." But it was as a truly great prose poet that Anderson took up the dormant literary tradition of mock oral narration, briefly revivified by Mark Twain, and transformed it afresh into a vibrant literary medium.

The book's narrator lacks the godlike knowledge and consequent arrogance of an omniscient author. Only to the extent that he artfully presents other grotesques, implying that he has attained an objective distance from them, will he transcend his grotesque configuration and justify his difficult effort to assume the role of artist rather than remaining a Winesburg zombie. The narrator, therefore, abjures sentimentality and pity as much as possible; his tenderness and sympathy are restrained and balanced with an astringent objectivity frequently brutal in contrast to the sufferings of his characters. The narrator's distance from his characters is established by reticence concerning physical details and by the use of a minimal amount of speech and scenic confrontation: the entangling possibilities of physical and dramatic immediacy are thus avoided. However, the narrator cannot help becoming subjectively involved. He observes, feels, digresses, analyzes, and generalizes. Yet he is often wrong, shortsighted, naive. He has become a major character in the tales who, like the symbolic objects liberally strewn about the pages of *Winesburg, Ohio*, must be metamorphosed into full meaning by the imaginatively stirred reader.

At the last, the narrator's stance of simple, artless sincerity revealing all is but a guise for artistic purpose and effect: all is actually given only as hint, clue, suggestion, implication, ambivalence, indirection. The covert truths proffered by Anderson never become didactic absolutes imposed by the narrator but remain implicit and open-ended. Each reader of the tales will grasp only as much of their essence as his individual insight is capable of apprehending.

Winesburg, Ohio is the first modern American expression of the wasteland theme later adumbrated in T. S. Eliot's *The Waste Land* (1922), F. Scott Fitzgerald's *The Great Gatsby* (1925), Hemingway's *The Sun Also Rises* (1926), John Steinbeck's *To a God Unknown* (1933), and Nathanael West's *Miss Lonelyhearts* (1933), the latter, like Hemingway's novel, greatly indebted to Anderson's model. Unlike most of the writers who followed, Anderson attempted to fructify his wasteland, which symbolized the world of provinciality, gentility, and business he had rejected spiritually in his flight from Elyria to Chicago in 1913.

Winesburg, Ohio had delineated the arid context of Anderson's first life. Having given it aesthetic form, he believed it imperative to create—again in art—the context of his new life. The aim had been formulated with yearning simplicity by George Willard, like the new Anderson an artistic creation: "In every little thing there must be order, in the place where men work, in their clothes, in their thoughts. I myself must be orderly. I must learn that law. I must get myself into touch with something orderly and big that swings through the night like a star. In my little way I must begin to learn something, to give and swing and work with life, with the law."

The difficulties Anderson faced were great, particularly since he was still working on the Winesburg tales during 1916 and 1917, when he began his quest for new definitions, and the mood of Winesburg pervaded him. There was nothing in Winesburg as he had portrayed it, with the exception of nature, to which he could return; the ties which bound men in community had withered; love had degenerated into conflict, sexual repression, and disappointing lust; familial relations mirrored the larger social emptiness; the traditional reliances of religious orthodoxy and ritual modes of cultural behavior were nonexistent. He had cast aside the illusions of business and the ugliness of the city. In every respect, then, he was free and unattached, young in situation and possibility, ready to make the world live up to its fruitful potentialities and become a habitable place for human beings.

In actuality, of course, the matter was not so simple. Anderson was in his early forties, exuberant but also physically and mentally weary. As he later granted in his *Memoirs,* the

Winesburg vision of his Ohio town had been harshly biased and he had too hastily rejected its few worthy attributes. It is apparent from the revelations in the early novels and letters of this period that he had been psychically maimed by the experiences of his first forty years. Nor, regardless of how much will he exerted, could he easily slough off the worldliness of his mind, or easily assume the role of newborn infant or virginal adolescent after the mature triumph of his repudiation of business and familial ties, after the even greater triumph of having transformed himself into an accomplished artistic creator. The record of Anderson's Progress as a new Adam is inevitably a compilation of noble effort, heroic attainment, and pathetic failure. As it must have been for one who, as he wrote in the poetic epigraph of "From Chicago" (*Seven Arts,* May 1917), was a "man child, in America, in the west, in the great valley of the Mississippi . . . a confused child in a confused world."

Henceforth, Anderson's art and life were inseparable. Instead of remaining hidden behind his work like James Joyce, Anderson made the problem of self-understanding the focus of his best work. He found it as necessary to write about himself as an artist as to work at his art: "While he is still young and pregnant with life it behooves the artist who would stand unashamed among men to make his contribution to the attempt to extend the province of his art. And as his struggle as an artist is and must be inseparably bound up with his struggle as a man, the attempt may fairly be said to fall under the head of an effort to extend the possibilities of human life." So opens "From Chicago," but it concludes humbly on a foreboding note so strong that Anderson self-consciously omitted the section when reprinting the piece in *Sherwood Anderson's Notebook* (1926): "I am looking forward to the coming of the new artist who will give us

... the beautiful and stirring story of the spirit that failed, just as the artist himself shall fail and who, like the Christ, on that dramatic night in the garden, must come at last to the facing of truth and know that he must always fail, that, even in keeping alive the memory of his struggle, all men shall fail." This tempering of egoism with limitation helped save Anderson from becoming, except briefly in the 1920's, a tiresome brayer of virtuous Selfhood in the manner of some of his less gifted imitators.

Mid-American Chants (1918), a collection of free-verse poems in the Whitmanian manner which Anderson began writing early in 1917, illustrates one phase of his attempt to fill his void. The poems are generally inept. Only a few manage coherently to unite their fragmentary rhapsodic ejaculations with the kind of sustained emotional energy, intellectual content, and symbolic structure present in Whitman's best poems. Anderson wanted to recreate the religious spirit and mythology of pagan Indian culture in the Ohio Valley before the culture's destruction by New England's pioneers. But he was insufficiently familiar with the details to do more than refer vaguely to the culture. On the other hand, when he did achieve a fragile identification, he blurred it with an alien prophetic exhortation and imagery derived from the Old Testament and Carl Sandburg. Not until Hart Crane wrote "The Dance" (*The Bridge*, 1930) were the primitive fertility rhythms of sacrifice, harvest, and rebirth celebrated in modern American poetry with the Dionysian richness Anderson sought to express.

Anderson was surprised that the editors of *Seven Arts*—one of whom, James Oppenheim, even wrote Whitmanesque poetry—frowned upon the poems later collected in *Mid-American Chants*. The apocalyptic spirit of the magazine, which found hope for an American Renaissance in "self-expression without regard to current magazine standards" and eulogized Anderson in the first issue as an emergent Whitman, had diverted him from the disciplined temper governing the Winesburg stories. It had encouraged him to assume the role of ebullient national bard and to find in the seeds, roots, stalks, and husks of corn— the recurrent symbol of the chants—a means of ordering his chaos. However, the excesses which *Seven Arts* encouraged as one product of its doctrines were actually abhorrent to men like Frank and Brooks. Their most fervent aim was to awaken an idealistic national art rather than to discard traditional standards of literary taste and accomplishment. Anderson's friendship with these men and his respect for their judgment declined in the heat of argument, though he maintained his intimacy with them for some years thereafter.

"An Apology for Crudity" (*Dial*, November 8, 1917) was a manifesto of his independent literary position which sniped at the formalism of his *Seven Arts* critics and others who had ridiculed several poems that had appeared in *Poetry* (September 1917). Significant literature, he asserted, could only come after a writer's immersion in the life of his times. Since "crudity and ugliness" were prime characteristics of American industrial society, modern literature must be affected by it. He rejected, consequently, the "intellectuality" and subtlety" of Henry James and William Dean Howells as ends in themselves, though he granted that both men were "American masters in prose." He linked himself to the tradition of Walt Whitman, Mark Twain, and Theodore Dreiser, who had not ignored the common.

But Anderson did not espouse realism. Vaguely he set forth the ideal of "subjective writing" as an alternative, the writer serving as an imaginative distiller of persons and experience. Later, in "A Note on Realism" (*New York Evening Post Literary Review*, October 25, 1924), he phrased his conception more concretely: "The life of the imagination will always remain separated from the life of reality. It feeds upon the life of reality, but it is not that life—cannot be. . . . Upon the fact in nature the imagination must constantly feed in order that the imaginative life remain significant. . . . The life of reality is confused, disorderly, almost always without apparent purpose, whereas in the artist's imaginative life there is purpose. There is determination to give the tale, the song, the painting Form— to make it true and real to the theme, not to life. Often the better the job is done the greater the confusion." Essentially, then, form and style were organic discoveries of imaginative creation, not pre-existent molds chosen in advance of the literary adventure.

Despite Anderson's impatience with the conventional novel and his recurrent effort to discover a "looser" form, his next major work failed to demonstrate any "experimental" characteristics. *Poor White* (1920) delineated the decline of the "pastoral golden age" in his Midwest during the 1880's and 1890's, the years of his childhood and adolescence. The book is crammed with information, for Anderson tried to anchor it in the facts of cultural, social, and economic history. Furthermore, he enveloped life in the Ohio town of Bidwell— which also appears in other post-Winesburg fiction—with a quiet charm derived from stable community relations, proximity to nature, intellectual curiosity and discussion, old houses, and streets shaded with old overhanging trees. Much of the vision is valid, but Anderson's nostalgia led him to idealize the town and its region until they became as exaggeratedly beautiful as Winesburg earlier had been exaggeratedly ugly. Yet this excessively rosy portrait of Bidwell was also aesthetically

sound, for it enabled Anderson to dramatize the emotional and social significance of its degeneration into Winesburg.

The corrupting agent in the agrarian paradise was industrialism, which had elevated materialism and turned men into mechanical monsters. Hugh McVey, a Huckleberry Finn-type from the Mississippi River town of Mudcat Landing, Missouri, symbolically embodies the process. With unsparing realism, young McVey is shown to be a shiftless and lazy "poor white," redeemed, however, by his tendency to daydream and transcend himself pantheistically in sky, earth, and water.

Orphaned, McVey lives with a family which indoctrinates him with the virtues of industry and profit. Gradually he becomes wholly mathematical in mind and mechanical in spirit, channeling his imagination into the invention of labor-saving agricultural machinery. The machines bring him financial success even though, ironically, they turn out to be unworkable and thus symbolically fraudulent. They involve the town in a fever of speculation, disrupting all patterns of behavior, all relations. The novel contains many vivid episodes of the degenerative transformation of characters into tormented grotesques when they are suddenly deprived of the self-fulfilling creative tasks of old. In all of Bidwell, the only creatures who remain virile and sentient are horses. McVey is also a grotesque, unable to consummate his marriage because of psychic impotence, roused finally from his dehumanization by the beautiful appearance of some brightly colored stones he has found. At the end, after a symbolic attack upon McVey by a maddened handicraftsman, Hugh's patient wife—a "new woman" given to thinking rather than feeling —is roused to maternal womanliness by his reversion to adolescent helplessness. The novel grinds to a confusing halt as Hugh, stirred by "the disease of thinking," is told by "his woman" of the forthcoming arrival of "a man child." This news is greeted mockingly by "a great whistling and screaming" from Bidwell's factories.

The style of *Poor White* is effectively elegiac and muted as befits the portrait of an unrecoverable past. It is also generally free of the grammatical errors and poor punctuation that had marred *Winesburg, Ohio* slightly and to a greater extent the earlier novels. *Poor White* was the high point of Anderson's novelistic career. However, it represented a mere refinement of the structure and materials of *Windy McPherson's Son* and *Marching Men* rather than a significant advance. All three novels are essentially accounts of the distortion of a man in youth, his subsequent involvement in a maturity of social fraud and emotional impoverishment, his attempt to attain self-fulfillment in escape and love with an unsatisfactory woman who symbolizes reason and convention rather than emotion and revolt, and the uncertainty of the man's future at the conclusion.

Undoubtedly these novels served Anderson as self-analysis. But the requirements of their objective form kept him from venturing deeply into a personal probing that would have brought him profoundly into himself and encouraged analytical subtlety and particularized detail. The novels come perilously close to being true-confession literature in which the apparent openness of the writing hardly conceals the complacent obduracy with which the author reiterates rather than explores the troubles from which he supposedly has escaped.

Anderson's next novel, *Many Marriages* (1923), exemplifies the impasse to which such writing could lead; with its publication—it was initially printed serially in the *Dial*—came the first strong reaction against Anderson by the newer generation of American writers.

Abandoning the chronological time sequence of the early novels, *Many Marriages* focused upon an extended moment of escape. This was given a past by means of flashbacks that vividly re-create the inhibition of feminine passion. But Anderson did little to set forth the positive hopeful quality of his masculine protagonist's passion beyond having him posture nakedly in presumably ritualistic fashion before a statue of the Virgin Mary. This ritual is neither primitive nor Catholic, for Anderson failed to provide any meaning for his key symbol, which he had picked up in *The Education of Henry Adams*. The result was a stasis, the temper of the Winesburg tales, that violated the thematic meaning of *Many Marriages* and revealed a disturbing lack of literary self-consciousness. What should have been a short story had been turned into a faulty novel.

Anderson published three more novels: *Dark Laughter* (1925), *Beyond Desire* (1932), and *Kit Brandon* (1936). All of them, like his preceding novels, have extraordinary scenes and passages whose high quality has been overlooked. These last novels also show that he endeavored to cope with the problems of extended narrative fiction in different ways; his solutions, however, were generally unsatisfactory, whether it was the attempt to portray the stream of consciousness in *Dark Laughter* or the device of having a central character relate her life story in an extended monologue in *Kit Brandon*.

Anderson's letters and writings from the mid-1910's until shortly before his death reveal that the objective novel, particularly the social novel, had interested him deeply only before the composition of the Winesburg tales. During the late 1910's, before the publication of *Poor White,* he began and abandoned several novels. After 1925, the pattern was repeated. His impulse was for expression in short forms: the poem, prose poem, and lyrical short story. But he was compelled, particularly since he had begun his career as a novelist, to continue writing novels. As late as 1933, for example, the publishing house of Scribners invited him to become one of its authors with the stipulation, according to Anderson, that the first of his books "must be either a novel or a continuous narrative."

It was not merely the pressure of publishers, as well as readers and critics, which pushed Anderson toward the novel against his natural inclination to work in shorter forms. Anderson shared the erroneous cultural belief that a novel is qualitatively as well as quantitatively more valuable than a short work. Had he been a younger man in the late 1910's and early 1920's, it is possible that he might have been able to develop the lyrical novel, a delicate form that would have best utilized his talents as it did those of Virginia Woolf, his admirer. But he had insufficient time in which to work slowly and perfect his art in every form. By 1919, at the age of forty-three, he was exhausted with the difficulty of earning his living as an advertising man and writing in his spare time. Not until 1922 did he finally leave the advertising business, convinced by the size of his earnings from books and magazines that he would be able to survive as a professional writer.

As it turned out, he was unprepared to work at the pace required of a professional writer whose contractual obligations force him to produce publishable materials on a regular basis. He wished to experiment, to work as the impulse to create arose, to make discoveries as any other young writer who still has his future ahead of him: Anderson believed that his life had begun in 1916 with the publication of his first book. Yet as a professional writer in the 1920's he allowed himself to publish whatever he wrote, regardless of whether or not he was proud of it. Thus he ironically was seduced by the same dream of success that he had repudiated in business.

Nevertheless, the bulk of Anderson's important creation is far greater than most critics and readers appear to have realized. His significant contribution to American literature begins with *Winesburg, Ohio* and includes many pieces of prose and poetry published in books and magazines from 1916 to 1941. To that body of work should be added the successful chapters and sections from generally unsatisfactory books, as well as the luminous autobiographical sketches compiled in the posthumous *Memoirs*.

One reason Anderson's writing has not received full recognition, apart from the disappointment aroused by his novels, is the uneven character of his books. Anderson's eagerness to publish, encouraged by editors and publishers, is partially responsible. For example, the two books which crystallized his fame as a short fiction writer in the early 1920's—*The Triumph of the Egg* (1921) and *Horses and Men* (1923)—are mixtures of quality and dross. In both books he included pages salvaged from discarded novels which were on the whole below the level of his current work. "Unlighted Lamps" and "The Door of the Trap" (*The Triumph of the Egg*) are sections of novels begun before 1913. "A Chicago Hamlet" (*Horses and Men*) is a portion of a 1918 novel; "An Ohio Pagan" and "Unused" in the same collection are parts of unpublished novels begun in 1920. A little more than half of *Horses and Men* thus belies the subtitle's description of the contents as "tales." Anderson's last collection of short fiction, *Death in the Woods* (1933), is similarly uneven. It should be noted, however, that the novel fragments frequently contain some of Anderson's most evocative writing. The pantheistic embrace of nature in "An Ohio Pagan," for example, has rarely been equaled in American literature.

Another reason for the relative neglect of Anderson's total accomplishment is the special nature of his talent. He wrote in an age which believed it could master the disorder of existence with patterns of order derived from myths and ideologies of the past or else with descriptions of objects and behavior that possessed the irreducible precision of scientific writing. Because Anderson did not adopt either one of these solutions, his reputation was severely damaged during the 1920's. A reassessment is now in order, for his alleged weaknesses ironically have become strengths which link him with some of the most vigorous currents in contemporary literature. Anderson's vision and method reappear triumphantly in recent American literature in the writing of Carson McCullers, Bernard Malamud, Flannery O'Connor, Tennessee Williams, Edward Albee, Saul Bellow, and John Hawkes. Anderson's pioneering conglomeration of the picaresque, the antiheroic, the grotesque, the passionate, and the rebellious is no longer puzzling nor is it a sign of irresponsible "mindlessness."

One of the most interesting discoveries to be made is that sentimentality is not one of the chief characteristics of Anderson's writing. When dealing with characters whose suffering and confusion he delineated at excessive length, failing to complicate and particularize their uniqueness or impart visible moral and intellectual significance to their predicaments, he did become pathetic and sentimental. Illustrations of his failure to claim the complex response of a reader are *Many Marriages* and "Out of Nowhere into Nothing."

But Anderson's critical temper conflicted strongly with his tendency toward acceptance and complacency. He could become exceptionally sharp, often brutal, in combating the impulse of quiescence. The lively battle he carried on elicited an amused, ironic attitude toward himself and his world. He often wrote satirically ("The Egg," 1920, and "The Triumph of a Modern, or, Send for the Lawyer," 1923) and often comically ("I'm a Fool," 1922, "There She Is—She Is Taking Her Bath," 1923, and "His Chest of Drawers," 1939). To have separated satire and comedy is misleading, however, for Anderson at his most humorous gives us that rare blend known as the tragicomic. When he achieved it, as in "The Egg," it rested in a delicate suspension of irony that looked back to the narrative voice of *Winesburg, Ohio*. Despite lapses into what Faulkner in 1925 described as an "elephantine kind of humor about himself," Anderson's vision remained deeply, incongruously tragicomic. Despite the dark years through which he passed in the late 1920's, this vision reemerged in his last decade of life, typically in his insistence in *Plays: Winesburg and Others* (1937) that the dramatized version of "The Triumph of the Egg" must be carefully directed in order to maintain a balance between comedy and tragedy; to play it either for "laughter" or "tears" alone would destroy the play.

Essentially Anderson was a lyric writer. Having accepted middle-class thought uncritically at first, then having rebelled against it, he feared that any other system of thought would be equally delusive, would limit and frustrate him, especially since reason tended to become abstract and to ignore the heart. "Feeling instinctively the uncertainty of life, the difficulty of arriving at truth," he resolved to remain "humble in the face of the great mystery" (" 'Unused,' " 1923). He might have been describing his own work when he wrote in *A Story Teller's Story*: "Dim pathways do sometimes open before the eyes of the man who has not killed the possibilities of beauty in himself by being too sure."

Anderson could be irritatingly blunt in stating his position, sneering at "slickness," "smartness," and glibness in all fields including literary criticism; thus he inevitably aroused charges of "mindlessness," "immaturity," and "distrust of ideas." Though he winced under the blows of increasingly harsh criticism, he unhesitatingly rejected ready-made truths of past and present. He turned his gaze inwards, searching for tentative explanations of mystery in the texture of his own emotional and social experience. His writings articulate the development of his perceptions of self in relation to the world, of the difficulties encountered on the way.

Anderson never abandoned the vision of himself as a poet despite the unfavorable reception of *Mid-American Chants*, as late as 1930 writing an extraordinary prose poem in "Machine Song" (*Perhaps Women*, 1931). From 1919 to 1927 he assiduously wrote prose poems which appeared in magazines and *The Triumph of the Egg* and were collected in *A New Testament* (1927). He regarded this work at the outset as "a purely insane, experimental thing . . . an attempt to express, largely by indirection, the purely fanciful side of a man's life, the odds and ends of thought, the little pockets of thoughts and emotions that are so seldom touched." The poems on the whole are inchoate, too vague and incoherent to communicate more than faint hints of subconscious existence. But they were valuable exercises nonetheless. When Anderson turned to prose during this period, he passed beyond the mere undisciplined expression of self and made skillful use of poetic techniques which he never forgot.

As in *Winesburg, Ohio*, the varying percep-

tions of a poetically conceived narrator animate and unify most of Anderson's best stories, quite a few of which are products of the 1930's. For the sake of convenient reference, I cite only those stories that are easily accessible in one of Anderson's three collections and *The Sherwood Anderson Reader* (1947), though any comprehensive view of his work must also take into account many of his fine uncollected stories still available only in magazines: *The Triumph of the Egg*: "I Want to Know Why," "Seeds," "The Other Woman," "The Egg," and "Brothers"; *Horses and Men*: "I'm a Fool," "The Triumph of a Modern, or, Send for the Lawyer," "The Man Who Became a Woman," "Milk Bottles," "The Man's Story"; *Death in the Woods*: "Death in the Woods," "There She Is—She Is Taking Her Bath," "In a Strange Town," "A Sentimental Journey"; *The Sherwood Anderson Reader*: "The Corn-Planting," "A Walk in the Moonlight," "The Yellow Gown," and "His Chest of Drawers." The first-person narrator sometimes merely introduces the monologue of another character, as in "The Other Woman" or "His Chest of Drawers." Only a few of Anderson's stories related from a third-person point of view possess high quality: "Senility" and "The New Englander" (*The Triumph of the Egg*), "Another Wife" and "Brother Death" (*Death in the Woods*), "Daughters" and "Not Sixteen" (*The Sherwood Anderson Reader*).

The uncertain, groping narrator of an Anderson story employs an art of suggestion to articulate his search for pattern and meaning in human existence. His experiences are fragmentary, incoherent, inexplicable. The chronological sequence of time may be interrupted and reversed by memories, inadvertent thoughts, gusts of emotion, and frustrated attempts at comprehension. Objects and people are haphazardly perceived, grotesquely distorted. Absurdly helpless, the narrator may succumb to impotence, give vent to explosive stirrings in his subconscious, flee the envelope of his body in mystical anguish or ecstasy, obsessedly focus upon trivialities such as a bent finger, find momentary relief in the muscular health and grace of animals.

Since the story is an articulation of the narrator's experience, its movement is repetitive and circular; it is not rounded off with a meaningful conclusion, for that would violate the narrator's integrity, his stance of wonder and search. Anderson's rejection of conventional plot and climax was aesthetically appropriate. So was his frequent representation of physical detail as incomplete image and generalized noun, his emphasis upon the musical sound of language before it becomes sense in order that he might portray the transformation of undifferentiated sensation and emotion into intelligible form.

The welter of sensuous and emotional perceptions is integrated—despite the powerful centrifugal impulse—by various unifying elements. The narrator maintains a consistent tone of voice. Whether youth or adult, light or serious, comic or satiric, critical or suppliant, he is also visibly interested and compassionate, anxious to discern the reality behind appearance. Moments in the story—episodes, sensations, repetitions—suddenly blaze up to give intense thematic illuminations. Objects, gestures, and events are encrusted with symbolic meaning. These symbols recur and invest the narrator's perceptions with deepened or new significance. Often these symbols are transformed into archetypal patterns of elemental human experience, such as sacrifice, initiation, and rebirth; Anderson's corn seed, for example, is a fertility symbol, its planting a ceremonial drama of death and resurrection.

Many of Anderson's stories, like his novels, are autobiographical either wholly ("In a Strange Town") or partially ("I Want to Know Why"). Presentation of a story from the first-person point of view encouraged an autobiographical concern. On the other hand, as a writer of autobiography, a form that fascinated him because of his vision of himself as "the American Man . . . a kind of composite essence of it all," he tended to fictionalize the details of his biography. This fusion of fact and fiction produced some of Anderson's finest lyrical prose. For example, "Death in the Woods," regarded as one of Anderson's best stories even by unfavorable critics, appeared as a third-person narrative (Chapter XII) in his autobiographical novel *Tar* (1926). In the same year, it also appeared as a story in the *American Mercury;* the name "Tar" had been replaced by "I" and third-person pronouns and other details revised to clarify the narrator's personal relations and experiences. "A Meeting South," the subtle account of Anderson's intimacy with Faulkner in New Orleans, conceals Faulkner under a pseudonym and was probably read as fiction in the *Dial* (April 1925). It reappeared the next year as an autobiographical sketch in *Sherwood Anderson's Notebook* and finally was identified as a story in *Death in the Woods*. Anderson's autobiographical writings, which compose much of his total work, must be taken into account before any definitive conclusions about his literary significance can be ventured.

A starting point might well be Chapters X and XI of *Tar,* portrayals of horse racing as brilliantly colored and airy as Raoul Dufy's watercolors of French tracks, written in a supple vernacular that captures motion and youth with clear-eyed verve. Another excellent piece is "The Nationalist" (*Puzzled America,* 1935), a satirical dialogue with "the rat king of the South" who wants Congress to abolish the law protecting snowy egrets from shooting by feather-hunters. " 'It isn't the money I am thinking about,' he said. There was a grave injustice being done. 'These egrets,' he said again, 'are not American birds. They are foreign birds and they come up here only to eat our American fish.' " Two sketches, "White Spot" (1939) and "Morning Roll Call" (1940), both published posthumously in *The Sherwood Anderson Reader,* are brilliant examples of his ability to express himself during his last years with the vibrancy that had been a basis for his distinction during the early 1920's.

"White Spot" and "Morning Roll Call" had been intended for *Sherwood Anderson's Memoirs,* a work left unfinished when he died on March 8, 1941, in the Panama Canal Zone while on an unofficial goodwill tour to South America. According to James Schevill, the book was faultily edited by Paul Rosenfeld. Such sketches as "White Spot" and "Morning Roll Call" were omitted; a few random magazine pieces more than a decade old were included despite their incongruous misrepresentation of the style and aim of the autobiographical sketches Anderson wrote during the late 1930's and which constitute most of the volume. Unfinished though the book is, however, it represents a fitting culmination of his career. All of his earlier concern with self-revelation and stylistic nuance bore fruition in charming, lyrical pages that leave one in awe at the resiliency of the human spirit as it copes with the mysteries of being in art.

The vivacity and insight of Anderson's memoirs are remarkable in view of the severe decline of his reputation in the mid-1920's and the lengthy emotional depression that affected him thereafter. To those critics who did not read his works attentively or at all after 1925, when *Dark Laughter* appeared, and to those who know Anderson's writing only on the basis of *Winesburg, Ohio* and two over-anthologized stories—"I'm a Fool" and "I Want

to Know Why"—the vibrancy of the memoirs will be truly inexplicable.

Perhaps Anderson should not have expected his work early or late to be wholly or widely appreciated. From the very beginning his literary reputation was shaky. Newspaper and magazine reviewers of his early books regularly oscillated between praise and blame, often mixing both.

Since Anderson was an avant-garde writer, however, a "little magazine" phenomenon, he was at first more enthusiastically received by young writers and critics interested in an American literature that was original, complex, unsentimental, and bold in dealing with taboo subjects such as sex. Thus young Hart Crane in 1921 wrote an encomium of Anderson's "paragraphs and pages from which arises a lyricism, deliberate and light, as a curl of milk-weed seeds drawn toward the sun. . . . He is without sentimentality; and he makes no pretense of offering solutions. He has humanity and simplicity that is quite baffling in depth and suggestiveness. . . ."

But before long even the recognition of the avant-garde was qualified or withdrawn. It generally began to misjudge and overlook Anderson's method and to conclude mistakenly that he was an elderly, provincial American realist because he wrote about the Midwest and praised Dreiser for his human sympathy and his frankness in the treatment of sex. Anderson's persistent criticisms of Dreiser's style as clumsy and of Sinclair Lewis' style as superficial were ignored. The epitome of ultimate avant-garde response to Anderson is best seen in the pages of the *Dial,* which published him frequently, printed laudatory statements, and early in 1922 bestowed upon him the first *Dial* award for distinguished service to American letters, then in the next few years directly and allusively in reviews and other forms of comment gradually formulated a negative attitude toward him.

Anderson's rejection by the avant-garde deepened a sense of estrangement from vital currents of modern literature that had begun earlier when his first prominent supporters—Frank, Brooks, Paul Rosenfeld—kept finding fault with his theories and writings. In such works as *A Story Teller's Story* (1924), *The Modern Writer* (1925), and *Sherwood Anderson's Notebook* (1926), he hopefully sought to define and justify his credo. He was not helped in this task by his antipathy to "talk" about literature and ideas or by his aversion to systematic exposition. Much of what he said had the nub of good sense but it was insufficiently clarified, overcast with a playfulness inappropriate for the occasion, and gave the impression of being narcissistic self-praise of an aesthetic phenomenon superior to traditional morality and critical judgment. Self-consciously ironic and derisive references to the "modern" began to appear in his fiction and articles. An attempt to demonstrate superior "modernity" in *Dark Laughter* was a fiasco: its style, supposedly an emulation of that in James Joyce's *Ulysses*, revealed a misunderstanding of the stream-of-consciousness technique; its rendition of expatriate American experience in Europe was ludicrously uninformed and unperceptive.

The strongest blows against Anderson's prestige and well-being came from young writers whom he had befriended. Hemingway, in whom Anderson had discovered "extraordinary talent" in 1921 and whose *In Our Time* (1925) had been published as a result of Anderson's efforts, parodied Anderson in *The Torrents of Spring* (1926). Faulkner, whose *Soldiers' Pay* (1926) had also been published following Anderson's efforts, less publicly but just as sharply ridiculed Anderson in the fore-

word to *Sherwood Anderson & Other Famous Creoles* (1926), a book published in a limited edition in New Orleans.

For the rest of his life, from the mid-1920's on, Anderson engaged in a quest for rediscovery of the talent which seemed to have atrophied. F. Scott Fitzgerald had written: "To this day reviewers solemnly speak of him [Anderson] as an inarticulate, fumbling man, bursting with ideas—when, on the contrary, he is the possessor of a brilliant and almost inimitable prose style, and scarcely any ideas at all." Anderson perceived, with utter rightness, that there is no style without form, no form without content, that ideas are no more important than the evocative enunciation of experience. He had traveled much during his early years as an advertising man and now he resumed his travels. His second marriage had ended in divorce in 1924, two years after he left the advertising business; his third marriage broke down in 1929. Restlessly he went about the country, observing men and women, listening, attempting to regain the equilibrium of mind, emotion, and voice that had earlier produced his particular artistic vision. The idea that a permanent home might provide stability attracted him. In 1926 he built a house in the mountains of southwestern Virginia; for several years beginning in 1927 he edited two newspapers in the nearby town of Marion, Virginia. Meanwhile he continued to write stories and articles, to struggle desperately with new novels. He was often stricken with black, destructive moods, on one occasion even threw the manuscript of an unpublished novel out of a hotel window, but persisted in his search for orientation. In 1930 he fell in love with his future fourth wife; their marriage was successful. Slowly he regained his self-confidence, his talent, and his sense of humor. These are embodied in writings which swell the enduring corpus of his work beyond that already produced by 1926, writings in which he returned to the common people and locales he had earlier portrayed with similar irony, pity, and understanding.

The ultimate test of a writer's permanence is the power of his words to rekindle generations other than his own. If that be granted, then Sherwood Anderson's stature as a major American writer seems established for decades to come. The "proper evaluation" for which Faulkner called in 1953 has been in progress ever since, and during the 1960's, with special impetus and great critical intelligence devoted to Anderson's rare talent. His works have been widely reprinted in translation abroad and new editions and collections continue to appear in the United States. With characteristic humility, Anderson himself had said in 1921 "that after all the only thing the present generation of men in America could expect to do is to make with their bodies and spirits a kind of fertilizing element in our soil." The issue of final grandeur and subsequent fame was a matter he left to others. Anderson's legacy has been wonderfully fruitful.

Selected Bibliography

WORKS OF SHERWOOD ANDERSON

NOVELS AND COLLECTIONS OF SHORT STORIES

Windy McPherson's Son. New York: John Lane, 1916. (Revised edition, New York: B. W. Huebsch, 1922.)

Marching Men. New York: John Lane, 1917.

Winesburg, Ohio: A Group of Tales of Ohio Small Town Life. New York: B. W. Huebsch, 1919.

Poor White. New York: B. W. Huebsch, 1920.

The Triumph of the Egg: A Book of Impressions from American Life in Tales and Poems. New York: B. W. Huebsch, 1921.

Horses and Men: Tales, Long and Short, from Our American Life. New York: B. W. Huebsch, 1923.

Many Marriages. New York: B. W. Huebsch, 1923.

Dark Laughter. New York: Boni and Liveright, 1925.

Beyond Desire. New York: Liveright, 1932.

Death in the Woods and Other Stories. New York: Liveright, 1933.

Kit Brandon: A Portrait. New York: Scribners, 1936.

POETRY AND PLAYS

Mid-American Chants. New York: John Lane, 1918.

A New Testament. New York: Boni and Liveright, 1927.

Plays: Winesburg and Others. New York: Scribners, 1937.

AUTOBIOGRAPHY AND OTHER PROSE

A Story Teller's Story: The Tale of an American Writer's Journey through His Own Imaginative World and through the World of Facts . . . New York: B. W. Huebsch, 1924.

The Modern Writer. San Francisco: Lantern Press, 1925.

Sherwood Anderson's Notebook. New York: Boni and Liveright, 1926.

Tar: A Midwest Childhood. New York: Boni and Liveright, 1926.

Hello Towns! New York: Liveright, 1929.

The American County Fair. New York: Random House, 1930.

Perhaps Women. New York: Liveright, 1931.

No Swank. Philadelphia: Centaur Press, 1934.

Puzzled America. New York: Scribners, 1935.

A Writer's Conception of Realism. Olivet, Mich.: Olivet College, 1939.

Home Town. New York: Alliance, 1940.

Sherwood Anderson's Memoirs. New York: Harcourt, Brace, 1942.

The Sherwood Anderson Reader, edited with an Introduction by Paul Rosenfeld, Boston: Houghton Mifflin, 1947.

The Portable Sherwood Anderson, edited by

Horace Gregory. New York: Viking, 1949. (Revised edition, 1971.)

Letters of Sherwood Anderson, edited with an Introduction by Howard Mumford Jones in association with Walter B. Rideout. Boston: Little, Brown, 1953.

Return to Winesburg: Selections from Four Years of Writing for a Country Newspaper, edited by Ray Lewis White. Chapel Hill: University of North Carolina Press, 1967.

The Buck Fever Papers, edited by Welford D. Taylor. Charlottesville: University of Virginia Press, 1971.

BIBLIOGRAPHIES

Sheehy, Eugene P., and Kenneth A. Lohf. *Sherwood Anderson: A Bibliography.* Los Gatos, Calif.: Talisman Press, 1960.

Rideout, Walter B. "Sherwood Anderson," *Fifteen Modern American Authors,* edited by Jackson R. Bryer. Durham, N.C.: Duke University Press, 1969.

Tanselle, G. Thómas. "Additional Reviews of Sherwood Anderson's Work," *Papers of the Bibliographical Society of America,* 56:358–65 (1962).

White, Ray Lewis. *Checklist of Sherwood Anderson.* Columbus, Ohio: Merrill, 1969.

————. "A Checklist of Sherwood Anderson Studies, 1959–1969," *Newberry Library Bulletin,* 6:288–302 (1971).

CRITICAL AND BIOGRAPHICAL STUDIES

Adams, Richard P. "The Apprenticeship of William Faulkner," *Tulane Studies in English,* 12:113–56 (1962).

Anderson, David D. "Sherwood Anderson after 20 Years," *Midwest Quarterly,* 119–32 (1962).

————. *Sherwood Anderson: An Introduction and Interpretation.* New York: Holt, Rinehart and Winston, 1967.

Asselineau, Roger, ed. *Configuration critique de Sherwood Anderson, la revue des lettres moderne,* Nos. 78–80 (1963).

Beach, Joseph Warren. *The Outlook for American Prose.* Chicago: University of Chicago Press, 1926.

Bishop, John Peale. "The Distrust of Ideas" [1921], in *The Collected Essays of John Peale Bishop.* New York: Scribners, 1948.

Burbank, Rex. *Sherwood Anderson.* New York: Twayne, 1964.

Chase, Cleveland B. *Sherwood Anderson.* New York: McBride, 1927.

Crane, Hart. "Sherwood Anderson," *Double-Dealer,* 2:42–45 (1921).

Dahlberg, Edward. *Alms for Oblivion.* Minneapolis: University of Minnesota Press, 1964.

Duffey, Bernard. *The Chicago Renaissance in American Letters.* Lansing: Michigan State College Press, 1954.

Faulkner, William. "Sherwood Anderson: An Appreciation," *Atlantic Monthly,* 191:27–29 (1953).

Fenton, Charles A. *The Apprenticeship of Ernest Hemingway.* New York: Farrar, Straus, 1954.

Fitzgerald, F. Scott. "How to Waste Material: A Note on My Generation," *Bookman,* 63:262–65 (1926).

Frank, Waldo. "Emerging Greatness," *Seven Arts,* 1:73–78 (1916).

Geismar, Maxwell. *The Last of the Provincials.* Boston: Houghton Mifflin, 1943.

Gregory, Alyse. "Sherwood Anderson," *Dial,* 75:243–46 (1923).

Herbst, Josephine. "Ubiquitous Critics and the Author," *Newberry Library Bulletin,* 5:1–13 (1958).

"Homage to Sherwood Anderson," *Story,* Vol. 19 (September–October 1941). (Contributions by James Boyd, Van Wyck Brooks, Theodore Dreiser, Waldo Frank, Julius W. Friend, Lewis Galantière, Harry Hansen, Henry Miller, Paul Rosenfeld, William Saroyan, Gertrude Stein, Thomas Wolfe, and others.)

Howe, Irving. *Sherwood Anderson.* New York: Sloane, 1951.

Phillips, William L. "How Sherwood Anderson Wrote *Winesburg, Ohio,*" *American Literature,* 23:7–30 (1951).

Rosenfeld, Paul. "Sherwood Anderson," *Dial,* 72:29–42 (1922).

Schevill, James. *Sherwood Anderson: His Life and Work.* Denver: University of Denver Press, 1951.

"Sherwood Anderson Number," *Shenandoah,* Vol. 13 (Spring 1962). (Articles by James K.

Feibleman, Frederick J. Hoffman, Jon S. Lawry, Walter B. Rideout, and Cratis D. Williams.)

"Sherwood Anderson Memorial Number," *Newberry Library Bulletin,* Second Series, No. 2 (December 1948). (Articles by George H. Daugherty, Waldo Frank, Norman Holmes Pearson, and Roger Sergel.)

"Special Sherwood Anderson Number," *Newberry Library Bulletin,* Vol. 6 (July 1971). (Articles by John H. Ferres, Walter B. Rideout, David D. Anderson, Welford D. Taylor, and an annotated checklist of an anniversary exhibit by Richard Colles Johnson.)

Sutton, William A. Four articles on Anderson's life from 1884 to 1896 and 1899 to 1907, in *Northwest Ohio Quarterly,* 19:99–114 (1947), 20:20–36 (1948), 22:39–44 (1950), 22: 120–57 (1950).

———. *The Road to Winesburg: A Mosaic of the Imaginative Life of Sherwood Anderson.* New York: Scarecrow Press, 1972.

Trilling, Lionel. *The Liberal Imagination.* New York: Viking, 1950.

Walcutt, Charles C. *American Literary Naturalism, A Divided Stream.* Minneapolis: University of Minnesota Press, 1956.

Warren, Robert Penn. "Hawthorne, Anderson and Frost," *New Republic,* 54:399–401 (1928).

Weber, Brom. "Anderson and 'The Essence of Things,'" *Sewanee Review,* 59:678–92 (1951).

White, Ray Lewis, ed. *The Achievement of Sherwood Anderson: Essays in Criticism.* Chapel Hill: University of North Carolina Press, 1966. (Selections by Waldo Frank, Francis Hackett, Rex Burbank, Bernard Duffey, William L. Phillips, M.A., Irving Howe, Edwin Fussell, Joseph Wood Krutch, Walter B. Rideout, James Schevill, Charles Child Walcutt, Frederick J. Hoffman, William Faulkner, Lionel Trilling, Malcolm Cowley, and David D. Anderson.)

Wright, Austin McGiffert. *The American Short Story in the Twenties.* Chicago: University of Chicago Press, 1961.

—BROM WEBER

Maya Angelou
1928–

Maya Angelou shares with the readers of her autobiographies an incredible journey that begins in a small town in Arkansas and stretches to the West Coast of Africa. Although Angelou is most familiar to her international audience for her series of autobiographies, she has excelled in other literary and personal modes as well. Reynolds Professor of American Studies at Wake Forest University in North Carolina since 1981, Angelou has been a poet, a filmmaker, an actress, a cabaret singer, a scholar, a dynamic lecturer, a nominee for both the Pulitzer Prize and the National Book Award—a woman so versatile that she belongs as much to popular culture as to the world of letters. Her poetic force is so widely recognized by African Americans that she was invited to read one of her poems at the Million Man March on October 16, 1995. This essay, while it occasionally touches on her connections with the media, is primarily concerned with the part Angelou has played in the American literary tradition.

It is as an autobiographer that Angelou has made her greatest impact on American literature, joining Richard Wright, Lillian Hellman, James Baldwin, Maxine Hong Kingston, Frederick Douglass, and other writers whose life stories have challenged and enriched the American ethos. So bewitching is Angelou's life-telling that Nancy Chick has called her a "twentieth-century Scheherazade," after the legendary storyteller who would each night tell the king a new story. By halting before each story's conclusion, Scheherazade kept the king in suspense and forestalled her execution. Like the thousand and one stories collected in the *Arabian Nights*, Angelou's five autobiographies are vivid and episodic narratives that accelerate or reduce their pace as the life winds and unwinds. By the mid-1990s, many of her admirers, anticipating that the pace would continue, suspected that a sixth volume was in the wings.

In her autobiographies Angelou proves to be an astute observer of self and society. Her recollections are grounded in the visual—in sights of shattered dolls, of filmy veils, and of Klansmen riding in the night. Her autobiographies are like a series of snapshots taken at different times from different angles that focus on major themes. For Angelou herself, life and work evoke another visual image, one derived from painting. In a 1977 *Black Scholar* interview, she told Robert Chrisman, then editor of *Ebony* magazine, "I try to live my life as a poetic adventure . . . , everything is part of a large canvas I am creating, I am living beneath."

Maya Angelou's poetic adventure began April 4, 1928, when she was born in St. Louis as Marguerite Johnson, daughter of Vivian (Baxter) Johnson and Bailey Johnson Sr. Soon after, the family moved to Long Beach, California, where her parents' troubled marriage ended in divorce. When she was three her father put Maya and her four-year-old brother Bailey on a train from California to Stamps, Arkansas, home of their paternal grandmother, Annie Henderson (generally called "Momma" in the narratives). For students of African American literature, these nearly abandoned children and this mighty grandmother are ingrained in the imagination by way of Angelou's first published autobiography, *I Know Why the Caged Bird Sings*.

As Angelou's life is best understood from her own autobiographical writings, this essay will reconstruct Angelou's story as she herself revealed it in *I Know Why the Caged Bird Sings* (1970), *Gather Together in My Name* (1974), *Singin' and Swingin' and Gettin' Merry Like Christmas* (1976), *The Heart of a Woman* (1981), and *All God's Children Need Traveling Shoes* (1986). These volumes, although disparate, are unified through a number of artistic features. While they follow conventional autobiographical technique in tracing the activities of the narrator, they also stretch over time and place to contain detailed portraits of other significant characters: Maya's first husband, Tosh Angelos; the Ghanaian chief and educator, Nana Nketsia; the Stamps "aristocrat," Mrs. Bertha Flowers; the American statesman, Malcolm X; the blues singer, Billie Holiday; her roommate, Alice Windom; and many other characters. Because of the vastness of her canvas, Angelou tends to underplay the traditional autobiographical device of individual development in favor of a more generalized technique; as Dolly McPherson has observed in her 1990 book, *Order Out of Chaos*, Angelou creates "rich portraits of a wide assortment of people, including description of the rhythms of their lives and the patterns of different environments."

This multiplicity of rhythms requires the reader to travel through several books to understand, for example, Maya's full attitude toward her mother or the entirety of her feelings about men. As an autobiographer, Angelou echoes in her structure the flexibility of the life processes. She constantly, although perhaps not always consciously, interrelates ideas, images, and characters within the five-volume structure. In her revision of traditional African American autobiography, Maya Angelou sets herself apart by extending the form, incorporating personal and historical materials into a continuing narrative that becomes a record of one black woman's life in America and Africa. From volume to volume there is a sense of historical change: in Jim Crow laws; in the Pan-African and civil rights movements; in black participation in theater; and countless other areas. By focusing on certain themes not ordinarily explored in more impersonal African American autobiographies such as those of Frederick Douglass or Gwendolyn Brooks, Angelou presents one of the closest looks in print at what it is to be an African American woman. She explores her womanhood in meticulous detail, finding both personal and cultural relevance in such diverse events as visiting her son's elementary school, preparing a dinner, or conversing with an African woman at a campfire. Sondra O'Neale writes that Angelou's attention to these "mundane, though essential, ordinary moments of life" are aspects of "superior autobiography." As we examine Angelou's autobiographies, their superior quality will become recognizable.

I Know Why the Caged Bird Sings is the first and still best-loved volume in the autobiographical series. *Caged Bird* begins with a symbolic prelude concerning Maya's fears of being stared at in church. Her emotions in this introductory section focus on her contempt for her black skin; like Pecola Breedlove in Toni Morrison's *The Bluest Eye*, she wishes for the privileges that come with being white. Jon Zlotnik Schmidt isolates this opening incident as one of several in which Maya feels abused and devalued because she is a black child who perceives herself as the "other" in a white world. Her "black ugly dream" introduces a motif which sets up the theme of racial displacement that occupies much of *Caged Bird* and of the subsequent volume, *Gather Together in My Name*.

The formal autobiography begins with Maya's recollection of traveling with her brother by train from California to Arkansas. Because Maya was three and Bailey was four they had tags around their wrists with notes "To Whom It May Concern" explaining their names and destination. These children, along with their stern grandmother, Annie Henderson, form an emotional pulse at the heart of *I Know Why the Caged Bird Sings*, a pulse which vibrates from the extended family into the community of Stamps, into its religious, social, and educational institutions. Uncle Willie, Annie Henderson's crippled son, is another key figure at the core of this narrative. In an early episode Uncle Willie is hidden in a potato bin to escape the attention of a white lynching mob; his humiliation gives Maya her first knowledge of racism.

Throughout much of *Caged Bird* Maya remains displaced, rejected in a racist society and all but abandoned by her mother, Vivian Baxter. In one of several reflective fantasies, the child imagines her mother lying in a coffin, dead, faceless: "since I couldn't fill in the features I printed M O T H E R across the O, and tears would fall down my cheeks like warm milk." The empty face of the mother is perceived through the imagination of a child who prints, who writes, who stares back. In the gap left by the absent mother Maya erects Momma Henderson: "I saw only her power and strength. She was taller than any woman in my personal world, and her hands were so large they could span my head from ear to ear."

I Know Why the Caged Bird Sings abounds in such moments of verbal force, where the metaphors perfectly correspond to the emotion, as in Momma's encompassing hands, as in the Christmas misery when Maya destroys the blond-haired doll her mother had sent her but preserves the other gift, a tea set, "because any day or night she might come riding up." The doll and the tea set seem to represent Maya's torn self, the angry child versus the ungrateful child—the doll destroyed in anger but the tea set saved in the hope of Vivian's return.

Another striking use of metaphor occurs in the confrontation between Annie Henderson and three "powhitetrash" girls who taunt her. The oldest of the girls brazenly performs a pantyless handstand before Momma's eyes. Symbolically, the white child unveils the power of her white sexuality in front of a woman who, though morally superior, is defenseless, being black, being the "other." Momma responds to her situation by quietly singing a hymn, her eyes toward Heaven. In his interpretation of this episode, Stephen Butterfield views Momma's silence as a victory in self-control, although, given the racist underpinnings of her response, her victory is ultimately a "consolation prize." McPherson reads this confrontation scene from Maya's perspective, seeing an example of "the kind of spiritual death and regeneration Angelou experienced during the shaping of her development."

Angelou presents a similar death of the spirit in describing her visit, with Momma, to a white dentist who would rather put his "hand in a dog's mouth than in a nigger's." The horrendous equation between "dog" and "nigger" recounts the history of dehumanization recorded by African American writers, from the first slave narratives to the "mad and hungry dogs" of Claude McKay's famous sonnet, "If We Must Die." Humiliated for herself, for her grandmother, for her culture, Maya retaliates silently in a fantasy of power where Momma's eyes burn "like live coals" and her arms grow to twice their length.

The most powerful emotional response in the

first autobiography, however, is Maya's negation of speech after being raped during a stay with her mother in St. Louis. The beautiful Vivian has a lover, Mr. Freeman, who befriends Maya and later rapes her. Angelou describes the episode in language that has been broadly acclaimed for its candor:

> Then there was the pain. A breaking and entering when even the senses are torn apart. The act of rape on an eight-year-old body is a matter of the needle giving because the camel can't. The child gives, because the body can, and the mind of the violator cannot.

After the rape Maya, ill from the shock and from the pain, is sent to the hospital, where she tells Bailey the rapist's identity. Mr. Freeman is tried and found guilty but inexplicably released the very day of his sentencing. Not long afterward Mr. Freeman's corpse is found behind a slaughterhouse, apparently kicked to death. Although the text suggests that Maya's uncles and grandmother were involved in Mr. Freeman's murder, this is never stated explicitly. After the trial and subsequent murder Maya, who has lied about her earlier sexual contact with Mr. Freeman, becomes mute so that the "poison" in her breath will not damage anyone else. Like Momma in the "powhite-trash" episode, the victimized child experiences a self-imposed "perfect silence."

Vivian Baxter, unable to charm her daughter into speech, sends both children back to Arkansas. Once again in the sanctuary of her grandmother's general store, Maya gathers strength from the African American community, whose values of self-determination and personal dignity help her to overcome her muteness. Maya gains special strength from Bailey and from Mrs. Bertha Flowers, a genteel black woman whose passion for reading helps Maya recover her speech—although Angelou, in a 1990 interview with Dolly McPherson, admitted that her "vol-

untary mutism" actually lasted "almost five years." Maya is eventually restored to speech, regaining her language through self-education and through formal training. Despite her crisis, Maya is able to graduate with top honors from the Lafayette County Training School in Stamps. Four years later she graduates from George Washington, a predominantly white high school in San Francisco, where she studies under Miss Kirwin, a "rare educator who was in love with information" and who had no "teacher's pets." While still in high school she receives a scholarship to study dance and theater at the California Labor School, also called the Mission School. Maya nonetheless remains insecure about her sexuality, so damaged has she been from the psychological consequences of the rape and the ensuing trial and murder. She develops negative images about her body; she thinks that her large bones, small breasts, and deep voice indicate that she is a lesbian. In order to disprove this notion she seduces a handsome neighborhood boy and becomes pregnant. At the end of *I Know Why the Caged Bird Sings*, Maya is a single mother, yet still herself a child, a mother afraid she might harm her baby. Maya's mother, Vivian Baxter, assuages this fear by firmly placing the infant in her daughter's arms.

In *Gather Together in My Name* (1974), Maya is a young mother pessimistic about her place in the American economy, and must face the disruptions that followed the Second World War. Her own tenuous world is steadied through caring for her son, Clyde. As *Gather Together in My Name* opens, Maya and Clyde (who will throughout this essay be known by his chosen name, Guy) are living in San Francisco with Vivian Baxter and her new husband. Maya seems unfocussed: "I was seventeen, very old, embarrassingly young, with a son of two months, and I still lived with my mother and stepfather."

In need of an income, Maya tries her skills at

several low-level jobs, including being a busgirl and a cook at a Creole restaurant. The tedium is alleviated when she falls in love with a man named Curly and experiences sexual pleasure for the first time in her life. The affair ends abruptly when Curly's girlfriend returns from San Diego.

Bailey, the beloved brother of *Caged Bird*, returns to San Francisco from merchant seaman's service and again plays a major role in Maya's life. He encourages her to go to Los Angeles, where she tries without success to live with relatives. At this stage Angelou fantasizes about "a juicy melodrama in which I was to be the star." Instead, she becomes a nightclub waitress and meets two lesbians, Johnnie Mae and Beatrice. In a dramatic scene Maya and the two women, acknowledged prostitutes, spend an afternoon smoking marijuana, dancing, and drinking Dubonnet. Maya convinces them to turn their house into a whorehouse, with Maya as madam. The partnership, so successful that Maya is able to buy a used Chrysler convertible, collapses when Johnnie Mae and Beatrice disobey the house rules.

Returning again to her mother, Maya applies for Officer's Candidate School and is accepted until the Army discovers that she had attended the California Labor School, which was "Communist." Maya then takes yet another minimal job, this time as a waitress at the Chicken Shack, where she meets a dancer, R. L. Poole, and auditions to be his partner. Although they become lovers and partners, the affair is over, as it was with Curly, when Poole's original woman returns.

The string of bad luck continues, next in Stockton, California, where Maya has yet another relationship with a man who manipulates her. L. D. Tolbrook is her father's age, married, and as Maya eventually discovers, a pimp. To please him Maya takes on her most degrading job; she becomes a prostitute. Through the language and the content of the whorehouse sequence, Angelou

captures the essence of a subculture of sex and drugs, thus being autobiographically faithful to the self she has become. In doing so she also, as a writer, observes areas of life that rarely find their way into mainstream American literature.

Angelou's arrangement with Tolbrook is interrupted when she learns that her mother is in the hospital and that her brother is deteriorating after his girlfriend's death from tuberculosis. In a reunion that recalls the intensity of *I Know Why the Caged Bird Sings*, Bailey and Maya promise to take care of one another. She feeds and nurtures him; he orders her to quit the business of being a prostitute.

But Bailey's dissipation seems to upset Maya. Although he is mentioned briefly in *Singin' and Swingin' and Gettin' Merry Like Christmas* for supporting Maya's decision to marry, the revered brother gradually disappears from the autobiographies and is rarely mentioned by the literary critics. In *The Heart of a Woman* one learns that Bailey, now aged thirty-three, is in prison for fencing stolen items. Maya's friend Martin Luther King Jr. consoles her: "We must save the Baileys of the world. And Maya, never stop loving him. Never give up on him. Never deny him." This compassionate advice appears to be the last reference to Bailey in the narratives.

Toward the end of *Gather Together in My Name* Maya nearly loses her son when the babysitter, Big Mary Dawson, kidnaps Guy and carries him off to Bakersfield. When Tolbrook refuses to help, Maya takes a bus, retrieves Guy, and returns to San Francisco.

Angelou's distressing second volume reflects the dangers faced by a young black teenager who attempts to take care of a baby in an economy that honors neither poor blacks nor unmarried women. In its explicitness, her self-portrait challenges the more general trend in American autobiography: to project the subject as a model of virtue and achievement, as in the self-righteous *Autobiography of Benjamin Franklin*; or, as in

Zora Neale Hurston's *Dust Tracks on a Road*, which, according to her biographer Robert Hemenway, "sacrifices truth to the politics of racial harmony."

It would have been difficult to predict that the author of *Gather Together in My Name* would become the Maya Angelou of the 1990s, regaled as a prototype for the empowerment of African American women. The early critics of *Gather Together in My Name* were mostly disheartened by this unexpected sequel to *Caged Bird*. Selwyn Cudjoe, for instance, was troubled by its shaky construction, while Lynn Z. Bloom objected to the less-suitable narrator, who lacked the "intuitive good judgment" displayed in *Caged Bird*. In its defense, Dolly McPherson argued that *Gather Together in My Name* is "an artistically more mature work than *Caged Bird*," and that its fragmentations reflect the "alienated fragmented nature of Angelou's life."

To a certain degree, the alienation in *Gather Together* is related to the geographical and spiritual absence of Annie Henderson, whose influence recedes as Maya's life becomes increasingly urban. Near the middle of the autobiography, Maya takes Guy to Stamps for a visit and discovers that she has become too racially liberated to accept Momma's protective regulations concerning whites. After Maya gets in trouble for talking impudently to two saleswomen, Momma slaps her and orders her to leave Stamps for Maya's and the baby's safety. It is to be their final meeting in the autobiographical series.

The climax of *Gather Together in My Name* occurs when an unexpectedly compassionate boyfriend, Troubador Martin, takes Maya, now smoking a lot of marijuana, on an unnerving tour of the underworld of heroin addiction. Troub makes her watch while he shoots up, makes her watch as the needle punctures a scab and "rich yellow pus flowed out and down his arm to the wrist." Maya's refusal, at Troub's advice, to do hard drugs marks the end of her irresponsibility and her inauguration of new standards that will help safeguard her and her son's survival. The book ends with a vow: "I had no idea what I was going to make of my life, but I had given a promise and found my innocence. I swore I'd never lose it again."

Despite its wildly celebratory title, *Singin' and Swingin' and Gettin' Merry Like Christmas* is fraught with conflicts: Maya's temporary separation from her son; her confused feelings about Vivian Baxter; her failed marriage to Tosh Angelos; her ambiguous assessment of her own motives and behavior; and the irrevocable loss of Annie Henderson.

Maya meets her husband-to-be, Tosh Angelos, when she is working as a salesgirl in a record store. Impressed by the young sailor's enthusiasm for jazz, she introduces him to Guy, who is immediately won over. Vivian Baxter, though, is opposed to Maya's marriage to a "poor white man." The marriage is initially satisfying until Maya begins to resent Tosh's demands that she stay at home and be the perfect housewife, the provider of suitable meals and "fabulous jello deserts." She is also bothered by what she senses to be the disapproval from others because of the interracial marriage.

When Tosh tells Guy that there is no God, Maya is furious. She retaliates by going on a secret quest that ends in her conversion at the Evening Star Baptist Church. Their differences grow until one day Tosh says he's "tired of being married." At this point Maya loses her affection for him, and the marriage of three years collapses.

Much of Maya's struggle in this third and most complex of the autobiographies concerns her private role as single mother versus her public role as a committed actress, one whose career makes it necessary to leave Guy for long stretches of time. Chosen to perform in a European tour of *Porgy and Bess*, Maya faces the realization that in leaving Guy with Vivian, she will repeat the hateful pattern established by her parents when they left her and Bailey in the hands of Momma Henderson. Her feelings are compounded by the fact that, as a young, black, single mother, she bears the ultimate responsibility for her son, whom she wants to support both emotionally (by being home) and economically (by being in Europe). In so concisely identifying the conflicts between working and mothering, Angelou offers her readers a model for understanding the problems that may arise when a woman attempts to fulfill both roles.

Maya returns from Europe to find her lonely son suffering from a skin disease that has psychosomatic origins. Promising never to leave him again, she takes Guy with her to Hawaii, where she has a singing engagement. The autobiography thus concludes with a reaffirmation of the mother-son bond that ended *I Know Why the Caged Bird Sings*.

Discreetly hidden in *Singin' and Swingin' and Gettin' Merry Like Christmas* is another narrative thread to which critics have paid little attention: the definitive separation from Momma Henderson. In the third autobiography, Momma, once the leading influence in Maya's development, vanishes from the texts. The powerful grandmother is dead, no longer able to comfort Maya with her strong hands or to influence Maya's actions. The record of Annie Henderson's death is perhaps the strongest emotional revelation of the five autobiographies. I emphasize the death of the grandmother now, as I did in my 1990 essay, "Singing the Black Mother," to underscore a problem that Angelou never comes fully to terms with in the autobiographical series: her ambivalent feelings toward those she loves, especially Annie Henderson. In her reminiscence about her grandmother's death, Angelou's style shifts from its usual conversational tone and becomes intense, religious, and emotional: "Ah, Momma. I had never looked at death before,

peered into its yawning chasm for the face of a beloved. . . . If I were as good as God's angels and as pure as the Mother of Christ, I could never have Momma's rough slow hands pat my cheek or braid my hair." This moving farewell, untypical of Angelou's more worldly autobiographical style, is overlooked by most critics.

Maya's elegy for her grandmother, which relies on gospel tradition, on the language of Bible stories, and on certain African American literary texts, especially on James Weldon Johnson's "Go Down Death—A Funeral Sermon," is related to a religious conversion previously experienced in *Singin' and Swingin'*. To Angelou the African American spirituals were "sweeter than sugar. I wanted to keep my mouth full of them . . ."; this image counters the negative images of the empty mother and wordless mouth depicted in *I Know Why the Caged Bird Sings*. Angelou's "singing" of the black grandmother in this extraordinary passage suggests a liberation from guilt and a loving reconciliation with Momma, an attempt, through religion, to mollify her ambivalence toward Annie Henderson by identifying with her traditions.

At the beginning of *The Heart of a Woman* Maya, amused by her beatnik appearance, is living with her son and four whites on a houseboat commune near San Francisco. When the situation wearies her, she manages to rent, through the intervention of white friends, a house in a segregated neighborhood. In this house she entertains the legendary Billie Holiday a few months before the singer's death. The record of their four-day friendship, with its portrayal of Holiday's moody anger and vivid language (both of which Guy dislikes), is one of the most memorable vignettes of the series.

After Guy experiences discrimination from the staff of the white school he is attending, he and Maya move to a mixed neighborhood. It is here that she starts to write: "At first I limited myself to short sketches, then to song lyrics, then I dared short stories.'' Following her decision to leave California for Brooklyn, New York, Maya joins the Harlem Writer's Guild. Through the encouragement and criticism of other African Americans—John Killens, John Clarke, Sarah Wright, and Paule Marshall among others—she begins to define herself as a writer. The act of writing contributes to her increasing maturity: ''If I wanted to write, I had to be willing to develop a kind of concentration found mostly in people awaiting execution. I had to learn technique and surrender my ignorance.''

Maya further expands her potential when she joins the off-Broadway cast of Jean Genet's play *The Blacks*. After hearing a sermon by Martin Luther King Jr., she and Godfrey Cambridge, also playing in *The Blacks*, plan a fund-raiser at New York's Village Gate. Called the Cabaret for Freedom, the fund-raiser is so successful that she is asked to be northern coordinator of King's organization, the Southern Christian Leadership Conference.

Several episodes, though, jar against these successes and recall the anxious motherhood of the earlier volumes. In the most striking of these, Maya returns from an engagement in Chicago to learn that Guy has gotten in trouble with a Brooklyn street gang. In order to protect her son, she confronts the gang leader and threatens to shoot his entire family if Guy is harmed. This confrontation represents the consummation of her maternal strength as she powerfully performs the role of mother and protector.

In *The Heart of a Woman* Maya finds power and happiness through her sexual experiences with Vusumzi Make, but becomes vulnerable to his male authority, as she had with Curly, L. D. Tolbrook, and other men in her past. She marries Make and they eventually move to Cairo, where he expects her to be the perfect African wife and homemaker. Against Make's wishes and Egyptian custom, Maya asserts her woman's will by

taking a job as an associate editor with the *Arab Observer*. The enlightened Angelou soon realizes that the marriage is unstable, that Make is too careless with money and too congenial with other women. The marriage ends bitterly when she becomes convinced of his infidelity.

With the heightened sensitivity that writing brings, Angelou becomes fully aware, for the first time, of her African heritage. As she begins to analyze the ambiguous relationship between being an African and being an African American, she discovers her connection with the African slaves who had been ''tied with ropes, shackled with chains, forced to march for weeks carrying the double burden of neck irons and abysmal fear.''

The problematic relationship with Vus Make; the commitment to Martin Luther King; the identification with the sorrows of Africa; the anguish she endures on realizing that her brother Bailey is in prison: these are some of the features that make *The Heart of a Woman* one of the most sensitive of her books. In it, claims Dolly McPherson, Angelou withholds nothing. ''Her writing here, describing her longings, doubts, and shortcomings, is raw, bare honesty.'' Yet *The Heart of a Woman* is at the same time a very public statement, informed by Angelou's affiliations with the Harlem Writer's Guild, the Cultural Association for Women of African Heritage, the Cabaret for Freedom, the Southern Christian Leadership Conference, and by her work as a political journalist.

Near the end of *The Heart of a Woman* the more private theme of motherhood is tragically reintroduced when Guy's car is hit by a truck outside of Accra, Ghana. As Maya stares at her son's pale face, she sees him ''stretched before me, stiff as a pine board, in a strange country, blood caked on his face and clotted on his clothes.'' Guy suffers a broken arm and leg but gradually recovers and during the act of physical healing grows toward a greater autonomy. In the last two paragraphs we find Angelou alone, testing her independence. She recognizes within herself an emergent new Maya, one emancipated from the role restrictions that had confined her in the earlier volumes.

Through the dramatic repetition of Guy's accident, Angelou ties the end of *The Heart of a Woman* to the beginning of her fifth autobiography, *All God's Children Need Traveling Shoes.* While her major concerns are Guy and his recovery from the car accident, she continues to explore the process of learning to give up her son, a process that accelerates when she discovers that Guy is having an affair with an American woman older than herself. When Maya threatens to punish him, Guy, in a reversal of roles, affectionately pats her head and says, ''Yes, little mother. I'm sure you will.'' Maya herself has a few flirtations in *All God's Children Need Traveling Shoes,* although she is more cautious than she had been with Vus Make. She has the wisdom to refuse the proposal of Sheikali, a wealthy importer from Mali, when he asks her to be wife number two and teacher to his eight children. Although she rejects Sheikali's offer, and despite her unhappiness with Tosh Angelos and Vus Make, Angelou does later remarry. Her third husband is Paul de Feu, a construction worker whom she met in England. In a 1990 essay Carol E. Neubauer mentions the third marriage, stating that the couple spent most of their seven years together on the West Coast.

One also finds, in *Traveling Shoes,* an increasing affirmation of sisterhood, a new respect for women that coincides with the vast political and social changes taking place around the world. She has two roommates, Vicki Garvin and Alice Windom, both of them businesswomen with master's degrees. Angelou also forms a very close friendship with Efua Sutherland, a flamboyant woman who founded the Ghanaian Society of Writers and who wrote tales of strong women such as Foruwa, the royal heroine of ''New Life at Kyerefaso.'' In one touching vignette, Angelou

recounts befriending Comfort Adday, a hairdresser and the victim of a voodoo spell put on her by a jealous woman. Maya loans Comfort the money to go to Sierra Leone, where she is promised a cure. Later Maya learns that Comfort is dead.

Initially alienated from Ghanaians by culture, language, and beliefs, Maya seeks solidarity by joining the fragile African American community. These expatriates, far from the United States, remain committed enough to stage a protest at the American Embassy in Accra as a show of solidarity with the spring 1963 March on Washington. The demonstration, which begins in a restrained, political manner, is soon transformed into ''Ole Time Religious stuff'' when the crowd learns of the death of W. E. B. Du Bois. Angelou writes, ''We were singing Dr. Du Bois' spirit, for the invaluable contributions he made, for his shining intellect and his courage. To many of us he was the first American Negro intellectual.'' The poignantly depicted reaction to the death of Du Bois is both an affirmation of Angelou's inherent attachment to the United States and an evocation of the eulogy to her grandmother in *Singin' and Swingin' and Gettin' Merry Like Christmas.*

All God's Children Need Traveling Shoes and, to a lesser degree, *The Heart of a Woman* seem to vacillate between a retained devotion to African American culture and a desire for commitment to the reincarnated African image—a desire to explore the language and customs of people who, while recognizably ancestors, neither welcome nor admire Americans. Maya first bridges the gap between these two cultures when, under pressure, she and her two roommates take in a young African boy named Kojo. This lovely child, with his dark skin and beautifully shaped head, reminds Maya of her brother Bailey. The three women assume Kojo is poor until, in one charming episode, his entire family, elegantly dressed, introduce themselves with gifts of yams and eggs from their prosperous farm. The encounter with

Kojo's family enables Angelou to move beyond her own concerns for Guy to a larger, almost cosmic theme—her affinity with mother Africa. Linda A. Myers describes this transformation from an American past to a Ghanaian present: Angelou is "able to be a spectator viewing her own past as a complex happening which has ended. Africa provides a renewal for a new pulse of life for her continuing journey."

Determined to immerse herself in the Ghanaian atmosphere of racial pride, Maya rents a car and ventures out alone to contemplate her newly discovered West African heritage. In her travels past Cape Coast and Dunkwa, she recognizes certain connections between her own traditions and those of her African ancestors, including their subjection to slavery, symbolized by the forts of Elmina Castle. She is both proud and amused when she is mistaken for a Bambara from Liberia. She makes friends with a Ghanaian woman, Patience Aduah, whose hospitality reminds her of Annie Henderson, who had aided African American travelers denied food and lodging in the Jim Crow era of segregation in Arkansas.

In Ghana, Angelou also encounters many of the African leaders and intellectuals who had come into power following the liberation: the dancer Grace Nuamah, the scholar J. H. Nketia, the poet Kwesi Brew, and the Ahanta Chief Nana Nketsia. Her initial meeting with Nana Nketsia is delightfully narrated, from the moment when his hesitant driver arrives at Maya's house to the moment when Nana, in a "passion of self-appreciation," affirms the superiority of his blackness. But the most memorable occasion of the volume is the meeting with Malcolm X, who had come to Ghana to speak against American racism following his historic trip to Mecca. Angelou's use of conversational dialogue in the Malcolm X segment lends an immediacy and humanity to a figure so often treated with reverential abstraction. Malcolm stresses the unity of all black people and chides Maya for her intolerance toward middle-class black groups: "When you hear that the Urban League or the NAACP is giving a formal banquet at the Waldorf Astoria, I know you won't go, but don't knock them. They give scholarships to poor Black children."

Angelou's breadth of experience with both people and places in *All God's Children Need Traveling Shoes* surely justifies the title, for she travels through major capitals and small villages, in Egypt and Ghana, in Italy and Germany. As her friend James Baldwin had done in his 1953 essay, "Stranger in the Village," so Angelou investigates the ambivalent role of the educated African American in Europe, offering a series of racially charged anecdotes that are softened by her tolerant humor. This combination of astute observer and experienced traveler has contributed tremendously to Angelou's success as an autobiographer.

Yet despite Angelou's commitment to the journey, *All God's Children Need Traveling Shoes* concludes in a leave-taking; she is leaving both the vigorous rhythms of Africa and her son, Guy, who remains in Accra to finish his degree. The final traveling scene is at the airport, as Maya prepares for her departure from Ghana and her return to the United States. Joyously celebrating her African and her American ancestries, Angelou reaches forth at journey's end to embrace the blues, gospel, and dance, and to bridge the distance between Ghana and the States. These positive fusions of African and American cultures inform much of Angelou's other work—the television scripts; her reflections on being a grandmother; her prose meditation, *Wouldn't Take Nothing for My Journey Now* (1993); and finally, the poems that illustrate the sweep of her literary interests.

In a 1986 essay published in *Woman's Day,* Angelou continues her narrative from the perspective of a grandmother. Her grandson, Colin, had been kidnapped by Guy's ex-wife. The essay recalls Maya's anxiety as she had tried to recover her missing son from his kidnapper, Big Mary, in *Gather Together in My Name.* One of the most interesting aspects of the essay is the feeling of autobiographical continuity as Angelou, now herself a protective grandmother, looks back to Momma Henderson. When Angelou reads Colin the *Brer Rabbit* tales and teaches him spirituals, she identifies with Momma Henderson: "My grandmother had done that for me and I wished to pass these treasures on to Colin." Later, in a moment of panic, Angelou writes, "I reached inside myself all the way back to my own grandmother and found enough reserve to keep from screaming." As in the first three volumes of her autobiography, Angelou, in the 1986 essay, still recognizes in the grandmother the cornerstone of the black community and the keeper of folk tradition.

As an autobiographer Angelou shares in a rich literary tradition of African American autobiography arguably initiated with the 1814 publication of *Gustavus Vassa, the African.* At the same time, however, she occupies a unique place within that tradition, as a number of critics observed in their enthusiastic response to *I Know Why the Caged Bird Sings.* In his 1975 essay George Kent, while he listed her affinities with Richard Wright, Anne Moody, Malcolm X, and others, argued that Angelou's narrative is singular in its distinctive attitude toward self, community, and imaginative form. Both Sidonie Ann Smith in 1973 and Stephen Butterfield in 1974 have compared *Caged Bird* to Richard Wright's *Black Boy,* finding similarities in those works' rendering of life in a small segregated southern town. Butterfield, however, ascribed Angelou's uniqueness as an autobiographer to her creation of a community where women support and respect one another. In a similar vein, Dolly McPherson, two decades later, credits Angelou's

originality to a "preoccupation with the effect of the community on the individual's achievement and retention of an integrated, acceptable self."

While each of these assessments is valid, the uniqueness of Angelou's voice can be further attributed to a number of additional factors, among them her intense examination of her own motives and desires; the complex relationship between her narrative structure and its re-envisioning of earlier forms such as the sermon, the spiritual, and the slave narrative; her singing of the black mother; and her unprecedented success in improvising the single-volume form into an extended, serial autobiography.

It is imperative to distinguish between the serial autobiography—practiced by Angelou, James Weldon Johnson, James Baldwin, and a few other African American autobiographers—with the more standard, single-volume autobiography produced by Zora Neale Hurston in *Dust Tracks on a Road;* or by Anne Moody in *Coming of Age in Mississippi;* or even by Richard Wright, whose 1945 *Black Boy* tells of childhood and adolescence, but whose 1944 political autobiography, *American Hunger,* is so distinct from his account of youth that the two works can hardly be considered parts of a series. And, while one could compare the autobiographical themes of Maya Angelou and Nikki Giovanni, with their emphasis on childbirth, black motherhood, and the family, Giovanni's *Gemini: an extended autobiographical statement on my first twenty-five years of being a black poet* is too brief a piece to convey the breadth that Angelou achieves in her series.

In the serial mode, with its prolonged and continuous narrative, problems arise that are not encountered in single-volume books, with their more ordered chronologies and established endings—although there are exceptions among modern writers, for instance Gertrude Stein, whose 1923 *The Autobiography of Alice B. Toklas* inverted the rules of standard autobiography. As a multivolumed autobiographer, Angelou had to face the technical challenges posed by that genre: when to convert present tense into past or future; how to orchestrate cross-references; how to preserve continuity without lapsing into repetition; how to sustain the theatrical tone; how to find the discipline to continue; where to let the texts die out; and where to begin again.

The serial biographer Angelou perhaps most closely resembles artistically is the dramatist Lillian Hellman, whose autobiographical sequence consists of four volumes: *An Unfinished Woman* (1970); *Pentimento* (1973); *Scoundrel Time* (1976); and *Maybe* (1980). The first of the series, *An Unfinished Woman,* won the 1970 National Book Award for Arts and Letters, the same year that *I Know Why the Caged Bird Sings* was published in a Book-of-the-Month Club edition. The likenesses proliferate. Both women rely on the language of theater as a method for staging first-person episodes. Both women emphasize the painting metaphor to describe their autobiographical method: Angelou's "large canvas" versus Hellman's "pentimento," a layering produced when a painter covers one image with another. Both are strong, independent, political writers who situate their biographies within both American and international settings. Both write with lucidity about the racial "other." Both have experienced enormous public recognition in their lifetimes.

Yet the parallels between Angelou and Hellman, delineated by Stephanie A. Demetrako-poulous in 1980 and by Ekaterini Georgoudaki in 1990, are disavowed by Angelou in an interview with Dolly McPherson in *Order Out of Chaos.* Generally, Angelou dislikes Hellman's autobiographical work, finding it to be "one-dimensional" or "romantic" or "self-centered" or "elitist." In her view Hellman invented blacks who are "cardboard characters." Further, Hellman "never represented a large group of people."

Angelou's objections to Hellman seem excessive. Perhaps they are reflections of differences in race or class or perhaps in lifestyle: Hellman's

teenage abortion, described in *An Unfinished Woman,* would have given her a different perspective from Angelou's, for whom the theme of teenage motherhood was so crucial. Angelou's objections seem even more emphatic when placed side by side with her affinity for the Chinese American. autobiographer Maxine Hong Kingston. Kingston's *Woman Warrior,* which traces the development and ancestry of a young Chinese American woman, has frequently been compared to *I Know Why the Caged Bird Sings*—by Stephanie A. Demetrakopoulous and, in 1991, by Helen M. Buss. Angelou enjoys the parallels with Kingston and even uses the phrase "woman warrior" in *Wouldn't Take Nothing for My Journey Now.*

For most reviewers, Angelou's work must be perceived within an African American feminist tradition. Joanne Braxton, for instance, claims not only that Angelou's literary ancestors are African American women writers but also that her autobiographical impulse "derives essentially from her celebration of the black women who nurtured her." A close study of *All God's Children Need Traveling Shoes* further reveals that her autobiographical roots, while planted in the literary traditions of African American women writers like Linda Brent and Zora Neale Hurston, are further nurtured by the soil of Mother Africa: an Africa first understood through the harrowing experience of the African American slave and then reframed through Angelou's residency in Egypt and Ghana.

In *All God's Children Need Traveling Shoes,* Angelou writes, "Many years earlier I, or rather someone very like me and certainly related to me, had been taken from Africa by force." Angelou's identification with slavery is both personal and formal; the slave narrative is an intuitive structure discernible in each of the five volumes but most prominent in the fifth volume. Set in West Africa, *All God's Children Need Traveling Shoes* echoes—as do all of the volumes—both the structure of traditional African American autobiographies and the structure of the slave narrative.

The slave narrative in its earliest form was the recollection by a former slave of her or his struggles in the journey from Africa to America and, once in America, from bondage to liberation. Many of these narratives were oral, translated into written words through the sponsorship of a white benefactor, although some narratives, written by slaves, celebrate the achievement of literacy as a major theme. (Frederick Douglass' *Narrative,* for example). William L. Andrews, an authority on the antebellum slave narrative, stresses the connection between freedom and literacy: ''In the slave narrative the quest is toward freedom from physical bondage and the enlightenment that literacy can offer to the restricted self- and social consciousness of the slave.''

Like the slave narrative, Angelou's autobiographies are informed by the motif of the journey and its opportunities for enlightenment. Her quest takes her from ignorance to consciousness, from muteness to articulation, from racial bondage to liberation. The narrator, in the course of her journey, crosses the racially imposed barricades of a southern town to travel to St. Louis, Los Angeles, Mexico, France, Israel, and at last to Africa and the Accra airport. Her journey thus mirrors the movement of the slave narrative, with its recalled journey from Africa to America, its catalog of hardships, and its promised ending in some sort of emancipation. For Maya Angelou the emancipation ensues in part from her continuous efforts as a writer, in part from her redefinition of self as mother and woman, in part from her profound rediscovery of her African heritage.

Through the autobiographical narrative form, Angelou found her own ''voice,'' whereas as an actress or singer she had given voice to other people's words, although often within the oral tradition of the African diaspora, as in her calypso performances described in *Singin' and Swingin' and Gettin' Merry Like Christmas.* In the 1986 essay, ''My Grandson, Home at Last,'' she mentions reading her grandson the *Brer Rabbit* tales. *Brer Rabbit,* one of several African American variants of a West African trickster tale, is also in some ways a slave narrative, the story of someone trapped, bound, but finally freed through his own ingenuity, his own skill with words (Toni Morrison uses the same image to great effect in *Tar Baby*).

In evoking the slave narrative, Angelou is not alone among her contemporaries; Hazel B. Carby claims that women's slave narratives ''haunt the texts'' of contemporary black women writers, repeating the themes of flight, servitude, rape, humiliation, poverty, and the separation of mother and child. In *Incidents in the Life of a Slave Girl* (1861), the best known of the slave narratives by women, Linda Brent (Harriet Jacobs) describes the anguish of this separation. Brent's first awareness of being a slave occurs at the death of her mother; much of Brent's quest involves her search for her daughter, Ellen, who was sold as a child to another master. In a section entitled ''The Children Sold'' Brent writes, ''I bit my lips till the blood came to keep from crying out. Were my children with their grandmother, or had the speculator carried them off? The suspense was dreadful.'' She compares this moment to ''the darkest cloud that hung over my life.'' The grandmother, like Momma Henderson of *I Know Why the Caged Bird Sings,* plays a crucial nurturing role in Brent's story. Her stabilizing function is common to both African American and West African societies, as Mildred A. Hill-Lubin has demonstrated in a 1986 essay on the grandmother.

Many contemporary African American women writers are engaged, like Angelou, in the process of re-envisioning the slave narrative from a mother's point of view. In *Beloved* (1987), a historical novel that owes much to the black autobiographical tradition, Toni Morrison reconstructs the narrative of a woman slave who murdered her baby to save it from white male violence. In her 1989 novel, *The Temple of My Familiar,* Alice Walker's heroine charts the dreadful journey into slavery, recalling ordeals that include the death of her mother and, afterward, the horrendous passage from Africa in a slave ship, where nursing mothers shared their milk with the starving children. Aunt Cuney, a mother figure in Paule Marshall's *Praisesong to the Widow* (1984), retells the narrative of Ibo slaves who crossed from West Africa to the shores of South Carolina. Marshall, Walker, and Morrison, like so many other African American women who have taken the journey, attest to the connection, only sometimes spoken, between their stories and earlier narratives of survival.

As an autobiographer, Angelou cannot insert herself into a fictionalized past. Nonetheless, the problems facing her as an African American woman echo those of the plantation system recreated by writers such as Morrison, Walker, and Marshall. Racial violence, loneliness, cultural isolation, rape, personal humiliation, silence, and separation from loved ones—all these can be found in Angelou's autobiographies. Fortunately, these negative experiences have often found relief through cultural constructs, among them the spiritual, signifying, playacting, the blues, black love, the folktale, farce, conversation, film, quilting, storytelling, and rap.

The theme of the journey, so prominent in the slave narratives, is reiterated in the title of Angelou's 1993 best-seller, *Wouldn't Take Nothing for My Journey Now.* The journey is philosophical rather than narrative, in the form of a series of short meditations resembling the *Analects* of Confucius (551–479 B.C.) but told from a female perspective and punctuated by an occasional poem. In this book Angelou offers advice that ranges from trivial matters like choosing clothing colors to profound issues dealing with death and racism. The book is at its most compelling when it is autobiographical, when it recounts episodes involving Bailey, or Clyde, or Vivian Baxter, or Annie Henderson. The sketch from *I Know Why the Caged Bird Sings* about how Momma sold chicken to factory workers is lavishly retold; the death of Momma Henderson, so emotionally narrated in *Singin' and Swingin' and Gettin' Merry Like Christmas,* is revived again in a musing on death, through the use of similar words and images.

At times Angelou recollects autobiographical moments that seem to have no direct bearing on the series. In one anecdote she describes being honored at Terry's Pub, a bar for "the black and hip in New York City," after being named the *New York Post*'s Person of the Week. She drinks too many martinis and, looking for a man, foolishly throws herself on a group of African American journalists. She tells them of her many skills in cooking, languages, and lovemaking, embarrassing not only herself but the five men as well. Tactfully escorted home by a friend, she sobers up and begins a meditation which takes her back to her first marriage to a Greek, Tosh Angelos, and to her subsequent unwillingness to form a relationship outside her race. This episode, seemingly detached from the five-volumed narrative, is nonetheless connected to it by way of attitudes, opinions, and specific associations with other self-revelatory embarrassments, for example her public confrontation of her husband Make's mistress in *The Heart of a Woman.* The pervasive autobiographical content helps to steer *Wouldn't Take Nothing for My Journey Now* away from a tendency to sermonize on proper conduct or virtue. Yet the sermonizing itself can be viewed as a reference to the African American tradition of preaching, exemplified by Martin Luther King, who figures so prominently in *The Heart of a Woman.*

The autobiographical perspective informs Angelou's poetry as well as her prose, although usually the poetry is more distanced in its revelation of the author's experience. Priscilla R. Ramsey discusses this distancing in a number of Angelou's love poems and speculates on the parallels between the poetic and autobiographical treatment surrounding her attachment to men. Joanne Braxton comments that most of the poetry "has some autobiographical content, and through much of it Angelou celebrates her dark womanhood."

Much of the autobiographical content, while it relies on the standard, first-person point of view, is veiled through the use of a persona or through an unspecified, presumably female position. In the poem "In Retrospect," for example, a lonely lover recalls the passing of last year's seasons:

Last year changed its seasons
subtly, stripped its sultry winds
for the reds of dying leaves. . . .

A similar perspective is presented in "I Almost Remember," where an unidentified older person recalls the "black / brown hands and / white thin yellowed fingers" of children who had slipped away, neglected.

In other poems, though, Angelou, in an approach comparable to the autobiographical segments of *Wouldn't Take Nothing for My Journey Now,* writes directly about her family: about her lame uncle in "Willie"; about her ancestral ties with her brother in "For Bailey"; about her roots, in "My Arkansas"; about her dauntless mother in "Call Letters: Mrs. V. B."

Of the various African American poets who have preceded her, Paul Laurence Dunbar receives the greatest acknowledgment; Angelou named *I Know Why the Caged Bird Sings* after a phrase in his 1896 poem, "Sympathy." The caged bird, symbolic of the chained slave, frequently reappears in Angelou's poems about racial injustice. Other poets who influenced her are Langston Hughes, Gwendolyn Brooks, and James Weldon Johnson. Angelou's flexible use of ballad form in poems like "The Gamut" or

"Remembering" is reminiscent of Hughes, the master of the "ballad-blues" structure in African American poetry, and of Brooks, who experimented with rhythm, race, and style in "the ballad of chocolate Mabbie" (1944) and other early poems. James Weldon Johnson, who was Annie Henderson's favorite poet, had an impact on Angelou in several of the spiritual poems, such as "Just Like Job" and "Thank You, Lord."

"On the Pulse of Morning" seized the imagination of America: first, because its unveiling was televised amidst the enthusiasm surrounding the Clintons of Arkansas; and second, because the poem offered hope for the dream of social change. Before Angelou, only one other American poet had been invited to read at an inauguration—this was Robert Frost, at the request of President John F. Kennedy in 1961. Written two decades earlier than the ceremony itself, Frost's "The Gift Outright" is politically conservative; its praise of the land moving "westward" pays no heed to the African Americans and Native Americans sacrificed to American expansionism. Angelou's ode, on the contrary, presents a litany of the oppressed: the Sioux, the Apache, the gay, the homeless, the Muslim, and others. It is a long poem—over one hundred lines as opposed to Frost's sixteen—written in a free form. At the inauguration, Angelou's theatrical rendering of "On the Pulse of Morning" was in a sense a culmination of the black oral tradition, returning to the roots of early African American literature in which former slaves like Frederick Douglass stood on podiums in cramped abolitionist meeting halls to articulate their concerns about the brutality of slavery.

There are three dominant images in the poem: the tree, the river, and the rock. The triple image evokes memories of a number of earlier British and American poems, including Walt Whitman's star / lilac / bird triad in "When Lilacs Last in the Dooryard Bloom'd," his elegy for Abraham

Lincoln. The Whitman poem, with its concerns for the president, its freedom of form and spirit, its controlling symbol of the bird, and its three-unit image patterns, may well have influenced "On the Pulse of Morning."

Of Angelou's images, each had appeared in her own earlier works, the river most prominently. In "Slave Coffle," from the 1983 collection *Shaker, Why Don't You Sing?*, the river of escape eludes the fingers of the doomed slave. In *Now Sheba Sings the Song,* a long poem modeled in part on the biblical lushness of Song of Solomon, all three metaphors are present: Sheba sees trees bending to weep for murdered slaves; she identifies with the eternal life of rocks and mountains; and she, as poet, has the power of breath to blow boats across the surface of the Mississippi and up the Nile.

Of the three metaphors that dominate "On the Pulse of Morning," the river is the one that has yielded forth a storehouse of associations for African American poets, both in the oral tradition of spirituals like "Roll, Jordan, Roll" and in the written poetry of James Weldon Johnson, Langston Hughes, Jean Toomer, and others. "On the Pulse of Morning" seems particularly reminiscent of the Hughes 1921 poem, "The Negro Speaks of Rivers," which anticipates Angelou's ode through its broad geographical focus and its celebration of the "ancient, dusky rivers" of the world. Angelou's poem also recalls a lesser- known work by Jean Toomer called "Brown River, Smile." Toomer also makes symbolic use of the river in order to praise other races—including the "great African races" and the "red races"—and, as Angelou would do six decades later, calls for a new day, crying for, in Toomer's words, a "new America / to be spiritualized by each new American." Like Hughes and Toomer before her, Angelou speaks for African Americans in their quest for peace and freedom, speaking through the voice of the sacred river:

Come, clad in peace,
And I will sing the songs
The Creator gave to me when I and the
Tree and the Rock were one.

In her crying of the river, Angelou at the same time cries the songs of her ancestors. In Ghana, with the help of her friends the poet Kwesi Brew and the folk specialist Efua Sutherland, Angelou made contact with African oral tradition and with contemporary African poetry. These connections are most dynamic in the undercurrents of animism (a belief that objects in nature can have souls or spirits) in "On the Pulse of Morning." Many traditional West African religions claim that the elements of nature are part of the spiritual life, and that skulls, trees, masks, and drums are capable of speech and cognition. One finds similar concepts in contemporary African poems: Leopold Senghor's "Prayer to Masks"; David Diop's "Africa, to My Mother"; and Birago Diop's "Vanity" are three examples. The speaking objects in Angelou's poem (the tree, the rock, and the river) underscore this ancient African belief, one that she describes and affirms in *Wouldn't Take Nothing for My Journey Now*: "all things are inhabited by spirits which must be appeased and to which one can appeal. So, for example, when a master drummer prepares to carve a new drum, he approaches the selected tree and speaks to the spirit residing there." Angelou's breadth of references to the African and African American traditions, epitomized by the oral elements of speech making and elocution inherent in both traditions, contribute to the vigor and credibility of her inaugural ode.

"On the Pulse of Morning" is finally an autobiographical poem, the work of a woman whose ability to recall and remember is remarkable. As in so many of her lyrics, the autobiographical voice is unspecified; here the river is speaking, but behind it one hears the poet / woman lamenting for her lost children and urging the survivors to build a new world, to "study war no more." "On the Pulse of Morning" is a poem made possible because of Angelou's accumulated knowledge—her struggles in Arkansas and California, her experiences as a traveler, her achievements in public speaking and acting, and her ability to transform the ideologies of her ancestors on this "bright morning" of hope. She took this same hope with her to Washington when she spoke at the Million Man March.

In *All God's Children Need Traveling Shoes* Angelou writes of her collective past: "Although separated from our languages, our families and customs, we have dared to continue to live. We had crossed the unknowable oceans in chains and had written its mystery into 'Deep River, my home is over Jordan.'" In her autobiographies other modes of transportation both replace and recall the slave ship and the boat over the River Jordan: the segregated train that brings Maya and Bailey from California at the beginning of *I Know Why the Caged Bird Sings;* the plane in *The Heart of a Woman* that flies Maya and Guy across the continent of Africa, from Egypt to Ghana; and the plane that will take her to America at the end of *All God's Children Need Traveling Shoes.* Angelou's narrative voyage, paramount in the autobiographies but evident in her poems and musings as well, opens up a powerful connection with the past for readers who have the freedom to travel with her.

Selected Bibliography

WORKS OF MAYA ANGELOU

AUTOBIOGRAPHIES

I Know Why the Caged Bird Sings. New York: Random House, 1970.

Gather Together in My Name. New York: Random House, 1974.

Singin' and Swingin' and Gettin' Merry Like Christmas. New York: Random House, 1976.

The Heart of a Woman. New York: Random House, 1981.

"Why I Moved Back to the South." *Ebony,* February 1982, pp. 130–134.

All God's Children Need Traveling Shoes. New York: Random House, 1986.

"My Grandson, Home at Last." *Woman's Day,* August 1986, pp. 46–55.

POETRY

Just Give Me a Cool Drink of Water 'fore I Diiie. New York: Random House, 1971.

Oh Pray My Wings Are Gonna Fit Me Well. New York: Random House, 1975.

And Still I Rise. New York: Random House, 1978.

Shaker, Why Don't You Sing? New York: Random House, 1983.

Poems: Maya Angelou. New York: Random House, 1986.

Now Sheba Sings the Song. With artist Tom Feelings. New York: E. P. Dutton, 1987.

I Shall Not Be Moved. New York: Random House, 1990.

Life Doesn't Frighten Me. With artist Jean-Michel Basquiat. New York: Stewart, Tabori & Chang, 1993.

The Complete Collected Poems of Maya Angelou. New York: Random House, 1994.

Phenomenal Woman. 1978. New York: Random House, 1995.

MEMOIR

Wouldn't Take Nothing for My Journey Now. New York: Random House, 1993.

BIOGRAPHICAL AND CRITICAL STUDIES

Andrews, William L. *To Tell a Free Story: The First Century of Afro-American Autobiography, 1760–1865.* Urbana: University of Illinois Press, 1986.

Arensberg, Liliane K. "Death as Metaphor of Self in *I Know Why the Caged Bird Sings.*" *College Language Association Journal,* 20:273–296 (1976).

Blackburn, Regina. "In Search of the Black Female Self: African American Women's Autobiographies and Ethnicity." In *Women's Autobiography*. Edited by Estelle Jelinek. Bloomington: Indiana University Press, 1980. Pp. 133–148.

Bloom, Lynn Z. "Heritages: Dimensions of Mother-Daughter Relationships in Women's Autobiographies." In *The Lost Tradition: Mothers and Daughters in Literature*. Edited by Kathy M. Davidson and E. M. Broner. New York: Ungar, 1980. Pp. 291–303.

Braxton, Joanne M. *Black Women Writing Autobiography: A Tradition Within a Tradition*. Philadelphia: Temple University Press, 1989.

Burgher, Mary. "Images of Self and Race in the Autobiographies of Black Women." In *Sturdy Black Bridges*. Edited by Roseann P. Bell, Bettye J. Parker, and Beverly Guy-Sheftall. Garden City: Doubleday, 1979. Pp. 107–122.

Buss, Helen M. "Reading for the Double Discourse of American Women's Autobiography." *A B: Auto-Biography Studies*, 6, no. 1:95–108 (1991).

Butterfield, Stephen. *Black Autobiography in America*. Amherst: University of Massachusetts Press, 1974.

Cameron, Dee Birch. "A Maya Angelou Bibliography." *Bulletin of Bibliography*, 36, no. 1:50–52 (1979).

Carby, Hazel V. *Reconstructing Womanhood: The Emergence of the Afro-American Woman Novelist*. New York: Oxford University Press, 1987.

Chick, Nancy. "Maya Angelou: A Twentieth Century Scheherazade." Master's thesis, University of Georgia, 1992.

Cudjoe, Selwyn. "Maya Angelou and the Autobiographical Statement." In *Black Women Writers (1950–1980): A Critical Evaluation*. Edited by Mari Evans. Garden City: Doubleday, 1984. Pp. 6–24.

Demetrakopoulous, Stephanie A. "The Metaphysics of Matrilinearism in Women's Autobiography: Studies of Mead's *Blackberry Winter*, Hellman's *Pentimento*, Angelou's *I Know Why the Caged Bird Sings*, and Kingston's *The Woman Warrior*." In *Women's Autobiography: Essays in Criticism*. Edited by Estelle Jelinek. Bloomington: Indiana University Press, 1980. Pp. 180–205.

Gates, Henry Louis, Jr. *Figures in Black: Words, Signs, and the "Racial" Self*. New York: Oxford University Press, 1987.

Gruesser, John C. "Afro-American Travel Literature and Africanist Discourse." *Black American Literature Forum*, 24, no. 1:5–20 (Spring 1990).

Hill-Lubin, Mildred A. "The Grandmother in African and African-American Literature: A Survivor of the Extended Family." In *Ngambika: Studies of Women in African Literature*. Edited by Carole B. Davies and Anne A. Graves. Trenton: Africa World, 1986. Pp. 257–270.

Kael, Pauline. "A Woman for All Seasons?" In *Critical Essays on Lillian Hellman*. Edited by Mark W. Estrin. Boston: G. K. Hall, 1989. Pp. 252–257.

Kent, George E. "*I Know Why the Caged Bird Sings* and Black Autobiographical Tradition." *Kansas Quarterly*, 7, no. 3:72–78 (1975).

Lupton, Mary Jane. "Singing the Black Mother: Maya Angelou and Autobiographical Continuity." *Black American Literature Forum*, 24, no 2:257–275 (1990).

———. Review Essay of *Order Out of Chaos* by Dolly A. McPherson. *Black American Literature Forum*, 24, no. 3:809–814 (1990).

McPherson, Dolly A. *Order Out of Chaos: The Autobiographical Works of Maya Angelou*. New York: Peter Lang, 1990.

Meyers, Linda Mae Zarpentine. "Maya Angelou and the Multiplicity of Self." Master's thesis, Morgan State University, 1995.

Neubauer, Carol E. "Displacement and Autobiographical Style in Maya Angelou's *The Heart of a Woman*." *Black American Literature Forum*, 17, no. 3:123–129 (1983).

———. "Maya Angelou: Self and a Song of Freedom in the Southern Tradition." In *Southern Women Writers: The New Generation*. Edited by Tonette Bond Inge. Tuscaloosa: University of Alabama Press, 1990. Pp. 114–142. Reprinted in *Contemporary Literary Criticism*, 77:21–32 (1990).

O'Neale, Sondra. "Reconstruction of the Composite Self: New Images of Black Women in Maya Angelou's Continuing Autobiography." In *Black Women Writers (1950–1980): A Critical Evaluation*. Edited by Mari Evans. Garden City: Doubleday, 1984. Pp. 25–36.

Raynaud, Claudine. "Rites of Coherence: Autobiographical Writings by Hurston, Brooks, Angelou, and Lorde." *Dissertation Abstracts International*, 53, no. 3:812A (September 1992).

Schmidt, Jan Zlotnik. "The Other: A Study of the Persona in Several Contemporary Women's Autobiographies.'' *College English Association Critic*, 42, no. 1:24–31 (1980).

Smith, Sidonie Ann. ''The Song of a Caged Bird: Maya Angelou's Quest after Self-Acceptance.'' *Southern Humanities Review* 7:365–375 (1973).

Stetson, Erlene. ''Studying Slavery: Some Literary and Pedagogical Considerations on the Black Female Slave.'' In *But Some of Us Are Brave*. Edited by Gloria T. Hull, Patricia Bell Scott, and Barbara Smith. Old Westbury and New York: Feminist Press, 1982. Pp. 61–84.

Starling, Marion Wilson. *The Slave Narrative*. Boston: G. K. Hall, 1981.

Weixlmann, Joe. ''African American Autobiography: A Bibliographical Essay.'' *Black American Literature Forum*, 24, no. 2:375–415 (1990).

MAJOR INTERVIEWS

Benson, Carol. ''Out of the Cage and Still Singing.'' *Writers Digest*, January 1975, pp. 18–20.

Chrisman, Robert. ''The *Black Scholar* Interviews Maya Angelou.'' *Black Scholar*, 8, no. 4:44–52 (January/February 1977).

Elliot, Jeffrey M., editor. *Conversations with Maya Angelou.* Jackson: University Press of Mississippi, 1989.

McPherson, Dolly A. ''An Addendum: A Conversation with Maya Angelou.'' In *Order Out of Chaos: The Autobiographical Works of Maya Angelou.* New York: Peter Lang, 1990. Pp. 131–162.

Neubauer, Carol E. ''An Interview with Maya Angelou.'' *Massachusetts Review* 28, no. 2:286–292 (Spring 1987).

Redmond, Eugene B. ''Boldness of Language And Breadth: An Interview with Maya Angelou.'' *Black American Literature Forum*, 22, no. 2:156–157 (Summer 1988).

Tate, Claudia. ''Maya Angelou.'' In *Black Woman Writers at Work*, edited by Claudia Tate. New York: Continuum, 1983. Pp. 1–11.

—*MARY JANE LUPTON*

W. H. Auden
1907-1973

"TRUE Love," W. H. Auden wrote, "enjoys twenty-twenty vision, but talks like a myopic." As a poet his central task was truthtelling, but he knew that his art obliged him to translate even the most painful and difficult truths into verbal artifacts of great complexity and beauty. The drama of his career grew out of the unresolvable conflict between his craftsman's impulse to construct memorable patterns of sound and feeling, and the ethical impulse to draw attention to the uglier world of fact. An artist who was constantly aware of the dangers of art, he knew that the potential danger of a work was often in direct proportion to its artistic excellence. The most beautiful and compelling works always invited their audience to conclude (he wrote) "that, since all is well in the work of art, all is well in history. But all is not well there."

The truth Auden was concerned to tell was neither the autonomous "truth of art" nor the inner psychological truths proclaimed by various poets and painters during the nineteenth and twentieth centuries. However moving, however personally authentic these "truths" might be, they could not be of much use to anyone other than the artists who originated them. What Auden was concerned with (after the first few years of his career) were truths that might be communicated and shared. He had no wish to limit access to his work to a sophisticated avant-garde audience, and he made no claim that he plumbed depths accessible only to poets.

These were democratic attitudes, but he had to teach them to himself, because his poetic predecessors held very different and more aristocratic views. The modernist poetic revolution of the early twentieth century, brought about by W. B. Yeats, T. S. Eliot, Ezra Pound, and D. H. Lawrence, was largely a revolution in poetic language. Its purpose (in the words of Stéphane Mallarmé translated by Eliot in *Four Quartets*) was "To purify the dialect of the tribe," to free language from tired conventions and trivialities, to give it clarity, directness, sincerity. But these admirable goals had certain limits. In the view of the modernists, poetry did not refer to a common world of shared experience, accessible to anyone who looked. Poetry and poetic language served as its own authority. What mattered was its intensity and clarity, and it was taken for granted that truthfulness would follow.

In fact something very different happened. When Auden began writing in the late 1920's, and began his efforts at truthtelling a few years later, the older generation offered little help in what he was trying to do. Eliot was struggling to break out of the isolation of his inner life; Lawrence was refusing to believe anything he couldn't feel in his solar plexus; Pound was arguing that the books Ezra Pound happened to

71

have read constituted the true liberal education on which society must be based; and Yeats was communicating with spirits—or wasn't, depending on how he chose to talk about it that day.

In the eyes of most modern critics and teachers of literature there is nothing wrong with any of this. Every literary period devises sets of critical theories and unexamined assumptions that will justify its poetic practice. The literary theory that rose in the wake of the great modernists—a theory that has an ancient and venerable ancestry—held that art was independent of what is ordinarily called truth. A poem was at best a "pseudo-statement," a model of what a true statement might be like. It did not have to be true to experience. Yeats wrote a poem to a friend whose hopes to bring art to the Dublin public had come to nothing, and advised her to find strength and confidence in her own self:

> Amid a place of stone,
> Be secret and exult,
> Because of all things known
> That is most difficult.

No one would question the rhetorical magnificence of these lines, and to anyone who has ever found consolation in the thought that the world fails to recognize one's secret inner merits—a thought that has consoled everyone who ever lived—the lines provide a thrill of self-congratulation. As poetry is taught in most classrooms or discussed by most critics, it doesn't matter at all that the lines are simply untrue, that exulting in secret is not the most difficult of all things known but the easiest, the most banal, and the most universal of self-delusions.

To Auden it did matter. Where Vladimir Nabokov, one of the last of the great modernists, wrote that "art is an intricate game of deception and enchantment," Auden disagreed: "In so far as poetry, or any of the other arts, can be said to have an ulterior purpose, it is, by telling the truth, to disenchant and disintoxicate." Auden found himself in the curious position of taking art more seriously than did those for whom art was the be-all and end-all, an independent realm with laws of its own. Auden saw that art could never be independent, because it persuades its readers to accept the attitudes it presents so beautifully—attitudes about relations and responsibility that are eventually translated into personal and political action, with results far less beautiful than any poem.

If the danger for the autonomous artist is the danger of losing touch with the real world, the danger for the truthtelling artist is that he will grow so concerned with the plain fact that he forgets about art, and becomes too boring for anyone to read. Auden survived this danger through his love of (in his words) "Riddles and all other ways of not calling a spade a spade . . . Complicated verse forms of great technical difficulty, such as Englyns, Drott-Kvaetts, Sestinas, even if their content is trivial . . . Conscious theatrical exaggeration. . . ." He packed his longer poems with as many complex verse forms as he could fit in—fifty-five in *The Age of Anxiety* alone—and then ended each long poem by, in effect, snapping his fingers to wake his readers from their aesthetic fascination. At the end of *For the Time Being* the narrator says of the poem's Christmas pageantry: "Well, so that is that. Now we must dismantle the tree, . . ." The end of *The Sea and the Mirror* admits that in this as in all other works of art the "effects" can never entirely succeed in persuading us of art's reality: "no piece of business, however unimportant, came off." The last pages of *The Age of Anxiety* echo the conclusion of *Finnegans Wake*, but where Joyce returns his reader to the start of the book in an endless insomniac cycle of reading and rereading, Auden restores his reader to "the actual world where time is real."

Auden's passion for truthtelling was a commitment to public service—a commitment not unlike that held generally by artists and writers up to the eighteenth century. It was only with the romantic revolution that artists began taking it for granted that they were necessarily opposed to society in all its forms, that personal integrity required the individual to reject all institutions. It is a law of intellectual history that a condition which one era regards as a rare calamity, a later era will accept as the norm. Thus the anxious isolation of Hamlet in a rotten society—for William Shakespeare a unique tragedy—becomes, a few centuries later, the conventional self-image of every well-to-do adolescent.

Like every young writer since the romantic era, Auden began by rebelling against his personal and literary ancestors, and he spent most of his adult life in voluntary exile from his native England. But through all his years of revolt and exile he remained a product of the English professional middle class, and he embodied its values in his poetry. Only in his late adolescence and early twenties did he think of his art in terms similar to those used by his modernist predecessors. If they were isolated, he felt, he would be even more isolated; such was the necessary course of history. But around the age of twenty-five, when his revolt changed character and became less personal than socialist, he made no effort to renounce his bourgeois upbringing. He read Karl Marx, he said later, in order to become a better bourgeois, not to destroy his society but to save it from destroying itself by its own injustice. The great modernists, when they thought politically at all, also held radical politics, but a radically nostalgic politics of the right, which denounced democracy in favor of the secure aristocracy of an idealized

or imaginary past. Auden's whole career, in contrast, was shaped by his sense of continuity between past and present, by his respect for his literary tradition and personal roots. Where the modernists saw all around them fragments and isolation and longed for some distant wholeness, Auden saw a complex and finally coherent present, with responsibilities that could not be deferred for the sake of an artist's beautiful dreams.

Wystan Hugh Auden was born on February 21, 1907, in the medieval city of York in the north of England, where his doctor father worked as a general practitioner. The following year the family moved to the industrial city of Birmingham, where Dr. Auden was appointed to the newly established post of school medical officer; later he became professor of public health at Birmingham University. Auden's mother had been among the first women to take an honors degree (in French) at London University. She then studied to be a nurse, intending to serve with missionaries in Africa, but gave up this plan when she met and married Dr. Auden. She and her husband were both children of Anglican clergymen. Dr. Auden held a detached intellectual attitude to religion, while Mrs. Auden held intense religious convictions and raised her children in the rituals of the High Church.

From his father, who was widely read in history, archaeology, and the classics, the young Auden learned the elements of science. From his mother he learned music, emotion, and religion. In later years he traced his homosexuality partly to his strong identification with his mother, an identification strengthened when his father was away from England with the Army Medical Corps during World War I. Isolated from other children by his mental precociousness and physical clumsiness, Auden devoted much of his childhood from the ages of six to twelve to constructing an imaginary private world. His fantasy was, however, made up from very real objects: "a limestone landscape mainly derived from the Pennine Moors in the North of England, and . . . an industry—lead mining." The character of his adult poetry was already implicit in the nature of his childhood imaginary world. His concern was not simply with the symbolic depths of the mines or the personal nostalgia of the lonely moors but also with the practical details of mining machinery, with the ways in which real means led to plausible ends. Later, as a poet, he would differ from predecessors like Thomas Hardy, Yeats, and Eliot in caring less for the intensities of solitary vision or the emotional power of rhetoric than for the ethical complexities of the world in which he and everyone else must choose and act. Once, he recalled of his childhood fantasy, "I had to choose between two types of a certain machine. . . . One type I found more sacred or 'beautiful,' but the other type was, as I knew from my reading, the more efficient. At this point I realized that it was my moral duty to sacrifice my aesthetic preference for reality or truth."

His adolescence brought a conventional adolescent rebellion. He discovered that he had lost the religious faith his mother had taught him and discovered his homosexuality (which his father eventually accepted, although his mother remained baffled and antagonistic). At school he had fewer difficulties than at home. He showed an aptitude for science and mathematics, but no more interest in literature than might be expected of any intelligent pupil. Until he was fifteen, he saw himself moving toward a career as a mining engineer, or something equally technical and scientific. Then a school friend, filling an awkward silence during a country walk, casually asked if he wrote poetry. He had never thought of doing so, but at that moment he recognized his vocation. Three years

later, at Oxford, when he introduced himself to Nevill Coghill, his English tutor, he explained that he intended to be a poet. The tutor observed that this would help with his English studies, by giving him insights into the technical side of the subject. "You don't understand at all," Auden replied. "I mean a great poet."

Both at school and at Oxford, Auden was an awesome if slightly comic figure to his contemporaries. His father's library had provided him with arcane knowledge of sex and psychoanalysis, and his intellectual assurance completed the effect. The saving comedy emerged in the extravagance with which he advanced his opinions, opinions liable to change at any moment. Poetically, though, he was little more than a highly competent provincial while he was at school and in his first year at Oxford. At fifteen he had pasticed William Wordsworth, then Walter de la Mare and other twentieth-century traditionalists. At sixteen he discovered Hardy and for more than a year read and imitated no one else. At seventeen he added Edward Thomas, then A. E. Housman, Robert Frost, and Emily Dickinson. Then, at nineteen, in 1926, he discovered T. S. Eliot's *The Waste Land* and discarded everything he had written earlier. For a few heady months he produced nothing but distilled Eliot. In spring, in his verse, "The itching lover weighed himself / At stations on august machines"; sunlight became "Inexorable Rembrandt rays, which stab / Through clouds as through a rotting factory floor." He proclaimed a severely "classical" poetic dogma to his friends: poetry, he said, must be austere, must ignore public issues and shared meanings, must virtually ignore its own subject, because the subject of a poem was merely the peg on which to hang the poetry.

It was another year before he began writing poems in a voice that he recognized as his own. In the summer of 1927, after his second year at

Oxford, when he was twenty, he wrote a poem he later titled "The Watershed." It marked the watershed between his juvenilia and his adult work and was the earliest poem he preserved between hard covers in his published volumes.

"Who stands, the crux left of the watershed," it opens, in radical ambiguity. Are the first two words interrogative or declarative? What is the missing word replaced by the comma? Is the crux a crossroads or a dilemma? And which of its two possible and antithetical meanings is expressed by "watershed"—a dividing line on high ground or a field on low ground? The poem makes all these matters clear in the lines that follow, but the obscurity of the opening, the way it seems to exclude the reader from the poem, proves, in effect, to be the subject of the lines that follow. The poem concerns a "stranger" who stands indecisively at a crossroads looking down over a ruined landscape, one who can never enter the land he observes, can never find the satisfaction he vaguely seeks. "Stranger, turn back again, frustrate and vexed:" commands the voice of the poem:

This land, cut off, will not communicate,
Be no accessory content to one
Aimless for faces rather there than here.
Beams from your car may cross a bedroom
     wall,
They wake no sleeper. . . .

In "The Watershed" and the poems of the next year or two, Auden entered the extreme psychological isolation Eliot had explored in "The Love Song of J. Alfred Prufrock" and went ever deeper, to the point where the observing mind and the observed world were not merely isolated but antagonistic. Guarded borders cross the landscape of these early poems, as in "No Change of Place," "Where gaitered gamekeeper with dog and gun / Will shout 'Turn back'." Even the features on a face, the mouth and eyes, seem "Sentries between

inner and outer." Any movement toward erotic satisfaction (in his early twenties Auden had little hope for any deeper love) is the act of a doomed spy or secret agent:

Control of the passes was, he saw, the key
To this new district, but who would get it?
He, the trained spy, had walked into the trap
For a bogus guide, seduced by the old tricks.

             . . .

     . . . They would shoot, of course,
Parting easily who were never joined.

Auden's style developed rapidly in these early years, but certain basic elements remained constant. A whole repertory of techniques preserved his isolation from his readers. Few poets have made so many threatening noises: "The game is up for you . . . It is later than you think"; "Before you reach the frontier you are caught." His obscurity became notorious, but it was only partly deliberate; in a journal entry he blamed it on his own laziness. What was entirely deliberate, however, was the baffling instability of his tone. He would shift within a few lines from lyric intensity to slapstick comedy, from solemn echoes of ancient epics to transient contemporary slang. There were superficial parallels between this style and the modernist styles of Eliot and Pound, but Auden's purposes were entirely different from theirs. Where *The Waste Land* and *The Cantos* echoed older forms to make an ironic contrast between a splendid hierarchical past and a depleted chaotic present, Auden emphasized the continuity between the anxiety and violence of ancient times and of today. Auden found in the past, not a better world, but disasters like those of the present: "The pillar dug from the desert recorded only / the sack of a city." Where Eliot and Pound tended to quote ostentatiously from the high style of the European renaissance, Auden moved further back into the past, to the sad dangerous world of Old English poetry and the

Old Icelandic sagas. And where Eliot and Pound always drew attention to their learned quotations, Auden, whose reading was wider than theirs, made no fuss about his use of earlier literature, no show of erudition. For example, a line quoted above, "Parting easily [two] who were never joined," is translated from an Old English poem "Wulf and Eadwacer." A phrase from "1929," another early poem, "love . . . gives less than he expects," is from Anton Chekhov's notebooks; a line about the "restlessness of intercepted growth" is from a book on psychology by Trigant Burrow; and there are hundreds of other examples. If a reader recognizes the source, all well and good; but however else Auden's earliest poems exclude their readers, they never do so by implying that the poet who wrote them is a learned sage whose knowledge lesser mortals can never share. For Auden throughout his career, a poet is one who handles words and poetic forms better than others do, never one whose vision and emotions are stronger or better than anyone else's.

Auden collected his earliest short poems in a book titled simply *Poems* (1930; second edition with slightly different contents, 1933; American edition, 1934). His longer works in this period were the brief play *Paid on Both Sides: A Charade* (printed in the various editions of *Poems*) and the long poem in prose and verse *The Orators* (1932; revised edition, 1934; included in the American edition of *Poems*). These books quickly established Auden as the major poet of his generation. No poet since Lord Byron achieved such wide fame so early in his career, but his work was widely misunderstood. Early reviewers and critics tended to read Auden's first books in light of the political concerns that entered his work only after 1932, concerns almost absent from his earliest poems, whose concerns were almost wholly psychological.

Paid on Both Sides is a compressed psychological tragedy, an expressionistic *Romeo and Juliet.* Two families in the north of England have been feuding for generations. The origins of the feud have long been forgotten, but as each generation transmits its hatreds to its children the cycle of murder and revenge continues. Abruptly, the son of one family breaks out of the cycle. He is cured of his hatred by a self-revealing dream that makes clear to him his willing complicity in the feud. Now he rides to the house of his enemies and proposes marriage to their daughter. Up to this point the play reflects the teachings of an American psychologist, Homer Lane, whose work Auden learned about during a year in Berlin (1928–1929) after finishing at Oxford. Lane taught the romantic doctrine that man was naturally good and that neurosis and disease could therefore be cured if one would only obey one's inner impulses. (Freud, in sharp contrast, distrusted the violent impulses of the id and welcomed the civilizing effects of sublimation.) The hero of *Paid on Both Sides* rejects parental repression and obeys his inner impulse to love. But although Auden briefly allowed his friends to believe he had embraced the optimism of Homer Lane, his play presents a darker and lonelier vision. The hero is murdered on his wedding day, to avenge a killing that he himself had committed before his cure, and the feud resumes.

The theme of *Paid on Both Sides* is the persistence of ancient hatreds into the present. Its style and setting evoke a comparable persistence of the past. The language ranges from the laconic manner and alliterative meters of Old English poetry to modern telegraphese and schoolboy slang. The hero's curative dream mixes patriotic speeches from World War I with passages from a psychology textbook and scraps of the traditional Christmas mummers' play of rural England. The title *Paid on Both Sides* is a scraping from *Beowulf,* from a line about a hard bargain, paid on both sides with the lives of friends.

The Orators, three years later, uses similar methods on a more elaborate scale. As in *Paid,* the setting often seems to shift even within a single sentence. As if in an optical illusion, the book's action takes place simultaneously in a boarding school, a primitive tribe, a suburban home, and a military airfield. This strange *sui generis* work, subtitled "An English Study," amounts to an anthropological survey of English society. As in more straightforward anthropology, Auden treats his subject apolitically, regarding his society not as the product of deliberate moral and practical choices (as its apologists would claim) but as the unconscious product of myth and ritual, a society powerless to understand itself or to change. The book's focus is the world of school, where the ruling bourgeois learn the rites and customs they will follow in later life. In the first of the book's three parts, "The Initiates," different prose voices record the initiation of a group of schoolboys into their tribal codes of behavior and belief; then into adolescent combativeness and sexuality; finally into middle-aged nostalgia for the lost glories of youth. The initiates are followers of a neurotic hero, whose thoughts, recorded in a "Journal of an Airman," make up the book's second part. The airman tries to organize society around hero worship but is destroyed by his own paranoia. What is especially unsettling about his journal is that it mixes Auden's own verses and opinions with passages designed to indicate the madness of its fictitious "author." (Auden later wrote that *The Orators* reads like the work of "someone talented but near the border of sanity" and guessed that his reason for writing it was partly therapeutic, "to exorcise certain tendencies in myself by allowing them to run riot in phantasy.") The third part of the book is a series of odes on various aspects of group life and hero worship, ending in a confession of frustration and defeat, and a mock prayer for change. A brief epilogue abandons the whole world described in the book for some unspecified other place that Auden can identify only by saying it is somewhere else:

"O where are you going" said reader to rider,

. . .

"Out of this house"—said rider to reader . . .

Around the time *The Orators* was published (1932), Auden began to think of this reader's destination in political terms. For a few months he thought he was in the process of what he called a "conversion to communism"—which never in fact took place. He wrote a few poems that adopted the voice of a communist (this was in the deepest phase of the great economic depression of the 1930's), but a communist of a very idiosyncratic kind, more concerned with a visionary community of love than with basic economic change. Auden was now working as a schoolmaster, but he found education, much as he enjoyed the work, a paradoxical task. "You cannot train children to be good citizens of a state which you despise." When he tried to write an epic poem that would portray the communist struggle for a different and better state, he abandoned it before it was half-finished. "No, I am a bourgeois. I shall not join the C[ommunist] P[arty]," he wrote in a letter to a friend. Yet the sense of isolation in which he began his career was growing intolerable, and he urgently needed a way out.

The lonely vigil of Auden's early years, his youthful contempt for the public realm, ended on a warm night in June 1933. That evening, he recalled, he was sitting on a lawn after dinner with three colleagues at the Downs School in Colwall, where he taught, when " . . . something happened. I felt myself invaded by a power which, though I consented to it, was irresistible and certainly not mine. For the first time in my life I knew exactly—because, thanks to the power, I was doing it—what it means to love one's neighbor as oneself." Thirty years later he identified the event as a "vision of agape," of religious charity and love. At the time, he thought he was finished with Christianity forever, and he said almost nothing about the experience—beyond asking one of his colleagues on that evening if the feeling had been shared, and learning that it was.

He was silent on the details or the cause, but for a short time his writings were suffused with a tone of exaltation unlike anything he had done before. In a poem written within days of the event, "A Summer Night" ("Out on the lawn I lie in bed, . . ."), he evoked the scene of some peaceable kingdom:

> Equal with colleagues in a ring
> I sit on each calm evening,
>   Enchanted as the flowers
> The opening light draws out of hiding
> From leaves with all its dove-like pleading
>   Its logic and its powers.
>
> That later we, though parted then
> May still recall these evenings when
>   Fear gave his watch no look;
> The lion griefs loped from the shade
> And on our knees their muzzles laid,
>   And Death put down his book.

As in his first political writings, he felt his class was doomed, that revolution was imminent—

> Soon through the dykes of our content
> The crumpling flood will force a rent

—but now he hoped that the love he felt on these evenings might survive as one of the strengths of the new order,

> As through a child's rash happy cries
> The drowned voices of his parents rise
>   In unlamenting song.

What is especially striking about this poem is its use of regular, almost jaunty meters in a tone of celebration and joy. The modernist poets, especially Eliot and Pound, had reserved serious subjects almost exclusively for free verse. Regular meters, if they could be used at all, were strictly for the purpose of satire or nostalgia, standing as a formal rebuke to the disorder of the modern world. Eliot wrote in 1917 that formal rhymed verse could now have only a limited role; it would not lose its place entirely, but "we need the coming of Satirist . . . to prove that the heroic couplet has lost none of its edge. . . . As for the sonnet I am not so sure." In the same 1933 summer when Auden began writing nonsatiric rhymed verse he also began writing not merely sonnets but whole sequences of sonnets. At first these preserved their conventional status as love poetry, but within a few years Auden was using sonnets for historical and mythical subjects on the largest possible scale; the sequence "In Time of War" (1938) extends without implausibility from the creation of the world to the present moment of crisis.

The whole character of Auden's work changed drastically after his vision of agape in 1933. Earlier he had assumed that his work must take the next logical step in the modernist revolution, extending the line laid down by Yeats, Pound, and Eliot. This early sense that he must work according to historical necessity, not by personal choice, had been encouraged by modernism itself, which took far more interest in the aesthetic intensity of the unique moment or the large determined cycles of history than it did in personal choice and the consequences of choice. Modernism emphasized formal innovation in art, but determined necessity in human affairs. Auden, in the mid-1930's, broke with modernism by restoring traditional meters in his art and by emphasizing freedom and choice in his vision of mankind.

When he wrote a love poem, such as the untitled one that begins "Fish in the unruffled lakes," the lover's beauty was important, but not as important as the lover's personal decision to love:

> ... I must bless, I must praise
> That you, my swan, who have
> All gifts that to the swan
> Impulsive Nature gave,
> The majesty and pride,
> Last night should add
> Your voluntary love.

"Swan," "majesty," "pride," and the poetic diction in which Auden sets these words—all derive from the love poetry of Yeats. But in acknowledging Yeats's preeminence as a love poet Auden corrected a crucial fault in Yeats's vision, his failure to take account of the voluntary quality of human relations. Elsewhere in the same poem Auden makes comparable references to "goodness *carefully* worn" and "Duty's *conscious* wrong" (italics added).

Because modernist poetry took little interest in choice and its consequences, the art to which it was most closely allied was the relatively static art of painting. In Yeats, Lawrence, Pound, William Carlos Williams, and Wallace Stevens, reality is most strikingly evoked by means of visual images. Auden deliberately broke this entangling alliance between poetry and painting, almost to the point of banishing visual images from his poetry entirely and replacing them with terms from the fields of ethics and morals, as in "Lullaby" (italics added):

> Lay your sleeping head, my love,
> *Human* on my *faithless* arm;
> Time and fevers burn away
> *Individual* beauty from
> *Thoughtful* children, and the grave
> Proves the child *ephemeral*:
> But in my arms till break of day
> Let the *living* creature lie,
> *Mortal*, *guilty*, but to me
> The *entirely* beautiful.

In all his writings from the mid-1930's Auden reiterated that the human world is the product of choices, not necessity. Where Yeats and Eliot dreamed in different ways of escaping from the world of time into the serenity of timelessness, Auden constantly turned back to the immediate problems of love and politics. Almost everything he wrote referred at some point to the difference between the world of nature and that of humanity. Both derived their energies from the life force that Auden called, after Freud's example, Eros. But in nature Eros made all the decisions for its creatures; animals and plants "knew their station and were good for ever." In individual men and women Eros has abdicated its authority to the individual will. Each of us is free to choose whether to "build the Just City" or to seek "the suicide pact, the romantic / Death." The instinctive powers of Eros insisted only on finding expression; in the human world they did not insist on any special kind of expression. If they were denied expression as love or art, they would emerge in distorted forms instead, as psychosomatic disease or the collective hatred of war.

So although Auden wrote more love poems during the 1930's than at any other time in his career, they were poems from which the shadow of political or personal disaster was seldom distant. "A Bride in the 30's," which began in the luxuriant erotic rhythms of a line like "Easily, my dear, you move, easily, your head," quickened, only a few stanzas later, to the martial beat of "Ten thousand of the desperate marching by / Five feet, six feet, seven feet high." It was not enough to withdraw from politics to the pleasures of the bed: "Hitler and Mussolini in their wooing poses" made an appeal not unlike the poet's to his love, and the poet knew it. Personal Eros could be as possessive and damaging as the political one. In another poem he recognized "How insufficient is / The endearment and the look" "Before the evil and the good."

The same kinds of choice that set the course of a personal life also set the course of nations. As on one hand the Great Depression exposed the weakness of capitalist society, and on the other the rise of fascism threatened to put an end to democracy, it seemed crucial to Auden and many of his contemporaries to become didactic artists, to educate their audience in the ways of responsible choice. Although Auden's sympathies were clearly socialist, he knew that he would violate his didactic purposes if he tried to dictate the choices others should make:

Poetry is not concerned with telling people what to do, but with extending our knowledge of good and evil, perhaps making the necessity for action more urgent and its nature more clear, but only leading us to the point where it is possible for us to make a rational and moral choice.

This principle was easier, at first, to enunciate than to follow. In the 1930's, too often for his own comfort, his sense of political urgency led him to try to tell people what to do, even when he was by no means certain what he ought to do himself.

His most important political works in the 1930's were commissioned by the Group Theatre of London. The Group had been founded in 1932 to pioneer modern stage techniques in England, and only later added political purposes to its aesthetic ones. Auden's first work for the Group was the playlet *The Dance of Death* (1933). On paper this seems a perfunctory trifle, but on stage, with music and dancing, it had a notable success. Auden had no use for the conventionally realistic theater of his day but did not wish to follow Yeats's withdrawal of poetic drama into the symbolic intensities of drawing-room theater. Instead, arriving independently at many of the techniques used by Bertolt Brecht, he adopted the styles of the cabaret, music hall, and revue in an attempt to establish a popular poetic drama, without the archaism or pomposity that damaged most of the recent efforts in that form. The ostensible subject of *The Dance of Death* is the decline of the middle classes, whose death wish and death throes are mimed by a dancer. The dancer and a chorus of singers and actors illustrate various bourgeois evasions of social change—romantic fantasy, mysticism, nationalism, fads in health and sex, with songs appropriate to each—until the dancer collapses. Karl Marx strides on stage to the tune of Mendelssohn's wedding march and pronounces the dancer dead of economic causes; and the play ends. The conclusion is a bit too abrupt and absurd to give much comfort to any committed Marxist, and Auden later called the play "a nihilist leg-pull." Through much of this period, when critics generally regarded Auden as a communist sympathizer, the newspaper of the Communist party, the *Daily Worker,* kept complaining about his severe lapses from party orthodoxy.

His next play, *The Dog Beneath the Skin* (1935), was the first of three written in collaboration with the novelist Christopher Isherwood. Again using techniques from music hall and cabaret, Auden now adopted a more straightforward didactic purpose. An improbable plot about a naive young hero's search for his village's missing heir (who is in fact disguised as the dog who tags along on the search) serves largely as an excuse for a satiric tour of Europe, modeled loosely on Voltaire's *Candide.* The play is designed to be an easy lesson in history. The village England of the opening scene is comfortably Edwardian, its characters singing in the rhythms of Gilbert and Sullivan. The hero's travels take him from Europe's tired old monarchies to its new lunatic fascism, introducing him along the way to decadent sexuality, the power of wealth and privilege, and a few hints of socialist revolution offstage. Finally he returns to his village, able at last to see the reactionary viciousness behind its innocent facade. As the play ends he and the village heir—now out of the dogskin—leave to join "the army of the other side." A chorus, which from the start has been explaining the action to the audience, now urges us to "Repent . . . Unite . . . Act." This triad of commands derives less from any political sympathy than from the closing exhortations in *The Waste Land* to give, sympathize, and control. The "army of the other side" and its purposes have never appeared on stage, except for one sympathizer who dies to the tune of a comic Wagnerian pastiche. The future liberator of English society, as Stephen Spender observed, is someone "whom the writers have not put in the picture because they do not know what he looks like, although they thoroughly support him."

Despite such ambiguities and cross-purposes, Auden was now generally accepted as a propaganda poet, a spokesman for his literary generation. He did his best to sabotage this impression in the next play that he and Isherwood wrote, but almost no one, possibly not even Isherwood, fully understood what he was doing. The play was *The Ascent of F6* (1936), a parable of the self-destructiveness of the pursuit of fame. Now the political satire has diminished to perfunctory gestures. The focus is on the psychology of the hero, superficially based on Lawrence of Arabia but ultimately a metaphoric self-portrait of Auden himself. The hero, Michael Ransom, is a mountaineer (metaphorically, an artist) who climbs mountains for the challenge of it but also partly as a neurotic release. Denied his mother's love in childhood, he is constantly seeking admiration as an adult. When the British government asks him to climb a peak on a colonial border for the sake of a propaganda victory, Ransom, despite his dreams of conquering that very peak, refuses to make his art serve a political cause. But when his mother adds her voice to those who insist he make the climb, his resistance fails. As he as-

cends the peak he is taken for a hero by the masses, who follow his efforts on radio and in newspapers; and he begins to dream of himself as a savior for mankind. But in conquering the mountain he destroys himself. His companions are seized with the nationalistic excitement of the race to the top, and he accedes to their wish to make the last part of the climb in a dangerous blizzard. He dies at the summit. Behind the story is Auden's conviction that the fame he had won for his political writing was a fatal temptation, that his propagandistic work, however much it delighted his audience, betrayed his art. When he wrote the play he was at the height of his fame, but he decided at that moment that he must someday leave England if he were to escape the temptations that he could not resist if he stayed.

In the months after finishing *F6* Auden kept away from direct political statements. He collected his poems of 1932–1936—toning down some of the politics of the earlier ones—in a volume that his British publishers titled *Look, Stranger!* (1936). Auden disliked the buttonholing tone of this and had the American edition titled *On This Island.* (He dedicated the book to Erika Mann, Thomas Mann's daughter, whom he married in 1935 in order to provide her with a British passport when the Nazis took away her German citizenship.) In a long poem written during the summer of 1936, *Letter to Lord Byron,* he adopted an urbanely ironic tone on politics, poetry, and himself—a comic tone but one entirely unlike the slapstick of *The Orators.* The poem keeps emphasizing the very real problems of society and art, both of which it discusses in materialist terms derived from Marx, but emphasizes also that artists are not the most likely source for solutions to these problems. Against the romantic and modernist dogma of the artist-hero, inspired by a deeper and sharper vision than his fellowmen, Auden's poem traces the artist's isolation to the rise of the *rentier* class in the eighteenth century, which made it possible for artists to devote their lives to writing what they wished, as they lived on their dividends—or starved heroically. Against the heroic stature he himself had begun to achieve among his contemporaries, Auden offers many stanzas of self-deflating autobiography—for example, about his Oxford days under the influence of Eliot and Eliot's quarterly magazine the *Criterion:*

All youth's intolerant certainty was mine as
   I faced life in a double-breasted suit;
I bought and praised but did not read
    Aquinas,
   At the *Criterion*'s verdict I was mute,
   Though Arnold's I was ready to refute;
And through the quads dogmatic words rang
   clear,
"Good poetry is classic and austere."

So much for Art. Of course Life had its
   passions too;
   The student's flesh like his imagination
Makes facts fit theories and has fashions too.

He wrote much of this poem in Iceland, where he spent a summer, partly as a holiday from European politics, partly to seek out the country of his distant ancestors. Auden's sense of the past tended to focus, not on the renaissance grandeurs or vague arcadias that modernism sought by the Mediterranean, but on the colder clarity and sanity of the North. To visit Iceland was to find a place where historical nostalgia was impossible, where the landscapes of the sagas remained unaltered. It was a cure, he hoped, for the political madness further south.

But while he was there he heard the first news of the Spanish Civil War. He had no doubt that Francisco Franco's invasion of Republican Spain was a trial run for a fascist war on the whole of Europe. There could be no es-
cape. Now political themes reentered his work, no longer with the old jokey ambiguities but in a tone of urgency and even despair. The great forces of history seemed to call everyone to action. Early in 1937 he went to Spain. He intended to drive an ambulance for the Republican forces but was instead put to work broadcasting propaganda. After two months he cut his journey short and returned to England. Only later did his friends realize that he had been profoundly disillusioned. Like many others who went to Spain hoping to serve an ideal, he found instead that the Republicans had divided into vindictive factions and the Stalinists were taking charge. He still regarded fascism as an absolute evil, but it was no longer possible to deceive himself that those who opposed one form of evil might not prefer another one instead. When he returned to England he wrote "Spain," a poem with grand rhetorical gestures and a concluding summons to action—one that he felt the urgency of the times demanded but in which he no longer believed:

The stars are dead; the animals will not look:
We are left alone with our day, and the time
    is short and
       History to the defeated
May say Alas but cannot help or pardon.

These lines are based on Auden's characteristic distinction between nature and man, and on his equally characteristic insistence on choice. But they also affirm that history will not pardon those who lose. If the final phrases are read metaphorically, they seem innocuous enough: history, they seem to argue, gives no second chance; we must act now. But Auden was not writing metaphorically when he used the word "pardon." This word and its fraternal twin "forgiveness" were gradually to become the crucial words in his poetic vocabulary. Both words pointed to that voluntary acceptance of another's imperfection, which, in both the personal and political realms, is essential to sympathy and love. To deny pardon to the defeated is, as Auden later charged against his own poem, "to equate goodness with success." In a ballad written about a year after "Spain," "As I Walked Out One Evening," he portrayed lovers who fantasized about their perfect loyalty to each other and their loved one's perfection—a fantasy that denied the need for forgiveness. But in answer to these doomed fantasies, the chiming clocks warn instead: "You shall love your crooked neighbour / With your crooked heart." The addition of the word "crooked" is not a denial of the biblical injunction but an explanation of what it means and how it must be obeyed.

Yet in his political writings in the late 1930's what Auden said was still often in conflict with his beliefs. *On the Frontier* (1938), the last of the Auden-Isherwood plays, is a tragedy of war and separation, ending with dying lovers reciting verses that sound very much like a Christian hymn to a better world, but Auden felt obliged to add some passages of versified propaganda. It scarcely mattered; the whole play was too tired and sketchy to mean much to its authors or audience. But a much finer book, Auden and Isherwood's *Journey to a War* (1939), a report in prose and verse on their visit to the Sino-Japanese War, is marked by a similar contradiction. Auden devoted all his skills to the sonnet sequence "In Time of War," tracing the whole history of mankind and the moral causes and effects of war but he then tacked on a verse "Commentary" that included propagandistic fantasies of civic unity in the face of a common enemy. The real state of "unity" in China between the Nationalists and the Communists was very different.

And when World War II finally began, "September 1, 1939" (a throwback to a manner he had otherwise abandoned earlier that year) included yet another denial of his convictions about the voluntary aspects of love:

> Hunger allows no choice
> To the citizen or the police;
> We must love one another or die.

This, like the conclusion of "Spain," seems perfectly reasonable, and when Auden discarded this stanza and then the whole poem he puzzled his critics. But the point behind the lines is that love is a hunger that must be satisfied, not a voluntary gift of mutual forgiveness. The equation of love with hunger struck Auden as a lie— memorable, stirring, but still a lie. He ended a poem of the 1950's, "First Things First," with the line: "Thousands have lived without love, not one without water."

By the start of 1939 Auden no longer found tolerable his public role as court poet to the English Left. He still made political gestures, but more from a wish to support his left-wing friends than from any deep convictions. Since writing *The Ascent of F6* he had spent much of his time traveling around Europe and then the world, as if searching for someplace other than England in which to live. When he and Isherwood were on the way back from the war in China, in the summer of 1938, they spent two weeks in America. They decided to return there permanently.

They sailed for New York in January 1939. In England their departure was widely felt as the end of an era. In America their arrival was hardly noticed—which was precisely what Auden hoped for. He later said that in England he always felt as if he were living among his family, and it was this sense of family obligation that led him to write in ways he considered dishonest and inauthentic. Even his politically charged writing fulfilled the expectations of his audience that a bright young man must be a rebel; and Auden knew furthermore that his political writings largely served as preaching to the converted and made no practical difference. In America, a nation that has never taken its writers as seriously as England takes its, he would be free from all temptation to please an audience that wanted to hear his familiar formulas.

A few weeks before he left for New York he was staying in Brussels, where he saw the Brueghels in the art museum. What he learned from these paintings was a rebuke to his own resonant calls to action. He realized that the most important events never occurred under a historical spotlight, never enjoyed the thrilling benefit of Yeatsian heroicizing rhetoric. The truth was less beautiful, more disturbing. Brueghel, in paintings like *The Massacre of the Innocents* and *The Fall of Icarus,* made this point quietly and exactly ("Musée des Beaux Arts"):

About suffering they were never wrong,
The Old Masters: how well they understood
Its human position; how it takes place
While someone else is eating or opening a
    window or just walking dully along;
            . . .
They never forgot
That even the dreadful martyrdom must run
    its course
Anyhow in a corner, some untidy spot . . .

In Brueghel's *Icarus,* for instance: how
    everything turns away
Quite leisurely from the disaster; the
    ploughman may
Have heard the splash, the forsaken cry,
But for him it was not an important failure;
            . . .
. . . and the expensive delicate ship that must
    have seen

Something amazing, a boy falling out of the
    sky,
Had somewhere to get to and sailed calmly
    on.

Earlier he had written about opposing ideological armies, with their pure causes. In "Spain," in stanzas dropped soon after he reached America, Franco's Nationalists were the manifestations of neurosis and fear, the People's Army the flower of tenderness and love. Now Auden could not be so self-congratulatory. Brueghel showed how we all turn away from suffering. The next step was to understand that we all cause it. In "Herman Melville," one of the first poems he wrote in America, Auden saw that "Evil is unspectacular and always human, / And shares our bed and eats at our own table. . . ."

Auden was beginning to immerse himself in American literature and the American language. Within a few months, in the long poem *New Year Letter*, although he wrote that "England to me is my own tongue," he could present this sweeping survey of American history and landscape as a backdrop for his continuing focus on the problem of choice:

A long time since it seems to-day
The Saints in Massachusetts Bay
Heard theocratic COTTON preach
And legal WINTHROP's Little Speech;
Since MISTRESS HUTCHINSON was tried
By those her Inner Light defied,
And WILLIAMS questioned Moses' law
            . . .
Long since inventive JEFFERSON
Fought realistic HAMILTON,
Pelagian versus Jansenist;
But the same heresies exist.
Time makes old formulas look strange,
Our properties and symbols change,
But round the freedom of the Will

Our disagreements center still,

     . . .

Here, as in Europe, is dissent,
This raw untidy continent
Where the Commuter can't forget
The Pioneer; and even yet
A *Völkerwanderung* occurs:
Resourceful manufacturers
Trek southward by progressive stages
For sites with no floor under wages,
No ceiling over hours; and by
Artistic souls in towns that lie
Out in the weed and pollen belt
The need for sympathy is felt,
And east to hard New York they come;
And self-respect drives Negroes from
The one-crop and race-hating delta
To northern cities helter-skelter;
And in jalopies there migrates
A rootless tribe from windblown states
To suffer further westward where
The tolerant Pacific air
Makes logic seem so silly, pain
Subjective, what he seeks so vain
The wanderer may die; and kids,
When their imagination bids,
Hitch-hike a thousand miles to find
The Hesperides that's on their mind.

Auden's early months in America, both in New York and on the travels that produced these lines, seemed filled with exhilarating renewals and also a calm sense of purposeful serenity. He gathered the poems he had written since 1936 in a volume entitled *Another Time* (1940), as if signaling that he had begun something new. "For the first time," he wrote a friend, "I am leading a life which remotely approximates to the way I think I ought to live."

Most important, perhaps, was that he had fallen in love. His earlier affairs had been, he knew, temporary and had done little to break through his personal isolation. In the spring of 1939 he met a college student named Chester Kallman, a young poet who offered the right mixture of personal similarities and differences that seemed to Auden essential for a faithful love. Auden had always disapproved of his own homosexuality on the grounds that it resulted in a species of narcissism, in which the loved object was a version of the lover himself. To counter this he had tried to love people who were different from himself, less intellectual and introspective, more physically confident. Now he recognized in Kallman someone who shared his passion for language, his wit, but who was different enough in class and background (American Jewish petit bourgeois) to prevent narcissism from taking hold. Auden thought of their relationship as a marriage, and the story of a marriage began to emerge in his poetry. In 1940 he wrote "In Sickness and in Health," a meditation on marriage that takes its title from the wedding service. Two years later he wrote "Mundus et Infans," about the birth of a baby, and "Many Happy Returns," about the upbringing of a young child. About twenty-five years later it was time for an "Epithalamium" written in a parental tone for the younger generation as it began its own marriages.

He also began, in 1939–1940, a slow return to the religion he thought he had abandoned. In Spain, in 1937, he had been surprised by his own disturbed feelings at the sight of churches closed or destroyed by the Republicans. "The feeling was far too intense to be the result of a mere liberal dislike of intolerance," he wrote later. Soon after his return from Spain he met the writer Charles Williams, who seemed to him, as to many others, an example of saintliness. The liberal tenets that Auden had taken largely for granted as the basis for progress and morals seemed almost overthrown by the rise of Hitler, who had come to power in one of the best-educated and intellectually sophisticated countries of Europe—despite the liberal assumption that education led directly to right actions. By what standards could he affirm that Hitler was absolutely wrong, that to oppose him was right? The answer seemed inevitably to have something to do with the moral absolutes of religion and the religious sense of original sin that made the lure of fascism comprehensible, not some strange violation of human nature beyond understanding. Religion proposed an ultimate moral truth that was real and absolute even if no human intelligence could fully encompass it.

Auden returned to Christianity largely by an intellectual process that involved matters like these, but he was helped along the way by his memories of the emotional beliefs of his childhood and by the personal example of figures like Charles Williams. His religious beliefs had almost nothing of the supernatural to them. Instead he found in religion an intellectual sense of the coherence of things, especially the relation of actions and consequences, a relation that is the basis of ethics. The moral law, he said, was not like a flawed human legal code but like the laws of physics or chemistry. Just as one did not violate the laws of physics by jumping out the window, one did not violate the moral law by committing murder. What the law determined in each case was the necessary consequence of a free action: the jumper lands with a thud, the murderer isolates himself from the human community, from all opportunity for trust and peace.

In the midst of his reconversion Auden wrote *New Year Letter* (published with other poems in *The Double Man,* 1941), the American passages of which were quoted above. This is a 1,700-line philosophical poem, moving, as Auden did in his conversion, from abstract speculation to personal prayer. By any standards, it is an astonishingly powerful and important poem. That the heir to Eliot's free-verse fragments should have said good-bye to all that

and written a poem in eighteenth-century couplets that included—without Joycean irony—the styles of history, criticism, and philosophy that modern poetry had mostly banished from its pages, and that he made it all work, seemed the most unlikely of all possible literary events. Yet the Augustan style of *New Year Letter* is consistent with a central aspect of Auden's earliest, most modern-sounding poems. It makes explicit the assumptions hidden in his earlier borrowings from Old English. In both cases he treated the past as something useful to the present, not as something lost or destroyed that now must be mourned. The poem joins romantic energy to Augustan decorum and is, in effect, Auden's *Faust.* Like Johann Wolfgang von Goethe's enormous drama, Auden's poem begins with a restless search among alternative ways of action and understanding; follows this with the temptations offered by "Poor cheated Mephistopheles"; then moves through vast ranges of history and myth (even versions of *Faust*'s "die Mütter," the source of all forms, in Auden's "The Terrible, the Merciful, the Mothers"); and ends with a hymn to the eternal feminine in the person of Auden's friend Elizabeth Mayer:

> Dear friend Elizabeth, dear friend
> These days have brought me, may the end
> I bring to the grave's dead-line be
> More worthy of your sympathy
> Than the beginning;
>
>   . . .
>
> We fall down in the dance, we make
> The old ridiculous mistake,
> But always there are such as you
> Forgiving, helping what we do.

Or, in Goethe's concluding words: "Das Ewig-Weibliche zieht uns hinan."

Auden's politics had changed with his religion. In his first reaction against his 1930's work he briefly espoused pacifism during the summer of 1939. But by early 1940 he wrote in a letter that he had "absolutely no patience with Pacifism as a political movement, as if one could do all the things in one's personal life that create wars and then pretend that to refuse to fight is a sacrifice and not a luxury." Although some English writers loudly charged him with fleeing the war by staying in America, Auden quietly went to the British embassy and volunteered to return. (He was told that only technically skilled people were needed.)

In New York, with no family to live among, Auden established a household of his own. Around 1940–1941 he lived in a large house in Brooklyn populated by artists and writers—at various times Carson McCullers, Louis MacNeice, Benjamin Britten, Richard Wright, Paul Bowles—where, in the midst of bohemian chaos, he took the role of bourgeois paterfamilias, banning politics from the dinner table, seeing to it that the rent was collected and paid. Much as he enjoyed New York, he decided that it was time to learn more of America and arranged to teach at the University of Michigan during 1941–1942, where the atmosphere might be more quiet.

In the summer before he left, the growing difficulties in his relationship with Kallman reached the point of crisis. While Auden had committed himself to sexual loyalty and faithfulness, Kallman was constitutionally unable to accept such domesticity, and in 1941 he began an affair with someone else. Auden was almost certainly alluding to his feelings about this when he wrote some years later that "providentially—for the occupational disease of poets is frivolity—I was forced to know in person what it is like to feel oneself in the prey of demonic powers, in both the Greek and Christian sense, stripped of self-control and self-pity, behaving like a ham actor in a Strindberg play." When the crisis abated he and Kallman agreed to have no further sexual relations with each other but to continue in many respects living as if in a marriage. For most of the rest of their lives they

shared the same household, and in later years they developed the domestic habits of long-married couples, routinely sharing errands, finishing each other's sentences.

The crisis left Auden's poetry with a new depth of feeling, less showy than much of his earlier work, more wise and self-aware. In Michigan, in 1941–1942, he wrote a Christmas oratorio, *For the Time Being,* intended for setting by Benjamin Britten. It was animated by popular styles and contemporary satire, but its Christmas celebration was shadowed by its "apprehension at the thought / Of Lent and Good Friday which cannot, after all, now / Be very far off." Auden once again used his technique of conflating, rather than contrasting, present and past in his version of the Christmas story. He explained the technique in a letter to his father:

Sorry you are puzzled by the Oratorio. Perhaps you were expecting a purely historical account as one might give of the battle of Waterloo, whereas I was trying to treat it as a religious event which eternally recurs every time it is accepted. Thus the historical fact that the shepherds were *shepherds* is religiously accidental—the religious fact is that they were the poor and humble of this world for whom at this moment the historical expression is the city-proletariat, and so on with all the other figures. . . . I am not the first to treat the Christian data in this way; until the 18th Cent. it was always done, in the Mystery Plays for instance or any Italian paintings. It is only in the last two centuries that religion has been "humanized," and therefore treated historically as something that happened a long time ago; hence the nursery picture of Jesus in a nightgown and a Parsifal beard.

After his year at Michigan Auden expected to join the U.S. Army but was rejected by the draft board for medical reasons in September 1942. He spent the rest of the war teaching at

Swarthmore College, where he wrote another long poem, *The Sea and the Mirror: A Commentary on Shakespeare's "The Tempest"* (this and his previous long poem were collected in book form as *For the Time Being*, 1944). The events of the poem occur after the end of Shakespeare's play, as Prospero makes a farewell speech to Ariel while packing to leave the island, and the other characters then report, as they sail home, what they learned there. The poem is Auden's most elaborate study in the range and powers of his art, a rebuke to the romantic idea of the autonomy of poetic imagination. Prospero, in his long opening poem, is the type of artist who cannot see anything except in terms of art (perhaps without intending to, Auden made Prospero into a poet like Wallace Stevens: "On walks through winter woods, a bird's dry carcass / Agitates the retina with novel images, / A stranger's quiet collapse in a noisy street / Is the beginning of much lively speculation"), and when he comments tartly on the other characters in the play he can see in them none of the depths he casually attributes to himself. Prospero sounds persuasive—the portrait is so vivid that more than one critic was trapped into reading it as Auden's self-portrait—but the rest of the poem shows how limited and ignorant his faith in the imagination has left him. In the middle section the other characters make their own speeches, culminating in a triumphantly beautiful villanelle for Miranda. But once we have been persuaded of the depths of this splendid sequence of poems, Auden brushes it aside as it had earlier brushed aside Prospero. In the third section Caliban speaks to the audience, reminding us at the start that the play we have seen, and the poem we have read, was all make-believe, all fiction: "If now," he begins, "having dismissed your hired impersonators with verdicts ranging from the laudatory orchid to the disgusted and disgusting egg, . . ." Auden's Caliban is the voice

of nature, of the energy and variety of life, of Eros itself. And since nature—as Auden emphasized in earlier years—has no personal voice of its own, it must speak in a borrowed one; hence Caliban's adoption of the most mannered of all English styles, the prose of the late novels of Henry James. This style allows for the greatest possible range of content and manner, from the vulgarly proverbial to the aristocratically ornate. Caliban uses his all-inclusive voice to record the failures not only of art but of all secular ambition and hope. He pictures us at the end in a moment of existential urgency, when "we do at least see ourselves as we are, neither cosy nor playful, but swaying out on the ultimate wind-whipped cornice that overhangs the unabiding void." Only at this moment (the idea derives from the New Testament via Kierkegaard) can the choice of religious faith be made and solid ground again rest under our feet. Only now can the ultimate order and coherence of the universe be acknowleged—and so "the sounded note is the restored relation." *The Sea and the Mirror* concludes with a love song spoken by Ariel, the disembodied voice of art, to Caliban, the solid disorder of life, as Ariel reminds Caliban that art has no real wish to be autonomous or self-sufficient, but knows that it depends on the flawed sad variety of mortal life for its very existence.

In 1945 Auden's *Collected Poetry* appeared. Critics had begun to charge that his earliest work was his best, so he arranged the book not chronologically or thematically, but by alphabetical order of first lines. This was an implicit challenge to critics to see whether they could tell by style alone whether one of his poems was early or late. Auden disliked the book's title—"collected" implied finality, which at thirty-eight he hoped was untrue—but the publisher insisted. Among the changes Auden made for this volume were wholesale deletions of political work, the breaking-up of *Paid on Both Sides* and *The Orators* into disconnected short poems (in later years, feeling less irritated by his younger self, he restored both works to their complete forms), and the addition of ironic, sometimes flippant titles to poems that had been untitled in earlier books. The volume eventually sold more than fifty thousand copies.

At the end of the war Auden left his Swarthmore job and worked for a few months with the U.S. Strategic Bombing Survey, in a unit of civilians and soldiers studying the effect of bombing on civilian morale in Germany. At first Auden thought the work a "statistical boondoggle" ("We asked them if they minded being bombed."). But his unit learned that morale increased as bombing did—a conclusion ignored by the military, who had to relearn it twenty years later in Vietnam.

Back from Germany, Auden settled again in New York, in Greenwich Village. There he worked at editing and reviewing, gave occasional lectures and, in the 1960's, went out across America on an annual reading tour. He and Robert Frost were the only poets able to make a living from their writing. Auden came to regard himself as one of a vanishing breed, the Man of Letters, who wrote not because he was devoted to the lonely discipline of his art but because his writing served a public function; Edmund Wilson was the closest parallel. In a late poem he referred to the audience of poets as "our clients"—in the same way doctors or lawyers have clients, who come to them for professional services they are trained to provide.

In New York, Auden finished the last of his long poems, *The Age of Anxiety* (1947). A "baroque eclogue" set in a Third Avenue bar, it records the intersecting thoughts of four characters—loosely embodying the four Jungian faculties of thought, intuition, feeling, and sensation—through an All Souls' Night that ends in varieties of religious negation and affirmation. The verse is Old English alliterative, but with modern idioms and adapted into a wide range of lyrical, narrative, and epigrammatic forms. This modification of the Old Icelandic drottkvaett is characteristic:

> Hushed is the lake of hawks
> Bright with our excitement,
> And all the sky of skulls
> Glows with scarlet roses;
> The melter of men and salt
> Admires the drinker of iron:
> Bold banners of meaning
> Blaze o'er the host of days.

As in the Welsh model, this identifies the four traditional elements by way of riddles: the lake of hawks is the air; the sky of skulls, earth; the melter of men, fire; and the drinker of iron, water, which rusts it.

Nineteen forty-eight through 1957 were the Mediterranean years of this least Mediterranean of poets. Every spring he closed his apartment in New York and spent about six months on the island of Ischia, near Naples. He deliberately chose a climate and culture with as little as possible in common with the Nordic landscapes he found most congenial. In "Good-Bye to the Mezzogiorno" (1958) he came "Out of a gothic North"

> In middle-age hoping to twig from
> What we are not what we might be next. . . .

He was too much the product of his English roots ever to settle in:

> If we try
> To "go southern," we spoil in no time, we grow
> Flabby, dingily lecherous, and
> Forget to pay bills: . . .

but his years in Ischia altered the character of his poetry and his beliefs.

In his early years in America he had focused virtually all his attention on the solitary choices of the individual mind. Now he wrote about the world of the flesh and about the world of the citizen, of mankind in landscapes and cities. The great personal questions of faith and doubt he had largely resolved. It was now time to write the poetry needed by an age in which the heroic vision of the romantic artist, alone with his imagination, had grown trivial. It was

in which the heroic image is not the nomad
wanderer through the desert or over the
ocean,
but the less exciting figure of the builder,
who renews the ruined walls of the city.

And to give a local habitation and a name to this solid and rooted figure, he began writing poems about the unheroic body. Poets in the romantic and modernist tradition had always found the body difficult to write about in any plausible way, probably because they were embarrassed by an aspect of themselves that—unlike the works of their imagination—they clearly did not make by themselves and that shared so many qualities with the common run of mankind. Eliot, until the last years of his life, hated the flesh and all it did. Lawrence, dying of consumption, fantasized the body as a repository of sacred energies that no real human body could ever have contained. Yeats found the body interesting only if ideally and impossibly beautiful or grotesquely ugly. Pound, until he was locked up, scarcely noticed the body at all. In contrast to all these, Auden saw that the body had rights of its own, that it was also an object which everyone put to use—"my accomplice now, / My assassin to be"—yet despite the isolating acts of the individual will the body does its best to recover, "restoring / The order we try to destroy, the rhythm / We spoil out of spite." It is "The flesh we die but it is death to pity" (to look down on as inferior to the mind) the one aspect of ourselves that sees through every lie we try to tell and suffers the strain of

our mental disorder. At the close of Auden's long historical meditation "Memorial for the City" (1949), the flesh itself speaks:

Without me Adam would have fallen
   irrevocably
   with Lucifer; he would never have been
   able
to cry *O felix culpa.*

. . .

I fell asleep when Diotima spoke of love; . . .

. . .

I was the just impediment to the marriage of
   Faustus with Helen; I know a ghost when I
   see one.

. . .

I was innocent of the sin of the Ancient
   Mariner; time after time I warned Captain
   Ahab to accept happiness.
As for Metropolis, that too-great city; her
   delusions are not mine.
Her speeches impress me little, her statistics
   less; . . .
At the place of my passion her photographers
   are gathered together; but I shall rise again
   to hear her judged.

Auden's one article of religious faith that stood beyond the world visible to science was his belief in the resurrection of the body at the end of time, a belief that took the body seriously and on the body's own terms.

"In Praise of Limestone" (1948) is Auden's calm hymn to a landscape that "dissolves in water," which in its pliability and change is an image for the body itself. It is a personal landscape as well, the Pennine Hills of his English childhood and the hills of northern Italy. He makes no spectacular claims for this small and local setting, which he knows has neither grandeur nor historical importance to recommend it. (Neither, of course, has the body.) What both limestone landscape and human flesh do, however, is rebuke the romantic poet's celebration of his mind and the scientific observer's concern for the inhuman spaces of atoms or galaxies. The scientist is right, his distant places are important. The poem recalls only that there is also a human landscape of responsibility and love.

The negative image of the human landscape of "In Praise of Limestone" is the "plain without a feature, bare and brown," of "The Shield of Achilles." This is a place—or a nonplace—where all identity and sympathy are absent, where nameless children grow who

> . . . never heard
> Of any world where promises were kept,
> Or one could weep because another wept.

Auden's verse form in much of his late work is largely a twentieth-century invention but one that stands outside the mainstream of modernism. He uses lines arranged by the number of syllables, without regular rhymes or regular patterns of stress. The form of "In Praise of Limestone" is alternating lines of thirteen and eleven syllables, with adjacent vowels (and vowels and *h*) arbitrarily counted as a single vowel, so that *the in-* or *-ly home* each count as one syllable only—a practice with a long classical ancestry. Thus:

> If it form the one landscape that we, the
>   inconstant ones,
>   Are consistently homesick for, this is chiefly
> Because it dissolves in water. Mark these
>   rounded slopes
>   With their surface fragrance of thyme and,
>   beneath. . . .

Auden learned syllabic verse from Marianne Moore, and it was also used by Robert Bridges and other poets earlier in the century but without Auden's range or depth. What syllabics made possible was a form that had all the regularity and order of traditional meters without in any way sounding archaic or anachronistic.

They permitted the formal pleasures of older poetry, but the understatement with which they asserted their formal properties allowed them to accommodate what Auden called the characteristic style of modern poetry, "an intimate tone of voice, the speech of one person addressing another person, not a large audience." When a poem required a relaxed tone of voice, long-lined syllabics provided room for expansiveness. When more intensity was needed, Auden tightened the form by using shorter lines and extensive internal rhyming:

> Simultaneously, as soundlessly,
>   Spontaneously, suddenly
> As, at the vaunt of the dawn, the kind
>   Gates of the body fly open
> To its world beyond, the gates of the mind,
>   The horn gate and the ivory gate
> Swing to, swing shut, instantaneously. . . .

These lines open a sequence of poems titled *Horae Canonicae*—canonical hours, the hours of daily prayer. After *The Age of Anxiety* Auden turned from long poems to connected sequences of shorter poems. The seven *Bucolics* of 1952–1953 concern different ways of life appropriate to different landscapes. The seven *Horae Canonicae* poems of 1949–1954 have a larger and more ambitious subject, the relation of individuals and their personal acts to the life of the city, and the necessary connection between civilized order and the violence needed to maintain it. (Auden published these and his other poems from his Mediterranean years in *Nones*, 1951, and *The Shield of Achilles*, 1955.)

Horae Canonicae is one of the great masterpieces of twentieth-century poetry. It has received little critical attention because it demands to be read in ways very different from those appropriate to the modernist tradition from Yeats to Wallace Stevens. Its concern is not the imposition of imaginative order on a passive world but the discovery of order that already exists in the world. In its disturbing emphasis on the price that must be paid for civilization, on the murderous violence that defends civil order, it is in the direct line of Vergil's *Aeneid* and Shakespeare's history plays. Aeneas, the hero who makes possible the peace and order of imperial Rome, yields at the end to the violent furor he is dedicated to oppose. In Auden's sequence the great civilizers—those with vocations for the arts and sciences, those who command laws and buildings to come into existence—are also those who provide the instruments and authority for the murder of the scapegoat victim, the banished outsider, without whose exclusion no community has ever constituted itself. Where Auden had earlier emphasized the element of choice that led to acts of love, now he examines the role of choice in murderous acts of will.

The sequence extends over an epic range. The first six poems cover the events of a single day—a Good Friday in the present that is simultaneously the day of the historical crucifixion, like the Christmas of *For the Time Being*—but extend also from the poet's birth to his death, from the rise to the fall of his city, from the evolution of man to the end of the species, and from the creation to the apocalypse.

All the beginnings occur in "Prime." This opening poem also establishes the theme of the isolating will. To draw breath—to choose to draw breath on first waking—is

> . . . to wish
>   No matter what, to be wise,
> To be different, to die and the cost,
>   No matter how, is Paradise
> Lost of course and myself owing a death. . . .

(The pun on "owing a debt" is originally Falstaff's.) In "Prime" the "I" of the sequence is still solitary. In "Terce" he is in transition between privacy and a public role. At this moment the hangman shakes paws with his dog and sets

out to work; the judge gently closes his wife's bedroom door and descends with a weary sigh. It is a neutral moment when our only wish is to get through the day without being called upon to do or choose anything in particular, to be left alone. But that modest wish has its fatal consequences, because someone always gets in the way, and there will be the wish to move him out of it.

The third poem, "Sext," opens with awed praise for those more devoted to vocation than themselves, "the first flaker of flints / who forgot his dinner, / the first collector of sea-shells / to remain celibate." Then it grimly acknowledges the city's need for those in authority, "very great scoundrels," but without whom "how squalid existence would be." It ends in a devastatingly level tone, describing the common crowd who gather at any scene of destruction, the crowd whom everyone can join ("Only because of that can we say / all men are our brothers,") and that worships only the brute fact of force. With all three groups in place, the crucifixion can happen. Those with vocation provide the instruments of murder; those in authority give the command; the crowd assents.

The fourth poem, "Nones," shows an emotional range and force, an ethical intelligence and depth, scarcely equaled in modern verse. It deserves more than the brief explication that is possible here.

A reader need have no interest at all in religion to feel the power of "Nones." Its emotional focus is the abrupt sinking realization—which occurs at some point in all human relationships—that one has done harm to another, perhaps inadvertently, that cannot now be undone. Whether it is a hurtful word thoughtlessly spoken or an angry act of violence, the act and its consequences are irrevocably *there*:

> What we know to be not possible,
>   Though time after time foretold

By wild hermits, by shaman and sybil
 Gibbering in their trances,
Or revealed to a child in some chance rhyme
 Like *will* and *kill*, comes to pass
Before we realize it. . . .

The shouting crowd that called for the victim's death has dissolved; each of those in it can blame the crowd, not himself. Nature, the realm of repetition and return, looks on in bewilderment at an act that, unlike the cyclical events of nature, cannot be repeated or reversed. (The modernist emphasis on cyclical history, as in Yeats or Joyce, or on the immediate moment, as in Williams or Stevens, or in a realm outside time, as in Eliot, excludes the whole subject of this poem from the world of modernist literature.) Every willed action seems to lead up to this definitive act of will. Every playful, apparently harmless, game of children or adults reveals its potentially fatal ending. We shall now,

 . . . under
 The mock chase and mock capture,
The racing and tussling and splashing,
 The panting and the laughter,
Be listening for the cry and stillness
 To follow after. . . .

Burdened by our own knowledge, we still "have time / To misrepresent, excuse, deny, / Mythify, use this event"; but its historical uniqueness, the real fact of murder, remains. "Its meaning / Waits for our lives." Meanwhile, "It would be best to go home, if we have a home"—all our fixities are in question—"In any case good to rest." And as we sleep "our dreaming wills" move through an ominous dream landscape of symbolic guilt and accusation:

 Through gates that will not relatch
And doors marked *Private*, pursued by
 Moors
And watched by latent robbers,

To hostile villages at the heads of fjords,
 To dark chateaux where wind sobs
In the pine-trees and telephones ring,
 Inviting trouble. . . .

And, at the same time, the sleeping body works undisturbed to restore order and wholeness to "our own wronged flesh." The language of the poem, up to this point rich in metaphor, for a moment becomes a language of plain fact as it describes the unpoetical workings of the body:

 . . . valves close
And open exactly, glands secrete,
 Vessels contract and expand
At the right moment. . . .

And the poem ends by rushing cinematically outward to the natural creatures, the unblinking hawk, the "bug whose view is balked by grass," the smug hens and shy deer, all awed by the fact of death, that sign of their own future which they, unlike man, cannot understand.

After the intensities of "Nones," the sequence relaxes somewhat. "Vespers," in prose, compares two fantasies of the ideal society, the innocent arcadia and ordered utopia, between which all real societies are built. "Compline" records the returns and endings of nightfall, of personal death and the end of the city, in a calm elegiac tone. And the sequence ends with the new dawn, in the early morning of "Lauds." After the encyclopedic range and intellectual rigor of the six preceding poems, it offers a simple musical promise of renewal and community:

The dripping mill-wheel is again turning;
Among the leaves the small birds sing:
In solitude, for company.

Auden intended to keep his summer house in Ischia at least until 1960, but when he won an Italian literary prize in 1957 his landlord tried to double his rent and Auden decided it was time to leave. He bought an eighteenth-century farmhouse in Kirchstetten, a small village thirty miles west of Vienna, and moved there the following year. He chose Austria, he said, because he loved the German language, because he wanted to be in a wine-drinking country, and because he wanted to be near an opera house. Opera was a taste he acquired from Chester Kallman, and in 1947 the two wrote the libretto for Igor Stravinsky's *The Rake's Progress*; later they wrote further libretti for Hans Werner Henze.

Auden's first years in Austria were among the happiest of his life. Once he stood in his garden and wept with joy at owning a home of his own. He wrote in 1958–1964 a sequence of twelve poems in celebration, *Thanksgiving for a Habitat*, the scale and exuberance of which suggests a house larger and grander than the rural domesticity of the Kirchstetten farmhouse with its low ceilings and dark rooms. Each room received a poem of its own, together with some general poems about the house itself, and each room is characterized, as in his earlier *Bucolics*, by special kinds of relationships, history, and rhetoric. In the study he recalls a dead friend, the poet Louis MacNeice, one of the many dead whose work survives in their influence on living writers; in the dining room he thinks of friends still very much alive; the cellar and attic evoke childhood memories; and so on through the living room, the guest room, the kitchen, the bath, and—the last and most difficult to write—the toilet. After the urban moralities of *Horae Canonicae* Auden narrowed his focus to the domestic and personal, but always in a historical and ethical context. Auden called *Thanksgiving for a Habitat* his first happy poems, the first he was able to write in the first person—that is, with all the quirks and details of his private existence on the visible surface of the poetry.

In the 1930's Auden had tried on the role of propagandist, had urged his readers to action. But he knew even then a poet had no more au-thority to recommend one or another course of action than anyone else did, and he renounced that role as false when he moved to America. In the 1950's and 1960's he again adopted a public role, but without a partisan label. As a poet he was in "loyal opposition," affirming the importance of personal choice in a mass society, but never, unlike his modernist predecessors, condemning his society as irredeemably corrupt or hopelessly inferior to some imagined past. He wrote as a democratic counterpart to the court poet of earlier times. With no pretense of writing as a leader or guide—he preferred to think of himself as a craftsman rather than as a bard—he commented on public events, bringing to light their historical and moral aspects. Much of his later poetry—in *Homage to Clio* (1960), *About the House* (1965), *City Without Walls* (1969), *Epistle to a Godson* (1972), and the posthumous *Thank You, Fog* (1974)—is deliberately "occasional," prompted by events ranging in scale from international invasions, political assassinations, and moon landings, to retirements, birthdays, and marriages.

Whatever their occasions, all these poems took as their central subject the use and misuse of personal relations and responsibility. What made love and responsibility possible, he suggested, was an awareness of the real outline and nature of things; the means by which love and responsibility were brought into being was personal speech. He distinguished between impersonal "linguistic codes," which may be found among birds and insects as well as man, and "speech," the conscious statement of personal choice, found only among individual people. To use speech is to use the first person, to take responsibility for what one says. Speech is the language of an "I" with a personal name, linguistic codes the language of an anonymous "he" or "she." Since all individuals are at the same time biological organisms with needs and functions common to all mankind, and unique persons differing from all others, everyone is capable of using both kinds of language. If I ask you the way to the train station, you will (I hope) answer in a linguistic code, giving me the same answer anyone else would give. But if I ask you what emotional associations the station has for you, you may (if you choose) answer in personal speech, telling me feelings and memories that no one else could possibly tell.

So—to return to a poem from the early 1950's—in "The Shield of Achilles," the barren warlike landscape is a place without responsibility or personal names:

> . . . congregated on its blankness, stood
>   An unintelligible multitude,
> A million eyes, a million boots in line,
> Without expression, waiting for a sign.
>
> Out of the air a voice without a face
>   Proved by statistics that some cause was
>   just
> In tones as dry and level as the place:
>   No one was cheered and nothing was
>   discussed. . . .

This is a scene on a twentieth-century version of the shield that Hephaestos, in the *Iliad*, casts at the request of Thetis, mother of the warrior Achilles. But in Auden's poem the names of the god and goddess are replaced by the anonymous "he" and "she" because they do not act, and it is their impersonality that brings about the barren impersonality on the shield's images:

> She looked over his shoulder
>   For vines and olive trees,
>
>   . . .
>
> But there on the shining metal
>   His hands had put instead
> An artificial wilderness
>   And a sky like lead.

Only in the final stanza do the proper names appear, together with the personal characteristics of their owners; but now it is too late. The smith god walks away from his creation; the goddess finally speaks, but in horror and revulsion; and the hero in whose name the shield was made has already chosen his death:

> The thin-lipped armorer,
>   Hephaestos, hobbled away;
> Thetis of the shining breasts
>   Cried out in dismay
> At what the god had wrought
>   To please her son, the strong
> Iron-hearted man-slaying Achilles
>   Who would not live long.

The ideas of language implicit in "The Shield of Achilles" became explicit in later poems. Writing on the occasion of the Soviet invasion of Czechoslovakia in "August 1968," Auden, whose home in Austria was only a few miles away, made a linguistic parable. He responded to the event in the terms that, as a poet, he understood best, and the point he makes is stronger than any direct propaganda:

> The Ogre does what ogres can,
> Deeds quite impossible for Man,
> But one prize is beyond his reach,
> The Ogre cannot master Speech.
> About a subjugated plain,
> Among its desperate and slain,
> The Ogre stalks with hands on hips,
> While drivel gushes from his lips.

The relation of personal speech to impersonal code, the contrast between the scale of the individual body and the inhuman scale of nature's remoter aspects, the importance of unique unrepeatable events in history as contrasted with the cycles of nature—it was this framework of ideas that made possible the special personal tone of Auden's later years. He wrote more and more directly about his personal experience, but unlike the younger confessional poets then emerging in America, he never suggested his experience was important because it was his.

He always made didactic use of it, as an example or warning. And he wrote about it in the deliberately unheroic miniature forms of haiku or haiku-sequences that he learned about by translating similar poems in Dag Hammar-skjöld's *Markings*:

> Money cannot buy
> The fuel of Love:
> But is excellent kindling.
>
> Our bodies cannot love:
> But, without one,
> What works of Love could we do?
>
> Thoughts of his own death,
> like the distant roll
> of thunder at a picnic.

A frequent topic in his later poems was his own aging, which was almost startlingly rapid in his late fifties and early sixties. "River Profile," written when he was fifty-nine, is a terrifying allegory of the growth and decline of the body in terms of a river's progress and an example of the great poetry of which he was still capable. The river's origin is a sexual storm ("head-on collisions of cloud and rock in an / up-thrust, crevasse-and-avalanche"); it first appears as a nameless stream; then it grows larger and stronger, until its middle age:

> Polluted, bridged by girders, banked by
>   concrete,
> now it bisects a polyglot metropolis,
> ticker-tape, taxi, brothel, foot-lights country,
> *à-la-mode* always.
>
> Broadening or burrowing to the moon's
>   phases,
> turbid with pulverized wastemantle, on
>   through
> flatter, duller, hotter, cotton-gin country
> it scours, approaching
>
> the tidal mark where it puts off majesty,

> disintegrates, and through swamps of a delta,
> punting-pole, fowling-piece, oyster-tongs
>   country,
> wearies to its final
>
> act of surrender, effacement, atonement
> in a huge amorphous aggregate no cuddled
> attractive child ever dreams of, non-country....

As the world of his poems drew inward from history and the city to the rooms of his house, and then to his aging body, Auden returned to the privacy of his beginnings. In 1972 he left his winter home in New York for a cottage provided by his old Oxford college, where he had been professor of poetry since 1956 (although he taught only three weeks of each year). He seemed to know he was near death: one of his last poems is ambiguously titled "Posthumous Letter to Gilbert White"; he wrote it only a month or two before he died. At the end his work took on a tone of elegiac gratitude as he recalled the culture and family that nurtured him. "A Thanksgiving" listed his debts to his literary ancestors, reviewing the whole course of his career. He named Hardy and Frost as his early masters, until

> Falling in love altered that,
>   now Someone, at least, was important:
>   *Yeats* was a help, so was *Graves.*
>
> Then, without warning, the whole
> Economy suddenly crumbled:
>   there, to instruct me, was *Brecht.*

And onward until the last poet named, Goethe, whose poem *"Gegenwart"* provided Auden with the meter for his.

Auden spent only one winter in Oxford. He found it lonely and provincial after his years in New York. Then, in 1973, he spent his usual summer with Kallman in Austria. When the time came to return to Oxford, he closed up his house and left for a weekend in Vienna before his flight. He died there in his sleep in the early hours of September 29, 1973. He was buried in the village cemetery of Kirchstetten.

A memorial plaque in the poets' corner at Westminster Abbey is engraved with the lines with which, in 1939, he concluded his elegy for Yeats. Writing less to Yeats than to the living poets of whom he was one, Auden celebrated the didactic powers of his art. In the world of time and of physical necessity, in the world of impersonal language, the poet still preserved the responsible freedom of personal speech. His task was to offer that spoken freedom to others:

> In the prison of his days
> Teach the free man how to praise.

Selected Bibliography

WORKS OF
W. H. AUDEN

COLLECTED EDITIONS

The Collected Poetry of W. H. Auden. New York: Random House, 1945. British edition: *Collected Shorter Poems, 1930–1944.* London: Faber and Faber, 1950. (Revised versions of most of Auden's earlier poems, with excisions.)

W. H. Auden. A Selection by the Author. Harmondsworth: Penguin/ Faber and Faber, 1958. American edition: *Selected Poetry of W. H. Auden.* New York: Modern Library, 1959. 2nd ed., New York: Vintage Books, 1971.

Collected Shorter Poems 1927–1957. London: Faber and Faber, 1966; New York: Random House, 1967. (Further revisions and excisions of earlier work, arranged chronologically.)

Collected Longer Poems. London: Faber and Faber, 1968; New York: Random House, 1969.

Collected Poems. London: Faber and Faber, 1976; New York: Random House, 1976. (Includes the two volumes listed immediately above, with some additional poems restored by Auden in later years and with the contents of his later volumes of short poems. Auden's final revised texts, with many early poems omitted.)

The English Auden. Poems, Essays, and Dramatic Writings, 1927–1939. London: Faber and Faber, 1977; New York: Random House, 1978. (Reprints the original versions, including all the poems that Auden printed in book form during his lifetime but omitted from his late collections.)

Selected Poems, New Edition. New York: Vintage Books, 1979; London: Faber and Faber, 1979. (Reprinted from the original versions, often differing from those in the *Collected Poems*, and including some omitted from the late collections.)

PROSE

The Dyer's Hand. New York: Random House, 1962; London: Faber and Faber, 1963.

Forewords and Afterwords. New York: Random House, 1973; London: Faber and Faber, 1973.

BIBLIOGRAPHY

Bloomfield, Barry C., and Edward Mendelson. *W. H. Auden: A Bibliography, 1924–1969.* Charlottesville: University Press of Virginia, 1972. (A full list of writings by and about Auden.)

BIOGRAPHICAL AND CRITICAL STUDIES

Blair, John G. *The Poetic Art of W. H. Auden.* Princeton, N. J.: Princeton University Press, 1965.

Carpenter, Humphrey. *W. H. Auden: A Biography.* New York: Harcourt Brace Jovanovich (in press).

Duchene, François. *The Case of the Helmeted Airman: A Study of W. H. Auden's Poetry.* London: Chatto and Windus, 1972.

Fuller, John L. *A Reader's Guide to W. H. Auden.* London: Thames and Hudson, 1970.

Greenberg, Herbert M. *Quest for the Necessary: W. H. Auden and the Dilemma of Divided Consciousness.* Cambridge: Harvard University Press, 1968.

Hynes, Samuel L. *The Auden Generation.* New York: Viking, 1977.

Johnson, Richard. *Man's Place: An Essay on Auden.* Ithaca, N. Y.: Cornell University Press, 1973.

Mendelson, Edward. *Early Auden.* New York: Viking (in press).

Spears, Monroe K. *The Poetry of W. H. Auden: The Disenchanted Island.* New York: Oxford University Press, 1963.

Spears, Monroe K., ed. *Auden: A Collection of Critical Essays.* Englewood Cliffs, N. J.: Prentice-Hall, 1964.

Spender, Stephen, ed. *W. H. Auden: A Tribute.* London: Weidenfeld and Nicolson, 1975.

Wright, George T. *W. H. Auden.* New York: Twayne, 1969.

—EDWARD MENDELSON

James Baldwin

1924–

Near the end of one of James Baldwin's most remarkable books, *No Name in the Street* (1972), the author discusses the doomed quest for love of the San Francisco flower children as symptomatic of the degeneration of American society. Suddenly, in one of those bewildering leaps in logic that characterize his social essays, Baldwin writes:

It has been vivid to me for many years that what we call a race problem here is not a race problem at all: to keep calling it that is a way of avoiding the problem. The problem is rooted in the question of how one treats one's flesh and blood, especially one's children. The blacks are the despised and slaughtered children of the great Western house—nameless and unnameable bastards.

In a quite literal historical sense, the statement has some validity. Uprooted from African culture, enslaved and transported, sexually exploited by owners and overseers, sold and resold in defiance of family ties, given the patronymic of the oppressor regardless of actual parentage, black people in America did appear, in Baldwin's historical perspective, to be bereft of legitimacy and identity. Alex Haley's *Roots* and Herbert Gutman's *The Black Family in Slavery and Freedom, 1750–1925* raise basic questions about this view, but Baldwin's adherence to it is based

not so much on the historiography of slavery as on a projection of autobiographical experience on the large screen of social and racial generalization. As the titles *Nobody Knows My Name* (1961) and *No Name in the Street* indicate, Baldwin is a writer obsessed by the theme of identity or its absence. Because his interrelated treatment of psychological and social issues derives so directly from his personal history, it is necessary to examine his early life with some care before moving to a consideration of his literary career.

Born in Harlem in 1924, James Baldwin had a singularly unhappy childhood. In 1927 his mother, Berdis Emma Jones, who worked as a domestic servant, married David Baldwin, a sternly authoritarian religious fanatic who had migrated from New Orleans to New York. Young James thus acquired a name but not a loving and supportive paternal figure. On the contrary, David Baldwin despised his stepson for his illegitimacy, his physical weakness and ugliness, and, later, his independence of spirit. The child's mother provided whatever compensatory affection she could, but her eight additional children born over the next sixteen years and her work in white people's kitchens left her little time to spend on her firstborn. Indeed, while she was scrubbing floors and dusting furniture downtown, young James was cleaning house and tending the growing brood of half brothers and half sisters uptown. In such a family situation it is little wonder that the future author's sexual development was ambiguous or that his major literary themes were to be the searches for love and identity.

If Baldwin's family life was emotionally difficult, its objective circumstances were economically tenuous and socially repugnant. Even with both parents working in menial jobs, the most that could be expected was physical survival. The squalor and vice of the slum neighborhood in which this survival had to be achieved left an indelible impression on young Baldwin's mind, first as evidence of the wages of sin, and later as the pathological symptoms of a racist society:

. . . visible everywhere, in every wine-stained and urine-splashed hallway, in every clanging ambulance bell, in every scar on the faces of the pimps and their whores, in every helpless, newborn baby being brought into this danger, in every knife and pistol fight on the Avenue, and in every disastrous bulletin: a cousin, mother of six, suddenly gone mad, the children parcelled out here and there; an indestructible aunt rewarded for years of hard labor by a slow, agonizing death in a terrible small room; somebody's bright son blown into eternity by his own hand; another turned robber and carried off to jail (*The Fire Next Time*).

From such nightmarish reality, some refuge was needed, some sanctuary offering spiritual and physical safety and emotional release. For the Baldwins this sanctuary was the storefront church where David Baldwin preached. In *No Name in the Street*, Baldwin speaks of his stepfather's "unreciprocated love for the Great God Almighty" as the major passion of his life. Mercilessly, he strove to inculcate his faith in all the members of his family, not always with complete success. His beloved youngest son by his

first marriage, Samuel Baldwin, rebelled in adolescence against his father's puritanical regimen and left the household at the age of seventeen.

If neither God above nor his favorite son on earth would reciprocate his love, the elder Baldwin must have felt, none should be lavished on young James, another man's son whose reliability, apparently unquestioning acceptance of Christian faith, and intellectual precocity served only to call to mind the absence of these qualities in Samuel. For James, religious faith was an effort to escape the dangers of the street, to placate his father, and finally to defeat him by excelling him in his own ministerial vocation. Whatever the motives, the intense emotional commitment to religion in his early life left James Baldwin an enduring literary legacy of religious subjects and imagery, a hortatory style, and high moral seriousness. Three of his books—*Go Tell It on the Mountain* (1953), *The Amen Corner* (1968), and *Blues for Mister Charlie* (1964)—deal explicitly with religious experience, and six others—*The Fire Next Time* (1963), *Tell Me How Long the Train's Been Gone* (1968), *No Name in the Street, One Day, When I Was Lost* (1972), *If Beale Street Could Talk* (1974), and *The Devil Finds Work* (1976)—derive their titles or epigraphs from spirituals or Scripture.

In contrast with the stresses of home and the emotionally depleting ecstasies of church, school offered Baldwin an arena for personal triumph removed from the awesome shadow of his domineering stepfather. Not that it provided physical safety, for the boy's diminutive size and mental superiority made him the easy target of schoolyard bullies; but the psychological support of his obvious intellectual prowess helped to sustain him in otherwise impossible circumstances. It also brought him to the favorable attention of Gertrude Ayer, the black principal of Public School 24 and something of a role model for young James, and of Orilla Miller, a white teacher who expanded his interests from books to the theater and befriended his family over a period of several years. A voracious reader, Baldwin finished his first book, *Uncle Tom's Cabin,* at the age of eight and moved quickly to *The Good Earth,* Dickens, Robert Louis Stevenson, Dostoevsky, and the Schomburg Collection of black literature and history. As he commented to Margaret Mead in 1970, "By the time I was thirteen I had read myself out of Harlem." He then began forays downtown to the main collection of the New York Public Library on Forty-second Street, the resources of which even his appetite for books was not likely to exhaust.

Baldwin's childhood thus developed simultaneously in two worlds—the actual world of home, street, church, and school, and the imaginary realm of book, play, and film. One of his mother's most characteristic recollections emphasizes this duality: "He'd sit at a table with a child in one arm and a book in the other." At Frederick Douglass Junior High School in Harlem and at DeWitt Clinton High School in the Bronx, Baldwin accelerated the creative efforts begun at Public School 24. Poems, plays, stories, and essays poured out, gaining him recognition as editor of *The Douglass Pilot* and *The Magpie* at Clinton. Encouraged by such gifted teachers as the poet Countee Cullen and Harvard-educated Herman W. Porter at Douglass, and Marcella Whalen and Wilmer Stone at Clinton, Baldwin longed to become a writer.

Before this ambition could be fulfilled, however, he had to confront related crises of sexual and religious identity. Baldwin has written at length of this period of his life, which began at age fourteen, in *The Fire Next Time* and, in fictional guise, in *Go Tell It on the Mountain.* The onset of puberty intensified the sense of innate depravity preached so incessantly by David Baldwin as axiomatic in his version of the Christian faith, and as especially applicable to his diabolically ugly stepson. The ranks of the fallen pimps and whores on Harlem streets bore vivid

testimony to the doom of those who yielded to the temptations of the flesh, now being felt so insistently by James and his suddenly adolescent acquaintances. Only through a transcendent religious experience, it seemed, could such a fate be averted. In this receptive frame of mind, Baldwin was led by his friend Arthur Moore to Mount Calvary of the Pentecostal Faith Church, whose pastor, the charismatic Mother Horn, received him warmly.

Later the same summer his salvation came:

One moment I was on my feet, singing and clapping and, at the same time, working out in my head the plot of a play I was working on then; the next moment, with no transition, no sensation of falling, I was on my back, with the lights beating down into my face and all the vertical saints above me.

The purging anguish and ecstasy of this experience temporarily relieved the pressure of Baldwin's developing sexuality. It led him also to the pulpit, where as a boy-minister he could be the catalyst for the salvation of others and where, more importantly, his histrionic gifts would outshine the more austere evangelical style of his stepfather. So long disadvantaged in his oedipal rivalry with David Baldwin, James could now vanquish him on his own religious field. As the young preacher's congregation grew during the three years of his ministry, his stepfather's followers dwindled in number, driving him closer to the paranoia that finally overwhelmed him.

Baldwin's success as a preacher was purchased dearly, not only in its effect on his stepfather but also in the inner conflict it produced in himself. At the very time that his ministry developed from the religious experience that simplified the moral issues of self, family, and environment, his intellectual and literary development was complicating his sense of reality. At the very moment of his seizure, he was devising the plot of a play; and in the parallel account of John

Grimes on "The Threshing-Floor" in *Go Tell It on the Mountain*, "a malicious, ironic voice" of his skeptical, secular intelligence provides counterpoint to the prayers of the saints. As this voice grew in volume, Baldwin's faith subsided. Leaving the pulpit and the church, he was to become a bitter critic of Christianity, of which the actual "principles were Blindness, Loneliness, and Terror, the first principle necessarily and actively cultivated in order to deny the two others" instead of the professed Faith, Hope, and Charity. The historical role of Christianity in aiding and legitimizing the enslavement of nonwhite peoples, as well as its stultifying effect on individual lives, was to receive his bitter condemnation.

His faith lost and his family situation deteriorating still further as his father sank into madness, but with his literary aspirations still intact, Baldwin in 1942 felt that he had to leave Harlem in order to survive. Joining his high-school friend Emile Capouya in New Jersey, he secured employment as a defense worker. He found himself in an extremely hostile racial environment. Except for some traumatic encounters with white policemen, Baldwin's direct experience with white racism in New York had been limited. In New Jersey, however, among native racists and white Southerners working in defense jobs, Baldwin, looking for a haven, found an almost ubiquitous hostility that seemed to confirm his stepfather's bottomless resentment of whites. "I learned in New Jersey," Baldwin wrote in the title essay of *Notes of a Native Son* (1955), "that to be a Negro meant, precisely, that one was never looked at but was simply at the mercy of the reflexes the color of one's skin caused in other people." From this exposure he contracted what he called a "dread, chronic disease, the unfailing symptom of which is a kind of blind fever, a pounding in the skull and fire in the bowels." His rage culminated in a violent confrontation in a Jim Crow diner at Trenton in which he was ready to murder or be murdered.

Called back to New York because of his stepfather's fatal illness, Baldwin was now more prone to understand the role of white racism in shaping the black condition. On the day after the funeral, August 2, 1943, which was also James Baldwin's nineteenth birthday, Harlem erupted in a riot occasioned by the shooting of a black serviceman by a white policeman. Black Harlem now seemed no more habitable for Baldwin than white New Jersey, for he had come to recognize the marks of oppression for what they were, not as the wages of sin. He concluded an *Esquire* essay on Harlem in 1960 with a solemn proclamation: "It is a terrible, an inexorable, law that one cannot deny the humanity of another without diminishing one's own: in the face of one's victim, one sees oneself. Walk through the streets of Harlem and see what we, this nation, have become."

Like many young Americans with artistic or literary ambitions, Baldwin was attracted by the legend of Greenwich Village. Perhaps here, he thought, free of Harlem's constraints of family and poverty and New Jersey's blatant racism, he could begin his career as a writer. Far from tranquillity, however, the Village provided an atmosphere more frenetic and fluid than anything Baldwin had known before. Racial and sexual problems persisted, not to speak of the effort required to maintain a hand-to-mouth existence while undergoing a literary apprenticeship. However precariously, though, Baldwin managed not only to survive his five years in the Village but also to make contacts that were to prove beneficial and to break into print for the first time in serious magazines.

Baldwin's first professional efforts, published in 1947, were book reviews for the *Nation* and the *New Leader*. In them he began to stake out areas and establish positions that were to characterize his early career. "Everybody's Protest Novel" (1949) is his most famous attack on the use of fiction as an instrument of social change, but two years earlier his reviews were attacking Maxim Gorky for his outmoded revolutionary zeal and Shirley Graham for her emphasis on racial uplift. He concluded his remarks on the latter's biography of Frederick Douglass: "Relations between Negroes and whites, like any other province of human experience, demand honesty and insight; they must be based on the assumption that there is one race and that we are all part of it." A year later he reviewed five novels of racial protest for *Commentary* with astringent hostility. While complaining of over-simplification and sentimentality in novels about race, Baldwin noted the centrality of sex in racial conflict. With much oversimplification of his own, he had asserted in a 1947 review of a novel by Chester Himes that "our racial heritage . . . would seem to be contained in the tableau of a black and [a] white man facing each other and that the root of our trouble is between their legs." The autobiographical implications here are clarified in his review of a book by Stuart Engstrand about repressed homosexuality and in the slightly later essay "Preservation of Innocence."

Rejecting overt racial conflict, though not race, as a literary theme and affirming the human pain and dignity of the homosexual, Baldwin was preparing himself for his first major creative efforts—*Go Tell It on the Mountain, The Amen Corner,* and *Giovanni's Room* (1956). Such attitudes were bound to bring him into eventual conflict with his literary idol, Richard Wright. When Baldwin met Wright in 1945, the older man read his manuscript, praised his talent, and helped him to secure a Eugene F. Saxton Memorial Trust Award, his first real literary recognition. In one of his several discussions of his friendship with Wright, Baldwin confesses that he viewed him as a father figure, David Baldwin having died only two years earlier. But for Baldwin a father figure was by definition what one rebelled against in order to establish one's own

identity. The explicit criticism of *Native Son* in "Everybody's Protest Novel" and "Many Thousands Gone," and the earlier implicit rejection of the Wrightian mode in the reviews of other works of protest fiction thus derive, as does all of Baldwin's work, from psychological pressures as much as from intellectual conviction. The overt rupture in the relationship between Baldwin and Wright occurred in France in 1949, but it had been inevitable from their first meeting in Brooklyn four years before.

Encouragement by Wright and Robert Warshow, editor of *Commentary,* was welcome to Baldwin and the recognition of publishing in major magazines was gratifying, but progress on his fiction (an overtly autobiographical novel and a novel about a bisexual based on the Wayne Lonergan case) was slow and the turmoil of his personal life continued. Plans to marry failed to develop because of his bisexuality, and the nervous strain of working, writing, and suffering in New York was depleting his energies and his morale. A friend had committed suicide by leaping from the George Washington Bridge, as Rufus was to do in *Another Country* (1962), Baldwin's novel based on his years in the Village. The protagonist of his first published short story, "Previous Condition" (1948), is a black actor suffering from a double alienation: as a black man he cannot identify with the white society that oppresses him; as an artist-intellectual he cannot identify with the black society from which he comes. No alternative now seemed available to Baldwin himself other than exile.

When Richard Wright went to Paris in 1946 as an official guest of the French government, he was lionized by such luminaries as André Gide, Roger Martin du Gard, Jean-Paul Sartre, and Simone de Beauvoir. His response to the beauty of the city and to the splendor of French civilization was unequivocally favorable. When his protégé, James Baldwin, arrived in Paris two and a half years later, he had some forty dollars in his pocket. Paris, he was to tell his biographer, "was awful. It was winter. It was grey. And it was ugly." Taken by a friend to Les Deux Magots, he ran into Wright, who helped him to find a cheap hotel. But, on the whole, life in Paris proved to be an even more precarious struggle for survival than life in New York. If prejudice against blacks was less intense than in the United States, prejudice against Arabs was ferocious. And prejudice against the poor and the powerless was a universal characteristic of the comfortable classes, as Baldwin was to learn from a humiliating episode, described in the essay "Equal in Paris" (1955), involving some stolen bedsheets and resulting in his brief imprisonment.

Various friendships helped to sustain Baldwin during these years, chief of them a close relationship with Lucien Happersberger, a seventeen-year-old would-be painter from Switzerland, who was to remain the writer's companion for many years and to whom *Giovanni's Room* is dedicated. It was on a visit to a Swiss village with Happersberger early in 1952 that Baldwin completed the manuscript of the novel on which he had been working for a decade. *Go Tell It on the Mountain* was published in May of the following year to critical acclaim. Still poor and hungry, the author was nevertheless definitely on his way. Two more books—*Notes of a Native Son* and *Giovanni's Room*—would appear before he returned to the United States to live in July 1957.

In the late 1950's the civil rights movement in the South was gaining momentum. The Supreme Court decision of 1954 outlawed racial segregation in public education, and at the end of the following year Martin Luther King launched a bus boycott in Montgomery, Alabama, that brought him to national attention. Throughout the South blacks were being reviled, brutalized, and murdered as white supremacists rallied their forces in opposition to racial change. Expatriation seemed

to Baldwin an evasion of his social responsibility. After two months in New York, he took a long trip to the South, his first, visiting Charlotte, Little Rock, Atlanta, Birmingham, Montgomery, and Tuskegee, and meeting numerous leaders, including Dr. King. In such essays as "The Hard Kind of Courage" (1958), "Letter from the South: Nobody Knows My Name" (1959), "Fifth Avenue, Uptown" (1960), "They Can't Turn Back" (1960), "The Dangerous Road Before Martin Luther King" (1961), and "A Negro Assays the Negro Mood" (1961), Baldwin addressed mainly white readers in an urgent plea for understanding and support of the black struggle. With *Nobody Knows My Name* and, especially, *The Fire Next Time,* he became a major spokesman for the movement.

Since the early 1960's Baldwin has been a genuine celebrity, lecturing throughout the country, appearing on television talk shows, conferring with Attorney General Robert Kennedy, gazing from the cover of *Time* magazine, writing for Broadway and Hollywood. Always restless, he has continued to travel from New York to Paris and the south of France, as well as to Turkey, Puerto Rico, and elsewhere. Both *Another Country* (1962) and *The Fire Next Time* were best sellers, allowing him to help his large family and still maintain a glamorous life-style. But Baldwin has never lost his sense of racial outrage. Indeed, such later works as *Tell Me How Long the Train's Been Gone, No Name in the Street,* and *The Devil Finds Work* subject American civilization to a more merciless examination than anything that preceded them, with small hope left for the healing power of love, upon which he once posited his faith. The deaths of the 1960's—Medgar Evers and Malcolm X and Martin Luther King and the Birmingham girls and so many others—have all but extinguished hope, Baldwin argued to Margaret Mead. Still, he returned in 1977 from St. Paul de Vence to the United States, renewing once more his contacts with the personal, racial, and social realities that have informed his fiction, his drama, and many of his essays.

The terrain of Baldwin's imagination encompasses four main sectors: church, self, city, and race. Naturally, the boundaries of these sectors are not always clearly defined, but they will serve as general areas on which his literary achievement can be mapped. In the chronology of his career, the church was his first major subject, for it had dominated his spiritual life at precisely the time in adolescence that his intellectual and creative life was beginning. Before moving to other subjects, he had to treat the crucial tension between the most absorbing of social institutions and the emergence of the autonomous self.

Go Tell It on the Mountain was Baldwin's first, and is still his "best," novel, his most perfectly achieved, most carefully structured, most tightly controlled. Ostensibly the story of a Harlem youth named John Grimes who undergoes a religious experience on his fourteenth birthday, the novel is also, almost equally, the story of John's stepfather Gabriel, a sternly fanatical zealot whose influence blights the lives of all who come near him. It is likewise the story of Florence, Gabriel's sister, and of Elizabeth, his present wife and John's mother. The various stories not only illuminate each other in their psychological intimacy, but also exemplify almost a century of black American social experience. Part One and Part Three are set in the present of the mid-1930's, but the middle section, twice as long as the other two parts combined, consists of extended flashbacks to the separate but related life stories of Florence, Gabriel, and Elizabeth, all of whom leave the South to live in New York, "the city of destruction." From the tales of slavery and emancipation told by the mother of Gabriel and Florence to the restoration of white supremacy to the great migra-

tion from the southern Egypt to the northern slums, the common denominators of the black social experience are revealed to be sex, race, and religion, precisely those elements with which John Grimes must come to terms if he is to achieve putative maturity and self-definition.

John's severe Oedipus complex propels him toward homosexuality. Although honoring the letter of his promise to Elizabeth to care for the material needs of her illegitimate son, Gabriel refuses to accept or love John, caught as he is in his dream of a regal procession of saints springing from his own loins. Pampered and protected by his mother, John lavishes his love on her. Ridiculed and rejected by his stepfather, he responds with fierce hatred. In repudiating Gabriel's overbearing cruelty, however, John tends to repudiate his overbearing masculinity as well. Symbolically emasculated by his stepfather, John turns to a slightly older, more virile youth, Elisha, for compensatory affection. Denied paternal love, John finds a homosexual surrogate.

Racially, John can achieve his identity only when he accepts his blackness without associating it with ugliness, dirt, and humiliation. Ashamed of his appearance, his color, his ghetto environment, he has longed for what he considers the cleanliness and order of the white world. Baldwin does not belabor the point, but his description of John's racial shame implies an indictment of the white racism responsible for it that is all the more telling because his protagonist does not make the connection. On the threshing-floor of the Temple of the Fire Baptized, however, John does come to a tentative racial self-acceptance when he hears a "sound that came from darkness"—the sound of the black past of suffering and victimization—"that yet bore such sure witness to the glory of the light."

John hears this sound in the mood of religious transport. Rejected as an Ishmael by his stepfather, who thinks of him as "the son of the bondwoman," and rejected because of race by the country and city of which he is a native son, he turns to God and to the fellowship of the saints. The religious milieu of the storefront church and its congregation is described in the most intimate detail. The power of the spirit becomes almost palpable; the psychological reality of the drama of sin and salvation is almost unbearable in the intensity of its presentation. John's ecstatic moment is valid and genuine, moving him through shame and hatred to love and temporary peace. Yet all the implications are that John will finally have to leave religion to engage the world, just as he must leave the Temple of the Fire Baptized to reenter the Harlem streets.

In its most conspicuous agent in the novel, Gabriel Grimes, religion becomes malevolent, an instrument of oppression. Therefore the ironic and skeptical voice speaking in John's ear in Part Three will eventually, the reader feels, bring him down from the mountaintop and into the world. *Go Tell It on the Mountain* is a carefully constructed novel about the black church that has penetrating characterization, an intensely poetic style, and fully realized psychological and social themes. It gives religion its due, but finally implies religious skepticism.

A more openly unfavorable view of religion appears in the play *The Amen Corner*, written in the summer of 1952 and first produced in the 1954–55 season at Howard University, under the direction of the poet-playwright Owen Dodson. The protagonist of this play is Margaret Alexander, a preacher who seems to be a composite of Mother Horn and Baldwin's stepfather. Like the former, she is a charismatic leader of her flock; like the latter, she is harshly fanatical, a "tyrannical matriarch" (Baldwin's phrase) to correspond to the tyrannical patriarch David Baldwin-Gabriel Grimes. The text of the sermon she delivers as the play opens is, ironically, "Set thine house in order," a favorite text of David Baldwin and Gabriel Grimes. Yet, like theirs,

her house is in fearful disorder: her son is in the process of leaving the faith for more worldly pleasures; her dying husband has returned home, after a long separation, to force her to face the consequences of her choices; and even her hold on her congregation is slipping as jealousies, rivalries, and suspicions begin to disrupt the fellowship of the saints.

Margaret's flaw in character, tragic in its results, is her effort to escape the anguish and pain of living in the world by embracing a religious faith that supersedes human love. Denying her function as woman, she has turned from her husband's arms to the sexual surrogate of religious enthusiasm in an impossible quest for purity. Baldwin sees clearly that this element of religion accounts for both its emotional richness and its betrayal of the primary relationships. Margaret advises a young woman in her congregation to leave her husband, as she had done, the better to serve God; and another member of the flock boasts, "I ain't never been sweet on no man but the Lord Jesus Christ." Betrayed by her followers, reproached by her husband, Luke, and disappointed by her son, David, who, like Baldwin himself, must leave his stifling environment to release his creativity, Margaret, in her very defeat, manages to attain a clarity of vision, however late, that constitutes a kind of triumph: "To love the Lord is to love all His children—all of them, everyone!—and suffer with them and rejoice with them and never count the cost!"

Substituting a humanistic for a supernatural faith, Margaret must confront her failure. David, rejecting his mother's mistake and acquiring his father's worldly vision, must leave his home, significantly in the same tenement as the church, to pursue the fulfillment of the self. Baldwin's own search for self is brilliantly set forth in several of his early essays, especially "Autobiographical Notes," "Notes of a Native Son," "Stranger in the Village" in *Notes of a Native Son,* and "The Discovery of What It Means to

Be an American'' in *Nobody Knows My Name*. It is also the theme of his first published short story, ''Previous Condition,'' and of his second published novel, *Giovanni's Room*. In the former, a black actor named Peter is put out of the room of a white friend by a racist landlady. Neither the friend nor Peter's white girl can offer much consolation, but neither can habitués of a Harlem bar to which Peter flees. ''I didn't seem to have a place,'' Peter ruefully recognizes, alienated as he is from both whites and blacks. Only by leaving the security of the group can the individual define the self, but the success of the effort is by no means assured and the process is necessarily painful.

The search for self is presented mainly in sexual terms in *Giovanni's Room*. Not as directly autobiographical as *Go Tell It on the Mountain*, Baldwin's second novel concerns white characters, principally those in a triangle relationship involving two expatriate bisexuals—David, an American, and Giovanni, an Italian—both living in Paris, and David's girl friend, Hella. Like Baldwin's first protagonist, David of *Giovanni's Room* struggles with questions of identity posed by his relationship to his parents. His mother having died when he was five, David suffers from a recurrent sexual nightmare involving her: ''her hair as dry as metal and brittle as a twig, straining to press me against her body; that body so putrescent, so sickening soft, that it opened, as I clawed and cried, into a breach so enormous as to swallow me alive.'' This disgust carries over into shame at his father's drunken affairs with women, the subject of shrill scolding by David's aunt. His father, moreover, has a kind of invincible American boyishness that inhibits the maturation of his son, who first resents, then pities, his father and his hapless love for him. A brief, bittersweet homosexual encounter with a boy named Joey compounds the confusion of the family situation. In what he explicitly calls an effort to find himself, recognizing in retrospect that

it was really a flight from recognition of the true nature of the self, David goes to France.

There he becomes involved first with Hella, an apprentice painter from Minneapolis who leaves him to travel through Spain in order to evaluate their relationship, and Giovanni, working as a bartender at a homosexual establishment presided over by Guillaume, a thoroughly corrupt and dangerously shrewd scion of an aristocratic French family. Like David, Giovanni is a bisexual moving inexorably toward homosexuality. Unlike David, he is willing to accept the imperatives of love, whatever form they take. David moves into Giovanni's small, cluttered room; but, despite the genuine affection of their relationship, he fears the prospect of becoming like Guillaume or Jacques, a businessman with a predilection for football players. This fear, this failure to commit himself fully to their love, constitutes a betrayal on David's part that drives Giovanni to desperation and finally to the murder of Guillaume. Apprehended, Giovanni awaits the guillotine while David, consumed by guilt, strives vainly to restore his relationship with Hella.

However different the circumstances, David's failure in *Giovanni's Room* is comparable with Margaret's in *The Amen Corner*. In both cases a culturally sanctioned and socially prescribed pattern—heterosexuality or Christianity—is followed in denial of the protagonists' responsibilities to the human beings they most love and to the deepest urgings of their own natures. Attempting to achieve security by accepting an externally imposed identity, they precipitate chaos. Rejecting the risks of recognizing the true self, they construct identities that are both specious and destructive.

Baldwin handles the homosexual theme in *Giovanni's Room* with dignity and restraint; but as a protagonist David lacks tragic stature, eliciting pity, perhaps, but hardly terror. A pattern of imagery recurrent in this novel and elsewhere in

Baldwin's work is that of drowning or being smothered or engulfed. David's dream of being swallowed alive in the embrace of his mother's decaying body reappears as his revulsion at Hella's female sexuality intensifies: "I was fantastically intimidated by her breasts, and when I entered her I began to feel that I would never get out alive." As Giovanni instructs David, "Women are like water," and the danger of drowning is always imminent. But David also perceives his life in Giovanni's room to be taking place under water. His sense of claustrophobia is acute. His problem, then, is not so much homosexuality or even bisexuality; it is asexuality, a disinclination to take the sexual plunge that can lead to emotional and psychic liberation. As he looks at his naked body in a mirror at the end of the novel, his language grows strangely theological: "I look at my sex, my troubling sex, and wonder how it can be redeemed . . . the key to my salvation." As is frequently pointed out in the novel, David's stunted self is an American self, tormented by puritanical attitudes that repress the psychic growth made possible only by undergoing the risks of love.

New York and Paris are the settings of *Go Tell It on the Mountain, The Amen Corner,* and *Giovanni's Room,* but the urban theme is muted to give full resonance to the interior conflicts of the protagonists. In the more socially conscious 1960's, Baldwin began to give greater attention to the relations between private anguish and collective despair. The city itself—New York in particular—with its inhuman living conditions, ethnic hatreds, commercial corruption, and moral disarray becomes a central concern, a fact readily apparent when the reader turns from Baldwin's earlier works to *Another Country.*

In *Go Tell It on the Mountain* and *The Amen Corner* most of the action takes place in a cramped flat or a small church; in *Giovanni's Room* the setting is again interior—the house in the south of France, Guillaume's bar, Giovanni's

or Hella's room. *Another Country* unfolds not only in apartments, pads, hotel rooms, bars, and restaurants, but also on rooftops, balconies, the George Washington Bridge, an airplane—all offering panoramic perspectives of New York—as well as on the streets in the shadows of the looming skyscrapers and in the subways rumbling below. The very first sentence locates the disconsolate Rufus Scott in the heart of the city, "facing Seventh Avenue, at Times Square," having just emerged after ten hours in the movies, trying to sleep in spite of the film, an importunate usher, and homosexual molesters. Rufus, we are told as he walks the hostile streets, is "one of the fallen—for the weight of this city was murderous—one of those who had been crushed on the day, which was every day, these towers fell." At the end of the long first chapter, he takes the subway from Fourth Street to 181st Street, traveling almost the entire length of the murderous city, and leaps to his death from "the bridge built to honor the father of his country."

In this city of the damned, the weather contributes to the general malaise. In early winter "a cold sun glared down on Manhattan giving no heat." In early spring "the wind blew through the empty streets with a kind of dispirited moan." The terrible New York summer, "which is like no summer anywhere," frazzles the nerves with its relentless heat and noise, intensifying hostilities and discomforts. Such a city, one of the characters realizes after returning from the more civilized milieu of Paris, is a place "without oases, run entirely . . . for money; and its citizens seemed to have lost entirely any sense of their right to renew themselves." In such an environment it is little wonder that the desperate search for love of the major characters is doomed, for the daily reality of their lives is conditioned by constant reminders of hatred and violence—graffiti, barroom brawls, schoolboy gang fights, racial enmity, casual sex, and prostitution. Baldwin's relentless portrayal of the horrors of New York confers a savage irony on the final words of the novel, which describe the entrance of a young Frenchman as "more high-hearted than he had ever been as a child, into that city which the people from heaven had made their home."

Another Country, then, is an ambitious effort to portray a city, calling to mind *Manhattan Transfer* or even *Ulysses*. In other ways, too, the scope of this work is larger, more expansive than Baldwin's writing of the 1950's. It is twice as long as *Go Tell It on the Mountain* and almost three times as long as *Giovanni's Room*. The plot is also much more complex, involving the interrelated lives of eight major characters. Rufus Scott, a black jazz musician fallen on evil days, commits suicide one-fifth of the way through the novel, but his memory persists in the minds of his friends, most of whom consider themselves to be in some degree responsible for his death.

Much of Rufus' immediate despair derives from his tormented affair with Leona, a good-hearted poor white refugee from the South whom he drives to a nervous breakdown. Rufus' best friend, Vivaldo Moore, an "Irish wop" from Brooklyn who lives in Greenwich Village and is struggling to write a novel, falls in love with Rufus' sister Ida, a beautiful but embittered girl mourning her brother but determined to survive in the urban jungle by any means necessary. Richard and Cass Silenski, the only married couple in the circle of Rufus' friends, are another oddly matched pair. In contrast with Vivaldo's struggle to create a meaningful work of fiction, Richard, his former teacher, publishes a commercially successful but artistically worthless murder mystery. This literary prostitution costs him the respect of his wife, a woman from an old New England family who admires Ida and Vivaldo. She then has an affair with Eric Jones, an Alabama-born bisexual actor who has left his younger lover, Yves, in France in order to resume his career in the United States. Eric had

earlier been involved with Rufus, and after Cass he makes love to Vivaldo while waiting for Yves to join him in New York.

These characters and relationships, all of them treated at some length, are necessary for the scope and diversity Baldwin is seeking, but they present a formidable challenge to his literary powers as he moves from one to another. Although *Another Country* does sprawl somewhat compared with the two earlier novels, the author shows considerable dexterity in rendering the individual stories so that they illuminate each other and develop a central theme.

This theme is the human craving for love and the difficulty of satisfying it in the city of New York. *"Do you love me? Do you love me? Do you love me?"* is the musical phrase "unbearably, endlessly, and variously repeated" by the saxophonist playing with Rufus at his last gig. Indeed, the question is repeated and considered by all the characters of the novel. The failure to find a satisfactory affirmative answer drives Rufus to suicide, Leona to a mental institution, Ida to the unloving arms of a television executive who can advance her career as a blues singer, Vivaldo to distraction and to Eric, Cass to Eric, Richard to wife-beating. Leona, Ida, Vivaldo, Cass, and Eric all realize that their love for Rufus was not strong enough to avert his fate. Their frenzied efforts to find what Rufus was unable to find are partly attempts to assuage their guilt. In this way Rufus, who dies at the end of the first chapter, becomes a central reference point for the other characters as the author unfolds his theme.

The other reference point is Eric Jones, who brings bisexual solace, if not quite love, to Vivaldo and Cass. He first appears in the first chapter of Book Two, naked in a garden, watching his lover, Yves, swimming in the Mediterranean. Many critics have noted the Edenic quality of the scene, contrasting sharply with the frenzied life of New York, and they have gone on to interpret Eric in quite favorable terms. Baldwin does indeed seem to feel sympathetic toward this character, who, though a southern white man, rises above racial and sexual categories to accept himself and others, even to reconcile the discords of his New York friends. Yet Baldwin also suggests reservations about Eric. The garden in which he sits is rented, and the images of flies and a stalking kitten likewise suggest a post-Eden world. Furthermore, his love for Yves is based as much on his memory of Rufus as on Yves himself, and he even questions the quality of his love for Rufus: "had it simply been rage and nostalgia and guilt? and shame?" Eric's love for Rufus is linked to his love for "the warm, black people" of his childhood. This undifferentiated love of black people comes near to being white racism inverted. As for Eric's love of Yves, one doubts that it can survive in New York. Certainly no sense of fidelity to it inhibits Eric in his ministrations to Cass and Vivaldo.

A certain authorial ambivalence toward Eric, then, somewhat qualifies his success in the role of reconciler in Book Two and Book Three of the novel. The relief he brings to Cass is only temporary; and as for Vivaldo, one feels that Ida is a far more effective catalyst of his maturation: "her long fingers stroked his back, and he began, slowly, with a horrible, strangling sound, to weep, for she was stroking the innocence out of him." As tortured as their relationship has been and will be, their love seems the most likely of any in the novel to provide the right answer to that endlessly repeated question.

The difficulty of achieving love in a destructive city is further explored in *Nothing Personal* (1964), for which Baldwin wrote a prose meditation to accompany a collection of striking photographs by his old high-school friend Richard Avedon, and in the superb short story "Sonny's Blues." First published in *Partisan Review* in 1957, "Sonny's Blues" prefigures some of the concerns of *Another Country*. Like Rufus,

Sonny is a jazz musician down on his luck and unable to secure the emotional support he needs from his family. Unlike Rufus, Sonny turns to heroin rather than suicide in response to his suffering. Also unlike Rufus, Sonny triumphs by transmuting, through musical expression, not only his own suffering but also that of his family and, by extension, his race in such a way as to redeem himself and simultaneously to expand his elder brother's moral awareness.

The story is narrated by Sonny's brother, a conventional, middle-class black man who teaches algebra in a Harlem high school and strives to remain detached from the pain surrounding him. As always in Baldwin's work, the effort to achieve security, to insulate oneself from the risks of living, is profoundly misguided. As the story opens, the brother, on his way to school, reads in a newspaper of Sonny's arrest on a heroin charge. After school he encounters a friend of Sonny's, funky and strung-out, who provides more information. The very way in which he learns of Sonny's trouble is a measure of his estrangement, his failure to be his brother's keeper.

This, precisely, was the charge imposed by his mother. Both parents had recognized the evil of the world, whether down home, where drunken white men ran down the father's brother in a car, or up North, where heroin and prostitution devoured so many of the young. Love and support were necessary to save one another from the pervasive darkness, or to enable one another to survive it. With their parents dead, Sonny's care devolves upon his brother, who cannot reconcile Sonny's commitment to jazz and the jazz life to his own bourgeois aspirations. Only his daughter's death from polio, by proving his own vulnerability, induces him to renew contact with Sonny. "My trouble made his real."

It is this community of suffering that constitutes the theme of "Sonny's Blues." Through a skillful reversal, Sonny becomes his elder brother's keeper; the teacher and the pupil exchange places. "Safe, hell!" their father had exclaimed. "Ain't no place safe for kids, nor nobody." Sonny teaches his brother this lesson, explaining that he can lapse at any time into his heroin habit. More effective than his words, however, is his music.

Indeed, it is music that links the black community in its response to suffering and its triumph over it. Throughout the story Baldwin plays riffs that prepare for Sonny's set at the end. As the elder brother and Sonny's friend talk at the beginning, they hear from a nearby bar "black and bouncy" music to which a barmaid keeps time. The brothers' uncle is carrying his guitar on the last night of his life. Sonny's idol is Charlie Parker, of whom the elder brother has never heard. Sonny plays the piano incessantly while living with the dicty family of Isabel, his brother's fiancée. The singing and tambourine beating of sidewalk revivalists bring together a diverse crowd of passersby in recognition of their brotherhood and sisterhood. Finally, the concluding scene in a downtown nightclub, in which Sonny and his jazz group achieve an ultimate musical expression of personal and racial suffering and survival, constitutes an experience for Sonny and his brother that is almost religious in its intensity and is certainly liberating in its effects. Baldwin's complete artistic control of language, point of view, and theme makes "Sonny's Blues" not only one of his finest personal achievements, but also a true classic of American short fiction.

The same cannot be said of *If Beale Street Could Talk*. Many of the familiar concerns and characters are present in this story of Tish and Fonny, young black lovers in conflict with a hostile urban society but sustained by their love for each other and the loving support of some members of their families. Falsely incarcerated on a charge of raping a Puerto Rican woman, Fonny must struggle to retain his sanity while

Tish, pregnant by him, struggles against time and a corrupt legal system to free her man before their child is born. In this effort she is aided by her parents and sister and Fonny's father, although Fonny's mother, an acidly sketched religious fanatic, and his sisters turn their backs on the trouble. Tish and Fonny recall Elizabeth and Richard of *Go Tell It on the Mountain*. Fonny, an illegitimate child, becomes a sensitive artist (a wood-carver) at odds with society, a recurrent situation in Baldwin's fiction with clear autobiographical overtones. In the abrupt conclusion of *If Beale Street Could Talk* the baby has been born and Fonny is out on bail, although his legal fate is still uncertain. Nevertheless, life has been renewed through love, despite all the malevolent forces of a corrupt and racist city.

It all seems too pat. The sentimentality that has always vied with Baldwin's artistic instincts seems to overcome them here, and the affirmative conclusion seems willed rather than inevitable. The point is debatable, of course, but another weakness, a serious failure in technique, seems beyond dispute. The narrative mode of *If Beale Street Could Talk* is first-person; the narrator is nineteen-year-old Tish. For the first third of the novel the narrative voice is carefully and consistently maintained. The use of Tish's voice seems to restrain the rhetorical excesses to which Baldwin's style is too often prone. After the reader has begun thoroughly to appreciate the narrative advantages of Tish's pungently colloquial voice, Baldwin suddenly lapses into his own language, point of view, and elaborate syntax in a passage dealing, significantly, with love and respect between men. Referring to women's response to such emotions, the author has Tish meditate:

The truth is that they sense themselves in the presence, so to speak, of a language which they cannot decipher and therefore cannot manipulate, and, however they make a thing about it, so far from being locked out, are appalled by the apprehension that they are, in fact, forever locked in.

Only two sentences earlier Tish was referring to "this fucked up time and place."

In the second half of the novel the exigencies of the plot require Tish to narrate episodes of which she has no firsthand knowledge: conversations between Joseph and Frank, the fathers of the lovers, or between her mother and their lawyer; her mother's trip to Puerto Rico in a fruitless attempt to gain the cooperation of the raped woman; Fonny in prison. On such occasions Baldwin forgoes any effort to work out his problem of technique. Instead, he awkwardly calls attention to it: "Joseph and Frank, as we learn later, have also been sitting in a bar, and this is what happened between them" or "Now, Sharon must begin preparing for her Puerto Rican journey, and Hayward briefs her." After an excellent beginning, then, Baldwin's technique breaks down in this novel. Despite brilliant individual scenes, an arresting conception, and a powerful indictment of urban corruption and racism, *If Beale Street Could Talk* does not fulfill its artistic potential.

As with any but the most escapist of Afro-American writers, race has been a major concern in almost all of Baldwin's books, *Giovanni's Room* and *Nothing Personal* constituting the sole exceptions. Beginning with the publication of *The Fire Next Time* in 1963, moreover, race and racism are the central issues in eight of the eleven published between then and 1976, and very important in two of the others (*Going to Meet the Man* [1965] and *If Beale Street Could Talk*). His attitudes have evolved from an effort at disengagement in his youth to fervent commitment to the redemptive power of interracial action for civil rights in the late 1950's and early 1960's to endorsement of black revolutionary nationalism in the late 1960's to a bitterly pessimis-

tic awaiting of retributive vengeance on the white racism of America that characterizes his position in the 1970's.

The Fire Next Time consists of two pieces previously published late in 1962: a brief letter to his nephew in the *Progressive,* and the long "Letter from a Region in My Mind," which appeared, incongruously, amid the advertisements directed to conspicuous consumers in the *New Yorker.* In the first Baldwin argues in a vein strikingly similar to that of Martin Luther King. Before blacks can be liberated from their condition, they must liberate whites from their racism by accepting them with love. In the second piece, retitled "Down at the Cross" when published in the book, Baldwin divides his meditation into three parts: an account of his youthful conversion, ministerial career, and rejection of Christianity because of the implausibility of its doctrines and the crimes committed in its name; a report on his meeting in Chicago with the Honorable Elijah Muhammad and a sympathetic assessment of the Black Muslims from a nonbeliever's point of view; and an analysis of American racial relations in the context of national history and contemporary international politics. In the final section Baldwin restates in a more tough-minded way the doctrine of his letter to his nephew. Because of the moral history of the West, black people are in a position to teach white people to give up their delusions of superiority and to confront the national political necessity to eliminate racism so as to survive the century.

The Fire Next Time concludes with a magnificent peroration, worthy in its rhetorical power of comparison with those of the Old Testament prophets so familiar to Baldwin's youth:

If we—and now I mean the relatively conscious whites and the relatively conscious blacks, who must, like lovers, insist on, or create, the consciousness of the others—do not falter in our duty now, we may be able, handful that we are, to end the racial nightmare, and achieve our country, and change the history of the world. If we do not now dare everything, the fulfillment of that prophecy, re-created from the Bible in song by a slave, is upon us: *God gave Noah the rainbow sign, No more water, the fire next time!*

If "Down at the Cross" is a stronger statement of Baldwin's position on racial issues than "My Dungeon Shook: Letter to My Nephew on the One Hundredth Anniversary of the Emancipation," the play *Blues for Mister Charlie* is stronger still. The racial protest is more vehement and the prospect of interracial cooperation much less likely. Indeed, the black and white inhabitants of the southern town in this play are so segregated by race and so polarized by the murder of a young black man that the pervasive mood is a hatred and tribal loyalty so fierce that love seems quite out of the question.

Yet for all its vitriolic language and abrasive emotions, *Blues for Mister Charlie* constitutes another effort by Baldwin to force white America to confront the plague of race so as to begin to overcome it. In his prefatory note Baldwin speaks of the necessity to understand even the most unregenerate racist, who is after all a product of the national ethos. He may be beyond liberation, but we can "begin working toward the liberation of his children." At the end of the play, Parnell James, the weak but well-intentioned white liberal who edits the local newspaper, marches alongside, if not quite with, the blacks, and at the end of the prefatory note Baldwin writes, in language recalling John's conversion in *Go Tell It on the Mountain:* "We are walking in terrible darkness here, and this is one man's attempt to bear witness to the reality and the power of light." *Blues for Mister Charlie* goes beyond anything that Baldwin had previously written in the racial outrage expressed, but it does not abandon hope for amelioration.

Based remotely on the Emmett Till case of 1955, the play treats the racial murder of Richard Henry, a young black man returned home after living in the North, by Lyle Britten, a red-neck store owner. As the play opens, a shot is heard and then the audience sees Lyle dump Richard's body with these words: "And may every nigger like this nigger end like this nigger—face down in the weeds!" The murder scene is presented in full at the end of the play, after Lyle has been found innocent of the crime by a racist court. Within this frame Baldwin explores various aspects of racial life and relationships in "Plaguetown": the leadership by Richard's father, the Reverend Meridian Henry, of a nonviolent campaign for civil rights, coping as well as he can with the impatience of black student activists; the ambivalent efforts of Parnell James, a longtime friend of the Reverend Henry, to secure justice while trying to reconcile his mutually exclusive friendships with the Reverend Henry and Lyle; the family life of Lyle Britten; Richard's inability to readapt to life in the South after living in the North and his growing love for Juanita, one of the students; the perversions of the judicial system. In probing the sources and ramifications of racism, Baldwin finds the sexual component to be central.

This is certainly true of Richard, Lyle, and Parnell. Richard is cast from the same mold as Rufus and Sonny. Like both of these characters he is a jazz musician. Like Rufus he attempts to achieve racial revenge through intercourse with white women, whose insatiable appetites prove too much for him. Like Sonny he attempts to ease the intolerable pressures of his life with dope. Even more than Rufus and Sonny he is proud and sensitive and tormented, too rebellious to survive anywhere in America, certainly not in the South after eight years of living in the North. Richard's specific torment originated in his reaction to the death of his mother, whom he believes to have been murdered by white men for resisting their sexual advances, and his shame at his father's acquiescence.

After experiencing white racism South and North, he has reached the conclusion that the only way black men can achieve power is by picking up the gun. To pacify his grandmother, however, he gives his own gun to his father, leaving himself unarmed for the fatal encounter with Lyle. This surrender of the gun, not without Freudian overtones, is clearly part of Richard's suicidal recklessness, as is his flaunting of photographs of his white women from his Greenwich Village days. His tense exchange with Lyle on their first meeting and their fight on their second are filled with sexual rancor. In the Britten store Richard flirts mildly and mockingly with Lyle's wife, Jo, Lyle joins the issue, and Richard impugns Lyle's potency. The sexual insult is repeated just before Lyle fires his first shot during their third encounter, and the dying Richard accuses Lyle not only of sexual jealousy of him but also of homosexual interest in him. The scene recalls Baldwin's early diagnosis that the root of American racial conflict lies between the legs of a white man and a black man confronting each other. Richard must act out his racial-sexual stereotype even if it means his death.

Lyle is equally a victim of the psychosexual pathology of racism. Aware of the need to make this character a man, not a monster, Baldwin presents him as an example of the banality of evil. On his first appearance in the play he is fondling his infant son, whom he loves, but strains in his sexual life immediately emerge in the ensuing dialogue with his wife, who complains of his excessive demands and implies his infidelity. His past affairs include one with a black woman whose jealous husband he murdered. His violence proceeds directly from the volatile combination of sex and race.

Even Parnell, a liberal intellectual of sorts and a bachelor, associates sexuality with blackness. Although his sexual life involves both white and black women, his tomcatting after the latter takes place with Lyle. Parnell's deepest feelings are directed toward a sensitive, poetic black girl whom he loved as a youth. It is her name, Pearl, that he utters during intercourse with white women. But Parnell's fascination with black sexuality is more amorphous than Lyle's. In a flashback soliloquy in the third act, Parnell thinks of this ruling passion of his life: "Out with it, Parnell! The nigger-lover! Black boys and girls! I've wanted my hands full of them, wanted to drown them, laughing and dancing and making love— making love—wow!—and be transformed, formed, liberated out of this grey-white envelope." Although the bisexual hint is not developed, Parnell may be viewed as a kind of soured Eric Jones, an Eric who stayed home. Like Eric, he thinks of heterosexual lovemaking as only a "calisthenic."

Blues for Mister Charlie makes brief and passing reference to other dimensions of racism— economic exploitation, political domination, social control—but these fade into insignificance compared with sex. Without underestimating the important role it does in fact play, one can say that the dramatist does overemphasize it. Here, as elsewhere in Baldwin, one feels that his psychological perceptions somewhat distort his social observations. They also compromise effective dramatic technique, for the flashbacks are too numerous, the soliloquies too introspective, the dialogue too discursive to constitute effective theatrical action, especially in Act Two and Act Three. One honors the attempt to avoid the easy commercial success of the superficial well-made play, but one must nevertheless note that the author's talents are more novelistic than dramatic.

In the title story of *Going to Meet the Man,* Baldwin moves beyond his portrayal of Lyle in presenting the sexuality of white racism. Overcome by impotence, a white southern deputy sheriff named Jesse lies in bed "one hand between his legs, staring at the frail sanctuary of his wife," whose name is Grace. Earlier in the day he has had an instant erection while beating a black activist in a jail cell. Now, lying in the darkness, he dreams back to his childhood, when at the age of eight he was taken by his parents to witness a lynching. There he stared at "the hanging, gleaming body, the most beautiful and terrible object he had ever seen till then." Still more beautiful and terrible than the phallic body was the phallus itself, which the boy watched as the emasculator severed it. The ritual filled the child with a great joy, reminiscent of the children in Claude McKay's poem "The Lynching," as well as with great love for his parents. Aroused by his dream, he turns to his wife with a surge of potency and takes her, moaning, "Come on, sugar, I'm going to do you like a nigger, just like a nigger, come on, sugar, and love me just like you'd love a nigger." The story has an undeniably powerful impact, but upon reflection the schematization and oversimplification of some complex psychological processes become apparent.

Of the other seven stories collected in *Going to Meet the Man*, "Sonny's Blues" and "Previous Condition" have been discussed. "The Rockpile" and "The Outing" clearly belong to the body of autobiographical material out of which *Go Tell It on the Mountain* comes. The homosexual theme is central to "The Outing" and also to "The Man Child," a curious, almost allegorical tale about white characters in an unspecified rural setting. Homosexual frustration and jealousy result in the murder of blond, eight-year-old Eric, the man child. Stark and haunting in its almost dreamlike simplicity, "The Man Child" is a memorable story, differing sharply from Baldwin's other fiction.

"This Morning, This Evening, So Soon" is a novella on the author's version of the international theme, looking back in some ways to *Giovanni's Room* and *Another Country*. Like the novels, this work contrasts the experiential wisdom of Europeans and blacks gained through suffering with the dangerous and destructive innocence of white America, to which the black protagonist must return from his European exile. Finally, "Come out the Wilderness" compares with the Ida-Vivaldo sections of *Another Country* in its exploration of the stresses in interracial heterosexual love. What drives Ruth and Paul apart in this story also accounts for much of Parnell's problem in *Blues for Mister Charlie*: "The sons of the masters were roaming the world, looking for arms to hold them. And the arms that might have held them—could not forgive." In the American racial context, the white search for sexual forgiveness of racial crimes seems doomed to perpetuate the sexual exploitation that was the greatest of those crimes.

Baldwin's ideological shift from nonviolence to at least the possibility of violence as a means of black self-defense reveals itself in *Blues for Mister Charlie* when the Reverend Meridian Henry places his dead son's gun on his pulpit under his Bible. An even more emphatic endorsement of violence as a legitimate weapon of the racially oppressed appears in the long novel *Tell Me How Long the Train's Been Gone*. In the concluding scene of this work the protagonist, Leo Proudhammer, agrees, still somewhat reluctantly, with his young friend-lover Christopher, a black nationalist, that, however outnumbered, "We need guns." Although in 1968 Baldwin could hardly expect to match the militance of the Black Panthers or Imamu Baraka or the martyred Malcolm X, the pressure of the times seemed to require some kind of affirmation of the nationalist position.

This nervous affirmation takes place at the end of the book as Leo, a highly successful actor, is completing his convalescence from a near-fatal heart attack suffered at the beginning of the book. The body of the novel moves back and forth in Leo's first-person narration between the present and the past of his memory. Although

Leo is a bisexual actor, not a writer, his Harlem background, his New Jersey and Greenwich Village experiences, and above all his temperament and personality indicate that he is quite clearly an autobiographical character. Indeed, *Tell Me How Long the Train's Been Gone* is Baldwin's most autobiographical novel, even if *Go Tell It on the Mountain* may be closer to the actual facts of his life, for he maintains virtually no aesthetic distance between himself and his protagonist. Their voices are all but indistinguishable.

The result is that the portrayal of Leo involves much material familiar to the regular reader of Baldwin, but sentimentalized far beyond anything that preceded it. Whatever the particular circumstances, Leo's overriding emotion is likely to be fear, as he confesses to the reader scores of times. Lying on his back in his dressing room after the heart attack, Leo realizes that his life "revealed a very frightened man—a very frightened boy." In his childhood he "was afraid" of the friends of his beloved brother Caleb. On the subways he "first felt what may be called a civic terror." Riding past his stop and becoming lost, he "became more and more frightened." Once, taking refuge from the rain in an abandoned house, he "squatted there in a still, dry dread." Stopped and frisked by policemen, he "had never been so frightened." When his father admonished him not to fear whites, he agreed. "But I knew that I was already afraid." After the return of Caleb from prison, Leo commiserated with his brother's suffering: "I listened, extended, so to speak, in a terror unlike any terror I had known."

As a young man he is also subject to "sudden fear, as present as the running of the river, as nameless and as deep." Alone in an apartment in New Jersey with a white woman, Leo is "really frightened." After their lovemaking he becomes "terribly, terribly afraid." Arrested by New Jersey policemen as a suspicious character, he finds it difficult "to keep my mortal terror out of my voice" and later to "control my fear." He feels his "bowels loosen and lock—for fear." After intercourse with another white woman, Barbara, whom he loves, he is "a little frightened," and on another occasion, on a mountaintop with her, he is "terribly afraid." As they descend, "my fear began to return, like the throb of a remembered toothache." Back in New York, living precariously, Leo notes that "terror and trouble" are the constants of his experience, but in his triumphant professional acting debut he decides that "all the years of terror and trembling . . . were worth it at that moment." Later, famous, he takes the young black Christopher into his apartment to live, and becomes "a little frightened."

Such all-pervasive, endlessly repeated pusillanimity finally becomes so tiresomely banal as to forfeit the reader's sympathy. It also tends to diminish the racial anger that Baldwin wishes to generate, for Leo's fear is clearly more personal than typical, even when he is being grilled by racist cops. Moreover, his dwelling on his fear is self-indulgent and self-pitying—and related to his racial self-hatred. If one compares Baldwin's use of fear in this novel with Wright's use of the same emotion in *Native Son,* one understands how poorly it serves Baldwin's purpose of racial protest.

Tell Me How Long the Train's Been Gone contains some effective scenes, especially in the Harlem sections, but the reader of Baldwin has encountered it all before: fear, bisexuality, the father figure, polemics against Christianity. That archetypal Baldwinian theme, the quest for love, naturally appears, both in memorable aphoristic form ("Everyone wishes to be loved, but, in the event, nearly no one can bear it. Everyone desires love but also finds it impossible to believe that he deserves it.") and in the most self-indulgently sentimentalized expression: "my terrible need to lie down, to breathe deep, to weep long and loud, to be held in human arms, almost any human arms, to hide my face in any human breast, to tell it all, to let it out, to be brought into the world, and, out of human affection, to be born again.'' On one occasion the protagonist chides himself, "Ah, Leo, what a child you are!'' Precisely. The reader may be willing to give love to a frightened child, but he tends to withhold it from a childishly narcissistic middle-aged actor who so clearly serves as a surrogate for the author himself.

A much tougher and more successful book is *No Name in the Street*, in which autobiography serves to reinforce rather than diminish the racial and social themes. Here Baldwin's personal tone is almost devoid of self-pity. He can even state that he must seem to an old childhood friend and to his mother "an aging, lonely, sexually dubious, politically outrageous, unspeakably erratic freak.'' Almost invariably he explores self in this book not to elicit compassion or to indulge his egocentricity, but to illuminate the situations of other individuals, to provide a personal context for social analysis, or to intensify emotionally his historical judgments. Thus his portrayal of his stepfather emphasizes his suffering and his efforts to maintain his dignity against overwhelming odds, not the pain he inflicted on his stepson. His account of his visit to his childhood friend to give him the suit he could no longer wear after Martin Luther King's funeral dwells on their estrangement, not in self-congratulation at his own comparative enlightenment but in rueful recognition of the moral and intellectual victimization inherent in his friend's struggle for economic position. His personal contacts with Malcolm X and his response to the assassination lead not into Baldwin's private sensibility, but to a charged indictment of the moral failure of the West.

Kaleidoscopically, *No Name in the Street* shifts back and forth between past and present, between personal experience and public significance. It is a method ideally suited to Baldwin's

talents as a polemicist. Always an emotional writer, he must make his historical arguments not with logically sequential development of a large body of evidence leading to carefully stated conclusions, but with powerful generalizations authenticated by the eloquence and intensity of feeling of their utterance and by the revelatory anecdote of vignette. The dangers of subjectivity so damaging to *Tell Me How Long the Train's Been Gone* are here avoided by careful control of tone and by using more mature self-knowledge as a way of understanding others.

In *No Name in the Street* Baldwin is no longer imploring his white readers to change their ways in order to avert the fire next time. No longer does he appeal to white liberals. His statement to a New York *Times* interviewer concerning his work in progress in the spring of 1972 applies equally to *No Name in the Street:* "There will be no moral appeals on my part to this country's moral conscience. It has none.'' Instead of moral exhortation, Baldwin now relies on more restrained rhetoric, on flatter statement. His mood is embittered, pessimistic, sad, somewhat tired. There is a terrible finality about his denunciations, whether of French oppression of the Algerians, the shameful compromises of American intellectuals with McCarthyism, the racist and sex-obsessed South, the unremitting international legal persecution of his friend Tony Maynard, the degradation of Watts, in Los Angeles, the war of the police against the Black Panthers, and, above all, the assassinations of his three friends—Medgar, Malcolm, Martin—dooming any hope of racial reconciliation in America.

All of these public issues receive extended discussion, but Baldwin also uses quick sketches of private madness to exemplify the public sickness, such as that of "a young white man, beautiful, Jewish, American, who ate his wife's afterbirth, frying it in a frying pan'' or that of a young black American believing himself to be a "Prince of Abyssinia'' and asking the author for a contribution of ten thousand dollars. Along with Malcolm X and Huey Newton and Angela Davis and George Jackson, all of whom he mentions approvingly, Baldwin takes the position that the evil of the West—its imperialism and racism—has irretrievably doomed it. "Above the thoughtless American head" he sees "the shape of the wrath to come." Of all the statements by black nationalists of the late 1960's and early 1970's, *No Name in the Street* is surely one of the most impressive.

Baldwin's remaining four books having race as the central theme are slighter works. *One Day, When I Was Lost* is a film scenario based on *The Autobiography of Malcolm X. The Devil Finds Work* examines American movies as they reveal racial attitudes. *A Rap on Race* (1971) and *A Dialogue* (1973) are transcripts of conversations with Margaret Mead in 1970 and with Nikki Giovanni in 1971. These conversations are provocative and spontaneous, but they add little to what has been said better elsewhere, especially in *No Name in the Street*. Baldwin's reliance on emotion and intuition in authenticating his historical judgments fares rather badly in comparison with Margaret Mead's ample and precise scholarly knowledge of apposite historical and anthropological facts. Her understanding of racism as a cross-cultural phenomenon makes Baldwin's attribution of it to the white West seem naive.

Deeply affected by the assassination of Malcolm X, Baldwin had first planned to write a play about him with Elia Kazan. Despite strong skepticism about Hollywood's ability to do justice to such a theme, Baldwin agreed to write a scenario instead of a stage play. Unable to adapt himself to life in southern California and unable to accept either the collaborative nature of writing for the movies or the specific changes in his script proposed by the studio, which he believed would seriously distort his sense of the meaning of Malcolm's life and death, he left Hollywood and the film was never produced. But Baldwin did publish the scenario, first in 1972 in a British edition and in the following year with his American publisher.

If Hollywood took indecent liberties with Baldwin's scenario, it can also be fairly said that *One Day, When I Was Lost* itself distorts in numerous ways the life story that Malcolm told to Alex Haley. Some of the changes were clearly dictated by the need to select episodes from a long and detailed biography to fit a cinematic format, and others resulted from legal complications arising from the dispute between the Nation of Islam and Malcolm's estate; but as Patsy Brewington Perry has demonstrated (O'Daniel, 1977), the effect is to oversimplify a complex personality and to narrow his message in a misleading way. By the use of recurring images, especially of fire, Baldwin emphasizes violence in American race relations and shames the white perpetrators of it. Nothing seems to have changed, the scenarist suggests, from the 1920's when Malcolm's Garveyite father was persecuted by the Ku Klux Klan, to the 1960's, when Malcolm's house was fire-bombed. *One Day, When I Was Lost* thus becomes yet another statement of despairing Baldwinian protest instead of the more optimistic and more complex testament produced by Malcolm and Haley.

In *The Devil Finds Work* Baldwin relinquishes the role of film writer for that of film critic, resuming that scrutiny of Hollywood's effort to deal with racial matters earlier undertaken in essays on *Carmen Jones* and *Porgy and Bess*. His concern is with cultural values and vacuities in films ranging from *The Birth of a Nation* to *The Exorcist*. The first of the three sections of *The Devil Finds Work* takes us back to the familiar ground of the author's childhood, when his extreme subjectivity made his moviegoing a means both of escaping from his stepfather's assaults on his personality and of coping with them. Ridiculed for protruding eyes, he took comfort in their similarity to those of Bette Davis. Indeed, young Baldwin's response to white stars depended on their approximation to blackness. Davis, Joan Crawford, Blanche Yurka (in *A Tale of Two Cities*), Sylvia Sidney, and Henry Fonda all appealed to him by confirming his sense of reality, by reminding him of people he knew or had seen on the streets of Harlem. Somewhat later, he saw his first play, the all-black *Macbeth* of Orson Welles, and later still *Native Son*. The stage confronted reality, Baldwin recognized, far more directly than the screen, for "the language of the camera is the language of our dreams."

In the first section Baldwin relates the films he saw as a child to the issues of self and race even though most of them are not overtly concerned with these matters. In the second section he analyzes films dealing explicitly with race relations: *I Shall Spit on Your Graves, The Birth of a Nation, In the Heat of the Night, In This, Our Life, The Defiant Ones,* and *Guess Who's Coming to Dinner.* In them he shows the unspoken assumptions, overt or covert racism, moral evasions, latent homosexuality, distortions of reality—a dispiriting but revealing analysis of the failure of film as a medium to treat the relation of whites and blacks seriously and honestly. In the third section Baldwin offers another example of the same failure in an extended analysis of *Lady Sings the Blues.* Not that Hollywood does much better on other serious themes, as he demonstrates in examining the refusal of *Lawrence of Arabia* to confront the ethnocentric violence of British imperialism, the viciously chauvinistic anti-communism of *My Son, John,* and "the mindless and hysterical banality of the evil presented in *The Exorcist.*"

As a film critic Baldwin lacks great technical expertise, although his working experience in Hollywood did provide him with a basic knowledge of the way movies are made. His main concern is with film as cultural expression and re-

flection rather than as artistic medium. Subjective, selective, digressive, and reductive as it often is, *The Devil Finds Work* offers a trenchant moral critique of the treatment of race in the movies.

James Baldwin can look back on a substantial literary career. He has written fifteen books and collaborated on three others. He is one of the best-known and most widely read of living American writers. He has been the subject of considerable critical attention: a biography, two serious critical studies, two collections of critical essays, and numerous articles in the scholarly and critical journals. Although he has not yet won a major literary prize, by most objective standards his work has earned him a secure, if not yet major, place in American literary history.

One feels, however, that Baldwin has not quite realized his full potential. His novels *Tell Me How Long the Train's Been Gone* and *If Beale Street Could Talk* lack the scope and power of *Another Country* and the literary finesse of *Go Tell It on the Mountain* or even *Giovanni's Room.* No subsequent short story has surpassed "Sonny's Blues," published in 1957. *One Day, When I Was Lost, The Devil Finds Work,* and *Little Man, Little Man* (1976—a children's book) are interesting minor efforts, but in them Baldwin seems to be marking time. Indeed, of his work in 1968–1978, only *No Name in the Street* can be said to equal the best work of the early phase of his career.

The pattern of Baldwin's literary development has been one of expanding perspectives as he has moved from the storefront church and the search for self to issues of life in the modern city and American race relations. In his essays he characteristically moves in the same direction, so that the concluding paragraph often enlarges the topic to global dimensions. He typically reveals the general significance of personal experience and infuses social or historical generalizations with intense individual feeling. His style has a capacity for genuine eloquence and elegance that recall William Faulkner and Henry James. Mark Schorer wrote that "we have hardly a more accomplished prose stylist in the United States today." With his thematic range, his intensity of feeling, his stylistic resources, the sense of structure apparent in his early fiction, he may yet write a truly major American novel.

Whether he does or not, Baldwin must already be counted among our masters of the personal essay, a genre he has regenerated for our time. And beyond any strictly literary estimate, James Baldwin must be reckoned one of the most urgent and inescapable of the twentieth-century witnesses to the racial agony that has been so tragic and so constant a factor in our national history.

Selected Bibliography

WORKS OF JAMES BALDWIN

BOOKS

Go Tell It on the Mountain. New York: Alfred A. Knopf, 1953.

Notes of a Native Son. Boston: Beacon Press, 1955.

Giovanni's Room. New York: Dial Press, 1956.

Nobody Knows My Name: More Notes of a Native Son. New York: Dial Press, 1961.

Another Country. New York: Dial Press, 1962.

The Fire Next Time. New York: Dial Press, 1963.

Blues for Mister Charlie. New York: Dial Press, 1964.

Nothing Personal. New York: Atheneum, 1964. (With Richard Avedon.)

Going to Meet the Man. New York: Dial Press, 1965.

The Amen Corner. New York: Dial Press, 1968. (First produced in 1956.)

Tell Me How Long the Train's Been Gone. New York: Dial Press, 1968.

A Rap on Race. Philadelphia: J. B. Lippincott, 1971. (With Margaret Mead.)

No Name in the Street. New York: Dial Press, 1972.

One Day, When I Was Lost. London: Michael Joseph, 1972.

A Dialogue. Philadelphia: J. B. Lippincott, 1973. (With Nikki Giovanni.)

If Beale Street Could Talk. New York: Dial Press, 1974.

The Devil Finds Work. New York: Dial Press, 1976.

Little Man, Little Man: A Story of Childhood. London: Michael Joseph, 1976.

UNCOLLECTED ESSAYS

"The Image of the Negro." *Commentary,* 5:378–80 (1948).

"Too Late, Too Late." *Commentary,* 7:96–99 (1949).

"Preservation of Innocence." *Zero,* no. 2:14–22 (Summer 1949).

"The Death of the Prophet." *Commentary,* 9:257–61 (1950).

"The Negro at Home and Abroad." *The Reporter,* 27:36–37 (November 1951).

"The Crusade of Indignation." *The Nation,* 7:18–22 (July 1956).

"On Catfish Row." *Commentary,* 28:246–48 (1959).

"Mass Culture and the Creative Artist: Some Personal Notes." *Daedalus,* 89:373–76 (1960).

"They Can't Turn Back." *Mademoiselle,* 51:324–25, 351–58 (August 1960).

"The Dangerous Road Before Martin Luther King." *Harper's Magazine,* 222:33–42 (February 1961).

"Theatre: On the Negro Actor." *The Urbanite,* 1:6, 29 (April 1961).

"The New Lost Generation." *Esquire,* 56:113–15 (July 1961).

"Views of a Near-sighted Cannoneer." *Village Voice,* July 13, 1961, pp. 5–6.

"As Much Truth as One Can Bear." *New York Times Book Review,* January 14, 1962, pp. 1, 38.

"Color." *Esquire,* 58:225, 2 (December 1962).

"Not 100 Years of Freedom." *Liberator,* 3:7, 16, 18 (January 1963).

"Letters from a Journey," *Harper's Magazine,* 226:48–52 (May 1963).

"James Baldwin Statement—Political Murder in Birmingham." *New America,* September 24, 1963, pp. 1, 4.

"The Creative Dilemma." *Saturday Review,* 8:14–15, 58 (February 1964).

"Why I Stopped Hating Shakespeare," *Observer,* April 19, 1964, p. 21.

"The White Man's Guilt." *Ebony,* 20:47–48 (August 1965).

"To Whom It May Concern: A Report from Occupied Territory." *The Nation,* July 11, 1966, pp. 39–43.

"Anti-Semitism and Black Power." *Freedomways,* 7: 75–77 (1967).

"God's Country." *New York Review of Books,* March 23, 1967, pp. 17–20.

"Negroes Are Anti-Semitic Because They're Anti-White." *New York Times Magazine,* April 9, 1967, pp. 26–27, 135–37, 139–40.

"The War Crimes Tribunal." *Freedomways,* 7:242–44 (1967).

"Sidney Poitier." *Look,* July 23, 1968, pp. 50–52, 54, 56, 58.

"White Racism or World Community?" *Ecumenical Review,* 20:371–76 (1968).

"Can Black and White Artists Still Work Together? 'The Price May Be Too High.'" New York *Times,* February 2, 1969, sec. 2, p. 9.

"Sweet Lorraine." *Esquire,* 72:139–40 (November 1969).

"Foreword." In Louise Meriwether, *Daddy Was a Number Runner.* Englewood Cliffs, N.J.: Prentice-Hall, 1970. Pp. 5–7.

"An Open Letter to My Sister, Miss Angela Davis." *New York Review of Books,* January 7, 1971, pp. 15–16.

"An Open Letter to Mr. Carter." New York *Times,* January 23, 1977, sec. 4, p. 17.

"Every Good-bye Ain't Gone." *New York,* December 19, 1977, pp. 64–65, 68, 70, 72, 74.

"James Baldwin Has a Dream." *Morning Courier* (Champaign-Urbana), April 27, 1978, p. 28.

CRITICAL AND BIOGRAPHICAL STUDIES

BIOGRAPHY

Eckman, Fern Marja. *The Furious Passage of James Baldwin.* New York: M. Evans, 1966.

CRITICAL STUDIES

Alexander, Charlotte A. *James Baldwin's Go Tell It on the Mountain and Another Country, The Fire Next Time, Giovanni's Room, Notes of a Native Son.* New York: Monarch Press, 1966.

Kinnamon, Keneth, ed. *James Baldwin: A Collection of Critical Essays.* Englewood Cliffs, N.J.: Prentice-Hall, 1974.

Macebuh, Stanley. *James Baldwin: A Critical Study.* New York: Third Press, 1973.

Moller, Karin. *The Theme of Identity in the Essays of James Baldwin; an Interpretation.* Gothenburg Studies in English series, 32. Atlantic Highlands, N.J.: Humanities Press, 1975.

O'Daniel, Therman B., ed. *James Baldwin: A Critical Evaluation.* Washington, D.C.: Howard University Press, 1977.

Weatherby. W. J. *Squaring Off: Mailer vs. Baldwin.* New York: Mason/Charter, 1977.

UNCOLLECTED ARTICLES

Allen, Shirley S. "Religious Symbolism and Psychic Reality in Baldwin's *Go Tell It on the Mountain.*" *CLA Journal,* 19:173–99 (1975).

Barksdale, Richard K. " 'Temple of the Fire Baptized.' " *Phylon,* 14:326–27 (1953).

Bell, George E. "The Dilemma of Love in *Go Tell It on the Mountain* and *Giovanni's Room.*" *CLA Journal,* 17:397–406 (1974).

Bigsby, C. W. E. "The Committed Writer: James Baldwin as Dramatist." *Twentieth Century Literature,* 13:39–48 (1967).

Bogle, Donald. "A Look at the Movies by Baldwin." *Freedomways,* 16:103–08 (1976).

Breit, Harvey. "James Baldwin and Two Footnotes." In *The Creative Present: Notes on Contemporary American Fiction.* Edited by Nona Balakian and Charles Simmons. Garden City, N.Y.: Doubleday, 1963. Pp. 5–24.

Bryant, Jerry H. "Wright, Ellison, Baldwin—Exorcising the Demon." *Phylon,* 37:174–88 (1976).

Burks, Mary Fair. "James Baldwin's Protest Novel: *If Beale Street Could Talk.*" *Negro American Literature Forum,* 10: 83–87, 95 (1976).

Charney, Maurice. "James Baldwin's Quarrel with Richard Wright." *American Quarterly,* 15:63–75 (1963).

Coles, Robert. "James Baldwin Back Home." *New York Times Book Review,* July 31, 1977, pp. 1, 22–24.

Cox, C. B., and A. R. Jones. "After the Tranquilized Fifties: Notes on Sylvia Plath and James Baldwin." *Critical Quarterly,* 6:107–22 (1964).

Dance, Daryl C. "You Can't Go Home Again: James Baldwin and the South." *CLA Journal*, 18:81–90 (1974).

Daniels, Mark R. "Estrangement, Betrayal & Atonement: The Political Theory of James Baldwin." *Studies in Black Literature*, 7:10–13 (Autumn 1976).

Dickstein, Morris. "The Black Aesthetic in White America." *Partisan Review*, 38:376–95 (1971).

Finn, James. "The Identity of James Baldwin." *Commonweal*, October 26, 1962, pp. 113–16.

Fischer, Russell G. "James Baldwin: A Bibliography, 1947–1962." *Bulletin of Bibliography*, 24:127–30 (1965).

Foster, David E. " 'Cause My House Fell Down': The Theme of the Fall in Baldwin's Novels." *Critique*, 13, no. 2:50–62 (1971).

Gayle, Addison, Jr. "A Defense of James Baldwin." *CLA Journal*, 10:201–08 (1967).

———. "The Dialectic of 'The Fire Next Time.' " *Negro History Bulletin*, 30:15–16 (April 1967).

Gross, Barry. "The 'Uninhabitable Darkness' of Baldwin's *Another Country:* Image and Theme." *Negro American Literature Forum*, 6:113–21 (1972).

Gross, Theodore L. *The Heroic Ideal in American Literature.* New York: Free Press, 1971. Pp. 166–79.

Hagopian, John V. "James Baldwin: The Black and the Red-White-and-Blue." *CLA Journal*, 7: 133–40 (1963).

Harper, Howard M., Jr. *Desperate Faith: A Study of Bellow, Salinger, Mailer, Baldwin, and Updike.* Chapel Hill: University of North Carolina Press, 1967. Pp. 137–61.

Howe, Irving. "Black Boys and Native Sons." *Dissent*, 10:353–68 (1963).

Jacobson, Dan. "James Baldwin as Spokesman." *Commentary*, 32:497–502 (1961).

Kim, Kichung. "Wright, the Protest Novel, and Baldwin's Faith." *CLA Journal*, 17:387–96 (1974).

Kindt, Kathleen A. "James Baldwin: A Checklist, 1947–1962." *Bulletin of Bibliography*, 24:123–26 (1965).

Klein, Marcus. "James Baldwin: A Question of Identity." In his *After Alienation: American Novels in Mid-Century.* Cleveland: World, 1964. Pp. 147–95.

Leaks, Sylvester. "James Baldwin—I Know His Name." *Freedomways*, 3:102—05 (1963).

Lee, Brian. "James Baldwin: Caliban to Prospero." In *The Black American Writer.* Edited by C. W. E. Bigsby. Volume 1. Deland, Fla.: Everett/Edwards, 1969. Pp. 169–79.

Levin, David. "Baldwin's Autobiographical Essays: The Problem of Negro Identity." *Massachusetts Review*, 5:239–47 (1964).

MacInnes, Colin. "Dark Angel: The Writings of James Baldwin." *Encounter*, 21:22–23 (August 1963).

Marcus, Steven. "The American Negro in Search of Identity." *Commentary*, 16:456–63 (1953).

Margolies, Edward. "The Negro Church: James Baldwin and the Christian Vision." In his *Native Sons: A Critical Study of Twentieth-Century Negro American Authors.* Philadelphia: Lippincott, 1968. Pp. 102–26.

Mayfield, Julian. "And Then Came Baldwin." *Freedomways*, 3:143–55 (1963).

McCarthy, Harold T. "James Baldwin: The View from Another Country." In his *The Expatriate Perspective: American Novelists and the Idea of America.* Rutherford–Madison–Teaneck, N.J.: Fairleigh Dickinson University Press, 1974. Pp. 197–213.

McCluskey, John. "If Beale Street Could Talk." *Black World*, 24:51–52, 88–91 (December 1974).

Meserve, Walter. "James Baldwin's 'Agony Way.' " In *The Black American Writer.* Edited by C. W. E. Bigsby. Volume 2. Deland, Fla.: Everett/Edwards, 1969. Pp. 171–86.

Moore, John Rees. "An Embarrassment of Riches: Baldwin's *Going to Meet the Man.*" *Hollins Critic*, 2:1–12 (December 1965).

Neal, Lawrence P. "The Black Writers' Role: James Baldwin." *Liberator*, 6:10–11 (April 1966).

Noble, David W. *The Eternal Adam and the New World Garden: The Central Myth in the American Novel Since 1830.* New York: George Braziller, 1968. Pp. 209–17.

O'Brien, Conor Cruise. "White Gods and Black Americans." *New Statesman*, May 1, 1964, pp. 681–82.

Pratt, Louis, H. "James Baldwin and 'the Literary Ghetto.' " *CLA Journal*, 20:262–72 (1976).

Roth, Philip. "Channel X: Two Plays on the Race

Conflict.'' *New York Review of Books,* May 28, 1964, pp. 10–13.

Sayre, Robert F. ''James Baldwin's Other Country.'' In *Contemporary American Novelists.* Edited by Harry T. Moore. Carbondale: Southern Illinois University Press, 1964. Pp. 158–69.

Scott, Nathan A., Jr. ''Judgement Marked by a Cellar: The American Negro Writer and the Dialectic of Despair.'' *Denver Quarterly,* 2:5–35 (Summer 1967).

Simmons, Harvery G. ''James Baldwin and the Negro Conundrum.'' *Antioch Review,* 23:250–55 (1963).

Spender, Stephen. ''James Baldwin: Voice of a Revolution.'' *Partisan Review,* 30:256–60 (1963).

Strandley, Fred L. ''James Baldwin: The Crucial Situation.'' *South Atlantic Quarterly,* 65:371–81 (1966).

———. ''James Baldwin: A Checklist, 1963–1967.'' *Bulletin of Bibliography,* 25:135 (1968).

———. ''James Baldwin: The Artist as Incorrigible Disturber of the Peace.'' *Southern Humanities Review,* 4:18–30 (1970).

———. ''*Another Country,* Another Time.'' *Studies in the Novel,* 4:504–12 (1972).

Thelwell, Mike. ''*Another Country:* Baldwin's New York Novel.'' In *The Black American Writer.* Edited by C. W. E. Bigsby. Volume 1. Deland, Fla.: Everett/Edwards, 1969. Pp. 181–98.

Wills, Garry. ''What Color Is God?'' *National Review,* 14:408–14, 416–17 (1963).

—KENETH KINNAMON

Amiri Baraka

1934 –

BORN Everett LeRoi Jones, on October 7, 1934, in Newark, New Jersey, Amiri Baraka is in 1980 a man whose literary and political growth is in midlife. However inaccessible and unpopular his work has been from a conventional standpoint, he has established himself as a writer of significant stature. With the vantage point of the racial outsider, he has passed through a series of painful and searching stages of growth. Strenuously resisting the artistic and cultural ideals of what he has called "mainstream" and "bourgeois" America, he offers in their stead radical social analysis, new cultural values, and a boldly innovative literature. In the process he has experienced a series of simultaneously disruptive and healing transformations—adjustments of major personal, artistic, and political importance.

From this perspective his writings can be usefully understood as the record of intense and ongoing changes. They began in the late 1950's with a confused but determined movement away from what he perceived as white-dominated lyric egotism, continued into the 1960's in the form of an emotional and cultural reintegration with the black world, and emerged in the 1970's as a complete ideological dedication to worldwide revolution. Through each phase Baraka has had to question closely his role as a writer and to find ways of making literary art

an effective instrument for defining his personal, cultural, and political goals. His remarkable achievements as a writer and activist—he came to regard the two roles as inseparable—bespeak a temperament marked by uncompromising energy and risk-taking modulated by intellectual and emotional resilience.

The son of Coyt LeRoi and Anna Lois Russ Jones, young LeRoi was raised in an urban black family with middle-class aspirations. Passing through the Newark public schools, he briefly attended Rutgers University on a science scholarship and then shifted to the more hospitable, if decidedly assimilationist, atmosphere of Howard University, majoring in English with a minor in philosophy and leaving in 1954 to join the Air Force. After nearly three years in the service, most of that time spent in Puerto Rico, he gravitated to New York City with certain distinct perceptions registered in his consciousness. "The Howard thing," he said in a 1964 interview with Judy Stone, "let me understand the Negro sickness. They teach you how to pretend to be white. But the Air Force made me understand the white sickness. It shocked me into realizing what was happening to me and others. By oppressing Negroes, the whites have become oppressors, ... convincing themselves they are right, as people have always convinced themselves."

Finding the intellectual and artistic atmosphere of the East Village section of the city to his liking, he took graduate courses in comparative literature at Columbia, worked for *Record Changer* magazine, and was generally absorbed into the Bohemian life-style. At a time when the advanced politics of race was distinctly anti-bourgeois and integrationist, Jones found the countercultural posture of the predominantly white "beat" community initially supportive.

In that congenial atmosphere he began to acknowledge the first impulses leading into his early poetry. In the reachable past were such established older-generation moderns as Ezra Pound, William Carlos Williams, and even T. S. Eliot, whom Jones subsequently dismissed as a "lovely . . . rhetorician." At the same time several groups of the new poets, for an interval, furnished a sustaining poetics: the Black Mountain School of Robert Creeley and Charles Olson offered workable poetic theories and techniques while the New York coterie of Allen Ginsberg, Gregory Corso, and others fostered useful social attitudes and emotional strategies. He participated in two of the numerous "little magazines" then proliferating in the East Village community, evanescent mimeographed issues with small circulation designed to promulgate the work of his literary friends: *Yügen,* founded and coedited with Hettie Cohen; and *Floating Bear,* coedited with Diane DiPrima. Jones married Hettie, a young Jewish coworker at the *Record Changer,* in October 1958, marking his furthest incursion into the white world. He was on the threshold of an arduous artistic and political struggle.

Although Jones needed to pull away from what he soon came to recognize as certain debilitating aspects of his "beat" identity, there were also strands in his early literary experiences that later tied up with his nationalist writings. In a 1960 radio interview with David Ossman he tells how William Carlos Williams alerted him to the importance of the spoken word: "how to write the way I *speak* rather than the way I *think* a poem ought to be written—to write just the way it comes to me, in my own speech, utilizing the rhythms of speech rather than any kind of metrical concept. To talk verse." While he learned about crafting verse from Pound's example, "how a poem should be made, what a poem ought to *look* like," it was Williams, he said, who showed him "how to get it in my own language." Just as meaningful were Charles Olson's pronouncements in *Projective Verse* (1959), stressing the efficacy of sound in poetry, letting the poetic line follow the dictates of breath, which, Olson says, "allows *all* the speech-force of language back in."

Jones pointedly entitled his own brief statement on poetics "How You Sound??" (1959). He emphasized the need for a voice that will recreate the sound of his private experience:

MY POETRY is whatever I think I am. (Can I be light & weightless as a sail?? Heavy & clunking like 8 black boots.) I CAN BE ANYTHING I CAN. I make a poetry with what I feel is useful & can be saved out of all the garbage of our lives. What I see, am touched by (CAN HEAR). . . . "Who knows what a poem ought to sound like? Until it's thar." Says Charles Olson . . . & I follow closely with that.

Such dicta anticipated the extraliterary modes of black music and speech at the center of the nascent black aesthetic that Jones began to delineate in the early 1960's as he wrote *Blues People.* For the time being, though, his attention to poetic voice was almost entirely self-directed, there being as yet no sense of his singular voice in relation to the collective voice of the black community.

Initially inviting, too, must have been the extent to which the "beat" subculture drew unabashedly upon black culture, canonizing bebop musicians like Dizzy Gillespie and Charlie Parker and making the socially estranged world of black music a conspicuous image for its own consciously chosen alienation. The black perspective, as understood by the white poets, was an appealing metaphor for disenchantment, as with Ginsberg's typical assertion in *Howl* that the best minds of his generation were "dragging themselves through the negro streets at dawn." As much as Ginsberg and others were touched by images of black culture, they were unable to appropriate black style as a workable model for poetic form.

Nor could Jones do so effectively until he freed himself from the influence of the moderns and the "new" poets. His first formulations of himself as a writer did not exclude the pressing awareness that he was black, but they did restrict the manifestation of blackness in his poetry of the late 1950's and early 1960's. When asked why the sense of "being a Negro" one finds in the poetry of Langston Hughes did not occur in his own work, Jones, in his "beat" guise, demurred: "I'm fully conscious all the time that I am an American Negro, because it's part of my life. But I know also that if I want to say, 'I see a bus full of people,' I don't have to say, 'I am a Negro seeing a bus full of people.'" In the poetry of *Preface to a Twenty Volume Suicide Note. . . .* (1961) and *The Dead Lecturer* (1964), as well as in *Blues People* (1963), his incisive social-historical interpretation of Afro-American music, Jones began a painstaking reassessment and slow moving out toward black self-identification as Amiri Baraka.

Preface to a Twenty Volume Suicide Note. . . . includes poems written between 1957 and 1961. The title suggests a posture common to much of the new poetry: that people are pressed to the brink of suicide by the internalization of popular myths and symbols that the poet must exorcise by a determined artistic in-

dividualism. With his own radio-prone youth much in mind, Jones typically assails the media heroes beamed into the American imagination—the inflated fictions of Tom Mix, Captain Midnight, and the Lone Ranger—along with the irrelevant serious art also produced by the same culture, "Great poets dying / with their strophes on." Such intrusions, damaging enough to acquiescent white perceptions, impinged even more menacingly on the mind of the vulnerable black artist. Jones's predicament was that he found himself beginning to question the efficacy of the new poetry, the vanguard literature of the very culture whose fantasies he was attempting to dissipate. Unlike Ginsberg, Jack Kerouac, and Creeley, he was much less certain that literary statement was an effective assertion of his integrity. So we see Jones at the beginning, laden with a cumbersome literary apparatus—prefaces and volumes bearing down heavily on his fragile "note."

"HYMN FOR LANIE POO," the second piece in the collection, satirically cuts into middle-class black pretensions fed by white-imposed stereotypes, fads, and beliefs. The ulterior responsibility, though, is identified in the final lines of the poem by an image that becomes a significant interpretive marker throughout *Suicide Note*:

> the huge & loveless
> white-anglo sun/of
> benevolent step
> mother America.

Throughout the poem the diffuse motioning toward whiteness is associated with the sun's penetrating light. By inverting this traditional life-giving symbol, Jones practices a strategy common to the black perspective: reversing the destructive meanings and values projected by the white world in order to buffer the besieged black psyche. The poem also implies that the values embodied in literary convention are part of the malign influence. A soothing aubade invites the poet into a lyrical acceptance of the sun as his ultimate genealogical source:

Each morning
I go down
to Gansevoort St.
and stand on the docks.
I stare out
at the horizon
until it gets up
and comes to embrace
me. I
make believe
it is my father.
This is known
as genealogy

The permeating image violates the poet's deepest privacies, seducing his sister ("Lanie Poo" was the nickname of Sandra Elaine, Jones's sister) into a "generation of fictitious / Ofays." The ironic hymn sets the general tone for the recurring condemnation of the insinuating American sun culture. In "ONE NIGHT STAND," dedicated to Allen Ginsberg, the poets are "foreign seeming persons" visiting the decaying city with their "Hats flopped so the sun / can't scald our beards. . . ."

Jones toys with other clever inversions to undermine popular sentimentalism, as in demonstrating that love can be "an evil word . . ." by turning it backward: "see, see what I mean? / An evol word. . . ." Two poems about his wife Hettie, which Baraka now understandably withholds from republication, propose a more painful romantic inversion by commenting wryly on the poet's interracial marriage. "FOR HETTIE" describes not only a woman who happens to be left-handed but one who has reversed the prevailing social order by taking a black husband and carrying a child whose paternity the poet questions. He impatiently mocks Hettie's left-handedness by accusing her of seeming to write backward, a style ironically

suggestive of his own literary countertactics. But the most telling reversal is genealogical, the poet's uneasy anticipation of their mixed-blood child. In "FOR HETTIE IN HER FIFTH MONTH" he observes his pregnant wife basking her womb in the sun's fading rays, foreseeing in the birth his complicity in the emergence of an absurd Hebrew-"beat" legacy.

Beyond the interracial quandary is an even more deeply felt emotional displacement in "THE BRIDGE." Under the inscription "(# for wieners and mcclure)," this lyric of disorientation and suicide is structured by musical metaphors into a sharp message for two of Jones's fellow poets, John Wieners and Michael McClure. Unable to return to his and their familiar melodies, the beginning or "head" of his song, he finds himself in disruptive motion along the bridging phrase where harmonic "changes" are unfamiliar:

you find yourself in its length
strung out along its breadth, waiting
for the cold sun to tear out your eyes.
        Enamoured
of its blues, spread out in the silk clubs of
this autumn tune. The changes are difficult,
    when
you hear them, & know they are all in you,
    the chords

of your disorder meddle with your would be
    disguises.

The old poetic values, Jones seems to assert to his friends, no longer apply: "& I have forgotten, / all the things, you told me to love, to try to understand, . . ." With the bridge leading only to the unknown and the song running out, he jumps into the "unmentionable black"—the territory to be charted in subsequent writings. A crucial turning point for Jones was his 1960 visit to Cuba with a group of black writers, to attend a commemoration of the revolutionary attack by Fidel Castro against President

Fulgencio Batista in 1953. It was Jones's first direct contact with Marxism—his own conversion would not occur for a decade. The political nature of the event awakened Jones to a new social and artistic sense of himself, an awareness recorded in the poem "BETANCOURT," dated July 30, 1960.

In the 1960 essay "Cuba Libre," reprinted in *Home* (1966), Jones describes his encounter with Señora Betancourt, a Mexican delegate to the celebration. An ardent Communist, she had attacked Jones as a "cowardly bourgeois individualist" when he defended his political neutrality on artistic grounds: "I'm a poet. . . . I'm not even interested in politics." The encounter deeply affected him, pointing up the inadequacy of his old poetic ways in the context of newly perceived Third World politics. The result is "BETANCOURT," his first politically informed self-criticism as a poet.

The poem repudiates his former work as the buffered perceptions of "some old man's poems" rotting in the "heavy sun, pure / distance. . . ." Using an image of poetic abnegation often repeated in *Suicide Note* and later in *The Dead Lecturer*, he dismisses the old poetic conventions: "Our gestures / are silence." Implicit is the sense that the new avant-garde poetry is now old and useless, leading Jones to conclude with a tenuous poetics of rejection:

> . . . (I mean I think
> I know now
> what a poem
> is) A
> turning away . . .
> from what
> it was
> had moved
> us . . .

Not yet perceiving aesthetic or political alternatives, Jones closes "Cuba Libre" by indicting himself and the "beats" as impotent old rebels:

"Even the vitality of our art is like bright flowers growing up through a rotting carcass." The last two poems in *Suicide Note* affirm this rejection of the old self while tentatively pointing to new but unrealized directions. The title "DON JUAN IN HELL" suggests that the poet's genealogy is still inclusive, a Europeanized man under an "unfamiliar sun." He is without a progenitor, "like / some son / lost his old dead father" and unable to actualize the "new man" trapped in his "old self." The poet concludes with notes not quite so suicidal that leave open the possibility of rebirth and future utterance. While "NOTES FOR A SPEECH" posits alienation—" . . . You are / as any other sad man here / american."—it is alienation from a new native land: "African blues / does not know me. . . . / Does / not feel / what I am."

Blues People and *The Dead Lecturer* were written in the early 1960's during approximately the same period of time, the tough-minded prose and expostulating poetry each representing in its own way Jones's thrusting past ineffectual suicide and mere rejection. *Blues People,* a lucid retrieval of Afro-American and African culture, traces through black music "the *path* the slave took to 'citizenship,'" delineating a usable heritage distinct from the European-American mainstream. Generally speaking, Jones was working within a well-established posture in black letters.

Early writers like W. E. B. Du Bois in *The Souls of Black Folk* (1903) and James Weldon Johnson in *The Autobiography of an Ex-Colored Man* (1912) had made concerted attempts to bring to light the particulars of Afro-American history and culture. Closer to Jones's time, Langston Hughes, Zora Neale Hurston, and Ralph Ellison had consciously sought ways to shape their writings in accordance with stylistic modes and symbols particular to the black tradition. In a more contemporary sense, though, Jones's strict commitment to the integrity of an

African genealogy linked him with the surge of cultural nationalism in the 1960's.

Blues People established Jones's seminal presence among such writers of the Black Arts Movement as Haki R. Madhubuti (Don L. Lee), Ed Bullins, Sonia Sanchez, and Ishmael Reed. Introducing the study as a "strictly *theoretical* endeavor," Jones fervently argues the premise of a sharp dichotomy between the African/ Afro-American and Western/European-American culture families. Within this dialectic he pursues the thesis that music, if properly interpreted, is central to an accurate understanding of black American reality:

... I am saying that if the music of the Negro in America, in all its permutations, is subjected to a socio-anthropological as well as musical scrutiny, something about the essential nature of the Negro's existence in this country ought to be revealed, as well as something about the essential nature of this country, *i.e.,* society as a whole.

Jones goes on to show how Afro-American modes of communication have been nurtured within a fluent non-Western tradition of improvised music, one markedly different from the prevailing scores and scripts of the media-oriented culture discredited in *Suicide Note.*

The important contribution of *Blues People* lies not only in its insistence on a clarifying cultural dialectic but also in the detailed presentation of African cultural values and musical styles transformed by the particular pressures of Afro-American experience. One concept articulated by Jones became a chief criterion of the new black aesthetics: African music, like all stylized African expression, is "functional." Because it grows out of commonplace social and religious circumstances in which all members of the community participate, music exists to fulfill a specific secular or spiritual function. Jones claimed that when viewed comparatively, the

tradition of Western fine arts, especially since the humanist Renaissance, is basically one of individual achievement—the inactive majority passively appreciating the artifacts created by a select few. If, as in *Suicide Note,* art and life had become disjunct, Jones had found the rationale for a restorative:

If we think of African music as regards its intent, we must see that it differed from Western music in that it was a purely *functional* music. . . . : songs used by young men to influence young women (courtship, challenge, scorn); songs used by workers to make their tasks easier; songs used by older men to prepare the adolescent boys for manhood, and so on. "Serious" Western music, except for early religious music, has been strictly an "art" music. One would not think of any particular *use* for Haydn's symphonies, except perhaps the "cultivation of the soul." . . . It was, and is, inconceivable in the African culture to make a separation between music, dancing, song, the artifact, and a man's life or his worship of his gods.

This was the beginning of a serviceable aesthetic that went beyond the nearly dysfunctional statement in "BETANCOURT" of what a poem was not, a "turning away . . . / from what / it was." If art comes directly from the experience of a people, and if, as *Blues People* clearly shows, that experience has obvious social implication, then the expression issuing from that experience will by definition have social—indeed, political—content. Thus armed with an intellectual basis for freeing himself from his apolitical "beat" pose, Jones in subsequent writings increasingly embodied the politics of cultural nationalism.

Blues People also identifies the important elements in African music and speech from which blues and jazz derive. Jones gives special emphasis to such stylistic features of vocal interpretation as polyrhythms, complex alterations in pitch and tone quality, improvisational rather than written expressions, and communal antiphony or call and response. These Africanisms survive in Afro-American music and speech, providing a particular expressive interpretation of the experience of the African being tested in the New World that was as valid for the black artist of the 1960's as for the slave three hundred years earlier.

From these African beginnings *Blues People* goes on to identify the generic forms and social meanings of Afro-American music as it has evolved to the present—shouts, field hollers, work songs, spirituals, blues, early jazz, swing, bebop, and rhythm and blues. These musical responses each represent "definite *stages* in the Negro's transmutation from African to American," and lead Jones to understand that "change," both social and stylistic, was a constant in both the historical fact of black reality and the expression of it: "there are certain very apparent changes in the Negro's reactions to America . . . and again, I insist that these changes are most graphic in music." After *Blues People* the concept of change became central to Jones's life and art. In accordance with the stages of growth and change in his personal consciousness, the personae in his poetry and drama shifted in posture from rage and victimization to the willful enactment of change.

The challenge for Jones was to find modes of expression as responsive to the representation of change as he understood black music to be. As a writer initially using the forms of written English, he must have felt at a distinct disadvantage in comparison with the fluent musicians and their music-related uses of Afro-American speech. In a chapter entitled "Enter the Middle Class," he deprecates the black literary tradition as not being informed with the same "legitimacy of emotional concern" one finds in coon shouts, the blues of Bessie Smith,

or bebop. With his own middle-class origins and recent literary allegiances no doubt weighing heavily, he sees the main function of literature as that of having eased the black writer into the bourgeois aspects of Western culture. Jones the poet was in the process of discovering that music was the primary black mode of expression, while the literature of black America was "essentially undistinguished." Although *Blues People* does not directly investigate the inadequacies of literary form, it validates in historical and aesthetic terms Jones's rejection of himself as a traditional poet. The implications of *Blues People* were apparent in *The Dead Lecturer* mostly through the poet's continuing struggle to escape Western literary formalism.

Although there are no sudden ideological or stylistic changes, the poems in *The Dead Lecturer,* written for the most part while *Blues People* was in the making, do represent forceful emotional siftings. As the title suggests, the poet, suffering the consequences of his attempted suicide, retains in many of the poems the degenerative images of sun, old age, and silence from *Suicide Note.* But from the vantage point of *Blues People* he can at least begin to acknowledge the potent artists—the makers of sound pictured in "SHORT SPEECH TO MY FRIENDS":

. . . these others, saxophones whining
through the wooden doors of their less than
gracious homes.
The poor have become our creators. The
black. . . .

Not yet able to incorporate flexible musical stylings into the contained print of his verse, Jones presented the old, fixed tradition as a parody of the very ideas and attitudes it embodies:

. . . the proper placement
of verbs and nouns. To freeze the spit
in mid-air, as it aims itself
at some valiant intellectual's face.

This defiant frustration is evident in a number of poems in *The Dead Lecturer.*

From this equivocal stance Jones began to challenge more directly the prevailing notion of the poem as a sanctuary of self-expression. Having tested the possibilities for isolated confession in such pieces as "THE BRIDGE," he now disclaimed such personalism even as he continued to indulge the lyric. Confronting the issue squarely in "Green Lantern's Solo," Jones broadly equates lyric egocentrism with a dangerously insular individualism. His intellectual acquaintances, he charges, are disconnected from the world of the living: "My friend, the lyric poet, / who has never had an orgasm. My friend, / the social critic, who has never known society. . . ." Launching into their puerile solo performances, the Bohemian poets and liberal thinkers represent for Jones the real evil, pursuing a convoluted sense of the truth that is indistinguishable from the lie:

What we have created, is ourselves
as heroes, as lovers, as disgustingly
evil. As Dialogues with the soul, with
the self, Selves, screaming furiously
to each other. As the same fingers
touch the same faces, as the same
mouths close on each other. The killed
is the killer, the loved the lover
and the islands of mankind have grown huge
    to include all life,
all lust, all commerce and beauty. Each idea
    a reflection of itself
and all the ideas men have ever had. Truth,
    Lie, so close they defy
inspection, and are built into autonomy by
    naive fools,
who have no wish for wholeness or
    strength. . . .

Writing in this unwholesome mode, the self-conscious poet is "The Liar," as Jones indicates in the title of the last poem in *The Dead Lec-turer:* " . . . Publically redefining / each change in my soul, as if I had predicted / them." In the final sardonic lines, the dead lecturer serves notice that his poetry has merely falsified his character: "When they say, 'It is Roi / who is dead?' I wonder / who will they mean?"

Lacking a cohesive ideology and aesthetic, one of the tentative strategies of *The Dead Lecturer* is to discredit the tradition of Western art. Jones's only "political" recourse is to strike directly against the pernicious individualism of the lyric, to use the form against itself because it serves no positive social function. In "A Guerilla Handbook," egocentric poets "Convinced / of the lyric" are reflexively trapped within the form, "knowing no way out / except description. . . ." In "Political Poem," near the end of the collection, Jones sees the poem as "undone" by its own irrelevance. Enshrouded in the lyric, he is left with only a "polite truth" and his ill-fated title role: " . . . like my dead lecturer / lamenting thru gipsies his fast suicide."

If *The Dead Lecturer* winds down in a series of politicized rejections of lyric individualism, there are several poems, conspicuous for their intensity, that move well beyond isolated self-accusations, toward a determined identification with the collective feelings of Afro-America. Taken together, they represent an important shift in focus that anticipates the eruptive dramatizations and terse explanatory preachings of the emerging nationalism in the plays soon to come.

This engaged sensibility first emerges in "A Poem For Willie Best," a substantial piece in eight sections. By ascribing a mythic stature to the suppressed feelings of the black victim, Jones breathes a drama of large dimension into the Hollywood character actor Sleep'n'Eat, who, along with Mantan Moreland in the 1930's, inherited the comic mantle of Stepin Fetchit. He sees in Best nothing less than the extreme racial distortion of all black men as deplorably fantasized and crucified by the "obscene invention" of the white imagination: "... The top / of a head, seen from Christ's / heaven, stripped of history / or desire." Restoring to Best an emotional and fleshly reality, Jones in effect proposes him as one of the valorous Blues People, seeking intimacy with his plight rather than stepping back to the safe satiric distance of such earlier poems as "HYMN FOR LANIE POO." The last two sections of the poem widen the scope of emotional possibilities even further, dignifying the victim's pain by revealing him as a "renegade / behind the mask." The tormented actor, "tired of losing," finally forces his vernacular anger through the habitual dialect: "'I *got* ta cut'cha.'" This is the germ of a new poetic voice, one already flexed in the play script for *The Toilet* (1967), that was intermittently tested in *The Dead Lecturer*.

The voice is strengthened by the mythic intensification of black music in "Rhythm & Blues," a poem that taps a deeper and more aggressive collective feeling. Although dedicated to Robert Williams, a Marine veteran who had been suspended as president of the Monroe, North Carolina, NAACP in 1959 for espousing militant self-defense (Jones had met him during the 1960 trip to Cuba), the poem addresses the response of a community rather than the predicament of an individual. At the center of that response is the percussive sound of rhythm and blues that forcefully expresses "a legitimacy of emotional concern," as he says in *Blues People,* not to be found in the silent passivity of written verse.

Jones imagines that the immediacy of musical statement not only gives form to feeling but also has the potential to heighten social awareness, perhaps even to the extent of moving people actively to resist their oppression, as Williams had done. As he makes this point through the poem itself, he questions the power of his own poetic art to have a similar effect:

> ... If I see past what I feel, and call
>   music simply "Art" and will
> not take it to its logical end. For the
>   death by hanging, for
> the death by the hooded political murderer,
>   for the old man dead in his
> tired factory; ...

Unlike the retrospective, page-bound verses of the poet, the improvised formulations of the musician are a projection of emotions as they occur, an unflinching, expressive reaction tantalizingly close to active retaliation:

>   ... There is no
> "melody." Only the foot stomped, the roaring
>   harmonies of need.
>   The
> hand banged on the table, waved in the air.
>   The teeth pushed
>   against
> the lip. The face and fingers sweating. "Let
>   me alone," is praise enough
> for these musicians.

By comparison, the poet feels his impotence: "I am deaf and blind and lost and will not again sing your quiet / verse. I have lost / even the act of poetry. ...."

In the throes of this inadequacy, Jones begins to vent his suppressed energies through the penetrating image of the scream, an imposing sound he increasingly associated with the emotional and expressive fluency at the core of black life: " ... our screams. / Of the dozens, the razor, the cloth, the sheen, all speed adventure locked / in my eyes." As amply illustrated in *Blues People,* it is a stylistic element central to the musical tradition (in shouts, hollers, work songs). It was especially developed by postwar rhythm and blues performers who "literally had to shout to be heard above the ... electrified instruments." As a matter of survival, "the human voice itself had to struggle, to scream, to be heard."

In "The Screamers," a 1963 sketch reprinted in *Tales* (1967), Jones portrays "the screamed riff" of rhythm and blues saxophonist Lynn Hope—heroicized by Jones as an ethnic historian and priest of the unconscious—pushing his listeners to the verge of active protest in the Newark streets. The scream is proposed as a fantastic mode of self-realization that anticipates political change: "We screamed and screamed at the clear image of ourselves as we should always be.... It would be the form of the sweetest revolution, to hucklebuck into the fallen capital, and let the oppressors lindy hop out."

Music takes on the same generative power in "Rhythm & Blues," but the ineffectual poetry is seen as distinctly subordinate to the amplified sounds:

> The
> shake and chant, bulled electric motion,
>   figure of what there will
>   be
> as it sits beside me waiting to live past my
>   own meekness. . . .

The ideal poetic voice, the poem implies, would be the impossible re-creation of music itself in printed form.

Two other poems address the broad issue of the creative force behind the security of black expression toward which Jones is working. Both are couched in strongly anti-white terms and both culminate in an appeal to Damballah, the loa of fertility—the first positive evocations in Jones's poetry of a revitalizing African genealogy.

"Crow Jane," in part an inverted parody of William Butler Yeats's "Crazy Jane," is the more traditional of the two. It is an all-out attack on what had become for Jones a pernicious social and racial presence—the white woman. The contained anxiety expressed toward the pregnancy of his white wife in "FOR HETTIE IN HER FIFTH MONTH" has grown here to the repudiation of an entire culture. Crow Jane is nothing less than the seductive force of white sexual and artistic supremacy that deflects the procreative and creative power of the black artist. Her capacity for destruction is fully realized in the character of Lula in the play *Dutchman* (1964).

The poem is a terse statement of liberation from "Mama Death," whose romantic allure no longer deceives Jones: " . . . Cold stuff / to tempt a lover. Old Lady / of flaking eyes. Moon lady / of useless thighs." Her patronizing reverse racism, the female counterpart of an attitude known as Jim Crow, is merely a ploy to flatter his intellectual vanity on " . . . some pilgrimage / to thought. Where she goes, in fairness, / 'nobody knows'. . . ." He is now sufficiently possessed of his black emotive power to define, and thereby control, her emasculating character: "Now / I am her teller."

In a closing ceremony entitled "The dead lady canonized," the poet celebrates in grim fleshly terms the passing of Crow Jane's influence. To ensure that her womb will no longer incubate "dead nouns" and "rotted faces," the stillborn progeny of his past, he calls upon Damballah to administer the healing benediction:

> . . . The lady is dead, may the Gods,
>
>   (those others
> beg our forgiveness. And Damballah, kind
>   father,
> sew up
> her bleeding hole.

A precarious balance of controlled nuance and roiling emotion, "Crow Jane" bristles with ironic interplay between the Western poetic style that Jones is trying to shuck off and the motif of Afro-American separatism that he is in the process of embracing.

A second poem, "BLACK DADA NIHIL-ISMUS," although not following in exact sequence, can be read as a counter piece to "Crow Jane." Released from its self-destructive fantasy of the white woman, the poetic voice now concentrates the psychosexual distortions of whites into an aggregate black male antagonist who converts these lurid stereotypes into a frontal assault on the "grey hideous space" that is the West. In what is perhaps Jones's most pungent cultural inversion, the absurd artistic and philosophical legacy of the white culture is conjured into a threatening black weaponry. In a later essay entitled "Philistinism and the Negro Writer" (1966) he contended that one way black people might confront "the denial of reality . . . institutionalized in America" would be to "turn crazy, to bring out a little American Dada, Ornette Coleman style, and chase those perverts into the ocean where they belong."

Accordingly, Jones forgoes the mincing intricacy one finds in the structure of "Crow Jane" and speaks in the hammering post-bebop voice of the musician-priest, challenging a collective black manhood to shake off its lethargy and enact into reality the preposterous racial mythicizing of whites. If still somewhat formal, the voice is flagrant, exerting through Afro-American tones a pressure that transcends conventional usage and literal meaning:

> . . . why you stay, where they can
> reach? Why you sit, or stand, or walk
> in this place, . . .
>
> . . . Come up, black dada
>
> nihilismus. Rape the white girls. Rape
> their fathers. Cut the mothers' throats.
> Black dada nihilismus, choke my
>   friends

And then, as if invoking the very style he cannot yet adequately express, he starkly incants the enriching aural images that will give black

definition and coherence to the destruction: "Black scream / and chant, scream, / and dull, un / earthly / hollering. . . ." Jones resolves the poem stylistically and culturally in a chanted appeal to Damballah, reaching for the still-distant but now retrievable African past through a ritual naming of victims and heroes of color (including his grandfather Tom Russ) who struggled in the New World:

> For tambo, willie best, dubois, patrice,
>   mantan, the
>   bronze buckaroos.
>
>   For Jack Johnson, asbestos, tonto,
>   buckwheat,
>   billie holiday.
>
>   For tom russ, l'overture,
>   vesey, beau jack,
>
> (may a lost god damballah, rest or save us
> against the murders we intend
> against his lost white children
> black dada nihilismus

"BLACK DADA NIHILISMUS" best encapsulates the racial anger welling up through the lyric self-confusion of the early poetry, an emotional force that Jones's sense of restricted poetic form could no longer adequately contain. The lyric would not be totally abandoned; rather, it would appear in later nationalist poetry in a more sparing and emotionally positive form.

Although Jones's next significant body of work was in the drama, where the impulses of his expanding racial consciousness could be given scope in proportion to their intensity, some of the emotional current was diverted into the less restricted space of the prose narrative. The quasi-autobiographical fiction of the early stories in *Tales,* and especially of the novel *The System of Dante's Hell* (1965), can in part be seen as a transition to the more cohesive development of black character in the plays. In fact, some of the figures briefly glimpsed in the novel—Ora, Skippy, Knowles, Love, and James Karolis ("He died in a bathroom of old age & segregation")—spurted to fuller growth in *The Toilet.*

The first portion of the novel, published as "The System of Dante's Inferno" in the magazine *The Trembling Lamb* (1959), not surprisingly reflects many of the stylistic and emotional contours of the early poetry. In a first-person voice cluttered with images of decay, silence, and death reminiscent of Ginsberg's cityscapes in *Howl,* Jones strings together fragmentary impressions of his youth in Newark: "The breakup of my sensibility.... Vegetables rotting in the neighbors' minds.... Drowning city of silence.... All dead." In a brief afterword he says he intended to create "association complexes" of sound and image that would interpret the "Hell in the head" of his growing up.

With its underground allegory, Dante's inferno provides a classic Christian veneer for the organization of Jones's version of Hell into various circles, ditches, and transgressors (heathen, wrathful, seducers) that lend ready identity to the chapter headings. The emotional impulses veer away from Dante's mythic intentions, though, to draw upon the particular Afro-American sense of the underground as the psychic hell of invisibility. A condition imposed by white myopia and dangerously internalized by the black victim, it is the "torture of being the unseen object," as Jones puts it, "and, the constantly observed subject." In this sense the novelist's vision is largely determined by symbolic perceptions long established in the black writing tradition: from the veil of the color line in Du Bois' *The Souls of Black Folk* to Richard Wright's subterranean guilt in *The Man Who Lived Underground,* Ralph Ellison's ambivalent anger in *Invisible Man* (with its own Dantean

descent into rhythmic emotional depths), and James Baldwin's relentlessly exposed psychosexual afflictions in *Another Country.* These works all deal with the anguish of native sons having to balance precariously the tensions of the "lower frequencies," as Ellison put it, and as Jones himself masterfully dramatized through the hurtling subway setting of *Dutchman.*

The portion of *Dante's Hell* written after 1959 takes on greater narrative continuity, pulling the expansive yet difficult prose into more coherent interludes of experience. Language intensity, sexual motifs, and the probing into feelings specifically black all predict important elements in Jones's early drama. "The Eighth Ditch" is in effect a self-contained play, an episode of homosexual seduction in which the protagonist in his naive Boy Scout guise is stimulated by a streetwise companion into an indiscriminate desire for the blues. Ambivalent representations of homosexuality (a sexual and emotional alternative widely accepted in the "beat" culture) briefly occurred in *The Toilet* and *The Baptism* before emergent black nationhood and manhood rhetorically equated the "faggot" with feckless white impotence.

In the last two sections the prose resolves into what Jones terms "fast narrative," quick-moving fusions of violent action and troubled self-consciousness. Appearing in roles Jones knew all too well, the protagonist is presented successively as a college boy and a young Air Force man whose enfeebled middle-class psyche is assailed and finally impregnated by surges of blackness that he uneasily begins to comprehend as his birthright. In "The Rape" he coolly leads on his buddies to attempt the rape of a drunken prostitute, only to have his puerile bravado shattered by her powerful curses: "She screamed, and screamed, her voice almost shearing off our tender heads. The scream of an actual damned soul."

In the final section, sporting his uniform with "bright wings" and secretly harboring his pretentious literary elegance ("I'm beautiful. Stephen Dedalus"), he visits The Bottom—the poor black outskirts of a southern town where he expects easy women and a good time. Instead, he finds himself descending into the deepest region of the black underground, into a "culture of violence and foodsmells" where the drinking, dancing, screaming denizens abuse him as an "imitation white boy." The Bottom is the Purgatory where the redemption of his blackness will begin in earnest. After an initiation of vivid cursing and sexual humiliation at the hands of a challenging young prostitute, he can slip out into the night and begin to recognize The Bottom as his own legacy: "The place was so still, so black and full of violence. I felt myself." But he soon finds that he has made only partial expiation. On his ascent he is accosted by three "tall strong black boys" in the menacing spirit of "BLACK DADA NIHILISMUS." To them he is still "Mr. Half-white muthafucka," an interloper in their world, and they proceed to beat him into a limbo of unconsciousness. In this condition he has a mixed vision of reading books and weeping followed by "negroes" dancing around his body, leaving him to continue the struggle for the blackness revealed in him in The Bottom.

Jones told Kimberly Benston in a 1977 interview that in *Dante's Hell* he was "writing defensively," trying to escape the white literary influences of Creeley, Olson, and Ginsberg through a consciously improvisational prose impelled by both stream-of-consciousness and jazz techniques, but that the content, in Marxist retrospect, was now to be criticized "for celebrating the subjective and the idealistic."

Celebration of black feelings and black values, though, was precisely what the confluence of cultural and political forces required and brought about in the 1960's. Not only were Third World nations of color in the process of radical change—the Cultural Revolution in China, the struggles for national independence in Africa, and, closer to home, the examples of Fidel Castro and Che Guevara—but black liberation was being irresistibly preached in the United States itself, first by Malcolm X on behalf of Elijah Muhammad and the Nation of Islam, and subsequently through the open paramilitary posture of the Black Panthers.

In this turbulent atmosphere Jones came of age as a strikingly innovative dramatist, discovering the voice of the play as far more appropriate, at least at the time, than the poetry for his burgeoning sense of cultural and political need. The play, after all, was itself a public and social occasion of sorts, offering up a usually willing audience for immediate interaction with the instructive ideas and feelings of the playwright—potentially an instrument of political influence. Furthermore, in accordance with the aesthetics defined in *Blues People,* the play was far more hospitable than the silence of poetry to the extraliterary modes of black expression. As Jones progressed from the somewhat conventional strategies of his first plays into the more ritual and communal theater of his nationalist period, he increasingly integrated vocal strategies, performed music, and the motions of dance into the representation of black experience.

Jones's first one-act efforts, *The Toilet* and *The Baptism* (both produced in 1964), were tentative gropings away from the concerns of the poetry, *The Toilet* being more provocative and successful for its concentrated speech force and realistic setting. The action is structured through energetic vernacular dialogue and assertive physical gestures exchanged by nine black youths who, in the aggregate, constitute the voice of the play. They are preparing to beat up a white boy, James Karolis, in the high school bathroom because they suspect him of making homosexual overtures to their leader, Ray Foots. The combination of racial animosity and aggressive speech vigorously dramatizes the black dada strain, causing some viewers to resent the language as overly obscene, the action as excessively stark. Ed Bullins, on the other hand, saw the play's "radical ... depiction of Black people" as fitting and precise "in a deep and profoundly revolutionary sense," affirming his own first uncompromising efforts to dramatize the intensities of black life in *Clara's Ole Man* (1965). If the style of *The Toilet* is exemplary, the presentation of Ray's confused feelings—he returns to cradle Karolis' bloodied head after his buddies have left—does not, in Jones's opinion, sufficiently clarify the black youth's entrapment by white sentimentality.

The Baptism, although set in a pretentious Baptist church, with the action taking place around an altar rather than a urinal, proposes similar themes and ambivalences in the form of a somewhat attenuated allegory. Both plays, for all their differences, are about the precarious struggles of black youth toward manhood in white America. Percy, a sincere young boy, naively tries to assert values of "humanity" and "charity" in the face of tangled sexual motivations and religious ideals as represented by the Minister and his deluded flock. Ironically, the presence of the Homosexual, whose cynical insights constitute the sanest voice in the play, at times threatens to overshadow the parable of Percy's thwarted manhood. Even though the knightly young protagonist is able to slay the Minister and congregation with his "silver sword," thereby signifying the promise of wholesome manhood, he is summarily whisked away by the laconic Messenger from the white world (on whose jacket is stenciled "The Man"). At the play's end, Jones pointedly resurrects the black Homosexual from Percy's carnage, leaving him casually to drift off to "cruise Bickford's," the sole emasculated survivor of

Christian hypocrisy and "The Man's" destruction.

Dutchman and *The Slave* (both produced in 1964) are more extensive dramas that crystallize the confused boyhood feelings of Ray and Percy into the full-blown rage of Clay and Walker, adult men conscious of the nature of their victimization. With these two plays Jones in effect broke from the tyranny of individualism implicit in white cultural values and began to place his art in the service of a collective black freedom. From an artistic standpoint this is nowhere more clearly noted than in a 1964 essay entitled "The Revolutionary Theatre" (reprinted in *Home*), in which the African-derived aesthetic of *Blues People* is catalyzed by the mounting pressure of political necessity. Change, as a social and stylistic process reflected in the development of black music, is now transformed into a conception to be willfully embodied and actively asserted by the black playwright: "The Revolutionary Theatre," Jones begins, "should force change; it should be change." The first phase, the essay makes clear, will necessarily involve alterations of consciousness in white, but especially in black, audiences, exposing the hatred inside "black skulls" so that "White men will cower," while at the same time moving the black victims "to look at the strength in their minds and their bodies."

If Clay in *Dutchman,* along with Walker in *The Slave,* and Ray in *The Toilet,* "are all victims," as Jones rightfully contends, they are portrayed at different stages of self-realization. Clay, the malleable college boy and would-be "black Baudelaire," hardens into a fiery preacher who reveals the relationship of sane black truths to absurd white illusions—a condition that the manic and fearful Ray can only intuit, or that the dazed initiate of The Bottom can only begin to grasp.

Dutchman, like *Dante's Hell,* melds Western

myth and legend into a usable black logic, creating a psychodrama that is unquestionably the most lucid and powerful of Jones's early plays. The portentous overtones are established before the dialogue begins, Jones introducing the nether-world setting as an ironic contemporary inversion of the Flying Dutchman: "In the flying underbelly of the city. . . . Underground. The subway heaped in modern myth."

Well-dressed and bookish, Clay is the doomed passenger on the rushing underground railroad, guilty of no crime but his blackness. He is destined, despite his respectable appearance, to be the repeated victim of America's most infamous social ritual—the lynching. Lula, the keeper of the ritual, is his white seductress and executioner, a perverse Eve who boards the train "eating an apple, very daintily." At heart she is the dramatic realization of Crow Jane, the tawdry purveyor of a hip Western rationalism calculated to prevent the suppressed rage of black manhood from bursting into insurrection. Having dispatched Clay and ordered his body thrown off the car, she makes an appropriate notation in her "notebook" and prepares to begin the ritual anew with another unsuspecting victim. Resonant with the psychosexual tension that motivates racial fear, she is a far more effective agent of white destruction than the Messenger in *The Baptism*.

While the deterministic ritual frame gives the play a solemn weight, the process of Clay's emotional awakening and climactic self-possession creates the dominant impression. Throughout the first scene Lula is clearly in charge, characterizing Clay to his face as "a well-known type" and easily manipulating him into feeling both flattered by her sexual attention and vaguely uncomfortable at taunts about his spurious middle-class aspirations. He is surprised when, at the end of the scene, she knowingly jokes that beneath his three-button suit and striped tie there lurks a murderer.

At the beginning of scene 2, as Lula becomes graphically suggestive about a rendezvous at her apartment ("I lead you in, holding your wet hand gently in my hand . . ."), it is revealed that her central concern—and Jones's—has all along been the question of Clay's "manhood." Impatient with his self-control, she finally draws his latent aggressions into the open by viciously insulting him with racial slurs and stereotypes. His response, a tirade addressed to both Lula and the whites in the audience, is a classic example of the "theatre of assault" Jones calls for in the essay. Clay's rage and capacity for retaliation are no longer deflected into subregions of feeling or coded into lies and devices, but consciously savored and directly expressed. Slapping Lula twice, he reveals himself to be the murderer she predicted:

I could murder you now. Such a tiny ugly throat. I could squeeze it flat, and watch you turn blue, on a humble. For dull kicks. And all those weak-faced ofays squatting around here, staring over their papers at me. Murder them too. Even if they expected it. That man there . . . (POINTS TO WELL-DRESSED MAN) I could rip that *Times* right out of his hand, as skinny and middle-classed as I am, I could rip that paper out of his hand and just as easily rip out his throat. It takes no great effort. . . . You don't know anything except what's there for you to see. An act. Lies. Device. Not the pure heart, the pumping black heart. You don't even know that. And I sit here, in this buttoned-up suit, to keep myself from cutting all your throats. . . .

But in the final analysis he cannot murder, it seems—and, ironically, because his pretensions as a poet make him vulnerable to the seduction of language. Through Clay, Jones states the predicament of the artist-activist, presenting in its most reductive form the conflict between the ineffective rhetorical gesture and the extreme revolutionary act. If the Charlie Parkers and the Bessie Smiths could have "killed some white people," Clay asserts, they "wouldn't have needed that music." At the same time he dismisses his own poetry as "Some kind of bastard literature . . . all it needs is a simple knife thrust. Just let me bleed you, you loud whore, and one poem vanished."

Here Jones has found, in substance, a representative black voice that the early poetry could not authenticate, a voice convincing by its intentions and intensities more than by its manner. (Clay's middle-American speech has only intermittent Afro-American nuances, as in the opening "hi're you?" to Lula, his class status setting him considerably apart from the collective voice in *The Toilet*.) And here, also, the voice suddenly wearies. Unable to assume the full responsibility for action that his explosion into consciousness dictates, Clay fatally lapses into his false intellectual security: "Ahhh. Shit. But who needs it? I'd rather be a fool. Insane. Safe with my words, and no deaths, and clean, hard thoughts, urging me to new conquests."

The visceral dramatization of racial conflict did not prevent *Dutchman* from being widely acclaimed or from winning the 1964 Obie Award for best off-Broadway play. It is undeniably good theater in the best conventional sense, with fast-paced dialogue, superb emotional timing, and compelling interaction between the two antagonists.

The Slave, although less engaging as theater, marks a transition from the intense but indecisive aggression of Clay to a more explicit radical consciousness in the character of Walker Vessels, one-time poet turned insurrectionary. As the black antagonist confronts his white ex-wife, Grace, in her tastefully furnished living room, he is a leader of the black revolution already in progress. His credentials are established at the very start: He is Lula's fantasy realized, having already killed whites and now appearing to Grace simply as a "nigger murderer"; and he has adopted a militant pragmatism of "use," akin to the functionalism described in *Blues People,* in place of the safe words of Yeatsian poetry and romantic idealism. Essentially, even though Walker admits the possibility "that we might not win," the political act has triumphed over the aesthetic statement, symbolizing his freedom from enslavement to Western civilization. The longish first act is mostly an ironic exchange of revolutionary ideology and liberal platitudes between Walker and his white adversaries, projecting more the sense of a play of ideas rather than of characters.

Although Walker's basic function seems to be the clear articulation of political freedom, his visit to Grace is motivated by the additional and unresolved question of what to do about the children of their interracial marriage. The end of the short second act focuses almost entirely on the destiny of his two half-white daughters, to whom he is tied emotionally and biologically. Amid the explosions and rubble of the race war he tells the dying Grace that he has killed them, even keeps shouting it after she dies, as if to convince himself it is so; yet the play ends ambivalently as the wounded rebel stumbles offstage to the sounds of a child "crying and screaming as loud as it can." Even as a dedicated revolutionary Walker is still a victim, still bearing the legacy of Crow Jane through the painful reminder of his and her mixed-blood children. Walker's appearance in the prologue "dressed as an old field slave," and his return to that identity when the play closes, suggest that the forces of racial determinism are very much at work and that slavery is still claiming its victims. Indeed Walker is the epitome of Jones's belief, as stated in "Philistinism and the Negro Writer," that his works ought to "identify and delineate the slave, the black man—the man who remains separate from the mainstream."

Jones had for some time been on the verge of

leaving Hettie and their two daughters, the inevitable divorce coming in August 1965 after a period of mounting pressure and change of the sort autobiographically reflected in *Dutchman* and *The Slave*. The separation was also cultural. Jones cut all ties with the East Village by moving to Harlem (where he briefly took charge of the Black Arts Repertory Theatre/School) and then back to New Ark—as he renamed it—in late 1965. He had indeed come home, as the title of his 1966 social essays attests, completing his transformation from literary assimilationist to black separatist. Including pieces written between 1961 and 1966, *Home* is a graphic exposition of Jones's changing perspective, what he calls "the sense of movement—the struggle, in myself, to understand where and who I am, and to move with that understanding." The final essay, "The Legacy of Malcolm X" (1965), perhaps best summarizes his arrival at a nationalist sense of politics and art:

... we know for certain that the solution of the Black Man's problems will come only through Black National Consciousness. We also know that the focus of change will be racial. (If we *feel* differently, we have different *ideas*. Race is feeling. Where the body, and the organs come in. Culture is the preservation of these feelings in superrational to rational form. Art is one method of expressing these feelings and identifying the form, as an emotional phenomenon.) In order for the Black Man in the West to absolutely know himself it is necessary for him to see himself first as culturally separate from the white man.

Jones completed his personal reintegration into the black world by marrying a black woman, Sylvia Robinson, in August 1966 and subsequently taking the name Imamu Amiri Baraka—meaning spiritual leader, prince, and blessed one—an affirmation of his religious

dedication to black nationhood. He founded Spirit House, a community center for political and educational activities, and launched himself vigorously into the political destiny of black Newark, including experiences as varied as his trumped-up arrest and conviction (overturned in a retrial) during the 1967 Newark insurrections and his later extensive assistance in the 1970 election of Kenneth Gibson as the city's first black mayor.

Baraka remained artistically productive despite the increased demands of his political and community activities. The plays collected in *Four Black Revolutionary Plays* (1969) and the late poems in *Black Magic* (1969) represent the major thematic and stylistic changes brought about by nationalism. Baraka's most succinct statement of the radical aesthetic embodied in these works is in a 1964 essay entitled "Hunting Is Not Those Heads on the Wall" (reprinted in *Home*). It crystallizes for literary use many of the stylistic implications of music suggested in *Blues People*. In contrast with the static art product of the Western tradition (the artifact, musical score, book), black art prizes the "lightning awareness of the art process" (any given instance or interval of creating), for which he coins the term "Art-ing." The hunter-artist is fulfilled by the experience of hunting-creating, not by the mounted trophy or the completed poem. To capture the immediacy and motion implied in Art-ing, the writer must favor the participle, as opposed to the nouns and object images of Western literature: "The clearest description of now is the present participle, ... Walking is not past or future. Be-ing, the most complex, since it goes on as itself, as adjective-verb, and at the moment of."

This predicate concept is consistent with both the politics of revolutionary change and the improvisational flow of Afro-American music: "I speak of the *verb process*, the doing, the coming into being, the at-the-time-of. Which is why we think there is particular value in live music, contemplating the artifact as it arrives, listening to it emerge." As an instance of spoken language in process, the play itself was the closest literary approximation of Art-ing, while ritual structure—the sense of mythic inevitability and ceremonial ongoingness as conveyed in *Dutchman*—was one of the effective Art-ing strategies within the play. *Experimental Death Unit #1* (1964), in *Four Black Revolutionary Plays*, aptly reflects the head-hunting metaphor through the ritual appearance of black soldiers marching in cadence to drums. The play closes as they sever the heads of Duff and Loco, two perverted white artists in the "beat" mold who lust after blackness, and mount them on pikes. They do not covet the bloody members as trophies but display them as symbols of the execution that must be ceremonially repeated until all whiteness is destroyed. Unlike Clay and Walker, the disciplined soldiers firmly control their own fate as we see them in the process of collectively defining their history.

The significant work in *Four . . . Plays,* though, is *A Black Mass*. Written in 1965 and first performed in Newark in 1966, it is addressed to black audiences, as all his subsequent nationalist drama would be. It is, in effect, a play about Art-ing and is appropriately dedicated to "the brothers and sisters of the Black Arts." Unlike *Dutchman* its mythic structure is exclusively black, taking for its source Yacub's History, the demonology of the Nation of Islam (fully narrated in *The Autobiography of Malcolm X*), which openly attributes black suffering to the white Beast. Jacoub, a somewhat altered version of the original Yacub, is the type of the black artist, and his error is in misunderstanding the nature and function of creativity.

The first half of the one-act play expostulates the basic conflict between the humane and spiritual tenets of black art through the black magicians Nasafi and Tanzil, as opposed to the de-humanizing aesthetics of the West practiced by the thoughtless renegade Jacoub. He compulsively channels his creative powers into the production of what he egotistically perceives as original form rather than honoring the inherent value of the creative process itself; the end product is a beast he falsely believes can be educated to serve black mankind. Through the questionings of his fellow magicians, Jacoub is revealed to favor the principles of fixed time instead of prediction and ongoingness, of rational abstractions rather than emotional and spiritual energy, and of personal aggrandizement rather than a concern for the collective welfare of the black world. He is, for all intents and purposes, a black artist brought down by the self-serving values of Western individualism.

With the appearance of the inarticulate and soulless white Beast itself, the play shifts abruptly from a forum of aesthetic ideas to a vivid theatrical. Though sexless and sterile, the Beast paradoxically unleashes its destructiveness through a kind of rape by contamination, perpetuating itself by transforming black victims into white Beasts through mere touch. True to the tradition of the lustful incursions of white slave masters, the first victim is a woman, Tiila, whose metamorphosis into a "deadly cross between black and white" strongly suggests the biological-sexual quality of the Beast's violation. Just before he is himself assaulted, Jacoub acknowledges his hideous error and consigns the Beast and its cohorts to "the evil diseased caves of the cold," as they are in Yacub's History. The narrator concludes the play by asserting that the beasts "are still loose in the world" and instructing that they must be exterminated by the Jihad, a holy war to be waged against the white world.

As the title implies, the play itself partakes of ritual, opening as the three magicians conclude a mass celebrating the black arts. The action then unfolds to expose the betrayal of this ritual, the revolutionary message being that black art has been, and is, vulnerable to destructive white influences. The artistic integrity of the play itself is preserved, though, by an infusion of music throughout the entire production. The stage directions particularly call for a performance by Sun-Ra, whose music is the essence of predicate motion, "the flow of *is*," says Baraka in "The Changing Same," a 1966 essay in *Black Music* (1967). At first the soothing "Music of eternal concentration and wisdom" as the mass is in progress, the sounds modulate to the more familiar rhythmic tensions of contemporary black music as Jacoub's treachery begins, "swelling, making sudden downward swoops, screeching." The ongoing music is powerfully present, not as mere background but as an integral part of the play's ritual quality. Music and language are fused, the formal intonations of speech enriched by Afro-American tonalities as the musicians punctuate the spoken lines in call-and-response fashion with their improvised phrasings. Upon the entry of the Beast, the script calls for "Sun-Ra music of shattering dimension," the screeching instruments and screams of the victims eliding into an amalgam of sound. This responsive interweaving of music and language splendidly epitomizes the predicate quality of Art-ing that the bare play script could not by itself achieve, an aesthetic strategy Baraka applied with even greater effect in *Slave Ship* two years later.

Two other plays, *Great Goodness of Life* (1966) and *Madheart* (1966), are instructional allegories without the informing musical cotext, although background music fades intermittently in and out of the dialogue in *Madheart*. Subtitled *A Coon Show, Great Goodness of Life* is a convoluted psychodrama about a bourgeois black father, Court Royal, who acquiesces in the execution of his insurrectionary son. The play confronts the audience's racial integrity with the emotional impact of this be-

trayal. More and more the plays took on this sort of didactic purpose, not simply showing victims but teaching black audiences the precise and often painful nature of their condition. "Art must serve to illuminate and educate," Baraka says in "Work Notes—'66," in *Raise Race Rays Raze: Essays Since 1965* (1971). The anatomy of Court Royal's buffered consciousness and the harsh exposure of the flawed Mother and Sister in *Madheart* typify Baraka's educational intentions, however disturbing to the playgoer: "Each aspect of black life must have light shed on it, must be analyzed must make the pain of recognizing the exact place of our crucifixion, the exact sloth and cowardliness, the precise ugliness and ignorance."

J-E-L-L-O (written in 1965), a ribald satire of the Jack Benny show in which Rochester instructively comes into possession of his blackness, was to have been a fifth play in the collection but was suppressed by the publisher as potentially libelous. In other plays of the late 1960's Baraka heeds his own call, stated in "What the Arts Need Now" (1967), in *Raise Race,* for "plays of all instance. Filling in and extending so-called 'reality.' . . . a post-American form. An afterwhiteness . . . where history is absolutely meaningful and contemporary." The plays have moved away almost entirely from any focus on palpable character, as witnessed in the figures of Clay and Walker, to key in on conditions and issues dramatically reified as Jacoub and Court Royal. *Police* (1968), *Home on the Range* (1968), and *The Death of Malcolm X* (1969) all deal with specific local and national black circumstances, unequivocally drawing racial-emotional lines in their explanation and interpretation of black reality.

Baraka's quintessential nationalist play, though, is *Slave Ship,* first published in *Negro Digest* in 1967, then separately in 1969, and reprinted in *The Motion of History and Other Plays* (1978). It is a powerful instance of what he defines in a 1967 essay entitled "The Need for a Cultural Base to Civil Rites & Bpower Mooments," published in *Raise Race,* as the prime function of black art: " . . . to get people into a consciousness of black power, what it is, by emotional example" rather than by "dialectical lecture." This is achieved in the play by an almost complete subordination of individual character and spoken dialogue to an irresistible vocal-musical rendering of the collective black presence. Subtitled *A Historical Pageant, Slave Ship* has as its ritual basis the intensity of expression and feeling born of the horrifying Middle Passage. African drum rhythms are combined with the screams of people torturously pressed into the hold of a ship, an experience of pure sound conveyed in total darkness during the first third of the pageant—the portentous historical beginnings of the Afro-American underworld vision. The audience is prepared at the onset to feel the pressing reality by hearing it, not by seeing it. Baraka orchestrates the sounds of Africa's abduction and bondage in the elaborate stage directions:

African Drums like the worship of some Orisha. Obatala. Mbwanga rattles of the priests. BamBam BamBamBoom BoomBoom BamBam.

Rocking of the slave ship, in darkness, without sound. But smells. Then sound. Now slowly, out of blackness with smells and drums staccato, the hideous screams. All the women together, scream. AAAAAIIIIIEEEEEEEEEEEEE.

The fragmentary expressions of fear, cursing, and appeals to African deities are bonded into emotional coherence by the ritualized screaming that marks the emergence of the black voice in the New World. The screaming then gives way to a "deathly patient" humming followed by strains of spirituals as the play shifts to its second phase, depicting slavery in America.

Here, lighting and dialogue are more pronounced, revealing the split consciousness of slave victims, some of whom shuffle and dance for their masters while others, like Nat Turner, plot uncompromising revolt against the white "Beast." In the final and contemporary phase of the pageant, the predominant sound is the aggressively clear screaming of a "new-sound" saxophone overriding the garbled nonsense speech of an integrationist preacher. Throughout, the African screams and voicings, especially through the recurrent motif of a mother calling for her lost child, Moshake, intersect the shifting sounds and historical changes as a persistent reminder of the enduring African spirit.

The pageant, in essence a processional of emotions, closes by celebrating the power of a unified black consciousness. All the members of the cast come together in a triumphant communion of Afro-American singing ("When We Gonna Rise") and dancing ("a new-old dance, Boogalooyoruba line") in a prelude to the eradication of whiteness. As a community in the fullest command of its expressive powers, they converge upon and kill the integrationist preacher and his white "boss," as if the political act could be accomplished by the very sounds and motions of Art-ing itself. In a final gesture of communal instruction, Baraka plays to the participatory expectations of his black audience by having them join with the cast in a continuation of the dance. When "the party reaches some loose improvisation," he jars the relaxed consciousness by throwing the severed head of the preacher onto the dance floor and dousing the lights. The final interruption and abrupt immersion in blackness force the playgoer to be aware that the struggle continues beyond the bounds of the play. In its fusion of terse speech fragments and vocal-musical improvisation into a unified play script, *Slave Ship* is significantly advanced in conception over the interacting dialogue text and musical performance of *A Black*

Mass. With the added dimensions of dance and audience participation, it stands as Baraka's most sustained and effective work of Art-ing.

"Sabotage," "Target Study," and "Black Art," the three books that make up *Black Magic* (1969), represent Baraka's continuing poetic activity between 1961 and 1967, while he was writing plays and flexing into nationalism. These poems begin (thematically if not chronologically) where *The Dead Lecturer* leaves off, developing toward predicate formulations of black spiritual integrity of the sort symbolized by the magicians Nasafi and Tanzil in *A Black Mass*. In the introduction Baraka dismisses his early poetry as preoccupied with suicide and death, "a cloud of abstraction and disjointedness, that was just whiteness." In contrast the poems of *Black Magic,* especially in the third book, strive for the "willpower to build" beyond whiteness in order to "force this issue," as he puts it, of transcendent black spirituality.

"Sabotage" (1961–1963), the first book, is a slow recovery from the old moribund misperceptions, the poet gathering his energies for the final breaking of all ties to the "superstructure of filth Americans call their way of life." In the third poem, "A POEM SOME PEOPLE WILL HAVE TO UNDERSTAND," the necessity for blotting out his "Watercolor ego" and "All the pitifully intelligent citizens / I've forced myself to love" is crisply stated: "Will the machinegunners please step forward?" His poetry still feels inert, though, and the actual breaking away is not easy. In "Citizen Cain" Baraka must prod himself: "Roi, finish this poem, . . . / . . . Your time is up / in this particular feeling. In this particular throb of meaning. / Roi, baby, you blew the whole thing." Although in "Letter to E. Franklin Frazier" he is isolated in a room ". . . where memory / stifles the present," he nevertheless sees himself, as he says in "THE PEOPLE BURNING," at a decisive and energizing turning point: " . . . It is

choice, now, and / the weight is specific and personal." He must turn the old death fixations into new life motions, the whiteness into blackness. The decadent white world and its hapless literature are virulently focused in "Sabotage" through metaphors of sexuality, tastelessness, and increasing anti-Semitic innuendo—"poets imagining / they are Shakespeare's hardon, . . . / . . . eating / into the strophe yard huge like empty Dachau. . . ."

There are indexes of wholesome change, though, the signs of personal and artistic rebirth parallel to the insights gleaned from *Blues People.* In "LEADBELLY GIVES AN AUTOGRAPH," music is exact and nurturing, opening up avenues of poetic expression. The poet is now assured by "The possibilities of music. . . . / . . . that scripture of rhythms," his voice no longer meek as it was in "Rhythm & Blues":

A strength to be handled by giants.

The possibilities of statement. I am saying,
    now,
what my father could not remember
to say. What my grandfather
was killed
for believing.

Foremost among the possibilities of poetic statement would be the bridging of personal feeling and broader social understanding. In a white-dominated world where everything is owned and objectified—God, people, time, language, as Baraka says in "Square Business"—his function would be to seek wholeness through subjectivity, through the expression of black feelings and spirit. In "The Bronze Buckaroo," at the end of "Sabotage," he is one of the "mutineers" in motion toward a more complete blackness, "Half way up the hill . . . / . . . and standing."

"Target Study" (1963–1965), Baraka says in the introduction, is in a more active mode, "trying to really study, like bomber crews do the soon to be destroyed cities. Less passive now, less uselessly 'literary.'" A twelve-line poem entitled "Ration" succinctly captures the spirit: "Banks must be robbed, / ... / The money must be taken / and used to buy weapons." As in "Sabotage," much energy is spent perverting shopworn symbols of American whiteness. The response here is more specifically keyed to avenge Jim Crowism, as opposed to the earlier exclusive repudiations of Crow Jane. Homosexual epithets abound (art is a "hairy" phallus, old artist friends "white drifting fairies," Uncle Sam "a queer," God "the baldhead faggot"), blatantly offensive sexual missiles aimed by the bombardier-poet to obliterate the presumption of white male omnipotence, establishing in its place a vision of manhood in accordance with the masculine dynamics of Black Power in the 1960's. Baraka's attitude reflects nothing more or less than the narrow sexual politics of the time, a racial rivalry perceived largely as a crisis of manhood. The opening poem, "Numbers, Letters," features the lean voice of a new man no longer " ... freakin' off / with white women, hangin' out / with Queens, ..." Unencumbered, he can speak straightforwardly, " ... Say what you mean, ... / ... and be strong / about it." The hesitations of "Sabotage" are all but gone:

I'm Everett LeRoi Jones, 30 yrs old.
A black nigger in the universe. A long breath
     singer,
wouldbe dancer, strong from years of fantasy
and study. All this time then, for what's
     happening
now. . . .

With this renewed sense of self, the poet urges the underground feelings of black manhood into visible realization. In "Ready Or Not," the bold print screams "BLACK MAN DREAMING OF MURDER / GET THE SHIT AND MEET ME / SOMEPLACE," as though addressing the Clays and Walkers of the 1964 plays. More and more reading his poems before receptive black audiences, Baraka had scant concern for the survival of "Ready Or Not" as a printed artifact. He implies in the final lines that the poem's chief function is the creation of consciousness at the moment of utterance: "This poem now has said / what it means, left off / life gone seconds ago". Some of the poems near the end of "Target Study" carp against the limits of written form. "Blank" states the ideal alternative of "live sound and image," formulations more readily embodied in the voices and gestures of the play. "THREE MOVEMENTS AND A CODA" exhorts open insurrection, the final lines defining the poem as an incomplete word-song awaiting its consummate formation through the extraliterary participation of the reader-listener: "These are the words of lovers. / Of dancers, of dynamite singers / These are songs if you have the / music"—no end punctuation but, rather, the expectation of the poem merging into whatever action might be induced in the responsive listener.

Such appeals to the essence of black manner and feeling culminate in "A Poem for Black Hearts." The poet elevates black self-identification and potential for action to mythic proportions in the name of Malcolm X, a contemporary black hero already a legend: "For Great Malcolm a prince of the earth, let nothing in us rest / until we avenge ourselves for his death. . . ."

In "Black Art" (1965–1966), the final and most substantial book in *Black Magic,* the reach toward a black spiritual essence is even more pronounced—the white madness almost fully displaced by the new black magic. The opening poem, "SOS," sets the prescriptive tone for collective integrity: "calling all black people, come in, black people, come / on in." Having summoned his audience, the poet-teacher firmly establishes in "Black Art"—one of Baraka's most often quoted poem-manifestos—the principle of what one might call the living poem, the poem indistinguishable from the natural world and, especially, from the live gesture of black assertion: "Poems are bullshit unless they are / teeth or trees or lemons piled / on a step. . . . / words of the hip world live flesh & / coursing blood. . . ." Clay's imprecation to Lula, that drawing her blood would cause one poem to vanish, is now the imperative aesthetic: " . . . We want 'poems that kill.' / Assassin poems, Poems that shoot / guns. . . ." In this terroristic manner, the poem represents the height of Baraka's anti-Semitism (" . . . dagger poems in the slimey bellies / of the owner-jews . . ."), with ethnocentric scattershot aimed at "wops," Irish cops, and non-black Negroes (" . . . girdlemamma mulatto bitches") as well. These are to be poems of exorcism, the purging of whiteness stated in literal terms in order to restructure black consciousness.

Ideally, the people themselves are the self-affirming artists, their lives the Art-ing:

> . . . Let Black People understand
> that they are the lovers and the sons
> of lovers and warriors and sons
> of warriors Are poems & poets &
> all the loveliness here in the world

Black statement is not to be an arty, individuated fact, but a collective participatory expression of poet and audience alike: "And Let All Black People Speak This Poem / Silently / or LOUD," he concludes.

The power Baraka wants to draw upon is perhaps best characterized in the essay "The Changing Same," in *Black Music*. As always, music is the exemplary medium, evidencing what the poet calls "the will of the expression." The musician-artist is in effect a priest whose sacred duty is to evoke spirituality: "This phenomenon is always at the root in Black Art, the worship of spirit—or at least the summoning of or by such force." In "Little Brown Jug" Baraka expresses the absolute equation of black selfhood, the song, and divinity—himself and all black people as the instrument (the little brown jug), the song, and the spirit force: " . . . Companion, of melody / rhythm / turned around heart runs / climbed & jumped screaming / WE ARE GODS, . . ." Several of the poems in "Black Art" are conceived as chants, invocations of spiritual energy—for example, "Sacred Chant for the Return of Black Spirit and Power." Where once "White evil" had prevailed (like the love once intellectually conceived as twisted to "evol" in *Suicide Note*), now the poet conjures positive spiritual inversions through the magical word power of the chant: "To turn their evil backwards / is to / live." So too has the once-evil Anglo-sun been restored and deified in the new righteous way of life, the poet proclaiming to his wife in "Stirling Street September" that " . . . for the sake of, at the lust of / pure life, WE WORSHIP THE SUN."

Some poems, like the aptly titled "Form Is Emptiness," press poetic convention to the limit in attempting to force the issue of spirituality. After a monotonous printed extension of chanted vowel sounds to evoke the gods of color (Rah, Damballah, Allah), the poet can only affirm the total inadequacy of the fixed poem to represent infinite deity: "is not word / is no lines / no meanings." In "Vowels 2," though, the extended chant is invigorated with images of motion and sound that simulate the ecstatic freedom of spiritual consummation, "the energy / the force" of godhead percussively summoned into emotional and bodily sensation by the preacher-poet. Difficult to read silently, the lines can be effectively sung out to project the rhythmic spell of a sermon whose text is black freedom. The poem that perhaps most gracefully captures the predicate principles of "Hunting Is Not Those Heads on the Wall" is "Death is the beginning of a new form." Black selfhood is offered in the ultimate form—the "new form"—of infinite motion working time-lessly toward complete self-possession and spiritual freedom. Participial forms combine with music images to create a flowing predicate style:

> of doing thinking feeling being
> forever endless in the instant
> we lean transformed into energy
> transformed into blurrd motion
> all that is transformed specks of fire
>
> . . .
>
> resolved in the silent beating of forever
>   divinity
> you are a portion of this
> you are the total jazzman
> a note on the horn
>
> . . .
>
> the universe is close to your lips
> blow it out

The poem collections following *Black Magic* show an intensification of spiritual concern and an emphasis on African origins rather than any further evolution in style. Baraka had come under the influence of Maulana Karanga's Kawaida doctrine in 1967, the full effects of which can be seen in the poetry of *In Our Terribleness* (1970) and *It's Nation Time* (1970). Carefully outlined in *Raise Race,* Kawaida is a program for black nationhood rooted in a seven-point African value system (unity, self-determination, collective work and responsibility, cooperative economics, purpose, creativity, and faith) that constitutes for Baraka a "religious creed." Although he soon abandoned Kawaida for Marxism, he saw its organizational features then as a distinct advance over the inspirational but unstructured teachings of Malcolm X. *In Our Terribleness* acknowledges Karanga as

"the master teacher" and at one point specifically directs that the "change" to nationhood take place by adhering to the seven principles. The main thrust of the poetry is toward a prophetic black future, sweeping the reader along in surges of black talk and preachment that make only occasional pro forma references to the white Beast—a romantic fusion of secular style and holy revelation extolling blackness.

The physical characteristics of *In Our Terribleness* as a book-artifact are in curious static tension with Baraka's predicate aesthetics. The title page is a hard, reflective silver, the 145 glossy leaves conspicuously unpaginated and black-bordered, the text in large, bold print and generously spaced. The poetry is combined with forty-three photographs by Fundi (Billy Abernathy), sometimes to caption the pictures but mostly unfolding as a dominant and independent sermon on *Some elements and meaning in black style,* as the book is subtitled. Baraka strains a bit to introduce the fixed images as Art-ing—"PAPERMOTION / PITCHAS . . ." he calls them—perhaps a tentative expression of his interest in cinematic techniques that influenced the plays of his Marxist period. The title itself symbolizes in poetic black language the integrity of style and culture that distinguishes black life for Baraka, an expansion of the Afro-American sense of the word "bad" as meaning good in the tested tradition of inverting white values: "Since there is a 'good' we know is bullshit, . . . / . . . We will be, / definitely, bad, bad, as a mother-fucker." Terribleness, then, is the ultimate goodness: "Our terribleness is our survival as beautiful beings." It is the essence of black life-style as expressed in the poem "LECTURE PAST DEAD CATS," the people exalted as a " . . . nation of super hip swift motional creation / . . . tone carriers of glowing magic" and the poet himself honored to be "one of the priests."

In "PRAYER FOR SAVING" Baraka exhorts the people to "Survive and Defend" the entire black tradition, evoking heroes and artists from Ray Robinson and Huey Newton to Claude McKay and John Coltrane, images to be immortalized in the collective black consciousness as "the together revelation of humanhood." He is most self-consciously Imamu (the title of Muslim priest or imam conferred upon him by Karanga) in the visionary poem "ALL IN THE STREET," where Allah speaks through the agency of the poet: " ... I am a / vessel, a black priest interpreting / the present and future for my people."

The same role is more confidently fulfilled in *It's Nation Time,* a compact, three-part service proclaiming the path to black nationhood. The first part, "The Nation Is Like Ourselves," is a litany urging unconverted "assimilados" to return to their blackness, preparatory to the inspirational message in "Sermon for Our Maturity." His congregation is now "the suns children / Black creatures of grace-" growing and expanding into an "Afro" space of "angelic definition." Baraka closes in the title poem, "It's Nation Time," by pressing the people to translate their newfound spiritual maturity into the necessary actions for building the black nation in the here and now.

This was the literary culmination of Baraka's nationalism, the final measure of the distance traveled from insurgent son to spiritual father—from Clay and Walker to the impassioned collective voice of *Slave Ship* and *In Our Terribleness.* As one of the prophet-teachers, Baraka also had a major hand in preparing the book that has become the primer of the Black Arts Movement, coediting *Black Fire: An Anthology of Afro-American Writing* (1968) with Larry Neal. A selection of essays, poetry, short fiction, and drama, it is a chronicle of 1960's nationalism comparable in importance with Alain Locke's documentation of the Harlem Renaissance in *The New Negro* (1925).

Abrupt as it might seem, Baraka's move to Marxism in the early 1970's was by no means a sudden turnabout. It was, rather, a continuation as well as an abandonment of certain facets of black ideology consistent with his sense of art and life as "The Changing Same." He is the same Amiri Baraka, but changed in discarding the religious pretense of the title Imamu; still a fervent spokesman for black people, but now with a worldwide revolutionary vision for all oppressed people; still an insurrectionary, but organizing against the international evils of capitalism and imperialism rather than the national tyranny of racism; still an artist of intensity, but keyed to structured gestures of political fact rather than the spiraling imagination of spirituality; still deeply committed, but to the discipline demanded by the "science of Marxism-Leninism-Mao Tse-tung Thought" rather than the program of Kawaida.

Although in the poem "HEGEL," from "Sabotage," he belittled the tedium of " ... trying to understand / the nightmare of economics," he subsequently described (in a published chapter from his unpublished 1973 autobiography "Six Persons") his own political conversion in hip Afro-Hegelian-Marxist terms: "But the class struggle yeh, then suddenly in 1971, and 2, and 3, fat gibber lip skunky funky declare the opening of the nigro pseudobourgeois hot foots.... Yeh its called, a 'qualitative leap.'" Although as late as 1969, Baraka was rejecting Marxist-Leninist "white ideology" as merely a violent form of integration, by 1973, under the influence of such African Marxists as Amilcar Cabral and Sekou Touré, we see his first distinctly postnationalist poem in "Afrika Revolution." The mother culture is no longer mythologized—made a "static absolute," as he would say self-critically of *Blues People.* Instead he enjoins African people all over the world "to make Revolution" against capitalism and imperialism. He sees change in political rather than metaphysical or aesthetic terms, the poetic voice frequently spare and didactically earnest: "The world must be changed, split open & changed / Transformed, turned upside down."

Baraka had altered his role from that of priest to the Leninist concept of the advanced worker, the socialist poet-instructor dedicated to "the education and organization of the proletariat." His literary subject is henceforth to be *Hard Facts*, as the poetry written during 1973–1975 is titled, not the ritual celebration of black magic. Instead of the former concern with "how you sound," he now stresses content, what you say. "Poetry," the introduction to *Hard Facts* begins, "is saying something about reality. It reflects the sayer's place in the production process, his or her material life and values." Following fundamental Marxism, Baraka conceives of himself as an artist-worker raising his audience's political and historical understanding of material reality. Moving from the concentrated if narrow sense of responsibility to black nationalism, he now accepts the broad premise of "a dynamic coalition of forces" against all forms of oppression. The keynote struck in most of his socialist poetry and drama is the pressing need to organize "a new revolutionary Marxist-Leninist party."

In the aggregate, *Hard Facts*—along with most of Baraka's subsequent Marxist poetry—addresses a black audience more than a multinational proletariat, his main concern continuing to be the political readjustment of black sensibilities. "WHEN WE'LL WORSHIP JESUS" speaks in a distinctly black voice charged with the energy of a preacher's rhetorical emphasis. It is a simple call to replace the anodyne of religion with a belief in science, knowledge, and revolution. Some poems isolate singular instances of black political regression, the prostitution of black integrity to bourgeois materialism and power by progressive people who in fact only represent the illusion of

change. These "attack pieces," as Baraka calls them in the introduction, are reminiscent of the corrosive voice in "Target Study." The satirical obscenities directed at poet Nikki Giovanni in "NIGGY THE HO" (transparently "Nikki the Whore") and the flaying of the mayor of Newark in "GIBSON" are exemplary. Even the hero of *Dutchman*, "Killed / by a white woman / on a subway / in 1964," is not allowed to rest in martyred peace. In "CLAY," that hero is derisively revived and then dispatched as "the first negro congressman" from Missouri: "we're not saying / that being dead / is the pre / requisite / for this honor / but it certainly helped make him / what he is / today"—an allusion to Congressman William Clay from St. Louis as well as a wry comment, no doubt, on the bourgeois acclaim accorded the play.

The most inventive piece of political instruction, one focused more on ideology than attitude, is "THE DICTATORSHIP OF THE PROLETARIAT." The poem is structured to desensitize the capitalist worker to the negative propaganda associated with the title phrase: "you hear that, the dictatorship / of the proletariat, and be scared / think somebody gonna hold you back / hold you down, . . ." The poem then encourages a correct resensitizing through clarification and gentle but firm repetition— ". . . Speak / of / the dictatorship until you understand it . . ."—concluding:

This is the dictatorship of the proletariat
the total domination of society by the working
    class

you need to hear that
you need to talk about that
you gonna have to fight for that

the dictatorship of the proletariat
think about that
the dictatorship of the proletariat

A lengthy explanatory passage near the end of the poem perhaps best exemplifies what Baraka called (in the 1977 interview with Benston) the "struggle form" he was attempting to realize in his poetry. An arhythmic discourse on proletariat rule, the unadorned lines in effect constitute a prose commentary patterned after the "short essay form" of the Chinese revolutionary democrat Lu Hsün—a form Baraka describes as a combination of "poetry and revolutionary observation."

Already a prolific essayist, as *Home* and *Raise Race* attest, Baraka feels more strongly than ever that the latitude of the essay and its emphasis on content are particularly suited, as he says, "to the kind of daily struggle I'm engaged in." And he is fully aware that this preference implies a relinquishing of at least some predicate quality in the rhythms of his poetry: "—I think the essay form could correspond to music *in places,* at a given moment. But I think it's less interested in the overall *sound* of words and more interested in *what* it's saying." This conscious tendency toward what might be called selected moments of expository poetry, however repressive it might seem to some of Baraka's more aesthetic-minded critics, is in some ways but a reversal of an earlier stylistic current one can observe in the infusion of poetry into the prose of *Dante's Hell, Tales,* and *Raise Race.*

Other poems have ideologically suggestive titles like "DAS KAPITAL" and "CLASS STRUGGLE," but concentrate on satiric description or poetic narrative to convey impressions of political reality rather than the clarification of doctrine. Instances of struggle form are limited to brief rhetorical calls for a revolutionary consciousness, as in "TODAY" and "RED AUTUMN." A central image is transformed yet again in "A POEM FOR DEEP THINKERS," the sun spiritualized in "Black Art" now but a symbol of romantic dissociation. Depicted as "Skymen," the nationalists are " . . . blinded by / sun, and their own images of things. . . . / . . . a buncha skies bought the loop-

dieloop program from the elegant babble of / the ancient minorities"—a sharp reassessment of his own Afro-American elegance. Baraka wants instead to write a "song of the skytribe walking the earth." The poem closes with a political revision of the salutation "hey my man, what's happening," the correct rejoinder hereafter to be: "meet you on the battlefield / . . . meet you on the battlefield." *Hard Facts* ends with a predicate call "FOR THE REVOLUTIONARY OUTBURST BY BLACK PEOPLE." Here the energies of black style and political expression converge in revolutionary climax: " . . . a spectrum of motion, . . . / We are poised in gradual ascendence to that rising" which is to be, as the poem concludes, "The violent birth process / of Socialism!"

Baraka's main dramatic work of the 1970's, a full-length play called *The Motion of History* (1975–1976), also conceptualizes motion as the political process leading inevitably to revolution. The play appears in *The Motion of History and Other Plays* (1978) with a shorter piece entitled *S-1* (1976)—after the abbreviated designation for the Criminal Justification, Revision and Reform Act, legislation Baraka interprets as dangerously repressive—and the previously published *Slave Ship.* In the introduction to the collection he mentions two earlier and still unpublished plays important to his development as a dramatist: *A Recent Killing* (1964), "about the U.S. Air Force," and *The Sidnee Poet Heroical* (subsequently published in 1979), which he says is "characterized by much petty bourgeois cultural nationalism." The two postnationalist plays in the volume, like the new poetry, "are vehicles for a simple message" aimed at the worker audience: "viz., the only solution to our problems . . . is revolution! And that revolution, socialist revolution, is inevitable."

Baraka is now concerned, as he told Benston, with a "theatre of ideas" that emphasizes an understanding of history rather than the "ahistorical worldview" fostered by his ritual drama, although in varying degrees such plays as *Dutchman* and, especially, *The Slave* and *A Black Mass* show an earlier need to deal with ideas as well. He acknowledges the influence of Bertolt Brecht, whose concept of "epic theatre" as a narrative social process arousing recognition and action is hospitable to both the nationalist plays and Baraka's present Marxist theater. Baraka sees the major change, as he says in the introduction, to be one from "the perceptual to the rational," from "the feeling and rage against oppression to the beginnings of actual scientific analysis of this oppression. . . ."

The Motion of History presents an analysis of two issues: the deliberate fostering of hostility between black and white workers by capitalism (an issue explored at length in the socialist writings of W. E. B. Du Bois) and the "recurrent rebellion" endemic to the history of the United States. Both the title and the action reflect Baraka's renewed sense of historical change through his engagement with dialectical materialism. "I began to understand very clearly," he explains to Benston, "that change is constant . . . that ultimately the motion of society and humanity is always onward and upward, from ignorance to knowledge, from the superficial to the in-depth and the detailed."

This is precisely dramatized in the play by the transformation of two apolitical emblematic characters, blandly designated Black and White, whose hedonism and ignorance buffer them from social injustice. In a quick montage of opening scenes (incorporating a movie screen and cinematic images, a technique used throughout the play), they suddenly merge into the stream of history by becoming James E. Chaney and Andrew Goodman, two of the three civil rights workers lynched in Mississippi in 1964. Act II moves back in time to the Hayes-Tilden compromise of 1876 that ended the Reconstruction, and from there to Bacon's Re-

bellion of 1676 in Jamestown, Virginia (represented as a spontaneous coalition of white indentured servants and black slaves rising up against the colonial ruling class). Curving forward toward the present in a kaleidoscope of episodes portraying black rebels in the 1800's (Nat Turner, Gabriel Prosser, Denmark Vesey, Harriett Tubman), Act III culminates in John Brown's insurrection at Harper's Ferry.

In the final and lengthy fourth act, the characters Black and White resurface to undergo their final changes in the strife-torn motions of the twentieth century. Their former bourgeois indifference is now a confused but earnest concern as they retrieve their different yet related heritages as Afro-American slave and Irish-American immigrant. The ultimate motion is their qualitative leap, embracing Marxism and fully clarifying the meaning of their common history of oppression under capitalism. Thus they assume a completely formed identity and naming as Lenny Nichols and Richie Moriarty, socialist factory workers united in the organization of a revolutionary Marxist party.

Baraka has moved from historical pageantry in *Slave Ship* to historical interpretation in *The Motion of History,* stressing that destiny is to be controlled by actions based on disciplined understanding rather than by confrontive rage. He now displaces separatism with a call for political unity among workers who understand that racism, black or white, is a capitalist strategy of control—not an acceptable rationale for determining human values. There is much explanatory monologue mixed with the dialogue, a play text more important for its content than for its style. The ultimate purpose is to clarify, through the example of Lenny and Richie, the need for a socialist revolution.

To this didactic end Baraka intercedes with the audience during the intermission after Act III to ask what they have learned from the play so far. His firm political hand always in evidence now, the stage directions call for "at least one plant in the audience" to guarantee the "correct" answers—that is, that the ruling class attempts "to keep the working-class people divided along national and racial lines," and that change will only come from "violent revolution" by the people. More structured than the participation improvised at the end of *Slave Ship,* this exchange is designed to raise consciousness through intellectual pressure rather than emotional shock. In the final scene, a meeting of the Red Congress, Baraka wants the audience to distinguish between the work of the artist and the work of the party activist, between the simulated reality of the play and the material reality in which they actually live:

RICHIE. . . . you know there's people like we was . . . looking at this like it was on a screen or on a stage. Got reality draped around them and won't step down into it and grab it up whole.

LENNY. That's what the party's for, to mobilize the great masses of people, to be a guide, a mobilizer, a leader, a clarifier, a fighter . . .

The strong voice of a woman concludes *The Motion of History,* anticipating an increasingly significant female dimension in Baraka's plays. The opening address to the Red Congress, delivered by Juanita Martinez, delegate from Puerto Rico (who otherwise has no role in the play), is the closing summons to the play viewer. In the struggle form of a short essay, her speech is Baraka's unabashed call for a "revolutionary party" based on "the correct political line" of "Marxism-Leninism-Mao Tse-tung Thought."

While *The Motion of History* interprets American rebellion as a precedent for accepting revolution, *S-1* (1976) is a more compact and somewhat slow one-act play that presents characters with a fully realized historical consciousness. Lil and Red Hall, black members of the Revolutionary People's Union (RPU), pick up where Lenny and Richie leave off, analyzing and actively resisting capitalist oppression in 1976. Numerous scenes take the form of party-line speeches, formal political debates, informal discussions, media interviews, and news broadcasts—a kind of running theatrical struggle form, a dialectic whose main purpose is to interpret the Criminal Justification, Revision and Reform Act as a fascist instrument of repression. The play ends with Red in jail (charged with treason under the deliberately vague provisions of the bill), proselytizing his fellow prisoners to accept "the formation of the party," while Lil and the RPU cadre attend a secret meeting of Marxist-Leninists preparing to unite as one central "Revolutionary Marxist-Leninist Communist Party." The pro forma presence of Juanita Martinez in *The Motion of History* is extended into the characterization of Lil Hall, who is equal with her husband as party strategist and political interpreter of events throughout *S-1.* She also provides the political theme song "America" that opens and threads through *S-1* (subtitled *A Play with Music in 26 Scenes*).

In a theater of ideas, music must supplement the play script "as background, to heighten the emotions . . . which is old, classic theater," Baraka now believes. It can no longer predominate as the direct expression of feeling inextricably linked to the text, as in *A Black Mass* or *Slave Ship.* The Liberation Singers in *S-1* who perform Lil's song are no doubt patterned after the Advanced Workers, a Newark group Baraka had recently been providing with political lyrics.

The protagonists of Baraka's Marxist plays are advanced workers like Lenny and Richie or Lil and Red. They function not as singular personalities but as representative commentators to enlighten the audience according to the discipline of Marxist-Leninist thought. Donna, the featured advanced worker of *What Was the Re-*

lationship of the Lone Ranger to the Means of Production? (1978), first printed in *Selected Plays and Prose of Amiri Baraka/LeRoi Jones* (1979), represents in part Baraka's acknowledgment of the issue of women's oppression in the larger context of the struggle against capitalism. A short satire set in a factory, the play is built around a continuous one-scene dialectical exchange between Donna, the no-nonsense voice of clarity, and the Masked Man and his chauvinist underling Tuffy, burlesques of the capitalist factory owner and his conspiratorial ally, the union bureaucrat.

This theatrical Lone Ranger is a culmination of the cowboy satirized throughout Baraka's works, the western hero who represents the extreme distortion of American values—"a butcher in a cowboy suit," as one poem puts it. While Donna serves mainly to interpret the madness of cowboy capitalism into sane political fact, she also directly confronts its offensive sexism. Resisting the masked owner's slick, wheedling efforts to co-opt the workers' political sensibility, she succeeds, like Lula in *Dutchman* but with a constructive motive, in drawing out her antagonist's real malevolence: the quick and easy readiness of the owner to murder in order to maintain control over the assembly line. The play ends with the striking workers going off to organize the party that will eventually put them in charge of the means of production.

Baraka's most recent poems are collected under the title "Poetry for the Advanced," poems written between 1976 and 1978 and published for the first time in *Selected Poetry of Amiri Baraka/LeRoi Jones* (1979). The poet begins by momentarily yielding his own voice, the entire introduction consisting of a quoted passage from Lenin that defines the advanced worker as the vanguard of the proletariat—as a representative of the "working-class intelligentsia." The voice of the worker-artist in the poetry, though, is confidently Baraka's own.

The elements of struggle form are inevitably there, but crafted so that on the whole they blend into a poetry that is stylistically, if not politically, advanced beyond *Hard Facts* (1976). There is more expressive power and less ideological self-consciousness—not less ideological intensity—as if some of the pressure of extended political exposition had been released into the plays. Predicate phrasings and musical motifs are much in evidence, and there is a firmer sense of the poet's personal place in the larger politicized scheme of reality.

The opening piece, "A POEM FOR ANNA RUSS AND FANNY JONES," equates his grandmothers' belief in a heavenly afterlife with the respectful concurrence that " . . . all society will / be raised to higher ground, a more advanced life" in this world. Their most natural humanity—and his—is lyrically shared by the masses of people: " . . . Your skin scraped off so the moonlight stings, so the swish of bird's wings / brings a message to the brain. . . . / . . . A link with the billions. . . ." Yet the "clear message" of crushing the "rule of the rich" by violent means " . . . cannot be hidden with lyricality / and mysticism. . . ." And so he concludes by gently and insistently implicating the traditional pacifism of his kinfolk in the people's revolution against the ruling class:

> . . . They huddle and plot
> our repression and pain. But
> just like the old stories grandmama, that ain't
> no big thing, we learned how evil wd act in
> Sunday School, and how the people, the
> righteous,
> wd always win!

Baraka is less than gentle in alluding to Allen Ginsberg as a "blind & crazy / metaphysical" prophet. Yet he acknowledges that his old "petty bourgeois" friend (himself no stranger to Marxism) had made a point back in 1956, when in the poem "America" Ginsberg said, "Go fuck yourself with your atom bomb." Baraka rejuvenates the protest, composing around the quoted line his own poem about America entitled "REPRISE OF ONE OF A. G.'S BEST POEMS," with Marxist variations on the repeated theme word "America."

Rendered somewhat in the manner of a popular song lyric, one imagines parts of the poem as suitable for performance by the Liberation Singers who in *S-1* sing Lil's socialist song "America." Baraka offers "REPRISE" as a "Hymn-poem," a thrust at the patriotic hymn "America" brightly animated at the end by Latin-accented snatches from the "America" of Leonard Bernstein's *West Side Story*. Where Ginsberg mainly gestures with lyric confusion and ironic nostalgia—"America I used to be a communist when I was a kid I'm not sorry"— Baraka flings out struggle taunts: "I'm a red pinko Commie / . . . a Marxist-Leninist / Whose ideology is / Marxism-Leninism-Mao Tse-tung Thought!" The repetitions and assertive refrains are similar to the song style of several other poems in the collection, making "REPRISE" more effective as a popular piece of music directed at worker audiences than as a fixed-print poem suitable for aesthetic analysis.

Baraka's musical intention in this regard is most evident in "LIKE, THIS IS WHAT I MEANT!," a song-manifesto defining the function of the poem for Marxist political purposes just as "Black Art" had earlier demarcated the poem from a strict nationalist view. The refrain "So that even in our verse" is used to unfold a series of short struggle quotations from Mao enlivened by a surge of interpolation and clarification from Baraka. Not only must poetry " . . . sing, laugh & fight," but, as with the message of the plays, "Poetry must see as its central task / building / a Marxist-Leninist / Communist Party / in the USA."

Carried along in the musical flow, the diction of political advance ("raging mass," "struggle erupts," "sweep forward," "human explosion") resolves in proposing the poem as a revolutionary song. Baraka parenthetically instructs the reader to "repeat as song" the final rallying refrain: "So that even / in our / verse / even in / our dancing / even in / our song / yeh / in our pure lover song / REVOLUTION!!!"

Song refrain and the back-up style of vocal groups typify "ALL REACTION IS DOOMED!!!," a poem weakened by hackneyed political invective (Nikita Khrushchev a "Fat bald head traitor," Trotskyites "those bedbugs made of vomit"), intrusions that would not stir all advanced readers. "AFRO-AMERICAN LYRIC" is the most stylized song-poem, utilizing refrains that encourage the listeners to "think" about and "study" revolution. Unlike the other song lyrics, it conspicuously features the manipulation of vowel sounds as rhythmically stretched and fondled by an urban soul singer. Pithy denunciation is wrapped in Afro-American predicate sound:

> society's ugly is the graspingclass
> its simple
> shit uh
> see-imm-pull
> see-im-pull
> Seeeeeeeeeeeee-immmmmmmmmm
>   pull
> Some See   -   im   -   pull
>   shit

As the sounds are turned over and given intense vocal inflection, the stylistic process presumably will crystallize political meaning for the singer-listener: that understanding material reality and the need for revolution is basically simple. As with some of the chant poems in "Black Art," these worker songs—political heirs to the earliest Afro-American work songs—are for the ear, not the eye. They suggest Baraka's increased willingness to accommodate the impulses of Art-ing to Marxist content, the augmenting of a spare poetic lyricism by the song lyric.

A number of poems work in more conventional ways to focus the expected political themes. "MALCOLM REMEMBERED (FEB. 77)" eulogizes Malcolm X in a montage of recent black nationalist history, presenting him as the "comrade" who was killed before his "final motion" into socialist revolution. In the short poem "PRES SPOKE IN A LANGUAGE," Baraka withholds direct ideological statement, poetizing the collective black sounds of saxophonist Lester Young—" . . . in the teeming whole of us he lived"—as an exemplary history of survival: "translating frankie trumbauer into / Bird's feathers / Tranes sinewy tracks / the slickster walking through the crowd / surviving on a terrifying wit." The poem fulfills its revolutionary obligation, and then only by implication, in the final line: "Save all that comrades, we need it."

If nationalism has been discarded, the pertinence of black culture has not. John Coltrane's "sinewy tracks" become "AM/TRAK," an ambitious poem whose rush of Art-ing almost overtakes the political conclusion. The poem is probably a subjective offshoot of "John Coltrane: Where Does Art Come From?," an unpublished Marxist analysis of black music that Baraka was writing in the late 1970's (a chapter of which appears in *Selected Plays and Prose*). The poetic expression of Coltrane's history and art is reminiscent of verse from "Black Art": "nigger absolute super-sane screams against reality / course through him / . . . / . . . the precise saying / all of it in it afire aflame talking saying being doing meaning." The political harnessing of this energy comes at the end, the music of Coltrane's "Meditations" touching the poet as a metaphor of struggle and study: "& it told me what to do / . . . / Live! / & organize / yr shit / as rightly / burning!"

This forceful emergence of Coltrane, a major inspiration for black poets in the 1960's, indicates that Marxism had not significantly displaced black culture in Baraka's art. It had only altered his interpretation of that culture. In "SPRING SONG," a recurrent symbol is once again changed in accord with Baraka's shifting perception of reality—the nationalist " . . . sun behind us, the day turned red,"—with musical pulsations reinforcing the political conceit at the end of the poem. The athletic "strides" of the advancing "black comrade" toward "the next hurdle," the qualitative leap, are likened to Coltrane's improvisations in the music of "Giant Steps":

> . . . the mass of people surging
> forward too, remind
> him of Trane—yeh Trane—you know that
> solo—Bee Dooo Bee Dooo Dooooo
> Dooo dooo   (Giant Steps)

The leap is completed in the autobiographical gesture of the last poem, "CHILD OF THE THIRTIES." Baraka stretches the child's game Red Rover into the same political image of the hurdle figured in "Spring Song," a motion that flows smoothly from the blues-blowing horn of the black musician:

> Red Rover, Red Rover, can you understand
> class struggle
>
>   . . .
>
> like the way your hand would reach your toe
> with the wood hurdle
> passing an 8th of an inch
> under your outstretched leg
> pass swift comrade, pass swift
> the way the everything do
> the way the all the things do
> the way the world is blew
> blue
> bluessssss

The musical note is ultimately political, the poem closing in a balance of metaphor and classic struggle statement: "Long Live Marx, Engels, Lenin, Stalin, Mao Tse-tung / Red Rover / Red Rover / You're over". This may or may not be LeRoi Jones's final motion. As he said many poems ago in *Suicide Note,* "the changes are difficult, when / you hear them, & know they are all in you." But as Amiri Baraka's subsequent experience has clearly shown, change is inevitable—indeed, is everything, as he says in "THE 'RACE LINE' IS A PRODUCT OF CAPITALISM": "all is, the only constant / is, / yeh yeh yeh, change!"

With Baraka's career as yet incomplete, summary is difficult. Comparable with Langston Hughes in stylistic finesse and with W. E. B. Du Bois in historical vision, Baraka is incomparably himself in creative scope and intellectual intensity. Always a hard critic of Western culture and the American way, he has wrenched from the bourgeois fine arts tradition—in the very process of rejecting much of its manner and many of its values—a commitment to the written word as a means of recording the personal and political struggles of one man: first speaking for himself, then for black people, and now for the proletariat. Most of all as a poet and playwright, but also as a writer of fiction and essays, his literary efforts have in common the quality of piercing inquiry—whether directed at himself or the world at large.

His questionable reputation with the critics is of little concern to Baraka. He measures his own achievement by the changes his writings have brought about in others. One reviewer has typically commented that in the Marxist poetry Baraka has "sacrificed artistic vitality on the altar of his political faith." Nothing could be further from the truth. In all the phases of his writing—whether "beat," nationalist, or Marxist—Baraka has shown a deep concern not only for attitudes and ideas but also for the effective adjustment of his aesthetics to the changing realities he tirelessly inscribes. Indeed, he is one of the important literary innovators working in the United States.

Selected Bibliography

WORKS OF AMIRI BARAKA (LEROI JONES)

BOOKS, PLAYS, PAMPHLETS

Preface to a Twenty Volume Suicide Note. . . . New York: Totem Press, 1961.

Blues People: Negro Music in White America. New York: William Morrow, 1963.

The Dead Lecturer. New York: Grove Press, 1964.

Dutchman and The Slave. New York: William Morrow, 1964.

The System of Dante's Hell. New York: Grove Press, 1965.

Home: Social Essays. New York: William Morrow, 1966.

The Baptism and The Toilet. New York: Grove Press, 1967.

Arm Yrself or Harm Yrself. Newark, N. J.: Jihad Productions, 1967.

Black Music. New York: William Morrow, 1967.

Slave Ship: A Historical Pageant. Negro Digest, 16, no. 6: 62–74 (April 1967). Reprinted Newark, N. J.: Jihad Productions, 1969.

Tales. New York: Grove Press, 1967.

Home on the Range. Drama Review, 12:106–11 (Summer 1968).

Police. Drama Review, 12:112–15 (Summer 1968).

Black Magic: Collected Poetry 1961–1967. Indianapolis–New York: Bobbs-Merrill, 1969. (Includes "Sabotage," "Target Study," and "Black Art.")

The Death of Malcolm X. In *New Plays from the Black Theatre,* edited by Ed Bullins. New York: Bantam Books, 1969. Pp. 1–20.

Four Black Revolutionary Plays. Indianapolis–New York: Bobbs-Merrill, 1969. (Includes *Experimental Death Unit #1, A Black Mass, Great Goodness of Life,* and *Madheart.*)

A Black Value System. Newark, N. J.: Jihad Productions, 1970.

In Our Terribleness (Some elements and meaning in black style). Indianapolis–New York: Bobbs-Merrill, 1970. (With Fundi/Billy Abernathy.)

It's Nation Time. Chicago: Third World Press, 1970.

J-E-L-L-O. Chicago: Third World Press, 1970.

Junkies Are Full of (SHHH . . .). In *Black Drama Anthology,* edited by Woodie King and Ron Milner. New York: New American Library, 1971. Pp. 11–23.

Bloodrites. In *Black Drama Anthology* (see immediately above). Pp. 25–31.

Raise Race Rays Raze: Essays Since 1965. New York: Random House, 1971.

Kawaida Studies: The New Nationalism. Chicago: Third World Press, 1972.

Spirit Reach. Newark, N. J.: Jihad Productions, 1972.

Hard Facts. Newark, N. J.: People's War, 1975.

The Motion of History. In *The Motion of History and Other Plays.* New York: William Morrow, 1978. Pp. 19–127.

The Motion of History and Other Plays. New York: William Morrow, 1978. (Includes *The Motion of History, Slave Ship,* and *S-1.*)

S-1. In *The Motion of History and Other Plays.* New York: William Morrow, 1978. Pp. 151–225.

"Poetry for the Advanced." In *Selected Poetry of Amiri Baraka/LeRoi Jones.* New York: William Morrow, 1979. Pp. 275–340.

Selected Plays and Prose of Amiri Baraka/LeRoi Jones. New York: William Morrow, 1979. (Includes the following previously unpublished prose: "I" [1973]; "National Liberation Movements" [1977]; "War/Philly Blues/Deeper Bop" [1978]; "The Revolutionary Tradition in Afro-American Literature" [1978].)

Selected Poetry of Amiri Baraka/LeRoi Jones. New York: William Morrow, 1979.

The Sidnee Poet Heroical. Berkeley, Calif.: Reed and Cannon, 1979.

What Was the Relationship of the Lone Ranger to the Means of Production? In *Selected Plays and Prose of Amiri Baraka/LeRoi Jones.* New York: William Morrow, 1979. Pp. 252–76.

WORKS EDITED BY BARAKA

Four Young Lady Poets. New York: Totem Press, 1962.

The Moderns: An Anthology of New Writing in America. New York: Corinth Books, 1963.

Black Fire: An Anthology of Afro-American Writing. New York: William Morrow, 1968. (With Larry Neal.)

UNCOLLECTED ESSAYS

"How You Sound??" In *The New American Poetry: 1945–1960,* edited by Donald M. Allen. New York: Grove Press, 1960. Pp. 424–25.

"Philistinism and the Negro Writer." In *Anger, and Beyond: The Negro Writer in the United States,* edited by Herbert Hill. New York: Harper and Row, 1966. Pp. 51–61.

BIBLIOGRAPHIES

There is no single completely up-to-date bibliography of Baraka's works or of criticism about Baraka. The best available sources are listed below.

Benston, Kimberly W. *Baraka: The Renegade and the Mask.* New Haven: Yale University Press, 1976. Pp. 278–83.

———, ed. *Imamu Amiri Baraka (LeRoi Jones): A Collection of Critical Essays.* Twentieth Century Views. Englewood Cliffs, N. J.: Prentice-Hall, 1978. Pp. 191–95.

Dace, Letitia. *LeRoi Jones: A Checklist of Works by and About Him.* London: Nether Press, 1971.

Hudson, Theodore. *From LeRoi Jones to Amiri Baraka: The Literary Works.* Durham, N. C.: Duke University Press, 1973. Pp. 198–209.

Sollors, Werner. *Amiri Baraka/LeRoi Jones: The Quest for a "Populist Modernism."* New York: Columbia University Press, 1978. Pp. 301–28.

BIOGRAPHICAL AND CRITICAL STUDIES

Baker, Houston A., Jr. "'These Are Songs if You Have The/Music': An Essay on Imamu Baraka." *Minority Voices,* 1:1–18 (1977).

Benston, Kimberly W. *Baraka: The Renegade and the Mask.* New Haven: Yale University Press, 1976.

———. "Amiri Baraka: An Interview." *Boundary 2,* 6:303–16 (Winter 1978).

———, ed. *Imamu Amiri Baraka (LeRoi Jones): A Collection of Critical Essays.* Twentieth Century Views. Englewood Cliffs, N. J.: Prentice-Hall, 1978.

Brady, Owen E. "Great Goodness of Life: Baraka's Black Bourgeoisie Blues." In *Imamu Amiri Baraka (LeRoi Jones),* edited by Kimberly W. Benston. Pp. 157–66.

Brecht, Stefan. "LeRoi Jones' *Slave Ship.*" *Drama Review,* 14:212–19 (Winter 1970).

Brown, Cecil M. "Black Literature and LeRoi Jones." *Black World,* 19, no. 8:24–31 (June 1970).

Brown, Lloyd W. "Comic-Strip Heroes: LeRoi Jones and the Myth of American Innocence." *Journal of Popular Culture,* 3:191–204 (Fall 1969).

———. "Jones (Baraka) and His Literary Heritage in *The System of Dante's Hell.*" *Obsidian,* 1:5–17 (Spring 1975).

Coleman, Larry G. "LeRoi Jones' *Tales*: Sketches of the Artist as a Young Man Moving Toward a Blacker Art." *Black Lines,* 1:17–26 (Winter 1970).

Costello, Donald P. "Black Man as Victim." *Commonweal,* 88:436–40 (June 28, 1968).

Cruse, Harold. *The Crisis of the Negro Intellectual.* New York: William Morrow, 1967. Pp. 355–68.

Dennison, George. "The Demagogy of LeRoi Jones." *Commentary,* 39:67–70 (February 1965).

Ellison, Ralph. *Shadow and Act.* New York: Random House, 1964. Pp. 247–58.

Fischer, William C. "The Pre-Revolutionary Writings of Imamu Amiri Baraka." *Massachusetts Review,* 14:259–305 (Spring 1973).

Hudson, Theodore R. *From LeRoi Jones to Amiri Baraka: The Literary Works.* Durham, N. C.: Duke University Press, 1973.

Hughes, Langston. "That Boy LeRoi." *Chicago Defender,* January 11, 1965, p. 38.

Jackson, Esther M. "LeRoi Jones (Imamu Amiri Baraka): Form and the Progression of Consciousness." *CLA Journal,* 17:33–56 (September 1973).

Jacobus, Lee A. "Imamu Amiri Baraka: The Quest for Moral Order." In *Modern Black Poets,* edited by Donald B. Gibson. Englewood Cliffs, N. J.: Prentice-Hall, 1973. Pp. 112–26.

Jeffers, Lance. "Bullins, Baraka, and Elder: The Dawn of Grandeur in Black Drama." *CLA Journal,* 16:32–48 (September 1972).

Lederer, Richard. "The Language of LeRoi Jones'
The Slave." *Studies in Black Literature,* 4:14–16 (Spring 1973).

Llorens, Davis. "Ameer (LeRoi Jones) Baraka." *Ebony,* 24:75–78, 80–83 (August 1969).

Mackey, Nathaniel. "The Changing Same: Black Music in the Poetry of Amiri Baraka." *boundary 2,* 6:355–86 (Winter 1978).

Margolies, Edward. *Native Sons: A Critical Study of Twentieth-Century Negro American Authors.* Philadelphia: J. P. Lippincott, 1968. Pp. 190–99.

Munro, C. Lynn. "LeRoi Jones: A Man in Transition." *CLA Journal,* 17:57–78 (September 1973).

Neal, Larry. "The Development of LeRoi Jones." *Liberator,* 6:4–5 (January 1966) and 18–19 (February 1966).

Ossman, David. *The Sullen Art.* New York: Corinth Books, 1963. Pp. 77–81.

Otten, Charlotte. "LeRoi Jones: Napalm Poet." *Concerning Poetry,* 3:5–11 (1970).

Phillips, Louis. "LeRoi Jones and Contemporary Black Drama." In *The Black American Writer,* vol. II, edited by C. W. E. Bigsby. Baltimore: Penguin Books, 1971. Pp. 204–19.

Pickney, Darryl. "The Changes of Amiri Baraka." *New York Times Book Review,* December 16, 1979, p. 9.

Schneck, Stephen. "LeRoi Jones, or, Poetics & Policemen, or, Trying Heart, Bleeding Heart." *Ramparts,* 6:14–19 (June 29, 1968).

Sollors, Werner. *Amiri Baraka/LeRoi Jones: The Quest for a "Populist Modernism."* New York: Columbia University Press, 1978.

Stone, Judy. "If It's Anger ... Maybe That's Good." *San Francisco Chronicle,* August 23, 1964, pp. 39, 42.

Taylor, Clyde. "Baraka as Poet." In *Modern Black Poets,* edited by Donald B. Gibson. Englewood Cliffs, N. J.: Prentice Hall, 1973. Pp. 127–34.

Tener, Robert L. "The Corrupted Warrior Heroes: Amiri Baraka's *The Toilet.*" *Modern Drama,* 17:207–15 (June 1974).

Williams, Sherley A. "The Search for Identity in Baraka's *Dutchman.*" In *Imamu Amiri Baraka (LeRoi Jones),* edited by Kimberly W. Benston. Englewood Cliffs, N. J.: Prentice-Hall, 1978. Pp. 135–40.

—WILLIAM C. FISCHER

Saul Bellow

1915-

PROBABLY the most significant American novelist to come to maturity in the 1950–60's has been Saul Bellow. Given critical acclaim early in his career for the beautifully wrought constructions of *Dangling Man* (1944) and *The Victim* (1947), he won national popularity with *The Adventures of Augie March* in 1953. The succeeding publications of *Seize the Day* (1956), *Henderson the Rain King* (1959), and the best sellers *Herzog* (1964) and *Mr. Sammler's Planet* (1970) widened the extent of this popularity, while stabilizing his reputation as a novelist of ranking stature. The first of the American Jewish writers to capture a large reading audience without departing from an American Jewish idiom, Bellow has been instrumental in preparing a way for other writers like Bernard Malamud, I. B. Singer, and Philip Roth. But his achievement has been impressive enough in its own right; he has developed a marvelously supple style of grotesque realism modulated by an ever-present sense of irony. However, the very success of his fictions may have drawn attention away from the intense moral seriousness of his concerns. In my attempt to expose the underlying substance of his work as a whole, I may appear at times to be denigrating his success. Nothing could be further from the truth. Bellow's achievement, it seems to me,

is so impressive and so relevant to our contemporary needs that only the most rigorous analysis and evaluation can suggest its prime importance or point to what I believe to be its most enduring qualities. And that his work possesses such qualities is what I shall try to demonstrate.

"Nobody truly occupies a station in life any more. There are mostly people who feel that they occupy the place that belongs to another by rights. There are displaced persons everywhere." These happen to be the words of Bellow's displaced millionaire, Eugene Henderson, but they could have been spoken by almost any of Bellow's characters, or, for that matter, by Bellow himself. As a pronouncement, of course, such a statement is hardly susceptible to proof, but it seems to me undeniable that Henderson's observation is one valid way of expressing a generally accepted "truth" of our time. Our current history has been a constant succession of massive dislocations in the scheme of our traditional social patterns; our incessant complaint is a nagging sense of anxious insecurity. And whether approached from a sociological or a psychological viewpoint, the problems raised by displaced persons and displaced personalities have become ever more common and ever more pressing. To put it largely, we might say that the events of the last fifty years have laid upon man an enormous lopsided burden of incomparable freedom without the balancing accompaniment of meaningful choices. The average citizen has been liberated from the daily siege of brutal physical labor; an abundance of the traditional luxuries has been lavished upon him; and yet he finds himself dangling in the midst of his new comforts without possessing a reason or a title for his occupancy. And thus, ironically enough, his new freedoms have increased the pressure of his responsibilities without adding a whit to his meager holdings of power or control. Under the weight of what can become an enervating sense of displacement, there develops a regular rhythm of steady frustration, spasmodically interrupted by sudden bursts of violence which are almost always vastly disproportionate to their activating causes. In this situation, neither rational analysis nor indignant censure seems particularly pertinent because the stresses themselves are almost wholly irrational. It is the rooted feeling of displacement that appears to be the immutable mark of our age and not the historical events that stand in antecedence to it.

I suppose that every serious artist of the mid-century has directly or indirectly addressed himself to this central problem, bringing to it his own strategies of interpretation and nomenclature. The catchwords have multiplied: the age of anxiety; the affluent society; the death of God; the discontinuity of tradition; the loss of self; the anti-hero; victims and rebels; picaresque saints and clowns of the absurd; radical innocence and unpardonable guilt; reactions of alienation and accommodation. Bellow's special position on this matter has been his unwavering conviction that man's fate and his opportunities for nobility are essentially no different today from what they

were two thousand years ago; and his achievement as a writer of fiction has been his patient capacity to deal with this central theme of displacement without being lured into the fashionable hysterics of either apocalyptic rhetoric or nostalgia. His own constant concern has been a single-minded attention toward defining what is viably *human* in modern life—what is creatively and morally possible for the displaced person that modern man feels himself to be. As his theater critic, Schlossberg, declaims in *The Victim*: "It's bad to be less than human and it's bad to be more than human. . . . Good acting is what is exactly human. And if you say I am a tough critic, you mean I have a high opinion of what is human. This is my whole idea. More than human, can you have any use for life? Less than human, you don't either."

Like Schlossberg, Bellow has a high opinion of what is "human." ("What is it, now, this great instrument? Played wrong, why does it suffer so? Right, how can it achieve so much, reaching even God?") But to isolate the problem is not the same as discovering solutions. The search for the "exactly human" is a direct plunge into the dark heart of our contemporary mysteries. After all, it may be that only the desire and the need to know are themselves human. "Who can be the earnest huntsman of himself when he knows he is in turn a quarry? asks Joseph of *Dangling Man*. Or, as Asa Leventhal differently poses the problem in *The Victim*: "The peculiar thing struck him that everything else in nature was bounded; trees, dogs, and ants didn't grow beyond a certain size. 'But we,' he thought, 'we go in all directions without any limit.'" The total reach of Bellow's work—seven novels, several plays, a handful of short stories and essays—constitutes his attempt to define habitable limits for contemporary man, within which he can rest secure and still seize hold of the day with a partial power and the responsibility for his employment of that power.

Men have traditionally been aware of their human limitations through the confining strictures of religion, society, or some sanctioned belief in an order, independent of man, discoverable in nature and natural processes. When these strictures are working properly, men may not be necessarily happy, but at least they have no difficulty in recognizing the exquisite balance between their obligations and their liberties. But such an almost spontaneous awareness is not possible for a man of Bellow's temperament and background. Born in Lachine, Quebec, in 1915, the youngest of four children—his parents had emigrated from Russia two years earlier—Bellow was raised in the Rachel Market section of Montreal. After the family moved to Chicago in 1924, he was educated in the public schools and attended the University of Chicago, taking his degree from Northwestern University in 1937 with honors in anthropology and sociology. In terms of family and childhood background, Bellow's is a specimen case of multiple dislocation—from the *shtetl* life of East Europe to Montreal to Chicago. In his early youth he received an orthodox religious education, but he emerged from the American university system with the preparatory training of a social scientist. The recurrent accent of his growing up would seem to be one of unremitting change, discontinuity, fluidity. The traditional sanctions of Jewish *shtetl* orthodoxy may have lingered artificially in the old Montreal ghetto, but they rapidly dissolved in the secularism and relative prosperity of Chicago in the 1920's and 1930's.

Here it is interesting to note the ambiguous roles that religion and family play in Bellow's works. There is a persistent, usually muted, religious referent in all his fictions, but Joseph, the dangling, waiting-to-be-drafted hero of

Bellow's first novel, is probably a fair spokesman for his author's rejection of any active adherence to a religious faith: "I did not want to catch at any contrivance in panic," Joseph says. "In my eyes, that was a great crime. . . . Out of my own strength it was necessary for me to return the verdict for reason, in its partial inadequacy, and against the advantages of its surrender." Twenty years later, Herzog reluctantly confesses: "Evidently I continue to believe in God. Though never admitting it." But this belief in God, common to all Bellow's protagonists, is merely an additional burden for them to carry. It increases their suffering of shame or guilt, without being in itself an alleviation of that suffering or a source of moral strength. Their belief in God may be slightly more than a mere religious sentimentality, but it is certainly a good deal less than a fundamental mode of defining what is legitimately human. Ritual has become incontrovertibly dissevered from daily behavior and the Bellow hero is driven to justify his own life—to press his actions into his own idiosyncratic rites of worship, since the traditional laws bear little relevance to his present needs. ("Herzog had been overcome by the need to explain, to have it out, to justify, to put in perspective, to clarify, to make amends.")

The persistent presence of "family" is likewise an ambiguous factor in Bellow's fictional world. Typically, his protagonists are products of fairly sizable families; frequently, one parent is dead or institutionalized. In their maturity the protagonists tend to live apart from their brothers and sisters, to marry one or more times, and to sire children on all their wives. But what is more to the point is that they are "family-minded" people. Reluctantly accepting the obligations of marriage and fatherhood, they worry about their children, they make sporadic efforts to understand and improve their relationships with their wives, they search the faces of their nephews and nieces for family likenesses, and they are subject to sudden overwhelming seizures of love for those who are connected to them by ties of kinship. And yet, in a perverse way, they manage to evade attachment to even their most intimate relatives and friends. The introspective point of view from which their fictions are usually narrated, as well as the arbitrary circumstances of plot, succeeds in isolating the protagonists as though they were genuine solitaries. Joseph spends the bulk of his days alone while his wife, Iva, works at the Chicago Public Library. Leventhal's wife is away helping her widowed mother move to Charleston when Kirby Allbee assaults the tenuous security of his life pattern. Augie March wanders through the terrain of his adventures in a thoroughly subjective and ultimately casual connection to the landscape. Tommy Wilhelm (*Seize the Day*) is legally separated from his wife and children. Henderson goes off to Africa by himself and Herzog ruminates on the past in his bachelor apartment in New York and in the peace and quiet of his abandoned house in Ludeyville. The "family" comes into actual existence only when the protagonist desires contact or aid; otherwise, except for the subplots in *The Victim* (in many ways, Bellow's most uncharacteristic novel) and in *Mr. Sammler's Planet*, family obligations exert no real demands on the protagonist. The family can be ignored or treated as a stable marginal presence unless the protagonist wills it to be otherwise.

And still the sense of family is one of the most urgent possessions in the life of the Bellow hero. Joseph recalls his early youth in St. Dominique Street in Montreal with such vividness as to conclude that it was "the only place where I was ever allowed to encounter reality." In a similar confessional mood, Moses Herzog discovers that his "heart was attached with great power" to the Napoleon Street of his boyhood: "Here was a wider range of human feelings than he had ever again been able to find." Nor are these the offhand comments of a nostalgia sentimentalized in tranquillity. The Montreal reminiscences in *Herzog* and the opening seven chapters of *The Adventures of Augie March* (the description of Augie's Chicago childhood and his relationships with Grandma Lausch, the Coblins, and the Einhorns) attain a density of texture and poignancy of emotion that are unequaled elsewhere in Bellow's writing. Similarly, and probably for the same reasons, the father-son confrontation in *Seize the Day* and the grotesque battle of "the brothers" (Leventhal and Allbee) in *The Victim* are the most cogent dramatic conflicts that Bellow has as yet managed to project.

In other words, the idea of family has much the same force in Bellow's work as does religion. It intrudes itself on the present as an ironically *un*usable past. It compels the memory of a way of life in which personality seemed not to be fragmented and isolated; in which men were integral parts of a congenial whole, able to share their griefs and joys spontaneously and directly, instead of carrying them onerously on their own shoulders. But more than a memory, it is also an unattainable standard of moral obligations. The "placed" child is father to the displaced man and the child holds the man accountable. A man must be *ehrlich*; he must be a *Mensch*. "Choose dignity," says Schlossberg. "Nobody knows enough to turn it down." Bellow's heroes yearn after dignity, but as soon as they catch themselves groping to achieve it, they are quick to mock their own attempts as comically futile. As Irving Malin has pointed out, there is a startling preponderance of *weight* and *deformity* imagery in all of Bellow's stories. His protagonists seem always to be laboring under immense loads and pressures from which they receive only momentary release. Here is Tommy Wilhelm, for example, in a fairly representative posture: "The spirit, the peculiar burden of his existence lay upon him like an accretion, a load, a hump. In any moment of quiet, when sheer fatigue prevented him from struggling, he was apt to feel this mysterious weight, this growth . . . of nameless things which it was the business of his life to carry about. That must be what a man was for." It is possible that this weight is precisely the measure of that amount of life which the Bellow hero is doomed to bear because the supporting structures of family and religion are no longer available to him. He has no option except to submit to the implacable judgments of his lost family and religious traditions, even though his radical displacement has made these standards impossible for him to live up to. He is alone and fragmented because there is no whole place for him. He cannot will his mind to cease posing impossible questions and each reiterated question riddles the temporary security of his life. And still he carries in his solitude a desperate need to realize the assurances of love which only participation in a communal life can provide. It is small wonder, then, that his spirit buckles and agonizes under such burdens.

It is in this sense, I suppose, that the Bellow hero can be justly termed a *schlemiel* type. If he is a victimized figure, he is a victim of his own moral sense of right and wrong—his own accepted obligation to evaluate himself by standards that will inevitably find him lacking. And it is for this reason that all Bellow's heroes are, like Joseph, "apprentices in suffering and humiliation." In what other way could they respond to their findings of spirtual deficiency without giving the lie to the possibilities of moral behavior? And not for them the "stiff-upper-lip" stoicism of American Protestantism. Bellow's heroes suffer intensely and rehearse

their agonies at operatic volume for all to hear. "I am to suffering what Gary is to smoke," says Henderson. "One of the world's biggest operations." But it would be a serious mistake to confuse this characteristic reaction of the Bellow hero with one of passive lamentation or self-pitying surrender. Even in his partly sincere and partly mock self-revilings, he is determined to believe that "human" means "accountable in spite of many weaknesses—at the last moment, tough enough to hold." And in final effect, none of Bellow's heroes actually resigns himself to his suffering. Painfully they climb again and again out of "the craters of the spirit," ridiculing their defeats with a merciless irony, resolved to be prepared with a stronger defense against the next assault that is sure to come.

Perhaps this aspect of Bellow's work has been the least appreciated by contemporary critics. Some have interpreted his thematic preoccupation with the sufferer as a device of compromise, a "making do," or accommodation—an argument which implies that Bellow is gratuitously surrendering the heroic ideal of a fully instinctual life to the expediency of flabby survival within the status quo. But this, it seems to me, is precisely to miss the moral point and to misread Bellow's deliberate irony. Trained in anthropology, Bellow is quite willing to regard the species *man* as merely one of the evolutionary products of nature and natural processes. But Bellow is determined to insist on the qualitative difference between *man* and the other sentient species that nature has produced. He may occasionally invest animals with "human" characteristics; and he is always careful to show that although his protagonists may loudly protest their innate "docility or ingenuous good will," brute animality resides deeply and subtly in their basic natures. The difference between the human animal and the brute, for Bellow, is a matter of essential kind rather than degree. As Augie March discovers, only "mere creatures look with their original eyes." For man is that creature who also creates himself. He has never owned "original eyes." His vision is filtered through the lenses of history and self-awareness. And it is because men do not possess "original eyes" that both the generous vision of love and the blindness of malice are fundamental human attributes which must be accounted for. It is not surprising, therefore, that those readers who find Bellow's heroes contemptibly self-conscious and alienated from nature are also the ones who must deny the efficacy of laughter as an anodyne for human misery.

The role of nature in Bellow's fictional world is thus far less significant than that of either religion or family. It has a prominence and a grandeur, to be sure, but it exists at a distance from the main struggles with which Bellow is concerned. His protagonists are urban-bred and urban-oriented. Their native habitat is the modern metropolis—cities of elevated trains, overheated apartments, traffic, universities and museums, slums and suburbs, city parks and anonymous cafeterias, the subway rumbling underfoot and the smog polluting the upper air. In the city the Bellow hero is almost at home; he can take the city for granted because he knows its ways—its bus routes, its expressway exits, the correct tip for the cabdriver, the right response to the newspaper vendor. And he knows as well the sudden absurd beauties which are a gratuitous by-product of its thriving ugliness. But he is at least equally responsive to the traditional attractions of nature also. He has an unusual competence in the names and habits of fish, birds, animals, and even insect life. Not only is he a devotee of zoos and aquariums, but he is a rapt student of trees and flowers, a follower of the seasonal changes in the foliage and the mysterious portents of weather. In fact

there are moments in Bellow's fiction which come very near to a wholehearted acceptance of some variety of nature mysticism. One remembers Leventhal discovering that "everything, everything without exception, took place as if within a single soul or person." But such instants of ecstatic revelation are, I think, ultimately incidental in Bellow's fictional world. His heroes feel a great sensuous joy in nature, but nature fails to become for them a dictionary or a bible of life. Nature remains always *outside*—a spectacle—for the Bellow protagonist; his unique individuality never becomes merged into its larger mystical embrace. As Herzog regretfully concludes, "I am a prisoner of perception, a compulsory witness." And the most intense and appreciative witness can never completely participate in what he is witnessing. He would have to possess "original eyes" in order to do that. Thus, for Bellow, nature remains an inexhaustible source of delight without becoming a dwelling place for the human spirit. It offers sensation, but not "truth"; endless mute instruction, but no sureties for the soul's search.

That Bellow has deliberately constructed his heroes along these lines is clear not only from his fictions, but also from his direct personal statements. In a review in 1951, he chides the American Jewish author for his reluctance to exploit the fullest depth of his cultural situation: "He [the Jewish writer] cannot easily accept the historical accident of being a Jew in America that is nonetheless among the first facts of his life. But this accident—the strangeness of discontinuity and of a constant immense change—happens to all and is the general condition. The narrowly confined and perfect unit of a man, if we could find him now, would prove to be outside all that is significant in our modern lives, lives characterized by the new, provisional, changing, dangerous, universal." And elsewhere he remarks,

"It is obvious that modern comedy has to do with the disintegrating outline of the worthy and humane Self, the bourgeois hero of an earlier age." Bellow's significance, it seems to me, is partly a consequence of his arrogant assumption that the historical accident which has formed his own special view of character can be universalized into an image of modern man. It is too early to judge Bellow's long-range success in this effort, but his warm reception, as well as his being given three National Book Awards, suggests that his arrogance may be amply justified.

Thus, the creation of a recognizable character type, the Bellow hero, is Bellow's major accomplishment. The faces and individual circumstances of this hero have varied from fiction to fiction. He has been rich and poor, well- and ill-educated; he has grown from youth to middle and old age, gone to war, multiplied his wives and mistresses, narrowed and extended his field of operations with the world. But when we compare the personae of his earliest published sketches in 1941 ("Two Morning Monologues") with his latest, we realize that the alterations in the hero are surprisingly superficial. He postures to a Dostoevskian rhythm in *Dangling Man*; he is clumsy and vulnerable in *The Victim* and *Seize the Day*; as Augie March, he affects the freewheeling manner of an unlikely reincarnation of Huck Finn; in the character of Moses Herzog, he absorbs all his previous roles in a comical apotheosis of despair; and in Artur Sammler, he walks a thin detached line above all his incarnations. The variations among the individual protagonists seem largely to be due to the expedients of their different dramatic settings. Any one of them could collapse into a paroxysm of welcome tears over a stranger's funeral bier. Any one of them could fulminate with the righteous rage of a Jeremiah and be capable of no greater violence than the spank-

ing of a fifteen-year-old niece. And any one of them could find himself knotted in impotent frustration, praying desperately: "For all the time I have wasted I am very sorry. Let me out of this clutch and into a different life. For I am all balled up. Have mercy." The Bellow hero is a composite of them all, a blend of Leopold Bloom and Stephen Dedalus, a cogent blur of modern man as comic sufferer. He is Jewish, an avid undisciplined reader with an erratic memory for assorted trivia and passages of moral exhortation, a city dweller oscillating between seizures of inarticulate yearning ("I want!") and "narcotic dullness." In a strange way he is the introspective inversion of the Hemingway hero, his most immediate Chicago predecessor. Like him, he is fearfully alone and afraid; like him, he struggles incessantly to achieve dignity and to impose a moral dimension upon life. But unlike him, he is cursed or blessed with a pervasive sense of irony; he is mistrustful of action, skeptical of heroics, painfully aware of the limitations of reason as only an intellectual can be, but unwilling, at the same time, to surrender himself to the dangerous passions of unreason.

Given such a concept of character, and given as well a desire to render this character into fictional form, Bellow has had serious technical difficulties in finding an adequate structure for his novels. His preoccupation with a single introspective consciousness has placed heavy limitations on the range and variety of his fictional world. And while these limitations recur throughout his work, they are most nakedly apparent in his first novel, *Dangling Man*, which is almost entirely the novel of Joseph's brooding. The awkward device of the journal form and the egotistical inward focus of Joseph's temperament inexorably determine the claustrophobically closed world of that novel. Nothing can enter this world save what Joseph chooses to allow, and since Joseph is not only a sedentary man, but also one who is not a particularly interested observer of anything that is outside himself, the resulting fictional world will be doubly closed. And this is precisely what happens. Joseph's wife, his father, his in-laws, his circle of friends, his mistress, his brother's family—in effect, the whole outside world of draft boards, winter, and a war raging around the globe—appear at the peripheries of his brooding vision in sudden surreal flashes of distorted life. And the effect of suffocation is further intensified because the novel lacks any real dramatic conflict except for the highly abstracted struggle that Joseph undergoes in the recesses of his own tortured spirit. In a way that might have been fatal to Bellow's art, *Dangling Man* is almost as much a brooding exposition on the ambiguities of directionless freedom as it is a novel at all.

But already there are evidences here of the brilliant techniques which Bellow will develop to enlarge and illuminate this obsessively closed world. From the beginning of his career, Bellow has been attracted by the disconnected gesture of the grotesque, the uninvestigated contortions of reality which constantly impinge, as it were, on the edges of our vision when we are concentrating primarily upon ourselves. A character like Mr. Vanaker, who leaves the bathroom door ajar when he goes to the toilet, who steals Joseph's socks and Iva's perfume, who throws bottles out of his window, will become one of Bellow's favorite strategies for stretching and lightening his restricted world. Mr. Vanaker is the first in a long line of grotesques, static representatives of the silent lives that exist on the margins of the Bellow hero's self-involvement. In that same novel, Joseph's father-in-law, Mr. Almstadt, is a similar conception. In the novels that follow, these dramatically and thematically unnecessary characters recur and proliferate, coming

tantalizingly close to the central protagonist without ever touching him. One thinks of Elena's mother in *The Victim*; of Augie's feeble-minded brother, George, of the Coblins and Padilla; of Mr. Perls and Mr. Rappaport in *Seize the Day*; of Lucas Asphalter and his monkey, of Nachman outside the cheese shop; of Eisen and the Gruner family in *Mr. Sammler's Planet*; of the taxi drivers and cigar vendors and innumerable insignificant encounters which the Bellow hero has in the course of his brooding days. Occasionally the disconnected grotesque may assume a more full-bodied substance in those rare instances when he enters vitally into the protagonist's life. Kirby Allbee, Dr. Adler, and perhaps Valentine Gersbach are examples of those whom the hero is forced to confront full face, from whom he cannot avert his eyes or his life, and who consequently take on real dramatic power because of this engagement. But, in general, the grotesque-as-actor is an exception in Bellow's fictional world. So powerfully and self-centeredly does the consciousness of the hero dominate and define the field of his contemplation that drama remains almost stifled in a succession of frantically mute gestures of grotesquerie which exist merely for their own sake, or to give the hero an opportunity for reminiscence or speculation.

Bellow's other device for creating an illusion of space is the introduction of the grotesque as spellbinding, marathon talker. All his life Bellow has been fascinated by authoritative orators of all varieties—by eloquent cranks, hucksters, confidence men, and city-park haranguers. He has experimented with the form of the monologue in an effort to capture the power of the obsessive speaker ("A Sermon by Doctor Pep"); he has interviewed the notorious "Yellow Kid" Weil, a man whose talent with words had earned him eight million dishonest dollars; and his attempt at a full-length play, *The Last Analysis*, is largely an extended speech in two acts by his ex-burlesque and TV ham comedian—turned sham Freudian—Philip Bummidge. Given the concept of a static protagonist, it becomes a natural fictional device for Bellow to surround this protagonist with gargantuan, hobbyhorse-riding theoreticians, with self-convinced "Reality-Instructors," as Herzog comes to define them. Beginning with Schlossberg in *The Victim*, such talkers appear again and again as one of Bellow's consistent resources for interrupting the closed concentration of his hero's endless broodings. Grandma Lausch, Einhorn, Mintouchian, Bateshaw—these are the speechmakers whom Augie describes as "those persons who persistently arise before me with life counsels and illumination throughout my earthly pilgrimage." The brilliant pseudo-Socrates, Dr. Tamkin, in *Seize the Day*; King Dahfu in *Henderson the Rain King;* Sandor Himmelstein and Simkin in *Herzog*; Govinda Lal in *Mr. Sammler's Planet*: their grotesque voices swell in volume or fall into inveigling whispers; they harangue, cajole, exhort, excoriate throughout Bellow's fictions. And, as in Dickens, these voices become compellingly alive on the printed page. For Bellow has the rare power of presenting characters who can talk themselves into life, and the best of his talkers achieve a magical reality beyond the echoes of their voices.

However—and this is a strangely paradoxical quirk in Bellow's fiction—they talk to deaf ears. Only in *The Victim* and *Seize the Day* does a genuine dialogue occur. The Bellow hero is a patient, willing, but heedless listener. He has "opposition" in him. The voices enchant him, but he learns nothing from what he hears. With Bellow's predilection for the first-person narrative focus and the "autobiographical tale," we would expect the curve of his hero's adventures to be cast in the form of the

Bildungsroman or "educational romance." That is, we would expect the hero to advance from some kind of innocence to experience, from a position of ignorance to one of knowledge. And we would suppose that the chorus of instructional voices must exert some influence on his progress toward his own acquisition of values. But this does not happen. In the first place, with the exception of Schlossberg's, the voices are patently unacceptable to the protagonist's temperament. They are either too Machiavellian or too crankishly eccentric for the hero to take them seriously. And in the second place, the hero never learns anything from his experiences anyway. To be sure, he goes through all the external forms of the educative experience, but he ends up in pretty much the same state as he began, just a little bit older perhaps and a little bit more weary. In an irony that may be even more bitter than Bellow had intended, the Bellow hero's fate *is* his character, and his character is his doom. His basic commitment to an ideal of amorphous possibility is so tenacious as to make both growth and acquired truth impossible.

A closer look at *The Adventures of Augie March* may make this more evident. The novel brings Augie from early boyhood to his postwar maturity as a black marketeer in Europe. Along the way, he has outgrown his family, the Depression, and Chicago; he has passed through his adventures with Thea and Caligula, survived war and shipwreck, temporized with several varieties of utopian dreams, and concluded his tale by describing himself winsomely as a "sort of Columbus of those near-at-hand." All his eloquent, self-assured instructors have been left behind, defined—and, therefore, finite—in the various formulas with which they have tried to struggle to an understanding with life. Grandma Lausch, Simon, Einhorn, Thea, Mintouchian—each has succeeded in creating a personality for himself, each has attempted to impose that personality on life, and each has been discarded by Augie as a kind of heroic failure. Augie alone refuses to formularize his existence. He has been everywhere and suffered everything; but he has learned no more than he knew already when he used to go to the Harrison Street dispensary for free eyeglasses. He has experienced grief, loss, and betrayal. He has grieved and betrayed others. He has listened to all the voices and he has himself speculated on life's deeper meanings. But in no real sense has he impressed a form on his experiences; in no real way has he shaped his life under the positive imprint of his character. For Augie is a strangely passive hero—and is this not true also of Moses Herzog, and even Henderson? People and life happen to Augie. He is readily responsive to women, but all his amorous liaisons are female-initiated. And, similarly, it is the "adoptional" quality that men sense in him and it is they who seek him out. In the long run, his "adventures" are little more than his blandly following the momentum of someone else's desires. And each episode comes to an end when the external initiator disappears from the scene to be replaced by his succesor. Augie's novel could have been legitimately concluded two hundred pages earlier, or, for that matter, it could have been continued almost indefinitely. Invention, not necessity, prescribed the duration of the form. And this is because the Bellow hero incarnates a curiously static immobility at the very center of his existence—a kind of metaphysical inertia which is firmly rooted in introspective despair.

But the first point to be noted here is that while Bellow has retained the traditional narrative structure for rendering a hero's growth from innocence to experience, he has cunningly discarded as irrelevant the substance of the dialectical terms. Augie comes very close to the pith of the problem when he says, "You

couldn't get the admission out of me that a situation couldn't be helped and was inescapably bad, but I was eternally looking for a way out, and what was up for question was whether I was a man of hope or foolishness." To be a "man of hope" when hope is unyoked to any faith or purpose save the involuntary buoyancy of the spirit is, I should think, to be a man of foolishness. Or if one is merely *pretending* the hope, it is to be a clown of despair. Bellow's realization that "innocence" and "experience" are outmoded terms—superfluous baggage left over from "the disintegrating outline of the worthy and humane Self"—is perhaps his most radical and subversive perception, but it deprives him of any dialectical resonance in his employment of the mythic structure of the quest. For the seminal image in all Bellow's fiction is not the image of a man seeking, but that of a man brooding in the midst of his solitude: of Joseph arguing wearily with the Spirit of Alternatives; of Herzog writing mental letters to the quick and the dead; of "Bummy" Bummidge conducting a psychoanalytical session with himself in which he plays the roles of both analyst and analysand. Only in *The Victim* and *Seize the Day* does the all-smothering act of brooding separate itself into genuinely interactive hostilities, and in both these fictions, Bellow can let his dramas work themselves out in the open without the deceptive disguise of a fruitless identity-quest or an account of a fabulous journey through the lion-haunted regions of the underconsciousness.

Perhaps there is no literary structure capable of making an effective drama of unpassionate, self-conscious brooding. Drama requires some vital collision between antagonistic powers, and a meandering discussion with the Spirit of Alternatives is simply too rational and wearily ironic to excite dramatic interest or suspense. Hence, Bellow's selection of the journal form for *Dangling Man* would seem to be the one best fitted to his personal eclectic preoccupations as a displaced and brooding intellectual. The journal convention requires and expects no tidy plot-design, nor any intrusive characters save the all-pervading personality of the journal writer himself. Its structure is almost completely a random one, subservient only to the mechanical movement of chronological time, punctuated by the arbitrary datings of its individual diary entries. It allows for the inclusion of barely relevant anecdotes, scenes briefly observed and biasedly rendered, reminiscences, fragmentary musings and theorizings, realistic and surrealistic effusions of attitude and opinion, expository arguments, hymns of lyrical invocation—indeed, it is open to whatever the writer is minded to inscribe in clear or murky mood. And the very haphazard quality of its form releases the writer from any obligation to deal with ultimate matters—with problems of destiny and eternity. That is, if the artist can be regarded in some sense as God-like in his creation of a structurally whole world, the journal writer is more a partaker in, than a creator of, a universe. He is free to pick and choose, start and stop abruptly; he is free to exploit the bits and pieces of his own personality without having to fix the place of man in the unshifting scheme of eternal values. And further, among its more obvious and practical functions, the journal may be the literary form in which a desperately lonely man can make his last-ditch effort to explode the constriction of his solitude and evade his imprisoning consciousness by attempting to communicate with another—even if that *other* is only himself.

At any rate, Bellow's choice of the journal form seems to have been responsive to some deep-seated urgency which has persisted throughout his writing career. In *The Adventures of Augie March,* and in *Henderson the Rain King,* he takes the traditional variant step away from the straight journal form to the autobiographical tale narrated in retrospect. Structurally, this merely means that the final diary notation of the journal is placed at the beginning rather than at the end, which gives the illusion of the form circling back on itself. The arbitrary dated entries are avoided, and there is a far greater narrative freedom in the treatment and compression of time sequences. So Augie declares the license of his idiosyncrasies at the beginning of his tale: "I am an American, Chicago born . . . and go at things as I have taught myself, free-style, and will make the record in my own way. . . ." And Henderson begins his tale by informing the reader that "the world which I thought so mighty an oppressor has removed its wrath from me. But if I am to make sense to you people and explain why I went to Africa I must face up to the facts." In *Herzog,* Bellow improvises brilliantly on the total resources of the journal form, carrying it, one would suppose, about as far as it can go. He succeeds in suggesting a duplicitously wide range of levels for his one brooding focus of narration; he reshuffles time sequences expertly, shifts Herzog's point of view from first- to third-person, employs the device of the fragmentary "mental" letters as a masterly bridge between solipsism and communication, and casts an ambience of irony over his entire construction. But if we are to understand properly what Bellow has accomplished, we must see that the silence which rests at the end of these three novels is the identical silence out of which the novels began. (*Herzog* concludes with the phrases "Nothing. Not a single word.") And in between these two silences, nothing has happened. The hero has been artfully displayed in a scintillating illusion of motion as a personality constitutionally invulnerable to change. For Augie was every bit as much a "Columbus of those near-at-hand" in his early Chicago days as he finds himself to be in the snow of Normandy. We know that the "wrath" of the world is only temporarily lifted from Henderson, who was born to be oppressed by it. And Moses Herzog ends as he began—a sentimentalist with a rigid heart, an adamant solitary who believes in the salvation of brotherhood.

To explain this without seeming to do disservice to Bellow's real achievements is difficult, because the weight of the analysis must necessarily appear more censorious than his successes deserve. But in this connection it is useful to examine the conclusions of Bellow's novels. No other elements of his work have been subject to more confusion and critical disapproval. Is Joseph's final abandonment of freedom and acceptance of regimentation to be read as a capitulation of the spirit or as an ironic defiance? What does the final meeting in the theater between Allbee and Leventhal *mean?* Is Tommy Wilhelm weeping for himself or for mankind? What is the purpose of the coda in *The Adventures of Augie March* —the scene where Jacqueline confesses her secret dream of Mexico and Augie laughs? What are we to make of the bearish Henderson galloping over the Newfoundland snows with his lion cub and the Persian boy? And should we see Herzog's final "peace" as the product of complete nervous exhaustion or as an attainment of harmony with the universe? The interpretative confusion is endless and I do not propose to offer a judicious settlement. But the habit of ambiguous conclusions suggests a radical deficiency in Bellow's capacity to bring his structures to an inevitable termination. In each of the finales, an implication is built into the plot action that the hero is at the point of surrendering, in some decisive way, his overweening and world-denying self-concern; the protagonist is frozen in a gesture

of readiness to embrace mankind. However, the dynamics of his character make such an embrace patently impossible. It is not enough to say—as all Bellow's heroes do resolutely say—that "I really believe that brotherhood is what makes a man human. If I owe God a human life, this is where I fall down. 'Man liveth not by Self alone but in his brother's face. . . .' " Correctly they diagnose the cause and fatal consequences of their isolation from their fellows; but only for the theoretician or the paralyzed dreamer is an accurate diagnosis sufficient in itself The Bellow hero—in this case, Herzog—continues: "The real and essential question is one of our employment by other human beings and their employment by us. Without this true employment you never dread death, you cultivate it. And consciousness, when it doesn't clearly understand what to live for, what to die for, can only abuse and ridicule itself."

Is this not explicitly the root problem of Bellow's fictional themes? His heroes are not, in the end, mere theoreticians of life's ironic cul-de-sacs; what they are best qualified to do is to recognize themselves as diagnosticians who suffer from their own acuity of vision and find no solution except to abuse and ridicule themselves. And what brings the Bellow hero to despair is the knowledge that with his temperament as a self-conscious intellectual and what Bellow has called "the mind's comical struggle for survival in an environment of Ideas," self-directed ridicule and abuse are the only options open to him. Or perhaps the despair is inherent in such a temperament and the self-ridicule is its principal means of expression. The Bellow hero is so keenly aware of the unceasing polarity of moods and human urgencies that his foreknowledge keeps him from either pursuing intensity with a full ardor or accepting without protest life's plateaus of quietude. Herzog despises the world's "potato love" and yearns after something finer and more dangerous, knowing at the same time that "intensity is what the feeble humanity of us can't take for long." Leventhal perceives within himself the dual desires to move and to be at rest, to risk everything and sacrifice nothing: "Everybody wanted to be what he was to the limit. . . . There was something in people against sleep and dullness, together with the caution that led to sleep and dullness. Both were there. . . ." From this viewpoint, Schlossberg's definition of "human-ness" can be interpreted as exactly that exquisite compromise between vegetable ("less than human") and ecstatic ("more than human") existence. But why should this cause the hero to despair? Because, under the honorific rationale of humanity, love, and moral dignity, this balanced compromise runs the inevitable hazard of exalting glandular dullness, acquiescence, and torpor as worthy life-goals.

This, as I take it, is the real force of Kirby Allbee's ranting criticism of Leventhal and the Jews in general: ". . . you people take care of yourselves before everything. You keep your spirit under lock and key. That's the way you're brought up. You make it your business assistant, and it's safe and tame and never leads you toward anything risky. Nothing dangerous and nothing glorious. Nothing ever tempts you to dissolve yourself. What for? What's in it? No percentage." In Bellow's other novels the same charge is more obliquely repeated in the accusation which the hero unfailingly directs at himself that he belongs "to a class of people secretly convinced that they had an arrangement with fate; in return for docility or ingenuous good will they were to be shielded from the worst brutalities of life." And the fact that the "arrangement with fate" is specious and ineffectual in no way deflects the bite of the accusation. Moses Herzog copies out the words of his daughter's favorite

nursery rhyme ("I love little pussy, her coat is so warm . . .") as a motto to revile himself with. And even Joseph catches himself up with the mocking revelation that he had "believed in his own mildness, believed in it piously." In their studied concern to be "exactly human" while avoiding "the worst brutalities" of human existence, Bellow's heroes cling to a pernicious closure of selfhood that tends to extinguish their most fundamental passions under the ashes of a bland passivity. And in full cognizance of what they have done to themselves, of what monstrous sin they have committed against God and mankind, they despair.

Several times Bellow has portrayed these fearful "brutalities" that exact such a heavy price for self-defense. They are imaged for Asa Leventhal in terms of his brief experience as a clerk in a lower-Broadway hotel for transients. His abiding fear is that he might fall in "with that part of humanity . . . that did not get away with it—the lost, the outcast, the overcome, the effaced, the ruined." These vague abstractions are more concretely rendered in a sordid street fight which Leventhal observes from his apartment-house window: "The scene on the corner remained with him . . . and he returned to it every now and then with the feeling that he really did not know what went on about him, what strange things, savage things. They hung near him all the time in trembling drops, invisible, usually, or seen from a distance. But that did not mean that there was always to be a distance, or that sooner or later one or two of the drops might not fall on him." Kirby Albee's disruptive invasion of his privacy is such a "drop." And its naked menace to Leventhal is terrifying and direct, not because it makes a victim of him—he has had an abundance of that experience!—but because it exposes him to himself as a passive victimizer. It closes the distance between the savage realities of the outside and the perilously taut artifices he has constructed to keep the world away from his timorous spirit. Similarly, such episodes as Mimi Villars' abortion or Stella's seedy intrigues with Oliver and Cumberland represent for Augie March the seamy life that rages beyond his fingertips—a savage order of life that his cool neutrality successfully ignores. A better illustration is the murder trial which Herzog witnesses as a courtroom visitor and which he is unable to watch without becoming physically sickened. The awful spectacle of calloused degradation (the defendant has killed her three-year-old son because he was a toilet-training problem and he cried a good deal) forces Herzog to realize that the power to act with passion bears within it the possibilities of such monstrous behavior as to make the term "human" equivalent to a cosmic insult. Better to dangle in brooding, self-centered passivity—to be guilty only to oneself—than to take the chance that opening a breach between oneself and the outside will automatically result in a fresh breeze of sweetness and light.

Thus the Bellow hero is entangled in an inextricable skein of vacillation and dread. The barriers which he erects to ward off the crudity and abandon of the external world can become as much a stultifying prison as a means of self-protection. To dangle uncommitted or to fall into the abyss—these seem to be his sole alternatives. And caught in that dilemma, deeply aware of the awesome dimensions of that abyss (the fate of the six million East European Jews is never very far from his mind as an example of what men can do with deliberation and self-righteousness), he can adequately express his anguish and outrage only in the accents of self-mockery and self-abuse. And thus, it seems to me, Bellow's curiously incomplete fictional structures reflect accurately the basic indecisiveness of his moral

position. Viewed in a harsh light, his final scenes may seem confused and contradictory —mere devices to terminate the fictional posturings of a brooding consciousness which lacks the moral energy to uphold a fully responsible position. But from a more sympathetic point of view they may be fruitfully ambiguous in that they leave his meanings honestly suspended between action and stasis, between commitment and withdrawal.

Of course there are those temperaments and philosophies for which sex may serve as at least a partial breakthrough from closed solipsistic brooding. Henry Miller, for example, is as much addicted to the form of the introspective journal as is Bellow. And the Bellow hero has doggedly explored the possibility of self-expansion through sexual union—but with generally negative results. The twice-married and multi-mistressed Herzog seems to sum up Bellow's conclusions on the matter when he says, "To look for fulfillment in another, in interpersonal relationships, was a feminine game. And the man who shops from woman to woman, though his heart ache with idealism, with the desire for pure love, has entered the female realm." This is an interesting statement, not only in its oddly ascetic insistence that "woman-shopping" be conducted on the idealistic level of "pure" love rather than "impure" sex, but in its implicit denial of the principles of brotherhood that we have earlier seen to be at the very heart of Bellow's philosophic perspective. It is a strange paradox that the Bellow hero should consciously reject fulfillment in "interpersonal relationships" even as he quotes with melancholy pleasure the dictum that "Man liveth not by Self alone but in his brother's face." In part there would seem to be a religious inheritance of female degradation that may be related to the traditional prayer that orthodox Jews recite every morning, offering thanks to the Almighty that they were born men and not women. At any rate, if the central problem of the Bellow hero is his ambivalent self-centeredness, then we must surely examine the role of the women with whom he shares his life. Moses Herzog, remembering the scene when his father returned to the Napoleon Street flat, his clothes torn and his face bleeding, thinks back on the giant figures of his earliest childhood and laments "Whom did I ever love as I loved them?" And in terms of our previous discussion, we can more clearly understand that the powerful emphasis of "family life" as the fundamental erotic influence on the Bellow hero will make all the later intrusions into his mature unfamilied life rootless and partial and lacking that greater adhesion which his idealism so desperately requires. If we recognize this, we should not be surprised to discover that Bellow's gallery of female characters tends to be composed of almost identical stereotypes, differing somewhat in ethnic background, erotic inventiveness, and the capacity for bitchiness; in other respects they will be similar, one to the other, whether they happen to bear the temporary title of wife or mistress.

Iva, Mary, Stella, Margaret, Frances, Lily, Daisy—it is impossible to keep the various wives separate and distinct. They are just *there* on those infrequent occasions when they appear in the novels. Unreal voices on the telephone, signatures on letters, additional elements of the prison furniture which surrounds the hero, exerting no significant stimulus on his behavior, and representing no real means by which he can escape himself. Nor are the mistresses any easier to distinguish from one another. Kitty, Sophie Geratis, Olive, Wanda, Zinka, Sono, Ramona—perhaps their names have a more romantic ring than those of the wives. They are all more or less acessible to the hero's uses in terms of the same function; and while they are sincerely enjoyed and ap-

preciated for their physical talents, they are clearly unrealized on any deeper level of engagement. But there are two exceptional women in Bellow's fiction; two distinct occasions when the hero is caught up in a love affair that goes beneath the superficialities of nuptial boredom or amorous release. These are the cases of Thea Fenchel in *The Adventures of Augie March* and Madeleine Pontritter in *Herzog*. These are both special encounters in Bellow's fiction; these are the only women who force the Bellow hero to rise to a qualitatively different kind of challenge than that of mere bedfellowship. And, inevitably, he fails both challenges.

Augie's surreal affair with Thea, which sweeps him away from labor-organization work in Chicago to an extended sojourn in the wilds of Mexico, entangling him in an exotic whirl where money is kept in the refrigerator and eagles are trained to hunt prehistoric lizards, can be easily misinterpreted. Nor, I think, is it entirely the reader's fault. Bellow goes out of his way to invest Thea with details of grotesque eccentricity, partly to conceal the nakedness of the demands which she makes on Augie. She wants simply to break out of her own prison of loneliness. She asks of Augie that he merge his life with hers in order that together they might create a world inside and secure from the demeaning outside world. This is most evidently seen when she rejects his plea for a second chance: ". . . I thought if I could get through to one other person I could get through to more. . . . Well, I believed it must be you who could do this for me. And you could. I was so happy to find you. I thought you knew all about what you could do and you were so lucky and so special. . . . I'm sorry you're here now. You're not special. You're like everybody else. You get tired easily." And although Thea's odd preoccupation with eagles and snakes may tend to make the reader discount her as a real woman, she must still be credited with an unqualified determination to follow a life of pure intensity. It is on this level that Augie fails her; he lacks the stamina to remain with her on the rarefield heights of an all-inclusive love. Afterwards, he himself wonders: ". . . was it true, as she said, that love would appear strange to me no matter what form it took, even if there were no eagles and snakes?" An affirmative answer to this question is implicit in all Bellow's fiction. Love *is* strange to the Bellow hero because it demands exactly that rejection of caution which Kirby Allbee propounded to Leventhal; it requires that the lover submit to the temptation to dissolve himself, to risk his primal security for something "dangerous" and "glorious." Perhaps because he has the least to lose, Augie comes closest of Bellow's heroes to success in such an all-consuming love; but he does tire easily ("My real fault was that I couldn't stay with my purest feelings") and he offers himself the dubious consolation that he who would pursue "an independent fate" must necessarily do without love.

The precise nature of Madeleine Pontritter's challenge to Herzog is more difficult to assess in this context because she is rarely presented full face in a direct dramatic situation. What we know of her must be gathered from the distorted fragments of Herzog's bitter recollections and from the pervasive pain which his memories engender in him. The actual outlines of her personality are concealed by the elliptical effects of the novel's narrative technique, and, then, further blurred by the assemblage of grotesque details which Bellow heaps upon her. Her frenetic family background, her impresario father, her theatrical conversion to Catholicism, the tomes of Slavic mysticism which she piles under the bed, the sense of absolute premeditation and treachery with

which she conducts the affair with Valentine Gersbach, her cold manipulation of the credulous Dr. Edvig—this overweighted accumulation of melodramatic matter and manner makes the reader suspicious of Herzog's capacity for distinguishing between an actual Madeleine and a Madeleine that he needs to portray to his own consciousness. What does seem to emerge with great reluctance from his reminiscences is the possibility that Mady offers the same kind of challenge to Herzog that Thea did to Augie. "Compared with her he felt static, without temperament," Herzog confesses at one point. Elsewhere he remarks that "Everyone close to Madeleine, everyone drawn into the drama of her life became exceptional, deeply gifted, brilliant. It had happened also to him." And in another place he says sarcastically that "The satisfaction she took in herself was positively plural—imperial." Superficially, it may very well be that Madeleine's overwhelming egotism is a sufficient explanation of her character, but if this is all she is, Herzog's anguish and fury at her infidelity and his loss seem surely disproportionate and misplaced. The domineering monstrosity whom Herzog consistently invokes in his memories—a Madeleine assembling herself for early Mass with the machined deliberation of an astronaut preparing for a launch; a Madeleine charming Professor Shapiro with herring, liver paste, a gaily adorned rear-end, and passionate talk of Tikhon Zadonsky and the younger Soloviëv; a Madeleine who expresses "a total will that he [Herzog] should die. . . . a vote for his nonexistence"—such a Madeleine could not have brought Herzog to the sterile depths of nervous exhaustion which the novel scrapes upon. It is as though there were something vitally important left out of Herzog's description of his life with Madeleine —a mosaic piece, as it were, without which the total portrait remains seriously incomplete

—compelling, perhaps, in its shocking grotesquerie, but finally unconvincing.

In other words, even though Herzog describes himself as being always under "the flavor of subjugation" to his second wife, the reader misses a scene which might display the two of them, equally loved and loving—and, hence, having equally something to lose. Whether the lack of such a scene is due to the repressive action of Herzog's instincts for survival or Bellow's failure as a novelist, such a scene might have redressed the balance in Madeleine's portraiture, making her less operatic in her ruthlessness and explaining more fully why Herzog suffers her rejection so intensely. This might then indicate that his deeper remorse is connected to the same realization of failure in himself that Augie should have felt, but did not feel. And it might have suggested that whatever love Madeleine did offer to Herzog was too "strange" and too costly for him to accept. That, for a second time, the challenge of a vivid self-effacing love was proffered to the Bellow hero, and for a second time his frozen psyche could not thaw itself sufficiently to accept. Nachman and his Laura drift away on the streets of Paris and Brooklyn, a shabby modern Paolo and Francesca, and Herzog counterpoints their destruction with a covert chronicle of his own unqualified defeat. For himself, such destruction is more than he can afford. In the end, love is a challenge which he deflects by translating it into the harmless world of metaphysical abstractions; he elects instead the pleasant performance of affectionate sex which he can control at a safe remove from the "distant garden where curious objects grow, and there, in a lovely dusk of green, the heart of Moses E. Herzog hangs like a peach."

Thus the Bellow hero returns ever to the prison of himself, uncommitted to religion, to society, to family, or to love, jeering impotently at himself for his bitter knowledge "that people can be free now but the freedom doesn't have any content." Once, in *Dangling Man,* he considers a narrow path of escape, the adolescent artist's classic rationalization for withdrawal and studied alienation. "The real world is the world of art and thought," writes a friend to Joseph. "There is only one worthwhile sort of work, that of the imagination." It would have been relatively simple for Bellow to have embraced the fashionable aesthetic standard of existence, bestowing upon his brooding intellectual heroes a measure of transcendent salvation from the rainbow shapes of order and harmony which it was within the power of their imaginations to create. But he has been too honest in his moral intransigency—too loyal, perhaps, to his early religious training—to have seized this facile egress from despair. As the comically conceived careers of Joseph, Henderson, Herzog, and Philip Bummidge teach us, "Humanity lives mainly from perverted ideas." To have accepted the primacy of a "world of art and thought" would have belied the deeper truth that man is a "throb-hearted character," a "strange organization" that will eventually die, a "most peculiar animal" that sometimes is filled with "an idiot joy" to which it must spontaneously exclaim, "Thou movest me." The Bellow hero has too much integrity of the flesh to try to escape himself in systems of thought or fancy that would deny his integral position in the sentient world. He has learned that his moods are subservient to the tidal undulations of his own blood, and over these he has no control. He knows that, in the end, his "balance comes from instability," and that such small intense joys as he may be blessed with when the spirit's sleep is burst will be inevitably followed by the shades of ever-returning despair. And for him there can be no permanent release from that despair—not in the exciting spume of theory or the framing of gaudy metaphors; not in a nostalgic clutching at a way of life that is forever lost; not in a rancid disgust at the mediocre quality of life that is at least available to him.

But such a summation of Bellow's fictional world makes too bleak a picture to do justice to the splendor of his achievement. For while I believe that I have been accurate in sketching the essential structure of that world, I have neglected to take into account the mollifying and humanizing effects of the humor which is so basic a part of Bellow's craft and life style. One recalls Philip Bummidge's proclamation of identity in *The Last Analysis*—a proclamation which is surely Bellow's as well: ". . . I formed my own method. I learned to obtain self-knowledge by doing what I best knew how to do, acting out the main events of my life, dragging repressed material into the open by sheer force of drama. I'm not solely a man but also a man who is an artist, and an artist whose sphere is comedy." From his earliest work to the present, Bellow's natural sphere has been comedy, and if it is true that his most significant recurrent theme has been despair, it is also true that this despair has been projected prismatically through a consistently comical lens. Walking across the fields of Normandy with his housekeeper, Jacqueline, Augie thinks of her dream of Mexico and bursts into laughter. "That's the *animal ridens* in me, the laughing creature, forever rising up," he thinks. "What's so laughable, that a Jacqueline, for instance, as hard used as that by rough forces, will still refuse to lead a disappointed life? Or is the laugh at nature—including eternity—that it thinks it can win over us and the power of hope? Nah, nah! I think. It never will. But that probably is the joke,

on one or the other, and laughing is an enigma that includes both." This laugh has always been present in Bellow's fiction as a double- or triple-voiced response to the mortal enigma of consciousness. The Bellow hero who mocks himself without mercy is, at the same time, mocked by the pittance of life which Bellow gives him to live. And yet the brute impersonality of life itself is also mocked; mind can always extract its human superiority over mindlessness—even when mindlessness assumes proportions that are as large as eternity. Humor is an enormously complex and problematical affair in modern literature, and one particularly protean and evasive in the work of a moral ironist like Bellow; here we can but point to some of its isolated effects without hoping to do more than suggest the larger ambience it may include.

Traditional satire and parody have not usually interested Bellow, nor has he been especially successful in their uses. The attempts, for example, to satirize a specific social group or idea—the Servatius party in *Dangling Man,* the Magnus family in *The Adventures of Augie March,* the Freudian hijinks of *The Last Analysis,* or the wilder inanities of hipsterism and radical revolt in *Mr. Sammler's Planet*—are, on the whole, rather labored and unconvincing efforts. Writers like Philip Roth and Bruce Jay Friedman have followed Bellow's lead and been far more effective with such satirical material. And similarly, although there is a sprinkling of parody in Bellow's work—most notably in *Henderson the Rain King*—this comic strategy is also clearly tangential to his central interests and talents. Bellow's dominant strength as a humorist has been his powerful sense of the grotesque and his accomplished capacity to communicate that sense to his reader. In *Dangling Man* Joseph remarks that "there is an element of the comic or fantastic in everyone," and Bellow, agreeing so completely with Joseph's perception that he sees Joseph himself as "fantastic," writes under the full ironic force of that conviction. That is, not only does the Bellow hero view the world in terms of the grotesque, but he is himself viewed in the same way. Bellow's art holds a deliberately warped mirror up to life and it is the task of the reader to focus the moral proportions as best he can. There are, of course, severe limitations in such an artistic perspective. As we have noted, this vision tends to freeze all action into a virtual paralysis, while it puts an inflated premium on passivity. It tends inevitably to shift values like love, faith, and truth from the turbulent immediacy of the real world into the placid realm of abstractions. And since it offers us the authority of the grotesque measured by the grotesque, it runs the danger of evading objective judgment almost entirely. But it does succeed in establishing a perverse buffer against the onslaught of despair, and such a defense is its major function.

It accepts despair as a basic reality of human life—perhaps the ultimate reality—but it deflects its enervating power through the agency of laughter, transforming despair into something that becomes the pragmatic equivalent of hope. At one point in *Seize the Day*, Dr. Adler chides Tommy Wilhelm for his sloppy, unheroic attitude toward life: " 'You make too much of your problems,' said the doctor. 'They ought not to be turned into a career. Concentrate on real troubles—fatal sickness, accidents.' " There is no question but that Dr. Adler is clinically correct in his diagnosis. His is the measured judgment of the real world, but Tommy and Bellow are humanly wiser than he. They are aware that the doctor's "truths" are irrelevant; that men's human lives are not lived in the real world; that terminal

sicknesses and accidents are not the real problems at all. These will, in due course of time, arrive, and they will dispense finality to man, but only a fool would expend his energies on fatalities that are impervious to the energetic action of the mind. What obsesses Tommy and all Bellow's heroes is the quality of the lives they are given to live—the porous quotidian texture which is squeezed between the accidents of birth and the fatal sicknesses which end in death. Submerging themselves in this texture, Bellow's heroes are in a constant froth of self-examination, checking the daily temperature of their happiness, measuring the degrees of deficiency in their self-fulfillments. This is the relentless focus of their brooding concerns. This is where they are most human and this is where they are most humorously treated by Bellow's art.

Indeed one might suggest that Bellow's humor rises to its most excruciating pitch when the despair bites closest to the bone. The opening forty pages of *Henderson the Rain King*, for example, voice an almost uninterrupted shriek of pain and outrage, and they are also among the most humorous pages that Bellow has written. Eugene Henderson, that grotesque amalgam of Holden Caulfield and Papa Hemingway, is purporting to explain why he has decided to go to Africa. Rich, and in vigorous health, Henderson has the material freedom to do what he will with his life; yet all he can effect with his millions and his magnificent incoherent ideals is to raise pigs on his ancestral Connecticut estate, take violin lessons in order to serenade his dead parents, shoot at cats under the table, and suffer the increasing stridency of the voice that bursts compulsively from his pent-up heart, "I want! I want!" Nor can one discount Henderson because he is eccentric and askew. His torment persuades us otherwise. He may be grotesque, but his sufferings are real and significant. As Joseph, an earlier prisoner of the same pinioning freedom, concluded many years before, ". . . reality . . . is actually very dangerous, very treacherous. It should not be trusted." Or, as Joseph explains more directly, "To be pushed upon oneself entirely put the very facts of simple existence in doubt." And the massive drift of twentieth-century life has pushed the Bellow hero upon himself entirely. The dissolution of the centripetal religious family-unit, the economic emancipation of the worker, and the creation of a mass affluent society have succeeded in isolating the individual imagination from both the sources and the goals of all belief. The Bellow hero is too honest to pretend that his situation is other than a displaced one. He is too desperate in his psychic needs to be able to accept the bland compromises that everyone around him seems to accept. But he is finally, at bottom, too human to be able to regard himself all that seriously. Too human, beause he is always aware that his is just one tiny life in an infinite multitude of lives and deaths. And so he suffers his real pains and mocks his torment with a single cry that is at once laughter and agony inseparably mingled.

The fact that Bellow has managed to view this plight of modern man as pathetic rather than tragic—probably because le also is too human to take himself all that seriously—is what has given him his characteristic comic methodology. For we must not forget his dictum that modern comedy has to do with "the disintegrating outline of the worthy and humane Self, the bourgeois hero of an earlier age." The Bellow hero is a specimen case of that worthy Self in the process of breakdown —a consciously quixotic blunderer who is designed to evoke his own and our laughter in his frantic efforts to avoid or absorb his own pain. And the special kind of humor which

makes this transaction of energies possible is exposed and released in Bellow's style. This, I believe, is the point where Bellow differs most significantly from the contemporary "black" humorists and nihilistic practitioners of "the absurd." While their works tend to extract a dark humor from the very senselessness of the inhuman condition, concentrating on the stark outrageousness of their fictional situations for their comic effects, Bellow's concern is directed toward the articulated human response to that condition—the verbal phrases and kinetic metaphors with which suffering man escalates implacable defeats into comic impasses which are, at least, barely tolerable. For, with the contemporary hostility against language and logic—against words as a mechanism of submission and compromise—Bellow has nothing to do. For him, man becomes human because he uses words. And, more than that, *style* is the final resort for the victim— his means of transcendence out of slavishness into a kind of comic heroism. This, of course, does not mean that Bellow is advancing a rhetoric which besmears reality—which gives the grandiloquent lie to life. Rather, it is an employment of language to define more accurately the crosscurrents which roil the spirit between a will to live and an awareness of death. For Bellow, neither demonic rhetoric nor silence can define the human condition correctly. Rhetoric invites dishonesty and silence cuts both below and above the level of the human. Bellow's notion of man is far too dependent on the miracle of rationality—on man's internal dialogue with himself—for him to be hostile to words. And hence, it is in his style that the complexities of his humor and his moral concern with the human unite and most persuasively develop.

And his prose style is a formidable instrument for his purposes. Eclectic, vital, raucous, it is unusually flexible in its different capacities. It delights in making grandiose catalogues—in chronicling the inventory of smells, tastes, and colors in a New York City delicatessen, or the three-dimensional turbulence of a modern city-scape, or the intellectual history of mankind gleaned erratically from the stacks of libraries and museums. This style of open-ended aggrandizement is one of Bellow's major devices for imparting a sensuous texture to his fictional world. But on the other hand, his style is equally adept at capsuling a welter of impressions into one firmly seized image in which the grotesque detail becomes comically, shockingly, irrefutably fixed in the prose: "Her lips come together like the seams of a badly sewn baseball." "And my face . . . is no common face, but like an unfinished church." Further, the tempo of Bellow's prose is susceptible to a large range of modulation. It can move at the "larky" pace of Augie's rambunctious recitation; it can lumber with the sullen clumsiness of Leventhal; or it can explode like firecrackers with the zany mock-hysteria of Henderson. It is comfortable with the logical rigors of formal exposition and, as I have already noted, it can be an acute mimic of the speech tones of the crank and the huckster. Perhaps it tends to become artificial and stilted in straight dramatic dialogue, and sometimes a little embarrassing in those lyrical flights where sentimentality escapes the realistic grip of the comic spirit; however, these awkwardnesses are relatively infrequent because Bellow's introspective focus tends to avoid both dramatic dialogue and untempered lyricism.

But whatever demands Bellow assigns to his style, that style is almost always under the controlling influence of a dominant oral tradition —that of spoken or argued Yiddish. The echo of a discernible human voice is deeply residual even in the most abstract of his prose passages; and that voice carries the ironic, chiding melody of the speech of the ghetto. In fact, it is entirely possible that the "voice" came first in Bellow's development as an artist—prior to his conscious shaping of thought or ideal. It is a voice which in its very rhythms mocks both speaker and the spoken, which has mastered a way of expressing lamentation and joy simultaneously, which loves to argue and analyze, which is balanced in a stance of aggressive defense at all times, which has a poised control over the affectionate insult, the cosmic curse, and the rare release of blessing. Bellow's prose and the life style which his fictions have figured forth are, in a sense, an expansion and extension of that brooding voice—a rich fusion of sophisticated erudition and earthiness which brings the full current of man's coursing blood into the world of mind and spirit, and which is careful to retain the sensual as the root metaphor of all experience. It is Bellow's style, thus, which subsumes and encompasses the direction and shape of his achievement as a writer. Rational, honest, ironic, cognizant of human limitations but struggling not to be cowed by them, it gropes and grapples and learns to accept itself as a deliberate comic thrust against life. It is, at the end, its own justification, but one severely fought for, and one which holds its victories as cheap because it knows well the heavy price it has had to pay for them. It is in his style that one can see Bellow's weaknesses as a writer—the narrowness of his scope, the solipsistic closure, the forfeits which his imagination has had to surrender to irony, and to the realism of mortal flesh. But his style is triumphantly a record of his remarkable strengths as well—his success in establishing and making viable an image of the human in the face of the dual tides of mechanism and brute animality that threaten to obliterate the very concept of humanity in their sweep. And it is here, I believe, that his finest achievement will be read and reckoned.

Selected Bibliography

WORKS OF SAUL BELLOW

NOVELS

Dangling Man. New York: Vanguard, 1944.
The Victim. New York: Vanguard, 1947.
The Adventures of Augie March. New York: Viking Press, 1953.
Seize the Day. New York: Viking Press, 1956.
Henderson the Rain King. New York: Viking Press, 1959.
Herzog. New York: Viking Press, 1964.
Mr. Sammler's Planet. New York: Viking Press, 1970.

PLAY

The Last Analysis. New York: Viking Press, 1965.

SHORT STORIES

"Two Morning Monologues," *Partisan Review,* 8:230–36 (May–June 1941).
"The Mexican General," *Partisan Review,* 9:178–94 (May–June 1942).
"Dora," *Harper's Bazaar,* 83:118–88 (November 1949).
"Sermon by Doctor Pep," *Partisan Review,* 16:455–62 (May–June 1949).
"Trip to Galena," *Partisan Review,* 17:779–94 (November–December 1950).
"Looking for Mr. Green," *Commentary,* 11:251–61 (March 1951). (Collected in *Seize the Day.*)
"By the Rock Wall," *Harper's Bazaar,* 85:135–205 (April 1951).
"Address by Gooley MacDowell to the Hasbeens Club of Chicago," *Hudson Review,* 4:222–27 (Summer 1951).
"A Father-to-be," *New Yorker,* 30:26–30 (February 5, 1955). (Collected in *Seize the Day.*)
"The Gonzaga Manuscripts," *discovery,* IV, edited by Vance Bourjaily. New York: Pocket Books, 1956. (Collected in *Seize the Day.*)
"Leaving the Yellow House," *Esquire,* 49:112–26 (January 1958).
Mosby's Memoirs. New York: Viking Press, 1969.

ARTICLES

"How I Wrote Augie March's Story," *New York Times Book Review,* January 31, 1954, p. 3.
"The Writer and the Audience," *Perspectives U.S.A.,* 9:99–102 (Autumn 1954).
"Isaac Rosenfeld," *Partisan Review,* 23:565–67 (Fall 1956).
"A Talk with the Yellow Kid," *Reporter,* 15:41–44 (September 6, 1956).
"Distractions of a Fiction Writer," *New World Writing,* 12:229–43 (New York: New American Library, 1957).
"Deep Readers of the World, Beware!" *New York Times Book Review,* February 15, 1959, p. 1.
"Some Notes on Recent American Fiction," *Encounter,* 21:22–29 (November 1963).
"The Writer as Moralist," *Atlantic Monthly,* 211:58–62 (March 1963).

CRITICAL AND BIOGRAPHICAL STUDIES

Alter, Robert, *After the Tradition.* New York: Dutton, 1969.
Axthelm, Peter M. *The Modern Confessional Novel.* New Haven, Conn.: Yale University Press, 1967.
Baumbach, Jonathan. *The Landscape of Nightmare.* New York: New York University Press, 1965.
Clayton, John J. *Saul Bellow: In Defense of Man.* Bloomington: Indiana University Press, 1967.
Detweiler, Robert. *Saul Bellow.* Grand Rapids, Mich.: William B. Eerdmans, 1967.
Donoghue, Denis. "Commitment and the Dangling Man," *Studies: An Irish Quarterly Review* (1964), pp. 174–87.
Dutton, Robert R. *Saul Bellow.* New York: Twayne, 1971.
Eisinger, Chester E. *Fiction of the Forties.* Chicago: University of Chicago Press, 1963.
Enck, John. "Saul Bellow: An Interview," *Wisconsin Studies in Contemporary Literature,* 6:156–60 (1965).
Fiedler, Leslie. *Love and Death in the American Novel.* Cleveland: World, 1962.
Galloway, David D. *The Absurd Hero in American Fiction.* Austin: University of Texas Press, 1966.

Gross, Theodore. *The Heroic Ideal in American Literature.* New York: The Free Press, 1971.

Guttmann, Allen. *The Jewish Writer in America.* New York: Oxford University Press, 1971.

Harper, Gordon Lloyd. "Saul Bellow: An Interview," *Paris Review*, 36:49–73 (Winter 1965).

Harper, Howard M., Jr. *Desperate Faith.* Chapel Hill: University of North Carolina Press, 1967.

Hassan, Ihab. *Radical Innocence.* Princeton, N.J.: Princeton University Press, 1961.

Kazin, Alfred. *Contemporaries.* Boston: Little, Brown, 1962.

Klein, Marcus. *After Alienation.* Cleveland: World, 1964.

Ludwig, Jack. *Recent American Novelists.* Minneapolis: University of Minnesota Press, 1962.

Malin, Irving, ed. *Saul Bellow and the Critics.* New York: New York University Press, 1967.

———. *Saul Bellow's Fiction.* Carbondale: Southern Illinois University Press, 1969.

Opdahl, Keith Michael. *Saul Bellow: An Introduction.* University Park: Pennsylvania State University Press, 1967.

Podhoretz, Norman. *Doings and Undoings.* New York: Farrar, Straus, 1964.

Poirier, Richard. "Bellow to Herzog," *Partisan Review,* 32:264–71 (1965).

Sokoloff, B. A. *Saul Bellow: A Comprehensive Bibliography.* Folcroft, Pa.: Folcroft, 1972.

Tanner, Tony. *City of Words.* New York: Harper & Row, 1971.

———. *Saul Bellow.* Edinburgh: Oliver & Boyd, 1965.

Weinberg, Helen. *The New Novel in America.* Ithaca, N.Y.: Cornell University Press, 1970.

Wisse, Ruth R. *The Schlemiel as Modern Hero.* Chicago: University of Chicago Press, 1971.

—*EARL ROVIT*

Gwendolyn Brooks
1917–

*A*T THE AGE of seventy, with the publication of *Blacks,* Gwendolyn Brooks set the terms for any and all discussion of her career as an American poet. Within a blue-black flexible binding, the volume's competing typefaces reflect the trajectory of her publishing career from the white New York world of Harper & Row to the black independent presses of Detroit and Chicago: Dudley Randall's Broadside Press; Haki Madhubuti's (Don Lee's) Third World Press; and her own Chicago-based publishing house, The David Company, which she named after her father. Dedicated to her parents, this collection of poems represents the poet's aesthetic *and* political response to her public life. The austere volume requires the audience to reconsider the essential Brooks and to remember that, for her, "Blackness / is a going to essences and to unifyings" ("To Keorapetse," in *Family Pictures*). Those essences and unifyings inform her decision to publish her own work. As she explained in an interview with D. H. Mehlem:

Satisfactions of publishing my own work: "complete" control over design, print, paper, binding, timing, and, not least, the capitalization of the word Black. . . . The current motion to make the phrase "African American" an official identification is cold and excluding. . . .

The capitalized names *Black* and *Blacks* were appointed to compromise an open, wide-stretching, unifying, empowering umbrella.

The freedom of self-publishing far outweighs what Brooks sees as the "Irks": "distribution, Storage, Printers." To review her career is to recognize the consistency of her wide-stretching, empowering, "do-right" vision even as her style has contracted and relaxed to accommodate her perception of shifting audiences and social urgencies.

Heir to the expectations of the Harlem Renaissance, Brooks continues to register aesthetically the racial identity crises of the African American poets who continue to marvel at Countee Cullen's "curious thing": "To make a poet black, and bid him sing!" By the late 1960's she had earned the regard of a new generation of black poets as she proclaimed, "True black writers speak *as* blacks, *about* blacks, *to* blacks" ("The Message of Flowers and Fire and Flowers," in Madhubuti's *Say That the River Turns*). Her formative years seemed to her then "years of high poet-incense; the language flowers . . . thickly sweet. Those flowers whined and begged white folks to pick them, to find them lovable. Then— the Sixties: independent fire!" Her daughter, Nora Brooks Blakely, contends that her mother "more than anything else . . . is a 'mapper' . . . delineat[ing] and defin[ing] the scenery of now"

("Three-Way Mirror," in Madhubuti's *Say That the River Turns*). Much of that present-tense scenery has remained remarkably constant as Brooks has charted the experience of being black in Chicago, in the United States (what she would finally call the Warpland).

Though Brooks saw the late 1960's as a time of political and artistic conversion—a time "to write poems that will successfully 'call' . . . all black people . . . *not* always to 'teach' [but] to entertain, to illumine"—a review of her early expectations suggests that she has been about this all along. Brooks grows impatient with politically aware readers who miss these urgent observations in her early work. In an interview with Claudia Tate, Brooks challenged Tate's assessment that her earlier works lacked "heightened political awareness." She explained:

I'm fighting for myself a little bit here, but not overly so, because I certainly wrote no poem that sounds like Haki's [Don L. Lee's] "Don't Cry, Scream". . . . But I'm fighting for myself a little bit here because I believe it takes a little patience to sit down and find out that in 1945 I was saying what many of the young folks said in the sixties. But it's crowded back into language like this:

> *The pasts of his ancestors lean against*
> *Him. Crowd him. Fog out his identity.*
> *Hundreds of hungers mingle with his own,*
> *Hundreds of voices advise so dextrously*
> *He quite considers his reactions his,*
> *Judges he walks most powerfully alone,*
> *That everything is—simply what it is.*

"The Sundays of Satin-Legs Smith"

My works express rage and focus on *rage*.

In fact much rage is "crowded back" in every gathering of Brooks's poems. And since the expression of anger, if it is righteous anger, is seldom devoid of the redemptive qualities of honor, pride, humor, or love, the absence of these correlatives is notable in Brooks's poetry.

A Gwendolyn Brooks poem offers language or voice to her imagined constituency: the "old-marrieds" of Bronzeville who live speechless "in the crowding darkness"; De Witt Williams; Mrs. Sallie, Pepita, and Melodie Mary in the Mecca; Lincoln West; the Near-Johannesburg Boy. She is at heart a partisan making audible the silent lives of her world: lives in Chicago and, later, Africa. She lends dignity to the individuals and their experiences by giving them names, descriptions—a place. "I don't start with the landmarks," she insists. "I start with the people" (*Report from Part One*). Nora Brooks Blakely sees her mother's poems as "entrances to the lives of people you might, otherwise, never know."

Finding a poetry suitable to aesthetic *and* social needs has troubled Brooks throughout her career. In competing dedication poems in "In the Mecca," "The Chicago Picasso," and "The Wall," she explores the primary tensions of her art and life not only as a black poet but also as a Chicago-based poet. Though all three are poems of commemoration, they nonetheless ask different and perhaps mutually exclusive questions of the poet. In "The Chicago Picasso," written in August 1967, the Seiji Ozawa–Mayor Daley–Picasso event forces the poet into an uncomfortable relationship with "Art":

> Does Man love Art? Man visits Art, but
> squirms.
> Art hurts. Art urges voyages—
> and it is easier to stay at home,
> the nice beer ready.
> In commonrooms
> we belch, or sniff, or scratch.
> Are raw.

The monumental art at the center of this poem is set against our animal nature; rather than consoling, this art "hurts." In fact, Brooks sees the folk as subservient to this overwhelming presentation of Culture: "But we must cook ourselves and style ourselves for Art, who / is a requiring courtesan.'' In an anthropological twist, the civilized / ''the cooked'' devitalizes the primitive / ''the raw.'' This dedicatory poem offers an ultimately sterile, disconnected view of music, art, and politics. Contrary to Carl Sandburg's characterization of the city as a ''Hog Butcher'' in his poem ''Chicago'' (1916), Brooks describes a world of gloss and success where art puts people in their place.

''The Wall,'' also written in August 1967, arises organically from the voices of people not very unlike the folk population of Edgar Lee Masters or Sandburg—except for their powerful blackness. The humility inspired by The Wall supplants the artificial reverence commanded by the Chicago Picasso. Here the poet celebrates, with the rhythmic fervor of Vachel Lindsay, a community in the making, as a slum wall is transformed into an object of reverence and art (the Wall of Respect):

> A drumdrumdrum.
> Humbly we come.
> South of success and east of gloss and glass are sandals;
> flowercloth;
> grave hoops of wood or gold, pendant
> from black ears, brown ears, reddish-brown
> and ivory ears;
>
> . . . .
>
> Women in wool hair chant their poetry.
>
> . . . .
>
> On Forty-third and Langly
>
> . . . .
>
> All
> worship the Wall.

This projection makes art a vital part of a community. In a curious way, Brooks has rerouted the magi and made their journey a solipsistic one. Here the object of reverence is culturally intrinsic; it is also worthy of respect. The Wall of Respect remains for Brooks an emblem of that

historical moment when she recalled ''hotbreathing hope, clean planning, and sizable black cross-reference and reliance'' (interview in *Tri-Quarterly*).

Brooks retains from those years of revolution and protest ''something under-river; pride surviving, pride and self-respect surviving.'' In spite of the flight of many black writers to major white publishing houses, she stands firm in her commitment (born of a time of revolution and nourished in the intervening years) to write for and be published by blacks. She in fact champions a segregated literary criticism. She explained to Tate:

I believe whites are going to say what they choose to say about us, whether it's right or wrong, or just say *nothing.* . . . We should ignore them. I can no longer decree that we must send our books to black publishers; I would like to say that. I have no intention of ever giving my books to another white publisher. But I do know black publishers are having a lot of trouble. . . .

We must place an emphasis on ourselves and publish as best we can and not allow white critics to influence what we do.

Although she achieved great success at the hands of what she came to regard as an enslaving culture (the Pulitzer Prize in 1950; Guggenheim Fellowships in 1946 and 1947), Brooks no longer courts the white literary establishment or those who indulge in ''literary 'hair-straightening.' ''

Making poems into verbal analogues of the Wall of Respect has done little to ease the tension in Brooks's mind between the desired audience (her people) and her actual audience (the academics of the college classroom). Norris Clark (echoing George Kent) suggests in ''Gwendolyn Brooks and a Black Aesthetic,'' ''It is precisely because Brooks's poetry fails to appeal to the black masses that it appeals aesthetically to the 'blacks who go to college.' '' The political atmosphere of the late 1960's made a poem like ''Riot'' a historical curiosity that survives without context. As Langston Hughes knew all too well, "Politics can be the graveyard of the poet. And only poetry can be his resurrection."

The monumental collection *Blacks* suggests that poetry has always resurrected Brooks. These poems' renewing observations of experience and people are products of "one who distills experience—strains experience" (Brooks's description of the poet). Amid stylistic shifts and historical cataclysms, Brooks keeps her look, her identity. She is a poet, unawed by wonder and comfortable with the stunning quotidian, who knows that, as she says in "The Artists' and Models' Ball":

Wonders do not confuse. We call them that
And close the matter there. But common things
Surprise us. . . .

Even as her poems verbally enact what Brooks calls "brav[ing] our next small business," her life mimics her aesthetic credo: "Live in the along."

This lifelong habit of attending to the available particulars was instilled during Brooks's "sparkly childhood, with two fine parents and one brother, in a plain but warmly enclosing two-story gray house" (*Report from Part One*). For Brooks, "Home meant a quick-walking, careful Duty-Loving mother" and a "father, with kind eyes, songs, and tense recitations" for his children. In dedicating *Blacks* to the memory of her "plain but warmly enclosing" parents, she paid tribute to her family as the original and sustaining force in her life.

Though her parents lived in Chicago, Brooks was born in Topeka, Kansas, on June 7, 1917. Both parents were descendants of blacks who had migrated to Kansas at the end of the Civil War; her father was the son of Lucas Brooks, a runaway slave. Her mother, Keziah Corine Wims, had returned home to her native Kansas for the birth of her first child. Prior to her marriage, Keziah Wims had attended Emporia State Normal School and taught fifth grade at the Monroe School in Topeka. She met David Anderson Brooks during the summer of 1914; they married in July 1916. David Brooks, a native of Atchison, Kansas, had moved to Oklahoma City at the age of nine and remained there until he finished his schooling—of the twelve children in his family, he was the only one to complete high school. He "got up at five o'clock to feed horses and to do other chores, so [he] could go to school." He attended Fisk University in hopes of a medical career but found that family obligations necessitated full-time employment. He became a janitor at the McKinley Music Publishing Company in Chicago. Gwendolyn recalled that though "not many knew of [her] father's lowly calling . . . SOMETHING . . . stamped [her] 'beyond the pale.' " In 1918, when Gwendolyn was sixteen months old, her brother, Raymond, was born. When she was three, the family moved from cramped quarters in Hyde Park to an apartment at Fifty-sixth and Lake Park Avenue. Here Gwendolyn and Raymond could play in the garden plot their mother tilled.

From her father, Gwendolyn acquired a love of "fascinating poetry" and "jolly or haunting songs" that he sang; her favorite was "Asleep in the Deep." Her mother also loved music, played the piano, and was often heard singing "Brighten the Corner Where You Are." The Brooks family encouraged the familiar, the repeatable. Holidays were occasions for well-loved rituals of cooking, singing, and decoration. Gift-giving days necessitated "the bake-eve fun" of baking and wrapping. In particular, Christmas was a time when "certain things were done. Certain things were not done."

One of the things "not done" in the Brooks household was Mother working outside the home. Father furnished "All the Money." Shortfalls in the family account meant that they ate beans and "would have been quite content to entertain a beany diet every day, if necessary . . . if there could be, continuously, the almost musical Peace [they] had most of the time." Home was nourished by her father's "special practical wisdom," which unerringly held the family together. He was a father who "really took time with his children."

Childhood was a time of dancing and dreaming—and writing. School offered little in the way of sweet society. Ostracized because of her appearance (too dark), her shyness, and her inability to "sashay," Brooks retreated into her world of home and imagination. Though her mother recalls her "rhyming at seven," Brooks dates the start of her poetic activity to her eleventh year. Her natural diffidence and her distaste for school-age pastimes like "Post Office" and "Kiss the Pilla" led young Gwendolyn to a discovery of her "in-life."

If Brooks's solitary childhood nurtured her writing, then her encounter with *Writer's Digest* fostered an alternative society as the fledgling poet discovered "*oodles* of *other* writers" who "ached for the want of the right word—reckoned with mean nouns, virtueless adjectives." When Brooks was thirteen, her father gave her a desk "with many little compartments, with long drawers at the bottom, and a removable glass-protected shelf at the top, for books." Here was a place to work, to dream, to reach. Her presiding spirit was Paul Laurence Dunbar (Langston Hughes recalled that "almost every Negro home had a copy of Dunbar"); Brooks wrote a poem every day under his portrait and studied "the Complete Paul Laurence Dunbar." In fact, Keziah Brooks predicted that Gwendolyn would become "the lady Paul Laurence Dunbar."

Brooks wrote daily and read widely. Traces of John Keats and William Wordsworth coexist in her writing with the more dominant voices of the Chicago school (Sandburg, Masters) and the Harlem Renaissance (Dunbar, Hughes, and Cullen). Cullen's *Caroling Dusk: An Anthology of Verse by Negro Poets* (1927) and Hughes's *The Weary Blues* (1926) made Brooks realize that "writing about the ordinary aspects of black life was important." After having endured the "coldness of editors, spent too much money on postage," she experienced her first publishing triumph in 1930, at the age of thirteen: *American Childhood* published "Eventide." Within three years the *Chicago Defender* was regularly accepting Brooks's poems for its column "Lights and Shadows."

By 1934, the year of her high school graduation, Brooks had written to and actually met James Weldon Johnson—the meeting occurred at the insistence of her mother, secure in her belief in Gwendolyn's talent. Johnson did not recall receiving any poems from the young poet, claiming he got "so many of them." He did suggest, however, that her talent would be best served by reading the modern poets. Already secure in her understanding of Hughes and Cullen, she began to read T. S. Eliot, Ezra Pound, and E. E. Cummings. Later that year, Keziah engineered another meeting, this time with Hughes. She "brought a whole pack of stuff" to his reading at the Metropolitan Community Church. Far from dismissing Gwendolyn, Hughes "read [her poems] right there" and declared that she "must go on writing." Though several of her teachers had urged her to continue writing so that she might, one day, be a poet, no classroom encouragement inspired her as much as did Hughes's making time for her work.

Brooks's studies came to an end with her graduation from Wilson Junior College (now Kennedy-King College) in 1936, leaving her to confront the working world. As an educated woman, she was ill prepared for the harsh conditions and humiliating nature of service work. Her flight from her first job as a maid led her to the Illinois State Employment Service—and an even less tolerable position: secretary to Dr. E. N. French, a "spiritual adviser" who sold "Holy

Thunderbolts, charms, dusts of different kinds, love potions" from the Mecca, the once "splendid palace, a showplace of Chicago" that was now "a great gray hulk of brick." Nothing in her early years had prepared Brooks for such a concentration of misery. These experiences resisted fictional treatment and continued to preoccupy her until they surfaced as the poems of *In the Mecca* (1968).

Membership in the NAACP Youth Council offered Brooks more than a community organization, for it was during a meeting at the YWCA on Forty-sixth and South Park that "the girl who wrote" met "a fella who wrote." Brooks writes that her "first 'lover' was [her] husband," Henry Lowington Blakely II. Blakely recalls "a shy brown girl . . . [with a] rich and deep [voice] . . . [whose] shining was inward . . . [and he] felt warm in that shining." On September 17, 1939, after "a nice little wedding" in her parents' home, Brooks felt "bleak when . . . taken to [her] kitchenette apartment . . . [and] the cramped dreariness of the Tyson." But soon that forbidding atmosphere yielded to the company and the togetherness of "mutual reading." A kitchenette was a place where a son could be "suddenly born" (as Henry Lowington Blakely III was on October 10, 1940), where that same son could "contract broncho-pneumonia," or where mice would come out of the radiators "in droves." For Brooks the kitchenette itself would become a controlling metaphor of her first collection of poems, *A Street in Bronzeville* (1945), as well as of her novel, *Maud Martha* (1953). Feeling that "marriage should get most of a wife's attention," she "scarcely put pen to paper" for a year after her son's birth.

In 1940 Brooks submitted "The Ballad of Pearl May Lee" to the poetry contest of the Negro Exposition. Over the objections of Hughes, the judges awarded the prize to Melvin Tolson, considering Brooks's poem "too militant." In 1941 Brooks and Blakely attended a poetry class at the South Side Community Art Center that was led by "socially acceptable, wealthy, protected" Inez Cunningham Stark. Stark wished to be considered "a friend who loved poetry and respected [her students'] interest in it." A reader for *Poetry* magazine, she gave all students a one-year subscription to the journal and "an education in modern poetry." The apprentice poets were serious and enchanted and diligent. And though some went home crying, many learned how to revise. Stark encouraged her students to read and study poetry, to avoid the easy technical device or cliché, to shun the obvious. Her critiques were "cool, objective, frank." Several of Brooks's Bronzeville poems were written under her guidance.

After winning a workshop prize (S. I. Hayakawa was a judge), as well as the 1943 Midwestern Writers' Conference poetry award, Brooks was encouraged to submit her first poetry manuscript to Emily Morison of Alfred A. Knopf (Hughes's publisher). Morison was impressed enough to counsel expanding the number of "Negro life" poems. Though Brooks took Morison's advice, she did not resubmit to Knopf but instead sent her manuscript to Harper & Brothers. There an editor showed it to the novelist Richard Wright, who applauded its genuineness and suggested expanding the collection, perhaps by adding a long poem. With the addition of "The Sundays of Satin-Legs Smith," *A Street in Bronzeville* was published in 1945.

In many ways the book marked the end of Brooks's innocent workshop years and the beginning of her career as a poet of national standing. From the generalizing indefinite article (*A*) and the subtitle (*Ballads and Blues*) to the closing sonnet sequence ("Gay Chaps at the Bar"), the poems both carry on the "tradition" and defy it. While the poems reflect the influence of the Harlem Renaissance writers and their use of dialect, they more often than not rely upon idiomatic expressions such as one might find in Robert

Frost. Like Frost, Brooks acts as a census-taker, recording the neighborhood's vital statistics and treating every entry with equal disinterest.

It is in this professional distance that Brooks's perceived realism resides. She charts the emotions without emotional display. The collection begins with a series of kitchenette vignettes, progresses to ballads and "The Sundays of Satin-Legs Smith," and ends with the sonnet sequence. More than a response to the South Side's kitchenette ethos or a continuation of the Chicago school of "folk nativist" poets (Sandburg, Masters, Edwin Arlington Robinson), *A Street in Bronzeville* begs for contextual examination as a 1945 reaction to a world of racial, class, and sexual tensions—and war. The black soldiers in these poems project more than masculine racial pride; they are a national challenge to racial relations.

Typical Bronzeville poems foreground the victims. Some are condemned to silence and "crowding darkness" ("the old-marrieds"), while others have life prematurely wrenched from them (the unborn of "the mother"; DeWitt Williams). Brooks is often relentless in the manner in which she captures the "fact" of Bronzeville, as in "the murder":

This is where poor Percy died,
Short of the age of one.
His brother Brucie, with a grin,
Burned him up for fun.

No doubt, poor Percy watched the fire
Chew on his baby dress
With sweet delight, enjoying too
His brother's happiness.

No doubt, poor Percy looked around
And wondered at the heat,
Was worried, wanted Mother,
Who gossiped down the street.

. . . .

No doubt, poor shrieking Percy died
Loving Brucie still,

Who could, with clean and open eye,
Thoughtfully kill.

Brucie has no playmates now.
His mother mourns his lack.
Brucie keeps on asking, "When
Is Percy comin' back?"

Though the poem is devoid of conventionally realistic detail, the governing impression is one of unerring fidelity to truth. As Brooks jostles us with familiar and pleasing words made terrible— "grin," "fun," "chew"—the repeated chorus of "No doubt" leaves the impression that *here,* in Bronzeville, this is the quotidian.

Many of the poems coalesce into a sharp-edged cast of acquaintances: Matthew Cole "in / The door-locked dirtiness of his room"; Sadie, who "stayed at home" while Maud "went to college" (anticipating Toni Morrison's *Sula* [1973]); the hunchback girl "think[ing] of heaven" (feminizing Dylan Thomas' "The Hunchback in the Park" [1942]); Mrs. Martin's Booker T., "[who] ruined Rosa Brown"; Moe Belle Jackson, whose husband "whipped her good last night" (echoing Billie Holiday's "Ain't Nobody's Business"). Still others require heroes—or antiheroes. "Queen of the Blues" not only updates Hughes's "The Weary Blues" but also reacts to an entire tradition of sorrow songs and folk seculars. "Ballad of Pearl May Lee" provides an early rationale for Brooks's 1951 essay "Why Negro Women Leave Home." Its savage narrator shares the rage and humiliation black women feel when their men "grew up with bright skins on the brain." With "Gay Chaps at the Bar," Brooks forsakes characterization for the sonnet sequence. As Cullen and Claude McKay had done before her, she finds an opportunity for argument in the form itself. The formal shift, from ballads and blues to sonnets, is not jarring; rather, it effects a kind of recessional. Questions of race, identity, and love as they trouble those "home from the front" lack the resolution the narrative poems have. The volume concludes with unexpected irony:

And still we wear our uniforms, follow
The cracked cry of the bugles, comb and brush
Our pride and prejudice . . .

. . . .

For even if we come out standing up
How shall we smile, congratulate: and how
Settle in chairs? Listen, listen. The step
Of iron feet again. And again   wild.

Patrons of poetry, familiar with Hughes and accustomed to Frost and Stephen Vincent Benét and Edna St. Vincent Millay, eagerly received the Bronzeville poems. Liberal readers, "comfortable" with the racial themes, neglected the harsh commentary that was contained within what Brooks herself called a "rather folksy narrative." *The New York Times Book Review* (November 4, 1945) found "the idiom . . . colloquial, the language . . . universal." *Poetry* (December 1945) praised her "capacity to marry the special qualities of her racial tradition with the best attainments of our poetic tradition"; *Saturday Review* (January 19, 1945) considered the poems to be a "poignant social document";
The New Yorker (September 22, 1945) praised the freshness of "her folk poetry of the city."

More important was the approbation of Brooks's peers. Cullen wrote to her on August 24, 1945, "I am glad to be able to say 'welcome' to you to that too small group of Negro poets, and to the larger group of American ones. No one can deny your place there." McKay followed with an equally congratulatory note on October 10: "[I] welcome you among the band of hard working poets who do have something to say." But it was Hughes's loving review in the *Chicago Defender* (September 1, 1946) that must have brought Brooks the greatest joy: "This book is just about the BIGGEST little two dollars worth of intriguing reading to be found in the book-

shops these atomic days. It will give you something to talk about from now until Christmas." Critics such as Houston A. Baker, Jr., Gary Smith, and George Kent agree that many of these poems were revolutionary in the way they dealt with race and sexual relationships; they disagree on whether Brooks was seeking to universalize the plight of her subjects.

In addition to the local success of *A Street in Bronzeville*, the book garnered numerous prizes for the poet. By time Brooks published *Annie Allen* (1949), she had won the *Mademoiselle* Merit Award (1945), Guggenheim Fellowships (1946, 1947), the American Academy of Arts and Letters Grant for Creative Writing (1946), and *Poetry*'s Eunice Tietjens Memorial Prize (1949). In the process she became a recognized writer and began to write reviews for the *Chicago Daily News* and the *Chicago Sun-Times*. This hometown work led to reviewing for Hoyt Fuller's *Negro Digest*, *The New York Times*, and the *New York Herald Tribune*. She "stopped reviewing because I decided that even a reviewer . . . should have read Everything." Brooks does recall that "while I Had At It, I was exuberant." Besides her excitement at receiving the packages of reviewer's copies, she relished the opportunity to share and support.

No matter how history recalls Brooks's literary contributions to the years 1941–1949, Brooks remembers the period as her "party era," a time when "party" became a verb. Unlike her solitary childhood and adolescent years, these were times when "merry Bronzevillians" put on the spread and "conversation was our 'mary jane.' " The best parties were at 623 East Sixty-third Street, Brooks's "most exciting kitchenette." Like Hughes, Brooks found her best material when "walking or running, fighting or screaming or singing" beneath her window. And as if to commemorate this shared vision, Hughes came to Brooks's exciting kitchenette for the party of the decade. Having finished at the Lab School in

Chicago, he chose her party for his farewell to Chicago and claimed that it was the "*Best* party . . . I've ever been given!" Brooks "squeezed perhaps a hundred people into our Langston Hughes two-room kitchenette party. Langston was the merriest and the most colloquial of them all. . . . He enjoyed everyone; he enjoyed all the talk, all the phonograph blues, all the festivity in the crowded air."

With *Annie Allen,* Brooks advanced beyond the loose vignettes and sonnets of the Bronzeville poems, preferring to trace the arc of a single character's life. Unable to ignore the war entirely, she dedicated the volume to Edward Bland, a friend whom she had first met in Inez Cunningham Stark's poetry class, and who had died in Germany in March 1945, and introduced it with the elegiac "Memorial to Ed Bland." The dedication and poem appear before the table of contents, as though separate from the rest of the collection. The bold captions and headline-like titles turn the contents page into a poem itself and make it clear that the poet is responding to literary as well as reportorial instincts in this collection. The opening sequence, "Notes from the Childhood and the Girlhood," though a bit more contracted than earlier poems, is familiar to readers of the Bronzeville collection. For these are poems where reality and imagination always collide. However "pinchy" the world, it "prances nevertheless with gods and fairies." The central sequence, a mock epic titled "The Anniad," contends with the literary world beyond the Chicago street noises. The hyperconscious lapidary language, the contracted lines, and the seven-line stanzas hurl Annie into an excessively ornamental and artificial world:

> Vaunting hands are now devoid.
> Hieroglyphics of her eyes
> Blink upon paradise
> Paralyzed and paranoid.

> But idea and body too
> Clamor "Skirmishes can do.
> Then he will come back to you."

Brooks, attempting a stylistic tour de force, seems to have tired of black vernacular structures and white strictures upon style and content. She succeeds on a stylistic level but overwhelms the ordinariness of her subject matter with that success. The work recovers in "Appendix to 'The Anniad'" and the final "Womanhood" sequences, where the narrative pulse is palpable and the style is Brooks's own. Mature Annie's laments—"People who have no children can be hard"; "What shall I give my children? who are poor?"—complement the expanded focus of these final sonnets.

If Brooks expected more of her readers, she had expected much more of herself. With *Annie Allen,* she sought to identify herself both with and against the tradition. These conflicting needs confused reviewers. The complexity of the volume caused many readers to complain that these weren't Bronzeville poems. But Phyllis McGinley, in *The New York Times Book Review* (January 22, 1950), saw that as an advantage. Singling out "The Anniad" for special praise, she claimed that Brooks was best when she forgot "her social conscience and her Guggenheim scholarship," thereby "creating unbearable excitement." In spite of the mixed reception accorded the collection, it was awarded the Pulitzer Prize in 1950. Though Brooks was the first black writer to win a Pulitzer in any category, she did not establish a precedent, merely a referent. It would be thirty-three years before another black woman would win (Alice Walker in 1983).

Some critics see *Annie Allen* as Brooks's first important work. Baker situates the collection in the greater swirl of modernism; in the book's echoing of Ernest Hemingway, Eliot, and Pound, it "join[ed] the mainstream of twentieth-century poetry in its treatment of the terrors of war."

Haki Madhubuti (Don Lee) reads its importance in a different way:

> *Annie Allen* (1949), important? Yes. Read by blacks? No. *Annie Allen* more so than *A Street in Bronzeville* seems to have been written for whites. . . . ["The Anniad"] requires unusual concentrated study. . . .This poem is probably earth-shaking to some, but leaves me completely dry. . . .
>
> There is an over-abundance of the special appeal to the world-runners. . . .

By the late 1960's, Brooks would join Madhubuti in his assessment of this successful period of her career. But for the moment, the Pulitzer brought with it public recognition and a national reputation.

The birth of her daughter, Nora, on September 8, 1951, convinced Brooks to leave the Kalamazoo, Michigan, home to which the family had moved in 1948. In spite of their wish to escape the racial tensions and claustrophobic conditions of inner-city life, the family returned to Chicago and by 1953 had their own home, at 7428 South Evans Avenue, near the University of Chicago. In "How I Told My Child About Race" (1951), however, Brooks recorded an unsettling experience. When she and her son were walking home, they were assaulted by stone-throwing young whites in that very "university district, mecca of basic enlightenment and progressive education. . . . The buildings, with their delicate and inspiring spires, seemed . . . to leer, to crowd us with mutterings—'Oh no, you black bodies!—no sanctuary here.' " This incident forced a mother to explain not what race is but why it is what it is. Long before Brooks would turn to the Pan-African movement for identity, she refused to drag "the subject of 'race' down for frequent examination and hammering, because [she thought] that children should be helped to view the samenesses among themselves and others."

In 1953 Brooks published her "autobiograph-ical novel," *Maud Martha*. Favoring the "nu-anceful, allowing" form of the novel over the memoir, she nonetheless reads herself into every page. Here "fact-meat" combines with "chunks of fancy" to build a narrative familiar to readers of her earlier works. Lower-class, vignetted titles echo strategies from the Bronzeville poems and prepare us for the dailiness of the lives within. Known faces and circumstances crowd the story of Maud's coming of age and young married life. A larger cast of kitchenette folks—Binnie, Mrs. Teenie Thompson, Mr. and Mrs. Whitestripe—is "real," as are many of the heroine's adventures. The slights and daily indignities ("the self-solace"), the masculine domination of Maud's every move, prompt what Brooks later called "woman rage." In "brotherly love," as she dresses a chicken, Maud's empathy is allowed to go beyond the human circumstances:

> But if the chicken were a man!—cold man with no head or feet and with all the little feather, hairs to be pulled, and the intestines loosened and beginning to ooze out, and the gizzard yet to be grabbed and the stench beginning to rise! And yet the chicken was a sort of person, a respectable individual, with its own kind of dignity. The difference was in the knowing. What was unreal to you, you could deal with violently.

Much later, as if anticipating the animal-rights movement, Brooks would reinforce this notion of chickens as "people": "people, that is, in the sense that we conceive people to be: things of identity and response."

Maud Martha received polite reviews that dismissed it with annoyance or faint praise. *The New Yorker* (October 10, 1953) complained that it was but a "series of sketches"; the *Southern Review* (October 1953) found it an "ingratiating first novel." Only the *Chicago Defender* (September 30, 1953) saw how the novel "struck at the twisted roots of racial antagonisms." In the wake of feminist criticism, some contemporary critics (particularly Mary Helen Washington and Patricia and Vernon Lattin) see it as a revolutionary work. Washington, attacking earlier views of the work as full of "optimism and faith," sees it instead as a work straining to contain its "bitterness, rage, self-hatred, and silence." Rarely in Brooks's oeuvre is there such a challenge to work against the pleasures of the narrative line and decode the savage "woman rage" just underneath. Here she uses the homey story to mask its own meanings, forcing the reader to translate not merely the black cultural context but the feminist context as well.

The rest of the 1950's were mostly spent addressing the needs of Brooks's children at home—and in verse. In 1956 *Bronzeville Boys and Girls* was published. These poems, juvenile reductions of her "adult" poems, are serious considerations of poverty, racism, and loneliness. Though offset by the lively rhythms and sound patterns, the sober vision of this childhood world remains. Reviewers, comfortable with their Gwendolyn Brooks "slot," tended to see the poems as universal expressions, rhythmic and simple. The *New York Herald Tribune Book Review* (November 18, 1956) explained the secret of the book: "Because Miss Brooks is a Negro poet, she has called these *Bronzeville Boys and Girls,* but they are universal and will make friends anywhere, among grown-ups or among children from eight to ten."

With the death of her mentor, Inez Cunningham-Stark, on August 19, 1957, and of her father, on November 21, 1959, Brooks assumed greater responsibilities in her life and art. She reconsidered early experiences in the hopes of writing another novel, the tale of an unfortunate, dark-skinned boy named Lincoln West. Though she published poetic versions of little Lincoln's life, she left the novel unfinished. She also hoped to tell the story of the Mecca and Dr. E. N. French but, like Lincoln's tale, this would have to await a poetic treatment. With two major collections be-

hind her, and having achieved a certain celebrity, Brooks entered a new decade, one in which she would become mentor to yet another generation.

With *The Bean Eaters* (1960), Brooks advanced to a new level of technical and aesthetic power as well as of social conscience. Originally entitled "Bronzeville Men and Women," the collection takes seriously what Kent sees as its association with Vincent van Gogh's *The Potato Eaters*. The world of these poems is one of poverty, dim spirits, and truncated hopes. Rather than presenting "acceptable" vignettes of blacks, these poems "massage the hate-[she]-had" as they address the world. Much of the book's drama draws upon Brooks's father's presiding spirit, evident in the opening "In Honor of David Anderson Brooks, My Father":

> A dryness is upon the house
> My father loved and tended.
> Beyond his firm and sculptured door
> His light and lease have ended.
>
> . . . .
>
> He who was Goodness, Gentleness,
> And Dignity is free,
> Translated to public Love
> Old private charity.

"Goodness, Gentleness, / And Dignity" abound in the life moments of *The Bean Eaters,* expanding upon what Stanley Kunitz praised as "the warmly and generously human" side of *Annie Allen.*

The Bean Eaters depends less upon its cast of characters for effect and more upon the depth of social and moral decisions it gives voice to. In this collection, language pulses and despair intensifies as Brooks searches beyond Bronzeville for meaning in the black experience. The topicality of this collection does not depend upon the war, but advances to consider the civil-rights news from the South. As the opening poem, "The Explorer," suggests, the volume works "to find a still spot in the noise. . . . a satin peace somewhere." But in the end the poems derive their energy from "Only spiraling, high human voices, / the scream of nervous affairs, / Wee griefs, / Grand griefs. And choices"— choices made, choices denied, choices "that cried to be taken." For the couple in "The Bean Eaters," the choice seems to have been one of acceptance of their lot:

They eat beans mostly, this old yellow pair.
Dinner is a casual affair.
Plain chipware on a plain and creaking
    wood,
Tin flatware.

Two who are Mostly Good.
Two who have lived their day,
But keep on putting on their clothes
And putting things away.

And remembering . . .
Remembering, with twinklings and twinges,
As they lean over the beans in their rented back
    room
        that is full of beads and receipts and
           dolls and cloths,
        tobacco crumbs, vases and fringes.

Brooks unassumingly intensifies the couple's poverty, relying upon the choral effect of "mostly" and the "ing" of participials and gerunds. However present-tense the action, the sheer routine of the couple draws the poem into memories of the detritus of their lives. While they seem never to have had any choices in their lives, they have endured. In startling contrast to this aged pair, the young toughs of "We Real Cool" opt for pool—and early death. Unlike the voice of Hughes's "Motto" ("I play it cool / and dig all the jive / That's the reason / I stay alive"), Brooks's pool players "left school . . . sing sin . . . thin gin . . . die soon." "Say the 'We' softly," says Brooks, because "the boys have no accented sense of themselves, yet they are aware of a semi-defined personal importance" (*Report from Part One*).

That ill-defined need for personal importance carries over to the topical poems "A Bronzeville Mother Loiters in Mississippi. Meanwhile, a Mississippi Mother Burns Bacon" and "The *Chicago Defender* Sends a Man to Little Rock." Although Brooks had always been engaged in the race crisis in America, she found in the Emmett Till case a terrifyingly comprehensible extreme of what she had witnessed in Chicago. The Till case at first seems so horrible as to warrant a literary analogue: "From the first it had been like a / Ballad." But, pursuing the literary whiteness and blackness, Brooks sees a literary and social worldview collapse as it relates to blacks:

    The fun was disturbed, then all but
    nullified
    When the Dark Villain was a blackish
    child
    Of fourteen, with eyes still too young
    to be dirty,
    And a mouth too young to have lost
    every reminder
    Of its infant softness.

With "terrifying clarity" the Till diptych reacts to both the murder and the acquittal of the accused murderer, exposing a world of racist inversions where "white" is "black" and "grown-ups" are "bab[ies] full of tantrums." The poem itself becomes an agent of the "meddling" North with its "pepper-words, 'bestiality,' and 'barbarism,' / and / 'Shocking.' " As in earlier poems of "woman rage," Brooks plumbs the distortion of sexuality in the case: chivalry as an excuse for murder. A chain of empathy is forged between women as the accused murderer's wife comes to hate the circumstances of her life:

Then a sickness heaved within her. Then
    courtroom Coca-Cola,
The courtroom beer and hate and sweat and
    drone,
Pushed like a wall against her. She wanted to
    bear it.
But his mouth would not go away and neither
    would the

Decapitated exclamation points in that Other
    Woman's eyes.

The only poetic resolution for Brooks is to
yield a severed, truncated verse—"The Last
Quatrain of the Ballad of Emmett Till"—to Mrs.
Till, a fellow Chicago mother: "She kisses her
killed boy. / And she is sorry." As the *ks* collide, love, sexuality, and death seem inextricably
linked.

The Chicago-Mississippi connections were
part of Brooks's neighborhood sensibility. The
Defender, in part responsible for the Great Migration of blacks from the rural South to Chicago after World War I, had made it a policy to
keep Mississippi on its front page. Lynching
was a metaphor for life in the South. For white
America, the Till case was the horrible exception; for Brooks and readers of the *Defender,* it
was the rule. These connections grew in generalization in "The *Chicago Defender* Sends a
Man to Little Rock." The reporter discovers a
place of families, baseball, concerts, hymns—
where evil wears a human face. Like the "ballad" of Till, the "saga" of Little Rock is a
"puzzle." The reporter unearths unmentionable
news: " 'They are like people everywhere.' "
In an unexpectedly Audenesque conclusion,
Brooks declaims, "The loveliest lynchee was
our Lord."

If *The Bean Eaters* was but a collection of
"Negro poems," reviewers might have been
more receptive. But in her extended poem "The
Lovers of the Poor," Brooks challenges race,
class, and "do-goodism." The ladies from the
Ladies' Betterment League mean well but know
little and care less about the root causes of the
poverty and race enslavement of the "voice-
less." They discover that

     . . . it's all so bad! and entirely too
    much for them.
The stench; the urine, cabbage, and dead
    beans,
Dead porridges of assorted dusty grains,

The old smoke, *heavy* diapers, and they're
    told,
Something called chitterlings. The darkness.
    Drawn
Darkness, or dirty light. The soil that stirs.

. . . .

They've never seen such a make-do-ness as
Newspaper rugs before!

More accustomed to "the nice Art Institute," the
ladies seek a less distressing project. Many readers, comfortable with the Southern civil-rights
poems, felt somewhat abused as Brooks turned
her lyric attack toward class indifference. Unlike
Hughes's "Dinner Guest: Me" ("I know I am /
the Negro Problem"), Brooks's "Lovers of the
Poor" are forced to visit the "Problem."

Whether in the alleys and tenements of Chicago or in the red dirt roads and shacks of
Mississippi, Brooks depicts a world where blacks
are always at risk. Unlike many topical poems,
these civil-rights pieces have survived their
inspiration.

Reviewers, uneasy with the book's topicality,
found comfort in identifying *The Bean Eaters* as
a collection of "social" poems, as if the category ameliorated their unease. Retrospectively,
critics have marveled at the way in which Brooks
turned "raw materials" into "artistry"; Baker
saw the Till sequence in a psychological and political light, claiming that it was "an evocation
of the blood-guiltiness of the white psyche in an
age of dying colonialism"; Jean Marie Miller, in
"The World of Gwendolyn Brooks," claimed
that "Brooks spans races in her poetry, not by
reaching for a pre-existing Western universalism, but by exploring and digging deeply enough
into the Black experience to touch that which is
common to men everywhere." In 1972 Madhubuti saw the major weakness of the book as its
"quiet confirmation of the 'Negro' as equal,"
failing to assess the enemies of blacks accurately.

The social turbulence of the 1960's asked
much of Brooks. On the one hand, she had

achieved fame as the most honored "Negro poetess" in America. On the other hand, the Pulitzer and Guggenheim awards came at the expense of her poems (who among her readers really heard the anger and despair?), and the success that seemed to be isolating her from her people concerned her on both a literary and a social level. As political challenges became more frequent, the media became increasingly chary in areas touching upon race. Early in 1962, Kent recounts in his biography of Brooks, New York radio station WNEW denied airtime to a musical setting of "Of De Witt Williams on His Way to Lincoln Cemetery" because of the word "black." The station's management claimed the reference would outrage "Negro" listeners. Brooks, following liberation movements in Africa, failed to believe that a word with such currency in Africa could give offense. At mid-career she saw this as an opportunity to emphasize her commitment to the greater political implications: "For seventeen years. Without ever detouring from my Business—which is being a writer. Many of the banners so brightly (and originally, they think) waved by today's youngsters I waved twenty years ago, and published sixteen years ago."

Brooks's need to share her work with the young led her to the classroom, informally at first and then professionally. Invited to read at the White House in 1962, Brooks used that and other public occasions to use fame for fortune so that she could fund programs and awards in creative writing. Her teaching career began in September 1963, when Mirron Alexandroff, president of Chicago's Columbia College, invited her to run a poetry workshop: "Do anything you want with it. . . . Take it outdoors. Take it to a restaurant—run it in a restaurant, a coffee shop. Do absolutely anything you want with it. *Anything!*" She accepted the challenge of trying "to enjoy this thing [she] had never done before." Appearing in her "new little professor's blue

suit," she sought to communicate what Inez Cunningham Stark had given to her: "the knowledge, the magic, the definitions" (*Report from Part One*).

The workshop at Columbia College led to more teaching, at Elmhurst College (Illinois), Northeastern Illinois State College, the University of Wisconsin–Madison, Columbia University, and the City University of New York. She found the excitement and challenge of teaching, and the freedom to experiment, most gratifying. But after suffering a small heart-attack on Christmas Day of 1971, she bade the classroom a "final Goodbye." Though uncertain whether writing can be taught, Brooks nonetheless believed that teachers can "explain the wonders" of poetry and "oblige the writing student to write." She met students' protestations and pleas—"Can't do it. CanNOT do it"—with a refusal to reconsider her demanding assignments, "telling them they were insulting their college and their own intellects." She provided tickets to "deputized" students so that they could attend poetry readings and report back to the class. She discovered the shared secret of teaching: "Such activities . . . enabled *me* to enjoy a class—and when I enjoyed it, almost without exception so did my students."

Teaching, coupled with the "news at home," encouraged Brooks to re-envision the work included in *Selected Poems* (1963). This gathering of poems cemented Brooks's critical reputation. *The New York Times* felt confident enough to claim that "Miss Brooks won a Pulitzer Prize in 1950 and deserved it." Reviewers in *Poetry* and the *Saturday Review* praised her idiomatic language, claiming it was the key to her ability to universalize and empathize. The praise showered on the volume overlooked the topical addition of "Riders to the Blood-Red Wrath." Written in 1963, the poem commemorated the Freedom Rides of 1961. The subject matter fairly rips at the poem's formal fabric:

My proper prudence toward his proper probe
Astonished their ancestral seemliness.
It was a not-nice risk, a wrought risk, was
An indelicate risk, they thought. And an excess.

With *Selected Poems* Brooks seems to have willed a formal closure to "Part One" of her writing career. Her relationship with Harper & Row would not end until after the publication of *The World of Gwendolyn Brooks* (1971), but that collection would strain to contain *In the Mecca*. Though she could but dimly perceive the direction her career would take, Brooks knew that her poetry had already taken her far beyond what was acceptable for a "Negro" poet in America.

As early as August 1962, Brooks had written to her editor at Harper & Row about her "Mecca" poem: "I can't give up on the thing; it has a grip on me." Readings, teaching, and family matters kept her from a full commitment to this nagging project. But it was not until she attended the Second Fisk University Writers' Conference in April 1967 that the requisite inspiration and political fire came to her. Used to being "loved" at readings and lectures, Brooks discovered that here, among the "New Blacks," she was "coldly Respected." Here Imamu Amiri Baraka (LeRoi Jones) shouted, "Up against the wall, Brother! KILL 'EM ALL!" And here Brooks met blacks understood by *no* whites, especially "professional Negro understanders." On December 28, 1969, a tribute to Brooks at Chicago's Affro-Arts Theatre continued her induction in the world of "New Blacks" as well as provided the meeting ground for her future biographer, George Kent. Schooled now by her juniors, she "enter[ed] at least the kindergarten of new consciousness" (*Report from Part One*). A year before the assassination of Martin Luther King, Jr., these blacks recognized the imminent collapse of integration as a social idea. Brooks heard the cry of Madhubuti's "New Integrationist," who sought "integration / of / negroes / with /

black / people." What did Brooks discover? Black pride? Cultural nationalism? "You may use any label you wish," she says (quoted in Kent, *A Life of Gwendolyn Brooks*). "All I know is when people started talking about Blacks loving, respecting, and helping one another, that was enough for me." The passive spectatorship of the Bronzeville poems was gone for good. It was no longer enough to share through description the circumstances of being black. Madhubuti writes, "Brooks' post 1967 poetry is fat-less. Her new work resembles a man getting off meat, turning to a vegetarian diet" (Preface to *Report from Part One*).

In the Mecca bears more than traces of the Fisk "fever." Buoyed by her poetry workshop with a Chicago street gang, the Blackstone Rangers, Brooks found the street energy necessary to complete her long-stalled "Mecca" work. The book-length poem is at once an indictment of racism and poverty symbolized by an apartment building, the "once splendid palace" at Thirty-fourth Street between State and Dearborn that had collapsed into a littered and dangerous ruin—and a mystery story. The narrative, "a mosaic of daily affairs," spins around the search for the lost Pepita, the youngest of Mrs. Sallie Smith's nine children. After a sharp-focused introduction to Mrs. Sallie's domestic sphere, the poem inches out into corridors of threat and dirt, dishonor and decay, tedium and nobility. Gangs threaten from without, poverty and craziness from within. Characters are at once particularized—we learn quickly to distinguish the voices of Loam Norton, Way-Out Morgan, Melodie Mary—and homogenized into a collective response to Mrs. Sallie's "Where Pepita?": "*Ain seen er I ain seen er I ain seen er* / Ain seen er I ain seen er I ain seen her.*"

Fractured narrative lines carry the news that many Meccans, as Melodie Mary knows, are as trapped as the rats and roaches that share their space. That Pepita has in fact been killed by a tenant, Jamaican Edward, seems at once incidental and central to the fury and frustrations of the Mecca: "Hateful things sometimes befall the hateful / but the hateful are not rendered lovable thereby." How like the aborted fetuses of "the mother"—those whose "births and . . . names . . . straight baby tears . . . and games" were stolen—is this "little woman [who] lies in dust with roaches"—who "never went to kindergarten . . . never learned that black is not beloved."

The "After Mecca" section both honors heroes, past and present, and severs ties with the old consciousness. Elegies for Medgar Evers and Malcolm X are celebrations of black manhood in the light of the new black nationalism. The monument of "The Wall" towers over that of "The Chicago Picasso" in terms of black pride and aesthetic significance. "Sermons on the Warpland" confronts the essence of Ron Karenga's assertion: "The fact that we are black is our ultimate reality."

Contemporary reviews reflect the ways in which Brooks's "blackening language" left many white readers uneasy and guilt-ridden. M. L. Rosenthal, in *The New York Times* (March 2, 1969), stunned by "the horrid predicament of real Americans whose everyday world haunts the nation's conscience intolerably," nonetheless found the poems (especially the title sequence) "overwrought." A reviewer in the *Virginia Quarterly* (Winter 1969) complained that Brooks was "more self-consciously a Negro than ever before. . . . It is a new manner and a new voice for Miss Brooks, better than her earlier work in its honesty, poorer in its loss of music and control." William Stafford in *Poetry* (March 1969) complained of excessively local references. Madhubuti saw value in this unease, claiming that "*In the Mecca* 'blacked' its way out of the National Book Award in 1968"—thereby creating a new aesthetic, a new identity, for Brooks (Preface, *Report from Part One*).

As poet laureate of Illinois (appointed in 1968), Brooks continued her creative-writing outreach programs for elementary and secondary students. Funding scholarships, prizes, and trips to Africa, she seemed intent upon making writing an agent of social change and black pride. In December 1969 she separated from her husband and "the hard, demanding state of marriage"; she saw the subsequent stage of her life as her "next future," in which she would write poems "that [would] somehow successfully 'call' . . . all black people: black people in taverns, black people in alleys, black people in gutters, schools, offices, factories, prisons, the consulate" (*Report from Part One*). Her husband, an ardent integrationist, failed to agree with "the new, young movements among blacks."

A year of nightmare inversions and violence, 1968 became the vortex of aesthetic and political conversion for many American poets. While Robert Lowell retreated into history and sonnets, Adrienne Rich shrugged off all formal constraints (marriage as well as poetic conventions) in search of a language capable of articulating the time. Rage of a lifetime, distilled in a year, led Brooks away from New York and Harper & Row to Detroit and Broadside Press. The relationship with Harper & Row had always been cordial, but as Madhubuti records, "Harper's never . . . pushed the work of Gwendolyn Brooks" (Preface, *Report from Part One*). *The World of Gwendolyn Brooks* (1971) ended her association with the white publishing world. She no longer believed that blacks could afford the individual acceptance proffered by white America; black success depended upon collective association and action.

Broadside Press brought the congenial editorial support of Dudley Randall as well as a radically different-looking Brooks book. *Riot* (1969), the dust jacket states, "is a poem in three parts . . . aris[ing] from the disturbances in Chicago after the assassination of Martin Luther King in 1968." The natural informality of the volume resides in the startling "Black Expression" frontispiece by

Jeff Donaldson, the open typeface and relaxed page layout, the manuscript-page insert—and the jacket photo of Brooks, "a sister who kept her natural." Never before had Brooks been as transparently confrontational as in "Riot," a poem where black anger is unleashed upon the "desperate" and wealthy John Cabot. Lacking the strong narrative fabric of such class-violence poems as "The Lovers of the Poor," "Riot" is pure revolt:

But, in a thrilling announcement, on It drove
and breathed on him: and touched him. In that
     breath
the fume of pig foot, chitterling and cheap chili,
malign, mocked John. And, in terrific touch, old
averted doubt jerked forward decently,
cried "Cabot! John! You are a desperate man,
and the desperate die expansively today."

John Cabot went down in the smoke and fire
and broken glass and blood, and he cried "Lord!
Forgive these nigguhs that know not what they
     do."

The class polarizations of the poem intensify the rage and poverty of the "sweaty and unpretty" blacks, the disgust and wealth of "John Cabot, out of Wilma, once a Wycliffe." Cabot serves as more than a class symbol; for Brooks, he is a failed white aesthetic. The "rightness" he represents might as well be the rightness of the Pulitzer committee, the Guggenheim jury, the editors at Harper & Row. "The Third Sermon on the Warpland," more deliberately topical than "Riot," seeks a local as well as a general sense of the riots.

A series of sharply focused chapbooks— *Family Pictures* (1970), *Aloneness* (1971), *Beckonings* (1975), and *Primer for Blacks* (1980)—record Brooks's swiftly evolving sense of African family identity. Her trips to East Africa (1971) and West Africa (1974) were a necessary completion of her developing appreciation for her African identity. In spite of her need for

assimilation in Kenya, she recognized immediately that she came bearing her "own hot just-out-of-the-U.S. smile." The "African Fragment" of *Report from Part One* (1972) charts a discovery both joyous and sad, for in Africa, Brooks encountered the fact of her lost culture: language, clothes, pride stripped away by the "Jamestown experiment." In 1973, reunited with her husband, she traveled to England. In the summer of 1974 they visited Ghana, England, and France.

As if to compensate for a heritage of deprivation, Brooks redoubled her efforts on behalf of the young. Poetry contests, scholarships, teaching about Africa and African Americans, travel grants so that the young might visit the "homeland"—Brooks made history, language, poetry into a continuum of race pride. The spirit of the Fisk conference pulsed life into Brooks's rescue missions. No longer was she content to describe despair; the time had come to avert despair. Tutored by raging youths at mid-life, she discovered things urgent and life-sustaining. Now it was her turn to save the young. In "To the Young Who Want to Die," she writes:

Sit down. Inhale. Exhale.
The gun will wait. The lake will wait.
The tall gall in the small seductive vial
will wait will wait:
will wait a week: will wait through April.
You do not have to die this certain day.
Death will abide, will pamper your
     postponement.
I assure you death will wait. Death has
a lot of time. Death can
attend to you tomorrow. Or next week. Death is
just down the street; is most obliging neighbor;
can meet you any moment.

You need not die today.
Stay here—through pout or pain or peskyness.
Stay here. See what the news is going to be
     tomorrow.

Graves grow no green that you can use.
Remember, green's your color. You are Spring.

Many of the works dedicated to children and adolescents—*Aloneness, The Tiger Who Wore White Gloves; or, What You Are, You Are* (1974) *Family Pictures,* and *Young Poet's Primer* (1980)—are in fact celebrations of the black family. As she explained in her address at Madhubuti's Twentieth Anniversary Conference on Literature and Society (December 1987):

I believe that writers should be writing more about the Black family. The Black family is really being hounded and hounded these days, and I feel we "ordinary" Black people shouldn't leave all the assessments of our essence to the likes of Bill Moyers, nor to Alvin Poussaint. We have tongues. We have calculating eyes.

In spite of pressure from feminist critics, Brooks has held the subject of the integrity of the black family above women's rights. She explained in an interview with Ida Lewis:

Relations between men and women seem disordered to me. . . . I think Women's Lib is not for black women for the time being, because black men *need* their women beside them, supporting them in these very tempestuous days.

Family Pictures offers a plausible trajectory for this life of new Pan-African imagination. For Brooks the hope begins with the individual life—even if that individual is the "Ugliest little boy / that everybody ever saw" ("The Life of Lincoln West")—and then, and only then, can it advance to heroes, young and old. Her message is consistent in "Speech to the Young":

And remember:
live not for the Battles Won.
Live not for The-End-of-the-Song.
Live in the along.

This commitment to a life of action rather than victory allows Brooks the freedom to savor the dedication of the Gwendolyn Brooks Junior High School (Elmhurst, Illinois) more than her reading at the White House. However pleasant the January 1980 reading with Robert Hayden and Stanley Kunitz, the November 1981 dedication was the very embodiment of her social program. As Madhubuti wrote, Brooks had become "a consistent monument in the real, unaware of the beauty and strength she had radiated." Honorary consultant to the Library of Congress in 1973, she served as a poetry consultant in 1985–1986. Somewhat inadvertently Brooks became a necessary reference for black *and* white readers.

In *to disembark* (1981) and *The Near-Johannesburg Boy and Other Poems* (1986) Brooks shuffled new poems in with old, providing a historical context for a younger audience. At the age of seventy her message remained quite clear: stay alive long enough to learn who you are—and, unlike the tiger who wore white gloves, learn to appreciate the fact that "what you are you are." Though she vehemently rejects the notion of "universal" elements in her work, preferring to see herself as an African poet writing for a global black audience, Brooks continues to attract a diverse readership.

She also continues to draw admiration and honors from old and new audiences. The larger American literary community has come around to Madhubuti's belief that Brooks is "a Living National Treasure." In 1987 she was elected an honorary fellow of the Modern Language Association. Since compiling *Blacks,* she has published *Gottschalk and the Grande Tarantelle* (1988). The collection includes "Winnie," a tribute to Winnie and Nelson Mandela, as well as the title-sequence "snapshot" of Louis Moreau Gottschalk. In an interview with Mehlem, Brooks explained the larger significance of the poem:

The title poem . . . does exactly what I wanted it to do. There—are—The—Slaves: you are aware of the horror of their crisis *and* you are aware of the fact that human beings *will* break away from ache to dance, to sing, to create, no matter how briefly, how intermittently.

In this poem Brooks sees herself as a "reporter," investigating the appropriation of black culture by greedy whites: "Gottschalk, Elvis Presley, George Gershwin, Stephen Foster, etc., have molded Black exhilaration and richness into money-making forms." She provides "the *scheduled* insinuation that other whites have done likewise."

Brooks maintains a schedule of readings, lectures, and workshops throughout the country. In addition, she is completing a book of poems about Mandela and seeing *Maud Martha* into a paperback edition and perhaps a film. She hopes to complete the second volume of her autobiography, *Report from Part Two.* In spite of current projects, *Blacks* remains the inevitable touchstone for Brooks's popular and academic audiences.

Feminists, black and white, hear in Brooks an early voice in the struggle for gender equality. Though citing her poems of "woman rage" and female circumstance, these critics are deaf to the poet's quarrels with their ideas. Black readers regard her work as generational and historically significant in that she bridges audiences from the Harlem Renaissance to the present. And to the broader general audience, introduced to her work by anthology pieces, Brooks represents a poet genuinely engaged in the urban family and class crises of the late twentieth century. Whether readers come to *Blacks* from the turmoil of race relationships in the United States or discover more about that unrest from her work, they will find a poet who, at the age of seventy-two, counseled herself, "Die / in use" ("Instruction to Myself").

Selected Bibliography

WORKS OF GWENDOLYN BROOKS

POETRY
A Street in Bronzeville. New York: Harper & Brothers, 1945.
Annie Allen. New York: Harper & Brothers, 1949.
Bronzeville Boys and Girls. New York: Harper & Brothers, 1956.
The Bean Eaters. New York: Harper & Row, 1960.
In the Mecca. New York: Harper & Row, 1968.
Riot. Detroit: Broadside Press, 1969.
Black Steel: Joe Frazier and Muhammad Ali. Detroit: Broadside Press, 1971.
Beckonings. Detroit: Broadside Press, 1975.
Primer for Blacks. Chicago: Black Position Press, 1980.
Black Love. Chicago: Brooks Press, 1981.
to disembark. Chicago: Third World Press, 1981.
Mayor Harold Washington and Chicago, the I Will City. Chicago: Brooks Press, 1983.
The Near-Johannesburg Boy and Other Poems. Chicago: David Company, 1986.
Gottschalk and the Grande Tarantelle. Chicago: David Company, 1988.
Winnie. Chicago: David Company, 1988.

PROSE
Maud Martha. New York: Harper & Brothers, 1953.
Report from Part One. Detroit: Broadside Press, 1972.

ESSAYS
"Poets Who Are Negroes." *Phylon,* 11:312 (December 1950).
"Why Negro Women Leave Home." *Negro Digest,* 9:26–28 (March 1951).
"How I Told My Child About Race." *Negro Digest,* 9:29–31 (June 1951).
"They Call It Bronzeville." *Holiday,* October 1951, pp. 60–64, 67, 112, 114, 116–117, 119–120.
"Perspectives." *Negro Digest,* 15:49–50 (July 1966).
"In Montgomery." *Ebony,* August 1971, pp. 42–48.

"Boys. Black: A Preachment." *Ebony*, August 1972, p. 45.
"Winnie." *Poetry*, 151:20 (October–November 1987).
"Keziah." *TriQuarterly*, 75:38–50 (Spring–Summer 1989).

WORKS FOR CHILDREN AND ADOLESCENTS

Family Pictures. Detroit: Broadside Press, 1970.
Aloneness. Detroit: Broadside Press, 1971.
The Tiger Who Wore White Gloves; or, What You Are, You Are. Chicago: Third World Press, 1974.
Young Poet's Primer. Chicago: Brooks Press, 1980.

COLLECTED WORKS

Selected Poems. New York: Harper & Row, 1963.
The World of Gwendolyn Brooks. New York: Harper & Row, 1971.
Blacks. Chicago: David Company, 1987.

EDITED WORKS

A Broadside Treasury. Detroit: Broadside Press, 1971.
Jump Bad: A New Chicago Anthology. Detroit: Broadside Press, 1971.
A Capsule Course in Black Poetry Writing. Detroit: Broadside Press, 1975. Edited by Brooks and others.

MANUSCRIPT PAPERS

The Gwendolyn Brooks Papers are at Atlanta University, Atlanta, Georgia.

BIBLIOGRAPHIES

Loff, Jon N. "Gwendolyn Brooks: A Bibliography." *CLA Journal*, 17:21–32 (September 1973).
Mahoney, Heidi L. "Selected Checklist of Material by and About Gwendolyn Brooks." *Negro American Literature Forum* 8:210–211. (Summer 1974).

Miller, R. Baxter. *Langston Hughes and Gwendolyn Brooks: A Reference Guide*. Boston: G. K. Hall, 1978.

BIOGRAPHICAL AND CRITICAL STUDIES

Baker, Houston A., Jr. "The Achievement of Gwendolyn Brooks." *CLA Journal*, 16:21–31 (September 1972). Reprinted in his *Singers of Daybreak: Studies in Black American Literature*. Washington, D.C.: Howard University Press, 1974. Pp. 43–51.
———. *Modernism and the Harlem Renaissance*. Chicago: University of Chicago Press, 1987.
Blakely, Henry. "How I Met Miss Brooks." In *Say That the River Turns*. Edited by Haki R. Madhubuti. Chicago: Third World Press, 1987. Pp. 4–6.
Blakely, Nora Brooks. "Three-Way Mirror." In *Say That the River Turns*. Edited by Haki R. Madhubuti. Chicago: Third World Press, 1987. Pp. 7–9.
Bloom, Harold, ed. *Contemporary Poets*. New York: Chelsea House, 1986.
Brooks, Keziah. *"The Voice" and Other Short Stories*. Detroit: Harlo Press, 1975.
Brown, Frank London. "Chicago's Great Lady of Poetry." *Negro Digest*, 10:53–57 (December 1961).
Christian, Barbara. "Nuance and the Novella: A Study of Gwendolyn Brooks's *Maud Martha*." In her *Black Feminist Criticism: Perspectives on Black Women Writers*. New York: Pergamon Press, 1985. Pp. 127–241. Reprinted in *A Life Distilled*. Pp. 239–253.
———. "Trajectories of Self-Definition: Placing Contemporary Afro-American Women's Fiction." In *Conjuring: Black Women, Fiction, and Literary Tradition*. Edited by Majorie Pryse and Hortense J. Spillers. Bloomington: Indiana University Press, 1985. Pp. 233–248.
Clark, Norris B. "Gwendolyn Brooks and a Black Aesthetic." In *A Life Distilled: Gwendolyn Brooks—Her Poetry and Fiction*. Edited by Maria K. Mootry and Gary Smith. Urbana: University of Illinois Press, 1987. Pp. 81–99.
Crockett, Jacqueline. "An Essay on Gwendolyn Brooks." *Negro History Bulletin*, 19:37–39 (November 1955).
Davis, Arthur P. "The Black-and-Tan Motif in the Poetry of Gwendolyn Brooks." *CLA Journal*, 6:90–97 (December 1962).

———."Gwendolyn Brooks: Poet of the Unheroic." *CLA Journal*, 7:114–125 (December 1963).

Fuller, James A. "Notes on a Poet." *Negro Digest*, 11:50–59 (August 1962).

Garland, Phyl. "Gwendolyn Brooks, Poet Laureate." *Ebony*, July 1968, pp. 48–56.

Gayle, Addison, Jr., "Gwendolyn Brooks, Poet of the Whirlwind." In *Black Women Writers, 1950–1980: A Critical Evaluation*. Edited by Mari Evans. Garden City, N.Y.: Anchor/Doubleday, 1984. Pp. 79–87.

Gould, Jean. *Modern American Women Poets*. New York: Dodd, Mead, 1984. Pp. 176–209.

Hansell, William H. "Gwendolyn Brooks' 'In the Mecca': A Rebirth into Blackness." *Negro American Literature Forum*, 8:199–207 (Summer 1974).

Harriott, F. "Life of a Pulitzer Poet." *Negro Digest*, 8:14–16 (August 1950).

Hudson, Clenora F. "Racial Themes in the Poetry of Gwendolyn Brooks." *CLA Journal*, 17:16–20 (September 1973).

Huggins, Nathan Irvin. *Harlem Renaissance*. New York: Oxford University Press, 1971.

Johnson, James N. "Blacklisting Poets." *Ramparts*, December 14, 1968, pp. 48–54.

Juhasz, Suzanne. " 'A Sweet Inspiration . . . of My People': The Poetry of Gwendolyn Brooks and Nikki Giovanni." In her *Naked and Fiery Forms: Modern American Poetry by Women—A New Tradition*. New York: Octagon Books, 1976; New York: Harper Colophon Books, 1976. Pp. 144–155.

Kent, George E. *Blackness and the Adventure of Western Culture*. Chicago: Third World Press, 1972. Pp. 104–138.

———."Gwendolyn Brooks' Poetic Realism: A Developmental Survey." In *Black Women Writers, 1950–1980: A Critical Evaluation*. Edited by Mari Evans. Garden City, N.Y.: Anchor/Doubleday, 1984. Pp. 88–105.

———. *A Life of Gwendolyn Brooks*. Lexington: University Press of Kentucky, 1990.

Kunitz, Stanley. "Bronze by Gold." *Poetry*, 76:52–56 (1950). (Review of *Annie Allen*.)

Lattin, Patricia H., and Vernon E. Lattin. "Vision in Gwendolyn Brooks's *Maud Martha*." *Critique*, 25:180–188 (1984).

Levine, Lawrence W. *Black Culture and Black Consciousness: Afro-American Folk Thought from Slavery to Freedom*. New York: Oxford University Press, 1977.

Madhubuti, Haki R. "Gwendolyn Brooks: Beyond the Wordmaker—The Making of an African Poet." In Brooks's *Report from Part One*. Detroit: Broadside Press, 1972. Pp. 13–30.

———, ed. *Say That the River Turns: The Impact of Gwendolyn Brooks*. Chicago: Third World Press, 1987.

Mehlem, D. H. *Gwendolyn Brooks: Poetry and the Heroic Voice*. Lexington: University Press of Kentucky, 1987.

———. *Heroism in the New Black Poetry: Introductions and Interviews*. Lexington: University Press of Kentucky, 1990.

Miller, Jean-Marie A. "Gwendolyn Brooks, Poet Laureate of Bronzeville U.S.A." *Freedomways*, 10:63–75 (First Quarter 1970).

———. "The World of Gwendolyn Brooks." *Black World*, January 1972, pp. 51–52.

Miller, R. Baxter. "Define the Whirlwind: *In the Mecca*—Urban Setting, Shifting Narrator, and Redemptive Vision." *Obsidian*, 4:19–31 (Spring 1978).

Mootry, Maria K., and Gary Smith, eds. *A Life Distilled: Gwendolyn Brooks—Her Poetry and Fiction*. Urbana: University of Illinois Press, 1987.

Ostriker, Alicia Suskin. *Stealing the Language: The Emergence of Women's Poetry in America*. Boston: Beacon Press, 1986.

Rampersad, Arnold. *The Life of Langston Hughes*. Vol. 2, *I Dream a World*. New York: Oxford University Press, 1988.

Redmond, Eugene B. *Drumvoices: The Mission of Afro-American Poetry*. Garden City, N.Y.: Anchor/Doubleday, 1976. Pp. 270–284.

Rivers, Conrad Kent. "Poetry of Gwendolyn Brooks." *Negro Digest*, 13:67–69 (June 1964).

Shaw, Harry B. *Gwendolyn Brooks*. Boston: Twayne, 1980.

Smith, Gary. "Gwendolyn Brooks's *A Street in Bronzeville*, The Harlem Renaissance, and the Mythologies of the Black Woman." *Melus*, 9:33–46 (Fall 1983).

Spillers, Hortense J. " 'An Order of Constancy': Notes on Brooks and the Feminine." *Centennial Review*, 29:223–248 (1985).

Washington, Mary Helen. " 'Taming All That Anger Down': Rage and Silence in Gwendolyn Brooks' *Maud Martha*." *Massachusetts Review*, 24:453–466 (1983).

Williams, Gladys Margaret. "Gwendolyn Brooks's Way with the Sonnet." *CLA Journal*, 26:215–240 (1982).

INTERVIEWS

Angle, Paul M. "We Asked Gwendolyn Brooks." Chicago: Illinois Bell Telephone, 1967. Reprinted in Brooks's *Report from Part One*. Pp. 131–146.

Brooks, Gwendolyn. "Interview." *TriQuarterly*, 60:405–410 (Spring–Summer 1984).

Hull, Gloria T., and Posey Gallagher. "Update on Part One: An Interview with Gwendolyn Brooks." *CLA Journal*, 21:19–40 (September 1977).

Lewis, Ida. "Conversation: Gwendolyn Brooks and Ida Lewis—'My People Are Black People.' " *Essence*, April 1971, pp. 27–31. Reprinted in Brooks's *Report from Part One*. Pp. 167–182.

Mehlem, D. H. "Humanism and Heroism." In her *Heroism in the New Black Poetry: Introductions and Interviews*. Lexington: University Press of Kentucky, 1990. Pp. 11–38.

Stavros, George. "An Interview with Gwendolyn Brooks." *Contemporary Literature*, 2:1–20 (Winter 1970). Reprinted in Brooks's *Report from Part One*. Pp. 147–166.

Tate, Claudia. "Gwendolyn Brooks." In her *Black Women Writers at Work*. New York: Continuum, 1983. Pp. 39–48.

— CAROLE K. DORESKI

William Cullen Bryant

1794–1878

THE poetry of William Cullen Bryant has always been difficult to place in an appropriate context. Because he was a poet of nature who found in the commonplace things of the natural world a source for reflection, critics often have sought to compare him with earlier poets who, like him, had developed their themes in descriptive poems of a philosophic cast. When his mature poetry was first published in pamphlet form in 1821, it was compared at once with that of William Cowper and, when a much enlarged edition was printed in 1832, with that of, among others, James Thomson and William Wordsworth. In the early nineteenth century this attitude was perhaps understandable. No poet of Bryant's stature had yet appeared in America, and critics were unsure of how to judge him. The persistence of this view into the twentieth century, however, does Bryant a serious injustice. Aside from the fact that no one poet could possibly bear close resemblance to writers so different as those with whom he has been compared, Bryant deserves to be seen on his own terms and valued for his accomplishments, however limited they may sometimes seem to be.

Every poet learns from the works of his predecessors. He imitates what he has read as he learns to write; and even when he has achieved his distinctive voice, he sometimes echoes lines or images from other poets that have stuck in his mind. Bryant is no exception. As a young man he was especially fortunate to have had at his disposal the volumes of English poetry that his father, Peter Bryant, himself the author of Augustan verse, had brought to their isolated home in western Massachusetts. They ranged from William Shakespeare, John Milton, and John Dryden through the major and minor poets of the eighteenth century—including such ''graveyard'' figures as Robert Blair, Beilby Porteus, and Henry Kirke White—to Wordsworth and the early Byron. The aspiring poet read much of it. We know from both his critical essays and his poetry that the range of Bryant's knowledge was broad. Illustrations and examples in his critical prose are drawn from Shakespeare and Milton, and certain lines in his verse echo familiar ones by Alexander Pope, Thomas Gray, and William Cowper. There are verses in ''Thanatopsis'' that resemble Blair's *The Grave,* and some in ''A Winter Piece'' that are unmistakably Wordsworthian.

The point is not, however, that such passages exist. They are always to be expected, and too much must not be made of them. Although they illustrate well the range of verse from which, under his father's tutelage, the young Bryant learned his craft, they are merely the last vestiges of those poetic masters from whom the young man quickly established his independence. Bryant was no imitator. Whatever he learned from his predecessors, the content and form of his poems are unmistakably his own. If he affirms an ordered world in his verse, it is not the deistic order of Thomson's *The Seasons;* if his poetic vision is fundamentally religious, it is not the evangelical Christianity of Cowper; if he maintains a close relation to nature and to nature's God, the two never merge into the pantheistic system of Wordsworth. Although Bryant no doubt learned to handle the blank verse form from reading the works of these and other poets who had made it an effective vehicle for contemplative poetry, his own blank verse does not resemble theirs in either movement or tone. Eclectic in his taste, he developed a point of view and mode of expression only partially conditioned by the poets he read.

At least as important were other elements in Bryant's education and training, especially the beliefs of two strong men who left an indelible impression upon him. One was his maternal grandfather, Ebenezer Snell, the stern Calvinist with whom the Bryant family lived for a number of years. The religious training the young boy received at his hands left such a mark upon him that Bryant the mature poet has sometimes been called a Puritan. This influence was strongly countered, however, by that of the poet's father. Peter Bryant, a medical man, was a much more liberal thinker and strongly influenced the boy toward the Unitarian thought that the poet eventually accepted. Both men, moreover, influenced his reading and writing. Bryant read the Scriptures and, at his grandfather's prompting, attempted to turn parts of the Old Testament into English verse. But he also read the classics, and under his father's guidance he began at an early age to write a kind of Augustan verse. It is almost as if, in the village of Cummington, Massachusetts, the budding poet was undergoing in small something of the intellectual experience of American society as a whole in the opening years of the nineteenth century.

As Bryant prepared to enter Williams College in 1810, he encountered yet another important intellectual system, Scottish associationist philosophy. Among the books he read were three by members of that ''common sense'' school: Dugald Stewart, Thomas Reid, and, most important, Archibald Alison, the aesthetician of the group. Unlike some earlier eighteenth-century thinkers, these philosophers accepted the external world as both real and knowable by the human mind. Because of its constitution, the mind, acting upon the impressions that came to it through the senses, could discern the qualities of that world and exert upon it the various modifications of thought. When disposed in the proper fashion, moreover, the mind could also perceive and be moved by the beauty and sublimity of the material world. The philosophy did not, of course, limit itself to nature; but examples drawn from the natural scene, from landscape gardening, and from landscape art are so important in Alison's *Essays on the Nature and Principles of Taste* as to make quite clear the aesthetician's deep interest in that aspect of material reality.

Because the aesthetic laid such stress not solely on the beauty and sublimity of the material world, but also on the essential truth to be found in it, the poet had of necessity to be a close observer of the external scene. The representation of nature in his verse had to be accurate. In no other way could he be sure that the meaning he perceived was true, or that he had been able to communicate it effectively to his reader. Since knowledge comes to the mind through sensory experience—primarily through sight and secondarily through hearing—visual and, to a lesser extent, auditory images must make up the bulk of the poem. The mind of the poet, then, acting upon the landscape, re-creates his vision in the poem; and if his sight be true and if his mind interpret the sensory images properly, he will draw from the natural scene a meaning that he will embody in his poem. Readers of that poem, moreover, will have the description before them expressed in suggestive language. If the poet has done his work well, they will perceive both the beauty and the truth he has discovered for them.

Such an aesthetic quite naturally had a profound effect on Bryant's poetry. The theory demanded that his material be drawn not from the poets he had read, but from what he had personally experienced among the hills and valleys of western Massachusetts. It gave him a point of view, that of a sensitive observer who consciously sought the beauty and truth to be found in the natural scene; and it gave him a source for his imagery in the sights and sounds he had witnessed in his rambles around his native countryside. Not all of Bryant's subjects, of course, are drawn from the natural landscape. His poems supporting the struggle for freedom in Greece and his long philosophic poem ''The Ages'' are obvious exceptions. But these and a few similar ones aside, the bulk of Bryant's poetry does indeed record his direct and continuing encounter with the natural world; and these are the poems by which his accomplishment must be judged today. In the best of this verse, he frees himself from his poetic masters, creates a vision of reality that bears little resemblance to theirs, and speaks in a poetic voice that is unmistakably his own.

Born November 3, 1794, in Cummington, Massachusetts, a village that had been settled for only some twenty-five years, William Cullen Bryant grew up in much the same fashion as most other boys in America. With his older brother, Austin, he attended the district school, where he received an education of the most elementary kind; and, although somewhat frail, he learned to work in his grandfather's fields as soon as he was able to handle the farm tools. Both winter and summer he rambled among the neighboring hills, and became from his earliest days, he later wrote, a keen observer of nature in all its various forms. During the stormy days and long evenings of winter, Bryant and his brother read the books in their father's well-chosen li-

brary, especially the *Iliad* in Pope's edition and, when they tired of Pope, the works of Sir Edmund Spenser, Cowper, and other English writers of verse and prose. Cullen, as he was called, was different from most boys, however, in showing signs of a strong intellectual bent. He began to compose verse as early as 1802, and wrote a poem for declamation at school in 1804 that attained such currency in the neighborhood that it was published in the Hampshire *Gazette* on March 18, 1807.

By that time the budding poet had written a goodly amount of juvenile verse—some, like his poem ''On the Late Eclipse,'' in pentameter couplets, but at least one, a version of David's lament over Saul and Jonathan, in blank verse. His skill increased markedly; and when his father saw some satiric lines of his on Thomas Jefferson, occasioned by the Embargo Act of 1807—an act that particularly hurt the commerce of New England—he encouraged his son to write more. The result was Bryant's first book, *The Embargo,* a satiric poem of 244 lines in heroic couplets, ''By a Youth of Thirteen.'' Peter Bryant arranged for its publication at Boston in 1808. The pamphlet was favorably reviewed by Alexander Hill Everett in the *Monthly Anthology* in June; and since the uproar over the embargo continued as supplementary acts were passed, the book quickly sold out. At his father's direction Cullen prepared a second edition, enlarged to 420 lines and including seven additional poems that he had written in 1807 and 1808. The new edition was published in February 1809, and this time the young man's name appeared on the title page.

Although only a piece of juvenile verse that Bryant never included in any collected edition of his poems, *The Embargo* merits at least a glance for what it tells us about its author in 1809. While the original poem was retouched by his father and another gentleman in Boston, it remains nonetheless a remarkable performance for so young a poet and illustrates well both the native talent he possessed and the degree to which it had already been disciplined. Its Federalist politics and Augustan style reveal the bent of mind and poetic taste of the young man, attitudes he would abandon during the period of intellectual and artistic growth that quickly ensued. And the revised edition clearly shows the skill with which Bryant was already able to criticize and improve his verse. The second edition smooths or removes some infelicities of language, expands his treatment of the sufferings of New England workers under the embargo, and sharpens and extends the satire on Jefferson and his supporters. Both versions attack Napoleon and France as the enemies of freedom, but in the second edition the title poem is followed by another, "The Spanish Revolution," that makes an additional attack on the French.

Because his son had shown such intellectual and artistic talent, Peter Bryant decided, despite his limited means, to give Cullen a college education. From November 1808 to October 1809, the young man studied the classics, first Latin with his uncle, Thomas Snell, in North Brookfield, and then Greek with Rev. Moses Hallock in Plainfield, Massachusetts. Cullen was a ready scholar and prepared himself so well in these languages, in mathematics, and in more general studies that he entered the sophomore class at Williams College in October 1810. He did not stay the year. Although he seemed to have enjoyed the literary society—the Philotechnian—to which he belonged, he was disappointed at the level of instruction; and, following the lead of his roommate, John Avery, he obtained an honorable dismissal during his third quarter so that he might prepare himself to enter Yale. His father's finances, however, would not permit the transfer. Although Austin was committed to farming, there were three boys and two girls younger than Cullen; and Peter Bryant had also to think of them. Instead of attending Yale,

therefore, the young poet was put to the study of the law, first with Samuel Howe at Worthington and later with William Baylies at West Bridgewater.

As always, Bryant worked diligently, completed his studies in four years, and was admitted to practice law in August 1815. He settled in Plainfield in December of that year but, a better opportunity presenting itself, he formed a partnership with George H. Ives at Great Barrington the following fall. Bryant remained there for almost nine years, pursuing a career that he did not really like. Yet he seems to have been successful. By May 1817 he was able to buy out his partner; his solitary practice succeeded; and over the next few years he held a number of elected or appointed offices, including town clerk and justice of the peace. It was in Great Barrington, too, that he met and courted Frances Fairchild. They were married on January 11, 1821; and the first of their two daughters, Frances, was born the following year. Bryant felt isolated in western Massachusetts, however; and although he met and associated with the Sedgwick family in nearby Stockbridge, he longed for more literary company than was available in Berkshire villages. What made its absence the more keenly felt was the rapid development of his poetic career.

Throughout the years of his education and legal training, Bryant had never stopped writing verse. As he mastered Latin and Greek, he tried his hand at translating Virgil, and later Sophocles and the Greek lyric poets. Indeed, the earliest of his poems, much reworked, that he included in his collected editions was "Version of a Fragment of Simónides," written while he was at Williams College. Bryant wrote a number of verse letters: to his brother Austin, to the Philotechnian Society at Williams, and later to his friend Jacob Porter (on the occasion of his marriage and, shortly thereafter, on the death of his wife). Most interesting of all, however, is a group of poems written while he was studying law. Many seem to record the vicissitudes of a romance between Bryant and a young lady from Rhode Island who had visited Cummington, while others, probably composed under the influence of the "graveyard" poets, show the young man's concern with and fear of death. Bryant was gradually freeing himself from his Augustan models. Under the influence of the associationist philosophers and of the Romantic poets, especially Wordsworth, that he had begun to read, he soon developed the mature voice of his best-known poetry.

The dates of Bryant's first important poems cannot be established precisely. The writing of "Thanatopsis" has been placed as early as 1811 and as late as 1815, and both the date and the occasion for the writing of "To a Waterfowl" have been the subject of some discussion. But if William Cullen Bryant II is correct in his arguments, we may reasonably consider 1814–1815 as the period of the poet's coming of age. During this time he composed initial versions of some of his best-known poems: the central section of "Thanatopsis," "The Yellow Violet," "To a Waterfowl," "Inscription for the Entrance to a Wood," and "I Cannot Forget with What Fervid Devotion." The difference between these and his earlier verses is marked. They clearly indicate the relation he had discovered between the mind of the poet and the natural world he observes, and they record the meanings that the discerning eye can discover in the external scene. Both "The Yellow Violet" and "To a Waterfowl" illustrate the analogical method by which, according to the Scottish philosophers, the mind could discover meaning through the impressions it received from the external world; and "Thanatopsis" and "Inscription" show the reflective mind deriving knowledge and comfort from its contemplation of nature.

In language and imagery, too, these poems mark a real advance over the juvenile verse. Al-

though some of the poems were later much revised to clarify the thought and remove some roughness in movement and tone, even the earliest versions indicate the progress Bryant had made in poetic diction. Never colloquial in his poetry, Bryant writes with an idiomatic freedom that does no violence to the natural patterns of educated language. Words like "russet," "illimitable," "primal," or "dissembled" sound natural in his verse; but he did learn from the new Romantic poets—especially Wordsworth and Robert Southey—to be, for the most part, precise and concrete in his imagery. Thus, although he may be guilty of such eighteenth-century diction as "the wingèd plunderer" in "Inscription," he also includes, in the early version of the poem, some sharply detailed descriptions of the external scene:

>   here from tree to tree
> And through the rustling branches flit the birds
> In wantonness of spirit;—theirs are strains
> Of no dissembled rapture—while below
> The squirrel with rais'd paws and form erect
> Chirps merrily.

Once he had achieved his characteristic voice, the way was open for him to develop his vision of the world in language well suited to its expression.

Bryant matured as a poet just at the time he was admitted to the practice of law; and at first he did nothing to advance his literary career, preferring to establish himself as a lawyer in Great Barrington. His father, however, acting upon the request of Willard Phillips, sent several of Bryant's poems to the *North American Review*. In September 1817 there appeared in the journal a four-stanza poem and a blank-verse fragment under the title "Thanatopsis," a name coined by one of the editors, and a "Fragment" that was later to become "Inscription for the Entrance to a Wood." These poems created a stir. Richard Henry Dana, who became Bryant's lifelong friend, could not believe that they had been written in America; and through some mistake "Thanatopsis" was attributed for a time to the poet's father. Early the next year Cullen sent the Simonides fragment and "To a Waterfowl" to the magazine, and the two appeared in March 1818. Although all the poems were published anonymously, Bryant had been introduced to some of the literati of Boston; and during the next few years he contributed some prose pieces to the review.

Despite this initial success, Bryant published no more poems at this time in the *North American Review*. He had also sent them "The Yellow Violet," but the poetry section was discontinued for lack of verse of sufficient quality and the poem was not printed. During the next few years, however, literary opportunities opened up for him. At Catharine Sedgwick's request Bryant contributed a group of five hymns to a Unitarian collection, in 1820, and he continued to write a few new poems. In the spring of 1821, he was surprised to learn that he had been elected to Phi Beta Kappa four years earlier, and was now invited to deliver the Phi Beta Kappa poem at the Harvard commencement in August. While he was writing this poem, moreover, he learned from Edward T. Channing that Dana was about to publish his own journal, *The Idle Man*. During the summer of 1821, Bryant completed and delivered a poem, "The Ages," on the cyclical vision of history; and during the summer and fall he sent Dana four poems for his journal: "Green River," "A Walk at Sunset," "A Winter Piece" (then called "Winter Scenes"), and "The West Wind."

But, most important of all, his friends in Boston—Channing, Dana, and Phillips—helped Bryant to publish a collection of his poems. The book is hardly more than a pamphlet, containing only eight poems in its forty-four pages: "The Ages," "To a Waterfowl," "Translation of a Fragment of Simonides," "Inscription for the

Entrance to a Wood," "The Yellow Violet," "Song" (later entitled "The Hunter of the West"), "Green River," and "Thanatopsis." This is the version of "Thanatopsis" that everyone knows, for while he was in Boston, Bryant wrote the introduction and conclusion that surround the now-revised section that had appeared in the *North American Review*. Slight as the book is, however, the publication of *Poems* (1821) was as significant an event in American literature as the appearance of Washington Irving's *The Sketch Book* (1819–1820) and James Fenimore Cooper's *The Spy* (1821). A truly American poetic voice joined theirs in prose; and if the book did not receive a wide circulation outside Boston, it was well reviewed by Willard Phillips in the *North American Review* and by Gulian C. Verplanck in the New York *American*. Bryant's reputation was spreading not only in America but also in England, where the eight poems were reprinted in *Specimens of the American Poets* (1822) and reviewed in *Blackwood's Edinburgh Magazine*.

Although Bryant had thus received considerable recognition both in the United States and abroad, he did not immediately pursue his poetic career. Quite the contrary. He remained in Great Barrington, practicing law. He may even have attempted, as he wrote in one of his poems, to break the spell of poetry and devote himself entirely to his profession. He did begin a satirical farce and a long narrative poem, but his output of poetry over the next two years was very slight. Late in 1823, however, yet another unexpected opportunity opened for him. In December of that year, Theophilus Parsons, editor of the *United States Literary Gazette*, asked him to contribute poetry on a regular basis. Since the payment offered—$200 a year—would increase his income substantially, Bryant readily accepted; and over the next two years he published some two dozen poems in that journal, including such important pieces as "The Rivulet," "An Indian at the

Burial-Place of His Fathers,'' ''Monument Mountain,'' and ''A Forest Hymn.'' In January 1826, moreover, a volume of poems selected from the pages of the *Gazette* and including Bryant's verses was published in Boston, thereby giving the poet added visibility in the literary world.

These years, 1824–1826, were a very important period in Bryant's life. They were undoubtedly the most productive that Bryant the poet ever had, but they also marked a crucial turning point for Bryant the man. Although well-established in Great Barrington, Bryant disliked the narrow community and was restive in his—to him—distasteful profession. He needed a larger arena for his talents, and his friends the Sedgwick brothers helped him find one. In April 1824 he visited Henry and Robert Sedgwick in New York, where he met James Fenimore Cooper, Fitz-Greene Halleck, Robert Sands, and Jared Sparks. During the following months, he considered the possibility of moving to that city. In January, Henry Sedgwick urged him to come down since a new literary review was under discussion and the owners wanted Bryant to be associated with it. Bryant made two trips, in February and March, but the negotiations took time; and it was not until May that he moved permanently to New York to be editor, with Henry J. Anderson, of the newly organized *New-York Review and Atheneum Magazine.* The first issue was dated June 1825.

Like most contemporary journals, the *New-York Review* was short-lived, lasting only a year. By the spring of 1826, Bryant was already making plans to merge it with the *United States Literary Gazette.* But before negotiations were complete, he took, in July, what he thought was to be a temporary job as editorial assistant on the New York *Evening Post,* an important city newspaper. Even after the merger of the magazines, which resulted in the *United States Review and Literary Gazette,* he divided his time between

newspaper and magazine. Bryant was responsible for only half of the literary journal. He selected the poetry and supplied the reviews of books from New York and points south, while Charles Folsom, in Boston, handled the material from New England. The *United States Review* was thus an attempt to establish a national magazine, published simultaneously in the two cities; but it, too, failed, the last issue appearing in September 1827. Thereafter, Bryant cast his lot with the *Evening Post.* He became joint editor in December, bought a one-eighth share in the firm, and began an editorial career that ended at his death, more than half a century later.

Bryant's first years in New York broadened his experience in ways that he could not have foreseen. He was soon caught up in the intellectual life of the city and began to associate with its leading writers and painters. In November 1825 he was elected to membership in Fenimore Cooper's Bread and Cheese Club, where he joined such writers as Halleck, Verplanck, and Sands, and such painters as Samuel F. B. Morse, Asher B. Durand, and Thomas Cole. Bryant was quick to support the young painters in their attempt to establish the National Academy of Design, where he later lectured on mythology. In the spring of 1826, moreover, he delivered a series of four lectures on poetry at the New York Athenaeum. Bryant had long been interested in the criticism of poetry. He had criticized Solyman Brown's *Essay on American Poetry* in 1818; he had published his famous essay ''On the Use of Trisyllabic Feet in Iambic Verse'' in 1819; and he had reviewed books of poetry. The lectures, however, gave him the opportunity to make a comprehensive aesthetic statement based on his knowledge of the Scottish philosophers, his wide reading in poetry, and his own poetic practice.

These years also provided Bryant with additional publishing opportunities. The two literary journals required a large amount of material; and in addition to his reviews, Bryant printed a number of poems, both old and new, in them. He even tried his hand at fiction, publishing three of his thirteen prose tales in these magazines. The journals were not, however, his only outlets. He joined his friends in a number of cooperative ventures. With Verplanck and Sands he helped to write a series of Christmas annuals, called *The Talisman,* published under the pseudonym Francis Herbert, in December 1827, 1828, and 1829. Bryant contributed poetry and prose, including short fiction, to all three, printing such well-known poems as ''The Past'' and ''To Cole, the Painter, Departing for Europe.'' In 1830 he contributed to *The American Landscape,* a book of paintings by his artist friends, engraved by Durand and with letterpress by the poet; and in 1832 he joined with Sands, William Leggett, Catharine Sedgwick, and James Kirke Paulding to publish *Tales of Glauber-Spa,* for which Bryant wrote two stories, ''The Skeleton's Cave'' and ''Medfield,'' his last attempts in the genre.

By far the most important event of these years, however, was the publication of the first collected edition of Bryant's works. The 1821 *Poems* had been merely a pamphlet. Now, ten years later, he selected eighty-nine poems, most of which had already appeared in print; revised them carefully, although not extensively; and published them in January 1832, in a book of 240 pages. Readers and critics were thus for the first time given the opportunity to read all of Bryant's mature poetry in one collection, and the book confirmed his position as the leading American poet of his time. Bryant wanted his book to be published in England and wrote to Washington Irving, then still living abroad, to enlist his help. Irving placed the work with a London publisher, added his own name as editor, and dedicated it to Samuel Rogers, the well-known British poet— all necessary, Irving wrote to Bryant, to call attention to the book in a depressed literary market. Bryant was pleased, and grateful to Irving

for what he had done. *Poems* (1832) was now before the entire English-speaking literary world, and the reviews on both sides of the Atlantic were generally favorable.

The publication of this volume marked the culmination of Bryant's career as a poet. Although the last edition of his works in 1876 contained more than double the number of poems of the 1832 volume, most of his best work was already behind him. An occasional later poem is worthy of note. ''The Prairies,'' written after his visit to Illinois in the spring of 1832 and published the following year, is probably the best. But poems like ''Earth'' and ''To the Apennines,'' written in Europe during his first trip abroad, and three blank-verse poems of the late 1830's and early 1840's—''The Fountain,'' ''Noon,'' and ''A Hymn of the Sea''—are also significant and should be mentioned. There were few years after 1832, however, in which Bryant wrote as many as six or eight poems; and as time passed, his annual production became very small. As new editions of his works appeared, Bryant incorporated into them the poems of the intervening years—four new poems in 1834, twelve in 1836, and only one in 1839—but since the bulk of each volume was essentially the same as that of 1832, there was little more to be said about his verse as a whole than had been elicited by the appearance of that volume.

Bryant did publish three completely new books of poetry: *The Fountain and Other Poems* (1842), a small collection of poems including parts of an unfinished long work; *The White-Footed Deer and Other Poems* (1844), ten new poems including both ''Noon'' and ''A Hymn of the Sea''; and *Thirty Poems* (1864), a small gathering that includes some of his Civil War verse. The poems from these volumes were also collected in the enlarged editions of his poetical works that appeared in 1847, 1855, 1858, 1871, and 1876, the last that Bryant himself brought out. None of these collections, it is fair to say, is so important as that of 1832, for none of them added appreciably to a poetic reputation that had peaked around then and was soon to be surpassed by that of the extraordinarily popular Henry Wadsworth Longfellow. The later books, including *Thirty Poems,* were well received; but it was Bryant the well-known, established figure who was being praised. He made no new departures in these books, remaining a poet of the early nineteenth century who lived to become an important newspaper editor who also occasionally wrote verse.

By 1832, Bryant was firmly established on the *Evening Post.* Editor in chief since 1829, he bought an increasing share in the business over the years, and soon found himself in comfortable circumstances. Bryant was not always happy in the editorial profession, but it supported him well and eventually brought him wealth. It also drew him deeply into politics. He had long since given up his youthful Federalist views to become an outspoken advocate of liberal causes, first among the Jacksonian Democrats and later, as the Civil War approached, with the newly founded Republican Party; and he wrote vigorous editorials in support of the positions that, under his guidance, the paper advocated. Moreover, Bryant's success on the *Evening Post* gave him the opportunity to indulge his love for travel. Over a period of some forty years, he made six voyages to Europe and the Near East; he traveled in the United States, to Illinois and the South; and he went to Cuba and Mexico. On most of these trips he wrote letters back to the *Evening Post,* many of which were collected in three volumes: *Letters of a Traveller* (1850), *Letters of a Traveller, Second Series* (1859), and *Letters from the East* (1869).

His position as editor of an important daily kept Bryant much in the public eye and, especially in his later years, he was frequently asked to deliver speeches on public occasions of both literary and civic importance. As well-known members of his generation died, Bryant was called upon to deliver memorial addresses for them: for Cole in 1848, Cooper in 1852, Irving in 1860, Halleck in 1869, and Verplanck in 1870; and he spoke on such occasions as the Burns centennial celebration in 1859, the laying of the cornerstone at the National Academy of Design in 1863, and the fiftieth anniversary of the Mercantile Library in 1870. A small collection of his speeches was published in 1873 as *Orations and Addresses,* a volume noteworthy mainly for gathering in one place the five major addresses on his friends in literature and the arts. Those on Cole, Cooper, and Irving are undoubtedly the most important. The poet felt called upon to comment on their works as well as their lives, and his critical judgments are of value both for what they say about the subjects themselves and for what they reveal about the poet's critical standards.

In his last years, too, Bryant engaged in several large projects. He wrote the introduction and helped select the material for a massive anthology of poetry, *The Library of Poetry and Song.* Bryant had earlier published a smaller collection, *Selections from the American Poets* (1840); but the new volume, published in 1871, included British as well as American works and soon attained a wide popularity. He also wrote introductions for both *Picturesque America; or, the Land We Live In,* published in two volumes (1872, 1874), and the multivolume *Popular History of the United States* (1878), written by Sydney Howard Gay. The most important work of Bryant's last years, however, was translation. From his earliest days he had translated Greek and Latin poetry, and his collected works contain a number of poems translated mainly from Spanish and German. In his old age he turned to Homer, making blank-verse translations of the *Iliad* (1870) and the *Odyssey* (1871–1872). Bryant found he could do this work without the strain that original composition entailed, and he sought in it a means to occupy himself after the death of his wife in 1866 had left him feeling like "one cast out of paradise."

Bryant remained active until the last weeks of his life. Strong of body and alert in mind, he kept busy not only with his newspaper work but also with his many other activities. Occasionally he would write poetry; and it is a testimony to his intellectual vigor that one of his last poems, "The Flood of Years," an imaginative treatment of life and death written in 1876, remains memorable. Bryant had lived a long and productive life. Although forced to earn his living by what he considered the drudgery of both law and journalism, he managed to keep his poetic fire alive and contributed both to the intellectual life of his city and to American literature as a whole. In his later years, of course, the exigencies of his profession forced him to mute his poetic voice; and he never completed the long poem he apparently attempted in the early 1840's. His accomplishment in poetry, however, is nonetheless significant. When Bryant died on June 12, 1878, in his eighty-fourth year, an important American poetic voice was stilled, one that had spoken truly of native things and, in its quiet way, had demonstrated to the English-speaking world that a distinctively American poetry had been born.

What is there in Bryant's verse that can be called specifically American? Certainly not the form. Although in his later years he experimented successfully with a number of lyric stanzas, Bryant was never an innovator in verse. He believed, as he wrote in his "Lectures on Poetry," that every apprentice in the art learns his craft from reading the works of those who have gone before him. Like the mathematician, the poet takes up his art at just the place where his predecessors left off; and if he has genius enough, he advances it just as far as he is able. Such a theory places great emphasis on both tradition and continuity in poetry. It leaves little

room for the kind of originality that breaks with the past and launches the art in a new direction. Those critics were right, therefore, who in the early reviews of his poems observed his relation to the English poets of the immediate past; and even though more perceptive ones also made it clear that he did not imitate those poets, knowledgeable readers have always recognized that Bryant's roots lie deep in the British poetry he had read and loved as a young man.

Both Bryant's philosophic stance and his aesthetic theory derive from a foreign source: Scottish associationist philosophy. Works by Dugald Stewart and Archibald Alison were extremely popular in the United States in those days: they were used as textbooks in the colleges, and they helped to form the aesthetic views of the first generation of American Romantic artists and writers. Along with other members of that generation, Bryant accepted as a matter of course both their realistic philosophy and its aesthetic corollaries. Their sensationalist view provided him with an epistemology that he never questioned, and he followed them in the moral and religious aspects of their belief. He found in Alison's treatment of the sublimity and beauty of nature an adequate explanation of the human response to the natural world, and he formed his taste around those aesthetic categories as they were illustrated and explained by Alison's treatment of both descriptive poetry and landscape art. Bryant even constructed his poems in accordance with those intellectual processes that the Scottish school had shown to be the means by which one learned from his impressions of external reality.

One finds the influence of these beliefs throughout Bryant's poetry. The sensationalist basis of his thought is apparent in the numerous images of sight, sound, and even smell that are everywhere in his verse. Most, of course, are visual. But the sounds of birds and insects, of rippling water and rustling trees are also present, as is the fragrance of those flowers that occasionally appear. Like the philosophers, Bryant believed that through the senses, the sympathetic observer could establish a proper relation with external reality. Not everyone, of course, would react in the same way to the natural scene, nor would the individual relate to it in the same fashion on different occasions. Although nature answers to the requirements of the mind, the mind itself, as Bryant wrote in "An Invitation to the Country," must actively participate in the process. The sights and sounds of the springtime are beautiful only when the observer "fondly" looks and listens. One must gaze at the world with "a loving eye" and breathe "with joy" the fragrance of April breezes, or the beauty and glory of nature will not be perceived.

On the properly disposed mind, therefore, the beauty and sublimity of the external world could have a salutary effect, answering, as the need might arise, to the gay or solemn mood with which one viewed the landscape. This was not, however, the only function of nature. Through correct perception of the external scene, the healthy rational mind could be led to an understanding of its meaning. Like the philosophers, of course, Bryant knew that sense impressions could sometimes be deceptive; and he occasionally included in his poems such phenomena as the delusive images of glittering light that so attract the dreamy youth in "Catterskill Falls" that he almost perishes, or the dim and misty landscape that leads the weary hunter to misinterpret reality and plunge to his death in "The Hunter's Vision." Indeed, the poet even plays fancifully with the concept in "A Day-Dream," where, gazing at rays of light quivering across the ocean floor, he imagines that sea nymphs rise from the waves and, in the murmuring of the waters, speak to him of the times when men believed in their existence. In all three poems, deceptive visual images, playing upon the imagination, influence the mind to perceive what is not actually there.

Such incidents are rare in Bryant's poetry. He more usually bases his themes on the philosopher's fundamental position that the objects of the world are both real and knowable. He can perceive the yellow violet and the fringed gentian, for example, not only as ephemeral flowers but also as entities that have certain specific and verifiable characteristics. In his part of the world, the yellow violet is a flower of April, blooming alone in the woods before the other flowers of spring appear; the fringed gentian is the last flower of autumn, blossoming when all others have died. Each has certain demonstrable qualities that help the poet to identify and place it in the general order of things. Bryant was an accomplished botanist, and sought to be scientifically exact in his descriptions of such plants. He saw no conflict between his scientific and poetic approaches to nature. Both were premised upon the belief that the natural world was real, that it could be reached and understood by the minds of men, and that reliable knowledge could be drawn from it of the utmost value to both the physical and the moral well-being of men.

It is precisely because he acted upon such beliefs that Bryant developed into a truly American poet. Once he had accepted the epistemological and aesthetic views of the Scottish philosophers, he found himself in a complex relation with nature; and the interaction between his mind and the objects that he perceived formed the intellectual and aesthetic basis for his poetry. The world Bryant observed could not be anything but American, for before his first trip to Europe in 1836, he had experienced no other; and the mind with which he perceived it, though necessarily influenced by the education he had received in Scripture, in classical and English poetry, and in Scottish philosophy, remained fundamentally American in its view both of external nature and of men and their institutions. This is not to say that Bryant and other Americans of his generation were totally different from their British contemporaries. But the process of change that had begun to work on the American character with the arrival of the first colonists had proceeded so far by the beginning of the nineteenth century that a distinctly American cast of mind had formed, and men born on these shores saw things through American eyes.

What they saw, moreover, was uniquely their own. The American landscape of the 1820's was markedly different from that of Europe, and Bryant sought to catch its quality and meaning in his art. The point is not that he wished to be nationalistic. He was willing to include European views in his work after he had experienced them, but his heart and mind were always with American nature because of what he had felt and learned in its presence. As he wrote in his sonnet "To Cole, the Painter, Departing for Europe," there is a brightness and a wildness in the American landscape, an expansiveness in its wide savannas and boundless groves, a solemnity in the uninhabited reaches of the wilderness that cannot be matched in Europe, where the hand of man, working through time, is seen in the houses, graves, and ruins of a thoroughly domesticated landscape. Bryant does not insist on the superiority of either; he stresses only the difference. But a man whose mind and art were formed in response to the wild, bright nature of his expansive country must always create an art that will reflect the values he derived from his experience.

This view of nature was not, of course, his only one, nor did Bryant rule out the presence of man in the American landscape. Most often, however, the human agents include such typically American characters as hunter, Indian, or independent farmer—there are no Wordsworthian leech gatherers or old Cumberland beggars in his verse—and his less expansive scenes frequently include some specific American locality or precisely described flora that the poet had observed. Yet it is not so much the presence of American things as the broad vision of real-

ity that is important in Bryant's verse. Each poem presents some aspect of it, but no poem contains it all. No one could, since each records an individual perception, a unique encounter between the mind of the poet and the external world. What Bryant might perceive one day was necessarily different from what he might see the next, for his mood would inevitably change and different aspects of the material world would catch his attention. Nonetheless, his fundamentally American bent of mind gave him a point of view that enabled him to maintain a consistent moral vision throughout his many poems.

To understand that vision, we must begin where Bryant did, with man's relation to nature. In composing his poems he sought, as he writes in his "Lectures on Poetry," "to shape the creations of the mind into perfect forms according to those laws which man learns from observing the works of his Maker," and to reveal to his readers "those analogies and correspondences which [poetry] beholds between the things of the moral and of the natural world." From the poet's point of view, he stands in a complex relation to nature and, through it, to God. Nature thus stands between the poet and the Deity, reveals to the former the moral truths of God, and provides the means through which the poet communicates those truths to his readers. The poet must first perceive those qualities in the natural landscape that have led him to his belief, and then re-create in his verse not merely a detailed description of the scene, but an evocation of its meaning. This he does by presenting a few suggestive touches and glimpses to awaken the imagination of the reader and fill his mind with delight. By this means the poet leads him to a perception of those truths that God has instilled in the natural scene.

Such a process must be premised upon a fundamentally innocent nature that does not itself deceive, and Bryant goes out of his way to establish the point. Though he believes in a fallen world, he writes, in "Inscription for the

Entrance to a Wood,'' that "the primal curse / Fell'' on an "unsinning earth,'' which, since it remains guiltless, still contains qualities that can ease the mind and heart of those who come to it from the "sorrows, crimes, and cares'' of the world of guilty men. "The calm shade'' brings "a kindred calm, and the sweet breeze'' carries a balm to the "sick heart.'' Bryant is seldom so explicit in developing the basis for his view. More usually he simply asserts the fact of an innocent nature. In "A Summer Ramble,'' for example, he describes the beautiful calm of a summer day, leaves his desk, and goes out amid "the sinless, peaceful works of God'' to share the season's calm; and in "The Firmament'' he carries the theme one step further by looking away from the earth to the "calm pure sphere'' of the skies, where he perceives "seats of innocence and rest.''

An innocent nature is a reliable one that can be depended upon in its communication of moral truth. It teaches, at times, by analogy. Simple flowers like the yellow violet and the fringed gentian, or birds like the waterfowl, lead the poet to an understanding of human behavior or to a perception of his place in the cosmos. Although he welcomes the yellow violet when he sees it blooming alone in the April woods, he ignores it when the gorgeous flowers of May appear; and the poet recognizes in this experience the sin of pride, which makes one forget his early friends when he climbs to wealth and social position. In a similar fashion the fringed gentian, blooming late in the year, when the woods are bare and the frost has come, makes him wish that when death draws near to him, he will similarly find hope blossoming in his heart. The famous "To a Waterfowl'' illustrates the same relation. The poet, like the bird, is moving through space to a new destination; and, perceiving his own situation reflected in its flight, he draws the moral conclusion that the God who directs the waterfowl unerringly to its destination will lead his steps aright.

Nature teaches in other ways as well. It is, for example, the measure of man and his accomplishments. Bryant does not always describe such small natural phenomena as wildflowers and birds. Sometimes he stresses the expansiveness of nature in both space and time. The opening lines of "Monument Mountain'' depict a spacious scene of rocky precipice and beautiful valley where the habitations of men are dwarfed to insignificance; those of "The Prairies'' describe a vast landscape that, stretching to the horizon, makes the lone man on horseback seem small indeed. "The Rivulet,'' on the other hand, measures man on a scale of time, for the little stream dances along its way unchanged, while the poet who played as a child along its banks already finds himself a grave man whose youthful visions have faded, and can foresee the day when he, "trembling, weak, and gray,'' will be an aged man. Indeed, after his death other children will mature and age near the spot, while the unchanging stream, "singing down [its] narrow glen, / Shall mock the fading race of men.'' In the presence of nature, man should perceive how small he is and how short his existence.

Man may react to this knowledge in a number of different ways. His initial response may be one of humility. The poet who feels "almost annihilated'' when he stands beside a "mighty oak'' in "A Forest Hymn'' reacts in a perfectly appropriate fashion, for the size and density of the centuries-old trees can only convince him of his own weakness and mortality and the vanity of human striving. On other occasions, however, the opposite response is proper. When the poet stands for the first time on the Illinois prairies and his "dilated sight / Takes in the encircling vastness,'' his "heart swells'' with the experience; when one looks out over the landscape from a lofty peak, as in "Monument Mountain,'' his "expanding heart'' feels kindred to the higher world to which he has been translated; and he experiences an "enlargement of [his] vision.'' All these reactions occur because the sensitive observer recognizes in nature the presence of an enormous power that, from one point of view, threatens to overwhelm him yet, from another, raises his spirit above the physical and gives him a glimpse of a brighter, happier sphere.

Both responses to nature derive from the poet's recognition that behind the spacious world lies the source of those truths to be discerned in it. Bryant's conception of God has always been the subject of some discussion. The poet's relation to Wordsworth might lead one to expect that he, like the English poet, would take a pantheistic view. But what one finds in his poems is something quite different. To be sure, in "A Forest Hymn" there is a brief passage that seems to imply that the forest flower may be

An emanation of the indwelling Life,
A visible token of the upholding Love,
That are the soul of this great universe.

But lines like these are rare in Bryant's poetry. His typical vision of God is that of a Creator who stands somewhat apart from His creation and reveals Himself not in, but through, it. The opening lines of the second section of "A Forest Hymn" are more typical. Here he addresses God as the "Father" who reared the massive trunks and wove the verdant roof above them, who looked "upon the naked earth" and raised forthwith all the "fair ranks of trees."

Precisely the same view appears in "The Prairies." As the poet looks across the "boundless and beautiful" unshorn fields, his mind turns to their Creator:

The hand that built the firmament hath heaved
And smoothed these verdant swells, and sown
    their slopes
With herbage, planted them with island-groves,
And hedged them round with forests.

Even when Bryant considers the physical world in terms of the geological processes that have formed its various features over eons of time, he sees as the ultimate cause of physical change that same God who initially created it. Thus, he begins "A Hymn of the Sea" with the lines:

The sea is mighty, but a mightier sways
His restless billows. Thou, whose hands have
    scooped
His boundless gulfs and built his shore, thy
    breath,
That moved in the beginning o'er his face
Moves o'er it evermore.

Bryant goes on to describe the changes that occur as the shores are worn away by waves and both coral reefs and volcanic islands form new land. Here too the hand of God is at work; and in a second echo of Genesis, Bryant writes: "Thou dost look / On thy creation and pronounce it good."

In Bryant's vision of reality, nature is both separate from and dependent upon a still-creating, still-sustaining Deity; but because the Creator may be known through His creation, God's qualities can be discerned in the physical world. The broad sweep of both space and time to be perceived in the universe bespeaks the infinity and eternity of Him who created it; the beauty and majesty of the natural landscape suggest the similar, though greater, qualities that He possesses. The light of God is revealed through the stars of the firmament, in "Song of the Stars," and His majesty in the mountains in "To the River Arve." The "grandeur, strength, and grace" of the trees, in "A Forest Hymn," suggest in small the similar qualities of God; and man, perceiving God's greatness in the surrounding forest, feels his spirit bowed "with the thought of boundless power / And inaccessible majesty." Indeed, once Bryant had established in his verse this fundamental vision of the external world as revealing the nature of God, any description of beauty or grandeur would carry with it the suggestion that the infinitely greater qualities of God were also being revealed.

But if the nature of God is made manifest in the external world, so too is His will, which, perceived by men, should lead them to moral action. For Bryant this is a crucial function of nature. He believes that fallen man, left to himself, is an easy prey to his passions, and that man as a whole in society creates endless conflict. While still a young man in Great Barrington, he had complained, in "Green River," that his occupation as lawyer had forced him to "mingle among the jostling crowd, / Where the sons of strife are subtle and loud"; and in "Autumn Woods" he longed to

> leave the vain low strife
> That makes men mad—the tug for wealth and
>   power—
> The passions and the cares that wither life,
>   And waste its little hour.

Later, in New York, Bryant returned to the same idea. His heart is oppressed with sadness, in "A Rain-Dream," because of the strifes and "tumults of the noisy world" where Fraud deceives and Strength overpowers his adversary. Evil, in Bryant's view, derives from the passions of men, which, if left unchecked, cause untold misery.

On a larger scale the same cause leads to war. As an early nineteenth-century American, Bryant was inclined to attribute aggressive war to the passions and greed of kings; and his poems on Europe frequently stress the horror of war and oppression that have characterized the past. Thus, in "Earth" he surveys the valleys of Italy that since early times have been the fields of war, where nations vanished, "driven out by mightier," and where free men fought each other until "strange lords" placed the yoke of servitude on all. To point up the folly of such struggles, and to affirm the peace that God wills for the world, Bryant sometimes juxtaposes a description of violent conflict and one of peaceful nature. In "To the Apennines" he recapitulates the long history of violence that has beset the Italian peninsula and pictures the shouting armies that have rushed together at the base of the Apennines. Be-

leaguered cities were destroyed, realms were torn in two, and commonwealths rose against each other and engaged in fratricidal war. Meanwhile, "in the noiseless air and light that flowed" around the mountain peaks, "eternal Peace abode."

The point of the contrast is not lost on some men. The poet recognizes, and tries to communicate to others, not only the folly of conflict but also its cure. He returns to the woods, in "A Forest Hymn," to reassure his "feeble virtue" in the presence of God; and he steals "an hour from study and care," in "Green River," to reestablish his peace of mind. In the peaceful stream he finds once again "an image of that calm life" he had previously found in his experience with nature. Many elements in the natural landscape can serve the same function. In "A Summer Ramble" the poet seeks peace in the calm of a summer day, while in "Lines on Revisiting the Country" he finds in the mountain wind a kind of "health and refreshment" that seems to come from heaven's own gates. Nature is thus an appropriate retreat from the conflicts of the world; but it is not merely an escape, nor does the poet seek only some vague influence from the natural scene. While it does provide an emotional calm, it also has a higher function in affirming the moral order that, in Bryant's view, is everywhere apparent in the harmony of nature.

Bryant was well aware that to most observers, the world did not appear to be a place of order and harmony. Even nature, unchanging as it may seem to be in comparison with human life, has undergone convulsive alterations in the geologic past; and wherever one looks in the present world, "eternal change," as Bryant wrote in "The Evening Wind," is clearly the law of nature. Like many another thinking man in the early nineteenth century, Bryant was fascinated with the problem of time and change, illustrated wherever he turned by the cycles of days, seasons, and years. And like many others, too, he sought some principle by which he might reconcile the endless manifestations of mutability that he perceived around him. He turned in one poem to the North Star as an apparently fixed element that could be read as a sign of "that bright eternal beacon" by which man might guide his life; but he needed some more general principle than this, some aspect of the external scene that, discernible throughout the natural world, could serve as an effective restraint on the passionate actions of men.

Bryant found that principle in the concept of ordered change. However mutable the world may be, change moves through constant patterns. The evening wind blows from sea to shore, but later returns from shore to sea; and the perceptive man will emphasize not the change, but the stable principle according to which change occurs. Thus, in "The Fountain" the poet writes of the many changes that have taken place around a woodland spring, itself a symbol of constant change. Yet something more than mutability may be seen in the flowing water. "Here the sage," Bryant writes,

Gazing into [the] self-replenished depth,
Has seen eternal order circumscribe
And bound the motions of eternal change,
And from the gushing of [the] simple fount
Has reasoned to the mighty universe.

Universal order is as apparent in the world as is the principle of mutability, and is more significant in that it reflects the unchanging nature of God. The lesson for man is obvious. He must learn to conform the order of his life to the order that lies at the heart of nature.

Some men, however, fail to perceive or heed the lesson that is writ large on the natural landscape. They continue their passionate struggle, unmindful of God or the message of peace and harmony He imparts to them through the ordered calm of nature. But if they will not learn from the milder aspects of the natural world, they may be influenced by the harsher. Bryant knew full well that nature could be frightening as well as reassuring, and he occasionally included its violent aspects in his work. In "A Forest Hymn" he depicts a tempestuous scene of thunder and lightning, of whirlwinds, and of pounding tidal waves that inundate the shore and destroy the cities. In scenes like these, he continues, prideful man lays by "his strifes and follies," recognizes his own incapacity, and acknowledges the power of God, Who rules the elements. The sublime aspects of the natural world are as important as the beautiful ones in leading men to a knowledge of how they should act, and the poet prays at the end of the poem that he may be spared the sterner aspects of God's power and learn from His "milder majesty" to order his life properly.

Yet even such warnings, Bryant believed, were sometimes not enough. In "A Hymn of the Sea" he carries the theme one step further by making a storm at sea the instrument of God's justice. Here an armed fleet is royally sailing to carry aggressive war to some unsuspecting realm, when "the fierce tornado" descends upon it. In a highly evocative passage filled with discord and violence, Bryant describes the destruction of the fleet, the vast ships whirled like chaff, sails rent, masts snapped, cannon thrust overboard, and the invading army "whelmed / By whirlpools or dashed dead upon the rocks." The instruments of power, violence, and oppression are utterly destroyed by the overwhelming force of the storm at sea; but the elements themselves are, after all, merely the instruments of a yet greater Power, who, in Bryant's view, may use them to teach a lesson to erring men. It ought to be a salutary one, and for a time it may be effective. But the poet offers scant hope that nations will change because of it. Although they stand in awe of what has happened to the invading fleet, they pause for only "a moment, from the bloody work of war."

The history of the world, as Bryant understood

it, certainly justified his conclusion. The record of the past was for the most part only a long series of wars and conflicts, as states and empires rose and fell, leaving only their ruins scattered across the landscape. His Phi Beta Kappa poem, "The Ages," recapitulates much of the record. He describes the ancient despotisms that flourished in the East, only to fall and leave behind a few monuments and tombs in the desert; he includes the decay of Rome as it sank, under the empire, into a state of guilt and misery; and he mentions the many nations that were "blotted out from earth, to pay / The forfeit of deep guilt." In "The Ruins of Italica," moreover, a poem Bryant translated from the Spanish of Francisco de Rioja, he presents the remains of the Roman city in Spain as an eloquent testimony to the emptiness of past glory. The palaces and gardens were all swept away with the Caesars, and Roman grandeur vanished from the earth as Trojan and Greek had disappeared before it. Such a record ought to be doubly instructive to men, to convince them that the glories of the world have always been, and still are, perishable, and to teach them that they should place their trust in other things.

This "ruins of empire" theme was a favorite among nineteenth-century writers and painters, both in the United States and abroad; and it so fascinated Bryant that he even developed it in an American context. The clearing of the forest and the supplanting of the Indian may have left no decaying monuments to past glories; but the historical process was, in a sense, little different from that recorded in Europe. The present American civilization was rising from the destruction of an earlier culture; and those involved in the process ought to be aware not only of what had happened in the past, but also of what might develop in the future. Bryant wrote several important poems on this theme. He imagines, in "The Fountain," the unrecorded history that has taken place around a woodland spring that once

flourished in the virgin forest. The Indian waged war in its vicinity, and hunters built their lodges near the spot. Then, after centuries passed, the white man came, cut the trees and plowed the ground; since that time a whole society has grown up around it. But change does not end with the present, and the poet muses on what additional changes—caused by man or nature—might lurk in the future.

Bryant depicts an even grander history, one more closely approximating the European version of the theme, in "The Prairies," where he tells of yet a third race, supplanted during the historical process in America—the Mound Builders, whom contemporary historians took to be a pre-Indian race. The mounds they left scattered across a large number of the eastern states were thus considered to be true ruins of a great historical past. Bryant describes their builders as "a disciplined and populous race" who constructed the mounds while the Greeks were erecting the Parthenon. He depicts their civilization as a relatively high one, brought down by the "warlike and fierce" redmen, who attacked and destroyed them. Now the Indians, too, have been driven away; and the white man is about to cultivate the fields where two previous cultures had once flourished. "Thus change the forms of being," Bryant writes:

Thus arise
Races of living things, glorious in strength,
And perish, as the quickening breath of God
Fills them, or is withdrawn.

The course of history in America resembles that in Europe, and contemporary men should heed the lesson it teaches.

That lesson involves both the present and the future. Men should not take pride today in what they know, from history, must eventually perish; but since men are by no means helpless in the world, what they do today can have some effect on the future. The basic question, of course, is whether the pattern must be continued unendingly, whether men must always succumb to their passions and forever repeat, as Bryant states in "Earth," "the horrid tale of perjury and strife, / Murder and spoil, which men call history." To Americans in the early nineteenth century, this question was crucial, for they saw their country as a young democratic state standing almost alone in a despotic world; and poets from Bryant to Walt Whitman viewed the United States as the hope of the future. America could serve that function only if it learned to avoid the mistakes of the past; but since, in Bryant's view, those mistakes had derived from the passionate nature of man, it remained an open question whether men in his day could acquire the self-control that would enable them to live in harmony, avoid conflict, and escape the age-old process of war and desolation that had overtaken all former people.

In his early poem "The Ages" (1821), Bryant had seemed hopeful that man in his time could change. "He who has tamed the elements," he writes, will not remain "the slave of his own passions"; he who can trace the course of celestial bodies will see God's will in His "magnificent works . . . / And love and peace shall make their paradise with man." Indeed, he ends the poem with the vision of a free and progressive America throwing off the last fetters of mankind and looking forward to a happy future. In later poems, however, Bryant sometimes appears to be less optimistic. In "Earth," for example, written in Europe some thirteen years later, he considers all the horrors that men have perpetrated and asks the obvious question of his "native Land of Groves" across the sea:

> a newer page
> In the great record of the world is thine;
> Shall it be fairer? Fear, and friendly Hope,
> And Envy, watch the issue, while the lines,

> By which thou shalt be judged, are written
> down.

There is an ominous tone to these last lines that contrasts sharply with the optimism of the earlier poem.

Bryant's uneasiness about the future derived, apparently, from his perception of what the historical process in America entailed. He knew, of course, that men of affairs in law and commerce were bound to be aggressive and contentious; and he always prescribed the untouched natural scene as the cure for passionate involvement in what are essentially trivial matters. But change in America involved the destruction of the wilderness; and by the early nineteenth century, American writers were beginning to warn their countrymen of the possible consequences of their actions. In "An Indian at the Burial-Place of His Fathers," Bryant makes a telling commentary on what had been happening. The Indian, who speaks the poem, visits the ancient burial ground of his tribe, from which they have long been driven; and in a series of contrasted pictures, he reveals the changes that the white man has made. In the first part of the poem, the contrast seems merely to indicate the two ways of life that the cultures created, the white man preferring the domesticated landscape of wheat fields and pasturage, while the Indian longs for the woods in which the warriors hunted. But there is more to the contrast than this.

The Indian sees a sign that the white man cannot perceive, and he predicts a future that resembles the European past:

> Their race may vanish hence, like mine,
>   And leave no trace behind,
> Save ruins o'er the region spread,
> And the white stones above the dead.

Because the white men have cut the trees and farmed the soil, the springs have dried up, and the rivers run "with lessening current." Hence, if the process continues, the lands for which the Indians were crushed may one day become "a barren desert." Although the words are placed in the mouth of an Indian, there can be no doubt that Bryant himself was aware of the danger. Toward the end of "The Fountain," after he has depicted all the changes that have taken place around the woodland spring, he considers the future and wonders whether, in historic time, men will not "seek out strange arts to wither and deform / The pleasant landscape which [the spring makes] green." If they do, the very aspect of the natural scene that could preserve them from their follies will have been destroyed.

Bryant thus faced a dilemma. Like many in his generation, he found value both in the untouched wilderness and in the strong democratic society that must come from its destruction; he lamented the passing of the Indian and foresaw the consequences that the despoliation of nature might entail, yet he could not condemn the rapid process of change that his generation of Americans, perhaps more than any other, was destined to experience. Bryant was well aware that the historical process could not be reversed. The continent would be settled and the face of the landscape would change. Yet, in the final analysis, his faith in America's future was so strong that he could face it with confidence. Even in "The Crowded Street," a poem that depicts the tide of humanity in all of its various aspects flowing through the city, he ends with the belief that however self-concerned these people may be and however aimless and wayward their course of action may seem, God holds them in His boundless love and guides "the mighty stream," of which they are but eddies, "to its appointed end." The providential view of history, in other words, informs Bryant's vision and gives him the faith that the process of change works ultimately for good.

For Bryant, as for many in his generation, the progress of history was toward human freedom; and since the United States was in the forefront of that movement, he could indeed look forward with confidence toward a time when God's will for man would be fulfilled. The basis for this belief was manifest in nature. Bryant saw in the unrestrained movement of the winds that spirit of freedom that must one day inspire the multitudes of Europe to throw off their chains, and he found in the mountains—both Alps and Apennines—an image of the liberty that had freed the Switzerland of William Tell and that would someday liberate Italy. Indeed, in "The Antiquity of Freedom," the poet finds in the peaceful woods of his native land a sign that the natural condition of man was originally freedom. Tyranny is later-born and, though powerful, "shall fade into a feebler age" while freedom waxes stronger. The battle is not yet over, for tyranny has become more subtle as it weakens; but the poet never doubts that the time will come when freedom shall triumph and a "new earth and heaven" be born.

Throughout his life Bryant supported the cause of freedom in his verse. He had celebrated the Spanish victory over the invading French in "The Spanish Revolution" (1808); and in "The Massacre at Scio," "Song of the Greek Amazon," "The Greek Partisan," and "The Greek Boy," he supported, like many a poet in his generation, the Greek struggle for independence. Although, unlike John Greenleaf Whittier and James Russell Lowell, he wrote little verse in support of the antislavery cause, there is "The African Chief," which details the destruction of the proud black man when he is captured and sold into slavery. The Civil War, of course, elicited Bryant's support of the federal government, "the gentlest sway / That Time in all his course has seen"; and he celebrated the emancipation of the slaves with an ode, "The Death of Slavery." The God "who marks the bounds of guilty power" had struck the shackles from the slave, who now "stands in his native manhood, disenthralled," while slavery itself, in these "better years that hasten by," is buried in the "shadowy past," with all those former wrongs of suffering and oppression from which so much of the world has been freed.

Bryant also counted on the ties of free trade to destroy the barriers that had arisen between men, and thus to unite the earth in one brotherhood. In "The Path" he imagines how a simple woodland path is linked to other paths and roads to make a vast network that binds all men together, and he praises the "mighty instinct, that dost thus unite/ Earth's neighborhoods and tribes with friendly bands." Like many another American in the nineteenth century, he sees in the physical links between men a sign of the higher association that will follow from them. Further, in "The Song of the Sower" Bryant pictures all the types of men who look to the sower's work for sustenance, and ends his poem with a vision of the grain going across the earth wherever "roads wind and rivers flow," to fill the marts of the ancient East and the tropical South. The image of peace and plenty that Bryant creates in this poem suggests the benefits that will flow when all men enjoy the blessings of liberty and neither barriers nor strife, caused by pride or spite, stand in the way of the peaceful interchange of goods between nations.

Bryant's philosophy of nature thus provided him with a comprehensive vision of reality that enabled him to write significantly about the American experience. Since close observation of nature could provide fallen man with the knowledge he needed to live successfully in the world, and since America was particularly blessed with broad expanses of forested hills and valleys that embodied the meanings that God intended for men to discern, Americans could learn from their native landscape the self-discipline necessary to control the pride and passions of their fallen nature and, thus, to live in freedom and peace. In building their country, of course, Americans incurred some risk that the result might differ little

from the experience of the past; and that prospect had to be faced. Time and change, however, could not be stopped. The westward expansion would go on at the expense of the Indian and of that wild, bright nature that Bryant valued so highly. Nonetheless, the poet found reason to hope that the change was being directed in such a way that a free American society would result and lead the world to that liberty and peace that he discerned in the natural landscape.

Bryant was not always so broadly philosophical in his verse. Although most of his important poems do develop one aspect or another of his vision, in a very few poems he wrote on highly personal subjects. Bryant was a man of strong emotions who kept them so firmly in check as to appear rather cold and severe, but he sometimes allowed his personal feelings to show through the medium of his verse. Of the several poems he wrote recording his youthful love for Frances Fairchild, he published only "Oh, Fairest of the Rural Maids," a poem in which he associates the beauty and innocence of the young girl with the analogous qualities of the natural scene in which she has lived. He also composed a few poems about her during his later years. In "The Life That Is," for example, written at Castellammare, Italy, in 1858, Bryant rejoices in her recovery from a serious illness that had threatened to take her life; and in "October, 1866," he expresses his grief and sense of loss at her death, which had occurred in July.

Bryant also treats the deaths of several members of his family. While composing "Hymn to Death" in 1820, he was shocked to learn of the death of his beloved father; he ended the poem with a tribute to the man who had taught him the art of writing verse and who had read and criticized all of his previous attempts at poetry. A few years later, in 1824–1825, he wrote two poems on his favorite sister, Sarah Bryant Shaw. In the first, "Consumption," he reconciles himself to the fact that his sister is dying; and in the very popular poem "The Death of the Flowers," he pays tribute to her after her death. Finally, in 1849, Bryant wrote "The May Sun Sheds an Amber Light" to commemorate his mother, who had died two years before in Illinois. In most of these poems—"Hymn to Death" may be an exception—Bryant exerts a firm control over the emotion he has experienced; and one feels that he published them not because of the personal meaning they had for him, but because he was satisfied that in each poem, the emotion had been given proper poetic expression.

The poems on the deaths of his wife and beloved members of his family are, moreover, important contributions to a subject that had fascinated the poet since his youth. Bryant had apparently had a real fear of death as a young man, had written a number of juvenile poems on the subject, and had read the British "graveyard" poets, who had dealt with it. One of his earliest poems—"Thanatopsis"—and one of his later—"The Flood of Years"—discuss the problem; and between these two there are many that, in one way or another, touch upon it. Poems on death, therefore, represent a significant part of Bryant's poetic output and deserve consideration both for themselves and for what they contribute to an understanding of his philosophy. From the latter point of view, the subject of death presented him with something of a problem. Because he based his philosophic position on the direct observation of nature and constructed his system of belief around it, Bryant would necessarily turn first to the material world for an understanding of the meaning of death. This he did, of course, in "Thanatopsis," where the voice of nature gives one aspect of that meaning.

What nature can say of death, however, must be limited to the physical. Since death is the natural end of all living things, it must simply be accepted as a matter of course. Beyond that, nature can say nothing about the ultimate significance of death; and the only comfort it can give is that all who have ever lived lie together equally in the common grave of earth. Critics have made much of the fact that no hint of immortality is given in the poem, and the omission is sometimes taken as a sign of Bryant's religious position at the time. It may well be. But Bryant himself had trouble identifying the voice that speaks the central section of the poem. In an early manuscript version of the introductory lines, he had made it his "better genius"; but this he rejected in favor of the present reading, in which the "still voice" comes from nature. The effect is to give a partial treatment of the subject, as if the poet would say: Here is the view that nature takes of the common fate of man, one that should give the observer courage to accept his personal end.

Seen from other points of view, however, death appears quite different. In human terms, as Bryant writes in "Hymn to Death," it can be seen as a deliverer who frees the oppressed and crushes the oppressor, or as the great leveler without whom the powerful of the earth would have enslaved the weak forever. Seen in yet other terms, as Bryant has it in "A Forest Hymn," death is not so triumphant as it sometimes appears to be. Though "all grow old and die," youth, "ever-gay and beautiful youth / In all its beautiful forms," perpetually presses "on the faltering footsteps of decay." Life mocks at death because it comes from God, Who has no end. From this intellectual position it is but a step to the affirmation of human immortality. Belief in an afterlife appears in some of the earliest of Bryant's poems—"Hymn to Death," for example—and is repeated in such later works as "Consumption," "The Past," and "The Future Life." In all of these poems, Bryant looks forward to another life, in which he hopes to meet again those whom he loved on earth.

As Bryant grew older, he turned increasingly to allegory to express his view of death and the afterlife, most frequently using the rather conventional image of passage down a road or stream into the unknown. In "The Cloud on the Way" he suggests the mystery of death by an image of mist into which all travelers disappear, and in "Waiting by the Gate" he depicts death as a portal through which everyone must pass. Both of these poems, moreover, show the strong Christian affirmation that appeared in Bryant's work as he grew older, for both suggest that on the other side one shall meet not only his departed loved ones but also "the Sinless Teacher" who died for men. In one of his last poems, "The Flood of Years," Bryant gave his final thoughts on death. The passing generations rise and fall on the crest of the flood of time, only to be overwhelmed and disappear in the ocean of the past. But all that is good and valuable shall be restored in an eternal present in which the process of change so familiar on earth will at last be reconciled in everlasting harmony.

Bryant, of course, was not alone in his intellectual position, nor was his mode of expression unique. Other writers and painters of his generation—James Fenimore Cooper and Thomas Cole are but two important examples—shared his religious vision of nature and expressed their related themes in strikingly similar ways. Both Cooper and Cole depict the beauty and sublimity of the American scene and suggest the moral meaning to be derived from its observation; they also take precisely the same view of human history and include the "ruins of empire" theme in their works. Bryant may thus be seen as both drawing upon a body of thought generally accepted by literate Americans in his generation, and addressing his works to an audience who shared many of his assumptions, approved the themes of his poetry, and took pleasure in their expression. From the historical point of view, therefore, Bryant must be considered an important member of the first generation of American Romantic artists; and his poetry may profitably be read as a significant statement of those intellectual, artistic, and moral values that character-

ized the cultural life of early nineteenth-century America. The success that Bryant achieved as a spokesman for his generation, however, may stand in the way of a proper appreciation of his poetic achievement today. His vision of nature was rapidly superseded by those of the transcendentalists, the symbolists, and the realists—for all of whom he had helped to pave the way—and to many readers of poetry in the twentieth century, both the themes he develops and his mode of expression may seem old-fashioned. Some will object, for example, to the touches of sentimentality that appear in a number of Bryant's poems or to the use of analogy in the development of his themes. To many readers today the analogies he draws will seem like moral tags appended to his verse, and it must be admitted that some of his analogies do not derive so closely from the descriptions that inspired them as one might wish. Finally, we may also note that Bryant's range was narrow and his development relatively slight. Once he had established his intellectual position and found his poetic voice, he wrote a body of verse that explored that position fully; but he did not often venture onto new ground.

Bryant's limitations as a poet are real, and cannot be gainsaid. He is not a major poet, but a very good minor one who can still be read with pleasure. In his favorite forms, the short lyric and reflective blank-verse poem, he is quite effective. At their best, as in "To a Waterfowl," his poems of analogy develop naturally and convincingly from observed phenomenon to philosophical conclusion; and his rolling blank-verse rhythms often strike the ear as most appropriate for his reflections upon the natural scene. These poems record the play of the mind across the external landscape; and as we read, we can watch the theme develop as the poet considers the meaning he finds in his observation. Bryant's mood changes, moreover, from poem to poem; and he evokes both gaiety and awe, peace and exhilaration in the movement of his verse, depending upon his bent of mind at the moment. Each poem is, after all, a new experience of nature; and since both he and the landscape change, it is natural that the tone of the poetry should vary. To Bryant's credit, he was often able to capture these changing moods well in his verse.

In content, too, Bryant remains a poet of some significance. Although his celebration of untouched nature comes from the preindustrial age of America, many of his themes are by no means out of date. He knew the cost that the settlement of the continent would entail—the destruction of the Indian and the despoliation of nature that would come with the westward expansion; and while he celebrated the democratic society that should result from the process, his knowledge of history and of the universal destruction of past civilizations made him aware that this nation, too, could perish. He depicted the passion, greed, and strife that he saw developing in the American cities; and he stressed the horrors that come from the selfishness and pride of human beings, especially in the form of war. He knew that the only cure was for men to recognize a power beyond their reach and strength, and he wrote of the need for humility if men were to lay by their follies. These are not minor themes. They were pertinent to the age in which he was writing and, considering what has happened since then, they cannot be considered irrelevant today.

Selected Bibliography

WORKS OF
WILLIAM CULLEN BRYANT

POETRY

The Embargo. Boston: printed for the purchasers, 1808. (Enlarged version with additional poems published 1809.)

Poems. Cambridge, Mass.: Hilliard and Metcalf, 1821.

Miscellaneous Poems Selected from the United States Literary Gazette. Boston: Cummings, Hilliard and Co., and Harrison Gray, 1826. (Contains twenty-three poems by Bryant.)

Poems. New York: Elam Bliss, 1832. (Republished, with new poems added, in 1834, 1836, 1839, 1847, 1855, 1858, 1871.)

The Fountain and Other Poems. New York: Wiley and Putnam, 1842.

The White-Footed Deer and Other Poems. New York: I. S. Platt, 1844.

Thirty Poems. New York: D. Appleton and Co., 1864.

Hymns. No place: no publisher, 1864.

Poems. New York: D. Appleton and Co., 1876. (The final collection in Bryant's lifetime.)

PROSE

Tales of Glauber-Spa. 2 vols. New York: J. and J. Harper, 1832. (Contains two stories by Bryant; other contributors were Robert Sands, William Leggett, Catharine Sedgwick, and James Kirke Paulding.)

Letters of a Traveller. New York: George P. Putnam, 1850.

Letters of a Traveller, Second Series. New York: D. Appleton and Co., 1859.

Letters from the East. New York: G. P. Putnam and Son, 1869.

Orations and Addresses. New York: G. P. Putnam's Sons, 1873.

MISCELLANIES

The Talisman for MDCCCXXVIII. New York: Elam Bliss, 1827.

The Talisman for MDCCCXXIX. New York: Elam Bliss, 1828.

The Talisman for MDCCCXXX. New York: Elam Bliss, 1829. (Bryant contributed poetry and prose to all three.)

TRANSLATIONS

The Iliad of Homer. 2 vols. Boston: Fields, Osgood and Co., 1870.

The Odyssey of Homer. 2 vols. New York: James R. Osgood and Co., 1871–1872.

COLLECTED EDITIONS

The Poetical Works of William Cullen Bryant, edited by Parke Godwin. 2 vols. New York: D. Appleton and Co., 1883; Russell and Russell, 1967.

Prose Writings of William Cullen Bryant, edited by Parke Godwin. 2 vols. New York: D. Appleton and Co., 1884.

The Poetical Works of William Cullen Bryant. New York: D. Appleton and Co., 1903. (The Roslyn ed.)

LETTERS

The Letters of William Cullen Bryant, edited by William Cullen Bryant II and Thomas G. Voss. Vol. 1: 1809–1836. New York: Fordham University Press, 1975. (Other volumes in progress.)

BIBLIOGRAPHIES

Blanck, Jacob. "William Cullen Bryant," in *Bibliography of American Literature*. New Haven: Yale University Press, 1955.

Phair, Judith T. *A Bibliography of William Cullen Bryant and His Critics, 1808–1972.* Troy, N.Y.: Whitston Publishing Co., 1975.

Rocks, James E. "William Cullen Bryant," in *Fifteen American Authors Before 1900,* edited by Robert A. Rees and Earl N. Harbert. Madison: University of Wisconsin Press, 1971.

Sturges, Henry C. *Chronologies of the Life and Writings of William Cullen Bryant, with a Bibliography of His Works in Prose and Verse.* New York: D. Appleton and Co., 1903. (Printed also in the Roslyn edition of the *Poetical Works*.)

CRITICAL AND BIOGRAPHICAL STUDIES

Allen, Gay Wilson. *American Prosody.* New York: American Book Co., 1935.

Arms, George W. *The Fields Were Green.* Stanford, Calif.: Stanford University Press, 1953.

Bigelow, John. *William Cullen Bryant.* American Men of Letters Series. Boston: Houghton, Mifflin, 1890.

Bradley, William A. *William Cullen Bryant.* English Men of Letters Series. New York: Macmillan, 1905.

Brown, Charles H. *William Cullen Bryant.* New York: Charles Scribner's Sons, 1971.

Callow, James T. *Kindred Spirits: Knickerbocker Writers and American Artists, 1807–1855.* Chapel Hill: University of North Carolina Press, 1967.

Conner, Frederick W. *Cosmic Optimism: A Study of the Interpretation of Evolution by American Poets from Emerson to Robinson.* Gainesville: University of Florida Press, 1949.

Duffey, Bernard. "Romantic Coherence and Romantic Incoherence in American Poetry," *Centennial Review,* 7:219–36 (Spring 1963); 8:453–64 (Fall 1964).

Godwin, Parke. *A Biography of William Cullen Bryant, with Extracts from His Private Correspondence.* 2 vols. New York: D. Appleton and Co., 1883; Russell and Russell, 1967.

Johnson, Curtiss S. *Politics and a Belly-Full.* New York: Vantage Press, 1962.

McDowell, Tremaine. *William Cullen Bryant: Representative Selections.* American Writers Series. New York: American Book Co., 1935.

McLean, Albert F., Jr. *William Cullen Bryant.* Twayne's United States Authors Series. New York: Twayne Publishers, 1964.

Nevins, Allan. *The Evening Post: A Century of Journalism.* New York: Boni and Liveright, 1922.

Pearce, Roy Harvey. *The Continuity of American Poetry.* Princeton: Princeton University Press, 1961.

Pritchard, John P. *Return to the Fountains: Some Classical Sources of American Criticism.* Durham, N.C.: Duke University Press, 1942.

Ringe, Donald A. *The Pictorial Mode: Space and Time in the Art of Bryant, Irving and Cooper.* Lexington: University Press of Kentucky, 1971.

Waggoner, Hyatt H. *American Poets from the Puritans to the Present.* Boston: Houghton, Mifflin, 1968.

Williams, Stanley T. *The Spanish Background of American Literature.* 2 vols. New Haven: Yale University Press, 1955.

—DONALD A. RINGE

Truman Capote
1924–1984

*I*N LATE 1959, Truman Capote came upon a brief article in *The New York Times* about the slaughter of a Kansas farming family. He showed it to William Shawn, editor in chief of *The New Yorker,* who agreed with Capote that it would make an intriguing story. Bennett Cerf, the Random House editor who was one of Capote's literary and high-society chaperons, lined up introductions to the Kansas academic community, and Capote was off to the Midwest, with his friend Harper Lee (author of *To Kill a Mockingbird*) along for the adventure.

The thirty-five-year-old writer, a precocious media darling and star of Manhattan's glamorous smart set, spent the next six years traveling back and forth to Kansas, working on a chronicle that became his tour de force, the best-seller *In Cold Blood: A True Account of a Multiple Murder and Its Consequences,* published in 1966. He became obsessed with this murder of an innocent heartland family and the characters of the killers. Capote used the event and the stories it generated as the basis for an appraisal of the American dream: *In Cold Blood* was a report from the front, a mid-twentieth-century update on what we were made of, on how we thought of ourselves as opposed to what we really were. Capote investigated, and reported, the state of American values and the composition of that mythicized collective figure who had spent a score of previous generations questing, pioneering, creating new worlds—that American who is "us," proudly singing our self-reliance and ourselves. His findings were unsettling.

Who was Capote to take this task upon himself, to present himself as an omniscient moral and cultural arbiter of twentieth-century America? When the short, effete, squeaky-voiced New Yorker arrived in Holcomb, Kansas, in the wake of the uncertain fear generated by the inexplicable murders, a few natives thought the strange-looking Capote himself might be the murderer, according to his biographer Gerald Clarke. In their eyes, said Harper Lee, "he was like someone coming off the moon." Although the Kansans he encountered first greeted Capote as little more than a flamboyant freak, later, as he worked his way into their confidence and their lives, they embraced him. Perhaps he could make right, or at least make sense of, what had happened to their world. Perhaps he was a visionary—the kind of twisted person who could explain the twisted world in which they lived.

Truman Streckfus Persons was born in New Orleans on September 30, 1924. His parents' marriage was in a constant state of turmoil. Truman's father, Arch Persons, was a schemer whose plans were rarely successful. His mother, born Lillie Mae Faulk, had little use for Arch.

He was only minimally present while Truman was growing up; a series of his mother's lovers were more prominent. While Truman's parents were indulging in their own little affairs, the young boy was left with relatives, usually his mother's endearing family, the Faulks, in Monroeville, Alabama.

In 1931, Lillie Mae asked Arch for a divorce so that she could marry Joseph Garcia Capote, a businessman who was more stable than Arch, and whose surname Truman had taken by 1933. While Joe and Lillie Mae provided a somewhat more secure home than Truman had had as a young child, he was still to have traumatic associations with the institutions of home and family, both real and fictional, throughout his life.

The Capotes lived in Greenwich, Connecticut, and New York City when Truman was an adolescent; his love affair with what he thought the most glamorous and exciting city in the world began at this time. At the age of eighteen he entered the world of contemporary belles lettres by securing a job as a copyboy at *The New Yorker*. Over the next few years, Capote worked to earn recognition as a rising young writer on other magazines, and to find a place for himself in New York's literary rat race. He applied himself to his writing passionately and intensively. Capote made the most of his winning social skills and the force of his personality: he was invited to write in residence at the prestigious Yaddo literary and artistic colony at the age of twenty-one, and he had indisputably arrived on the scene with a highly publicized and controversial best-seller by the time he was twenty-four.

Over the next three and a half decades, Capote left his imprint across what he considered to be civilized society. Based in New York, he made extensive forays into the world's most exotic resorts. His career, begun in fiction, was similarly far-reaching in style and subject. His circle took in hundreds of the world's most famous celebrities, among whom he traveled sometimes triumphantly, but sometimes disastrously. His two most significant romantic associations were with the critic Newton Arvin, from 1946 until 1949, and with the writer Jack Dunphy, from 1949 until Capote's death.

By the time of his death (in Joanne Carson's Los Angeles mansion) on August 23, 1984, from severe debilitation caused by drugs, alcohol, and emotional exhaustion, he had established a persona, what might be called a media presence, that linked together his eclectic written works, and at the same time somehow transcended them. Capote's pathetic decline at the end of his life—when he found himself embittered, out of control, creatively blocked—reflects the devastating personal toll his work exacted and provides an ironic counterpoint to his meteoric rise in youth.

Truman Capote's writing taught Americans something about who we were. He wrote of the country's heroes (Marilyn Monroe, Marlon Brando, Humphrey Bogart) and of its common folk (the Kansans). He captured the American landscape—the Midwest, Manhattan, New Orleans—as well as the glamorous international scene—the Mediterranean, Moscow, Haiti—as they appear to the urbane American adventurer. He wrote of his childhood in the South, portraying a vivid sense of that region and its people, and at the same time offering a moving psychological portrait of modern American childhood and adolescence, with its anxiety, instability, hostility, and loneliness. Though Capote drew closely on his own childhood experiences—his unloving and abusive parents, the odd relatives he traveled among, trying to find a home—he parlayed this into a more generalized contemporary portrait of the vagaries and pain of the modern American family.

He wrote of American aspirations at their most elementally capitalist and consumerist, as he looked at Tiffany's, Fifth Avenue, the Upper East Side, and the Four Seasons, and at their most depraved and destructive, as he looked at death row, and also as he eavesdropped on what people were actually saying at the Four Seasons. He flitted within high society, entranced with the trappings of the elite and their culture, embracing them but then turning on them just as fiercely in vicious-spirited exposés of their hypocrisy and idiocy.

America affirmed, during a decades-long fascination with this character, that he did indeed know where to look to find its story. The public followed him wherever he went, devouring piece by piece his idiosyncratic dissection of contemporary society. Capote's own relationship with the public was both productive and destructive: he loved the clamoring approval of the crowds, the media, the glitterati, yet he was also susceptible to frequent breakdowns, to addictive and self-destructive behavior, to the fear of failing to live up to the public's expectations. He shared with his character Holly Golightly, in *Breakfast at Tiffany's* (1958), frequent susceptibility to "the mean reds": "You're afraid and you sweat like hell, but you don't know what you're afraid of. Except something bad is going to happen, only you don't know what it is." He was quite capable of humiliating himself in numerous ways, coast to coast, in front of millions.

Capote's success covered a realm extending from fiction to journalism, from books to magazines, from plays to musicals to movies to television documentaries, from serious literary efforts to black-tie parties that dominated the society pages. In the course of his eclectic literary and cultural career, the bizarre pervasive character of the writer himself always preceded him and infused whatever he was undertaking. Capote's mark on American letters is inseparable from the relationship of this writer-character to American culture at large—the extent to which the public trusted him (and the extent to which he was successful) at taking the American pulse, with a wider range and scope and in more mul-

tifaceted ways than any other writer, artist, or intellect had demonstrated.

Capote's canvas extended to wherever Capote himself wanted to go and could get in. He was commercially motivated to a certain extent, and he took on some dubious projects because the price was right. But he was more strongly drawn to novelty—novel venues from Kansas to Kyoto, and whatever might be for him a new way of capturing those venues—and to fame. In novels, novellas, fragments of novels, nonfiction, short stories, and magazine pieces—all copiously gathered into various published collections—as well as in his films, Capote mixed freely on his canvas parties, places, failed projects (scripts and ideas that otherwise never came to fruition), and, especially, people: family, lovers, tormentors, and many alter egos, people who were real or fictional, or fictional people who were thinly disguised real people. In his final literary effort, published in 1987 as *Answered Prayers: The Unfinished Novel,* he retells his own adventures, as he had done in his numerous travel pieces; he shares a lifetime of accumulated gossip, as he did in smaller doses with Monroe in "A Beautiful Child" (1955) or with Brando in "The Duke in His Domain" (1957); he explores the glamorous intrigues and seamy underside of the cosmopolitan life, as he had done in *Breakfast at Tiffany's* and numerous stories. The glittering people who compose the worthies of the world in Capote's eyes recur throughout his work: Eudora Welty, Colette, Jackie Kennedy, Greta Garbo, Jane Bowles, Cecil Beaton.

Capote, like many writers, was fond of telling the same story over and over, examining it each time from a slightly different approach or perspective, and that narrative is a strong connective force among his disparate undertakings. When he tells various versions of his life story, he always wrestles with the pervasive issue of his sexuality, its formation and development—he did this in his first published work, *Other Voices,*

Other Rooms (1948), and continually thereafter. The story that Capote retells is generated by, and is about, loneliness. It is the story of how a talented yet troubled man writes the world around him. "I'm an alcoholic. I'm a drug addict. I'm homosexual. I'm a genius," was Capote's oft-repeated self-description, as resonant a mantra as Timothy Leary's "Tune in, turn on, drop out."

Capote's triumph was that he wrangled his Ur-story into a fascinating spectrum of smart reports from the cutting edge of American culture that his audience watched as eagerly as they watched Capote himself. He came across as a kind of freak, but never enough so that he repelled for long. His readers felt warmly toward him, as toward a mascot, and they were always ready to take him back into their hearts, to see what adventure he was up to next. He was not a writer-hero like Ernest Hemingway, Norman Mailer, or Jack Kerouac, with whom Americans vicariously identified; rather, his audience necessarily distanced themselves from him. One of his last incarnations, as the fey crime boss Lionel Twain in the tedious Neil Simon film *Murder by Death,* was his least dignified, his silliest; still, it only added to the mythic allure of his persona. Like Leary, and other cultural commentators such as Andy Warhol and John Lennon, Capote transcended the social stereotype of the writer-artist-intellectual, achieving a prominence that was transcultural and far-reaching.

Capote's far-flung aspirations translate into a career that defies simple summation. Charting the various phases, periods, genres, and manifestations of his work, his different focuses, would quickly result in a graphic confluence of arrows, overlaps, and free-floating escapades. Capote's work begins with his southern fiction: his first novel, *Other Voices, Other Rooms,* published when he was twenty-three, as well as *The Grass Harp* (1951), which he adapted as a musical, with little success, and an assortment of short stories such as "My Side of the Matter" (indebted to Eudora Welty's "Why I Live at the P.O."), "Children on Their Birthdays," and "A Tree of Night," collected in the 1949 *A Tree of Night and Other Stories.*

Capote's southern fiction, with its element of southern gothic and of a troubled South, is firmly in the tradition of Flannery O'Connor, Eudora Welty, Carson McCullers, and, less strikingly but still notably, of William Faulkner and Tennessee Williams. Capote's South is a land of haunting spaces and shadows. As Joel, the young protagonist of *Other Voices, Other Rooms,* first sees the landscape through which he will journey, he finds it "lonesome country; and here in the swamplike hollows where tiger lilies bloom the size of a man's head, there are luminous green logs that shine under the dark marsh water like drowned corpses." A thick folkloric milieu of southern ghosts and tragic seers reinforces the pervasive gothic. The settings, Noon City and Skully's Landing, symbolically accentuate the boy's "psychological journey from day into night, from the active aboveground world into the underground world of dreams," writes Clarke These dreams become nightmares as Joel settles in at Skully's Landing: Capote writes of his protagonist, "At thirteen Joel was nearer a knowledge of death than in any year to come."

The Grass Harp takes its name from the eerie atmosphere described by its narrator, Collin, at the beginning of that novel:

[Past] a glaring hill of bonewhite slabs and brown burnt flowers [in the Baptist cemetery] begins the darkness of River Woods. It must have been on one of those September days when we were there in the woods gathering roots that Dolly said: Do you hear? that is the grass harp, always telling a story—it knows the stories of all the people on the hill, of all the people who ever lived, and when we are dead it will tell ours, too.

Capote's landscapes are evocative and fecundly storied. He begins to discover in his early writing, and will violently confirm by the time he gets through Kansas, that the American landscape is hostile, exciting but dangerous; it cannot be confidently controlled or navigated. It reveals the stories of the dead and of the horror of their deaths, of the unfulfilled chaotic lives that terminate in the certain bleak closure of these deaths which powerfully dominate the landscape.

Capote's gothic panorama is largely peopled by grotesques: Cousin Randolph in *Other Voices, Other Rooms* is the most resonant of these. Inhabiting a gaudy room of faded gold and tarnished silk that subtly sickens Joel ("It all made him feel as though he'd eaten too much candy"), Randolph lamely tries to imitate a Wildean decadent, but his actual experience is without any of the requisite trappings, except for a vague memory of an orgiastic Mardi Gras. His posturing appears hollow, even to the young Joel, and yet Randolph represents Joel's (and thus, Capote's) fate. Ihab Hassan writes, he has "all the unpredictability and perverted innocence which qualify him for becoming the mentor and lover of Joel" (*Radical Innocence: Studies in the Contemporary American Novel*, Princeton, N.J. [1961], p. 241). Eventually, Randolph is seen exposed, weakened, pathetically lonely. His one-time affiliation with prizefighter Pepe Alvarez provides a moment of potential greatness, a kind of homosexual (per)version of a Hemingway tableau, but Randolph's inability to connect, his uncomfortable fate as a social misfit, shatters that moment: "One night Pepe came to the house very drunk, and proceeded with the boldest abandon to a) beat Dolores [another member of a loosely organized "family" in which Randolph only temporarily belongs, whom Pepe loved as Randolph loved Pepe] with his belt, b) piss on the rug and on my paintings, c) call me horrible hurting names, d) break my nose, e and f and otherwise." Randolph's eventual incarnation is

as a feeble transvestite, dressed as Dolores and pining after Pepe.

Capote's panorama of southern grotesques includes characters like Miss Roberta, who initiates Joel on his journey and points him toward Noon City: "She had long ape-like arms that were covered with dark fuzz, and there was a wart on her chin, and decorating this wart was a single antenna-like hair"; Zoo, the servant at the Noon City home, with an elongated neck that made her "almost a freak, a human giraffe," a magnet for horrific violence, knife assaults, and gang rape; a carnival freak show, with a four-legged chicken, a two-headed baby floating in a glass tank, and a Duck Boy flapping his webbed hands. In "My Side of the Matter," the narrator verbally assaults his wife's aunts, who have poisoned her mind against him: "Eunice is this big old fat thing with a behind that must weigh a tenth of a ton. . . . [Olivia-Ann] is a natural-born half-wit and ought really to be kept in somebody's attic. She's real pale and skinny and has a mustache." In "Children on Their Birthdays," the young protagonist Miss Bobbit lives in a boardinghouse with the alcoholic Mr. Henderson, who "would charge to the top of the stairs and bellow down to Mrs. Sawyer that there were midgets in the walls trying to get at his supply of toilet paper. They've already stolen fifteen cents' worth, he said." That story opens in the finest form of Capote's gothic grotesque: "Yesterday afternoon the six-o'clock bus ran over Miss Bobbit. I'm not sure what there is to be said about it."

Capote's grotesqueries are not absolute or immutable: in the wings, there are always, providing kindness, various incarnations of the character of Sook Faulk, a much older cousin of Capote's who, though seen by her family as childlike and simple, lavished loving companionship on the young boy when no one else did. There are also families, and a degree of caring that comes from these families, tentative and sometimes twisted though they are.

In *The Grass Harp,* this "family" includes a crotchety old judge and Riley, a charismatic young man, who are drawn to comfort and protect Collin and Dolly (the characters based on Capote and Sook); yet the group can exist together only when they flee up into a tree, removing themselves from society and living, literally, above it in a tree house. The sheriff and townspeople clamor beneath trying to disrupt and sunder this family. Eventually they succeed in bursting Capote's untraditional family, which had temporarily transcended the limitations of an imperfect social setting. Since Collin and Dolly are not allowed to live in the tree house, they must subsist in the mundane real world, where Dolly cannot endure. Collin needs Dolly as Capote needed Sook; the older woman is the one who hears and sees the supernatural beauty of things, like the stories from the grass harp. (Later, in *The Thanksgiving Visitor,* published in 1967, Sook tells the young Capote, "Chrysanthemums . . . are like lions. Kingly characters. I always expect them to *spring.* To turn on me with a growl and a roar." And Capote writes, "It was the kind of remark that caused people to wonder about Miss Sook, though I understood that only in retrospect, for I always knew just what she meant.") Capote badly needs this spirit, this companion. Sook saw that everyone, even young Truman, has a kind of specialness within him, the kind of specialness that materializes only up in the trees and only if there is a Dolly figure to bring it out, as she does for the Judge and Riley as well. Capote's fantasy vision in this novella approaches a surreal appraisal of what a boy must do to survive in the South. Collin's perspective sharply presents the lonely desperation of a young boy who must depend on the kindness of strangers (though Joel, like Capote himself, finds this kindness no more satisfying than did Blanche DuBois), and if not the kindness then the strangeness of strangers.

Capote retains fertile memories from his southern boyhood odyssey, and his southern world is one that scares, threatens, and represses the young boys who are trying to make sense of it, trying to discover their selves, their roles in life, amid a generally hostile or disquieting cast of characters. The hero is predominantly uncomfortable, embarrassed, awkward in this world where he does not fit. In *Other Voices, Other Rooms,* this sensibility is epitomized when Joel is asked, "Why are you so fidgety? Must you use the bathroom?" He replies, " 'Oh no.' He felt all at once as though he'd wet his pants in public. 'Oh no.' " The quintessential adolescent fear of being wrong and ridiculous permeates Capote's southern literature, and a similarly elemental fear resonates throughout his career.

That fear is closely linked with loneliness, which throughout Capote's writing generates a clear sense of otherness. The "other" of *Other Voices, Other Rooms* represents the people and places where Capote and his characters cannot live. Capote knows that comfortingly "normal" voices and rooms exist, but his sensibility cannot reach them. Little Sunshine, a bizarre hermit in that book, whose nickname reveals that not much hope peeks through and whose creation of "a charm guarantee no turrible happenins gonna happen" inflames Joel's desire for such an amulet, stays in his swampy gothic home in an abandoned hotel because "it was his rightful home. . . . If he went away, as he had once upon a time, other voices, other rooms, voices lost and clouded, strummed his dreams." William L. Nance writes in *The Worlds of Truman Capote,* "For Joel, as for Little Sunshine, home is a decayed and forbidding place, but it must be accepted, even if it should prove to be presided over by the devilman." The otherness—an alternate and more palatable reality—is dimly perceived, but can never be attained.

Capote's protagonists are thus doomed to a spectrum of manifestations of lonely isolation. When Collin arrives to stay with his aunts in *The Grass Harp,* Dolly says, "I told Verena you would be lonesome." In "Master Misery," Sylvia lives with her married sister, who asks her, "Doesn't it make you lonesome seeing how happy we are?" In "Shut a Final Door," "Walter was alone and very lonesome in New York." In "Miriam," Mrs. H. T. Miller's "interests were narrow, she had no friends to speak of." In *Breakfast at Tiffany's*, Holly Golightly receives letters from soldiers that "were always torn into strips like bookmarks. . . . *Remember* and *miss you* and *rain* and *please write* and *damn* and *goddamn* were the words that recurred most often on these slips; those, and *lonesome* and *love*." However painful, lonely, or misfitting the grotesque reality may be, it is one that is destined to endure for Capote.

Not fitting, not belonging, is the tragic bane of all Capote's characters, from Joel and Collin to Holly and Perry Smith (one of the murderers from *In Cold Blood*). In "Shut a Final Door," Walter is the New York urbane cosmopolitan manqué; after the failure of his personal relationships and his professional aspirations, he collapses in the arms of a fellow sufferer: " 'Hold me,' he said, discovering he could still cry. 'Hold me, please.' 'Poor little boy,' she said, patting his back. 'My poor little boy: we're awfully alone in this world, aren't we?' " These words might serve as an epigram to the whole of Capote's work, and to his life. "Hold me" is a plea Capote never stopped making. There were always characters in his writing and people in his life who could pat the lonely man's back and try to soothe him, but the soothing is never completely successful. Capote's heroes inescapably remain "awfully alone." Capote's world of troubled Southerners—tormented crippled misfits, always at least bordering on the grotesque—resembles McCullers' world in *The Ballad of the Sad Cafe* (1943), or John Kennedy Toole's in *A Confederacy of Dunces* (1980). His characters are not as self-expository or voluble as those in many of Williams' or Faulkner's worlds, but they

seek the same kind of communion (however tenuous and fragile) and family unity (which is somewhat achieved, but always tentatively).

Other Voices, Other Rooms is a bildungsroman: Joel travels to Skully's Landing incomplete, in search of his father and trying to find himself as well; but what does he learn? From Jesus Fever and Little Sunshine he tries to learn the ways of the South, its people, its gnosis; from Idabel and Florabel he tries to learn how to play with and interact with his peers; from Randolph, Miss Amy, and his paralyzed father he tries to learn his background, his family heritage; from Zoo he tries to learn how to be cared for. From this array of characters who are themselves very unstable, Joel attempts to wrench out some sense of meaning, some human connection. He needs to learn the archetypal human endeavors: how to go on a quest, however eerily unpromising it seems; how to recognize and attain an amulet; how to commune with one's father. Joel must learn these things, however unfulfilling and even irrelevant they may seem to the world around him. This learning is never completely successful—the others are too weird and too firmly limited in their own worlds, their own inadequacies. Nevertheless, one gets what one can from what is available; Joel, like Holly Golightly, like Kansas killer Perry Smith, and like Capote himself, learns how to scrounge for scraps.

Joel's adolescence is certainly not far removed from the twenty-three-year-old author's own. Capote, like Joel, was shunted around to various family members in the South as he was growing up, few of whom cared much for him or paid him much attention. Their distorted lives resembled, to a young boy, the ones he creates in his fiction. Joel's last name is changed from his father's, Sansom, to Knox, after his parents' divorce, making his search for his paternal legacy that much more difficult; this parallels Capote's name change in adolescence.

Adolescence, as depicted in the portrait of Joel, is certainly a scary prospect, but also, in a Joycean way, full of vast epic and artistic potential. Joel's fragmentary memories of youth are very much in the tempo of *A Portrait of the Artist as a Young Man* (1916):

He hadn't had a proper hour's rest since leaving New Orleans, for when he closed his eyes, as now, certain sickening memories slid through his mind. Of these, one in particular stood out: he was at a grocery counter, his mother waiting next to him, and outside in the street January rain was making icicles on the naked tree limbs. Together they left the store and walked silently along the wet pavement, he holding a calico umbrella above his mother, who carried a sack of tangerines. They passed a house where a piano was playing, and the music sounded sad in the grey afternoon, but his mother remarked what a pretty song. And when they reached home she was humming it, but she felt cold and went to bed, and the doctor came, and for over a month he came every day, but she was always cold, and Aunt Ellen was there, always smiling, and the doctor, always smiling, and the uneaten tangerines shriveled up in the icebox; and when it was over he went with Ellen to live in a dingy two-family house near Ponchartrain.

In spite of the dense gothic setting, and the oppressive forces of painful memory and an uncongenial present atmosphere, the adolescent sustains a degree of innocence that can lift him at least somewhat above this world; in spite of its decadence, the world is rich with character that can be potentially transmuted into art or, perhaps, repressed into art. In this bildungsroman Joel learns how to be Truman Capote when he grows up, just as the unpromising Stephen Dedalus must learn how to become James Joyce; Capote knows that this may not be a very comforting lesson, but it is one that embodies a kind of noble endurance. As he creates the characters of Joel, Idabel, and Randolph, Capote is locating himself somewhere among them—trying to define his sense of gender and sexuality, of goals and personality and relations to others. However tenuously, Capote works out in *Other Voices, Other Rooms* whatever strengths he will carry into his young adult life.

If the first item in Capote's oeuvre is southern fiction, item one-prime might be the author's later literature of nostalgic reminiscence. Even after Capote turned from writing about the South to writing about the chic, cosmopolitan world in which he moved as an adult, the powerful experiences of his southern childhood remained strong in his imagination. *The Thanksgiving Visitor* and *A Christmas Memory* (first published in 1956 and reissued as a boxed volume a decade later) are heavily influenced by the same southern voice of Capote's early fiction, but they are also importantly autobiographical, capturing the warmth of his relationship with his adored cousin Sook and also the anxiety of a young child who knows that he is terribly lonely and that he is fated to continue a lonely life because he does not fit in. These singular stories represent the essence of the Capote-as-character theme, which occupies much of his other work.

It is a bit hard to imagine Capote as his younger self in the episodes he describes from his rural Alabama childhood in *The Thanksgiving Visitor*: working on the farm, rising from bed at 5:30 A.M. for a breakfast of fried squirrel, fried catfish, and hominy grits. But the relationship between Truman and Sook rings true—again, an unlikely but vital affiliation. Another character, Capote's schoolmate Odd Henderson, is also an important type in Capote's writing. Odd is a tormenting bully, an underprivileged child whom Sook forces a reluctant Capote to invite for Thanksgiving. Odd, who repays Sook's kindness by trying to steal a cameo brooch from the bureau in her bathroom, seems much like the character of Dick Hickock, the meaner of the killers from *In Cold Blood*. Capote views this kind of personality as capable of enormous evil—the young Truman in *The Thanksgiving Visitor* has nightmares about Odd's meanness to him—but such a character nevertheless has a tender aspect: Sook tells Capote that Odd's mother views him as a tremendous help. (Hickock's parents, too, seem to have drawn strength from their son, however evil he was.)

This small portion of kindness is not meant to mitigate the dominant evil of the character, but, Capote knows, it is nonetheless something he must come to terms with. People are not unilaterally composed of any single characteristic—they are confusing bundles of contradictory traits. This story demonstrates Capote's vision of the complexity of morality and personality, especially cruel personalities. Odd represents the kind of character who is not just abstractly mean but specifically oppressive to Truman, reminding the young hero of his own deficient socialization; as troubled as Odd is, society is actually more likely to accept Odd than Truman:

Once, when he had me pinned against a wall, I asked him straight out what I had done to make him dislike me so much; suddenly he relaxed, let me loose and said, "You're a sissy. I'm just straightening you out." He was right, I was a sissy of sorts, and the moment he said it, I realized there was nothing I could do to alter his judgment, other than toughen myself to accept and defend the fact.

Capote cannot condemn Odd for the torment he inflicts; self-debasingly, he seems to accept that the way of the world is to be subjected to such torment, given his own misfitting character. Odd speaks in the other voices from other rooms that are absolutely closed to Truman, and Truman's fascination with Odd echoes his obsession with the Kansas killers.

Still, despite the confusion that surrounds the young man, Sook is a respite. In *A Christmas Memory*, Capote depicts an episode of unmitigated warmth, as he tells how he and his cousin—referred to simply and touchingly only as "my friend"—collect nuts and berries in the woods and buy whiskey from the bootlegger Mr. Haha Jones for their annual ritual of making fruitcakes on a budget of $12.73 in loose change, carefully hoarded over the year. The portrait is uncharacteristically delightful: the elderly cousin and the seven-year-old boy get soused, as part of the ritual, drinking from jelly glasses the two inches of whiskey left over after the cakes are done. They distribute their thirty-one cakes in a way that reflects, again, the way Sook and Capote scrounged to form a makeshift network of "family":

Who are they for?

Friends. Not necessarily neighbor friends: indeed, the larger share is intended for persons we've met maybe once, perhaps not at all. People who've struck our fancy. Like President Roosevelt. Like the Reverend and Mrs. J. C. Lucey, Baptist missionaries to Borneo who lectured here last winter. Or the little knife grinder who comes through town twice a year. . . . Is it because my friend is shy with everyone *except* strangers that these strangers, and merest acquaintances, seem to us our truest friends? I think yes.

Even the gloomy Mr. Haha Jones softens in the face of this enterprise, and donates the whiskey in exchange for a fruitcake (with an extra cup of raisins in it as a reward). The pair wonders if Eleanor Roosevelt will serve the cake they sent her at dinner.

Breakfast at Tiffany's marked the beginning of Capote's literary fascination with wealth, parties, the elite, and the general atmosphere of panache that pervaded Manhattan, and it captures his equal fascination with the underside of this cosmopolitan world, the failure or absence of much that it promised, to which he was never oblivious. Gore Vidal asserted that Capote "abducted Isherwood's Sally Bowles for *Breakfast at Tiffany's*"; certainly, Capote creates an updated version of Berlin's famously cosmopolitan atmosphere. In a similar vein were Capote's continuing stream of New York stories (such as "Miriam," about the oppressive loneliness of Manhattan, and "Shut a Final Door," about proto-yuppies in Manhattan's fast lane, both in *A Tree of Night*) and such portraits as "New York" and "Brooklyn" in *Local Color* (1950); "A House on the Heights" in *The Dogs Bark: Public People and Private Places* (1973); and "Hello, Stranger," which details the fascinating stories of sordid humanity that come out over cocktails at the Four Seasons, and "A Day's Work," both in *Music for Chameleons* (1980).

Like Capote's southern writing, his cosmopolitan writing was drawn from a universe he knew intimately. While he was generally more successful in the sophisticated international world than in the South—famous and financially rewarded, more accepted, better (though certainly not perfectly) fitting—this writing retains a sense of Capote's lonely alienation and failure of human communion; perhaps this is an inescapable remnant of his youth. Holly Golightly represents a kind of transcendence for Capote's protagonists, because unlike Joel or Collin she is beautiful, gregarious, adored; she seems able to control her own life, which is filled with rich, exotic men (like the handsome Brazilian José Ybarra-Jaegar—intelligent, presentable, important) and the thrilling power brokers of the underworld (Sally Tomato, the crime boss who pays Holly a hundred dollars a week to visit him in Sing Sing and take back "weather reports" to his "lawyer") who seem willing to do anything for her. Money seems to materialize effortlessly for her: whatever she wants can be attained by taking a few trips to the powder room (financed luxuriantly by her escorts). For Holly, Tiffany's is a cosmopolitan refuge, a dazzling array of consumerist allure that, she believes, transcends sordid reality: "Nothing very bad could happen to you there, not with those kind men in their nice suits, and that lovely smell of silver and alligator wallets." She dreams of waking up one morning and having breakfast at Tiffany's—then she will know she has attained her version of nirvana.

Ultimately, though, Holly cannot write her own fantasy life, cannot escape her constraining past. Tiffany's is only a jewelry store—it doesn't serve breakfast, and it doesn't sell contentment. Holly's abandoned husband, Doc Golightly, materializes from Tulip, Texas, and unravels the image she has fabricated in Manhattan, showing that one cannot simply wish away one's dreary past and its responsibilities. Nor can she control the present—the Sally Tomato ploy turns out to be a conduit for drug-smuggling information, and the police catch up with Holly. After she is arrested, the media reports reflect the image Holly has created of chic cosmopolitan allure. DRUG RING EXPOSED, GLAMOUR GIRL HELD, read the tabloid headlines, with exotic stories about "the beautiful movie starlet and café society celebrity . . . highly publicized girl-about-New York . . . arrested in her luxurious apartment at a swank East Side address." But Holly's neighbor, the narrator, a struggling young writer entranced by her wild life—an incarnation of Capote, of course—sets the story straight, again, like Doc, exposing the distorted unreality of Holly's cosmopolitan facade: "She was not arrested in her 'luxurious apartment.' It took place in my own bathroom. . . . '*Here* she is: the wanted woman!' boomed Madame Spannela. . . . 'Look. What a whore she is.'"

Holly's world does not endure, though it was certainly exciting while it lasted, tingling with erotically sensual allure (which Audrey Hepburn toned down in the popular film version to a kind of teasing adolescent playfulness). Holly snags none of her dashing men; she cannot even sustain a relationship with her cat, which she refuses to name because that would imply responsibilities and permanence, and her life is not stable enough for that. She escapes from the law, from the clutches of society, running off to Buenos Aires in search of more rich men to sucker, but she has lost her allure, and she is far from Tiffany's; she looks more clearly like a moneygrubbing tramp. On the way to the airport, she abandons her cat in a rainstorm in Spanish Harlem. Having done this, though, she immediately realizes the pointlessness of leading her life as she has, with no connections. Unable to find the cat herself, she makes the narrator promise to return for it, which he does—finding it, after weeks of arduous searching, settled comfortably "in the window of a warm-looking room." He does not take care of the cat as he had pledged, since someone else, clearly, is already doing so. But simply by tracking down one of the loose ends Holly had left hanging, the narrator atones for at least a small part of his friend's reckless existence. Determined to ensure the cat's safety, he struggles to sustain a kind of communion and responsibility that Holly's hollow and emotionally barren cosmopolitanism did not allow.

In this story, Capote reflects on his own perceptions of his world. There is just a bit of Sook in Holly, in the sometimes uncritical rapport she establishes with the young man who is very different from herself, and in the loosely familial and supportive connection the two share. Holly, for a time, calls the narrator Fred—the name of the beloved brother she had abandoned in Texas. But more important, Holly is, at various times, both alter ego and ego for Capote. Though the narrator is only in the background of Holly's life, he is forcefully present as the recording and judgmental voyeur. Her careless adventure is not exactly his, but he does here confront the troubling morality, to which Holly is oblivious, of the cosmopolitan world. Unlike Holly, he will never be

able to dispense with or repress its contradictions. Nance points to "the role of this story in Capote's gradual transition from fiction to nonfiction," writing that "he had moved from a private dream world to one that was identifiable, topical, even journalistic." *Breakfast at Tiffany's* does indeed embody the kind of journalism Capote takes up for the rest of his career: not because it has the same detached, objective perspective that characterizes his later style, but rather because of the author's role as a burrowing investigator out to get the story, out to expose what underlies the story he is reporting.

The cosmopolitan sensibility in *Breakfast at Tiffany's* evokes Capote's personal, extraliterary indulgence in the cosmopolitan life, his role as a publicity hound and social climber. Capote's courting of the public eye began with his first book, *Other Voices, Other Rooms,* or, more precisely, with the book's dust jacket. The boyish author lies supine on a sofa, oozing sensuality; later he told Lawrence Grobel, "I guess it assumes that I'm lying on the sofa and more or less beckoning somebody to climb on top of me." This "exotic photograph," he said, was "the start of a certain notoriety that has kept close step with me these many years." Capote's audience raised its eyebrows not simply at the photo or the book, but at the combination of the two. This set a pattern that was to endure throughout Capote's career—the writer's fascinating personality was always complexly intertwined with his text.

Cosmopolitanism, for Capote, manifested itself in a network of people and places. Clarke's biography meticulously describes how Capote sought out the best of these: the richest, the most socially alluring and well-connected, the most celebrated, the cutting edge. He lived in a symbiotic relationship with the people he latched onto: he traveled with them, visited their estates and retreats, flew with them on their private planes and cruised on their yachts, and parlayed connection into connection.

His modus operandi was to attach himself to glamorous, wealthy young women. He served as adviser and confidant; he was sensitive, understanding, nonthreatening, and they relished his companionship as a respite from the catty turmoil of their upper-class lives. Capote provided consolation, amusement, and sometimes even mentorship; he helped women improve their social skills and connections, and he had a good sense for women's fashion. Despite a calculating aspiration for social connections on Capote's part, often such attachments involved true and deep friendship as well. Sometimes Capote connected also with the husbands through the wives: the most famous example of this was his relationship with Barbara ("Babe") Paley and her husband, CBS founder William S. Paley. Other famous people in his coterie included Lee Radziwill, her sister Jaqueline Kennedy (and, through her, her husband John), Joanne Carson (who was then married to Johnny Carson), Carol Marcus Saroyan Matthau (wife of William Saroyan and, later, Walter Matthau), Oona O'Neill Chaplin (Eugene O'Neill's daughter, who was married to Charlie Chaplin).

These people provided Capote with entrée to the beautiful places of the world. He drew on the energy of these locations, writing numerous shorter portraits of them and using them as backdrops for his larger efforts, but also seeming to have an almost compulsive need simply to *be* in such settings, in case something happened, to see who else was there. His haunts included the elite restaurant and hotel scene (the Four Seasons, Sardi's, the Plaza) in the 1950's and 1960's, the Hamptons and Palm Springs in the 1960's and 1970's, and later, perhaps most obsessively, the most fashionable New York bars and discos, especially Studio 54 (and inside that disco, the place of honor, the deejay's booth, where the crème de la crème congregated by spe-

cial invitation), in the last frenzied years of his life.

Manhattan (annexing a slice of Brooklyn Heights) was the center of the universe by Capote's cosmopolitan standards and lent him a strong dose of creative energy. He wrote as a young man in "New York":

It is a myth, the city, the rooms and windows, the steam-spitting streets, for anyone, everyone, a different myth, an idol-head with traffic-light eyes winking a tender green, a cynical red . . . a place to hide, to lose or discover oneself, to make a dream wherein you prove that perhaps after all you are not an ugly duckling, but wonderful, and worthy of love.

Capote had thoroughly exploited his childhood in the South for his early writing; in New York, he found a Pandora's box of new material. New York as a subject posed a bigger challenge, which later in his life often led to considerable writing blocks. The city sometimes forced him to flee, and eventually overwhelmed him, as it psychologically overwhelmed Mrs. H. T. Miller in "Miriam." That short story, about an incomprehensible young girl (or an apparition of one) who haunts an Upper East Side widow, is one of the few instances in Capote's writing in which no communion—no connection, however tentative—can be achieved. New York, at its worst, can be omnipowerfully squelching. Still, it was the site of Capote's most vivid challenges and triumphs. Even *In Cold Blood*, his most famous work, though a story of Middle America, was commissioned by and first published in *The New Yorker*; it owes as much to the city that nurtured that magazine, and that nurtured Capote, as it does to small-town Kansas.

The Black and White Ball stands as a fantastic example of Capote's personal flair and his presence in the national spotlight. Capote threw the fabulously decadent affair for five hundred of his closest friends at the Plaza Hotel in November

1966. The list of invited guests, as printed in *The New York Times*, covered a range of celebrities including Sammy Davis, Jr., Jackie Kennedy, Mrs. W. Vincent Astor, Richard Burton, Oscar de la Renta, Noel Coward, Averell Harriman, Lillian Hellman, Christopher Isherwood, and the Baron and Baroness Guy de Rothschild, as well as some of the friends Capote had made in Holcomb, Kansas, like Alvin Dewey, the Kansas Bureau of Investigation's lead investigator on the Clutter murder case. The party was a real-life event but one that became transformed as it entered the national media into something that looked more like a scene out of Capote's fictional world of glitz. The American public devoured the spectacle: media reports of the ball were infused with ornate accounts of manners evocative of Edith Wharton's stylish turn-of-the-century affairs and intrigues.

Those who weren't invited were crushed. Those who did come flew in from all over the country and made a tremendous commotion over their hairdos, their costumes (black was prescribed for men, black or white for women), and their masks—Halston and Adolfo were deluged with orders for personalized masks, for which they charged hundreds of dollars. *Time* magazine reported that Capote boasted of having spent a mere thirty-nine cents on his mask, only to be undercut by Theodore Roosevelt's eighty-two-year-old daughter Alice Roosevelt Longworth, who had shopped around and paid thirty-five cents.

As Capote's cosmopolitan connections and literary success became stronger, he broadened his scope to take on projects such as adapting works for plays, musicals, and movies; he also wrote screenplays. Neither a 1954 musical based on his short story ''House of Flowers'' nor a 1952 play based on *The Grass Harp* were well received. His film adaptation (with William Archibald) of Henry James's *The Turn of the Screw*, titled *The Innocents* (1961), was disappointing, and his

film scenario for *The Great Gatsby* was rejected. Film productions of *Breakfast at Tiffany's* and *In Cold Blood* were lucrative for Capote, and his publicized presence at the filming of *In Cold Blood*, on location in Kansas, heightened the connection between his roles as writer and media figure. Among his most successful ventures was his work on the offbeat John Huston film *Beat the Devil* (1954). In this film noir parody of the Graham Greene variety of spy film, Capote imbues his characters with an exotic Mediterranean flair, and Robert Morley, Humphrey Bogart, and Peter Lorre are amusingly insouciant in their roles. It was Capote's disclosure of his friendship with Bogart, dating from the production of the film, that broke the ice in his first interview with the murderer Perry Smith, who idolized the actor.

An important ingredient in the hodgepodge that constitutes Capote's cosmopolitan world is his sexuality. It is difficult to determine whether Capote's homosexuality is more pertinent as a biographical or as a literary issue; probably, as with most aspects of the writer, its role is intertwined in both the personal and literary spheres, and cannot be placed neatly on either side. Capote is one of America's most important authors to be openly gay throughout his career, and while his writing is by no means purely ''gay literature,'' Capote's sexuality infused his writing to much the same degree that it defined his life. In his southern literature, this sexuality is a bit more closeted, probably reflecting some of Capote's own uncertainty and the confused hostility that his homosexuality encountered in the South. The young Capote had experienced numerous manifestations of homosexuality in himself and around him, like Joel Knox in *Other Voices, Other Rooms*, who, as a young boy, ''had witnessed many peculiar spectacles, . . . most puzzling of all, two grown men standing in an ugly little room kissing each other.'' Joel is stereotypically effeminate, as was Capote himself: "He was too pretty, too delicate and fair-skinned, . . . a girlish tenderness softened his eyes, . . . his voice was uncommonly soft." Joel's relation to Cousin Randolph, who is flamboyantly gay, probably illustrates the young Capote's view of homosexuality: he sees that what he is destined to become will make him a target of scorn; he sees that gay life can be lonely and difficult, especially if one is flamboyant (as Capote must have known he would be) and surrounded by people who are already uncompassionate. While Randolph is the only person in Skully's Landing who serves as any kind of role model for Joel, he is a satirically caricatured model, and the others in the family attempt to repress Randolph's manifestations of his homosexuality in front of the boy (again, Capote knows what will be in store for him). As Randolph squeezes Joel's hand, Joel knows that if there is any communion to be gleaned in this family, it will have to involve Randolph; he accepts this communion on one level, but at the same time, "holding hands with Randolph was obscurely disagreeable, and Joel's fingers tensed with an impulse to dig his nails into the hot dry palm." Joel mirrors Capote's ambiguity about his sexuality: not about whether he is gay, of which there is no question, but about what it means to be gay.

The narrator in *Breakfast at Tiffany's* is able to remain essentially detached from Holly's world because it is heterosexual, and he is not. Much of Capote's writing from this period embodies a muted but unapologetic homosocial sensibility. In "A Diamond Guitar," one of three short stories published with *Breakfast at Tiffany's*, Mr. Schaeffer is the elder statesman of a prison farm to which a young Cuban named Tico Feo is brought:

Mr. Schaeffer glanced up at the boy and smiled. He smiled at him longer than he had meant to, for the boy had eyes like strips of sky. . . . Looking at him, Mr. Schaeffer thought of holidays and good times.

Such loaded glances are Capote's usual method of vaguely implying the love of men for men. Later in this story, Capote is more specific:

Soon Tico Feo was allowed the honor of having a bed near the stove and next to Mr. Schaeffer. . . . Except that they did not combine their bodies or think to do so, though such things were not unknown at the farm, they were as lovers.

In "Shut a Final Door," Walter's encounter is less kind:

I was in a bookshop, and a man was standing there and we began talking: a middle-aged man, rather nice, very intelligent. When I went outside he followed, a little ways behind: I crossed the street, he crossed the street, I walked fast, he walked fast. This kept up six or seven blocks, and when I finally figured out what was going on I felt tickled, I felt like kidding him on. So I stopped at the corner and hailed a cab; then I turned around and gave this guy a long, long look, and he came rushing up, all smiles. And I jumped in the cab, and slammed the door and leaned out the window and laughed out loud: the look on his face, it was awful, it was like Christ. I can't forget it.

Clearly, Walter has some kind of homosexual inclination, which he represses here. Still, Walter and Capote are aware of the suffering of the anonymous follower: he is a Christlike martyr to the world's cruelty. In nearly every one of Capote's stories can be found a moment of gay awareness, sometimes positive, often suppressed or crushed (as between Randolph and Pepe in *Other Voices, Other Rooms*), and, especially earlier in his career, frequently oblique (as with Vincent in "The Headless Hawk" [1946], who takes "rather female pride in his quarters").

In *In Cold Blood*, the sexuality of both killers is troubling. Dick Hickock is at least a potential rapist, child molester, and exhibitionist. Perry Smith seems, loosely, to have the same kind of attraction for Dick as described in Capote's early muted portraits of homosexuality; he is drawn to Dick (and frequently dreams of a life involving a strong tie with him), and jealously resentful of Dick's reckless heterosexuality. Capote himself seems to have a keen tenderness for Perry and his unresolved sexuality. Perry, on his way to the gallows, kissed Capote on the cheek and said, ''Adios, amigo.'' Capote later reported that Perry said to him, ''Good-bye. I love you and I always have.''

By the time he published *Music for Chameleons*, Capote's references to homosexuality had become forthright and explicit. In ''A Beautiful Child,'' he describes a one-night stand he had with Errol Flynn; in ''Then It All Came Down,'' he reports uncensored his subject's vivid description of gay sex in prison; in ''Hidden Gardens,'' his interviewee recounts a joke—the kind of gay humor that perhaps appeals to Capote's campy persona: Jesse James storms onto a train and shouts, '' 'Hands up! We're gonna rob all the women and rape all the men.' So this one fellow says: 'Haven't you got that wrong, sir? Don't you mean you're gonna rob all the men and rape all the women?' But there was this sweet little fairy on the train, and he pipes up: 'Mind your own business! Mr. James knows how to rob a train.' '' In *Answered Prayers* Capote offers an especially unfettered portrait of homosexuality in the world of the sophisticated set.

Capote was writing during a time when it was acceptable, marginally, for a gay man to discuss his sexuality, not in terms of general gay rights or acceptance, but as one eccentric artsy fag. A stereotypically capricious gay atmosphere was acceptable; the reality of the largely closeted and suppressed gay world was not. Homosexuality in Capote's writing is not very real—nor does it reflect the chaotic tribulations of Capote's love life: he had two long-term and relatively satisfying relationships, but numerous others that generally proved difficult and uncontrollable. Rather, Capote's sexuality is parodically distanced from what is assumed to be a ''normal'' (heterosexual) audience. As perhaps America's most prominent openly gay celebrity of the 1950's and 1960's, Capote might be criticized as too campy, too effete, too confirmative of prejudicial stereotypes about gays. His writing was probably not very helpful to the contemporary gay community, as was, for example, James Baldwin's more socially conscious *Giovanni's Room* (1956), nor did it ever attempt to provide a thorough overview of some part of the gay world, as did Hubert Selby's *Last Exit to Brooklyn* (1964). Capote does not pave the way for other homosexual writers or readers—in his writing, homosexuality is a fact, and accepted, but in a way that relates only to Capote himself. Still, he lived his life on his own terms, and underneath the cultivated facade of quivering, limp-wristed effeminacy was a core of strength that allowed him to act and be seen exactly as he wanted to be—never to mask his personality, however ridiculous it might seem.

Capote worked with two important photographers, Richard Avedon and Cecil Beaton. Capote wrote the text for Avedon's 1959 collection of celebrity photographs *Observations* (in which he appeared himself in a puckish pose), helping the photographer capture the personalities of such figures as Isak Dinesen, Ezra Pound, and Mae West. Beaton was a longtime close friend, and some of his masterful skill at capturing people's inner personalities with a photographically objective precision seems to have rubbed off on Capote; as Capote's work matured, he relied less on the grotesquely surreal personality portrait and more heavily on closely detailing the lives, the speech, the literal behavior of his subjects.

Such detailing is evident in the passage on Dinesen from *Observations*:

The Baroness, weighing a handful of feathers and fragile as a *coquillage* bouquet, entertains callers in a sparse, sparkling parlor sprinkled with sleeping dogs and warmed by a fireplace and a porcelain stove: a room where she, an imposing creation come forward from one of her own Gothic tales, sits bundled in bristling wolfskins and British tweeds, her feet fur-booted, her legs, thin as the thighs of an ortolan, encased in woolen hose, and her neck, round which a ring could fit, looped with frail lilac scarves.

Capote was working harder, more carefully, to evoke a vision that was not simply a psychologically internalized memory, but one that could stand as a public statement—one that was still, of course, imbued with a subjectively judgmental atmosphere, but an atmosphere that was meant to be shared more widely, more accessibly. In portraits of celebrities such as Louis Armstrong, Marilyn Monroe, and Humphrey Bogart, Capote presents (with a bit of his own recasting) what these people look like, or should look like, to the world at large. His choice of subjects in *Observations* reflects his cosmopolitanism, and this combined with the power he saw in photography moved Capote on to another important phase of his writing, that of nonfiction prose.

Two extremely successful journalistic enterprises in 1956 set the stage for Capote's best-known work, *In Cold Blood*. Both *The Muses Are Heard* and "The Duke in His Domain" were commissioned for *The New Yorker*. *The Muses Are Heard* is a meticulous account of a touring production of *Porgy and Bess* behind the iron curtain, the first of its kind ever undertaken by an American company. In the preface to *Music for Chameleons* he wrote:

I conceived of the whole adventure as a short comic "non-fiction novel," the first. For several years I had been increasingly drawn toward journalism as an art form in itself. . . . Journalism as art was almost virgin terrain, for the simple reason that very few literary artists ever wrote narrative journalism.

In his description of the traveling, the rehearsals, the interpersonal relationships and squabbles of the actors, the behind-the-scenes diplomatic and theatrical arrangements, there is nothing stylistically fascinating or overwhelming. In places, Capote's prose clearly has been whipped into line by the hand of a *New Yorker* editor, to conform with the magazine's timelessly immutable style. But Capote's report is eloquent, careful, sharply paced. What he must have gotten out of the exercise was simply the experience of writing about real people, their characters, their interplay, their small but compelling intrigues: the discovery that there *is* a story sitting right out there in real life.

In "The Duke in His Domain," Capote refines his journalism with an extended close focus on one character, Marlon Brando. Capote shows himself adept at getting a personally revealing interview out of an actor notorious for his unwillingness to sit for such portraits. He captures Brando as a spoiled tyrant, egotistical, rambling disconnectedly, unusually confessional ("The last eight, nine years I've been pretty mixed up, a mess pretty much"), and protectively isolated, like a duke in his domain, from the outside world.

In both these reports Capote is present, somewhat more forcefully than is the background narrator in *Breakfast at Tiffany's*. He refines the character of author as insightful voyeur, the canny recorder who sets out for his readers, with just a small dose of guidance, the artifacts that compose whatever cultural milieu he chooses to define. In the 1950's and 1960's, he wrote nonfiction pieces in many of the same magazines in which he had earlier published short stories, thus establishing a connection between the two kinds of writing and the different voices he used for each. He wrote essays, travel pieces, and profiles for popular magazines—*Life, Harper's Bazaar, Mademoiselle, Redbook, Vogue, Esquire*—that people read in beauty shops and in their living rooms, magazines that purported to capture the life and times of contemporary America and Americans. Seemingly effortlessly, he turned out the vintage portraits and insights that could come only from a man who had soaked up life as he had, and, like Hemingway and Fitzgerald, Capote could not help inscribing himself in his writing as a character somehow more interesting than anyone else he wrote about. His style is marked by a kind of subtle omniscience, a savoir faire that is almost, but not quite, pompous, elitist, cosmopolitan. It is clear to his readers that his writing *could be* all these things, but that it is purposely, though not condescendingly, tailored to appeal to the curiosity of the middle-class masses.

In the preface to *Music for Chameleons* he said that writing *In Cold Blood* was "like playing high-stakes poker; for six nerve-shattering years I didn't know whether I had a book or not." In 1966, Capote found himself with a book that burst into the national consciousness. Two cold-blooded killers, Dick Hickock and Perry Smith, fascinated the writer and his audience in the same way that Milton's Satan fascinated Romantic readers: in their evilness, they stand out as immensely more compelling than their victims, four members of a comfortable Kansas farming family who, as Capote inspects them, end up looking like caricatures of a hackneyed ideal. Herb Clutter is a bourgeois petty tyrant, running his farm with an outdated puritanical rule. He forbids the use of tobacco, but his children sneak cigarettes; he ruthlessly fires any workers on his farm found with alcohol. Capote, himself an alcoholic and a drug addict, is drily but insistently sarcastic about what pass for Mr.

Clutter's upstanding, noble virtues. Capote exploits the dark irony of the Clutters' lives with almost comic shamelessness. He describes pillows in Nancy's room bearing the legends HAPPY? and YOU DON'T HAVE TO BE CRAZY TO LIVE HERE BUT IT HELPS; as Mr. Clutter takes out a life-insurance policy on the day he will die, Capote records the insurance agent telling him, "From the looks of you, from what the medical report tells us, we're likely to have you around a couple of weeks more."

Clutter makes a show of pluralist tolerance, but intrusively and domineeringly forces his daughter Nancy to ease out of her relationship with her boyfriend, Bobby Rupp, because he is Catholic. Mrs. Clutter is psychologically frail; the details are not precise, but she resembles a nineteenth-century "neurasthenic," spending her days a virtual invalid in bed, while the rest of the family tiptoes around the house and tries not to jar her nerves or confront her condition. Mr. Clutter, who no longer sleeps with his wife, seems vaguely responsible for her condition.

Kenyon and Nancy are all-American kids, riding horses, active in 4-H; on the day of their deaths, Nancy takes time out from an activity-filled day to teach a younger neighbor how to bake a cherry pie; the night before, she had starred as Becky Thatcher in a student production of *Tom Sawyer*. They live in a home that Capote finds sterile, tacky, homogeneous, as he dissects it:

spongy displays of liver-colored carpet intermittently abolishing the glare of varnished, resounding floors; an immense modernistic living-room couch covered in nubby fabric interwoven with glittery strands of silver metal; a breakfast alcove featuring a banquette upholstered in blue-and-white plastic. This sort of furnishing was what Mr. and Mrs. Clutter liked, as did the majority of their acquaintances, whose homes, by and large, were similarly furnished.

As Capote inspects and reconstructs their lives, their wholesomely American sensibilities seem like a mask for a crumbling inner world. Mr. Clutter plants a grove of fruit trees on his farm, an emblem of "the paradise, the green, apple-scented Eden" that, Capote informs us, the farmer strove to create. That image sets up Capote's pervasive irony, for *In Cold Blood* is about the failure of this paradise, about the brutal expulsion from this Eden—for the Clutters and, symbolically, for the American audience that envisioned the Clutters as the consummate representatives of themselves. While the portrait of prelapsarian life in Holcomb is steeped in the smug comfort of 1950's America, Capote is filtering his narrative through the much more cynical perspective of the 1960's—after the Kennedy assassination, in the throes of cold war paranoia. In the postmortem that he conducts on the Clutter family, the mass murder seems almost a secondary cause of death. Primarily, the American dream has become malignant; the murders are almost a symptom, rather than the cause, of the Clutters' demise.

In the early sections of the book, Capote perversely juxtaposes the lives of the Clutters and their killers. He introduces the killers by writing, "Like Mr. Clutter, the young man [Perry Smith] breakfasting in a café called the Little Jewel never drank coffee." With macabre insistence, Capote's narrative repeatedly jumps back and forth from the Holcomb family to the killers on their adventure to murder the Clutters. Capote forcibly conjoins their fates as he describes the central event of the story, the "four shotgun blasts that, all told, ended six human lives." His underlying thesis is that Dick and Perry are as integral a part of the American dream as are the Clutters, if not more so. *In Cold Blood* captured the American imagination in its methodical analysis of the disintegration of the American dream. The Clutters may surround themselves with the outward trappings of this dream, but they are

slaughtered on page 72, and Capote's story has hundreds of pages to go.

The place to look for that story, Capote finds, is with the people who smashed the dream, Dick and Perry. They are, simply, more exciting than the Clutters; they are the people we must inspect to understand the future of American society, its hopes and values. Though the dream has gone bad for them, they are excellent practitioners (or perhaps victims) of some fundamental American sensibilities. They are daring, imaginative questers journeying through rough but challenging territory—across the Kansas heartland to kill the Clutters, and then all across America as they flee. The American landscape as mediated by the Clutters and their farm community is classically noble ("a white cluster of grain elevators rising as gracefully as Greek temples are visible long before a traveler reaches them"), but is brought to life only by the killers: "Until one morning in mid-November of 1959 [the day of the murders], few Americans—in fact, few Kansans—had ever heard of Holcomb." Capote writes that, in 1959, "the last seven years have been years of droughtless beneficence"; the rejoinder is implicit: seven years of lean will follow—the seven years in which the killers are caught, tried, and then await execution; the seven years in which Capote, with Dick and Perry's assistance, works on capturing their story and exploring its implications. The landscape is charged, and at its most vital, as Capote follows Dick and Perry through it, foraging for equipment for the murder and later escaping into its complex labyrinth as they flee from Kansas. Dick and Perry can read the land, can live off the land; the Clutters' physical environment is stagnant—cluttered.

Time and again, the two killers demonstrate how versatile their understanding of the local country is: Dick schemes elaborately and cunningly to cash bad checks to finance their journey, playing confidence games on shopkeepers and locals; in one instance, Perry poses as a bridegroom, with Dick as best man, to win the confidence of a clothing-store clerk—a calculating, untraditional re-creation of the American "family." The epitome of Dick and Perry's fruitful interaction with the landscape comes in a touching scene involving two hitchhikers the killers pick up while they are on the lam: a young boy and his frail grandfather, on a torturous quest of their own to find their family and a place to settle. The two "couples" join together briefly and get along well. The boy and his grandfather finance their journey as resourcefully as do Dick and Perry: they collect bottles from the roadside and redeem them for the refund money. Contrary to what one might expect of cold-blooded murderers running from the police, Dick and Perry eagerly assist and join in the search for bottles, driving slowly through the vast Texas countryside and stopping to pick up empties:

Dick was amused, but he was also interested, and when next the boy commanded him to halt, he at once obeyed. The commands came so frequently that it took them an hour to travel five miles, but it was worth it. The kid had an "honest-to-God genius" for spotting, amid the roadside rocks and grassy rubble, and the brown glow of thrown-away beer bottles, the emerald daubs that had once held 7-Up and Canada Dry. Perry soon developed his own personal gift for spying out bottles. . . . It was all "pretty silly," just "kid stuff." Nevertheless, the game generated a treasure-hunt excitement, and presently [Dick], too, succumbed to the fun, the fervor of this quest for refundable empties.

Capote shows in this scene the challenge of mining the landscape, and its fecundity—the quartet eventually comes up with $12.60 (coincidentally close to the $12.73 Capote and Sook scrounged in *A Christmas Memory*), which they split, and which provides the starving questers with a banquet at a roadside restaurant. The travelers are living off litter, the

dregs of the landscape; but with its "brown glow" and "emerald daubs," this landscape can be as evocative, as beneficent, as any nineteenth-century transcendentalist landscape portrait. As in James Fenimore Cooper's or Walt Whitman's visions of untamed country offering up plenty and adventure, Capote's adventurers, on the margin of society, appreciate and exploit the treasures of a familiar territory that has itself become marginal. The boy teaches the murderers some scavenging tricks, just as Natty Bumppo and the Indians shared with each other the secrets of the land, and this sharing, this appreciation and understanding of nature, becomes the basis of human communion.

Perry and Dick, in fact, exhaust the American landscape they have been milking: their ultimate goal is a home in Mexico. Perry fantasizes about living in Cozumel, which is, according to a magazine article he had committed to memory, "a hold-out against social, economic, and political pressure. No official pushes any private person around on *this* island." From his memories of John Huston's movie *The Treasure of the Sierra Madre,* Perry has latched onto the notion of prospecting for gold in Mexico. Ironically, Perry realizes that one must forsake America if one is to attain the quintessentially American fantasies of individualism and instant self-made wealth in the mid twentieth century.

Dick and Perry have vivid hopes and dreams—unrealizable, but for that reason all the more dramatic and enthusiastic. They seek to control their own destinies through their own initiative. Their approach may be demented and evil, but Capote essentially eschews any moralistic sensibility as he probes for the archetypal American narrative he sees lurking in these events. The moral vacuum of Capote's story (perhaps a legacy of his southern gothic and grotesque vision) evoked a stunned and furious reaction on the part of some: Stanley Kauffmann wrote in *The New Republic* (January 22, 1966):

It is ridiculous in judgment and debasing to all of us to call this book literature. Are we so bankrupt, so avid for novelty that, merely because a famous writer produces an amplified magazine crime-feature, the result is automatically elevated to serious literature?

Hilton Kramer, in the *New Leader* (January 31, 1966), wrote that the book "is not what the language of fiction, the medium of a significant art, always is: the refraction of a serious moral imagination"; this "deficiency . . . stands out on every page." But most readers devoured the story, affirming it as compelling and important without stopping to think of its moral implications. This itself is a sign that Capote was right about the devolution, or irrelevance, of American morality.

Perry's mother is a full-blooded Indian, Capote notes—perhaps the author sees this story as the Indians' revenge on the white usurpers. In any event, Capote seems to imply that the American ideal is catching up with itself, destroying itself, and that a society capable of producing people like Dick and Perry deserves what it gets. Their fantasies, after all, are simply those ingrained by their society: they go on their crime and murder spree because they want a little money, a good life, a way to celebrate themselves. Perry, especially, wants family and human communion, which elude him as, Capote implies, it had eluded the Clutters. If anything, Capote seems to view Perry as more thoughtful than the Clutters, because Perry at least realizes the nature of his deprivation and takes steps to do something about it. He dreams of setting up a kind of home with a friend—at times he thinks about doing this with his sister's family or with other friends from prison, but eventually he settles on Dick. Perry is doing exactly what Capote had always had to do—to search for some sense of communion, however untraditional, to overcome the bad hand that society had dealt him.

Capote's sympathies are with Perry, who is physically deformed (from leg injuries he received in a motorcycle accident) and who feels condemned to remain a social misfit. Capote has denied many critics' suggestion that on some level he was in love with Perry, having spent years visiting and corresponding with him before his execution. "I didn't love either one of them, but I had a great understanding for both of them, and for Perry I had a tremendous amount of sympathy," Capote told Lawrence Grobel. In his reportage, Capote scrutinizes the killers' letters, diaries, and psychiatric reports, trying to get as deeply inside their minds as he can, because he knows that this is where the story is, the journalistic scoop on the state of the American dream. Capote visits the two devotedly on death row, bringing back to the world their observations and impressions and seeming to envision them as the gurus, or philosophers, of their age.

The Black and White Ball of 1966, which Capote organized as a celebration of the end of his seven years of work on *In Cold Blood,* marks an important climax in Capote's life. He had been catapulted into the public eye, where he would remain prominently for the rest of his life, unchallenged as a public icon and with his character firmly set. At the same time, his writing never again reached the heights it had up to that point; this realization made him increasingly depressed and self-destructive, psychologically and physically, as his addictions escalated out of control. Bruce Bawer, in "Capote's Children," explains the disappointment many in the literary establishment felt about Capote's writing after *In Cold Blood*:

The appeal of much of this work has relatively little to do with its literary merits. Capote, in his zeal to write "nonfiction novels" and "nonfiction short stories," may well have thought that he was being faithful to "what is *really* true," but all he was doing, in actuality, was neglecting his obligation as a literary artist to create, to order, and thereby to serve not merely personal and superficial truths but universal ones. It is an obligation to which Capote was attentive for so long, and which he fulfilled with such distinction, that his ultimate renunciation of it (manifestly well-intentioned though it may have been) is particularly disheartening.

The author of *In Cold Blood* became a kind of popular media expert on crime and the mind of the criminal—"Then It All Came Down," an interesting short profile of Robert Beausoleil, a member of the Manson clan, features the same kind of incisive rapport with the murderer that marked *In Cold Blood.* In *Handcarved Coffins,* collected in *Music for Chameleons,* Capote revisits the territory he mapped out in *In Cold Blood,* exploring a series of unsolved murders. The pervasive compulsion (of the criminals, and of the detectives as well) is familiar ground. These murder cases are more intriguing and complex than the Clutter case, but the detective work is less successfully captured than in Capote's masterwork. Though *Handcarved Coffins* is subtitled *A Nonfiction Account of an American Crime,* Capote errs by contriving to bring this narrative closer to the realm of mystery fiction; his crisply eerie buildup milks the suspense of the crime drama, but what Capote misses here are the much more fascinating real-life implications of murderous evil that he had earlier captured so deftly. Capote's credentials as an authority on crime were also exploited in his collaboration on a 1972 television prison drama, *The Glass House,* and in a documentary on capital punishment, *Death Row, U.S.A.,* which was so grim that ABC decided not to air it.

To match the success of *In Cold Blood,* Capote had an idea for a different sort of masterpiece, a final tour de force that would stun the American audience. What endures of this idea is a loose but provocative story, published in installments in *Esquire* in the 1970's and then posthumously as the unfinished novel *Answered Prayers.* For this undertaking, Capote turned to his favorite subject, himself—the character of the writer in the fast world of Manhattan, the New York publishing scene, and the arena of the cosmopolitan elite. Some critical opinion holds that the work would have been devastatingly and resoundingly successful. James Michener predicted that Capote would be well remembered into the twenty-first century if he ever finished the book. Clarke wrote that the fragments "contain some of the best writing he ever produced," and Max Lerner asserted in the *New York Post* (April 28, 1976) that Capote writes, in what appeared of the novel, "as if he were the Saint-Simon of our times, writing the annals not of the Court of the Sun God at Versailles, but of New York and Paris, of the salons and hotels and the Left Bank. 'This is how it was,' he seems to be saying to later generations."

What came to be published of this work are three chapters (out of a projected eight or more) and a bizarre series of publishing anecdotes reflecting Capote's diminishing grasp on his life and his talent. To placate the demands of publishers for whom Capote missed over a decade of deadlines, he offered incredible accounts of lost or stolen chapters (Joseph Fox, his editor, speculates that Capote may have destroyed drafts of some chapters), and sometimes claimed to have finished the book and handed it over to Random House.

The fragments that were published, in any case, were quite enough to cause a well-publicized furor among those members of Capote's smart set whose lives were ruthlessly exposed, parodied, and dissected in the catty and contemptuous roman à clef. Capote in fact maintained in an interview with Grobel that the stories were "not intended as any ordinary roman à clef, a form where facts are disguised as fiction. My intentions are the reverse: to remove disguises, not manufacture them.'' Many of his closest friends cut him out of their lives, never to reestablish ties. Grobel writes that they ''were suddenly slapped awake with the realization that a writer among them—especially one as sharp and perceptive as Capote—was dangerous. Doors he had spent a lifetime prying open were now beginning to close on him.'' In a loose picaresque narrative focused on a very Capote-like young writer, P. B. Jones, and a glamorous society star, Kate McCloud (a composite portrait of Capote's rich confidantes), *Answered Prayers* presents luridly detailed and smutty stories of male prostitution, cheap sexual encounters, literary politics, international social warfare, and celebrity foibles.

In the decade before his death in 1984, Capote published two more collections of essays and stories that were competent and well received: *The Dogs Bark* and *Music for Chameleons*. Both feature the standard mix of cosmopolitan atmosphere, nonfiction portraits and essays, finely worked stories, and additional snippets of Capoteana; some of these were new; more were recycled. *Music for Chameleons* ends with an ''interview'' by Truman Capote of Truman Capote, about the personality and experiences of, naturally, Truman Capote. The writer, at the end of his career, believes more firmly than ever that he has become his most interesting creation; the character he has created embodies everything else he has written. But Capote is not oblivious to the weaknesses inherent in the self-obsession he has nurtured. The interviewer tells the subject at the end, ''I love you''. The subject replies, ''I love you, too.'' And then,

TC: Zzzzzzz
TC: Zzzzzzzzz
TC and TC: Zzzzzzzzzzz

The interviewer falls asleep. The subject falls asleep. TC and TC, interviewer and subject, merge into the composite figure of ''Truman Capote.'' Public and private faces of the author-character, conjoined finally in one unified entity, as they tended to do throughout Capote's career, drift peacefully and harmlessly off to sleep, exhaustedly out of the limelight.

Selected Bibliography

WORKS OF TRUMAN CAPOTE

PROSE
Other Voices, Other Rooms. New York: Random House, 1948.
A Tree of Night and Other Stories. New York: Random House, 1949.
Local Color. New York: Random House, 1950.
The Grass Harp. New York: Random House, 1951.
The Muses Are Heard. New York: Random House, 1956.
Breakfast at Tiffany's: A Short Novel and Three Stories. New York: Random House, 1958.
Observations: Photographs by Richard Avedon; Comments by Truman Capote. New York: Simon & Schuster, 1959.
A Christmas Memory. New York: Random House, 1966. First published in 1956.
In Cold Blood: A True Account of a Multiple Murder and Its Consequences. New York: Random House, 1966.
The Thanksgiving Visitor. New York: Random House, 1968. First published in 1967.
One Christmas. New York: Random House, 1983.
Answered Prayers: The Unfinished Novel. New York: Random House, 1987. Separate chapters first published in 1975 and 1976.

ANTHOLOGIES
Selected Writings. New York: Random House, 1963.
The Dogs Bark: Public People and Private Places. New York: Random House, 1973.
Music for Chameleons. New York: Random House, 1980.
A Capote Reader. New York: Random House, 1987.

DRAMA

The Grass Harp. New York: Random House, 1952.

House of Flowers. New York: Random House, 1968. With Harold Arlen.

Trilogy. New York: Macmillan, 1969. With Eleanor Perry and Frank Perry.

FILMS

Beat the Devil. Columbia Pictures, 1954. Screenplay by Capote.

The Innocents. 1961. Screenplay by Capote and William Archibald.

Truman Capote's Trilogy. Allied Artists, 1969.

Murder by Death. Columbia Pictures, 1976. Featuring Capote.

WRITING FOR TELEVISION

The Glass House. CBS, February 4, 1972.

Truman Capote Behind Prison Walls. ABC, December 7, 1972.

Crimewatch. ABC, May 8, 1973, and June 21, 1973.

BIBLIOGRAPHIES

Bryer, Jackson R. "Truman Capote: A Bibliography." In *Truman Capote's "In Cold Blood": A Critical Handbook*, edited by Irving Malin. Belmont, Calif.: Wadsworth, 1968.

Stanton, Robert K. *Truman Capote, A Primary and Secondary Bibliography*. Boston: G. K. Hall, 1980.

BIOGRAPHICAL AND CRITICAL STUDIES

Bawer, Bruce. "Capote's Children." *The New Criterion*, 3, no. 10:39–44 (June 1985).

Clarke, Gerald. *Capote: A Biography*. New York: Simon & Schuster, 1988.

Garson, Helen S. *Truman Capote*. New York: Frederick Ungar, 1980.

Grobel, Lawrence. *Conversations with Capote*. New York: New American Library, 1985.

Heyne, Eric. "Toward a Theory of Literary Nonfiction." *Modern Fiction Studies*, 33, no. 3:479–490 (Autumn 1987).

Inge, M. Thomas, ed. *Truman Capote: Conversations*. Jackson: University Press of Mississippi, 1987.

Malin, Irving, ed. *Truman Capote's "In Cold Blood": A Critical Handbook*. Belmont, Calif.: Wadsworth, 1968.

Nance, William L. *The Worlds of Truman Capote*. New York: Stein & Day, 1970.

Reed, Kenneth T. *Truman Capote*. Boston: Twayne, 1981.

Siegle, Robert. "Capote's *Handcarved Coffins* and the Nonfiction Novel." *Contemporary Literature*, 25, no. 4:437–451 (Winter 1984).

—RANDY MALAMUD

Willa Cather
1873–1947

"LIFE BEGAN FOR me," Willa Cather once said, "when I ceased to admire and began to remember." Her artistic power was also born when she moved from admiration to memory, but this was a long process. Cather began writing fiction as an undergraduate at the University of Nebraska in the early 1890s; in her first novel, *Alexander's Bridge,* published in 1912, she was still an admirer, patterning her story after the high-toned psychological fiction of Henry James—whom she described as the "mighty master of language." But in *O Pioneers!*—published just a year later, in 1913—Cather "hit the home pasture," as she told her friend Elizabeth Sergeant. Now her creative process had tapped into the deep wellspring of memory, and after that, her fiction would soar.

O Pioneers! was her literary breakthrough: in it she returned to the Nebraska cornfields of her childhood and invented a character new to American fiction, a strong, creative woman who is not rebuked for her independent-mindedness, unlike the heroines created by Nathaniel Hawthorne and Henry James. Cather continued to take what she called the "road home" in *The Song of the Lark* (1915), her novel of a woman artist's emergence from a Western background much like Cather's own, as well as in *My Ántonia* (1918), the novel that most extensively draws on, and explores, the creative power of memory.

Cather's early novels were hailed as bringing a fresh voice to American fiction by such prominent critics as H. L. Mencken and Edmund Wilson. She kept writing and her literary reputation continued to rise throughout the 1920s: she won the Pulitzer Prize in 1923 for *One of Ours* (1922), received honorary degrees from major universities, and was elected to the National Institute of Arts and Letters. In the 1930s, when left-wing critics attacked her for "escapism," Cather's literary reputation slipped momentarily. But her creativity continued to flow, and she published a novel or a collection of short stories every two or three years until 1940, an extraordinary record of productivity coupled with continuing literary excellence. She suffered no dry spells, not even when politically motivated critics slighted her work, confounding F. Scott Fitzgerald's famous dictum, "There are no second acts in American lives." Cather's discovery of the deep force of her creative powers in *O Pioneers!*—after twenty years of apprenticeship—had opened the floodgates.

CATHER'S REPUTATION AND APPEAL

The novels she wrote during those years are not only still valued, they are read. What is extraordinary about Willa Cather is her continued enjoyment of critical esteem combined with a wide popular readership. After suffering slightly during the 1930s and 1940s, Cather's literary reputation began to rise again in the 1970s and 1980s as new critical approaches—feminist criticism, cultural studies, gay and lesbian studies, among others—found new depths and resonances in her fiction. Her complete works were published by the Library of America in the 1990s.

Her work appeals to different kinds of readers because it can be read on so many levels—her prose is supple, pure, and readable, always in the service of the story, and yet resonant with what Cather called "the inexpressible presence of the thing not named." Some readers believe that this beautifully ambiguous phrase refers to the lesbian narrative she could not tell directly. It also suggests the power given the text by what has been omitted—and by those ineffable truths that can only be suggested by language, not directly captured.

Once viewed simply as a celebrator of the American landscape and the heroic past, Cather is now considered a writer who employs a complex and shaded emotional palette and whose work explores the darker tones of American life—violence, greed, change, loss—as well as the power of the creative imagination, which she sees possessed by pioneers as well as artists, women as well as men. Cather's fiction, even when somber, is not pessimistic. Against the forces of pettiness, materialism, and mortality, she places the human desire to make meaning through work, family, religion, art, domestic crafts, and—perhaps most important to her—storytelling.

NEBRASKA GIRLHOOD AND EDUCATION

Willa Cather was first introduced to storytelling during her rural Virginia childhood. Although we associate her with Nebraska, she was born on December 6, 1873, in the small farming community of Black Creek in Virginia's Shenandoah Valley,

the eldest child of Charles and Mary Virginia Cather. She eventually would be the older sister to six brothers and sisters. She recalled her earliest delight with narrative taking place when women came to the Cathers' farmhouse, Willow Shade, to help out with canning, preserving, and quilting, and told stories that enthralled Cather as a listening child. Later, Cather would pay tribute to this first exposure to women's creativity in her last novel, *Sapphira and the Slave Girl* (1940).

In 1883, when Willa was nine years old, Charles Cather decided to leave sheep farming behind, and the family left Willow Shade to join Charles' brother and parents, who were farming on the Nebraska Divide. Cather at first found the transition from Virginia's green, sheltered landscape to the raw openness of the Nebraska prairies a painful one. She almost died, she later said, from homesickness and did not know how she had survived being "thrown out" into a country as "bare as a piece of sheet iron."

Eventually Cather came to love her new home, which proved to be a rich source of material for soul-making. The prairies' wide expanses gave her a sense of freedom rather than annihilation, and her exhilaration with the West's open spaces lasted a lifetime. "When I strike the great open plains, I'm home," she would say. "That love of great spaces, of rolling open country like the sea—it's the grand passion of my life."

Helping Cather to feel at home were the immigrant farmers who had come to the American Midwest to start over; like the young Cather, they were surviving the trauma of uprooting and resettlement. She was surrounded by a far more varied ethnic mix of people than in the more homogenous culture of the Shenandoah Valley, Scandinavians, French, Russians, Germans, and Bohemians farmed alongside native-born Americans. European settlers "spread across our bronze prairies like the daubs of color on a painter's palette," she said later, bringing vitality and shading to a "neutral new world."

In many of her novels and short stories she recorded the lives of Nebraska's immigrant settlers, who introduced her to the cultures and histories that first directed her gaze from America to Europe. Throughout her life, Cather remained sensitive to the processes of uprooting, transplantation, and resettlement: the move to Nebraska stamped her creative imagination forever. Time and again, her novelist's imagination was drawn to individuals and groups who leave one home for another: a slave girl who escapes to Canada; a professor who finds himself unable to leave his old house; the immigrants who settle the Nebraska Divide; the French settlers in seventeenth-century Quebec; the Spanish and French missionaries in the American Southwest; the Native Americans who migrated to the Southwest and built their homes into the cliffs of Arizona and New Mexico. When she wrote these stories, she was concerned not with simple survival but with the capacity of human beings to create spiritual and emotional meaning in their new landscapes—to make the strange become familiar and to make houses become homes.

Charles Cather did not take to farming, and in 1884 the family moved into the small prairie town of Red Cloud, where he found work in real estate. Willa Cather's awakening imagination found many resources in the town; she attended a school where she found supportive teachers, acted in amateur theatricals, attended plays, studied Greek and Latin with a town storekeeper, apprenticed herself to the town's two doctors, and found neighbors who introduced her to European literature. She formed close friendships with the Miner girls, Carrie and Irene, and found herself drawn to the daughters of the immigrant farm women, "hired girls" like Annie Sadilek (later the model for Ántonia) who found work in town.

But even as she formed such friendships, Willa Cather herself was repudiating Victorian girlhood. In 1888, when she was fourteen years old, she rejected the constraints of "namby-pamby" femininity by cropping her hair to crew-cut length, donning male attire, and proclaiming herself "William Cather, Jr.," and "William Cather, M.D.," reflecting her ambition to be a doctor. "The old country doctor and I used to talk over his cases," she said. "I was determined then to be a surgeon."

Cather's desire to be a doctor illustrates her repudiation of conventional gender roles: she scorned the nineteenth century's "cult of true womanhood," which celebrated the supposedly innate female virtues of purity, piety, submissiveness, and domesticity. As "William," she could envision a heroic future for herself and imagine leaving the domestic sphere her culture assigned to women. Given the fact that Victorian society imagined "woman" and "artist" as conflicting, incompatible identities, Cather was also clearing space for her creative emergence.

Ultimately, Willa Cather would leave William Cather behind and manage to integrate the identities of woman and artist by redefining "woman." This was a necessary part of her artistic journey, since as long as she repudiated women she was repudiating herself, and denial is not a powerful source of creativity. Had Cather never moved beyond male identification, she would not have become the writer we read today—one who does not imitate male writers but who speaks in her own voice.

Although the teachers and mentors Willa Cather found in Red Cloud offered support for a gifted rebel, the town was limited and confining, the source for the repressive Black Hawk in *My Ántonia* where the "tongue of gossip" keeps people in line. Cather's burning need to escape gave her another theme to explore in her fiction, the story of an unconventional self, at war with confining, soul-numbing mediocrity, the story she tells in "Paul's Case," *The Song of the Lark,* and *One of Ours.*

In September 1890 Cather happily moved to Lincoln and enrolled as a second-year student in the Latin School, the two-year preparatory school of the University of Nebraska. She eventually graduated from the university in 1896. In Lincoln, Cather found her interests moving from medicine to literature, and she began writing book and drama reviews for local newspapers; she also published her first short story, "Peter," in a Boston magazine. She also wrote several stories that appeared in the college literary magazine.

Although discovering herself as writer, as a critic the young Cather declared that womanhood and art were incompatible. She wrote contemptuous dismissals of women writers and declared her fondness for the "manly" ideology of masculinity that was popular during the 1890s. "As a rule," she wrote, "if I see the announcement of a new book by a woman, I—well, I take one by a man instead. . . . I have noticed that the great masters of letters are men, and I prefer to take no chances when I read." Cather did acknowledge some exceptional women writers. She admired "the great Georges, George Eliot and George Sand, and they were anything but women, and there was Miss [Charlotte] Bronte who kept her sentimentality under control, and there was Jane Austen who certainly had more common sense than any of them and was in some respects the greatest of them all." Even here, however, Cather suggests that femininity and literary greatness are incompatible, since the "great Georges" were "anything but women." And her literary advice to young women writers reveals her connection of aesthetic excellence with masculine values: "When a woman writes a story of adventure, a stout sea tale, a manly battle yarn, anything without wine, women and love, then I will begin to hope for something great from them."

Among her friends and fellow students at the university were Dorothy Canfield (later Dorothy Canfield Fisher) and Louise Pound. Canfield became a novelist and judge for the Book-of-the-Month Club, and remained Cather's personal and literary confidante over the years. Cather's friendship with Pound was more important to her emerging romantic nature. Cather did not remain friends with Pound, who became a well-known folklorist and linguist, perhaps because this was a love relationship which, once broken, could not be repaired.

Although not all Cather's biographers and critics regard her as lesbian, some do, often approaching Cather's writing from the critical frameworks offered by feminist and queer theory. Some readers of Cather's fiction concentrate on her need to conceal her lesbian desire by writing heterosexual "cover" stories that hide the subversive homosexual subtext. These readers argue for example, that in *My Ántonia* the narrator, Jim Burden, is a mask for a female consciousness, and unable to develop or express his love for Ántonia because he is really a stand-in for the lesbian author. Certainly camouflage has a place in Cather's writing, but we need to be careful, as we explore the impact of concealment on her creative process, not to minimize her imaginative reach. Like all great writers, she possessed a creative imagination that allowed her to create a variety of characters different from herself; the connection between any writer's life and art is never simple or direct.

When she first began writing fiction in the 1890s, however, Willa Cather did not yet possess a great novelist's transformative power. Her apprenticeship fiction in general cannot be distinguished from the average fiction of the day. Many of her early stories are based on popular formulas or are derived more from her reading than from her own observations. Occasionally, however, signs of the mature Willa Cather appear, as in her first published story, "Peter," which was based on the first tragic tale Cather heard when she came to Nebraska: disheartened by a long, cold winter, Francis Sadilek, a Bohemian immigrant farmer, killed himself. Later Cather would rework "Peter" in describing the death of Mr. Shimerda in *My Ántonia*, but her first fiction has its own grim power: "In the morning Antone found him stiff, frozen fast in a pool of blood. They could not straighten him out enough to fit a coffin, so they buried him in a pine box."

EARLY STORIES

Ironically enough—given her views of women's sentimental writing—Cather's first job was editing a woman's magazine, the Pittsburgh *Home Monthly,* which she took over in the summer of 1896. She did a good job, but still enjoyed satirizing the magazine's domestic content in her letters home: it was the worst trash in the world, she wrote a Lincoln friend, all babies and mince pies. During her ten years in Pittsburgh, she worked as editor, newspaper woman, and high school teacher of English and Latin. These were productive years, professionally and personally. Cather wrote book and drama reviews for the Lincoln and Pittsburgh papers, placed several short stories in national publications (among them *Scribner's, McClure's,* and *Cosmopolitan*), and in 1903 published a collection of poems—largely languid, imitative verse—called *April Twilights.* Her fiction caught the attention of the powerful S. S. McClure, editor of *McClure's* magazine, who published her short story collection *The Troll Garden* in 1905.

Some of the stories in *The Troll Garden* are in her Jamesian mode, such as "The Marriage of Phaedra" and "Flavia and Her Artists," in which the young writer shows off her familiarity with classical references and gives her two-dimensional characters stilted dialogue. (" 'I meant, madam,' said the novelist conservatively, 'intellectual in a sense very special, as we say of men in whom the purely intellectual functions seem almost independent.' ") But two stories with Western settings, "A Wagner Matinee" and "The Sculptor's Funeral," foreshadow Cather's return to her Nebraska material in *O Pioneers!*

In the brilliant "Paul's Case," Cather looks back at an earlier self—William Cather, Jr.—as she portrays another imaginative, sensitive youth at odds with a repressive society. Paul's enemy is Presbyterian Pittsburgh, an emotionally and aesthetically bankrupt world that he flees, preferring the fairytale beauty of the concert hall and theater. Forbidden these realms by his father and put to work as a bank messenger, Paul steals money to finance a trip to New York, the Waldorf, and the Metropolitan Opera, but he cannot escape "the tepid waters of Cordelia Street." "Paul's Case," the high-water mark of Cather's early fiction, reflects her training with such writers as Gustave Flaubert and Anton Chekhov. Long the favorite of critics, this was Cather's first choice as well, and in later years the only story she allowed to be anthologized.

Cather's maturing craft and steady productivity were owed in part to the happy domestic life she found in Pittsburgh. In 1899, she met Isabelle McClung, the daughter of a wealthy and prominent judge. The two women were drawn together by their shared interests in literature, the arts, and the theater. They began a lifelong intimacy; Isabelle remained the romantic love of Cather's life, even after they separated in 1916. In 1901, Cather began living with Isabelle and her family, and the McClung home became a nurturing space where she could combine intimacy with creativity, taking over an unused sewing room as a study and writing room.

Just as Isabelle fostered Cather's writing, so she helped her to reconcile creativity with womanhood. Isabelle was a beautiful, elegant woman who enjoyed wearing fine clothes as well as buying them for her friend. Under Isabelle's tutelage, Cather became more interested in elegant styles of women's dress. In later years Cather would purchase fabrics, furs, and hats from Bergdorf Goodman and have dresses custom-made. She preferred royal and theatrical clothing—velvets and silks, turbans and feathers, which became signs of female power to her.

JEWETT'S ADVICE

In 1906, Cather accepted a job offer from S. S. McClure and moved to New York City to begin work at *McClure's* as a staff writer. In 1908, she became managing editor and began sharing an apartment with Edith Lewis, a Nebraska acquaintance who was working in advertising, although she made frequent trips back to Pittsburgh to stay with Isabelle. These were years of heady accomplishment during which Cather succeeded in the male world of publishing and journalism. But they were also years of exhaustion and eventual depression when she feared her literary powers, drained by the work of editing, were not maturing. Although she struck others as energetic, confident, and self-assured, she progressively felt depleted and unsure of her literary talents. Because her work involved securing and editing other people's manuscripts, she was enabling other people to write while she was silencing herself. McClure had ceased to flatter Cather as a fiction writer, suggesting to her that her true talents were in journalism—vocational wisdom that would keep her working for him.

In 1908, Cather wrote a discouraged and depressed letter to Sarah Orne Jewett, the Maine author of *The Country of the Pointed Firs,* who would be the maternal mentor of Cather's fiction. With all her energy absorbed by work she did not want to be doing, after a day in the office she simply did not have the resources to write, she told Jewett. She was in her thirties and should be a better fiction writer than she was—her literary talents, she feared, were declining, not advancing. (Cather decided to turn the clock back for her 1909 *Who's Who* entry, listing her birth date as 1875, as if that way she could give herself more time to develop as a writer.)

In December 1908, Jewett sent Cather the most important letter she ever received. "I think it became a permanent inhabitant of her thoughts," Edith Lewis observed. It is a wonderful letter—a letter of both encouragement and warning. The older writer was concerned that Cather's demanding work was impeding her literary development, and she had the delicate task of letting the younger

woman know she was concerned about her literary growth without disheartening her.

> My dear Willa,—
> I have been thinking about you and hoping that things are going well. I cannot help saying what I think about your writing and its being hindered by such incessant, important, responsible work as you have in your hands now. I do think it is impossible for you to work so hard and yet have your gifts mature as they should. . . . In the "Troll-Garden" the Sculptor's Funeral stands alone a head higher than the rest, and it is to that level you must hold and take for a starting-point. You are older now than that book in general; you have been living and reading and knowing new types; but if you don't keep and guard and mature your force, and above all, have time and quiet to perfect your work, you will be writing things not much better than you did five years ago. This you are anxiously saying to yourself! but I am wondering how to get at the right conditions.

The "right conditions," Jewett thought, were a protective and nurturing solitude: "To work in silence and with all one's heart, that is the writer's lot; he is the only artist who must be a solitary, and yet needs the widest outlook on the world." So Jewett encouraged Cather to find a "quiet place near the best companions (not those who admire and wonder at everything one does, but those who know the good things with delight!)."

Jewett ended her letter with a lovely reassurance that could hearten any writer: she assured Cather that she had been "growing" even when she felt "most hindered." Later Cather would dedicate *O Pioneers!* to Jewett, acknowledging her maternal role in her literary emergence.

Cather took a leave of absence from the magazine in 1911 and spent three months in a quiet farmhouse in Cherry Valley, New York, with Isabelle McClung, always the guardian of her friend's creativity. There she revised the manuscript of what was to be her first novel, *Alexander's Bridge.* But this novel was still in her Jamesian mode, an "external" story, she said later, that did not spring from her deepest self.

In later years Cather liked to disown *Alexander's Bridge*, viewing it as a failed, conventional beginning. But she was too hard on her first work. Not only was the novel more self-expressive than she acknowledged, but also its acceptance for publication by Houghton Mifflin bolstered her self-confidence and helped her to take a creative risk with her next novel. The seeds of her Western fiction were already flowering during her Cherry Valley sojourn: "The Bohemian Girl" is a story of adulterous love and defiance of convention set on the Divide, its protagonists drawn from the immigrant groups who peopled Cather's home landscape. And "Alexandra," the story of a Swedish woman farmer, would lead directly into *O Pioneers!*.

O PIONEERS!

Cather's restorative vacation at Cherry Valley, where she had found the "quiet center of life" Jewett had hoped for her, gave her the courage to take an even longer break from *McClure's* in 1912. She decided to take a journey to the Southwest, and this would be the turning point in her creative life.

While visiting her brother Douglass, exploring canyons and Indian cliff dwellings, hiking and camping, Cather spent a good deal of time with a young Mexican named Julio who told her local legends and myths and took her to the Painted Desert. Cather's letters to her friend Elizabeth Sergeant describing Julio show her romantic infatuation with him—they are joyous, glowing, exuberant. Later he would contribute to the portrait of Spanish Johnny in *The Song of the Lark*.

Cather was always captivated by the Southwest's desert landscape and the Indian cultures she found there. Like other writers and artists who gravitated to New Mexico and Arizona during the first decades of the twentieth century—the novelists D. H. Lawrence and Mary Austin, the photographer Laura Gilpin, the writer and literary figure Mabel Dodge Luhan—Cather admired Pueblo civilization. Communal, religious, and mystic, the Southwest Indians' culture seemed a healthy counterpoint to the increasing materialism and isolation of American life.

Cather was particularly moved by the pots and vessels the Indian women had shaped to hold grain and water. She felt inspired by "women who, under conditions of incredible difficulty and fear of enemies had still designed and molded . . . beautiful objects for daily use out of river-bottom clay." In the cliff-dweller's civilization, unlike her own, woman and artist were not conflicting identities. Following so soon after her creative inheritance from Sarah Orne Jewett, Cather's discovery of the Indian women potters strengthened her association of femaleness with creativity, and helped her to create the artist-heroines of her next two novels, Alexandra Bergson and Thea Kronborg.

On her way back East, Cather stopped off in Red Cloud to see friends and family. She was in time for the wheat harvest, a communal activity she had not witnessed in several years. She enjoyed this return to her homeland, soaking herself "in the scents, the sounds, the colours, of Nebraska, the old memories."

By October Cather was resettled in Isabelle McClung's house in Pittsburgh, ready to begin writing. Stories began to emerge that she had not planned, a sign that she was letting material emerge from her unconscious. She began a short story set in Nebraska called "The White Mulberry Tree," a tale of tragic love, and all of a sudden something seemed to explode inside her and this new story entwined itself with "Alexandra," the Cherry Valley story, giving her the novel she had not known she was going to write.

When she left Pittsburgh for New York she had a draft of *O Pioneers!* with her. Later Cather described this submission to her creative intuition as "the thing by which our feet find the road home on a dark night, accounting of themselves for roots and stones which we had never noticed by day." In composing *Alexander's Bridge*, Cather had consciously shaped the story, but this time she found she had "less and less power of choice" in determining the direction of her narrative: "It seem[ed] to be there of itself, already molded."

Even at the time, Cather knew this novel marked her breakthrough into literary originality. She sent a copy of *O Pioneers!* to her childhood friend Carrie Miner in Red Cloud, writing this inscription on the flyleaf:

> This was the first time I walked off on my own feet—everything before was half real and half an imitation of writers whom I admired. In this one I hit the home pasture and realized I was Yance Sorgeson and not Henry James.

The novel begins with a section called "The Wild Land," evoking the harshness of the Nebraska Divide in the 1880s, before white settlers have made their mark:

> The dwelling-houses were set about haphazard on the tough prairie sod; some of them looked as if they had been moved in overnight, and others as if they were straying off by themselves, headed straight for the open plain. None of them had any appearance of permanence, and the howling wind blew under them as well as over them. . . . But the great fact was the land itself, which seemed to overwhelm the little beginnings of human society that struggled in its sombre wastes.

Recalling the harsh landscape of "A Wagner Matinee" and her early *Troll Garden* stories—as well as the grim land "as bare as a piece of sheet iron" the young Cather confronted in 1883—this "disheartening" country is one where human beings have not been able to write their story:

> The roads were but faint tracks in the grass, and the fields were scarcely noticeable. The record of the plow was insignificant, like the feeble scratches in stone left by prehistoric races, so indeterminate that they may, after all, be only the markings of glaciers, and not a record of human strivings.

Cather begins her next section, "Neighboring Fields," after a sixteen-year gap. Now we see the cultivated, inscribed land:

> From the Norwegian graveyard one looks out over a vast checker-board, marked off in squares of wheat and corn; light and dark, dark and light. . . . From the graveyard gate one can count a dozen gayly painted farmhouses; the gilded weather-vanes on the big red barns wink at each other across the green and brown and yellow fields. . . . The Divide is now thickly populated.

Taking her title from Whitman's poem of settlement, "Pioneers! O Pioneers!," Cather tells the bold, epic story of emigration, westward expansion, and manifest destiny, and, despite her fascination with Southwestern native culture, fails to recognize that Nebraska was not a blank, uninscribed land before white settlement in the 1870s and 1880s. And yet hers is a story with a difference: to use Adrienne Rich's term, *O Pioneers!* is a "revision" of the male-authored American story of the pioneer experience. The novel's hero, and the person responsible for this transformation of the land is a woman, Alexandra Bergson—a woman who wants to work with the land rather than against it.

Alexandra's father does not succeed in his pioneer venture, Cather suggests, because he has no sympathy for Nebraska's landscape: he has come to conquer, not cultivate, and so he makes "little impression upon the wild land he had come to tame." Alexandra succeeds as a farmer because she combines traits her society divided between "female" and "male." Unlike her father and brothers, she loves the land, coming to sense poetry and beauty in its soil. Yet even while giving Alexandra a maternal, even erotic connection with the land, Cather grants her shrewd business sense and agricultural pragmatism. Alexandra experiments with new farming techniques, confers with other farmers, buys up the land others are deserting and expands her holdings. Alexandra's successful use of both "male" and "female" traits reflects

Cather's own challenging of the polarized gender identities.

If the novel had ended with Alexandra's success, it would have been interesting enough, a kind of feminist rewriting of the westward expansion story—the national myth that ascribed the creation of culture and the conquering of the frontier to men—and a reassessment of the violence and greed that often accompanied the land's settlement. But when Cather intertwined "The White Mulberry Tree" with "Alexandra," she produced an even richer, darker novel than that, complicating the American myth of progress with the tragic lovers' subplot.

Some of Cather's readers have criticized her for writing an episodic novel in which the lovers' subplot is imperfectly integrated into the whole, but she had good reasons for intertwining the two stories—both are stories about passion. Alexandra channels her passionate energies into the land; her younger brother Emil and Marie, the Bohemian wife of the disgruntled farmer Frank Shabata, channel theirs into romantic love, with disastrous results.

The novel ends on a muted note: Alexandra, grieving and depressed after the lovers' murder, will marry her childhood friend Carl Linstrum, but this is not the romantic ending of the sentimental women's fiction Cather disliked. "When friends marry, they are safe," Alexandra observes, and the reader is left wondering about the submerged emotions the protagonist is still guarding.

Alexandra's last words are unusual ones in an American novel of that era: "I am tired," she tells Carl. "I have been very lonely." Fatigue and loneliness are very much part of American life, but generally are not acknowledged by a protagonist at a novel's end. Cather, as the narrator, goes on to conclude her novel with a paean to the Nebraska Divide—"Fortunate country, that is one day to receive hearts like Alexandra's into its bosom, to give them out again the yellow wheat, in the rustling corn, in the shining eyes of youth!"—but

this odd spiritual recycling does not outweigh the sadness and loss with which Cather concludes Alexandra's story, and which give the novel its depth and resonance.

Cather's editor at Houghton Mifflin, Ferris Greenslet, was impressed with the novel and told his colleagues it would establish Cather as a "novelist of the first rank." Most reviewers agreed, singling out her use of American materials and settings. A *New York Times* critic praised Cather for creating a "new mythology" with this story of a "goddess of fertility" who is "American in the best sense of the word," and the Lincoln *Sunday State Journal* reviewer, Celia Harris, commended Cather's "extraordinary" and "beautiful" book, particularly applauding Cather's move from her denser, more convoluted early style to simple, unaffected prose.

In drawing on her own memory and imagination, Cather had indeed taken more command of the language, leaving her stilted Jamesian structure behind. Writing of her own country and people, she knew what words to use. When a college professor criticized Cather's use of the word "globule" instead of "dewdrop," Cather was not intimidated. She defended her choice "stoutly," remembered her friend Elizabeth Sergeant, saying that dewdrops "could be of several shapes," but only "globule" described the "firm round drop found on prairie grass."

THE SONG OF THE LARK

Willa Cather never returned to the staff of *McClure's*. After *O Pioneers!* was published, she wrote a few freelance articles for the magazine and ghostwrote S. S. McClure's autobiography, which appeared in the magazine under his name with the acknowledgment "I wish to express my indebtedness to Miss Willa Sibert Cather for her invaluable assistance in the preparation of these memoirs." This was the last time Cather would publish something for which she did not receive full recognition.

One of Cather's freelance articles, "Three American Singers," gave her an idea for her next novel, *The Song of the Lark* (1915). Cather had long been interested in opera and considered the divas who dominated the stage the epitome of the female artist. She interviewed three of America's most famous divas—Louise Homer, Geraldine Farrar, and Olive Fremstad, a Swedish-born immigrant who had also grown up in the Midwest. Cather and Fremstad became friends, and the singer helped the writer to imagine the character of Thea Kronborg.

Cather sensed the connection between her own recent transition from the short story to the novel and Fremstad's bold decision to extend her vocal range from contralto to soprano—thereby preparing herself to take on opera's most central and dramatic female roles. Fremstad's strength was supposed to be in her lower tones, according to music critics, but she believed that the "Swedish voice is always long" and extended her upper range "tone by tone, without much encouragement." "I do not sing contralto or soprano," Fremstad told Cather. "I sing Isolde. What voice is necessary for the part, I will produce."

As the author of *O Pioneers!* who had also produced the voice she needed for the part, Cather delighted in the correspondences she saw between herself and Fremstad, as well as the similarities between Fremstad and the immigrant farm women she had known in childhood. In *The Song of the Lark*, Cather combined her story and Fremstad's in creating Thea, the singer who discovers the power of her voice after a liberating sojourn in the Southwest. The strongest autobiographical source for the novel, though, was the emergence of Cather's own voice as a writer in *O Pioneers!*: Cather's new self-confidence allowed her to see the parallels between herself and Fremstad, and in a sense *Song* is the story of Cather's creative journey to *O Pioneers!*

The Song of the Lark is a *künstlerroman*, the story of an artist's awakening to her own talent, traditionally a male story—but here the portrait is of the artist as a young woman. At the time Cather was writing her novel—the fall of 1914 and spring of 1915—she was exuberant and self-confident, telling Ferris Greenslet that she thought so well of her book that she had better not give him her opinion, but she knew he would not be publishing a novel like it every day.

In 1932, when Cather wrote a new preface for an English edition to the novel, she was less happy with it. *The Song of the Lark* is Cather's longest novel: she describes not only Thea's artistic emergence, but also devotes a lengthy section to her artistic life after she becomes an acclaimed opera singer. Cather felt she had made a mistake in doing so: "Success is never so interesting as struggle," she wrote, "not even to the successful." In the latter half of the novel, she acknowledged, her story becomes "paler," and she wished she had "disregarded conventional design" and ended the novel with Thea's discovery of her voice, rather than with her triumphs at the Metropolitan Opera. Later in her career Cather endorsed the values of understatement and suggestion—"the novel démeublé," or the unfurnished novel—and *The Song of the Lark* struck her as too heavily upholstered, given the sparer literary aesthetic she adopted.

Although the latter part of the novel, showing the professional success brought by Thea's spiritual revelation, is too naturalistically detailed, it does show Cather rewriting earlier patterns in American fiction that had kept "woman" and "artist" separated, or that had punished the woman artist with silence or death (as in Kate Chopin's *The Awakening*, published just sixteen years earlier). Cather was engaging in re-vision in *The Song of the Lark*, just as she had in *O Pioneers!*, creating a new story for the gifted female protagonist, suggesting the comfort she had attained in reconciling womanhood with art. Cather was well aware that she was writing an inspiring woman's story: she urged Ferris Greenslet to advertise the novel in women's colleges like Smith, Mount Holyoke, and Bryn Mawr, knowing that the students would admire Thea's defiant success.

Cather dedicated *The Song of the Lark* to Isabelle McClung, including a poem evoking the nurturing, creative space Isabelle had created for her in Pittsburgh, and in their relationship:

> On uplands,
> At morning,
> The world was young, the winds were free;
> A garden fair,
> In that blue desert air,
> Its guest invited me to be.

But shortly after the novel was published, Isabelle's father died, the Pittsburgh house was sold, and Cather lost both a home and a creative sanctuary. She liked her New York apartment, she told a friend, but it did not feel like home in the way Isabelle's house did—a safe, protected space. Then, a few months later, came even more terrible news: Isabelle announced her upcoming marriage to violinist Jan Hambourg. Cather at first was devastated by this apparently unexpected turn of events. Writing to her friend Dorothy Canfield, she said that the change in her life was irrevocable, the loss overwhelming. When she talked with Elizabeth Sergeant about Isabelle's marriage, her eyes were "vacant," her face "bleak." "All her natural exuberance had drained away," Sergeant remembered.

The winter of 1915–1916 was grim: marked by the "loss of old friends by death and even by marriage," Cather admitted to a friend. Isabelle's marriage was a kind of death. Throughout the winter and spring Cather remained grieving and depressed. She had an idea for a new novel—a novel that would become *My Ántonia*—but she had no interest or desire to begin it. Her creative force seemed as vacant as Nebraska's winter landscape would to Jim Burden.

In the summer of 1916 she traveled west, staying in New Mexico—always a landscape of renewal for her—and visiting her brother Roscoe in Wyoming. Isabelle's marriage was still hard, she wrote a friend, but the rest of the world was still there. Then she returned to Red Cloud for several months, feeling that she had left the grim winter of her soul behind in the Rockies. In Red Cloud she renewed attachments to family and friends, including Annie Sadilek—once one of the "hired girls" who had worked for American-born families, now a farm woman with several children, and the inspiration for Cather's next novel.

MY ÁNTONIA

When Cather returned to New York in the fall of 1916, *My Ántonia* was ready to emerge, and she wrote steadily and well for several months. Then she found a new summer retreat to replace Pittsburgh—the Shattuck Inn in Jaffrey, New Hampshire. She and Edith Lewis spent several weeks there in the summer of 1917. Cather pitched a tent in a friend's meadow, and this became the morning retreat where she wrote.

My Ántonia was the most aesthetically daring novel Willa Cather had yet written. In returning to memories of her childhood and youth in Nebraska, she crafted a novel that was experimental in both form and content. "I knew I'd ruin my material if I put it in the usual fictional pattern," Willa Cather said. *My Ántonia* is a drama of memory. Narrated by Jim Burden—who, like Cather, was transplanted in childhood from Virginia to Nebraska—the novel tells the story of Ántonia Shimerda, the Bohemian immigrant girl who preoccupies Jim's imagination throughout his life.

Retrospectively narrated, the novel evokes the intensity of his frontier childhood and of Ántonia's vitality, but always with a sense of loss, for Jim has not found emotional or spiritual fulfillment in his adult life. Because, according to Cather's narrative design, Jim not only narrates but also *writes* the story we read, we sense that for Jim loss is a spark for creativity.

During the act of recalling Ántonia and "the country, the conditions, the whole adventure of our childhood," the past comes alive for Jim, as he often tells us. "I can remember exactly how the country looked to me," he says, and "All the years that have passed have not dimmed my memory of that first glorious autumn." Phrases like "I can see them now" or "they are with me still" recur throughout the novel. "They were so much alive in me," Jim says, speaking of the memories of Black Hawk friends that remain vivid after he has left for Lincoln, "that I scarcely stopped to wonder whether they were alive anywhere else, or how."

Like memory, which is a collection of separate and sometimes unconnected images, *My Ántonia* is told through vignettes (sometimes widely separated in time), inset stories, and word pictures that, taken as a whole, make up a photograph album of the past. There is no conventional love story (Ántonia deserved better than that *Saturday Evening Post* treatment, Cather said), no linear dramatic action, no single conflict and resolution.

While early readings of the novel tended to view it as an elegiac, nostalgic narrative of the frontier, later readings have taken account of the novel's darker, more disturbing material—such as the suicide of Mr. Shimerda, Peter and Pavel's story of the bride fed to the wolves, Wick Cutter's attempted rape of Jim (posing as Ántonia), Ántonia's seduction and "disgrace" as an unwed mother, Jim's erotic fantasy of Lena carrying a "curved reaping hook," and, winding its way through the novel, the sexual allure of the working-class, immigrant "hired girls" who distract Black Hawk's middle-class young men.

Some critics see sexual fear underlying the novel, pointing to the fact that Jim, although preoccupied with Ántonia and Lena, never achieves a satisfactory sexual and emotional relationship with either one. Others see the novel as a feminist critique of male-authored stories and myths about women, pointing out that Jim, as the narrator, has the power to silence the female characters and to represent them in limiting ways. His celebration of Ántonia as a stereotypic Earth Mother, a "rich mine of life" who produced "sons that stood tall and straight" is an example of his restricted representation of the women in the novels. Still other readers see Cather as perpetuating, rather than challenging, limiting male views of women. And others regard Cather as the lesbian writer who uses Jim as the unconvincing mask to hide her own desire.

My Ántonia has attracted such contradictory interpretations because of its unusual narrative structure. In contrast to Cather's three previous novels, which were all narrated in the third person, *My Ántonia* has a first-person narrator, Jim Burden, who not only tells the story but also *writes* it. We find out that he is the author in the unusual preface, in which an unnamed narrator—a writer who is assumed by most critics to be a stand-in for Willa Cather—meets Jim Burden on a train. The narrator and Jim are childhood acquaintances and "old friends," having grown up in the same Nebraska town, and their conversation drifts back to "a central figure, a Bohemian girl whom we had known long ago and whom both of us admired. . . . To speak her name was to call up pictures of people and places, to set a quiet drama going in one's brain." At the end of the trip, the two agree to write down their memories of Ántonia, and months later Jim brings the narrator his manuscript. "My own story was never written," the narrator of the preface tells us, "but the following narrative is Jim's manuscript, substantially as he brought it to me."

The narrative ambiguities here, given the autobiographical nature of the novel, are intense. Are we supposed to think that the narrative reflects Jim's views, and so are we to distinguish Cather from her narrator? Or is Cather to be identified with Jim? And just what does "substantially" mean: has the narrator of the preface, who can be read as Cather, made editorial alterations that we are supposed to catch? Because critics' decisions about authorial distance have varied so much—some believing that Cather is identified with Jim, others that she is ironically distant—they have constructed such contradictory readings.

My own view is that Cather's authorial distance wavers in this narrative: at times she seems merged with Jim, as when he evokes the beauty of the Nebraska landscape; at times she is the author self-consciously detaching herself from a fictional character with limited, unreliable views. This complex relationship between author and narrator gives us a novel that is rich with ambiguity and that yields no simple or unified interpretation.

In addition to the biographical details they share—the Virginia homeland, the Nebraska childhoods, the move East in adult life—Jim and Cather are most similar in the sources of their creativity—loss, change, memory. "Some memories are better than anything that will happen to you again," Jim says, and many of his memories, like Cather's, are the stories he recalls, and shapes, from his past. In addition to the novel Cather creates and the story Jim writes, there are several inset stories—the Bohemian folktales Ántonia tells; the story of Pavel and Peter that she tells him; the Widow Steavens' narrative of Ántonia's romantic betrayal; the stories Ántonia and her children tell while they are looking at photographs of the past. Without loss and absence, the novel suggests, these stories would not come into being.

Of all her fiction, *My Ántonia* was the novel about which Cather cared the most deeply; she invested herself from the start in the book's production, stating her preferences for the colors of the cover and the book jacket, the typeface, the weight of the paper. Even more important, she commissioned a series of line drawings from the Bohemian artist W. T. Benda to illustrate her manuscript, and fought to keep them in the text when Houghton Mifflin balked at the price. She

also gave her publisher strict instructions about design and placement, and when Houghton Mifflin dropped the illustrations for a cheap 1930 reprint, Cather considered this an unauthorized edition. Later she fought to keep her novel out of paperback and away from the movies: she did not want mass production to cheapen "her" Ántonia.

In her correspondence with Greenslet over the next several years, much of it concerned with defending the novel's integrity, Cather invariably refers to *My Ántonia* as "she" rather than "it." Her novel appears in these letters as a living, breathing woman, vulnerable to being exploited by a publisher who views her as a commercial object. She was particularly outraged when Houghton Mifflin wanted to publish excerpts from the novel in an anthology and produced a reduced text for classroom use—such cutting and packaging was a brutal trade, she told Greenslet, and in 1938 she won his agreement to continue protecting *Ántonia's* integrity.

ONE OF OURS

Houghton Mifflin's stinginess with the Benda illustrations—they agreed to pay only for eight, not the twelve Cather wanted—convinced her that it was time to leave her publisher. Like many authors, at first Cather was thrilled to be published by such a venerable house, but soon came to feel that her work was not being sufficiently promoted, advertised, and valued. As good reviews accrued for *O Pioneers!* and *The Song of the Lark*, she thought Houghton Mifflin was refusing to acknowledge her growing literary stature, a belief not dispelled when her editor told her that *My Ántonia* might have significant sales as a children's book.

Cather's growing belief in the literary power and commercial potential of her fiction led her to leave Greenslet and Houghton Mifflin after the publication of *My Ántonia* for Alfred A. Knopf, who was just starting a new publishing company. In Knopf, Cather found a man who believed that novels should be beautifully designed, aesthetically rich, and commercially successful; like Cather, he did not see why art and financial reward should be contradictory. Cather's confidence in her new publisher was justified: throughout the 1920s and 1930s her satisfaction with the appearance and marketing of her novels increased along with their sales and her royalties. *My Ántonia* had been published in 1918 in a first edition of only 3,500 copies, and Cather earned only $1,300 in the first year of publication, $400 in the second. In September 1922, by contrast, Knopf published *One of Ours* in an edition of 15,000 copies; 40,500 copies were in print by November. The following year Cather earned $19,000 in royalties, quite a sum for 1923.

In the fall of 1920, Knopf published *Youth and the Bright Medusa*, a short story collection that included the *Troll Garden* stories—with some revisions—as well as four new stories with New York settings. Meanwhile Cather was working on a manuscript she called *Claude*. When she finished it a year later, she reluctantly agreed with Knopf's suggestion that it be retitled *One of Ours*.

In *One of Ours* (1922), Willa Cather took the risk of writing a war novel, inspired not by her former advice to write a "manly battle yarn," but by loss—the novel originated in the death of her nephew G. P. Cather, killed in 1918 at Catigny. After reading his letters to his mother Cather felt compelled to tell his story; as she wrote her friend Dorothy Canfield, she felt a kind of blood-identity with her nephew, and she spent the next four years in what she later termed a perfect companionship with the novel's protagonist Claude Wheeler, an imaginative rendering both of her nephew and of a male figure whom she came to regard as her other self. Some of her was buried with her nephew in France, she told Canfield, and some of him was living in her. Given her psychic bond with her fallen nephew, Cather felt that she possessed the authority, as well as the inspiration, to invade male literary territory and write a war novel. Although she knew this was a problematic genre for a woman writer, she felt claimed by her subject, claimed by a story that demanded to be told.

Her nephew, who had seemed to her to be a discontented country boy, found dignity and purpose in his death, she thought—testimony to the transforming power of war. David Hochstein, a young violinist whom she knew slightly, likewise seemed to have been mysteriously ennobled by his experience in battle. After reading Hochstein's letters to his mother, published after the war, Cather observed that "something very revolutionary had happened in Hochstein's mind; I would give a good deal to know what it was!"

One of Ours was in part inspired by Cather's desire to "know what it was" that happened to her nephew and soldiers like Hochstein. In addition to reading her nephew's and Hochstein's letters to their mothers, she had many conversations with returned soldiers, some of whom she interviewed in the hospital, some of whom she invited to her Bank Street apartment; and, one summer in Jaffrey, she came across a military doctor's journal that became the source of book 4, "The Voyage of the *Anchises*."

Although as a woman and a civilian Cather was removed from the experience of war, her letters to Dorothy Canfield show how strongly she identified with G. P. Cather and, by extension, with the American soldier. In addition to describing her sense of empathy with her nephew, Cather stressed their shared dislike of Nebraska's constricted life and desire for escape. She invested Claude with her own desire to flee bourgeois oppression, her distaste for materialism, and her quest for authentic, creative selfhood. Cather did not feel that by augmenting her character with her own motivations she was falsifying the experience of her cousin or other American farm boys who believed they would play more exciting parts in the theater of war than in the fields at home.

Although Cather won the Pulitzer Prize in 1923 for *One of Ours,* it is not her best novel, and has attracted criticism from male writers and critics who found the novel to be a woman writer's romanticized, inauthentic view of modern combat.

But such critics of the novel miss an antiromantic subtext: scattered around the margins, among the minor characters we find weakness, infantilization, disease, amputation, and dismemberment as Cather surrounds Claude with disfigured and mutilated men. Near the end of the novel Cather introduces her most grotesque image of dismemberment, the hand of a German corpse that keeps reaching out of the earth, refusing to stay buried.

The imagery of mutilation undercuts the surface plot of heroic masculinity, and may also have reflected Cather's awareness that she was a woman writer venturing into hostile literary territory. Throughout her life Cather associated creative power with the hand—she wrote all her drafts by hand, employing a secretary to type them for her, in turn correcting typed drafts by hand. Yet she frequently suffered from pain and paralysis in her right hand, which at times prevented her from writing. Images of mutilation in her fiction frequently occurred at times of professional and personal stress, so the soldiers lacking fingers, hands, and arms that we find in the margins of the text may not just reflect the realities of war, but also the woman author's anxiety about attempting the male-defined genre of the war novel.

Cather had anticipated criticism before the novel came out, and in a letter to Canfield imagined rescuing Claude from the text. Even if the book fell down, she told Canfield, she would want to save Claude: he could jump from the book as from a burning building, and she would catch him in a blanket. All her letters to Canfield reveal her deep emotional connection with Claude: when she finished proofreading, she wrote, she felt as if she were putting away a dead lad's things.

She was distressed by negative reviews: she had been deeply involved with this novel, with Claude, and with G. P. Cather and the American soldier. The Pulitzer, welcome as it was, did not fully make up for the criticism. In the summer of 1923, Cather went to France to visit Isabelle and her husband, hoping to work on a new novel, but she suffered a painful attack of neuritis in her right arm and shoulder and was unable to write.

A LOST LADY AND *THE PROFESSOR'S HOUSE*

In 1922 Cather published "The Novel Démeublé," (the unfurnished novel) in the *New Republic,* her statement of aesthetic principles of selection and refinement that would guide all her later fiction: "Out of the teeming, gleaming stream of the present [the novel] must select the eternal material of art."

A Lost Lady, published in the fall of 1923, was such a novel. It tells the story of the charm, decline, and resilience of Marian Forrester, the "lost lady" of the title, wife of Sweet Water, Nebraska's captain of industry, the banker Captain Forrester. The novel is narrated in the third person, but located squarely in the center of consciousness of Niel Herbert, a local boy who becomes entranced with Marian's magical grace. Niel's narrative presence is not always reliable. Some readers of the novel have assumed Cather's identification with Niel's perspective—in particular, when he links Marian Forrester's decline, after her husband's death, into sexual and economic dependence on the evil realtor Ivy Peters with the decline of the West from pioneer splendor to commercial squalor.

But such readings do not take into account the irony with which Cather surrounds the romantic, rhapsodizing Niel, showing us how his seemingly pure worship of his "lady" conceals a sexual urge he does not acknowledge. When he embarks on a morning pilgrimage to Marian's bedroom, carrying flowers as a sacred offering, Cather surrounds him with an eroticized nature—"wild roses, with flaming buds, just beginning to open"—that tells the reader the story of his unconscious yearnings. When Niel, holding his bouquet of "half awake" roses finds his lost lady, half awake, in bed with her lover Frank Ellinger and throws the roses into the mud, thinking "Grace, variety, the lovely voice . . . all this was nothing," we are not supposed to join him in his castigation of Marian, but to see how, in his limited emotional repertoire, he has turned the virgin into the whore.

In contrast to the heroines of Cather's pioneer novels who did devote themselves to what she called "something complete and great" *My Ántonia*—the land, art, the family—Marian Forrester seems weaker, given her dependence on men's economic protection, and Cather seems to be retreating from an earlier, more feminist, stance. But in fact she was enlarging her canvas and her sympathies. Her later novels, beginning with *A Lost Lady*, show her ability to understand the mixture of power and dependence in women who could not leave the marriage plot behind, women more like her mother than like herself.

Throughout 1924 Cather was hard at work on *The Professor's House*, a novel drawing on her experience of the Southwest as well as her own entrance into mid-life. She turned fifty in 1923, and her protagonist, Godfrey St. Peter, is trapped in what we would now call a mid-life depression, a time when the structures and relationships that have defined him have lost their savor and yet he is unable to move on.

Published in 1925, *The Professor's House* reflects Cather's penchant for narrative experimentation. The novel is structured like a triptych. The first section, "The Family," describes the professor's reluctance to leave the comfortable house where he and his wife have raised their family and where he has written his books in an attic study. His thoughts keep going back to Tom Outland, his brilliant and charismatic student who was killed in the war, and with whom he seems to have shared the most profound relationship of his life. In the second section, Outland's diary tells the story of the summer he spent on the Blue Mesa in Colorado in the cliff-dweller ruins. Cather wanted this section—set in the light and air and space of the Southwest, in sharp contrast to the professor's dark, enclosed study and confining life—to open her novel outward, letting the fresh air from the Blue Mesa blow away the cobwebs and the trivialities. In the final section, Godfrey St. Peter reminisces in his attic study, drawn by the lure of Tom Outland's memory and the freer aspirations of his own younger self. He forgets to turn off an old, defective gas heater and falls asleep, nearly dying from the fumes. He is rescued by the housekeeper, Augusta, a primal woman of the earth. Cather then gives *The Professor's House* an unusual ending for an American novel: the protagonist is neither renewed nor destroyed, but accepts his need to live "without delight," and lets go of his yearning for passionate intensity, whether joy or grief.

Some critics of the novel find its three-part structure unsuccessful, finding "Tom Outland's Story" to be an unintegrated disruption. But Tom's evocation of the cliff-dwellers' houses reminds the reader of what the professor's contemporary American life is missing—houses that were homes, meant for shelter, not status, and grouped together to signify and create community.

DEATH COMES FOR THE ARCHBISHOP

Both *A Lost Lady* and The *Professor's House* show Cather more and more concerned with the issues of the second half of life—not with issues of achievement, but with issues of meaning. Cather followed this direction in her novella *My Mortal Enemy* (1926), a sharp, bleak little book that gives us a woman who believes, too late in life for change, that she has taken the wrong path. Myra

Henshawe eloped with a German "freethinker" and was disinherited by her wealthy uncle. When she is old and ill, living in a shabby rented apartment, she regrets her choices: "It's been the ruin of us both," she tells her still-devoted husband. "We've destroyed each other. I should have stayed with my uncle. It was money I needed. We've thrown our lives away." In *My Mortal Enemy* Cather delivers the death-blow to the sentimental love plot perpetuated by nineteenth-century women writers: the fairy-tale story of courtship and marriage that ended, always, happily. Here Cather begins her story years after the ending of the romance and shows her heroine suffering the consequences of a romantic gesture— all very well when she was young, but not satisfying when she is old. The stories that give hope in the first half of life, Cather suggests, may not be adequate for the second.

At this time Cather was encountering the dark fact that while the first half of life ends, if we are lucky, in some sort of individual accomplishment, whether marriage, motherhood, or professional success, the second half of life ends in death. In 1926 she spent time with her sick mother in Red Cloud, and although her mother did not die for five more years, the long process of her decline had begun. Cather was now fifty-three, and in her mother's illness she could see foreshadowed her own death. In 1922 she and her parents had been confirmed in the Episcopal Church in Red Cloud (the family had been Baptist) and Cather grew more and more interested in the ways in which the Catholic Church had preserved spiritual stories over time, stories that offered people a meaningful connection to something larger than the self.

In 1925, when she was staying in Santa Fe, Cather came across a rare book, *The Life of the Right Reverend Joseph P. Machebeuf* by a priest named William Howlett. Father Machebeuf had been the boyhood friend and co-worker of Archbishop John Baptist Lamy, the first Roman

Catholic bishop of New Mexico, and his biography told the story of the missionary priests in the Southwest. The discovery of this book—like the intertwining of "Alexandra" and "The White Mulberry Tree"—was an inner catalyst, sparking Cather's growing interest in matters spiritual. She stayed up late reading Howlett's book and by the next day she could see the design of *Death Comes for the Archbishop* in her mind. "Without these letters in Father Howlett's book to guide me, I would certainly never have dared to write my book," she said later. Writing her book, returning to the purity and danger of pioneer times, was like "going back and playing the early composers after a surfeit of modern music." In a sense, *Death Comes for the Archbishop* was an open window—as if Cather wanted to dwell, for an extended period, in the bracing spiritual landscape of "Tom Outland's Story."

The novel itself is like a series of saints' legends, lacking the principles of conflict and resolution thought essential to the novel. The greatest mystery in this novel is not human motivation, but the link between the visible and invisible worlds; Cather returns to an earlier time when even the land is read spiritually, when signs are taken for wonders. When the Bishop is taking a solitary journey by horseback through the red hills of New Mexico, he comes upon a juniper in the shape of a cross. Understanding it to be a message from God, he concludes that it is time to pray.

If the novel can be said to have a plot, it is the plot of a spiritual Western—the bishop gradually brings the order and civilization of European Catholicism to this land of mixed cultures, a transformation signified by the building of his French-inspired cathedral in Santa Fe. And yet this novel, like *My Ántonia*, has elements of unintegrated darkness, suggesting Cather's awareness that Native American religions and cultures are not so easily erased by Catholicism, the religion of the colonizers. We see this subterranean resistance to spiritual colonization most clearly in the "Stone Lips" sequence, when the archbishop and his Indian guide Jacinto take refuge in a cave to escape a blizzard. The archbishop feels uncomfortable in this underground refuge, which is, he suspects, a chamber used by the Indians for "pagan" rituals. As in *My Ántonia*, Cather is interested in what stories are told, and what stories are silenced. The stories told by Native American religions are literally driven underground by the triumph of the archbishop's cathedral, and the economic, social, and religious power it signifies.

But this observation of the silencing power of a dominant religion itself seems underground in the novel. Cather did not consciously set out to remind us of the stories that were lost by the victories of the missionary priests; the story of Jacinto's cave seems a tale told by her unconscious, and it is not fully integrated into the novel. This subversive undercurrent only makes *Death Comes for the Archbishop* more interesting and complex, riven with chasms and fissures like the New Mexico soil itself. "Trust the tale, not the teller" is D. H. Lawrence's guide to reading American literature, and this dictum seems especially helpful in the case of this novel.

Death Comes for the Archbishop was published by Knopf in September 1927, the fifth novel Cather had completed since her move to Knopf in 1922. Her new publisher nourished her creativity, but equally important was the supportive life that she and Edith Lewis had fashioned together. After Isabelle McClung's marriage, Cather shared more and more of her life with Lewis. The two developed a social life as a couple, hosting Friday afternoon open houses at their Bank Street apartment. Gradually, Bank Street became the creative sanctuary Cather needed, and Lewis the companion to her creativity, accompanying her on summer writing sojourns in Jaffrey, and later to the cottage Cather had built on Grand Manan Island. Lewis was the ideal writer's partner—supportive when needed, deferential to her friend's talent, offering her companionship as well as "solitude without loneliness."

ART AND POLITICS

Death Comes for the Archbishop gained glowing reviews, but Cather did not have long to relish them. The next few years would be hard ones, marked by death and loss and grieving. In the summer of 1927 her father suffered a heart attack, and he died in March of 1928. At the same time Cather's apartment building on Bank Street was torn down to make room for a subway, and she and Edith Lewis moved to the Grosvenor Hotel on Fifth Avenue, a move intended to be temporary but one that lasted for five years. Then, near the end of 1928, her mother had a stroke that left her partially paralyzed. During the spring of 1929 Cather stayed with her mother in Long Beach, California, and she found it painful and sad to be with this once-powerful woman, now dependent and speechless. She tried to work on *Shadows on the Rock*, but found it hard to concentrate. She was beginning to feel, she told Dorothy Canfield, a good deal like a ghost. Her mother died in August 1931; a month later, *Shadows on the Rock* was published. Reviews were unenthusiastic, but sales reached 160,000 by Christmas.

Although *Shadows* is set in seventeenth-century Quebec, the central relationship—between the apothecary Euclide Auclair and his daughter Cécile—evokes Cather's lost bond with her father. At the same time we see her reflecting on the power of mother-daughter inheritance in Cécile's fidelity to her dead mother's housekeeping traditions, "all the little shades of feeling which make the common fine." The French settlers in Quebec have much in common with Cather's Nebraska pioneers and artists: they too are bringing their culture to a remote, inhospitable place, keeping alive the past through story, legend, and ritual. Given Cather's interest in cultural continuity and emotional connection, the recipes Cécile's mother passes on have as much weight in maintaining civilization as do the legends of the martyrs.

Many of Cather's reviewers, however, were not pleased with her juxtaposition of domestic and religious ritual, what Lionel Trilling termed her "mystical concern with pots and pans." Although Cather's novels continued to be praised in journals such as *Saturday Review* and *Commonweal*, during the 1930s they found increasing disfavor with left-wing critics who believed that art should grapple with the stern social, political, and economic realities of the time. Newton Arvin complained in *The New Republic* that Cather wrote as if "mass production and technological unemployment and the struggle between the classes did not exist" and so she failed to "come to grips with the real life of her time."

Such attacks on Cather reflect a conflict over art and politics: her critics were judging her work using a 1930s standard of politically correct writing, one that Cather ignored. Sexual politics were also at work: her critics were male, and throughout the 1930s and 1940s they not only referred to her as a "feminine" writer, as if that made her second-rate. They also established a set of metaphoric equivalences among "feminine," "romantic," and "small," a circle of associations that led them, seemingly inevitably, from "woman" to "minor."

Faced with such criticism, Cather could have tried to please the reviewers and write against her own grain. But she kept to her own course, as Sarah Orne Jewett might have advised. In 1932 she published *Obscure Destinies*, a collection of three lovely Nebraska stories that are among her best writing. One of them, "Old Mrs. Harris," is the most autobiographical story Cather ever wrote. In this story, concerned with the legacy of love and power and misunderstanding that connects a grandmother, mother, and daughter, Cather portrays her female relatives, and her own younger self, with compassion and reflective understanding. Doubtless prompted by her mother's death,

the story shows Cather coming to terms with her own past.

In the fall of 1932 Cather and Lewis finally moved from the Grosvenor Hotel to an apartment on Park Avenue, and Cather was happy to be reunited with all the belongings she had kept in storage for five years. Shortly after they moved in their former French housekeeper came back to cook for them: "It was like beginning to really live again," Lewis recalled. Soon after they were settled, Alfred and Blanche Knopf gave Cather a phonograph and she bought dozens of records, enjoying this return to the pleasures of music. "Perhaps it was in part the happiness of living again in an atmosphere of music—she heard scarcely any music during the Grosvenor period—that gave Cather the theme of *Lucy Gayheart*," Edith Lewis speculates. Cather's story of a musically gifted young girl who subordinates her talent to her romantic infatuation with a famous singer seems like a pale revisiting of *The Song of the Lark*. Cather began writing the novel in a state of fatigue and "she did not attack it with any great vigour or enthusiasm," Lewis remembers, and *Lucy Gayheart* does read like a novel she decided to write rather than one she *had* to write. The novel was published in 1935, a difficult year for Cather—Isabelle McClung Hambourg, ill with a kidney disease, was in New York for medical treatment, and Cather devoted most of her time to her ailing friend, who did not have long to live.

SAPPHIRA AND THE SLAVE GIRL

Cather was now in her late sixties, not sure how much longer she would live herself and thinking about beginnings and endings. Perhaps inevitably, her imagination began to drift back to her Virginia origins. In the spring of 1938 she visited her childhood home in Black Creek with Edith Lewis. The trip had a particular poignancy, Lewis remembers, as if Cather were seeing into the past itself. Willow Shade, her old home, had become "so ruinous and forlorn that she did not go into it," but this sad transformation, "instead of disheartening her, seemed to light a fierce inner flame that illumined all her pictures of the past." When she returned to New York, the story of *Sapphira and the Slave Girl*, her only novel set in Virginia, came flooding out. "She could have written two or three *Sapphiras* out of her material," Lewis recalls, "and in fact she did write, in her first draft, twice as much as she used. She always said it was what she left out that counted."

More deaths and losses blocked her progress on the novel—her brother Douglass and Isabelle McClung Hambourg both died in October 1938. But Cather kept working, finding it even more urgent to listen to the lost voices of the past. Knopf published *Sapphira and the Slave Girl* on December 6, 1940, Cather's sixty-seventh birthday.

Set in 1850s Virginia, the novel concerns the tangled relationships among a group of women—a slaveholding mother, her daughter, and the slave girl whose escape the daughter aids. Reading the novel now, when we are attuned to questions of race and gender, we can see how daring a novel *Sapphira* was for its time, as well as the ways in which Cather still perpetuates demeaning racial stereotypes. But in the face of her critics Cather was publishing a novel centered on women and set in the nineteenth century, a decision she must have known would not please the left-wing reviewers.

The independence Cather showed in writing *Sapphira* during her decade of trouble with critics is evident also in the novel's unusual form. This apparently conventional historical novel ends with an unusual epilogue. Instead of continuing the novel's fiction, the epilogue is a personal essay in which Cather tells the story of the real-life event that gave rise to her novel—the reunion she, as a child, had witnessed between an African American mother and daughter. The daughter had escaped from slavery, fleeing to Canada, and in the late 1870s the young Cather was present when the daughter returned and saw her mother for the first time in more than fifteen years.

In a sense, Cather ends her last novel by telling, in her own voice, the story of her creative process: the childhood memory of a mother-daughter reunion giving rise to her last novel. This mixing of the genres of fiction and memoir, although common today, was unusual in 1940. And because Cather was criticized for being too limited and feminine, it was also a daring move to end her novel with a self-exposing autobiographical narrative. Yet it seemed to her that her fiction demanded a personal conclusion, and she did what she felt her material required.

THE FORMER HALF

"The world broke in two in 1922 or thereabouts," Willa Cather once said, saying she belonged to the "former half." She was referring to her increasing distaste for a modernizing American culture that she found materialistic and soulless. But if we take the phrase another way, it can help us understand the difference between the first and the second halves of Cather's life, as well as the shift in her fiction that began with *A Lost Lady*, her first novel published after the turning point in 1922.

During the first half of life, she was living what we might call the child's story. Looking ahead toward individual accomplishment, she saw life as an ascending curve, seemingly without end, or ending in the drama of personal success. But once Cather entered the second half of life—a period that began after Isabelle's marriage in 1916 and became entrenched in the early 1920s—she recognized that the end of life was not individual accomplishment but the obliteration of the self in death. Earlier novels like *O Pioneers!*, *The Song of the Lark*, and—to an extent—*One of Ours* tell versions of the hero's plot: linear, chronological narratives in which a sensitive individual triumphs over limiting circumstances. But beginning with *A Lost Lady*, Cather was telling more muted, darker stories, creating novels in which individual achievement is far more qualified. Myra Henshawe faces a lonely and poverty-ridden old age; Godfrey St. Peter resigns himself to a limited domestic existence; the archbishop does not live to see his cathedral built.

But Cather's later novels in a way are more satisfying than her early ones, which partake too much of the American myth of progress. Her later novels acknowledge the darkness that is part of human life but they also celebrate the light—the human ability to make meaning from experience, often in the form of stories. Stories take many guises in Cather's fiction: they can be the simple conversations farm people have with each other; the myths and religions that structure the worlds of Native Americans, Mexicans, and Anglos in New Mexico; the rituals of cooking and housekeeping that are passed down from mother to daughter in Quebec; the music that inspires Lucy Gayheart; and the inherited folktales and legends that Cather received from the old women in Virginia that underlie *Sapphira and the Slave Girl*.

There are common threads, however, that weave together Cather's more optimistic early fiction and her darker later fiction. Dorothy Canfield Fisher declared that the theme of all Cather's work was escape, and Cather agreed. By "escape" the two writers meant transcendence, or the escape from limiting circumstances to a purer realm of spirit and meaning. What Cather meant by "escape" is perhaps best expressed in *Death Comes for the Archbishop*. Cather is describing Archbishop Latour's love for the air of desert countries—dry, light air that one "could breathe only on the bright edges of the world, on the great grass plains or the sage-brush desert." The desert air for the archbishop is what the creative process was for

Willa Cather—a force larger than the self, into which the soul expands.

> That air would disappear from the whole earth in time, perhaps; but long after his day. He did not know just when it had become so necessary to him, but he had come back to die in exile for the sake of it. Something soft and wild and free, something that whispered to the ear on the pillow, lightened the heart, softly, softly, picked the lock, slid the bolts, and released the prisoned spirit of man into the wind, into the blue and gold, into the morning, into the morning!

Willa Cather's last years, which coincided with the outbreak of World War II, were not easy ones. Subject to failing health, the deaths of family and friends, painful neuritis in her right arm, fearing for the survival of European civilization, she confessed to a friend that sometimes she just did not want to live in the world. She could only write infrequently, given the pain in her right arm. Dictating was impossible: she needed the physical act of writing in order to see the pictures the words made. Trying to dictate a novel, she said, was like trying to play solitaire without looking at the cards.

But she and Edith Lewis maintained some of the old rhythms of their life together. They could not travel to Grand Manan during World War II, so they spent summers at the Asticou Inn at Northeast Harbor, Maine, sharing a "charming cottage" with a fireplace. It often rained torrents, Lewis remembered, but Cather was happy to sit by the fire and read.

During this last period Cather's life was diminished, as it is for most people in old age. But she still could take satisfaction from small pleasures. As Lewis recalled,

> In the last year, it was the little things one lived in; the pleasure of flowers; of a letter from an old friend in Red Cloud, the flying visit of a young niece . . . the glory of great poetry, filling all the days. She turned

almost entirely to Shakespeare and Chaucer that last winter, as if in their company she found her greatest content, best preferred to confront the future.

Willa Cather died from a cerebral hemorrhage on April 24, 1947, in her New York City apartment. Edith Lewis carried out her wishes, and she was buried in Jaffrey, New Hampshire, within sight of Mount Monadnock, close to the field where she had written much of her fiction. On her gravestone is a quote from *My Ántonia*: "That is happiness, to be dissolved into something complete and great."

Selected Bibliography

WORKS OF WILLA CATHER

POETRY
April Twilights. Boston: Gorham Press, 1903.
April Twilights and Other Poems. New York: Knopf, 1923.

NOVELS AND SHORT STORIES
The Troll Garden. New York: McClure, Phillips, 1905.
Alexander's Bridge. Boston: Houghton Mifflin, 1912.
O Pioneers! Boston: Houghton Mifflin, 1913.
The Song of the Lark. Boston: Houghton Mifflin, 1915.
My Ántonia. Boston: Houghton Mifflin, 1918.
Youth and the Bright Medusa. New York: Knopf, 1920.
One of Ours. New York: Knopf, 1922.
A Lost Lady. New York: Knopf, 1923.
The Professor's House. New York: Knopf, 1925.
My Mortal Enemy. New York: Knopf, 1926.
Death Comes for the Archbishop. New York: Knopf, 1927.
Shadows on the Rock. New York: Knopf, 1931.
Obscure Destinies. New York: Knopf, 1932.
Lucy Gayheart. New York: Knopf, 1935.
Sapphira and the Slave Girl. New York: Knopf, 1940.
The Old Beauty and Others. New York: Knopf, 1948.

ESSAYS
Not under Forty. New York: Knopf, 1936.

Willa Cather on Writing. New York: Knopf, 1949.
Willa Cather in Europe: Her Own Story of the First Journey. Lincoln: University of Nebraska Press, 1984.

COLLECTIONS
Willa Cather's Collected Short Fiction, 1892–1912. Introduction by Mildred R. Bennett. Lincoln: University of Nebraska Press, 1965.
The Kingdom of Art: Willa Cather's First Principles and Critical Statements 1893–1896. Edited by Bernice Slote. Lincoln: University of Nebraska Press, 1966.
The World and the Parish: Articles and Reviews, 1893–1902. 2 volumes. Edited by William M. Curtin. Lincoln: University of Nebraska Press, 1970.
Uncle Valentine and Other Stories: Willa Cather's Uncollected Short Fiction 1915–1929. Edited by Bernice Slote. Lincoln: University of Nebraska Press, 1973.
Early Novels. New York: Library of America, 1987.
Later Novels. New York: Library of America, 1990.
Stories, Poems, and Other Writings. New York: Library of America, 1992.

OTHER WORKS
Bohlke, L. Brent. *Willa Cather in Person: Interviews, Speeches, and Letters*. Lincoln: University of Nebraska Press, 1986.

BIBLIOGRAPHY

Arnold, Marilyn. *Willa Cather: A Reference Guide*. Boston: G. K. Hall, 1986.
Crane, Joan. *Willa Cather: A Bibliography*. Lincoln: University of Nebraska Press, 1982.
Lathrop, JoAnna. *Willa Cather: A Checklist of Her Published Writing*. Lincoln: University of Nebraska Press, 1975.
O'Connor, Margaret Anne. "A Guide to the Letters of Willa Cather," *Resources for American Literary Study* 4: 145–172 (Autumn 1974).

CRITICAL AND BIOGRAPHICAL STUDIES

Bennett, Mildred R. *The World of Willa Cather*. Lincoln: University of Nebraska Press, 1961.

Bloom, Harold, ed. *Willa Cather*. New York: Chelsea House, 1985.

Brown, E. K., and Leon Edel. *Willa Cather: A Critical Biography*. New York: Knopf, 1953.

Carlin, Deborah. *Cather, Canon, and the Politics of Reading*. Amherst: University of Massachusetts Press, 1992.

Daiches, David. *Willa Cather: A Critical Introduction*. New York: Collier, 1962.

Fischer, Mike. "Pastoralism and Its Discontents: Willa Cather and the Burden of Imperialism," *Mosaic: A Journal for the Interdisciplinary Study of Ideas* 23: 31–44 (Winter 1990).

Fryer, Judith. *Felicitous Space: The Imaginative Structures of Edith Wharton and Willa Cather*. Chapel Hill: University of North Carolina Press, 1986.

Gelfant, Blanche H. "The Forgotten Reaping-Hook: Sex in *My Ántonia*." *American Literature* 43: 60–82 (March 1971).

Harrell, David. *From Mesa Verde to* The Professor's House. Albuquerque: University of New Mexico Press, 1992.

Lee, Hermione. *Willa Cather: Double Lives*. New York: Pantheon, 1990.

Lewis, Edith. *Willa Cather Living*. New York: Knopf, 1953.

Middleton, Jo Ann. *Willa Cather's Modernism: A Study of Theme and Technique*. Rutherford, N.J.: Fairleigh Dickinson University Press, 1990.

Millington, Richard H. "Willa Cather and 'The Storyteller': Hostility to the Novel in *My Ántonia*." *American Literature* 66: 689–718 (December 1994).

Murphy, John, ed. *Critical Essays on Willa Cather*. Boston: G. K. Hall, 1984.

O'Brien, Sharon. *Willa Cather: The Emerging Voice*. New York: Oxford, 1987.

O'Brien, Sharon. "Becoming Non-Canonical: The Case against Willa Cather." *American Quarterly* 40: 110–26 (1988).

Reynolds, Guy. *Willa Cather in Context: Progress, Race, Empire*. New York: St. Martin's Press, 1996.

Robinson, Phyllis. *Willa: The Life of Willa Cather*. New York: Doubleday, 1983.

Rosowski, Susan. *The Voyage Perilous: Willa Cather's Romanticism*. Lincoln: University of Nebraska Press, 1986.

Schroeter, James, ed. *Willa Cather and Her Critics*. Ithaca, N.Y.: Cornell University Press, 1967.

Schwind, Jean. "The 'Beautiful' War in *One of Ours*." *Modern Fiction Studies* 30: 53–72 (1984).

Sergeant, Elizabeth Shepley. *Willa Cather: A Memoir*. Philadelphia: Lippincott, 1953.

Skaggs, Merrill Maguire. *After the World Broke in Two: The Later Novels of Willa Cather*. Charlottesville: University Press of Virginia, 1990.

Slote, Bernice, and Virginia Faulkner, eds. *The Art of Willa Cather*. Lincoln: University of Nebraska Press, 1974.

Stouck, David. *Willa Cather's Imagination*. Lincoln: University of Nebraska Press, 1975.

Urgo, Joseph R. *Willa Cather and the Myth of American Migration*. Urbana: University of Illinois Press, 1995.

Woodress, James Leslie. *Willa Cather: A Literary Life*. Lincoln: University of Nebraska Press, 1987.

Woods, Lucia. *Willa Cather: A Pictorial Memoir*. Text by Bernice Slote. Lincoln: University of Nebraska Press, 1973.

—SHARON O'BRIEN

Raymond Chandler

1888–1959

*T*HAT WE HAVE a dominant American-based tradition of "hard-boiled" detective fiction, as opposed to the classic English tradition of brilliant amateur sleuths deciphering clues in country manor houses, is due in large part to Raymond Chandler. That the detective story has, at its best, become a vehicle for character analysis, social commentary, exploration of stylistic possibilities, and experiments with point of view is due in large part to Raymond Chandler. That theoretical critics such as Roland Barthes, F. R. Jameson, and Geoffrey Hartman have taken a serious professional interest in detective fiction is due in large part to Raymond Chandler. That all this should be so is ironic because Raymond Chandler always felt a greater affinity with English life and culture than with American; it is ironic because he came to professional writing late in life, settling on crime fiction as a relatively quick and easy way to make money after alcoholism and the Great Depression had ended his career as an oil executive; and it is ironic because, despite his eventual desire to create art rather than formulaic detective stories, he hated abstract, intellectual discussions of literature, which made him intensely uneasy. In other words, little in the outward events of Raymond Chandler's first forty-four years would lead one to predict the accomplishments of the next twenty-seven, or their lasting influence.

*   *   *

Chandler was born in Chicago on July 23, 1888, to an Irish mother and a Pennsylvania Quaker father whose own ancestors had come from Ireland in the seventeenth and eighteenth centuries. His father, Maurice, was an alcoholic, as Chandler would become. Possibly some of Chandler's self-loathing in later years resulted from his following the pattern of a man he despised as "an utter swine." Raymond never again saw his father after his parents divorced when he was seven. He and his mother, Florence, then moved to England, where they lived in Upper Norwood, a suburb south of London, with her sister Ethel and, in Chandler's words, his "stupid and arrogant grandmother." Natasha Spender, Chandler's close friend at the end of his life, recounts in *The World of Raymond Chandler* (1978) that the mother and son "were made to feel like disgraced poor relations." At an early age Chandler assumed the role of his mother's protector by absorbing the humiliations and "moralizing condescension" meted out by his female relatives.

In 1900 the household moved to Dulwich, a fashionable suburb in South London, so that Raymond could attend Dulwich College, a well-known public (i.e., private) school. There he studied classical and modern subjects with schoolmasters who instilled a respect for clear prose as well as the Christian and classical virtues. The defiantly old-fashioned morality of Philip Marlowe, Chandler's greatest creation, has its roots in Dulwich, as Chandler later acknowledged in claiming that his classical education gave him a surprisingly good "basis for writing novels in a hard-boiled vernacular." The approach to writing he learned at Dulwich also had a lasting influence. Instructors would require the boys to translate Latin passages into English and then, at a later date, to translate their English back into Latin. Chandler followed the same method in teaching himself the craft of detective fiction, first reducing stories by Dashiell Hammett and others he admired to a skeletal plot outline and then rewriting them in his own style.

Chandler graduated from Dulwich with vague ambitions of being a writer, but his family decided on a career in the civil service instead. After a period of study in France and Germany, he returned to London in 1907, became a naturalized British subject, and took the six-day civil service examination. Out of six hundred candidates he placed third overall, first in the classics. He gained a record-keeping job in the Naval Stores Branch but resigned after six months to pursue his writing, much to the dismay of his family.

After a poor stint as a reporter for the *Daily Express,* Chandler joined the staff of the liberal *Westminster Gazette.* His writings there show a dualism that characterizes his novels. Between 1908 and 1912 he published twenty-seven sentimental, idealistic, yearningly romantic—and not especially good—poems with such titles as "The Unknown Love," "The Perfect Knight," and "Time Shall Not Die"; he also published a series of satirical sketches.

By 1912, Chandler was frustrated with his lack of genuine literary accomplishment, despondent over a failed love, and upset by the suicide of a friend whom he considered a greater talent. He borrowed five hundred pounds from his uncle and sailed for America. The trip changed the course of his life. On board he met Warren and Alma Lloyd, he a Yale Ph.D. in philosophy and she a sculptor. Chandler accepted their invitation to visit them in Los Angeles, where they owned a family oil business. Warren helped Chandler get a bookkeeping job at the Los Angeles Creamery and brought him into the lively intellectual circle centered around Friday night gatherings at the Lloyds'. Among the regular guests were Julian Pascal, a distinguished composer and pianist, and his wife Cissy, who was to become Chandler's wife despite being eighteen years his senior.

Shortly after the United States entered World War I, Chandler enlisted in the Canadian Army because, as he later explained it, "it was still natural for me to prefer a British uniform." In June 1918, a German artillery attack killed every man in his unit except him. Aside from one brief sketch recounting the horror of a soldier "alone in a universe of incredibly brutal noise," he never directly treated the experience in his writing and rarely spoke of the war. Only years later, in *The Long Goodbye* (1953), did he touch upon it tangentially in the war-ravaged figure of Terry Lennox.

When the war ended, Chandler was thirty and rootless. He drifted down the West Coast from Vancouver, where he had been discharged, eventually returning to Los Angeles and renewing his friendships there. He also fell in love with Cissy Pascal, a vibrant and cultivated woman who looked much younger than her forty-eight years. After her divorce from Julian in 1920, she lived with or near Chandler until they married in 1924, following the death of Chandler's mother, whom Chandler had been caring for and who had strongly opposed the relationship.

By this time, Warren Lloyd had helped Chandler become an auditor in the Dabney Oil Syndicate, where Lloyd's brother was a partner. In the early 1920s about one-fifth of the world's crude oil came from the Los Angeles area. Boom times, hard work, aptitude, and a series of fortunate circumstances propelled Chandler to a vice-presidency and a thousand-dollar-a-month salary well before the end of the decade. Gradually, though, his life started to unravel. His rapid rise occasioned jealousy, and his tough, autocratic business style bred enemies. Cissy, approaching sixty, was frequently ill and now obviously much older than her husband, who began appearing alone at public functions and having office affairs. With the onset of the Depression, Chandler developed a terrible drinking problem, eventually disappearing on binges for weeks at a time. He frequently threatened suicide and attempted it at least once. In 1932 he was fired. He found himself at forty-four a broken man—an alcoholic with no job, no prospects, little money, and an aging, sickly wife. At this miserable juncture, having little left to lose, he decided to do what he had always wanted to do: write.

Chandler started with poems and fictional sketches. The one surviving example of these initial attempts is ''Beer in the Sergeant Major's Hat, or The Sun Also Sneezes,'' an affectionate parody of Hemingway. Such self-indulgent fun, however, would not pay the rent. Chandler knew that he had to find a more serviceable vehicle. Even while desperate, he disdained writing for such slick magazines as *Cosmopolitan* and the *Saturday Evening Post* because of ''their fundamental dishonesty in the matter of character and motivation.'' But he was drawn to pulp fiction when he realized that ''I might be able to write this stuff and get paid while I was learning.''

He chose *Black Mask,* one of the best pulp magazines, as his outlet. Under the editorship of Joseph T. ''Cap'' Shaw, it favored stories that, compared with the industry standard, emphasized character development over intricate mechanical plotting, analysis of human behavior over analysis of carefully embedded clues. Among its regular contributors were Erle Stanley Gardner and Dashiell Hammett, who became Chandler's major influence.

In particular, Chandler valued Hammett for blazing a trail away from the detective-story-as-tale-of-ratiocination derived from Edgar Allan Poe. Hammett's stories were less concerned with demonstrating the exercise of deductive powers than with exploring a human response to living in a corrupt, dangerous modern world. As Chandler wrote in 1944, in ''The Simple Art of Murder,'' Hammett ''took murder out of the Venetian vase and dropped it in the alley.'' He put the language of the alley in the mouths and minds of his characters. He used detail and observation to reveal mood and character. Most of all, he wrote stories one would want to read even if the last chapter were missing.

And yet Chandler felt that he could exceed Hammett as a stylist, that he could make language resonate in a way Hammett could not, that he could say things Hammett ''did not know how to say, or feel the need of saying.'' His ambition was to write serious fiction using the detective-story format, ''to exceed the limits of a formula without destroying it.'' His method, adapted from Dulwich, was to prepare a detailed synopsis of a story he admired and then rewrite it in his own words.

Soon he began to develop plots that were his own, albeit somewhat formulaic. He continued in his method of writing and rewriting each story, as he would throughout his career, often starting all over again if he was unsatisfied with any part of it. After spending five months rewriting ''Blackmailers Don't Shoot,'' he submitted it to *Black Mask.* Shaw paid him $180, one cent a word, and Chandler's first story was published in December 1933. Although it is not merely the ''pure pastiche'' and ''goddamn pose'' Chandler later called it, neither is it the piece of polished perfection that *Black Mask* deemed it. The story is interesting, though, not only for introducing characteristic elements but also for showing how far Chandler progressed by the publication of *The Big Sleep* in 1939.

"Blackmailers" is a rather confused jumble of double and triple crossings among a set of Hollywood types. The rising star's career is threatened by her earlier romance with the racketeer, a plot device that recurs in *The Little Sister* (1949). If blackmailers don't shoot, everyone else does. As is typical of the early fiction, violence and gunplay take the place of the detailed descriptions and characterization of the novels. The detective Mallory is a rudimentary Marlowe—tough, honest, independent, persistent, and smart enough to see farther into the mystery than he was supposed to. His repartee, though, lacks something of Marlowe's wit: "Do that again and I'll put a slug in your guts, copper. So help me, I will." Nor is there any of the startling poetry with which Marlowe conveys his inner world. The third-person limited point of view does not allow us to see into anyone's mind, much less the detective's, and the characters seem like flat cutouts set artificially moving on collision courses, hardly the recognizably human figures of the novels who are driven by complex and antithetical needs.

An important trait of Chandler's narratives is already apparent, though: a degree of irresolution in a genre in which the convention is to tie up every loose end, to fit every piece of the puzzle into place. It is never fully clear who did what or why. Mallory does not even know whether he will return home to Chicago or stick around Hollywood. Chandler kept him in Hollywood, where he developed quickly into one of the most original and significant creations in detective fiction.

Four years and a dozen stories intervene between "Blackmailers Don't Shoot" and "Red Wind," which appeared in the January 1938 issue of *Dime Detective Magazine*. Philip Marlowe is now Chandler's first-person narrator, a dimensional man with a gift for observation and a need

for reflection, a poetic streak and a self-deflating humor, a romantic idealism and a cynical pessimism about the world and human nature. Most of all, he has a penchant for stepping into trouble almost accidentally, and then deliberately stepping in further. Part of his motivation is curiosity, part is knight errantry. As in the novels, his impulse to shield the lady in distress causes him to risk physical danger and also professional suicide by incurring the enmity of the law. The main plot device, a scheme to steal jewelry in order to sell it back to the owner, figures in *Farewell, My Lovely* (1940), and the necklace that symbolizes a tragic once-in-a-lifetime love is central to the mystery of *The Long Goodbye*. And of course blackmail is the spring, as in most of Chandler.

Despite his rapid development and regular publication, the years of pulp fiction were hard ones for Chandler. Even in the best of them, he never earned more than a tenth of his salary as an oil executive. He and Cissy moved constantly from one furnished apartment to another. The compulsive rootlessness at least gave him firsthand knowledge of a wide variety of locations in and around Los Angeles. He was, however, starting to find the short fiction artistically as well as financially unrewarding. Chandler had used the stories to learn and practice his craft—to experiment with tone, subject matter, narrative construction, point of view, and characterization, especially of his detective. But the magazine format's demand for constant action forced him to downplay his real strengths, extended dialogue and vivid description, and to stress his acknowledged weakness, plotting. He was ready to paint more freely, and on a larger canvas.

Chandler began writing *The Big Sleep* in the spring of 1938 by "cannibalizing" earlier stories, especially "Killer in the Rain" and "The Curtain." By stitching together existing materials, he could spend less time on plot construction and more on building links between different scenes through development of character and setting. He found the method so congenial that he employed it for several of the later novels, though never again with such ease. *The Big Sleep* was completed in three months. Published in 1939, it sold extremely well for a first novel and relieved Chandler's financial distress. It also established Chandler as an important writer, not merely of detective stories but of fiction. The dimensions that the pulp format could not accommodate are evident from the opening of chapter one. Philip Marlowe arrives at the Sternwood mansion sporting a powder-blue suit with matching accessories and a cockiness tinged with wry self-mockery: "I was neat, clean, shaved and sober, and I didn't care who knew it."

Marlowe then describes the setting, observing and interpreting details in such a way as to foreshadow the action, establish a pattern of imagery and symbolic reference, and comment ironically on his own character and situation:

> Over the entrance doors, which would have let in a troop of Indian elephants, there was a broad stained-glass panel showing a knight in dark armor rescuing a lady who was tied to a tree and didn't have any clothes on but some very long and convenient hair. The knight had pushed the vizor of his helmet back to be sociable, and he was fiddling with the knots on the ropes that tied the lady to the tree and not getting anywhere. I stood there and thought that if I lived in the house, I would sooner or later have to climb up there and help him. He didn't seem to be really trying.

The bound lady proves to be Carmen Sternwood, although as befits the modern debasement of the paradigm her hair is cut short and a pornographer is using naked photos of her for blackmail.

The knight is fumbling and ineffectual, even comically anachronistic, but Marlowe recognizes that he will probably find himself in the role. This early he reveals his salient trait: he is torn between a romantic idealism—manifested in a chivalric code of honor, service, and self-

sacrifice—and a cynical, world-weary pessimism about human nature, societal corruption, and the efficacy of individual action. Later in the story, fending off the naked Carmen, he looks down at the chessboard on which he is playing a game against himself and thinks, "The move with the knight was wrong. Knights had no meaning in this game." But he keeps trying to play it.

Most of Marlowe's complexities spring from this dualism, none more so than the remarkable range of voices and styles in which he speaks, observes, and reflects. At times he sounds like Hemingway, a writer Chandler admired and Marlowe had read: "I braked the car against the curb and switched the headlights off and sat with my hands on the wheel." In the next sentence he sounds more like Fitzgerald: "Under the thinning fog the surf curled and creamed, almost without sound, like a thought trying to form itself on the edge of consciousness."

One might say that Chandler had not yet digested his models very thoroughly or settled on his own voice, except that the voices persist throughout his fiction and correspond to fundamental divisions in Marlowe's nature, divisions that make him a complex, absorbing character and a very unusual private eye: "At seven-twenty a single flash of hard white light shot out of Geiger's house like a wave of summer lightning. As the darkness folded back on it and ate it up a thin tinkling scream echoed out and lost itself among the rain-drenched trees." The passage begins as if by Joe Friday and ends as if by John Keats. The precise notation of the time of the event is typical of a detective, but the movement into poetic descriptions of sensory impressions is not.

Raymond Chandler is a stylist attentive to nuance, figurative language, symbolic imagery, and poetic tropes; his great achievement is to create a detective who is himself just such a stylist. Marlowe clearly enjoys exploiting the possibilities for verbal play that his role as narrator affords. He specializes in startling similes: the rapidly failing General Sternwood "spoke again, slowly, using his strength as carefully as an out-of-work showgirl uses her last good pair of stockings." Outside the Sternwood mansion "the sunshine was as empty as a headwaiter's smile." Although not likely to be mistaken for a metaphysical poet, Marlowe has a predilection for what Samuel Johnson called "heterogeneous ideas . . . yoked by violence together."

In his more poetic moods, Marlowe also has a penchant for synesthesia, or the description of one sensory experience in terms of another sense, as in "thick silence folded down." When given to irony or self-mockery, Marlowe employs a vast repertoire of techniques ranging from comically inflated descriptions to terse, surprising zeugmas in which a word bears the same grammatical relation to two or more sentence elements but with a very different meaning in each case. For example, in tailing a car through traffic, Marlowe is forced "to make a left turn and a lot of enemies"; later he goes to bed "full of whiskey and frustration." He is certainly not above using a pun to undercut a serious mood. Before the echo of the thin, tinkling scream lost itself among the rain-drenched trees, Marlowe was out of the car and running to the pornographer Geiger's house. Inside he found Carmen drugged and naked before a large camera and Geiger shot dead. Geiger's murderer had fled with the plateholder containing the photographic images of Carmen. Says Marlowe, "I didn't like this development."

That such effects are Marlowe's and not just Chandler's is shown by Marlowe's self-consciousness about them. On first hearing Mona Mars's "smooth silvery voice" he thinks, "It had a tiny tinkle in it, like bells in a doll's house. I thought that was silly as soon as I thought of it." The description of Mona's voice, which does nothing to forward the action but characterizes her, is exactly the dimension Chandler wanted to gain in moving from the short story to the novel. But if his main purpose was to characterize Mona, he could have omitted or replaced a simile he found wanting; his only reason for keeping it and including Marlowe's commentary is to characterize Marlowe as a man with the ability, and the need, to craft the story he tells. When questioned by General Sternwood, Marlowe reluctantly divulges, "I'm thirty-three years old, went to college once and can still speak English if there's any demand for it. There isn't much in my trade." Hence the laconic outer self. But the inner self demands it, as evidenced by Marlowe's very telling of the tales.

Nor will Marlowe's inner self let him leave apparent problems and injustices alone, even if he endangers himself or exceeds the scope of his job in pursuing them. The General hires Marlowe only to investigate what are presented as his daughter Carmen's gambling debts. Suspecting that these may be initial attempts at blackmail, Marlowe presses further, ultimately uncovering the connection between Carmen and Geiger. Geiger's murder draws Marlowe in further to the world of racketeer Eddie Mars, who seems to have some illicit hold on Vivian Regan, Sternwood's first daughter. Vivian had been married to a bootlegger, Rusty Regan, who disappeared without word some months before Marlowe is retained by the General—disappeared with the wife of Eddie Mars, so the rumor goes and the police apparently believe. The General, who had come to love Rusty as a son, was particularly hurt by his abrupt departure.

In due course, Geiger's homosexual roommate kills the man who he thinks killed Geiger and who did steal the photographic plates. Marlowe recovers the photos, concealing a murder and suppressing evidence for a time so that Carmen is not mentioned in the police reports and the General is thus spared knowledge of her activities. Marlowe has done his job, above and beyond the call of duty, and has $500 coming. "The smart thing for me to do was to take another drink and forget the whole mess. That being the obviously smart thing to do, I called Eddie Mars'' and pursued the matter of Rusty Regan without permission from the General. Several killings later, it turns out that the psychotic Carmen had murdered Rusty for rejecting her sexual advances, just as she had tried to shoot the temptation-proof Marlowe. Vivian was forced to enlist the aid of Eddie Mars in the cover-up, and he has been, in her words, bleeding her white. The phrase is not just a cliché. On his first visit to the Sternwood mansion, Marlowe registered something in the color scheme of Vivian's room: ''The white made the ivory look dirty and the ivory made the white look bled out.'' Such use of symbolic detail is the mark of Chandler's distinction, and one of his self-conscious narrator's few satisfactions. Another is that the General will die without ever knowing the truth.

But these are lonely satisfactions. Marlowe's inner self has no company—no fellow professional to share his understandings with, no woman to share his life or even his bed. His rigid code of fidelity to his employer has made him deny the dangerous but alluring Vivian. Mona Mars, whose naive faith in her husband powerfully attracted him, disappears after helping him escape Eddie's hit man. Marlowe never sees her again. The novel ends with a feeling of unfulfillment, of irresolution, that is unusual for the detective story. We do not know whether Vivian will have Carmen committed to an institution or how Marlowe will deal with Eddie Mars. And Marlowe himself seems far less assured than the self-confident, nattily attired detective who came ''calling on four million dollars'' just a few days earlier. The irony in his voice is not from wisecracks but from brooding over what it means to be ''sleeping the big sleep.'' He has solved the case, but as a result he has pulled himself, and us, deeper into the intractable mystery of human evil.

In February 1939 Chandler wrote to Alfred A. Knopf that ''*The Big Sleep* is very unequally written. There are scenes that are all right, but there are other scenes still much too pulpy. . . . To acquire delicacy without losing power, that's the problem.'' Throughout the year Chandler attempted to master the problem while working simultaneously on two books drawn from earlier stories. For one he cannibalized ''Try the Girl'' and ''Mandarin's Jade''; after several entire rewrites and title changes, *Farewell, My Lovely* was published in 1940. At first less commercially successful than *The Big Sleep,* it received highly favorable reviews and is still considered one of Chandler's best; Chandler himself called it his own favorite, although he had not then written *The Long Goodbye.*

The novel begins with Philip Marlowe in a bad neighborhood, having failed to locate a runaway husband. He observes an enormous, gaudily dressed white man enter a black-run gambling hotel. Moments later someone sails across the sidewalk and lands in the gutter. Marlowe crosses the street and stands before the double doors thinking, ''It wasn't any of my business. So I pushed them open and looked in,'' thus precipitating the chain of events that constitutes the story. The giant, Moose Malloy, has just been released from prison after serving time for robbery and is returning to the site of a club where his girlfriend Velma Valento used to sing. Velma may still have the stolen money, but Moose is searching out of love, not greed. Marlowe witnesses Moose kill the manager, who tried to eject him before he found what he was after. Since the man was black, the police don't care much about the murder. They would, however, like to track down Moose and Velma. To earn himself a little goodwill, Marlowe agrees to help the police look for Velma. His search takes him to Jessie Florian, the alcoholic widow of the owner of the club where Velma sang. After getting her drunk, he takes potential evidence to give to the police and then, disgusted with himself, withdraws from the case. So he thinks.

A Lindsay Marriott calls to offer him a job—accompanying Marriott while he buys back a jade necklace that was stolen from an unnamed lady. They drive to a remote canyon, where Marlowe is struck from behind and knocked out. Anne Riordan arrives on the scene; she had seen the headlights and, like Marlowe, couldn't resist investigating. Marriott has been murdered and his money for the necklace stolen. Left behind, though, is his cigarette case containing marijuana cigarettes. By the time Marlowe is functioning the next day, Anne has traced the theft report on the necklace to Helen Grayle and arranged for a meeting. Marlowe cuts open one of the reefers and finds the card of "Jules Amthor, Psychic Consultant." Warned off the case by Lieutenant Randall, he instead calls Amthor and arranges to see him about Marriott. On a hunch, he checks the title on Jesse Florian's property and finds that it is held by Marriott. Marlowe visits the Grayle mansion, where Helen Grayle outdrinks and nearly seduces him, interrupted only by the awkward appearance of her aged husband.

Marlowe now becomes entangled in a series of bizarre misadventures that suggest a broad conspiracy against him. Finally, while Moose is hiding in Marlowe's apartment, Marlowe confronts Helen with his suspicions: she is Velma; she set up Moose after the robbery; and she killed Marriott because he knew her secret. The business with the necklace was just a ruse; Marriott thought he was leading Marlowe into an ambush. Velma had been willing to pay Marriott a little blackmail, given her husband's tremendous wealth, but when Marlowe began nosing around Jesse Florian's she decided to sever the connection with her past. Moose emerges, still smitten and apparently willing to forgive. Velma fatally shoots him and then flees. Three months later she is captured in Baltimore, where she is working as a club singer, by a cop who recognizes her from the old days. She kills the policeman and then herself.

Again, deliberately, the ending is untidy. Marlowe and the reader look for a satisfactory explanation that links all of the different characters and subplots, but there isn't one. The linking principle appears to be not conspiracy but rather coincidence operating within a milieu of corruption. We don't learn exactly how various characters, such as Amthor and Marriott, are connected to one another. We don't know what finally happens between Marlowe and Anne, last seen making her play for him. We don't know what motivated Velma to shoot herself rather than return for a trial she would probably have won, given her husband's money, Moose's violent history, and the lack of evidence connecting her to Marriott's murder. Marlowe speculates that she may have decided to "give a break to the only man who had ever really given her one. . . . An old man who had loved not wisely, but too well." Randall replies sharply, "That's just sentimental." Marlowe agrees that he is probably wrong, and so this story too ends with the unanswerable mystery overshadowing the solution of the crime. Closure, as Roland Barthes observes of modern fiction, is "simultaneously set up and disappointed."

And again, this sense of unfulfillment describes Marlowe's life. He is without friendship. Lieutenant Randall is a tough, shrewd, principled cop whom Marlowe comes to respect, yet when Marlowe tries to compare their indefatigable but futile efforts to those of a stubborn pink bug in Randall's office, "He didn't know what I was talking about." No doubt he missed the allusion to Othello too. Marlowe is also without love. Anne, who is clearly offering it to him, is bright, lively, curious, and attractive, yet Marlowe reflexively distances himself from her while shielding her from trouble. He is the chivalric knight seeking the unholy Grayle, and his code seems to include chastity as well as integrity and the pursuit of justice: the "nice little girl," as he calls Anne, is not to be violated, and he will not let himself be violated by the woman without virtue, although she might tempt him.

Another possibility has occasionally been suggested: Marlowe's, and Chandler's, repressed homsexuality. Both at various times voice their aversion to homosexuals, but of course aversion can be the mind's own disguise for what it does not want to acknowledge. Natasha Spender has said that she and others who knew about Chandler's life assumed that such might be the case. Chandler, however, had numerous heterosexual affairs, despite doting on Cissy, and is never known to have been with a man. The homosexuals in his fiction appear as stereotypes whom Marlowe generally disdains. But despite his expressed attitudes, Marlowe is often oddly unguarded in his appreciation of male beauty—of Carol Lundgren, Geiger's lover in *The Big Sleep,* of Jules Amthor, of Lindsay Marriott, and of others. Much has been made especially of his first encounter with Red, a man he meets by chance on the Bay City waterfront and feels suddenly drawn to: "His voice was soft, dreamy, so delicate for a big man that it was startling. . . . I looked at him again. He had the eyes you never see, that you only read about. Violet eyes. Almost purple. Eyes like a girl, a lovely girl. His skin was as soft as silk. Lightly reddened, but it would never tan." Much has also been made of the vehement disgust that Marlowe occasionally shows toward female sexuality, as when he "savagely" tears his bed to pieces after expelling the seductive Carmen from it.

The matter of Chandler's or Marlowe's sexuality cannot be definitively settled. Like his author, the detective remains a complex and lonely man, often divided from others by being divided within himself and isolated by a fear of intimacy masked as self-reliance. When Red asks Marlowe whether he might need help finding Moose, Marlowe replies: "I need a company of marines. But either I do it alone or I don't do it. So long."

Marlowe also reveals a deep ambivalence about wealth. On the one hand, he is as responsive to fine furnishings as he is to the charms of the women or men he cannot let himself have. In particular, he often describes interiors with a sensitive and well-informed eye. He does so partly because he is a trained observer who records and analyzes details for their significance; he also does so simply because his aesthetic side responds to beauty. On the other hand, Marlowe regards the trappings of wealth with cynicism and suspicion, knowing that they are a facade behind which to hide evil. Chandler pronounced that he and Marlowe "despise" the upper classes "because they are phoney." Marlowe takes a grim Puritanical pride in the shabbiness of his office and apartment, which he touts as emblems of his honesty. Of course his office is in Hollywood, a latter-day Vanity Fair that delivers a world of sumptuous, seductive illusions. This same Hollywood began to take an interest in Marlowe: in 1941 RKO bought the film rights to *Farewell, My Lovely.* Chandler sold them for only $2,000.

The early 1940s were difficult years for Chandler. Cissy's health was bad and money a constant worry. Distracted from his work by the war, he was attempting to finish *The Lady in the Lake,* the novel he had been writing along with *Farewell, My Lovely.* When frustrated, he would turn to one of several short stories and yet another novel. This one, not drawn from earlier material, was completed first and published in 1942 as *The High Window.* Its theme, a strong person's selfish manipulation of the weak, is reminiscent of Nathaniel Hawthorne and Henry James, one of Chandler's idols. Again, the rich are the source of evil. So keen is Chandler's resentment that the book has a shrill tone and melodramatic edginess. Chandler attempts to leaven this tone with humorous scenes and, of course, Marlowe's wisecracks, but the novel has an uneasy feel to it, and Chandler was not especially happy with the result. It had, he wrote to his publisher, Blanche Knopf, "no action, no likable characters, no nothing. The detective does nothing."

Chandler exaggerates the faults. Marlowe is kept busy and does ultimately expose a number of wicked schemes, but many critics have complained that the book seems misanthropic in its absence of admirable or even decent specimens of humanity. The most sympathetic of a very unsympathetic lot is Merle Davis, Mrs. Murdock's neurotic, guilt-ridden, and emotionally abused secretary who becomes this novel's lady in distress. *The High Window* is really two stories that are somewhat awkwardly woven together: the story of how Mrs. Murdock psychologically bullies Merle into believing herself responsible for the death of Mrs. Murdock's first husband, Horace Bright, some eight years earlier, and the story of a scheme to counterfeit an antique gold coin, the Brasher Doubloon, stolen from the collection of Mrs. Murdock's deceased second husband. The connection between the two stories is Louis Vannier, who planned the counterfeit scheme and who is also blackmailing Mrs. Murdock with some very improbable evidence of her guilt in the death of Horace Bright, a photograph he happened to be shooting from across the street exactly as she pushed her husband out of a high window. Just as implausible are Mrs. Murdock's ability to convince Merle that she had pushed Mr. Bright because he was threatening her sexually, or even Mrs. Murdock's reason for doing so, given Vannier's evidence.

Naturally, Marlowe knows nothing of all this when he is first summoned to the Murdock house. Mrs. Murdock suspects that her unsuitable daughter-in-law, a nightclub singer named Linda Conquest, has stolen the coin from her late husband's collection. She wants Marlowe to find Linda, get the coin back, and make her agree to an uncontested divorce—all without police, publicity, or the knowledge of her son Leslie. Marlowe is, if anything, flintier than ever. He insists on hav-

ing it known that he will do things his way and according to his rules. When the formidable Mrs. Murdock insists that the matter "be handled with delicacy," he replies, "If you hire me, you'll get all the delicacy I have. If I don't have enough delicacy [to frame Linda if necessary], maybe you'd better not hire me."

> MRS. MURDOCK: "You don't like me very well, do you?"
> MARLOWE: "Does anybody?"

Once more, Marlowe's curiosity and persistence compel him to delve further than he was hired, or desired, to go. He thus becomes the catalyst who precipitates actions based on hatreds, fears, and greeds that had been hanging in delicate, uneasy suspension for years.

As in earlier cases, many of Marlowe's breakthroughs come not from methodical ratiocination in the manner of Poe's Dupin or Conan Doyle's Holmes but from flashes of insight, hunches based on what makes sense in human terms. The same instinct that led him (in *Farewell, My Lovely*) to equate Helen and Velma or to sense (in *The Big Sleep*) that a spurned Carmen had killed Rusty Regan operates again here, along with a keen eye for interiors: feeling that the painting of a man in doublet and hose leaning out of a high window does not fit the decor of Vannier's room, Marlowe inspects the backing and finds the photograph that connects the threads of the case.

Marlowe sends Merle Davis back to her parents, freeing her from Mrs. Murdock's tower but not her spell: the girl cannot absorb the evidence of Mrs. Murdock's guilt or her own innocence. Satisfaction, a sense of closure, still eludes Marlowe. He feels as though "I had written a poem and it was very good and I had lost it and would never remember it again." He sees the moonlight "cold and clear, like the justice we dream of but don't find." And again, he seems alone in his search. He makes a heartfelt attempt to explain his code to Lieutenant Breeze, who shrugs it off as a rationalization for bending the law. The novel ends with Marlowe alone, playing out a chess game by the grandmaster José Raúl Capablanca. ''Beautiful cold remorseless chess, almost creepy in its silent implacability.'' This degree of closure achieved, Marlowe looks at himself in the mirror: '' 'You and Capablanca,' I said.''

The Lady in the Lake, published the next year, 1943, cannibalizes Chandler's earlier short stories ''The Lady in the Lake'' (1939), ''Bay City Blues'' (1938), and ''No Crime in the Mountains'' (1941). Chandler had been working on it intermittently since 1939 while he and Cissy moved about from Los Angeles and Santa Monica to Riverside and Big Bear Lake. Similarly, the story bounces back and forth between the environs of Los Angeles and Bay City (Santa Monica) and the fictional mountain retreat of Little Fawn Lake. Chandler made the interweaving narrative lines so tangled and complicated that critics have suspected him of parodying the genre's demand for intricate plots and its reliance on coincidence. It is Chandler's story of mistaken identity, an elaborate bit of legerdemain and misdirection that keeps everyone, including Marlowe, looking the wrong way until the end. The novel begins, as usual, with Marlowe's being hired to handle a fairly routine matter. Businessman Derace Kingsley last saw his wife Crystal a month ago at their mountain cabin. Soon after he received a telegram saying that she was going to Mexico to get a divorce and marry playboy Chris Lavery. Given their troubled relationship, Kingsley is willing to let the matter go until he bumps into Lavery, who denies any knowledge of it.

The inner Marlowe feels himself aging, an empty life passing him by, but the outer Marlowe is still the same man who in his younger days was fired by the district attorney's office for insubordination. He is deliberately abrasive, as if trying to establish his own toughness and independence. ''I don't like your manner,'' says Kingsley after a Marlovian wisecrack. ''That's all right,'' Marlowe replies, ''I'm not selling it.'' Kingsley retains him, and Marlowe immediately becomes enmeshed in a larger and more dangerous web than anyone suspected. In the critic William Stowe's phrase, Marlowe's brand of detection is more akin to hermeneutics than to semiotics: rather than decode signs to explicate a set and preexisting reality, he alters events by the very act of investigating them and creates more questions by his questioning.

Not that he is happy in his role as catalyst: every line of inquiry produces a new death. On discovering Lavery's body, he thinks ''murder-a-day Marlowe.... They have the meat wagon following him around to follow up on the business he finds.'' Lavery, it turns out, had found the body of the wife of his neighbor, Dr. Almore, a drug-dispensing physician who had treated Crystal for alcoholism. The death was ruled a suicide, but a cover-up involving Bay City cop Lieutenant Degarmo is rumored. Dr. Almore's nurse, Mildred Haviland, has also disappeared.

At Little Fawn Lake, Marlowe interrogates the caretaker, Bill Chess, whose wife Muriel ran away the same night that Crystal vanished. They see something in the lake that proves to be the decomposed body of a woman. A distraught Chess identifies it as Muriel's. Many twists and reversals later, it turns out to be Crystal's. She was murdered by Mildred Haviland, who had been having an affair with Almore and had murdered his wife. She then fled to Riverside leaving Almore and her husband, Lieutenant Degarmo, to manage the cover-up. There, as Muriel, she met and married Chess, leaving him when she could make Crystal's death appear to be her own. She happened to encounter Lavery on the way, whom she knew slightly from his visits to Crystal at the lake, and seduced him into accompanying her to El Paso, where she sent the telegram to Kingsley. Ultimately, the distraught Degarmo murders her.

Marlowe unravels this tangled skein at the end of the novel in a manner that parodies, or at least patterns itself on, the disclosure scene in the classic detective story. With the chief suspects and the local constable in attendance, he delivers a fifteen-hundred-word step-by-step account of how it all happened, even employing such stock phrases as "That disposes of motive, and we come to means and opportunity." Parody seems likely since Marlowe has already mocked several developments in the case as crime-novel clichés. Moreover, Chandler complained to his publisher that American audiences did not recognize the burlesque in his work. One would like to think that the interlocking farfetched coincidences here are offered in this spirit. The motivation for much of the important action, though, also seems strained and implausible, and the ending is oddly abrupt. The previous novels close with some kind of summary meditation by Marlowe. This one stops with Degarmo—whom Marlowe and the sheriff have strangely allowed to escape—being shot by wartime sentries as he drives away. Marlowe sees them reach into the car and lift something out: "Something that had been a man." The end.

Just as Marlowe felt himself becoming older and more spent, less equal to the task, so Chandler was prone to despondency during the writing of *The Lady in the Lake.* Depressed by the war, he volunteered for officer training in the Canadian Army but was rejected because of his age. Cissy turned seventy in 1940. And although Chandler the man was hardly gregarious, Chandler the writer was as isolated in his profession as Marlowe the detective was in his. Chandler did not publish another piece of fiction for six years. Hollywood, the setting for his stories, became the setting for his life. Having already sold the film rights to *Farewell, My Lovely* (released as *Murder, My Sweet*) and *The High Window* (released as *Time to*

Kill), he was asked in 1943 to collaborate with Billy Wilder on a script for James M. Cain's *Double Indemnity.* Wilder found him "one of the greatest creative minds" he had worked with, but also "kind of acid, sour, grouchy," always suspicious of being patronized. Chandler called the experience "agonizing." Still, the movie was a great success, earning an Oscar nomination for the screenplay and establishing Chandler as a screenwriter in demand.

Somewhat like Marlowe, Chandler continued to be acerbic toward industry people in high places but open and helpful to the powerless, especially young writers. He began to drink again and to have affairs. He loved Cissy, but she was seventy-three and he was surrounded by young women. His working relationships with directors, producers, and studio heads continued to be difficult. While working on an original screenplay for *The Blue Dahlia* in 1945, he took offense at the offer of a bonus to finish the script on time, regarding it as both a bribe and a sign of doubt about him. He became so distraught that he could not work unless drunk. The studio had to arrange for secretaries and doctors to attend him and for two limousines to stand ready at all times to run household errands or deliver finished copy. The screenplay was completed, but it was not Chandler's best, and he was upset at alterations made during the filming. Although pleased with Howard Hawks's *The Big Sleep* (1946), starring Humphrey Bogart and Lauren Bacall, with a screenplay by William Faulkner and Leigh Brackett, he was very unhappy with Robert Montgomery's filming of *The Lady in the Lake* (1947), on which he collaborated.

Soon afterward, the Chandlers moved to La Jolla, where Chandler hoped to finish a new novel, *The Little Sister,* which was finally published in 1949. He stopped to write a screenplay, tentatively titled *Playback,* that dispensed with both Marlowe and the Los Angeles setting. Neither he nor the studio was satisfied with the product, and it was dropped. But as Chandler wrote to his London publisher, he was becoming bored with Marlowe, who was "getting self-conscious, trying to live up to his reputation among the quasi-intellectuals." Chandler frequently complained about the work in progress, writing, for example, to the *New York Herald-Tribune* reviewer James Sandoe, "It's the only book of mine I have actively disliked. It was written in a bad mood and I think that comes through." Reviews of the book were mixed, depending on how the reviewer responded to its cynical, misanthropic tone.

Despite being overly complicated and melodramatic, *The Little Sister* has the typical Chandler strengths of sharp dialogue and skillful use of language. It also marks Chandler's only artistic attempt to address the phenomenon of Hollywood. The film industry would seem to be a natural subject for him, with its ready-made themes of richly fabricated illusion masking a grim reality, of underhanded power struggles and manipulations, of personal excess leading to scandal and blackmail. Curiously, despite his experience as an insider, Chandler made little use of it. Marlowe had occasionally commented that cops or gangsters or nightclub owners were patterning themselves after B-movie figures. Once Linda Conquest (in *The High Window*) shot back, "And what about the wise-cracking snooper with the last year's gags and the come hither smile?" But only in *The Little Sister* does Chandler more fully explore the meaning of the film industry, which becomes the backdrop for the action, the basis for thematic treatments, the source of key characters, and the frame of reference by which the characters define and interpret one another.

The story opens with a bitter-sounding Marlowe putting off a potential client with insults and complaints about his depression. When she tells him he talks too much, he replies, "Lonely men always talk too much." The client is Orfa-

may Quest, whose name lends credence to Chandler's claim that he was "spoofing more and more" to counter his boredom with the detective-story format. Marlowe, who complains, "I don't want to work. I don't want anything," finally takes the case because "I was just plain bored with doing nothing." Orfamay has come from Kansas seeking her brother Orrin, who has stopped writing home. In attempting to find him, Marlowe steps into a plot to blackmail rising film star Mavis Weld over her romantic attachment to a midwestern racketeer come to Hollywood under a new identity. His investigation provokes a string of murders, by gun or ice pick, stemming from greed, fear, and sexual jealousy. Aside from being overly complicated, the plot relies on a number of extremely implausible coincidences and finally begins to undermine itself when characters' later actions subvert the rationales for their earlier ones.

Of interest, though, are Chandler's dark humor and grisly absurdity, bordering on surrealism. Marlowe finds a key piece of evidence inside the toupee of a dead man with the ice pick still protruding; he then puts the hairpiece "carefully back on the dead egg-bald head" of "Dr. Hambleton, retired (and how) optometrist," who is sporting "the new style in neckwear." Such are the light-hearted moments. Also of interest is Marlowe when serious, Chandler's portrait of a strong man standing frightened before an abyss of depression as he senses his inner reserves draining away after years of futile striving: "I felt as if I had spent my life knocking at doors in cheap hotels that nobody bothered to open." Alone, he has to keep interrupting his embittered litany to reign himself back—"Hold it, Marlowe, you're not human tonight." Finally he asks, "Why would I be?" He has no answer. Nor does he find any by solving the interlocking crimes: "Sometimes when I'm low I try to reason it out. But it gets too complicated." A displaced Puritan looking for truth behind the visible signs, he is overmatched by a world consisting of vanity and illusion, where even death seems strangely haphazard and baseless, arising from nothing more substantial than the aped conventions of B-movies.

Two chapters in *The Little Sister* suggest that Chandler was chafing under the limitations of the genre. Neither has anything to do with advancing the story. Chapter 13 consists of Marlowe's ruminations on the Hollywood movie culture. Chapter 30 is Marlowe's fantastic encounter with an elfin cop who says his sole function at the police station is to "establish a mood." This he does at night so that he can spend his days playing Mozart and Bach. He can also handle guns and cards with preternatural dexterity. Marlowe looks away when another cop enters the room and turns back to find him gone.

Chandler wrote in letters and notebooks of his desire to create a work of fantasy. He never accomplished that goal, but he had a more attainable one—what he described in a 1949 letter as "a novel of character and atmosphere with an overtone of violence of fear." He interrupted this project for what proved to be his final attempt at screenwriting, an adaptation of Patricia Highsmith's *Strangers on a Train.* Chandler and the director Alfred Hitchcock were constantly at odds over how best to tell the story, and finally the script had to be rewritten by Czenzi Ormonde. Sulking over the film's success, Chandler declared his break from a medium that typically requires "no contribution from the audience but a mouthful of popcorn."

Cissy's health deteriorated during these years, and Chandler, now approaching sixty-five, suffered frequently from bronchitis, chronic sore throats, and skin allergies so severe that he required morphine to endure them. He forged ahead with the writing, though, and finished *The Long Goodbye* in July 1953. It is his most ambitious work, an attempt to examine the charac-

ters and the society in which they live; to confront the difficult and sometimes contradictory aspects of his own personality; to explore the possibilities for morally significant action; and especially to consider the nature of friendship and love. "I don't care whether the mystery was fairly obvious," he wrote in May 1952, "but I cared about the people, about this strange corrupt world we live in, and how any man who tries to be honest looks in the end either sentimental or plain foolish."

Again, Marlowe is the prime example. He initiates the adventure by helping a drunken man after the woman with him drives off in disgust. The man turns out to be Terry Lennox, a physically and emotionally scarred British war veteran with whom Marlowe forms an unprecedented bond. The woman is Sylvia, his ex-wife and daughter of the ultra-rich newspaper magnate Harlan Potter. To Marlowe's disgust, Terry remarries Sylvia and allows himself to become a "kept poodle." Disapproval drives Terry away until he appears one morning at Marlowe's, distraught and carrying a gun. He asks Marlowe to take him to the Tijuana airport and Marlowe agrees, despite the obvious advantages of remaining uninvolved. Saying good-bye, Terry hints that he has killed Sylvia. In spite of persistent and at times brutal interrogation by the police, Marlowe will not compromise his friend, whom he does not believe capable of the violent murder even after seeing what purports to be a confession Terry wrote before shooting himself in a Mexican hotel.

Marlowe suspects that Potter is behind a frame-up and begins to investigate, his only client being allegiance to his friend's memory. Around this time Marlowe is enlisted by Eileen Wade to find her husband Roger, a writer of historical romances who has disappeared after inexplicable episodes of alcoholism and threatened violence. Marlowe succeeds but senses that Eileen has another agenda. He becomes uncharacteristically involved in their personal lives, learning that Eileen had lost the man she loved in the war and discovering that Roger had been having an affair with Sylvia Lennox. Roger is killed by a gunshot to the head. The police rule it suicide, but the circumstances are suspicious.

Marlowe ultimately determines that Terry Lennox was Eileen's lost love and first husband. She found him again, accidentally, after he had become a drunken idler married to Sylvia. That more than Sylvia's affair with Roger drove Eileen to murder. Terry let himself be blamed to protect her and to atone for Sylvia's unhappiness, and Harlan Potter assisted to avoid scandalous publicity. Roger tried to live with the secret but was beginning to break; Eileen killed him when Marlowe began peering into the cracks. Exposed, she takes an overdose of Demerol. The official finding is accidental death. Marlowe, inviting the wrath of all the powerful forces intent on maintaining the public fiction, leaks a copy of Eileen's suicide note to the press, clearing Terry's name.

At the end of the novel, Terry reappears, almost unrecognizable after plastic surgery, and explains how he faked his death. Marlowe feels used. Recognizing that Terry's easy acquiescence to a self-indulgent, amoral life contributed to Sylvia's death and that his complicity in the cover-up led to Roger's and Eileen's, Marlowe is forced to choose between his moral code and his companion. In an especially poignant closing scene, Marlowe rejects Terry's attempt to restore their friendship.

The Long Goodbye is Chandler's most autobiographical novel, containing what many have recognized as three different self-portraits. Terry Lennox in this scheme is the lost, alienated, self-pitying side of Chandler—always the outsider—who could never again see life steadily and see it whole after the trauma of war. Roger Wade is the middle-aged writer, grappling with alcoholism and self-disgust, who feels a mixture of defensiveness and contempt for the genre that brought

him success. And Marlowe is the hybrid cynic-romantic, the lonely idealist whose unbending standard isolates him. Though not without sympathy, it is this Chandler that prevails and passes judgment on the others.

Marlowe is again the most complex and interesting character, whether as a self-portrait or in his own right. He is again the man who will show dogged devotion for a few dollars a day but cannot be bought at any price, and he spends much of the novel refusing money that he doesn't feel he has earned on his own terms. He is again a man with strong physical desires and a strong aversion to the physical. Sitting poolside, he "carnally" watches a girl with "a luscious figure." But actually he is drawn by the ethereal elements of the scene and repulsed by the carnal. As she dives, "spray came high enough to catch the sun and make rainbows that were almost as pretty as the girl." Out of the pool, she "wobbled her bottom" over to a man who pats her thigh. "She opened her mouth like a firebucket and laughed. That terminated my interest in her."

Marlowe's squeamish recoil from vulgarity is immediately juxtaposed with the arrival of "a dream" whose "hair was the pale gold of a fairy princess" and whose "exquisitely pure" smile excites a four-hundred-word disquisition on different types of blondes. Marlowe concludes, "The dream across the way was none of these, not even of that kind of world. She was unclassifiable." She is Eileen Wade, and it takes Marlowe most of the novel to realize what underlies his romantic vision. In their one approach to a sexual encounter, Marlowe reacts with a mixture of erotic passion and startled aversion. "Saved" by circumstance, he deliberately drinks himself unconscious.

Chandler has previously used romantic paradigms to structure his fiction or characterize Marlowe. In *The Long Goodbye* he explores the darker side of romanticism. The self-destructive Roger wishes "to cease upon the midnight with no pain," then contemptuously assumes that the allusion to Keats will be lost on Marlowe. It isn't. Alluding to the same stanza in "Ode to a Nightingale," Marlowe recognizes in Eileen the morbid romanticism of one who kills because she is "in love with death." She had idealized her wartime love with Terry into an absolute that could bear no worldly stain. In her note she writes, "He should have died young in the snow of Norway, my lover that I gave to death. . . . The tragedy of life . . . is not that beautiful things die young, but that they grow old and mean. It will not happen to me."

Despite what he learns of Eileen, Marlowe follows her example—twice. He too rejects the Terry who returns to him tainted; and like Eileen, he is hurt more by the loss of the past than by the loss of a future. Near the end of the novel Marlowe has an intense one-night love affair with Linda Loring, Sylvia's sister. She represents the future, offering marriage in place of "the loneliness of a pretty empty kind of life." In delivering her to Marlowe, Linda's chauffeur questions him about the meaning of key lines from T. S. Eliot's "Love Song of J. Alfred Prufrock," the poem of a frightened, lonely, aging man's failure to reach out. Marlowe made better use of Keats: he dismisses the insights of "Prufrock" and rejects Linda's offer, saying he's "spoiled by independence." In reality, he fears the dwindling of their passion into stale indifference. Like Eileen, he would rather have it die young. After sending Linda away, he "pulled the bed to pieces and remade it," just as he had done after rejecting Carmen Sternwood (in *The Big Sleep*) years earlier. "To say goodbye is to die a little," he tells himself. He is choosing a little of the romantic death that Eileen took in full measure.

Cissy Chandler died on December 12, 1954. Her husband, then sixty-six, was devastated. Through their difficulties, he had adored her and relied on her to give his life meaning. Two months after her death he attempted suicide and had to be hospitalized. Before his own death five years later, he would be hospitalized several more times for suicidal depression or alcoholism. In April 1955 he traveled back to London, where he was sustained by Natasha and Stephen Spender and a circle of their friends who formed a "shuttle service" to watch him through the worst times. According to Natasha, when Chandler was not threatening suicide "his fantasy seemed entirely to be used in acting out romantic Don Quixote illusions" of shielding his protectors from imaginary dangers.

For more than two years after Cissy's death, Chandler was unable to produce any sustained writing. But with the help and encouragement of Helga Greene, who became his literary agent, he reworked *Playback* into a novel that reinstated Marlowe and southern California—this time "Esmeralda" (La Jolla) rather than Los Angeles. Published in 1958, it is Chandler's last and least-regarded novel, an anomaly in many ways. For one, it is a mystery without a murder, or, given the rather confused plotline, something of a muddle without a murder. Marlowe is hired by attorney Clyde Umney to trail a young woman and report on her whereabouts. He completes his assignment but becomes curious about her plight; naturally, he pursues the matter.

Marlowe's chivalric code of duty and aversion to money bring matters to a comic pass when he and the woman, Betty Mayfield, argue about the terms of his employment. She wants to pay him $5,000 to go away and leave her alone. He holds out for $500 so that he can protect her as his client. He tells the exasperated Betty, "It isn't money I want. It's some sort of understanding of what the hell I'm doing and why." In the end, he refuses any money from anyone. When Clark Brandon, a racketeer trying to go legitimate, asks how much he owes for Marlowe's services, Marlowe replies, "Nothing. I just want to know what happened." Chandler's own distrust of money is also intact. The prosperous facade of Esmeralda's Grand Street hides the squalor of Polton's Lane, "the back yard of elegance," immediately behind. In one of the book's most powerful scenes, Marlowe must go there to find the junkie night attendant for the parking lot of Brandon's luxury hotel. The man has hanged himself in the privy.

The attitudes toward sex have relaxed, however. Chandler had previously said that he wanted his detective to be a catalyst, not a Casanova, and Marlowe typically imposed rigid restrictions on himself. Here he has affairs with both his client, Betty, and Umney's secretary, Helen Vermilyea. Still, he remains the "ferocious romantic" Chandler described himself as being. Marlowe does not want to make love to Helen in the bed he shared with Linda: "I had a dream here once, a year and a half ago. There's still a shred of it left. I'd like it to stay in charge." Something of Eileen Wade (in *The Long Goodbye*) survives in Marlowe and Helen, who also views love in absolute terms: "I'll never see you again and I don't want to. It would have to be forever or not at all." Ironically, their uncompromising romanticism commits them to a life alone.

Or so it would seem. Marlowe returns to the emptiness of his rented house and thinks, "Alcohol was no cure for this. Nothing was any cure but the hard inner heart that asked for nothing from anyone." Then, through what Vladimir Nabokov dubbed "*deus ex telephonica,*" Marlowe is suddenly saved. Linda calls from Paris and begs him to marry her. He accepts, so long as *he* can pay for the plane ticket. When he hangs up, "the empty room . . . was no longer empty. . . . The air was full of music." This ending has been criticized for being tacked on and overly sentimental. Certainly it represents the wish fulfillment of the man who confessed to Helga Greene while working on the book, "the older I get, the more desperately I long for the presence of someone I love, to hold her and touch her . . . nothing else is any good at all." He told *Newsweek* (July 21, 1958), "I thought it was time Marlowe was given something worth having. . . . You see, there's a lot of him in me, his

loneliness." Chandler began another novel, with Marlowe married to Linda and chafing under their lifestyle in Palm Springs. *The Poodle Springs Story,* later completed by Robert B. Parker and published as *Poodle Springs,* was to be structured as "a running fight interspersed with amorous interludes," but the years of depression and alcoholic abuse overtook Chandler before he could finish it. He died in La Jolla on March 26, 1959.

Two weeks later, an abridged version of "The Pencil" appeared in the *London Daily Mail* as "Marlowe Takes on the Syndicate." It contains much that is characteristic of Chandler and Marlowe. At the end, several key points remain unresolved and the fates of several characters, including Marlowe and Anne Riordan, are left open. He is beginning to long for the kind of life he could have with her, but his code is still an impediment: "I'm too shop-soiled for a girl like you." When last seen, they aren't making plans for the future but rather puzzling over the unexplained elements of the case. "What I like about you," Anne says, "is that when you don't know an answer you make one up." What a temptation for an uncompromising, compulsively scrupulous detective, and what a useful expedient for a mystery writer with higher aspirations than plotsmithing.

Marlowe and Chandler were both impatient with the limits of the genre they lived in. While hiding from hit men who are seeking to "pencil him out," Marlowe buys a crime story and tries to read himself to sleep. Bad move. "The paperback scared me so badly that I put two guns under my pillow. . . . Then I asked myself why I was reading this drivel when I could have been memorizing *The Brothers Karamazov.*" No doubt Chandler would rather have been writing something along those lines. He fell short of his grandest ambitions, but he triumphed in his dream of exceeding the limits of the detective formula without destroying it. Instead he transformed it, preparing the way for successors such as Robert B. Parker and Ross Macdonald. He created a character who stands firmly in the tradition of American loner heroes such as Leatherstocking, Ishmael, Huck Finn, and Nick Adams—a character who, as Chandler observed in his notebook, represents the ''American mind; a heavy portion of rugged idealism, a dash of good hard vulgarity, a strong overtone of strident wit, an equally strong undertone of pure sentimentalism, an ocean of slang, and an utterly unexpected range of sensitivity.''

Thus equipped, Philip Marlowe became a remarkably acute instrument for viewing and recording a complex, disturbing world in transition. Through his eyes and voice, Raymond Chandler delivered matchless portraits of Los Angeles at a critical juncture in American history, registering as only a cynical romantic could the loss of an old order and the uncertain beginnings of a new one. The assessment of W. H. Auden stands: Chandler's works ''should be read and judged not as escape literature, but as works of art.''

Selected Bibliography

WORKS OF RAYMOND CHANDLER

NOVELS

The Big Sleep. New York: Knopf, 1939; London: Hamish Hamilton, 1939.

Farewell, My Lovely. New York: Knopf, 1940; London: Hamish Hamilton, 1940.

The High Window. New York: Knopf, 1942; London: Hamish Hamilton, 1943.

The Lady in the Lake. New York: Knopf, 1943; London: Hamish Hamilton, 1944.

The Little Sister. Boston: Houghton Mifflin, 1949; London: Hamish Hamilton, 1949.

The Long Goodbye. London: Hamish Hamilton, 1953. Boston: Houghton Mifflin, 1954.

Playback. Boston: Houghton Mifflin, 1958; London: Hamish Hamilton, 1958.

SHORT STORIES

''Blackmailers Don't Shoot.'' *Black Mask*, December 1933.

''Smart-Aleck Kill.'' *Black Mask*, July 1934.

''Finger Man.'' *Black Mask*, October 1934.

''Killer in the Rain.'' *Black Mask*, January 1935.

''Nevada Gas.'' *Black Mask*, June 1935.

''Spanish Blood.'' *Black Mask*, November 1935.

''Guns at Cyrano's.'' *Black Mask*, January 1936.

''The Man Who Liked Dogs.'' *Black Mask*, March 1936.

''Noon Street Nemesis'' (republished as ''Pick-up on Noon Street''). *Detective Fiction Weekly*, May 30, 1936.

''Goldfish.'' *Black Mask*, June 1936.

''The Curtain.'' *Black Mask*, September 1936.

''Try the Girl.'' *Black Mask*, January 1937.

''Mandarin's Jade.'' *Dime Detective Magazine*, November 1937.

''Red Wind.'' *Dime Detective Magazine*, January 1938.

''The King in Yellow.'' *Dime Detective Magazine*, March 1938.

''Bay City Blues.'' *Dime Detective Magazine*, June 1938.

''The Lady in the Lake.'' *Dime Detective Magazine*, January 1939.

''Pearls Are a Nuisance.'' *Dime Detective Magazine*, April 1939.

''Trouble Is My Business.'' *Dime Detective Magazine*, August 1939.

''I'll Be Waiting.'' *Saturday Evening Post*, October 14, 1939.

''The Bronze Door.'' *Unknown*, November 1939.

''No Crime in the Mountains.'' *Detective Story*, September 1941.

''Professor Bingo's Snuff.'' *Park East*, June–August 1951; *Go*, June–July 1951.

''Marlowe Takes on the Syndicate.'' *London Daily Mail*, April 6–10, 1959; also published as ''Wrong Pidgeon.'' *Manhunt*, February 1961. Reprinted as ''The Pencil.''

ESSAYS

''The Simple Art of Murder.'' *Atlantic Monthly*, December 1944.

"Writers in Hollywood." *Atlantic Monthly,* November 1945.

"Critical Notes." *Screen Writer,* July 1947.

"Oscar Night in Hollywood." *Atlantic Monthly,* March 1948.

"The Simple Art of Murder." *Saturday Review of Literature,* April 15, 1950. Revised version of the December 1944 *Atlantic Monthly* article.

"Ten Per Cent of Your Life." *Atlantic Monthly,* February 1952.

CORRESPONDENCE AND OTHER WORKS

The Blue Dahlia. Carbondale: Southern Illinois University Press, 1976. Reprint of Chandler's 1945 screenplay.

Chandler before Marlowe: Raymond Chandler's Early Prose and Poetry, 1908–1912. Edited by Matthew J. Bruccoli, introduction by Jacques Barzun. Columbia: University of South Carolina Press, 1973.

The Notebooks of Raymond Chandler and English Summer: A Gothic Romance. Edited by Frank MacShane. New York: Ecco, 1976.

Raymond Chandler on Writing. Boston: Houghton Mifflin, 1962.

Raymond Chandler Speaking. Edited by Dorothy Gardiner and Katherine Sorley Walker. Boston: Houghton Mifflin, 1962 [1977]. Contains excerpts from Chandler's letters and the surviving fragment of *The Poodle Springs Story.*

Selected Letters of Raymond Chandler. Edited by Frank MacShane. New York: Columbia University Press, 1981.

COLLECTED EDITIONS

The Simple Art of Murder. Boston: Houghton Mifflin, 1950. Contains selected stories and the essay "The Simple Art of Murder."

Killer in the Rain. Edited by Philip Durham. Boston: Houghton Mifflin, 1964. Contains selected short stories.

The Midnight Raymond Chandler. Edited by Joan Kahn. Boston: Houghton Mifflin, 1971. Contains *The Little Sister, The Long Goodbye,* and selected short works.

Raymond Chandler: Stories and Early Novels. Edited by Frank MacShane. New York: Library of America, 1995. Contains early magazine fiction, *The Big Sleep, Farewell, My Lovely,* and *The High Window.*

Raymond Chandler: Later Novels and Other Writings. Edited by Frank MacShane. New York: Library of America, 1995. Contains *The Lady in the Lake, The Little Sister, The Long Goodbye, Playback,* the screenplay for *Double Indemnity,* and selected essays and letters.

ARCHIVES AND BIBLIOGRAPHIES

Department of Special Collections, Research Library, University of California at Los Angeles. Contains manuscripts, notebooks, translations, memorabilia, and Chandleriana.

Bruccoli, Matthew J. *Raymond Chandler: A Checklist.* Kent, Ohio: Kent State University Press, 1968.

———. *Raymond Chandler: A Descriptive Bibliography.* Pittsburgh: University of Pittsburgh Press, 1979.

BIOGRAPHICAL AND CRITICAL STUDIES

Beekman, E. M. "Raymond Chandler and an American Genre." *Massachusetts Review* (Winter 1973): 149–73.

Durham, Philip. *Down These Mean Streets a Man Must Go: Raymond Chandler's Knight.* Chapel Hill: University of North Carolina Press, 1963.

Gross, Miriam, ed. *The World of Raymond Chandler.* New York: A & W, 1978.

Jameson, Fredric. "On Raymond Chandler." *Southern Review,* 6:624–650 (1970).

MacShane, Frank. *The Life of Raymond Chandler.* New York: Dutton, 1976.

Merling, William H. *Raymond Chandler.* Boston: Twayne, 1986.

Newlin, Keith. *Hardboiled Burlesque: Raymond Chandler's Comic Style.* New York: Brownstone, 1984.

Pendo, Stephen. *Raymond Chandler on Screen: His Novels into Film.* Metuchen, N.J.: Scarecrow, 1976.

Pollock, Wilson. "Man with a Toy Gun." *New Republic,* May 7, 1962, pp. 21–22.

Porter, J. C. "End of the Trail: The American West of Dashiell Hammett and Raymond Chandler." *Western Historical Quarterly* (October 1975):411–24.

Reck, T. S. "Raymond Chandler's Los Angeles." *Nation,* December 20, 1975, pp. 661–663.

Ruhm, Herbert. "Raymond Chandler: From Bloomsbury to the Jungle—and Beyond." In

Tough Guy Writers of the Thirties. Edited by David Madden. Carbondale: Southern Illinois University Press, 1968.

Speir, Jerry. *Raymond Chandler.* New York: Ungar, 1981.

Thorpe, Edward. *Chandlertown: The Los Angeles of Philip Marlowe.* New York: St. Martin's, 1983.

Wolfe, Peter. *Something More Than Night: The Case of Raymond Chandler.* Bowling Green, Ohio: Bowling Green State University Press, 1985.

SELECTED WORKS OF GENERAL RELEVANCE.

Auden, W. H. "The Guilty Vicarage." *Harper's,* May 1948.

Barzun, Jacques, and Wendell Hertig Taylor. *A Catalogue of Crime.* New York: Harper & Row, 1971.

Hartman, Geoffrey H. "Literature High and Low: The Case of the Mystery Story." In *The Fate of Reading and Other Essays.* Chicago: University of Chicago Press, 1975.

Macdonald, Ross. *On Crime Writing.* Santa Barbara, Calif.: Capra, 1973.

Most, Glenn W., and William W. Stowe, eds. *The Poetics of Murder: Detective Fiction and Literary Theory.* San Diego: Harcourt Brace Jovanovich, 1983.

Poirier, Richard. *A World Elsewhere: The Place of Style in American Literature.* New York: Oxford University Press, 1966.

Symons, Julian. *Bloody Murder: From the Detective Story to the Crime Novel: A History.* London: Penguin, 1972.

—PETER L. COOPER

John Cheever

1912–1982

JOHN CHEEVER was born May 27, 1912, in Quincy, Massachusetts, the son of Frederick L. and Mary Liley Cheever. His father's family traced their origins to Ezekiel Cheever, who came to Boston in 1637 and made so distinguished a career as an educator and a politician that Cotton Mather preached a funeral sermon in his praise. Cheever's father, a shoe salesman, was hit hard by the depression; but the diminutive Mary Cheever, an Englishwoman, salvaged the family finances by putting down her copy of *Middlemarch* (a book she claimed to have read thirteen times) and opening a gift shop. Soon after, Cheever left home in company with his older brother Fred. "I'd be damned," he recalled, "if I'd be supported by a gift shop."

He was further spurred toward early independence by being expelled from Thayer Academy, for smoking and laziness, when he was seventeen. That was the end of John Cheever's formal education but the beginning of his literary career, for it led to his first story, "Expelled," a jaundiced look at the illiberalism and hypocrisy of prep school life, which Malcolm Cowley accepted for the *New Republic* in 1930. Here he retells his own tale from behind the thinnest of fictional veneers; and many subsequent stories and novels also refer back, with more or less exactitude, to his own experience and to his family and its origins in New England. *The Wapshot Chron-*

icle, for example, draws directly on that heritage. Yet Cheever rightly insists that his "fiction is not cryptoautobiography," for a remarkable inventiveness distinguishes his writing from the merely documentary. Invention is a gift he has always had, rather, as he puts it, "like having a good baritone voice." In grade school his teacher would call on him to concoct tales for the entertainment of the other pupils, and young John learned to spin out his stories at length to avoid returning to classroom routine. He decided early to cultivate this gift and was ready to follow his muse when he was expelled from Thayer and family tensions became insufferable. He could go ahead and be a writer, his parents decided in their quirky moralistic way, so long as he promised never to think of becoming rich or famous.

Cheever moved first to Boston, and then to New York, where he lived in grubby surroundings and took odd jobs—doing book synopses for Metro-Goldwyn-Mayer, teaching writing at Barnard—to keep himself alive. As the 1930's wore on, he started to place his spare, tightly structured stories in *Atlantic, Hound and Horn, Story, Yale Review,* and, beginning in May 1935, the *New Yorker*. Harold Ross's young magazine was then looking for fresh material, and made a lasting find in Cheever. Of his more than 200 stories, half appeared originally in the

New Yorker. William Maxwell, another *New Yorker* hand, once described Cheever as a "story-making machine"; and it was through his repeated appearances in the magazine that he became known as a writer worth watching.

In March 1941 Cheever married Mary Winternitz, the daughter of a Yale medical school dean; they had three children: Susan, Benjamin Hale, and Federico.

Cheever's first book of stories, *The Way Some People Live,* came out in the spring of 1943, while he was serving in the army. There are thirty stories in the collection, most of them only a few pages long. The prose is plain-spoken and straightforward, lacking the rhetorical flourishes that characterize his longer fiction. At times the endings seem pat and the ironies come too easily; but there are brilliant moments that serve as talismans of his developing talent. Here as later Cheever invariably manages to be interesting. Here as always he possesses an uncanny ability to capture place, the furnishings and landscape and customs and talk that make a particular environment come alive. The actual settings range from down Maine, along the Northeast corridor to Washington, D.C., with most of the action centered in Boston, Newburyport, New York, and Westchester County.

In theme the stories fall into three nondiscrete groupings: love—the struggle between the sexes conducted by young marrieds and unmarrieds; money—the bitterness and caution of parents and grandparents fallen on evil times after relative affluence; and war—the ambiguous feelings of young men confronted with an unpleasant and unavoidable challenge. More narrowly, Cheever reveals some of his private preoccupations. Husbands are uxorious: one poor lead-footed chap takes dance lessons to please his wife, who may not be home when he gets there. Brothers are close, perhaps too close: two brothers separate upon realizing that they can only confront life directly if they go their separate ways. And emo-

tions are communicated through the senses: "Where have I seen you before? he wanted to ask her. . . . And yet he knew that he had never seen her before. It was like being thrown back to a forgotten afternoon by the taste of an apple or the odor of woodsmoke." But there is no going back to the past, for the idyllic locations of one's youth have become tearooms and boardinghouses.

With the publication of *The Enormous Radio and Other Stories,* in 1953, Cheever fulfilled the promise he had demonstrated in his first book. It is the best of his six collections of stories. Nearly all of the fourteen stories are brilliantly honed; and two of them—"Goodbye, My Brother" and "The Enormous Radio"—rank with the best short fiction of this century. Cheever continued to delineate the difficulties of married couples and to evoke the agony of reduced circumstances; he also included stories that persuasively render the life, upstairs and downstairs, of another environment, the Upper East Side apartment building. The stories are much longer, the characters more fully realized; and for the first time he invaded the world of the mysterious and miraculous that his later work was increasingly to inhabit.

Superficially, "Goodbye, My Brother" concerns the family reunion of the Pommeroys at Laud's Head, their summer place on the Atlantic. There are Mrs. Pommeroy and her four grown children: Chaddy, the eldest and favorite; Diana, who has had a series of lovers; the unnamed narrator, who teaches at prep school; and the youngest, the universally disliked Lawrence. Lawrence is afflicted with a baleful view of life. His sister used to call him "Little Jesus," his mother "The Croaker." He looks rather like the Puritan cleric they had all descended from, and derives his dourness from grandparents and great-grandparents "who seemed to hark back to the dark days of the ministry and to be animated by perpetual guilt and the deification of the scourge.'' Throwing off this mantle of ''guilt, self-denial, taciturnity, and penitence'' has been a trial of the spirit for all the Pommeroy siblings, but only Lawrence has failed. His life has consisted of a series of departures from people and places that did not measure up to his standards of probity. His mother, he concludes, is an alcoholic. Diana is promiscuous, and so is Chaddy's wife. Chaddy is dishonest. The narrator is a fool. The house will fall into the sea within five years. The cook should join a union. He has only come back to say goodbye to his family.

While Lawrence goes about morosely criticizing everyone, his wife ruins her days washing clothes with ''expiatory passion,'' and his children stay inside because they have spied a snake under the doorstep. Lawrence's piety and capacity for being judgmental make life especially miserable for the narrator, whose own cheerful frame of mind is in exact opposition to his younger brother's.

Lawrence does not like the sea; to the narrator, it represents ''the rich green soup of life.'' Where Lawrence detects decay, the narrator finds beauty. Lawrence lives in the country of morbidity, the narrator in that of joy. Finally, during a walk on the beach the narrator confronts his saturnine brother, and in exasperation bloodies his head with a blow—a foreshadowing of Ezekiel Farragut's murder of his similarly awful brother in *Falconer*. Lawrence is not badly hurt, but packs up and decamps with his unhappy brood, leaving the others to swim in the purifying waters of the Atlantic, ''naked, unshy, beautiful, and full of grace.''

Cheever relies on the consciousness of the narrator throughout, so that many of Lawrence's most odious thoughts are not articulated by him, but instead, are attributed to him by the narrator. It is as if the two brothers, in their total opposition, formed two halves of the same mind, and Cheever were setting down the story as a way of exorcising the dark spirit within. The narrator

knows that his mother and sister and older brother have their faults, but refuses to let that realization dim his own joyous response to the world. ''Oh, what can you do with a man like that?'' he asks of Lawrence. ''What can you do? How can you dissuade his eye in a crowd from seeking out the cheek with acne, the infirm hand; how can you teach him to respond to the inestimable greatness of the race, the harsh surface beauty of life . . . ?''

But Cheever is no Pollyanna. In ''The Enormous Radio,'' he cuts beneath that gleaming surface to reveal the festering decay. Jim and Irene Westcott meet the statistical average reported in alumni magazines of the better Eastern colleges. They have been married for nine years, have two young children, and go to the theater 10.3 times a year. They live in an apartment house near Sutton Place and have a maid; and someday they hope to move to Westchester. The vicissitudes of life seem to have barely touched them. Irene is ''a pleasant, rather plain girl with soft brown hair and a wide, fine forehead upon which nothing at all had been written.'' Although Jim's hair is graying, he still wears the same kind of clothes he wore at Andover, and cultivates an ''intentionally naive'' manner. But when Jim brings home a new, ugly, enormous radio to fill Irene's idle hours, he introduces a serpent into their apparent Eden.

The radio has magical powers, and instead of playing Beethoven quartets, it picks up the conversation emanating from the other flats in the apartment building. Together the Westcotts listen in on a nanny reading to her charge, an uproarious cocktail party, ''a monologue on salmon fishing in Canada, a bridge game, running comments on home movies of what had apparently been a fortnight at Sea Island, and a bitter family quarrel about an overdraft at the bank.'' At first this is amusing, but when Irene overhears demonstrations, in brutal language, ''of indigestion, carnal love, abysmal vanity, faith, and despair,'' she is astonished and troubled. In the elevator, she stares at her fellow tenants, wondering which one had overdrawn, which one was worried about her health, which one had told her maid not to serve the best Scotch to anyone who does not have white hair. The members of the Salvation Army band on the street corner, playing ''Jesus Is Sweeter,'' now seem ''much nicer'' to her than most of the people she knows.

Irene eavesdrops on increasingly more unpleasant matters, until one night Jim comes home to find her crying and disheveled. ''Go on up to 16-C, Jim!'' she screams. ''Mr. Osborn's beating his wife.'' Jim arranges to have the radio fixed instead, and they go to bed reassured that their own life is not as terrible and sordid and awful as the lives of their neighbors. But the next day they have a quarrel—about money, of course—and in an access of rage Jim shouts a litany of her secret sins:

''Why are you so Christly all of a sudden? What's turned you overnight into a convent girl? You stole your mother's jewelry before they probated her will. You never gave your sister a cent of that money that was intended for her— not even when she needed it. You made Grace Howland's life miserable, and where was all your piety and your virtue when you went to that abortionist?''

Together these two stories represent the poles of Cheever's dual vision. On the one hand he detests hypocrisy and repudiates attempts such as that of the Westcotts to shut out evil through calculated naiveté. On the other, he equally detests the lugubrious, and celebrates both ''the abundance of created things'' and the human capacity for love.

In an interview shortly after publication of *The Enormous Radio and Other Stories,* Cheever argued for the contemporary appropriateness of the short story form. The vigorous nineteenth-century novel, he remarked, had been based ''on parish life and lack of communications.'' The short story, by comparison, was ''determined by moving around from place to place, by the interrupted event,'' and so was ideally suited to an era of perpetual wanderings and communications bombardment.

Cheever's next book, however, was his first novel, *The Wapshot Chronicle* (1957). Its opening evocation of St. Botolphs, a decaying Massachusetts town, focuses on the kind of old-fashioned organic community that characteristically served as the background for the nineteenth-century novel. But the characters soon scatter; and Cheever follows them about, producing an episodic quality that offended more than one reviewer.

Read *The Wapshot Chronicle* for its comic flavor, they advised, or for its luminous style, its brilliant scenes, its ''inexhaustible flow of inventiveness''—but do not expect coherence, for, as one critic charged, the book was ''held together largely by spit and wire.'' In fact, the novel is organized, although loosely, around its two finest creations: the town of St. Botolphs and the character of Leander Wapshot.

The first chapter paints the old New England seaport, no longer the thriving village it once was, against the backdrop of the annual Fourth of July parade. St. Botolphs is populated largely by eccentrics: Cousin Honora Wapshot, who burns her mail unread; the exhibitionist Uncle Peepee Marshmallow; Doris, the male prostitute; Reba Heaslip, the antivivisectionist spinster; and banker Theophilus Gates, who keeps a ''For Sale'' sign on his front lawn as a poormouth gesture, although he has no intention of selling his home. Sarah Wapshot, wife of Leander and mother of two sons, Moses and Coverly (whose own adventures are later to be told), rides at the lectern on the Women's Club float during the parade, a symbol of prominence earned by her devotion to good works. She is the sort of woman who manages to retain her dignity even when small boys throw firecrackers and the horses bolt, turning the parade into a shambles. Meanwhile her husband, Leander, does ''not mind missing his wife's appearance in the parade.''

St. Botolphs is not heaven; but it tolerates and cares for its own. It is a fictional place, Cheever insists, made up of fragments from Quincy, Newburyport, and elsewhere that obviously lie close to the author's heart. Odors carry its nostalgic appeal. The downtown offices smell of dental preparations, floor oil, spittoons, and coal gas; the beach evokes the scent of lemons, wood smoke, roses, and dust. Cheever skirts sentimentality in establishing the town and its inhabitants through the device, common for him, of descending from the marvelous to the mundane, as for example, in the catalog of Sarah's civic accomplishments:

It was she who had organized a committee to raise money for a new parish home for Christ Church. It was she who had raised a fund for the granite horse trough at the corner and who, when the horse trough became obsolete, had had it planted with geraniums and petunias. The new high school on the hill, the new firehouse, the new traffic lights, the war memorial—yes, yes—even the clean public toilets in the railroad station were the fruit of Mrs. Wapshot's genius.

When the Wapshot boys leave to seek their fortunes (''Why do the young want to go away?''), the narrative shifts repeatedly from Moses to Coverly to the pithy journal of Leander; but St. Botolphs serves as a reference point throughout.

The well-favored Moses lands a top secret job in Washington, where he is exposed to the social-political pecking order. At an embassy concert he sees three bedraggled old women sneak in at intermission to seize abandoned concert programs and sneak out triumphantly. ''You wouldn't see anything like that in St. Botolphs.'' A man in Moses' boardinghouse has kept a graph of his social progress during his two years in Washington. He has been to dinner in Georgetown eighteen times, to the Pan-American Union four times, to the X embassy three times, to the B embassy once, to the White House once. ''You wouldn't find anything like that in St. Botolphs.'' Moses ventures to his cousin Justina's mansion in Clear Haven, a marvel of eclectic ostentation, in order to court the beautiful and unpredictable Melissa. To reach his lover at night, he must traverse the roofs of the castle. You wouldn't find anything like that in St. Botolphs, either.

The travels of the worrisome Coverly take him first to New York, where he is exposed to a myriad of new sights: high buildings, dachshunds, parking meters, a man in suede shoes, a woman blowing her nose on Kleenex. But he is most startled by the fineness of the sky above the caverns of Manhattan, for he had come to feel ''that the beauties of heaven centered above'' his home. In a funny scene, Coverly flunks his interview with a company psychiatrist and loses the job he had been promised. He studies computers, instead, and goes off to serve at a missile base near Remsen Park. Instead of softball games or band concerts, the administration sponsors rocket launchings on Saturday afternoons; whole families eat sandwiches, drink beer, and ''sit in bleachers to hear the noise of doom crack and see a fire that seemed to lick at the vitals of the earth.'' Remsen Park is a new community established for those who work at the missile base; and life there is both orderly and unfriendly. But Coverly sometimes feels homesick for St. Botolphs, ''for a place whose streets were as excursive and crooked as the human mind.''

Both Moses and Coverly marry and produce male heirs, thus ensuring themselves a bequest from rich Cousin Honora. The real hero of the novel, however, is their father, Leander Wapshot. Descended from sea captains, he is reduced to piloting a decrepit excursion launch from St. Botolphs to the amusement park across the bay at Nangasakit. Leander loses even that dubious eminence when his boat founders in a storm and, dredged up, is turned into "The Only Floating Gift Shoppe in New England" by Sarah. Bereft of occupation and desperate for esteem, he issues calls for help; but only the maid and Coverly respond. (Leander loves his older son Moses more, and had wanted Coverly aborted.) In the end he wets his wrists and temples, a gesture that might look like a man making the sign of the cross, and swims ritually to his death in the sea he loves.

Leander is no ordinary failure. Some of his ancestors had been schoolteachers instead of shipmasters, and he has inherited their talent for instruction. He has taught his sons such manly skills as how "to fell a tree, pluck and dress a chicken, sow, cultivate and harvest, catch a fish, save money, countersink a nail, make cider with a hand press, clean a gun, sail a boat, etc." As a rite of initiation, he takes each of his boys on fishing trips in the wilds of Canada. He attempts to instill in Moses and Coverly his own deep respect for ceremony as a stay against contemporary chaos:

He would like them to grasp that the unobserved ceremoniousness of his life was a gesture or sacrament toward the excellence and continuousness of things. . . . The coat he wore at dinner, the grace he said at table, the fishing trip he took each spring, the bourbon he drank at dark and the flower in his buttonhole were all forms that he hoped his sons might understand and perhaps copy.

The most important lesson Leander teaches, however, has to do with love.

When Coverly's wife Betsey runs home to Georgia, he feels his maleness compromised by homosexual stirrings. In distress he writes his father for reassurance, and the old man responds with a Chaucerian tale of how he himself had disposed of a homosexual pursuer by dumping the contents of a chamberpot on his head. "All in love," he reminds Coverly, "is not larky and fractious." Coverly imagines attending a school of love that would include classes on the moment of recognition; symposia on indiscriminate erotic impulses; courses on the hazards of uxoriousness; and lectures on that hairline boundary where lovers cease to nourish and begin to devour one another. "It would be a hard course for Coverly . . . and he would be on probation most of the time, but he would graduate." Love might immensely complicate life—women make things difficult for all the Wapshot men—but the alternative is unthinkable.

Leander's life has been touched with tragedy, but he faces his fortune with an attitude of joyous acceptance. Appropriately the novel ends not with his watery suicide, but with Coverly's discovery, in a copy of Shakespeare, of his father's final note of instruction to his sons:

Never put whisky into hot water bottle crossing borders of dry states or countries. Rubber will spoil taste. Never make love with pants on. Beer on whisky, very risky. Whisky on beer, never fear. Never eat apples, peaches, pears, etc. while drinking whisky except long French-style dinners, terminating with fruit. Other viands have mollifying effect. Never sleep in moonlight. Known by scientists to induce madness. Should bed stand beside window on clear night draw shades before retiring. Never hold cigar at right-angles to fingers. Hayseed. Hold cigar at diagonal. Remove band or not as you prefer. Never wear red necktie. Provide light snorts for ladies if entertaining. Effects of harder stuff on frail sex sometimes disastrous. Bathe in cold water every morning. Painful but exhilarating. Also reduces horniness. Have haircut once a week. Wear dark clothes after 6 P.M. Eat fresh fish for breakfast when available. Avoid kneeling in unheated stone churches. Ecclesiastical dampness causes prematurely gray hair. Fear tastes like a rusty knife and do not let her into your house. Courage tastes of blood. Stand up straight. Admire the world. Relish the love of a gentle woman. Trust in the Lord.

Leander's catalog, which begins with such subjects as liquor, sex, clothes, and sleep, rises to a triple command to his sons: to love the natural creation, to love a good woman, and to love God.

With its blend of gusto and nostalgia, ribaldry and acceptance, *The Wapshot Chronicle* may strike some as not serious enough, basically an entertainment. That charge cannot be brought against Cheever's sequel, *The Wapshot Scandal* (1964), for here the presiding spirit is demonic. In "Homage to Shakespeare," one of Cheever's early uncollected stories, the narrator's grandfather detects "gleaming through the vanity of every incident . . . the phallus and the skull." Similarly it is degrading lust and the fear of death that dominate *The Wapshot Scandal*. But the difference between the two novels, as George Garrett has observed, may be measured in olfactory terms, for those smells that so often provide sensuous enjoyment in *Chronicle* have virtually disappeared in *Scandal*.

Cheever's second novel opens like the first with an idyllic small-town scene. It is snowing in St. Botolphs on Christmas eve. The carolers make their rounds, stopping along the way for hospitable sustenance. Honora Wapshot provides them with hot buttered rum and her customary recitation by heart of Emerson's "Snow-Storm." All is neighborly, it seems to Mr. Jowett the stationmaster, who, despite his railroad pass, has never wanted to travel far. In St. Botolphs, he thinks, "everybody was going home, and everybody had a home to go to. It was one place in a million. . . ."

Cheever finds ways to blur this idealized picture, however. Not everyone is motivated by the Christmas spirit alone. Trees are being trimmed by the decorously clad all over town, but the widow Wilston and Alby Hooper, an itinerant carpenter, have been drinking bourbon for two days and wear nothing at all while decorating theirs. The minister, Mr. Applegate, has also been tippling, and hearing the singing of the carolers, he "felt his faith renewed, felt that an infinity of unrealized possibilities lay ahead of them, a tremendous richness of peace, a renaissance without brigands, an ecstacy of light and color, a kingdom! Or was this gin!"

Foreboding death also casts its shadow over the holiday celebration. The reclusive Mr. Spofford, unable to give his kittens away, tries to drown them but, instead, falls into the river himself. No one hears his cries for help, and "it would be weeks before he was missed." In addition the tone of the narrator undercuts the rosiness of the scene, as Cheever adopts the disinterested voice of a social historian. Twice in the first three pages he insists on his distance from his subject by referring casually to "the time of which I'm writing." But the time is manifestly the present, or rather, only last year, for the novel ends on the following Christmas, when Coverly comes back to a diminished St. Botolphs: Mr. Jowett is nowhere to be found, and only four worshippers attend Mr. Applegate's Christmas eve service. Yet, for the moment, the town stands as a beacon of hope and love against which the historian assesses the ills of modern life. A young girl who has left home calls her parents from Prescott's drugstore in St. Botolphs, assuring her mother that she is not drunk. Outside the carolers sing "Good King Wenceslas," but the voice of the wandering girl, "with its prophecy of gas stations and motels, freeways and all-night supermarkets, had more to do with the world to come than the singing on the green."

St. Botolphs, although it has not ceased to exist, represents our better past. But the inescapable present takes over, for the chief character of the novel, as one reviewer has observed, is the twentieth century itself—or more precisely the post-World War II years. In an anthology published in 1959, Cheever indicated his disenchantment with the age. The decade, he wrote, had begun with great promise, but halfway through the 1950's

. . . something went terribly wrong. The most useful image I have . . . is of a man in a quagmire, looking into a tear in the sky. I am not speaking here of despair, but of confusion. I fully expected the trout streams of my youth to fill up with beer cans and the meadows to be covered with houses; I may even have expected to be separated from most of my moral and ethical heritage; but the forceful absurdities of life today find me unprepared. Something has gone very wrong, and I do not have the language, the imagery, or the concepts to describe my apprehensions. I come back again to the quagmire and the torn sky.

In *The Wapshot Scandal,* he tried to put those inchoate apprehensions down on paper.

Once again Moses and Coverly go out into the world, but the attack on modernity implied in *The Wapshot Chronicle* now takes an overt form. Cheever castigates the surface absurdities of the way we live: wearing wash and wear shirts to the drive-in movie, uttering debased language, and being pursued by the demons of avarice and lust. But the malaise lies still deeper.

Coverly is assigned to the missile base at Talifer, most of which is concealed beneath the cow pasture of what once was a farm. There remain

a house, a barn, a clump of trees and a split-rail fence, and the abandoned buildings with the gantries behind them had a nostalgic charm. They

were signs of the past, and whatever the truth may have been, they appeared to be signs of a rich and a natural way of life.

Talifer, by contrast, epitomizes artificiality. For reasons of security the place is never mentioned in the newspapers; it has no public existence. As in Remsen Park, the resident scientists and technicians are persistently unfriendly. Betsey Wapshot plans an elaborate cocktail party, sending out dozens of invitations, but only four people attend: she and Coverly, and the bartender and maid she has hired. Talifer seems to her as "hostile, incomprehensible and threatening as the gantry lines on the horizon."

In charge of operations is the brilliant Dr. Cameron. He is perceptive enough to realize that a "highly advanced civilization might well destroy itself with luxury, alcoholism, sexual license, sloth, greed and corruption." Civilization, he feels, "is seriously threatened by biological and mental degeneration." But he is unperturbed by the danger of nuclear holocaust; and he dispassionately carries out his task, which is to plot the end of the world. At a congressional hearing, Cameron is confronted by an old senator who speaks from the past on behalf of the future.

"We possess Promethean powers," he reminds the scientist, "but don't we lack the awe, the humility, that primitive man brought to the sacred fire? . . . If I should have to make some final statement, and I shall very soon for I am nearing the end of my journey, it would be in the nature of a thanksgiving for stout-hearted friends, lovely women, blue skies, the bread and wine of life. Please don't destroy the earth, Dr. Cameron," he sobbed. "Oh, please, please don't destroy the earth."

Moses and Melissa inhabit another environment entirely, the New York suburb of Proxmire Manor. But even in this comfortable and predictable suburb, technology prevails. Gertrude

Lockhart is driven to drink, adultery, and suicide by her inability to cope with the persistent breakdown of the modern conveniences—plumbing, heating, washing machine, and refrigerator—that presumably are intended to make existence less rather than more complicated. And Melissa, bored by the empty round of social life, and suddenly obsessed by intimations of mortality, commits the unpardonable sin of taking the grocery boy Emile for a lover.

It is appropriate that Emile should be so employed, for a supermarket motif runs through the novel. All across America people feed on frozen meat, frozen french fried potatoes, and frozen peas; but when blindfolded they cannot identify the peas, and the potatoes taste of soap. The supermarket where these viands are sold seems, in "A Vision of the World" (a story written at about the same time), to be the product of another civilization entirely. You would need a camera, the narrator of that story suspects, "to record a supermarket on a Saturday afternoon," for our language, which was based on "the accrual of centuries of intercourse," was traditional and except for "the shapes of the pastry, there was nothing traditional to be seen at the bakery counter. . . ." Promotional jargon substitutes for the language we've inherited. In *The Wapshot Scandal,* an entire family converses in advertising slogans while lunching at an airport restaurant:

"My!" the mother exclaimed. "Taste those bite-sized chunks of white Idaho turkey meat, reinforced with riboflavin, for added zest."

"I like the crispy, crunchy potato chips," the boy said. "Toasted to a golden brown in health-giving infrared ovens and topped with imported salt."

"I like the spotless rest rooms," said the girl, "operated under the supervision of a trained nurse and hygienically sealed for our comfort, convenience and peace of mind."

"Winstons taste good," piped the baby in his high chair, "like a cigarette should. Winstons have *flavor.*"

This is amusing, but it also serves as a foreshadowing of our last glimpse of Melissa, reduced to unhappy exile.

She travels to Rome through the intervention of Emile. As an employee of a supermarket, he is charged with the distribution of plastic eggs containing prizes. There are five golden eggs worth vacations in European capitals, and he places the egg for the trip to Rome on Melissa's lawn. Later he comes to Europe himself, where Melissa "purchases" him during a slave auction on the island of Ladros. They live together in Rome, but are snubbed by even the dregs of expatriate society. Melissa is last seen with her hair dyed red, bewilderedly seeking some solace from the blows life has dealt her while shopping at the American supermarket on the Via delle Sagiturius:

No willow grows aslant this stream of men and women and yet it is Ophelia she most resembles, gathering her fantastic garland not of cornflowers, nettles and long purples, but of salt, pepper, Bab-o, Kleenex, frozen codfish balls, lamb patties, hamburger, bread, butter, dressing, an American comic book for her son and for herself a bunch of carnations. She chants, like Ophelia, snatches of old tunes. "Winstons taste good like a cigarette should. Mr. Clean, Mr. *Clean,*" and when her coronet or fantastic garland seems completed she pays her bill and carries her trophies away, no less dignified a figure of grief than any other.

The force driving Melissa to moral degradation is the fear of death. Indeed, the imminence of death pervades *The Wapshot Scandal.* Cheever ingeniously states the theme by way of an experiment in scientific approaches to literature. To while away his time at Talifer, Coverly feeds the poetry of John Keats into a computer, and in violation of all laws of probability (the author announced in front matter that all the characters in his book were fictitious, as was much of the science) the most frequent words in Keats's vocabulary spell out a message in verse for 1960, not 1820: "Silence blendeth grief's awakened fall/ The golden realms of death take all/ Love's bitterness exceeds its grace/ That bestial scar on the angelic face/ Marks heaven with gall."

The beautiful Melissa succumbs to her own bestiality after encountering a series of harbingers of death. A despicable old man, "craning his neck like an adder," follows her home. The doorbell rings, and when it is the grocery boy and not her frightening pursuer, she feels her first stirrings of desire for Emile. Later she goes to town for a glimpse of Emile's mother, who works in a florist shop. A man comes in to order flowers for his deceased sister, and Melissa is visited by a premonition of her own death:

The image, hackneyed and poignant, that came to her was of life as a diversion, a festival from which she was summoned by the secret police of extinction, when the dancing and the music were at their best. I do not want to leave, she thought. I do not ever want to leave.

She learns that Gertrude Lockhart has hanged herself. She is afraid of the ubiquitous modern killer, cancer. (One of Coverly's co-workers has twenty-seven friends who are dying of cancer, none having more than a year to live.) And so Melissa determines to dance, drink, and fornicate while she may. Sex makes her feel alive. (It serves a similar function for Dr. Cameron, for only in the arms of his mistress, a Roman tart, can he feel "the chill of death go off his bones.") So Melissa drifts in the current of her lust. At the end she walks in the Borghese Gardens, "feeling the weight of habit a woman of her age or any other age carries from one country to another; habits of eating, drinking, dress, rest,

anxiety, hope and, in her case, the fear of death."

But there are better ways of facing death. About to board an airplane, Coverly reads in the afternoon paper of a jet crash in which seventy-three persons died. His own flight is delayed because of engine trouble. When he finally boards, the lady sitting next to him is obviously terrified; and with good reason, as it turns out. The plane is robbed by skyjackers, who announce over the intercom that the passengers are "helpless." Everyone sits silent with fear, "sixty-five or seventy strangers, their noses pressed against the turmoil of death." But then a woman sitting forward begins to sing "Nearer, My God, to Thee" in her common church soprano; others join in, and even those not knowing the words come in strong on the refrain. "They sang more in rebelliousness than in piety; they sang because it was something to do. And merely in having found something to do they had confounded the claim that they were helpless." The fear of death need not conquer all.

Love—unlike the carnal urgings of Melissa or Dr. Cameron—provides an alternative to lust. Young Miles Howland and Mary Perkins of St. Botolphs have become lovers, but they plan to marry in the spring. Miles, an innocent choir boy, cannot believe that he has sinned, since he can "at the same moment praise his Saviour and see the shape of his lady's foot."

Another way of confronting death is offered by Cousin Honora, whose fate is contrasted to Melissa's. (Far more than any other Cheever novel, *The Wapshot Scandal* devotes itself to women.) The eccentric old lady refuses to pay bus fares, but sends the bus company a check once a year. To the government, however, she sends nothing; and when the Internal Revenue's computer finally catches up with her, she flees to Italy. Although she and Melissa are in Rome at the same time, they do not see each other and, indeed, would not have much to say if they did.

Honora has a place she belongs to, and finds permanent expatriation inconceivable. She cheerfully accepts extradition and returns to St. Botolphs, where she drinks whiskey, refuses food, and manages to die a happy though impoverished death. Her scandal is more forgivable than Melissa's, for her tax delinquencies have not been motivated by self-concern. Always the resident philanthropist of St. Botolphs, Honora's last request is that Coverly provide Christmas dinner for the residents of the Home for the Blind. He does so after rescuing Moses, now totally alcoholic, from the widow Wilston.

Coverly's problem, articulated in the first novel, is "to build some kind of bridge between Leander's world and that world where he sought a fortune." In the sequel the problem becomes more acute—and it is clearly Cheever's problem as well. The dignity of the blind at their Christmas feast helps somewhat, for despite their cruel handicap they "seemed to be advocates for those in pain; for the taste of misery as fulsome as rapture, for the losers, the goners, the flops, . . . for all those who fear death." So does the ghost of Leander, for he once more issues his benediction from beyond the grave, this time through a note found in his wallet: "Let us consider that the soul of a man is immortal, able to endure every sort of good and every sort of evil."

That final grace note comes hard after the novel's evocation of evil. Cheever is on record that writing *The Wapshot Scandal* cost him some pain: "I never much liked the book and when it was done I was in a bad way." And despite its dark power, the novel is Cheever's least successful, being flawed by certain inconsistencies of character and tone: Dr. Cameron is sympathetic in one scene, despicable in the next; one is not sure whether the downfall of Gertrude Lockhart is to be taken comically or seriously; a character's name unaccountably changes; and St. Botolphs sometimes takes on an improbably rosy hue.

In *The Wapshot Scandal*, the suburb of Proxmire Manor functions as setting less than one third of the time. In Cheever's stories of this period, however, the suburb is the preeminent point of focus. *The Housebreaker of Shady Hill and Other Stories* (1958) consists of eight stories about the inhabitants of Shady Hill. This commuter suburb is a kind of Winesburg, Ohio, a gallery of grotesques living amid the manicured lawns and impeccable interiors.

Money and drink are the worms in the apple. Johnny Hake falls on hard times and steals $900 from a neighbor. Cash Bentley, longing for his youth, breaks a leg hurdling furniture at a party, and then is killed in midhurdle when his wife Louise misaims the starting gun. Francis Weed, survivor of a plane crash in "The Country Husband"—the best of the stories—falls in love with the babysitter, before being restored to his normal lack of emotion by woodworking and common sense. Young Amy, worried about her parents' excessive drinking, empties gin bottles in the sink. The Crutchmans lead a compulsively frenetic social life. Mean Mr. Baker gets his comeuppance from a secretary he seduced and then fired. Will Pym, sure that his wife is deceiving him, knocks down her suspected lover. Marcie Flint, a neglected housewife, takes up civic affairs, including one with a socially unacceptable fellow from the much-scorned "development" nearby.

Some People, Places & Things That Will Not Appear in My Next Novel (1961) and *The Brigadier and the Golf Widow* (1964) are two other story collections containing penetrating depictions of suburban life. "The Death of Justina," in the first, provides a link between the two Wapshot novels. The setting is Proxmire Manor, whence Moses commutes to the city to write commercials for a tonic called Elixircol. Justina comes for a visit and dies quietly after a luncheon party. The trouble is that Proxmire Manor, in its unsuccessful attempt to eliminate "the thorny side of human nature," has decreed that no one may die in Zone B. To obtain an exemption to this idiotic rule and have the old lady buried, Moses is forced to summon up the most vigorous arguments. Meanwhile, at the office his tyrannical boss insists on more and more copy praising the virtues of Elixircol. Moses composes black comedy, instead ("You have been inhaling lethal atomic waste for the last twenty-five years and only Elixircol can save you"), then turns out a Madison Avenue version of the 23rd Psalm and goes home, presumably jobless, to start drinking again.

Afflicted with a strong sense of his heritage, Moses cannot accommodate himself to the contemporary:

There are some Americans who, although their fathers emigrated from the Old World three centuries ago, never seem to have quite completed the voyage and I am one of these. I stand, figuratively, with one wet foot on Plymouth Rock, looking with some delicacy, not into a formidable and challenging wilderness but onto a half-finished civilization embracing glass towers, oil derricks, suburban continents and abandoned movie houses and wondering why, in this most prosperous, equitable, and accomplished world—where even the cleaning women practice the Chopin preludes in their spare time—everyone should seem to be so disappointed.

The note Moses strikes is one of sadness. Like Cheever himself, he might be criticized for not getting angry enough.

A more ambitious story, and one of the author's best, is "The Swimmer" from *The Brigadier and the Golf Widow*. It was "a terribly difficult story to write," taking Cheever many times longer than his usual three-day gestation period. The narrative itself is deceptively simple. Neddy Merrill, apparently in the prime of a prosperous and attractive life, sets out one Sunday to cross eight miles of suburban space by water—or, more specifically, by way of "that string of swimming pools, that quasi-subterranean stream that curved across the county." He decides to name this stream after his wife Lucinda. The journey becomes for him a quest undertaken in the spirit of "a pilgrim, an explorer, a man with a destiny." But reality—the whistle of a train, the main highway that must be crossed on foot—keeps intruding. As his trip proceeds, Neddy becomes increasingly weak and cold with fatigue, and the neighbors whose pools he swims in become progressively more insulting. Finally he arrives home, exhausted, to find that his house is boarded up and his wife and four daughters have moved on.

So artfully has Cheever wrought this story that one is liable on first reading to miss the implied progression from day to night, summer to winter, vigorous manhood to old age. Neddy Merrill's Sunday swim thus represents the downward course of his life, as he falls victim to financial and alcoholic problems. But the story takes on mythic overtones as well, with its timeless themes of journey and discovery (as Frederick Bracher has observed) combining the patterns of the *Odyssey* and "Rip Van Winkle." Upon finishing "The Swimmer," Cheever did not write another short story for a long time; but he began work on *Bullet Park* (1969), his most pervasive examination of suburbia.

His concentration on suburban settings came naturally enough, following his move from New York City to Ossining on the east bank of the Hudson, a move he, like many another, made to ensure better schools for the children. Certain critics of an urban cast of mind did not easily forgive Cheever's shifting his fictional milieu from Manhattan to suburbia. Suburbia and its denizens, they maintained, were too dull and bland to constitute fit subjects for fiction, although Cheever himself finds Ossining in some ways "wilder than the East Village."

Since 1945, American fiction has been prone to demographic lag, with most major writers concerning themselves with the city while the out-migration to the suburbs reached and passed its peak. Cheever is one of the few good writers (John Updike and Philip Roth are others) who have dealt with suburbia seriously and without sneering. The woman who saves Plaid Stamps and dreams of the prizes they will someday bring her may be mistaken to do so, but she is indisputably real; and Cheever refuses to dismiss her as a figure of farce. Not that he glorifies suburban life-styles; quite the reverse. "God preserve me," the narrator of "The Trouble of Marcie Flint" comments,

from women who dress like *toreros* to go to the supermarket, and from cowhide dispatch cases, and from flannels and gabardines. Preserve me from word games and adulterers, from basset hounds and swimming pools and frozen canapes and Bloody Marys and smugness and syringa bushes and P.T.A. meetings.

But Cheever has always insisted that his purpose is not to be a social critic or a defender of suburbia. "It goes without saying that the people in my stories and the things that happen to them could take place anywhere." He aims, instead, for accurate and interesting portrayals of the way we live now, and seeks the universal in the particular.

If not a social critic, Cheever is clearly distressed by the continued trashing of America. From the beginning his writing has bespoken his delight in the creation, his sensuous rapport with nature. One of the reasons he left prep school, according to his first published story, was that he was tired of seeing spring "with walls and awnings to intercept the sweet sun and the hard fruit." He wanted to go outdoors "to feel and taste the air and be among the shadows." This boyhood yearning has lasted all his life. Now in his sixties, he still cuts firewood, bicycles, skates, skis, walks, sails, and swims. Indeed, he invests nature with religious correspondences reminiscent of the Transcendentalists. "The trout streams open for the resurrection. The

crimson cloths at Pentecost and the miracle of the tongues meant swimming." One trouble with southern California, in his view, is that the trees there are not indigenous but imported.

In his fiction since 1960 Cheever has frequently warned against the hazards presented in the unequal struggle between nature and technological progress. The symbols that stand for such heedless progress are almost invariably associated with transportation. One excellent story, "The Angel of the Bridge," specifically focuses on the relationship between modern means of travel and the dispiriting quality of contemporary existence. The story is built around three phobias. The first is that of the narrator's seventy-four-year-old mother, who came from St. Botolphs and who insists on skating on the Rockefeller Center rink at the lunch hour, "dressed like a hat-check girl." She used to skate in St. Botolphs, and she continues to waltz around the ice in New York City "as an expression of her attachment to the past." For all her seeming bravado, however, she panics and is unable to board an airplane. The second phobia is that of the narrator's successful older brother, who because of his fear of elevators ("I'm afraid the building will fall down") is reduced to changing jobs and apartments. Finally, the narrator himself, who had felt superior to both his mother and his brother, finds that he is quite unable to drive across the George Washington Bridge because of an unreasonable, unshakable conviction that the bridge will collapse. On a trip to Los Angeles (for he does not mind flying), it comes to him that this

terror of bridges was an expression of my clumsily concealed horror of what is becoming of the world. . . . The truth is, I hate freeways and Buffalo Burgers. Expatriated palm trees and monotonous housing developments depress me. The continuous music on special-fare trains exacerbates my feeling. I detest the destruction of familiar landmarks, I am deeply troubled by the misery and drunkenness I find among my friends, I abhor the dishonest practices. And it was at the highest point in the arc of a bridge that I became aware suddenly of the depth and bitterness of my feelings about modern life, and of the profoundness of my yearning for a more vivid, simple, and peaceable world.

His problem is temporarily resolved when a young girl hitchhiker, carrying a small harp, sings him across a bridge with "folk music, mostly." "I gave my love a cherry that had no stone," she sings, and he can for the moment negotiate the trip across the Hudson, the sweetness and innocence of the music from the past restoring him to "blue-sky courage, the high spirits of lustiness, and ecstatic sereneness."

In *Bullet Park* the principal characters seek a similar angel to restore them to spiritual and psychological health. Once more, the dominant symbol for their ills comes from the world of transportation. Railroads, airlines, and freeways—which shrink space, distort time, and confuse perceptions—stand for a deep psychological alienation. Cheever's contemporary suburbanites are terrified by the hurtling freeway automobiles, high-speed trains, and jet airplanes that make it possible for them to sleep in Bullet Park, work in New York, and fly across the continent on a business call.

This emphasis grows naturally out of the concentration on the journey motif in "The Swimmer." The concept of life as a journey dates to the earliest legends; but in Cheever's work the theme is obsessive. His characters are forever in transit. The dominant metaphor is that of the risky journey that modern man takes each day. There are some who manage to miss the "planes, trains, boats and opportunities," but such derelicts are the exception. Normally, the Cheever protagonist has, in the eyes of the world, "made it." The house in Bullet Park

stands as emblem of his success, as does the daily trip into the city.

Although his plight may be extreme, Neddy Merrill is symptomatic of the restless and rootless denizens who inhabit Cheever's suburbs. "The people of Bullet Park," for instance, "intend not so much to have arrived there as to have been planted and grown there," but there is nothing organic or indigenous or lasting about their transplantation. The evenings call them back to "the blood-memory of travel and migration," and in due time they will be on their way once more, accompanied by "disorder, moving vans, bank loans at high interest, tears and desperation." They are, almost all of them, only temporary visitors, and they find themselves, most of them, in the same commuter train every morning.

To underline the rootless quality of Bullet Park, the narrator once more, as in *The Wapshot Scandal,* adopts the pose of an anthropologist looking back on what is, in fact, current American society. Although it is not raining, Eliot Nailles turns on his windshield wipers. "The reason for this was that (at the time of which I'm writing) society had become so automative and nomadic that nomadic signals or means of communication had been established by the use of headlights, parking lights, signal lights and windshield wipers." For the power of speech, for face-to-face communication, contemporary society substitutes mechanical symbols. One character in the book is convinced that her windshield wipers give her "sage and coherent advice" on the stock market; Nailles is urged by the diocesan bishop "to turn on [his] windshield wipers to communicate [his] faith in the resurrection of the dead and the life of the world to come."

The technology of rapid movement (which is both a cause and effect of the development of places like Bullet Park) attempts, in short, to provide a convenient, painless substitute for the true affirmation of one's spiritual faith. Lent passes; and only Nailles remembers the terrible journey of Paul of Tarsus:

"Thrice was I beaten with rods, once was I stoned, thrice I suffered shipwreck, a night and a day I have been in the deep; in journeyings often, in perils of waters, in perils of robbers, in perils by mine own countrymen, in perils by the heathen, in perils in the city, in perils in the wilderness, in perils in the sea, in perils among false brethren; in weariness and painfulness, in watchings often, in hunger and thirst, in fastings often, in cold and nakedness."

But what possible analogy can be drawn between the trials of Saint Paul and the seemingly placid lives of Eliot and Nellie Nailles in Bullet Park?

Eliot Nailles, the principal figure in the novel, is a middle-aged businessman with a job he would rather not talk about. Educated as a chemist, he is employed to merchandise a mouthwash called Spang. He is kind and uxorious; a conventional family man with old-fashioned values. If he had the talent, he would write poems celebrating his wife Nellie's thighs. He loves her, as he loves their only child, Tony, possessively and protectively; his love is "like some limitless discharge of a clear amber fluid that would surround them, cover them, preserve them and leave them insulated but visible like the contents of an aspic." He thinks "of pain and suffering as a principality, lying somewhere beyond the legitimate borders of western Europe," and hardly expects any distressing foreign bodies to penetrate his protective fluid.

But suburbia offers only false security. Neither Nailles nor Nellie nor their son Tony, a high school senior, can escape the ills of modern society. Nellie goes to New York to see a matinee in which a male actor casually displays his penis; outside the theater college youngsters carry placards proclaiming four-letter words; on a bus one young man kisses another on the ear. She returns from her disconcerting afternoon "bewildered and miserable." In an hour, she thinks during the train ride home, she will be herself again, "honest, conscientious, intelligent, chaste, etc. But if her composure depended upon shutting doors, wasn't her composure contemptible?" She decides not to tell Nailles about her experience, and it is just as well; absolutely monogamous and faithful himself, he is shocked and disturbed by promiscuity or homosexuality.

Thus, nothing much to trouble Eliot Nailles comes of Nellie's day in the city. The case is quite different when Tony, suffering through a prolonged spell of depression, refuses to get out of bed or to eat normally. Physically, there is nothing wrong with the boy; psychologically, he is consumed by a sadness that is impervious to the ministrations of the family doctor, a psychiatrist, and a specialist on somnambulatory phenomena. After Tony has been in bed for seventeen days and it appears he will not survive his depression, Nailles also breaks down and finds himself unable to ride the commuter train without a massive tranquilizer.

The locomotive, screaming across the countryside, was the preeminent machine invading the nineteenth-century American Garden of Eden. We have constructed an Atropos, a fate that will soon slip beyond our control, as Thoreau warned. Do we ride upon the railroad or the railroad upon us? Emerson wondered. Dickinson's iron horse, paradoxically "docile and omnipotent," stuffed itself on nature as it hooted its way to its stable door. And Hawthorne, in "The Celestial Railroad," made it clear (as the folk song affirmed) that you can't get to heaven in a railroad car.

But the railroad has been supplanted in the mid-twentieth century by other, more frightening technological monsters. Take, for example, the jet airplane, which enables one "to have supper in Paris and, God willing, breakfast at home, and here is a whole new creation of self-knowledge, new images for love and death and the insubstantiality and the importance of our affairs.'' This is no conventional paean to the wonders of progress, for ''God willing'' emphasizes the risk attendant upon jet travel, and if the ''affairs'' that send us hurtling across oceans and continents are truly insubstantial, without body, they are hardly important enough to justify the trip.

Just how trivial these affairs are, in fact, is emphasized in Cheever's much anthologized ''The Country Husband.'' Francis Weed survives a crash landing on a flight from Minneapolis to New York, and later that same evening he attempts, unsuccessfully, to interest someone—his wife, children, neighbors, friends—in what happened. Nothing in his suburb of Shady Hill ''was neglected; nothing had not been burnished''—and the residents want things to stay that way. They do not wish to hear of disasters, much less disasters narrowly averted; they shut tragedy, especially potential tragedy, out of their consciousness. Cheever's fiction tries to wake them up, to point to the thorns on the rosebushes, to call attention to the hazards of the journey.

Trains play a somewhat ambiguous role in Cheever's gallery of horrors. To the extent that they are reminiscent of a quieter past, they summon up a certain nostalgia. ''Paint me a small railroad station then,'' *Bullet Park* begins, and not by accident, for the ''setting seems to be in some way at the heart of the matter. We travel by plane, oftener than not, and yet the spirit of our country seems to have remained a country of railroads.'' The train mistily evokes loneliness and promise, loss and reassurance:

You wake in a pullman bedroom at three a.m. in a city the name of which you do not know and may never discover. A man stands on the platform with a child on his shoulders. They are waving goodbye to some traveler, but what is the child doing up so late and why is the man crying? On a siding beyond the platform there is a lighted dining car where a waiter sits alone at a table, adding up his accounts. Beyond this is a water tower and beyond this a well-lighted and empty street. Then you think happily that this is your country—unique, mysterious and vast. One has no such feelings in airplanes, airports and the trains of other nations.

A romantic aura envelops any journey, by night, along the tracks of the continent. But in the small railway station at Bullet Park, designed by an architect ''with some sense of the erotic and romantic essence of travel,'' the windows have been broken, the clock face smashed, the waiting room transformed into a ''warlike ruin.''

The train trip is one thing; commutation is something else. The commuter station is the site of the sudden death, one morning, of Harry Shinglehouse, who is introduced and disposed of within a few sentences. Shinglehouse stands on the Bullet Park platform with Nailles and Paul Hammer (who has determined, in his madness, to crucify Tony Nailles), waiting for the 7:56, when ''down the tracks came the Chicago express, two hours behind schedule and going about ninety miles an hour.'' The train rips past, its noise and commotion like ''the vortex of some dirty wind tunnel,'' and tears off into the distance. Then Nailles notices one ''highly polished brown loafer'' lying amid the cinders, and realizes that Shinglehouse has been sucked under the train.

The next day, troubled by his memory of this incident and by Tony's refusal to get out of bed, Nailles misses his usual connection, takes a local that makes twenty-two stops between Bullet Park and Grand Central Station, and finds that he has to get off the train every few stops to summon up the courage to go on. ''Nailles's sense of being alive was to bridge or link the disparate environments and rhythms of his world, and one of his principal bridges—that between his white house and his office—had collapsed.'' To restore this sense of continuity and to alleviate his commutation hysteria, Nailles begins taking a massive tranquilizer every morning that floats him into the city like Zeus upon a cloud. When the pills run out, however, he discovers that the doctor who prescribed them has been closed down by the county medical society and desperately turns to a pusher to get a supply of the gray and yellow capsules. Even after Tony is miraculously restored to health by the unlikely savior, Swami Rutuola, Nailles continues each Monday morning, ''to meet his pusher in the supermarket parking lot, the public toilet, the laundromat, and a variety of cemeteries.'' And even after Nailles, with the help of the Swami, manages to rescue Tony from crucifixion, ''Tony went back to school on Monday [these are the final words of the novel] and Nailles—drugged—went off to work and everything was as wonderful, wonderful, wonderful, wonderful as it had been.''

Cheever's suburbanites drink, smoke, and party a great deal, while their children stare fixedly at television. Clearly, they stay drugged to ward off reality. After having a few drinks with the neighbors who come to commiserate with her over her husband's suicide, Mrs. Heathcup ''almost forgot what had happened. I mean it didn't seem as though anything had happened.'' On his way to Europe to see his mother, Paul Hammer drinks martinis to cross the Atlantic in a drunken haze, and then goes directly to a pub when he is delayed in London. He is a victim of the economy that his mad mother, once a militant socialist, characterizes as having degenerated ''into the manufacture of drugs and ways of life that make reflection—any sort of thoughtfulness or emotional depth—impossible.'' It is advertising, she maintains, that carries the pernicious message:

''I see American magazines in the cafe and the bulk of their text is advertising for tobacco,

alcohol and absurd motor cars that promise—quite literally promise—to enable you to forget the squalor, spiritual poverty and monotony of selfishness. Never, in the history of civilization, has one seen a great nation singlemindedly bent on drugging itself.''

If she were to go back to the States, she tells her son, she would crucify an advertising man in some place like Bullet Park in an attempt to ''wake that world.'' Hammer takes over her mission, changes his victim from Eliot Nailles to his son, and fails only because he pauses for a cigarette before immolating Tony on a church altar.

The use of drugs also facilitates driving on the freeways and turnpikes that represent, in Cheever's fiction, the most damnable pathways of contemporary civilization. Despairingly he watched the construction work on Route 9 obliterate the landscape near his Ossining home, and determined to ''write about that, too.'' In *Bullet Park* and later stories, he did. Among the machines in his garden, none is so cruel or so terrifying as the bulldozers and road builders that have gouged out unnatural and inhuman roads. Dora Emmison, for example, cannot negotiate the New Jersey turnpike unless she is drunk:

''That road and all the rest of the freeways and thruways were engineered for clowns and drunks. If you're not a nerveless clown then you have to get drunk. No sensitive or intelligent man or woman can drive on those roads. Why I have a friend in California who smokes pot before he goes on the freeway. He's a great driver, a marvelous driver, and if the traffic's bad he uses heroin. They ought to sell pot and bourbon at the gas stations. Then there wouldn't be so many accidents.''

Fifteen minutes after this speech, well fortified with bourbon, Dora is killed in a crash on the turnpike.

The suicide rate aside, the most shocking statistic in *Bullet Park* has to do with casualties on the highway; these "averaged twenty-two a year because of a winding highway that seemed to have been drawn on the map by a child with a grease pencil." A story in *The World of Apples* (1973) vividly portrays the cost of that technological wonder, Route 64. One Saturday morning Marge Littleton loses her husband and children when their automobile is demolished by a gigantic car carrier. She begins an unsuccessful campaign against widening the highway. Then, upon recovering from her bereavement, she marries a "handsome, witty, and substantial" Italian who is decapitated by a crane as he drives down Route 64 in his convertible. Subsequent to these tragedies, curious accidents begin to occur on the highway. Three weeks after his death "a twenty-four wheel, eighty-ton truck, northbound on Route 64 . . . veered into the southbound lane demolishing two cars and killing their four passengers." Two weeks later another truck "went out of control at the same place" and struck an abutment; the two drivers "were so badly crushed by the collision that they had to be identified by their dental work." Twice more trucks swerve out of control at the same spot; in the last case the truck comes to rest peacefully in a narrow valley. When the police get to the oversized vehicle, they discover that the driver has been shot dead; but they do not find out that Marge did the shooting. Finally, in December "Marge married a rich widower and moved to North Salem, where there is only one two-lane highway and where the sound of traffic is as faint as the roaring of a shell."

Marge Littleton's personal vendetta hardly provides the harried suburban traveler with a practical way of expressing his objections against heedless technological progress. Nor is there consolation in the prayers of the drunken Mr. Applegate, in *The Wapshot Scandal*, for "all those killed or cruelly wounded on thruways, expressways, freeways and turnpikes . . . for all those burned to death in faulty plane landings, mid-air collisions, and mountainside

crashes . . . for all those wounded by rotary lawn-mowers, chain saws, electric hedge clippers, and other power tools."

Cheever seems to suggest that progress will not only kill large numbers of human beings but will also destroy the quality of life for those who survive. The world that Moses and Coverly Wapshot leave St. Botolphs to conquer is symbolized by the vast Northern Expressway that takes them south, "engorging in its clover leaves and brilliantly engineered gradings the green playing fields, rose gardens, barns, farms, meadows, trout streams, forests, homesteads and churches of a golden past." Similarly, Bullet Park's Route 61, "one of the most dangerous and in appearance one of the most inhuman of the new highways," is a road that has "basically changed the nature of the Eastern landscape like some seismological disturbance," a freeway on which there are at least fifty deaths each year. The simple Saturday drive on Route 61 becomes warlike, and Nailles fondly recalls the roads of his young manhood:

They followed the contours of the land. It was cool in the valleys, warm on the hilltops. One could measure distances with one's nose. There was the smell of eucalyptus, maples, sweet grass, manure from a cow barn and, as one got into the mountains, the smell of pine. . . . He remembered it all as intimate, human and pleasant, compared to this anxious wasteland through which one raced the barbarians.

Significantly, it is the mountains that Nailles's son inchoately longs for as he lies in deep depression. Nailles rouses him from bed one morning, takes him to the window, shows him how beautiful it is outside, and tells him that "everything's ahead of you. Everything. You'll go to college and get an interesting job and get married and have children." But Tony sinks to the floor and then howls out, "Give me back the mountains." What mountains? The White Mountains in New Hampshire that he and his father climbed together one summer? The Tirol where, Nailles later remembers, he had been so happy climbing the Grand Kaiser and the Pengelstein? Tony does not know (and will not know until the Swami Rutuola's cure) that the mountains are symbolic.

The Swami had first discovered his ability as a healer while employed to clean the washrooms at Grand Central Station. There he had been accosted very early one morning by a desperate man who was certain he was going to die momentarily. The Swami took him up to the concourse where they gazed at the "great big colored picture that advertises cameras" and which showed a man and a woman and two children on a beach, "and behind them, way off in the distance, were all these mountains covered with snow." Then he had asked the dying man "to look at the mountains to see if he could get his mind off his troubles," and the therapy had worked. As part of his treatment for Tony, Rutuola recites "cheers of place" for pleasant, unspoiled places: "I'm in a house by the sea at four in the afternoon and it's raining and I'm sitting in a ladderback chair with a book in my lap and I'm waiting for a girl I love who has gone on an errand but who will return." These cheers, and others, miraculously restore Tony to health.

In a malaise similar to Tony's, Paul Hammer is overtaken "on trains and planes" by a personal *cafard,* or carrier of the blues, whom he can escape only by summoning up images that represent to him "the excellence and beauty" he has lost. The first and most frequent of the images that counterpoint the realities of Bullet Park is that of a perfect, snow-covered mountain, obviously Kilimanjaro. In attempting to ward off the *cafard,* Hammer also calls up a vision of a fortified medieval town that, "like the snow-covered mountain, seemed to represent beauty, enthusiasm and love." Occasionally he glimpses a river with grassy banks—the Elysian fields perhaps—though he finds them difficult to reach and though it seems "that a railroad track

or a thruway [has] destroyed the beauty of the place."

In Tony's malaise, in Rutuola's cheers, in Hammer's visions, Cheever expresses his yearning after unspoiled nature and his conviction that mankind can stand only so much technological progress. Now that the walls of the medieval town have been breached, the Elysian fields invaded by freeways, space obliterated and time brought very nearly to a stop, Cheever joins Mark Twain in lamentation that "there are no remotenesses, anymore."

Bullet Park takes chances with the reader's willingness to suspend disbelief. As always Cheever observes the sorry emblems of our actual world with minute faithfulness. No one understands the surfaces of suburbia better than he. But then he whisks us off to the surreal, where Paul Hammer casually plans his homicide ("Have you ever committed a murder?" one chapter innocently begins) and the Swami Rutuola cures arthritis and sadness by means of chants. The plot of the novel, one reviewer complained in exasperation, could only be described as Gothic, for on "nearly every page, someone is doing something highly improbable for a remarkably obscure reason."

Cheever recognizes the tendency toward the incredible in his later work. But he argues that if the reader "truly believes he is standing on a rug you can pull it out from under him." Furthermore, he knows that no such rug is secure, that at any moment it could mysteriously ascend. In a 1960 article, "Writing American Fiction," Philip Roth maintained that in times like ours literature could not compete with the craziness of life. Cheever takes the opposite position and attempts to set down the mad things that do happen, without explanation or apology.

The creative power of the Swami Rutuola had been prefigured in "A Vision of the World," one of the stories in *The Brigadier and the Golf Widow.* The quotidian world here presented is chaotic, but a succession of characters find solace through a dream in which someone utters the magical eight-word phrase, "porpozec ciebie nie prosze dorzanin albo zyolpocz ciwego." These nonsense syllables are associated with the good things in life; and among the good things are those that the Swami and Tony Nailles had celebrated by chanting: not merely places, but such abstractions as love and honor. At the end of the story the dejected narrator travels to Florida where a pretty woman appears to him in a dream. The ghost seems absolutely real to him, "more real than the Tamiami Trail four miles to the east, with its Smorgorama and Giganticburger stands, more real than the back streets of Sarasota." She speaks the mysterious eight words, and he awakes to speak eight words in his own tongue: " 'Valor! Love! Virtue! Compassion! Splendor! Kindness! Wisdom! Beauty!' The words seem to have the colors of the earth," and as he recites them he feels his hopefulness mount until he is "contented and at peace with the night."

Cheever's belief in the magical power of dreams and chants stems from his heritage. He was brought up on mythology, which he calls "the easiest way to parse the world." And his Episcopalianism provides him with "a metaphor for ecstasy" and an opportunity, once a week, to get down on his knees and thank God "for the coming wonder and glory of life." From the first his work has carried resonances from Greek myth and the Bible. But these resonances penetrate deepest into his most recent fiction—*Bullet Park,* the stories in *The World of Apples,* and most of all his novel *Falconer* (1977).

Even *Bullet Park* is, as John Gardner observed, "a religious book, affirmation out of ashes," for Tony Nailles is saved from death and restored to health. *Falconer* offers a still more powerful affirmation, achieved from still less promising materials. Gone are the brilliantly evoked backgrounds—New York apartment, Yankee village, exurban retreat—that characterized Cheever's earlier fiction. The action of *Falconer* takes place, instead, within the prison of that name, and within the confused but entirely human head of forty-eight-year-old former professor Ezekiel Farragut, a heroin addict who has known those other environments—before his incarceration he lived in Indian Hill, Southwick, Connecticut, a place undescribed in the novel but surely resembling Bullet Park, Shady Hill, and Proxmire Manor—yet ends up behind walls ("fratricide, zip to ten, #734-508-32").

The name Ezekiel—Zeke for short—reminds us of Ezekiel Cheever, who founded the family line in New England. There are other echoes as well. The potential for fratricide underlay "Goodbye, My Brother." And the immediate cause of Zeke's murderous attack on his brother Eben—who had twice tried surreptitiously to dispose of Zeke—was Eben's insistence that their father had wanted Zeke aborted. This charge turns out to be true, just as it was true of Leander Wapshot. But the Captain Leander of the Wapshot books is diminished in *Falconer* to a ne'er-do-well father who "neglected his son and spent most of his time tacking around Travertine harbor in a little catboat." Similarly, Farragut's mother represents a rather jaundiced version of Sarah Wapshot. In her salad days, Zeke thinks, she might easily have interrupted his breast-feeding to play a rubber of bridge. Mrs. Farragut like Mrs. Wapshot is eventually forced into trade, although she runs a gas station rather than a gift shop. Thus the word "mother" evokes for Farragut "the image of a woman pumping gas, curtsying at the Assemblies and banging a lectern with her gavel." Another part of his mind calls up the Degas painting of a woman with a bowl of chrysanthemums that symbolized the serenity of "mother." Try as he will, Zeke cannot reconcile the two images.

His beautiful and intolerable wife Marcia stands at the end of a line of similar women in

Cheever's fiction that traces back to Melissa Wapshot, and includes the chilling portrait of Jill CHIDCHESTER Madison—as she reports herself to the alumnae magazine of her alma mater, one of the Seven Sisters—in "An Educated American Woman." Determined to fulfill herself in travel, civic works, and a biography of Flaubert, Jill ignores her nice but bewildered ex-halfback husband and neglects her son Bibber, who dies of pneumonia. Farragut is bound in matrimony to the still more monstrous Marcia. She is narcissistic and prefers her Italian lesbian lover to him. When she comes to visit Farragut in prison, she pulls her hand away from his touch. During their brief conversation she remarks that "it's nice to have a dry toilet seat" in his absence; comments that prison has turned his hair becomingly snow white in less than a year; tells him that he has ruined her life; and explains that it would be unwise to let their son come to see him.

Such is the background that leads Farragut to drugs—his addiction carries to a logical conclusion the drugging motif in *Bullet Park* and other stories of suburbia—and to the final degradation of prison. Cheever taught writing for a couple of years to inmates at Sing Sing prison, in Ossining. That exposure helped him bring his mastery of place to bear on Cellblock F, where the bars "had been enameled white many years ago, but . . . worn back to iron at the chest level, where men instinctively held them." He also brings to life such inmates as Chicken Number Two, a tattooed folk-singing former jewel thief; Tennis, an airplane hijacker who expects, any week now, to "leap the net" to freedom; and Cuckold, who insists on telling in excruciating detail how often his wife betrayed him before he "iced her" one night, "by mistake." Presiding over them is the obese guard Tiny, who slaughters dozens of cats—prison population: two thousand inmates, four thousand cats—after one makes off with his London broil. Farragut himself provides the en-

tertainment on another day when the guards decide to withhold his methadone fix and watch the "withdrawal show."

Bestiality and sadism flourish in Falconer Prison, yet Farragut manages to achieve redemption there: he works off his self-pity in a series of indignant letters; he kicks his drug habit; and he manages to find love, both carnal and caring.

His physical lover is Jody, a young prisoner who casually seduces him. Although Farragut does not understand why, there is no doubt that he feels the same passion for Jody that he had felt, on the outside, for dozens of women. He waits for the squeak of his basketball sneakers just

as he had waited for the sound of Jane's heels on the cobbles in Boston, waited for the sound of the elevator that would bring Virginia up to the eleventh floor, waited for Dodie to open the rusty gate on Thrace Street, waited for Roberta to get off the C bus in some Roman piazza, waited for Lucy to install her diaphragm and appear naked in the bathroom door, . . . waited for the end of the thunderstorm that was frightening Helen. . . .

When Jody escapes, Farragut is temporarily bereft. But the urgings of the flesh are transformed into a more humane and compassionate love. In a moving scene, Chicken Number Two is revealed as the most desperately solitary of all the prisoners. The authorities decide to ameliorate tensions behind the walls by arranging to have pictures of the inmates taken before a large decorated tree and sent for Christmas to whatever address they designate. When his turn comes, Chicken Number Two opts to send his picture to *Mr. and Mrs. Santa Claus. Icicle Street. The North Pole.* Later, when Chicken falls ill, Farragut takes him into his cell and cares for him until he dies, a final act of charity that leads to his own escape. Farragut gets away (after a priest mysteriously comes to bless him in his cell) by zipping himself into the death sack intended for Chicken Number Two. Once outside he meets a stranger on a bus who presents him with a raincoat. All of this is deeply implausible, as are the circumstances of Jody's escape.

Confinement is the theme of the novel, and the prison serves as a metaphor for the confinements we visit upon ourselves. Yet Cheever, who has said that he knows "what it feels like inside a strait jacket," attempts in *Falconer* to express his "conviction of the boundlessness of possibility." What he asks us—persuades us—to believe is that miracles can and do happen.

The greatest miracle of all, and the one most taken for granted, is the wonder of the natural world. In prison Farragut yearns for the blessing of blue skies, now virtually denied him. "The simple phenomenon of light—brightness angling across the air—struck him as a transcendent piece of good news." He gains a sense of oneness with the earth when permitted to mow the prison lawn. Why, he wonders, do people on television "all stay in one room, quarreling, when they could walk to the store or eat a picnic in the woods or go for a swim in the sea?" The drug he finds in the ecstacy of release from confinement is "a distillate of earth, air, water and fire." What this novel demonstrates is that Cheever, for all his skill at realistic evocation of person and place, has become essentially a spiritual writer—worshipful toward the creation, unafraid to believe in the unbelievable things that may occur once we learn to love one another. Zeke Farragut ends *Falconer* unequivocally: "Rejoice, he thought, rejoice."

The radiance shining through the gloom of *Falconer* is characteristic of the mixture of light and dark in Cheever's works. "Oh, what a beautiful story, it's so sad," his agent once told him about a new piece of fiction. "All right," Cheever answered. "So I'm a sad man"—and not merely sad, but at times almost apocalyptically so in nightmare stories such as "The Enormous Radio" and novels like *Bullet Park*. Yet he remains a writer with double vision, as keenly aware of the promise and the beauty of life as of its disappointment and degradation. In fact, it is that sense of promise, the celebration of hope amid the ruins, that ordinarily prevails in his fiction. Essentially, he is a comic writer, one who celebrates and affirms the rapture of existence.

Cheever's comedy is fully capable of making his readers laugh out loud. And it may be that to some extent Cheever's "marvelous brightness," as Alfred Kazin wrote, represents an effort to cheer himself up. Certainly he derives affirmation from unprepossessing materials. But the author himself attributes his fictional attitude to another motive. "One has an impulse to bring glad tidings to someone. My sense of literature is a sense of giving, not a diminishment." He has aimed, in his writing, "to make some link between the light in the sky and the taste of death." Death will intrude, but light remains the goal. "Man's inclination toward light, toward brightness, is very nearly botanical—and I mean spiritual light. One not only needs it, one struggles for it." This set of mind suits ill with the lugubrious tone of much modernist writing, with what Gardner calls "the tiresome modern fashion of always viewing the universe with alarm, either groaning or cynically sneering."

Nor has Cheever's critical reputation benefited from the periodical company he has kept. Despite his novels, he is still regarded by many as the quintessential *New Yorker* story writer. The stories in that most successful of middle-class, middlebrow magazines are supposed to run to a pattern: they focus on a single incident, but in the telling suggest echoes from the past and omens for the future. The settings are regional, most often New York or its suburbs—"The Connecticut Story," William Van O'Connor called it. The hero—or rather protagonist, for there are no heroes in *New Yorker* stories—is characterized by his sensitivity; he is a man of feeling, not of action. Plot is unimportant; and readers sometimes complain that "nothing happens" in these stories. Certainly little happens at the end; and it is said that to get a *New Yorker* ending, one need only cut off the last paragraph of a more conventional one. The stories in the magazine may instruct, but they must entertain.

The *New Yorker* has served as patron to John Cheever for four decades, although he has rarely written "a *New Yorker* story"—elegant, charming, inconsequential—since his first book was published in 1943. In the later stories characters are fully fleshed out, plots are more complicated, violence smolders or erupts, and the setting shifts at times to overseas locations, particularly to Rome. Yet so pervasive is the power of the stereotype and so well known Cheever's connection with the magazine that as recently as 1973 Kazin remarked that "The *New Yorker* column is still the inch of ivory on which he writes."

Furthermore, Cheever suffered temporary critical ostracism when *Time* magazine, that still more pervasive voice of middle-class values, proclaimed his virtues in a March 1964 cover story. The story was headed "Ovid in Ossining," but it "offered Cheever to the world"— in John W. Aldridge's phrase—"as a kind of crew-cut, Ivy League Faulkner of the New York exurbs, who could be both artistically sincere and piously right-thinking about the eternal verities": a Faulkner one could count on, for one knew the territory. What was good enough for *Time* tended to alienate critics such as the one who observed, accurately enough, that "if Cheever were Swift, *Time* would be more worried about him." By sticking to his desk (or rather a series of desks, for he habitually works on each new book in a different room of his house), Cheever has managed to write his way out of the ill effects of such middlebrow praise. He tries to avoid taking the issue of critical acceptance too seriously; he often arranges to be out of the country when a book is scheduled to appear. Only in the case of *Falconer* has he submitted to the invasion of the writer's privacy so hungrily sought by the practitioners of publicity.

In any case, he has earned his share of more meaningful recognition. *The Wapshot Chronicle* won the National Book Award for fiction in 1958. *The Wapshot Scandal* was awarded in 1965 the still more prestigious Howells medal of the American Academy of Arts and Letters for the best work of fiction published during the previous five years. (In accepting, Cheever wondered with characteristic acuity about the wisdom of dividing American fiction into half-decade periods.) All along he has been a writer's writer, admired by such fellow craftsmen as John Gardner, John Hersey, Joan Didion, George Garrett, and Joseph Heller. Someone once referred to John Updike as his disciple, a classification that ignores both the independent achievements of each man and the real friendship between them.

Cheever's work refuses to fit comfortably into any critical pigeonhole, a fact that is demonstrated by the variety of writers to whom he has been compared. He has reminded some, for example, of such social observers as Marquand and O'Hara, a categorization he repudiates: "The fact that I can count the olives in a dish just as quick as John O'Hara doesn't mean that I am O'Hara." He has been likened to Nabokov for their mutual capacity to turn the cultural artifacts of contemporary life to artistic purposes. He resembles Fitzgerald, it has been asserted, for the luminosity of his prose and for that "extraordinary gift for hope," that "romantic readiness" that he shares with Jay Gatsby. In the best work of both writers, one always knows "what time it is, precisely where you are, the kind of country." "If he has a master," Elizabeth Hardwick observed, "it is probably F. Scott Fitzgerald."

Cheever has been called the "Chekhov of the suburbs," and is most like the Russian master, perhaps, in his knack for making patently ridiculous characters seem somehow winning. He has been compared to Hawthorne for possessing a sense of history—an awareness not merely of the pastness of the past, but of the pastness in the present. He is like Faulkner, it has been observed, in bringing to life a particular plot of American ground—the New York suburb, rather than the Mississippi county. And he seems like Kafka to yet another reader, for in their fiction the shadow of the sinister can fall across the outwardly commonplace landscape in the blink of an eye. Indeed, the multiplicity of such comparisons suggests that Cheever is right in denying that he belongs to any particular American literary tradition, other than the abiding one of individuality.

There is general agreement about Cheever's shortcomings. He is better at the particular scene than at stringing scenes together. His tightly wrought short stories are generally superior to the novels, which tend toward the episodic in their looseness of structure; and perhaps because of Yankee reticence, he has not always plumbed the depths of his characters. He inveighs against contemporary ills—the standardization of culture, the decline in sexual mores that tends to confuse love with lust, the obliteration of nature by the engines of technology—but blurs his outrage with blue-sky endings.

Cheever's merits far outweigh such shortcomings, however. He has achieved an "amazing precision of style and language," and is capable of lyrical moments reminiscent, once again, of Fitzgerald. He possesses "a remarkably acute nose" for the fascinating situation, "a remarkably acute ear" for the thing said in context. Memory and imagination are blended into a remarkable comic inventiveness. His genius is the "genius of place." His greatest gift is "for entering the minds of men and women at crucial moments." No other writer "tells us so much"—this from Didion—"about the way we live now." Furthermore, he is not for nothing a

descendant of the Puritans, and his writing is invariably grounded on firm moral bedrock.

Cheever knows that fiction is not meant to provide lessons, but "to illuminate, to explode, to refresh." Still, the journeys his characters undertake are fraught with moral perils, and he judges those who fall by the wayside according to conventional and traditional standards. Those led astray are inflexibly punished, banished from enjoyment of the natural world that lies around them. But he is an "enlightened Puritan" of the twentieth century; and for him the greatest, most saving virtues are those he wishes for in himself and his children: love and usefulness.

Cheever finds solace in his work; and his greatest pleasure comes in shutting himself off in a room to get a story down on paper. At such moments he feels he is practicing his rightful calling. For when writing, he is invested by a

. . . sense of total usefulness. We all have a power of control, it's part of our lives; we have it in love, in work that we love doing. It's a sense of ecstasy, as simple as that. The sense is that "this is my usefulness, and I can do it all the way through."

Selected Bibliography

WORKS OF JOHN CHEEVER

The Way Some People Live. New York: Random House, 1943.
The Enormous Radio and Other Stories. New York: Funk & Wagnalls, 1953.
The Wapshot Chronicle. New York: Harper, 1957.
The Housebreaker of Shady Hill and Other Stories. New York: Harper, 1958.
Some People, Places & Things That Will Not Appear in My Next Novel. New York: Harper, 1961.

The Wapshot Scandal. New York: Harper & Row, 1964.

The Brigadier and the Golf Widow. New York: Harper & Row, 1964.

Bullet Park. New York: Knopf, 1969.

The World of Apples. New York: Knopf, 1973.

Falconer. New York: Knopf, 1977.

The Stories of John Cheever. New York: Knopf, 1978.

CRITICAL AND BIOGRAPHICAL STUDIES

Aldridge, John W. "John Cheever and the Soft Sell of Disaster," in *Time to Murder and Create*. New York: David McKay, 1966. Pp. 171–77.

Auser, Cortland P. "John Cheever's Myth of Men and Time: 'The Swimmer,' " *CEA Critic*, 29:18–19 (March 1967).

Baker, Carlos. "Yankee Gallimaufry," *Saturday Review*, 40:14 (23 March 1957).

Bracher, Frederick. "John Cheever and Comedy," *Critique: Studies in Modern Fiction*, 6:66–78 (1963).

———. "John Cheever: A Vision of the World," *Claremont Quarterly*, 11:47–57 (1964).

Breit, Harvey. "In and Out of Books," *New York Times Book Review* (10 May 1953), p. 8.

Broyard, Anatole. "You Wouldn't Believe It," *New Republic*, 160:36–37 (26 April 1969).

Burhans, Clinton S., Jr. "John Cheever and the Grave of Social Coherence," *Twentieth Century Literature*, 14:187–98 (1969).

Burt, Struthers. "John Cheever's Sense of Drama," *Saturday Review of Literature*, 26:9 (24 April 1943).

Clemons, Walter. "Cheever's Triumph," *Newsweek*, 89:61–62, 64 (14 March 1977).

Corke, Hilary. "Sugary Days in St. Botolphs," *New Republic*, 150:19–21 (25 January 1964).

Cowley, Susan Cheever. "A Duet of Cheevers," *Newsweek*, 89:68–70, 73 (14 March 1977).

DeMott, Benjamin. "The Way We Feel Now," *Harper's*, 228:111–12 (February 1964).

Didion, Joan. "The Way We Live Now," *National Review*, 16:237–38, 240 (24 March 1964).

———. "*Falconer*," *New York Times Book Review* (8 March 1977), pp. 1, 22, 24.

Donaldson, Scott. "The Machines in Cheever's Garden," in *The Changing Face of the Suburbs*, edited by Barry Schwartz. Chicago: University of Chicago Press, 1975. Pp. 309–22.

Esty, William. "Out of an Abundant Love of Created Things," *Commonweal*, 66:187–88 (17 May 1957).

Fiction of the Fifties: A Decade of American Writing, edited by Herbert Gold. Garden City, N.Y.: Doubleday, 1959.

Firth, John. "Talking with John Cheever," *Saturday Review*, 4:22–23 (2 April 1977).

Gardner, John. "Witchcraft in Bullet Park," *New York Times Book Review* (24 October 1971), pp. 2, 24.

———. "On Miracle Row," *Saturday Review*, 4:20–24 (2 April 1977).

Garrett, George. "John Cheever and the Charms of Innocence: The Craft of *The Wapshot Scandal*," *Hollins Critic*, 1:1–4, 6–12 (1964).

Gaunt, Marcia E. "Imagination and Reality in the Fiction of Katherine Anne Porter and John Cheever: Implications for Curriculum." Ph.D dissertation, Purdue University, 1972.

Geismar, Maxwell. "End of the Line," *New York Times Book Review* (24 March 1957), p. 5.

Gilman, Richard. "Dante of Suburbia," *Commonweal* 64:320 (19 December 1958).

Grant, Annette. "John Cheever: The Art of Fiction LXII," *Paris Review*, 17:39–66 (Fall 1976).

Greene, Beatrice. "Icarus at St. Botolphs: A Descent to 'Unwonted Otherness,' " *Style*, 5:119–37 (1971).

Hardwick, Elizabeth. "The Family Way," *New York Review of Books*, 1:4–5 (6 February 1964).

Hassan, Ihab. *Radical Innocence: Studies in the Contemporary American Novel*. Princeton, N.J.: Princeton University Press, 1961. Pp. 187–94.

Hersey, John. "Talk with John Cheever," *New York Times Book Review* (6 March 1977), pp. 1, 24, 26–28.

Hicks, Granville. "Literary Horizons: Cheever and Others," *Saturday Review*, 41:33, 47 (13 September 1958).

Hyman, Stanley Edgar. "John Cheever's Golden Egg," in *Standards: A Chronicle of Books for Our Time*. New York: Horizon, 1966. Pp. 199–203.

Janeway, Elizabeth. "Things Aren't What They Seem," *New York Times Book Review* (5 January 1964), pp. 1, 28.

Kazin, Alfred. *Bright Book of Life*. Boston: Atlantic-Little, Brown, 1973. Pp. 110–14.

Kees, Weldon. "John Cheever's Stories," *New Republic*, 108:516–17 (19 April 1943).

Kendle, Burton. "Cheever's Use of Mythology in 'The Enormous Radio,' " *Studies in Short Fiction*, 4:262–64 (1967).

Malcolm, Donald. "John Cheever's Photograph Album," *New Republic*, 136:17–18 (3 June 1957).

McPherson, William. "Lives in a Cell," *Washington Post Book World* (20 March 1977), pp. 111–12.

Nichols, Lewis. "A Visit with John Cheever," *New York Times Book Review* (5 January 1964), p. 28.

Nicol, Charles. "Salvation in the Suburbs," *Atlantic*, 223:96, 98 (May 1969).

Oates, Joyce Carol. "The Style of the 70's: The Novel," *New York Times Book Review* (5 June 1977), pp. 7, 40–41.

"One Man's Hell," *Time*, 77:103–04 (28 April 1961).

"Ovid in Ossining," *Time*, 83:66–70, 72 (27 March 1964).

Ozick, Cynthia. "America Aglow," *Commentary*, 38:66–67 (July 1964).

Peden, William. *The American Short Story: Front Line in the National Defense of Literature*. Boston: Houghton Mifflin, 1964. Pp. 45–55.

Ray, David. "The Weeding Out Process," *Saturday Review*, 44:20 (24 May 1961).

Rupp, Richard H. "Living in the Present: American Fiction Since 1945," in *Celebration in Modern American Fiction*. Coral Gables, Fla.: University of Miami Press, 1970. Pp. 16–25.

———. "John Cheever: The Upshot of Wapshot," *Celebration*. Pp. 27–39.

Schorer, Mark. "Outstanding Novels," *Yale Review*, n.s., 32:xii, xiv (Summer 1943).

Scott, Winfield Townley. "John Cheever's Country," *New York Herald Tribune Book Review* (24 March 1957), pp. 1, 9.

Scully, James. "Oracle of Subocracy," *Nation*, 200:144–45 (8 February 1965).

Segal, David. "Change Is Always for the Worse," *Commonweal*, 81:362–63 (4 December 1964).

Shapiro, Charles. "This Familiar and Lifeless Scene," *Nation*, 208:836–37 (30 June 1969).

Sheed, Wilfrid. "Novelist of Suburbia: Mr. Saturday, Mr. Monday and Mr. Cheever," *Life*, 66:39–40, 44, 46 (18 April 1969).

Ten Harmsel, Henrietta. " 'Young Goodman Brown' and 'The Enormous Radio,' " *Studies in Short Fiction*, 9:407–08 (1972).

Valhouli, James N. "John Cheever: The Dual Vision of His Art." Ph.D. dissertation, University of Wisconsin (Madison), 1973.

Warnke, Frank J. "Cheever's Inferno," *New Republic*, 144:18 (15 May 1961).

Wink, John H. "John Cheever and the Broken World." Ph.D. dissertation, University of Arkansas, 1974.

—SCOTT DONALDSON

Stephen Crane

1871-1900

SOME writers work their way up to popularity in a long and difficult climb; others hit upon success almost overnight. Stephen Crane's early attempt at literary creation, his novel *The Red Badge of Courage*, met with triumphal acclaim in 1896, but he only lived long enough to enjoy a few years of controversial fame.

Experimenting in various media—journalism, fiction, poetry, playwriting—Crane was for his contemporaries above all a picturesque figure of the world of the press. His professional commitments kept him in close touch with the life of his country, and he explored slums and battlefields with unabating eagerness, seeing war in two brief conflicts in 1897 and 1898. The conjunction of highstrung temperament and obstinate neglect of his health brought Crane's life to an early close, when he was not yet twenty-nine.

During the two decades following his death, in 1900, he was to be almost forgotten. Then in 1923 Thomas Beer published an impressionistic biography which served to focus attention on Crane once more, and *The Work of Stephen Crane* (1925–27), edited by Wilson Follett, made most of his writings available to a scholarly audience. This limited edition contained laudatory prefaces by creative writers such as Amy Lowell, Sherwood Anderson, H. L. Mencken, and Willa Cather, a few assessments by professional critics, and reminiscences by fellow journalists. Crane's reputation was also enhanced by the faithful support of some of his friends, especially Edward Garnett, Joseph Conrad, H. G. Wells, and Ford Madox Hueffer, later known as Ford Madox Ford. The thirties saw in him a champion of the cause of the common man, and the forties continued to fit him into a realistic tradition; in the next two decades he has appeared to critics primarily as a symbolist, but a wide range of interpretations has confronted the student with a mass of conflicting scholarship. In 1950 John Berryman's *Stephen Crane* established him as an American classic. The Modern Library edition of *The Red Badge of Courage* came out the following year with a preface written by R. W. Stallman, whose extensive work on Crane, climaxed by his monumental biography in 1968, has aroused much enthusiasm and controversy. D. G. Hoffman's *The Poetry of Stephen Crane*, a very lively and perceptive study, appeared in 1957. Since 1951 there has also been a steady outpouring of articles, dissertations, monographs, and reprints. When, in the summer of 1966, a *Stephen Crane Newsletter* was founded and began to be issued regularly by Ohio State University, Stephen Crane had come into his own.

Stephen Crane had deep roots in the soil of New Jersey and was extremely proud of his American heritage. One of his ancestors bearing the same name had, according to Crane, "arrived in Massachusetts from England in 1635." The man who wrote *The Red Badge of Courage* was, on his father's side, descended from a long line of sheriffs, judges, and farmers, and another Stephen Crane had been one of the leading patriots of New Jersey during the Revolution; in his mother's family, as he humorously put it, "everybody, as soon as he could walk, became a Methodist clergyman—of the old, ambling-nag, saddle-bag, exhorting kind."

Born in a Methodist parsonage in Newark, New Jersey, on November 1, 1871, Stephen was the fourteenth child of Jonathan Townley Crane, D.D. He grew up in various parsonages in New Jersey and New York State, his father being, according to the custom of his church, shifted from one charge to another every two or three years. The death of Dr. Crane in Port Jervis, New York, in 1880 brought this itinerancy to a close. Still a child when his father died, Stephen always cherished his memory.

After the death of her husband Mrs. Crane returned to Newark for a while, but soon made a permanent home in Asbury Park, New Jersey, which was a new stronghold of American Methodism. There she settled in 1883 and, that same year, was elected president of the Woman's Christian Temperance Union of Asbury Park and Ocean Grove. Frequently lecturing in neighboring towns, she occasionally traveled to distant cities as a delegate of that organization. A well-educated woman, she also dabbled in journalism to eke out her meager resources and reported on the summer religious meetings on the New Jersey shore, contributing mostly to the *New York Tribune* and the *Philadelphia Press*. She suffered from mental illness for some months in 1886 and was to die in 1891. Her religious zeal did not inspire a similar response in Stephen and he left the fold of the church; but he remained dominated by fundamental religious precepts and patterns—charity, fraternity, redemption, and rescue—which he usually kept at an earthly level.

At the age of fourteen he left Asbury Park to go to the Pennington Seminary, a Methodist academy in New Jersey, and thus attended a school over which his father had ruled for ten years (1849–58). He did not complete the four-year course there but transferred in the middle of the third year to Claverack College and Hudson River Institute, a semi-military Methodist school near Hudson, New York. He stayed there from January 1888 to June 1890. His university education lasted only one year: it began at Lafayette College, a Presbyterian institution at Easton, Pennsylvania, where he spent the autumn term of 1890, and ended at Syracuse University the following June. All these schools stressed religious and classical studies, and at no time did the young man feel any sympathy for these two branches of knowledge. He was already a rebel resolutely hostile to formal education and preferred to study "humanity."

Crane suffered both from his mother's moral severity and from her physical neglect of him, but in Asbury Park he enjoyed a happy freedom near the "soft booming sound of surf." The deaths of his father, his sister Agnes, his brother Luther, and finally his mother must have made his childhood and adolescence a period of many severe trials. Three of his older brothers played the part of father-substitutes, offering either material assistance or a questionable but attractive model. William, who became a lawyer in Port Jervis in 1881, and Edmund, a man of limited education but of generous heart who, in 1894, settled at Hartwood, near Port Jervis, often helped the young man in his financial difficulties at the beginning of his literary career. Jonathan Townley Jr.'s bohemian tastes exerted a powerful influence on his younger brother; almost twenty years older than Stephen, he was in the late 1880's the coast correspondent of the *New York Sun*, the *New York Tribune*, and the Associated Press in Asbury Park and so a well-known regional journalist. Stephen, as early as 1888, began helping him in his reportorial work on the New Jersey shore. His oldest sister, Nellie, who then kept an art school in Asbury Park, may have introduced Stephen to the world of color and prepared him for an aesthetic exploration of his environment.

Stephen Crane's sensitivity was thus early aroused and developed through a gradual training of his faculty of observation: Methodism forced him to probe his own soul, journalism taught him how to note facts with accuracy, and art provided his craving for reality with chromatic patterns.

After publishing a few pieces in *Cosmopolitan* and the *New York Tribune*, a paper for which he wrote his "Sullivan County Sketches," boyish tales of the woods, in the early part of 1892, he was fired by the *Tribune* for an ironic article about a parade of workers in Asbury Park, and became a free-lance journalist in New York. (This brief report had expressed, in the tone of a sententious aesthete, his mild amusement at the sight of "an uncut and uncarved procession" of men with "principles" marching past a "decorous" throng of "summer gowns" and predatory Asbury Parkers.) Then began his apprenticeship in bohemianism in the metropolis, where he lived with struggling young artists. Occasional visits to his brothers Edmund and William helped him keep from starving; they provided him with handy refuges where he could escape from the hardships and turmoil of New York. His pride, however, prevented him from making frequent use of them. In 1893 he published his first book, *Maggie: A Girl of the Streets*, under a pseudonym and at his own expense. The audacity of the subject did not deter Hamlin Garland and W. D. Howells from praising that novel, but they were almost the only critics to notice it. They both encouraged him to write proletarian sketches, some of which appeared in the Boston *Arena* and others in the *New York Press*, enabling him to attain some financial security. His picture of the big city was centered around the life of the underprivileged in their ordinary setting, the southern tip of Manhattan.

Gradually acquiring self-reliance, experience, and ambition, he immersed himself in the most significant venture of his literary life, the writing of *The Red Badge of Courage*, an imaginative reconstruction of a Civil War battle; it was first printed in an abbreviated form as a newspaper serial distributed by the Bacheller Syndicate in December 1894. The success of the story led to an assignment as roving reporter in the West and Mexico at the beginning of 1895. When he came back in May, his first volume of verse, *The Black Riders*, had just appeared in print and proved that the young man was impelled by the spirit of religious and social rebellion. Appleton published *The Red Badge* as a book in New York in October 1895, and the London firm of Heinemann included it in its Pioneer Series at the end of November. Warmly received by English reviewers, it soon became a popular novel in the United States as well and its tenth American edition was issued in June 1896.

In that year Crane's celebrity reached a

peak. All at once praised, parodied, and harshly criticized, he found it difficult to cope with success. Going from one apartment to another in New York and probably from one girl to another, he ended up challenging the impregnable metropolitan police force on behalf of a prostitute who claimed she was being unjustly harassed. Then, rushing into escape, he accepted a commission to report the insurrection in Cuba against Spanish rule, but his ship sank off the coast of Florida on January 2, 1897, and he returned to Jacksonville, where before sailing he had met Cora Howorth (known there as Cora Taylor), the proprietress of the Hotel de Dream, a somewhat refined house of ill-fame. She had already been married twice and, at the time of her first meeting with Crane, was thirty-one years old. They were to live together for the rest of his life. His previous adventures with women had been inconclusive episodes. At the age of twenty he had fallen in love, at Avon-by-the-Sea, a resort near Asbury Park, with a certain Helen Trent, who was already engaged. In 1892 a love affair with a young married woman, Lily Brandon Munroe, enlivened his summer in Asbury Park and inspired some of his more moving love letters. Nellie Crouse, a provincial maiden whom he met at a social tea in New York, flirted with him by mail but finally rejected him. In 1896 he started sending money to Amy Leslie, a former actress now past her prime who had become a drama critic for the *Chicago Daily News*. He kept doing so until January 1898, when she succeeded in having a warrant of attachment issued against him to recover $550 of the $800 she had allegedly given him in 1896 to deposit for her. The details of their relationship remain somewhat obscure but, in November 1896, when he set out for Florida, he was probably fleeing from her as well as from the New York police.

The year 1896 was not marked by any really new work from his pen, except his "Tenderloin" sketches for the *New York Journal*: Crane was too busy with his public and private life. *Maggie*, made respectable by the success of *The Red Badge* and slightly revised, came out under his real name, accompanied by another tale of the slums, *George's Mother*, which had been completed in November 1894. A volume of war stories, *The Little Regiment*, appeared in New York late in 1896 and in London in February 1897.

Crane's longing for adventure had apparently been only whetted by the shipwreck off Florida, in which he nearly lost his life; periodically the urge to see violent action was aroused in him. The Greco-Turkish War, which he covered in a disappointing manner for the *New York Journal* and the *Westminster Gazette*, took him to Europe in the summer of 1897; his bad health interfered with his reportorial duties in Greece, but he saw enough fighting to conclude on his return to London that *"The Red Badge* [was] all right."

Obviously conscious of the impossibility of introducing his "wife"—there is no record of a marriage ceremony—to his family, and still afraid of retaliatory action by the New York police, he decided to stay on in England after the Greek war was over. His shipwreck had inspired him to write a brilliant short story, "The Open Boat," which *Scribners* printed in June 1897. About the same time he published *The Third Violet*, a novel based on his experiences in the highly contrasted worlds of Hartwood, New York, and New York City. Crane's stay in England did not provide the writer with a fresh batch of literary topics but it did enable him to see his own life in a new perspective. Many of his western adventures and several accounts of urban poverty went into a volume published in 1898 under the title *The Open Boat and Other Stories*. This volume, which contains seventeen tales, gives a sample of Crane's best talent. His meeting with Joseph Conrad brought him into contact with a writer whose aesthetics was very close to his own. In his "villa," situated on the borderline between Oxted and Limpsfield, Surrey, where he settled in the fall of 1897, Crane was not far from Ford Madox Hueffer and Harold Frederic. A few English Fabians, the Sydney Oliviers and the Edward Garnetts notably, lived in the vicinity.

In 1898 he was hired by Pulitzer to write for the *New York World* and, seeing war for the second time, reported the Spanish-American conflict, which left deep scars on his body and mind; the symptoms of the tuberculosis that was to prove fatal had already set in. In the fall he lingered in Havana, where he served as special correspondent for the *New York Journal* and wrote the first draft of a novel, *Active Service*, based on his Greek assignment.

Early in 1899 he was back in England and, because of harassing creditors in Oxted, decided to move from Surrey to Sussex, his new English residence being the medieval manor of Brede Place situated near Rye on the charming Sussex coast. There his literary production reached a peak, but his efforts to avoid bankruptcy proved vain in the face of a rising tide of debts and recurring signs of failing health. He kept writing doggedly, now coaxing, now threatening his literary agent, James B. Pinker, from whom he tried to obtain more and more advances, and even the best work of this period shows the effects of haste and worry. Drawing upon his recent experiences, he completed a series of eleven fictional and autobiographical accounts of the Cuban war, which were posthumously collected in *Wounds in the Rain* (1900). He also wrote thirteen children's stories which first appeared in *Harper's Magazine* and were assembled in book form after his death under the title *Whilomville Stories* (1900). In the course of 1899 three other books

saw print: a volume of verse, *War Is Kind*, containing a variety of poems whose composition embraced a period of seven years; *Active Service*, a novel which he himself regarded as second-rate; and the American edition of *The Monster and Other Stories*. Reminiscing about his family's role during the Revolutionary War, he composed three "Wyoming Valley Tales" and, creating an imaginary country, chose it as the setting for a series of archetypal battles, the "Spitzbergen Tales," which began to appear in English and American magazines in 1900.

Taking a mild interest in Cora's passion for entertaining, he watched streams of guests come to visit him in his dilapidated mansion, among whom were some distinguished writers (Conrad, Wells, Henry James) and many parasites. He decided or was persuaded by Cora to arrange a Christmas party for his literary friends, producing an original play for the occasion. The play was very aptly called *The Ghost* and, in spite of a widely advertised collaboration with famous English and American authors, most of it was written by Crane himself. During the festivities he almost died of a lung hemorrhage. He was to drag on for a few more months, his body and his brain gradually weakening, but he went on writing to his deathbed. With the help of Kate Lyon, Harold Frederic's mistress, he turned out a series of articles on nine great battles of the world for *Lippincott's Magazine*, outlined the plot and wrote the first twenty-five chapters of *The O'Ruddy*, a picaresque novel of the eighteenth century with an Irish hero and an English setting. But it was left uncompleted when Crane died on June 5, 1900, in Badenweiler, Germany, where Cora had seen fit to take him in the idle hope of a miraculous recovery from tuberculosis. Crane's friend Robert Barr agreed to write the final chapters of the novel which, after picaresque ups and downs, was eventually published in New York in October 1903.

The inescapable trait of Crane as a writer is his desire to express his own mind candidly, regardless of accepted opinion, conventions, and satirical attacks. The world first appeared to him with the colors, shapes, and sounds of the Psalms and of Wesleyan hymns, and he unconsciously made frequent use of the rhythms and imagery of Biblical stories. His parents' participation in charitable work encouraged his interest in slum life, and he soon discovered, through his own deep concern with the mainsprings of fear, a strange curiosity about war.

In Crane's generation "low life" was a subject of reportage, fiction, and melodrama. When he moved into this area of literature he did so with the seriousness, the intentness, and the acuteness of a minister's son who had received his training as a journalist. Even if he did not know New York well at the time he wrote *Maggie*, he must have caught by then a few glimpses of the poorer districts of the American metropolis, which was so close to Asbury Park where he lived between his stays at boarding school or college.

The approach to slum life of Crane's first novel was new in that it did not preach and did not encourage "slumming"; it simply aimed, he said, to "show people to people as they seem[ed] to [him]." Maggie is the daughter of the Johnsons, a family of poor tenement dwellers living on the lower East Side of Manhattan. A large part of the story is devoted to drinking bouts, and Maggie's home is the scene of a daily fight for survival. We thus attend the growth and brutal extinction of the heroine, who has "blossomed in a mud-puddle" to become a "pretty girl" strangely undefiled by her surroundings. She tries to escape the de-grading atmosphere of her home by working in a collar-and-cuff factory, but soon discovers the dull routine and corruption of the sweatshop. Then Pete, a commonplace bartender, comes into her life, and to Maggie he seems to be "a supreme warrior," "a knight." He takes her to dime museums, beer gardens, and theaters, and thus satisfies her vague and romantic longings for culture and refinement. Seduced and abandoned by her lover, rejected by her drinking mother and callous brother on "moralistic" grounds, Maggie finally turns to prostitution. Shortly afterwards, "upon a wet evening," she abruptly ends her life in the East River while in the distance "street-car bells [jingle] with a sound of merriment."

The problem this story hinges on is not primarily a social one, and Crane is not merely content with studying the causes and consequences of prostitution. Mainly concerned with the "soul" of the young prostitute, he tries to challenge the beliefs of Sunday school religion. Can an "occasional street girl" be expected to end up in Heaven, irrespective of the indignant frowns of "many excellent people"? The answer is never made explicit in a narrative brimming over with irony, but it could not be other than positive. Maggie falls because "environment is a tremendous thing in the world," because she herself is romantic and weak, and also because nobody is interested in her fate. She, however, redeems herself by committing suicide, her only possible escape from a life of moral degradation. By doing so she undergoes an ironic purification in the foul waters of the East River while her brother Jimmie, who had "clad his soul in armour," and her mother, who belatedly "ferg[ave]" her, are allowed to continue their degenerate lives of vice and hypocrisy in the human jungle to which they are perfectly adapted.

As a first novel *Maggie* revealed on the part

of the author a deep seriousness and the powerful urge to gain an audience. It posited the imperative need for a new ethical code and, through a consistent use of irony, debunked the false values worshiped by society and exposed the part played by collective passivity in the destruction of innocence. "Indifference is a militant thing," Crane commented in a story of 1897; this idea is implied throughout *Maggie*. Much of this early Crane is reminiscent of the young Zola's passion for social rescue, which found its most moving expression in *La Confession de Claude* (1865). The critics who wonder whether *Maggie* should be called a tragedy or a melodrama raise a fruitless issue, because the book is undeniably filled with pity and fear, and Howells was right when he discovered in it "that quality of fatal necessity which dominates Greek tragedy."

George's Mother is a companion piece to the drama of the New York prostitute, and it takes up again the problem of the corruption of innocence, this time in the person of a young workingman, George, who has recently settled in New York and lives in a tenement with his widowed mother, a very religious woman. The path leading to George's physical and moral destruction opens early in the story when he meets a former acquaintance, a certain Jones, who introduces him into a circle of alcoholics. He thus misses work one day and invents a lie as an excuse for his absence. His mother, who tries to keep him from drifting, induces him to go with her to a prayer meeting which only "prov[es] to him again that he [is] damned." Plunging more resolutely into drink and dissipation, the young man inflicts great moral torture upon his mother, who finally dies, worn down by disappointed expectations. The last scene shows her in the grips of her death agony, while her son, hastily called to her bedside, suddenly feels "hideous crabs crawling upon his brain." This book shows more the interest in abstract ideas than in real people; it demonstrates the baneful effects of Sunday school religion upon George, who seeks refuge from it in drink, and the failure of this primitive faith to succor the mother in her sorest need. It also points to the impossibility of communication between human beings. The power corruptive influences and environment exert on immature minds is here again illustrated. This rather flimsy novel raises a number of issues but solves none, and throughout are heard distinct echoes of Crane's conflict with his own mother.

The confined world of *George's Mother* could easily be contrasted with the maelstrom of life in Crane's New York City sketches, which he ranked among his "best work." He started his field study in the poorer districts of southern Manhattan, observing the motley streams of passers-by on Broadway, breadlines, crowds gathering outside cheap lodging houses, jingling streetcars, fires, Italian fruit vendors, tramps, policemen, and here and there his camera eye stopped on a detail, a "tiny old lady" lost in "the tempest of Sixth Avenue," or two children fighting for a toy. His sympathy drew him instinctively to the cause of the common man, but he was more inclined to study the actual working of minds than the possible consequences of economic systems. In his study of the "Tenderloin," undertaken for the *New York Journal* in 1896, he calls up a picture of restaurants, dance halls, and opium dens where, beneath the superficial gaiety, slumbers the fire of an ever-present violence.

His technique in these city sketches follows three main patterns: that of the journey of initiation, exemplified by "An Experiment in Misery" and "An Ominous Baby"; that of canvas painting, in "The Men in the Storm," "An Eloquence of Grief," and "The Auction"; and that of the parody, in some of his "Tenderloin" stories. The reporter-errant selects a certain situation which becomes a pretext for a psychological study of urban conflicts. To him "the sense of city [was] battle."

How did Crane's war novel, *The Red Badge of Courage*, come into being against this background of urban literature? The book is not an ordinary Civil War novel. Although the theme is the baptism of fire of a Union private, Henry Fleming, during the battle of Chancellorsville, the tone is psychological rather than military. Its main characters are most of the time designated as figures in an allegory, "the tall soldier," "the loud soldier," "the tattered man," "the man of the cheery voice"; and the protagonist, usually referred to as "the youth" in the early chapters, only acquires his full identity in Chapter XI.

The author's observation of "the nervous system under fire" is conducted on the level of Henry's restless mind; before the battle we witness the premonitory misgivings of this farm boy in uniform; then comes his moment of reassurance after a first onslaught of the enemy has been repulsed. A second attack launched against his side causes his sudden panic and flight. Driven by shame to wander on the fringe of the battlefield, he seems to be helplessly floating in a nightmarish atmosphere; this, for our cowardly private, is the beginning of a journey of expiation. He meets a "tattered soldier" whose wounds and embarrassing questions increase his sense of guilt. The two men are caught up in the procession of wounded soldiers who make their way to the rear. Among them they see Henry's friend, Jim Conklin, the mortally wounded "tall soldier" who, after horrible sufferings climaxed by a gruesome "danse macabre," dies under their petrified gaze. After this shattering experience Henry abandons the "tattered man" whose very presence seems to him an accusation. Retreat-

ing Union soldiers fly past him, and one of them, whom the youth tries to question, knocks him down with the butt of his rifle, ironically giving him the "red badge of courage" he had been longing for. After regaining consciousness Henry meets a man with "a cheery voice" who takes him back to his regiment and, from then on, the protagonist's attitude is altogether changed. He feels full of aggressive but specious self-confidence and, because he does not reveal the real cause of his wound, derives much unmerited respect from his fellow soldiers for his ostensibly courageous conduct. The last chapters show him turning into a daredevil, fighting at the head of his unit during a victorious charge, but at the end of the story—which is no pamphlet for recruiting officers—Henry's regiment finds itself recrossing the river it had crossed a few days before and thus going back to its previous position on the other bank of the Rappahannock as if nothing had happened. Henry's first impression had been right after all: "It was all a trap."

A constant ironic counterpoint aims to debunk the traditional concept of glorious war. The whole thing seems absurd: generals shout, stammer, and behave childishly on the battlefield; Henry's wound confers upon him a spurious glory; Wilson, the "loud soldier," has become as meek as a lamb in the last chapters, and the whole tumult has resulted in no gain of ground for the Union forces and no loss for the Confederates. What remains in the mind of the reader is a series of confused movements with, from time to time, "men drop[ping] here and there like bundles" and, in the protagonist's "procession of memory," sad nerve-racking images suddenly blurred with a sense of relief when the "sultry nightmare [is] in the past."

Like all the great classics of literature *The Red Badge of Courage* speaks of different things to different minds. However, only an oversimplified interpretation could see in Henry's final charge the proof that he has become, as he himself thinks, "a man." The pattern of this book is that of a spiritual journey, but the final goal remains in doubt when we reach the conclusion: "Over the river a golden ray of sun came through the hosts of leaden rain clouds." The youth, in his baptism of fire, has acquired self-knowledge and experience, but a radical change has not taken place within him: he remains, in his heroic pose at the end, just as grotesque as the fearful "little man" he was at the beginning. The dialogue he has been carrying on with his own conscience often contains overtones of legalistic chicanery: it is a constant search for excuses to justify his cowardly conduct. Occasional flashes of inner sincerity are defeated by his attempts to demonstrate that what he did was logically and morally valid, but his arguments would fail to convince anyone and only add to his torment. Through a series of excruciating experiences which follow his shameful act he manages to keep his secret and even to rise in stature in the eyes of his regiment. But, instead of closing the book with a reassuring epiphany, the author preserves the ironic structure throughout. Henry's conscience is still disturbed when the book ends, and his concealed guilt spoils "the gilded images of memory."

The Red Badge of Courage contains the account of a half-completed conversion. It is only in a satellite story entitled "The Veteran" that Henry pays the full price for his "sin" and goes through the final stage of his itinerary of redemption. Then, by belatedly but unequivocally confessing his lack of courage on the battlefield, he purges himself of his former lie. In the last scene of "The Veteran," determined to save two colts trapped in his burning barn, he plunges into the flames never to come out, thus making a gesture of genuine and unconventional bravery. Rejecting his previous

irony, Crane presents here a real conversion, grounded on cool, selfless determination and not on spurious enthusiasm, as was Henry's sudden reversal of mood on the battlefield.

In Crane's war novel religious imagery prevails, centered on an itinerary of spiritual redemption which leads not to eternal salvation but to a blissful impasse. Alone in the middle of the forest the hero discovers the imaginary "chapel" with its "columnlike" trees where a "hymn of twilight" is heard. When the "tall soldier" dies, wildly gesturing in his final agony, he seems to resemble "a devotee of a mad religion"; most significant in the same creative process is Henry's illusion after his cowardly flight: he looks for "a means of escape from the consequences of his fall" and, unable to reach redemption through mere introspection, returns to "the creed of soldiers." But his final charge does not purge him of his guilt in spite of a temporary exultation due to the repression of his fear; "the ghost of his flight" and "a specter of reproach" born of the desertion of "the tattered man" in his sorest need keep haunting the youth at the close of the book. Some obvious similarities with the theme of concealment in Hawthorne's fiction can also be noted: "veil" metaphors and similes clustered around the character of Henry Fleming keep recurring in the narrative. In Chapter I the hero "wish[es] to be alone with some new thoughts that [have] lately come to him"; in Chapter VII he "cring[es] as if discovered in a crime" and, under the burden of his hidden guilt, soon feels that "his shame [can] be viewed." But an ironic glimmer of hope reappears in his consciousness when he imagines that "in the battle blur" his face will be hidden "like the face of a cowled man."

Beside this procession of religious images there appears here and there a scattering of scenes with animal characters which seem to be fables in miniature. The style abounds in symbolic rabbits, squirrels, horses, cows, and snakes which form a conventional bestiary by the side of a Christian demonology swarming with monsters directly borrowed from Biblical literature.

Another facet of this book is its consistent use of legalistic terminology. A dossier is being minutely, if inconclusively, revealed to us: the youth of this story approaches his problem of fear in a logical manner and determines to "accumulate information of himself"; at first he tries to "mathematically prove to himself that he [will] not run from a battle." Then, after experiencing his shameful flight, he acts as his own lawyer and attempts to present a convincing defense of his case: "He had done a good part in saving himself, who was a little part of the army. . . . His actions had been sagacious things. They had been full of strategy. They were the work of a master's legs." A strong ironic coloring, one of the main characteristics of Crane's style in the whole book, can easily be detected here. Henry is constantly trying to show his actions to advantage; when he returns to his regiment after his cowardly escape, he even considers using the "small weapon"—a packet of letters—which Wilson in a panic had left in his hands before the battle. This "exhibit" would, Henry thinks, "prostrate his comrade at the first signs of a cross-examination."

The mechanistic imagery of *The Red Badge of Courage* already adumbrates the development of Crane's war motif in his writings after the Cuban conflict of 1898, and serves to highlight the complexity and destructiveness of modern war: "The battle was like the grinding of an immense and terrible machine to him. Its complexities and powers, its grim processes, fascinated him. He must go close and see it produce corpses."

If military courage had been one of the values pitilessly probed in *The Red Badge of Courage*, it also furnished the central topic for a satellite story entitled "A Mystery of Heroism." Private Fred Collins ventures into no man's land under the pretext of procuring some water for his company; but in fact his action has been prompted by the desire to prove himself that he is not "afraid t' go." After being "blindly . . . led by quaint emotions" he returns unscathed to his lines, but the author wastes no sympathy on his "heroic" deed. "Death and the Child' deals with the same theme, the scene being now the Greco-Turkish war of 1897; the central character, a war correspondent, soon sees his battle fury die out and, instead of fighting by the side of the soldiers of his mother country, flees and encounters a child who asks him this embarrassing question: "Are you a man?"

In his reporting of the same war and of the Cuban conflict Crane fell in with the conventions of his time and did not aim at more than ordinary journalistic style. But when reworking his factual accounts of battles and recollecting his war experiences in tranquillity he achieved the spare and severe economy of *Wounds in the Rain* (1900), a moving and realistic adaptation in fiction of his own adventures with the American forces sent to Cuba in 1898. His protagonist then ceased to be a dreamy amateur like Henry Fleming in *The Red Badge* or Peza in "Death and the Child," and the figure of Private Nolan, the regular, as anonymous and unromantic as any true regular, stood out in the foreground. Crane was now dealing with war as a special trade, and his soldiers at work were shown to be "as deliberate and exact as so many watchmakers." In "The Price of the Harness" he went beyond the phantasmagoria of his early definition of war and made of "a great, grand steel loom . . . to weave a woof of thin red threads, the cloths of death," the essential metaphor of his battle symbolics. Henceforth, in the logbook of the war correspondent, what had been in *The Red Badge* a "monster," "a dragon," or a "blood-swollen god," gradually came down to the lowly estate of "death, and a plague of the lack of small things and toil." Crane could not have gone any further in deglamorizing that image of "vague and bloody conflicts" which had once "thrilled [Henry Fleming] with their sweep and fire."

A gradual reduction of the concept of war to the archetype can be found in Crane's later stories, if we leave aside as mere pot-boiling and unoriginal work his *Great Battles of the World* (1901). It is in the "Spitzbergen Tales" that the war metaphor is suddenly brought down to its essentials, the taking of a coveted hill, the storming of a redoubt, or a burial scene on the front line. The typical hero of most of these stories is no longer a private but a non-commissioned or low-ranking officer, the problem of conduct being then studied in an almost abstract context and the main issue being the duty of the responsible professional toward his command. Primarily concerned with war as a personal test, Crane avoided the approach of the historian, that of the strategist, and deliberately worked out that of the moralist.

To him war, in its various manifestations, was the alpha and omega of human life, essentially a testing ground, but adventure could be a fair substitute. Sent to the West and Mexico by the Bacheller Syndicate as a roving reporter early in 1895, he drew upon his tour for a few outstanding stories. His shipwreck off the coast of Florida in January 1897 furnished material for "The Open Boat," a tale which won immediate recognition and found in Conrad and H. G. Wells two faithful admirers. The latter even went so far as to say about it: "[It is], to my mind, beyond all question, the crown of all his work."

Stephen Crane depended on adventure, vicarious or real, as fodder for his imagination.

He had to *feel* intensely to *write* intensely. As soon as the pace of his life became relaxed because of illness and a general weakening of his spiritual energy, he was compelled to turn to his childhood reminiscences, also fraught with intense emotions, or to an archetypal war metaphor in order to write successfully.

The short stories "The Blue Hotel," "The Bride Comes to Yellow Sky," and "The Open Boat" outline his personal attitude toward the literary utilization of experience. Although fond of exotic settings and people, Crane is not a local colorist. The colors of his adventures are the colors of his soul. For example, the real fight that he saw in a saloon in Lincoln, Nebraska, which is supposed to have been the germ of "The Blue Hotel," was transmuted by him into a moral study on the theme of collective and individual responsibility. The narrative in this tale is conducted on two levels, straight storytelling and ironic counterpoint. A Swede who has lived for ten years in New York and is now traveling in the West experiences forebodings of violent death and is eventually justified in his fear, since he meets his doom at the hands of a professional gambler. Crane, however, succeeds in keeping up the suspense by leading his main character into ominous situations at the Palace Hotel which are ironically deflated and prove harmless to the frightened hero. Once the latter feels that all danger is over and is about to celebrate his escape from the hotel in a neighboring saloon, he is stabbed to death by a gambler whom he wanted too insistently to befriend. Crane here comes back again to an analysis of fear. In the Swede's mind this feeling follows a pattern similar to that of Henry's itinerary in *The Red Badge*: from timidity to unrestrained arrogance. Both Henry and the Swede are intoxicated, the former with a belatedly discovered battle fury, the latter with repeated drinking. Crane also explores the comic overtones of violence, and notes the grotesque fall of the Swede's body, "pierced as easily as if it had been a melon." The protagonist obviously brought about his own destruction, but the writer is not just censuring one man's attitude, and the easterner, Mr. Blanc, who acts as point-of-view character, declares: " 'We are all in it! . . . Every sin is the result of a collaboration.' " Once again the creator of *Maggie* stigmatized the unpardonable sin, indifference: no one had done anything to prevent the final denouement from taking place. The hotel-keeper and the bartender had provided drink; the other "collaborators," Johnnie excepted, since he had been most active in arousing the Swede's anger, had each exhibited a different form of passivity.

"One Dash—Horses" is another study of fear, this time in a Mexican setting. In its gaudy and alluring garb this tale reads like a direct transcript of experience, but the narrative is not limited to the account of a thrilling manhunt; Crane is more interested in exploring the psychological springs of fear and the power of illusion. The young American and his guide are afraid of the Mexican bandits, and the latter are terrorized by the thought of the mounted police—the "rurales"—but it is an abstract stereotype of the traditional enemy which causes this feeling in both cases. The Mexican bandits prove to be playthings in the hands of the gods, and the arrival of a group of prostitutes scatters to the winds their plans of murder and plunder; later on, when their lust has been appeased and they have resumed the chase, a detachment of rurales frightens them away without firing a single shot. The real power of the story lies in its subtle use of irony and in its cascading evocations of fear in a western-style pursuit.

In "The Bride Comes to Yellow Sky" Crane reached a peak in his exploration of the humorous overtones of fear. A favorite of the author

himself and of many of his admirers, "The Bride" raises the western story to the level of the classic by consistently applying to a trite but dramatic situation the powerful lever of irony. It deals with a very unromantic event, the homecoming of a town marshal after his wedding with a plain-looking and timid bride. This town marshal is afraid of nothing except public opinion and, since his marriage was secretly arranged, he fears the hostile reaction of the inhabitants of Yellow Sky, an obvious projection of Crane's own predicament in his life with Cora. When, after walking through the deserted town, the couple reach the door of their home, they meet Scratchy Wilson, the local outlaw. A bloody encounter to come, we might think, but in fact nothing happens: the outlaw is defeated by the mere sight of the town marshal seen for the first time as a married man and walking home unarmed. "Defeated by a woman's mute presence" might have been the headline for such a story if it had been printed in a "yellow" newspaper. Crane thought that "The Bride" was "a daisy," and he was right. From beginning to end this charming tale proves that the whole mystique of the wild West was for him nothing but a game, and he enjoyed watching this game in its closing stages.

But no judgment of Crane's ability as a storyteller can be reached without a proper assessment of "a tale intended to be after the fact" entitled "The Open Boat," which relates the concluding phase of an almost fatal adventure. The newspaper report he sent to the *New York Press* in January 1897, immediately after his shipwreck, gave a detailed account of every episode excluding the "thirty hours" spent in an open boat. It took a few weeks for the definitive story to crystallize in his mind as a parable of human existence. We follow the ordeal of four survivors during their long wait in a lifeboat, their desperate attempts to reach the shore after their ship has sunk. Finally the captain decides to risk steering the frail dinghy through the breakers: the four men—the captain, the cook, the oiler, and the correspondent—have, each of them, felt the "subtle brotherhood" born of their shared distress and struggle. Once in the breakers the boat is overturned and the oiler is killed. The other three set foot safely ashore. Crane never wrote a more orderly tale: the correspondent, acting as point-of-view character—although he is also a participant—helps to bring the main facets of the story into focus. We learn much about the transformation of his mind in the crucible of experience. This shipwreck is for him a journey leading from cynicism to humility. But here again Crane retains the ironic approach, especially when he shows the correspondent's indignation leveled at the serene indifference of God. "Shipwrecks are *apropos* of nothing" puts into a nutshell the meaning of the whole story. There is the world of facts on one side and the world of ideas and literature on the other, but facts as such do not exist to *prove* anything. However, some lessons can be drawn from the chaos of experience if men manage to be "interpreters." Crane's message here is one of endurance, brotherhood, and stoic acceptance of man's fate; his vision of the universe is one in which man appears frail and insignificant when isolated but surprisingly strong in a united effort. Ruthlessly debunking all the conventional views about heroism, he seems to imply that the only courage worthy of esteem is unobtrusive, silent, and more self-denying than self-assertive.

The true power of this story comes from a style which, in descriptive passages, is almost that of a prose poem. The dialogue, spare and accurate, gives balance to the general tone. According to Edward Garnett, Crane's art at its best was "self-poising as is the art of the perfect dancer." Joined to the grace of the dancer we find in this tale of human frailty a superb control of emotion which makes it a masterpiece of classical art, the epic flow of the narrative being constantly tempered and toned down by gentle touches of irony.

There always remained in Crane, as Alfred Kazin has pointed out, "a local village boy." Essentially American in his stance, although a rebel against many things American, he willingly spoke about his experience of the small town. Far from idealizing his vision, he set it against the background of his urban and cosmopolitan environment and judged it unemotionally.

The Crane brothers loved the countryside of Sullivan County, New York, where they fished, hunted, rode horses, and camped during the summer months. The hills, mountains, and valleys of this still rather wild area form a recurrent image in many of Stephen Crane's stories, poems, and prose poems. Although he used this background indirectly in his fiction, he made of it the infrastructure of his vision of the world.

The Third Violet (1897) reflects a deep attachment to the colors and shapes of Sullivan County. It exploits both the popular theme of the "summer hotel" and Crane's own experience at the Art Students' League in New York. In this novel the author has captured some of the flavor of bohemianism, but his treatment of this subject lacks originality. *The Third Violet*, which won very little applause from critics except for Ford Madox Hueffer, is saved from mediocrity by contrasting vignettes of rural and urban life. This book hints at the difficult struggle of young artists with the commercial values of their age: Hawker, a young painter, goes to Sullivan County where his farmer parents live; he is merely in search of peace and inspiration but, in a neighboring hotel, the summer has brought adventure in the shape of a rich New York heiress, Miss Fanhall. It is love at first sight, and the novel abounds in meetings and vapid conversations between the two lovers and a few other characters, a "writing friend" of Hawker's called Hollanden, a rival in love, named Oglethorpe, who is the irresistible rich suitor, and a group of irresponsible young artists belonging to Hawker's circle in New York. Among the latter stands out a rather colorful young model in love with Hawker, Florinda. We close the book unconvinced by the plot which, with the gift of a final violet symbolizing the reconciliation of the two lovers, seems to be heading for a conventional epilogue. Crane did not want his novel to end tragically, as his real-life romance with Nellie Crouse had done.

"The Monster," a story set in a rural background, can be regarded as one of the most important of his short works. It is centered on the disastrous consequences of a generous action: a doctor's son has been rescued from his burning house by a Negro servant, Henry Johnson, whose face is "burned away." Out of gratitude the doctor decides to nurse his heroic servant and insists on keeping him in his reconstructed house, but the sight of the "monster" frightens everyone in the neighborhood; the doctor soon becomes an object of opprobrium and loses much of his practice. A deputation of influential citizens tries to persuade him to compromise with public opinion and asks him to turn Henry over to an institution, but the doctor remains adamant. The last scene shows him returning from his rounds and finding his wife crying over the teacups of guests who have not come. This brilliant exposition of village mores is enhanced by symbolic touches which, in the laboratory scene during the fire, reach a climax with the lurid vision of threatening and fantastically colored shapes. Besides the fear born of physical danger, the author probes the blind unreasoning panic generated by the sight of the harmless and horribly maimed Negro, and the many anxieties caused by public opinion. He has also, by the very choice of his protagonist, indicated that true heroism is not the privilege of the whites alone.

Crane began reminiscing about his early youth when he had used up the store of material born of his adult experience. Port Jervis, New York, was the nucleus around which the *Whilomville Stories* took shape. It is "any boy's town," but also a very specific one within reach of New York City, yet quite provincial and sleepy with its backdrop of fields, rivers, hills, and forests, a place where boys and girls can roam at peace except when under the ferule of their school or Sunday school teachers. The fields are close by and the farmers' slow and benevolent manner offers a sharp contrast with the "barbarous" habits of the villagers who give tea parties, launch into charitable campaigns, and, in the summertime, entertain relatives from the city.

The rural life depicted by Crane is more civilized than that Mark Twain had evoked before him; it is less sentimentally reconstructed than the *Boy's Town* of W. D. Howells. Abhorring as he did the "Little Lord Fauntleroy" craze which had swept his country in the 1880's, Crane did not hesitate to show us real children. He is aware of their tastes and distastes and conscious of their cruelty—at times they appear to him as "little blood-fanged wolves." In fact, more than a picture of childhood, he gives a picture of town life, since the children project an image of their parents' world stripped to its essentials. Although fond of the company of youngsters and a great favorite with his nieces, Crane was not holding a brief in favor of youth. To quote Robert Frost out of context, he "lov[ed] the things he love[d] for what they [were]"; his children were, like their adult counterparts, charmingly deluded in their vision of the world, and we can safely smile at their innocent pranks, for Crane did not allow them to give free rein to their worst instincts. At the critical moment something happened: a bully relented or an adult came into view, and none of these little dramas of the backyard turned into a real tragedy.

By profession a journalist and a writer of fiction, Crane had a higher regard for his poetic endeavors than for the rest of his literary work. He preferred his first volume of verse, *The Black Riders* (1895), to his *Red Badge of Courage* because "it was a more ambitious effort. My aim was to comprehend in it the thoughts I have had about life in general while 'The Red Badge' is a mere episode in life, an amplification."

But he did not observe the traditions and conventions of poetic expression respected by most of his contemporaries, except isolated rebels like Walt Whitman and Emily Dickinson. Alfred Kazin has called Crane "our first *poète maudit*," and such a label fits him to perfection, for he regarded poetry, more than prose, as a vehicle for ideals generally unconventional or iconoclastic.

It is easy to find models for the patterns if not for the tone of Crane's early verse. He had obviously read Biblical parables, and some of the work of Emily Dickinson, Whitman, Ambrose Bierce, and Olive Schreiner, but his poetry remained essentially the expression of his own vision.

The sharpness and brevity of the sixty-eight pieces forming his *Black Riders* remind many readers of Emily Dickinson's great verbal economy. Like that of the poetess of Amherst his voice was one of protest. His own rebellion went against the God of the Old Testament, and he strove to debunk a cluster of false values, especially ambition, conformity, worldly wisdom, military glory, and tradi-

tional religion. The universe pictured by Crane in his poetry has elements of pessimism which have caused some critics to regard it as naturalistic, but the poet also exalts the positive virtues of love, endurance, and self-reliance. Crane feels a great admiration for the "little man" who keeps facing the mountains fearlessly, for the lonely individualist who "sought a new road" and "died thus alone," for "they said he had courage." The first themes of his poetic vision radiate from a central concern, the problem of man's relation with God. Even earthly love can be poisoned by the idea of sin, and man must free himself from his obsessive fear of God and from the network of illusions woven by his imagination. Crane's rebellion was sound, but the occasionally crude phrasing of his protest and the printing of the volume in small capitals made it fair game for the parodists.

His second book of poetry, *War Is Kind* (1899), contained thirty-seven poems: fourteen of these had already been printed between 1895 and 1898; a group of ten love poems called "Intrigue" and some of the remaining pieces belonged to a second poetic output. The iconoclastic note had not died out and the author went on debunking the outward forms of religious ritual:

> You tell me this is God?
> I tell you this is a printed list,
> A burning candle and an ass.

But his poetry gradually became more concrete and more socially oriented. Instead of dealing with abstract imaginings, vague and remote parables, it drank deep from the fountain of experience. His bitter satire on the popular glorification of military courage in such a poem as "War Is Kind" (which, although the initial piece in the second volume, belongs to the first period) had been expressed along general lines. With the "The Blue Battalions" and the poems inspired by the Spanish-American War, Crane did not hesitate to present war as the utmost form of God's playful fancy and violently denounced the exploitation of "patriots" by "practical men" as well as the imperialistic overtones of America's help to the Cuban rebels.

Several poems stigmatized other forms of exploitation of man by man. The gaudy and showy splendor of the mansions of the new rich aroused his metaphoric ire with a vision of

. . . a crash of flunkeys
And yawning emblems of Persia
Cheeked against oak, France and a sabre,
The outcry of old beauty
Whored by pimping merchants
To submission before wine and chatter.

And he ironically rejected the basic injustice of laissez-faire economics:

Why should the strong—
—The beautiful strong—
Why should they not have the flowers?

If the theme of love had, in the poems of the first poetic manner, taken on few romantic dimensions except in the sheltering gesture of a woman's "white arms," the second volume of verse and some posthumous poems enable us to probe deeper into Crane's house of love. "On the desert" and "A naked woman and a dead dwarf" fly the banner of Baudelairean decadence most clearly and remind us of "La femme et le serpent" and, as has been recently pointed out, of a prose poem by the French symbolist entitled "Le fou et la Vénus." "Intrigue," the last section of *War Is Kind*, represents Crane's attempt to bring into focus the many components of his love poetry: sensuality, sin-consciousness, and jealousy form the dark side of man's central passion, but Crane's

bitter lyricism is spoiled by hackneyed romantic imagery, skulls "with ruby eyes," cracked bowls, castles, temples, daggers, and specters.

He discovered a better instrument for his highly sensitive nature in the prose poem. "The Judgment of the Sage" and "The Snake" are true fables, and the same ingredients are found in them as in his verse; but whereas the verse rejects all traditional rules (rhyme, regular meter, and very often stanzaic form), the prose poems retain a classical mode of expression. They remind us of Baudelaire's utilization of the same medium, but here again Crane's manner remains distinctly his own. He thus studied some archetypes, those of charity, material success, earthly conflict or cosmic battle. "The Judgment of the Sage," which raises the ghost of a Kantian dilemma, briefly tells us the story of a vain quest, that of worldly wisdom. Should we practice charity "because of God's word" or because the beggar is hungry? Crane does not solve this riddle; God seems to play with man his eternal game of hide-and-seek and keeps him on the run. "A Self-Made Man" parodies the Horatio Alger type of success story. " 'To succeed in life . . . the youth of America have only to see an old man seated upon a railing and smoking a clay pipe. Then go up and ask him for a match.' " "The Voice of the Mountain" and "The Victory of the Moon" are focused on the conflict between man and a mysterious cosmic power which can occasionally be defeated by "the little creature of the earth." With "The Snake" the inevitable fight for survival is brought to its emotional climax: the two most antagonistic creatures in the world, man and the snake, confront each other in a ruthless duel in which the principals fight with equal arms, the snake with its venom and man with his stick. If the snake is defeated it is not for lack of courage. Thanks to a clever manipulation of language

Crane combines in a unified whole the simplicity of the fable, the logical structure of the sermon, and the raciness of the tall tale.

His poetry at times foreshadows Imagism, as Carl Sandburg pointed out in his "Letters to Dead Imagists," but some pieces of the second volume of verse show a tendency to explode the small abstract capsule of the early poems. It is difficult to say where Crane's real poetic genius lies, whether in his spare, concise parables, in his longer symbolistic compositions, or in his prose poems. He worshiped brevity as the first tenet of his literary creed, but he was also touched by the wave of decadent aesthetics that Copeland and Day, his publishers, who were also the American publishers of the *Yellow Book,* had helped to introduce into the United States. There was, however, too much love of moral integrity in Crane for him to become a true decadent. In his verse he often displayed the pathetic agony of a fallen albatross, but the prose poem was perhaps the literary instrument whose scope and subtle rhythm best suited his genius.

Crane's style has a certain number of idiosyncrasies: it is primarily the language of a writer in transition betraying an inner conflict between a romantic tradition and realistic impulses. He began with what he called his "Rudyard-Kipling style" and the "Sullivan County Sketches" contain the germs of most of his future work, displaying as they do a love of abstraction and a systematic use of color, patterning the narrative with structural irony, and building up an oneiric atmosphere laden with threat. It is a gradual mastery of form that we witness in the passage from the style of the early years to that emerging between 1894 and 1898.

Impelled by a desire to control the deep stirrings of his soul, he soon declared that he wished "to write plainly and unmistakably, so that all men (and some women) might read and understand." Crane's literary aesthetics was close to that of the French master of the short story, Guy de Maupassant. According to the author of *Pierre et Jean,* "Les grands artistes sont ceux qui imposent à l'humanité leur illusion particulière." Such a position might very well have been defined by Stephen Crane, who wanted the writer to tell the world what "his own pair of eyes" enabled him to see and nothing else. Maupassant's universe, however, differed significantly from Crane's: whereas the French writer often indulged in an excess of sensual evocations, Crane preserved throughout his writing career the viewpoint of the moralist and usually conveyed his ethical comments by means of ironic counterpoint.

He was deeply conscious of man's littleness and of God's overbearing power. Man's wanderings on the earth were pictured by him as those of a lonely pilgrim in a pathless universe. Crane's phraseology comes directly from the Bible, the sermons, and the hymns which had shaped his language during his youth. The topography of his stories, where hills, mountains, rivers, and meadows appear under symbolic suns or moons, is, to a large extent, an abstraction fraught with religious or moral significance. With its "monsters" of various kinds and its "dragons," the demonology of *The Red Badge of Courage* evinces a truly apocalyptic quality. In Crane's best work the imagery of the journey of initiation occupies a central position and reaches a climactic stage with some experience of conversion. He did not accept, it is true, the traditional interpretation of the riddle of the universe offered by the Methodist church. Nevertheless he constantly used a Christian terminology, and the thought of "sin" inspired his characters with guilty fears and stirred up within them such frequent debates with a troubled conscience that it is impossible to study his achievement outside a religious tradition.

But he did not remain a prisoner of the stylistic patterns which he derived from his revivalist heritage. New York street life very early made an impact on his language, which thus acquired its liveliness and its ability to picture violence in colorful terms. Crane's dialogues abound in expletives, in stereotyped phrases, in phonetic transcriptions of common verbal corruptions and dialectal idiosyncrasies. Yet they never fall into the trap of overspecialization. His ear was good, whether he listened to Irish, German, Italian, or Cuban immigrants in New York, to farmers in Sullivan County, or to Negroes in Port Jervis, but he never tried to achieve a perfect rendering of local dialect. In *The Red Badge of Courage* he used dialogue to introduce some degree of differentiation between Henry Fleming and his comrades but, on the whole, Crane's characters all speak one language which is Crane's own, a youthful and casual version of the American vernacular of the 1890's often heard in artists' studios and among students.

Language is in the mouths of his central characters a stylized medium carrying universal overtones, and this trait reveals an essential aspect of his fictional techniques, namely the dramatic approach. He tried his hand several times at playwriting and, although his various attempts in this literary genre were of modest stature, he was naturally inclined to work out his tales and some of his verse in terms of stage stylistics. He completed three very slight plays. *At Clancy's Wake* (1893) is a one-act sketch which brings to life the hilarious moments of an Irish wake in New York; *The Blood of the Martyr* (1898) satirizes in three brief acts German imperialistic policies in China. Another attempt at playwriting was his "Spanish-Amer-

ican War Play," unpublished in Crane's lifetime but recently included in *The War Dispatches of Stephen Crane* (1964): this two-act drama gives a mildly amusing but superficial picture of stereotyped national traits against the background of a real conflict that the author had seen at first hand. Only a fragment of the text of "The Ghost"—his English play—has reached us so far and it is difficult to take seriously what was meant to be a mere Christmas entertainment. All his other attempts at playwriting were abortive.

What remains most striking in Crane's style considered as a whole is a concern for brevity and a constant use of irony which serves a twofold purpose: it provides his best work with tightly knit thematic structures and reveals his tacit belief in a rigid set of values which condemns indifference and conformism, and extols moral courage and integrity.

Seen in the perspective of the years which have elapsed since his death, Crane's work is surprisingly modern. His influence on the war literature of the twentieth century in England and America has been very significant. Many of Hemingway's novels and short stories disclose a similar preoccupation with "the moral problem of conduct" and obvious stylistic affinities; distinct echoes of *The Red Badge* can be heard in *A Farewell to Arms*. In England we could trace recurring correspondences in the work of Joseph Conrad and Ford Madox Ford. Ford, like Conrad, had been a good friend of Crane's during the last three years of his life, and both defended his literary and moral reputation in magazine articles or prefaces after his death. The plight of the isolated hero, which became a favorite theme of Conrad's, stemmed directly from *The Red Badge of Courage*. Obsession with the fear of showing a white feather haunted the soul of the author of *Lord Jim* as much as that of the creator of Henry Fleming. In his own fiction Ford Madox Ford used complex techniques and mixed many strands of life, but some of the most dramatic scenes in *A Man Could Stand Up,* which are mere vignettes of life at the front, remind us in their bare and rugged prose of deliberately unpoetic descriptions of war in *The Red Badge.* Like Crane, Ford emphasized "the eternal waiting that is War" and the crippling effects of noise on a battlefield. And, in order to describe the subtle change taking place in a soldier's mind, he used almost Cranean terms.

Among the pioneers of the "free-verse army" Crane is often neglected by anthologists or literary critics. Yet he gave to the poetry of his country the patterns and rhythms of an "exasperated prose" that foreshadows modern poetic expression.

Carl Van Doren wrote in 1924: "Modern American literature may be said, accurately enough, to have begun with Stephen Crane." This statement needs to be qualified, but Crane was one of the leading figures of protest of his generation and thus showed the way to American liberalism. His influence in the field of the novel has affected a mode of thought rather than literary techniques, if we leave aside his synesthetic use of imagery which survives almost intact in F. Scott Fitzgerald. Crane's impact has been felt mostly in the genre of the short story, for which he displayed a personal preference. "The Blue Hotel," "The Bride Comes to Yellow Sky," and, above all, "The Open Boat" are some of the finest models of American literary achievement in this genre, and the greatest successes of Faulkner, Sherwood Anderson, Hemingway, Fitzgerald, and other modern American short story writers hark back to these models. Accuracy in details, conciseness, and effective rendering, framed and supported by an ironic structure, are now frequently regarded as essential re-

quirements by American practitioners of the short story.

Most of Crane's work could be explained in terms of his religious background, and he always betrays, even in his most sportive mood, the serious preoccupations of the born moralist. However, his slum stories, instead of aiming to move the reader by exaggerated pathos and convert him to the cause of reform, wish to convert him to the cause of psychological truth; social implications are left for the reader to discover but are not explicitly stated. When dealing with his main theme, war, he gradually worked out a revolutionary stand, doing away with externals and reducing human conflict to a classic drama of internal forces struggling with elemental powers. From Henry Fleming in *The Red Badge* to Timothy Lean in the "Spitzbergen Tales" the itinerary of heroism evolves from a path sprinkled with doubtful victories to a road doggedly followed with a sturdy and silent acceptance of personal responsibility; diseased and action-hampering introspection eventually gives way to selfless and unassuming patterns of affirmation. "The Open Boat" contains a plea for human solidarity and *Wounds in the Rain,* in spite of a persistent and depressing background of military servitude, discreetly affirms the superiority of collective to individual prowess. A subtle feeling of warmth and brotherhood pervades the later studies of Crane on war; even "The Upturned Face," a macabre piece which describes a burial scene on the front line, places the reader in the midst of an ultimate manifestation of soldierly brotherhood.

It is in the novel of manners that Crane's achievement is at its lowest ebb. He did not try to study complex human relationships born of urban settings but dealt with a few basic themes, rivalries between lovers, or conflicts between generations and social classes. Often unable to provide his puppets with life, he proved his mastery in the art of reproducing informal dialogue. He experimented in the field of the picaresque novel—a medium he had already used in several short stories—but *The O'Ruddy* cannot be regarded as a genuine offspring of his mind since Robert Barr gave this novel its conclusion and ultimate form.

Crane's identity runs no risk of being drowned in a backflow of imitators, because his style remains his own. His unerring eye for color, his brilliant use of synesthetic effects, his love for the potent metaphor made him controversially famous in his lifetime and now stamp him as a truly original artist. His sometimes erratic grammar no longer shocks us, while his cinematic techniques have come into their own.

It was his aim to underline elements of absurdity in human life, and his work contains disquieting overtones for sedate minds. His was a voice of dissent which rejected the ostensibly impregnable soundness of historical Christianity, the conventional vision of a well-ordered society and that genteel tradition of culture which never left drawing rooms and libraries. Crane inherited the New England habit of individual assertion. He fits well into the American liberal tradition and can, in some respects, be regarded as a spiritual son of Emerson. Any form of dogmatism in any field of human life seemed to him both childish and harmful to what he valued above everything else, the integrity of the human soul. No problem could, according to him, ever find a definitive solution and he had certainly listened to Emerson's advice: "Congratulate yourself if you have done something strange and extravagant, and broken the monotony of a decorous age." This sentence adorned a beam in one of the studios of the old Arts Students' League building in New York where Crane lived sporadically in 1893 and 1894. Above and be-

yond this cult of nonconformism is another idea of Emerson's which involves the deeper regions of the soul: "Always do what you are afraid to do." Crane put this motto into practice so consistently that he wrecked his health and seriously endangered his moral reputation in his own country.

His recent popularity, essentially due to a revival of critical interest during the 1950's, should help prepare the ground for a clearer assessment of Crane's achievement. To our generation he can still teach moral integrity, a revised conception of courage, and psychological truth, all the more effectively because he did not resort to traditional didactic devices. He can also show modern prose writers the flexibility of the English language and encourage them to make linguistic experiments and create a language free from any excessive tyranny of the past, perfectly in tune with the spirit of the age and yet retaining the robust vitality which is the trademark of the classic.

Selected Bibliography

WORKS OF STEPHEN CRANE

NOVELS

Maggie: A Girl of the Streets (A Story of New York), by Johnston Smith (pseud.). N.p. [1893]. (Revised edition, *Maggie: A Girl of the Streets*. New York: Appleton, 1896.) There have been three recent reprints of note: one edited by Joseph Katz (Gainesville, Fla.: Scholars' Facsimiles and Reprints, 1966); another by Maurice Bassan (*Stephen Crane's Maggie, Text and Context*, Belmont, Calif.: Wadsworth Publication, 1966); and another by Donald Pizer (San Francisco: Chandler, 1968).
The Red Badge of Courage. New York: Appleton, 1895.

George's Mother. New York and London: Edward Arnold, 1896.

The Third Violet. New York: Appleton, 1897.

Active Service. New York: Frederick A. Stokes, 1899.

The O'Ruddy. New York: Frederick A. Stokes, 1903.

The Complete Novels of Stephen Crane, edited by Thomas A. Gullason. New York: Doubleday, 1967.

SHORT STORIES AND SKETCHES

The Little Regiment and Other Episodes of the American Civil War. New York: Appleton, 1896.

The Open Boat and Other Stories. New York: Doubleday and McClure, 1898.

The Monster and Other Stories. New York: Harper, 1899. (Contains only "The Monster," "The Blue Hotel," and "His New Mittens.")

Whilomville Stories. New York and London: Harper, 1900.

Wounds in the Rain. New York: Frederick A. Stokes, 1900.

Great Battles of the World. Philadelphia: Lippincott, 1901.

The Monster. London: Harper, 1901. (Contains "The Monster," "The Blue Hotel," "His New Mittens," "Twelve O'Clock," "Moonlight on the Snow," "Manacled," and "An Illusion in Red and White.")

Last Words. London: Digby, Long, 1902.

Men, Women and Boats, edited with an introduction by Vincent Starrett. New York: Boni and Liveright, 1917. (Contains seventeen stories and sketches.)

A Battle in Greece. Mount Vernon, N.Y.: Peter Pauper Press, 1936. (Contains a reprint of the battle sketch which appeared in the *New York Journal* of June 13, 1897.)

The Sullivan County Sketches, edited by Melvin Schoberlin. Syracuse, N.Y.: Syracuse University Press, 1949.

The Complete Short Stories and Sketches of Stephen Crane, edited by Thomas A. Gullason. New York: Doubleday, 1963.

The New York City Sketches of Stephen Crane and Related Pieces, edited by R. W. Stallman and E. R. Hagemann. New York: New York University Press, 1966.

Stephen Crane: Sullivan County Tales and Sketches, edited by R. W. Stallman. Ames: Iowa State University Press, 1968.

WAR DISPATCHES

The War Dispatches of Stephen Crane, edited by R. W. Stallman and E. R. Hagemann. New York: New York University Press, 1964.

POETRY AND PLAYS

The Black Riders and Other Lines. Boston: Copeland and Day, 1895.

A Souvenir and a Medley. East Aurora, N.Y.: Roycroft Printing Shop, 1896. (Contains seven poems, as well as a sketch entitled "A Great Mistake" and a fifteen-line piece printed in capitals, "A Prologue," which reads like stage directions.)

War Is Kind. New York: Frederick A. Stokes, 1899.

At Clancy's Wake, in *Last Words*. London: Digby, Long, 1902.

The Collected Poems of Stephen Crane, edited by Wilson Follett. New York: Knopf, 1930.

The Blood of the Martyr. Mount Vernon, N.Y.: Peter Pauper Press, [1940]. (A play originally printed in the Sunday magazine of the *New York Press* on April 3, 1898.)

Drama in Cuba, in *The War Dispatches of Stephen Crane*, edited by R. W. Stallman and E. R. Hagemann. New York: New York University Press, 1964.

The Poems of Stephen Crane, a critical edition by Joseph Katz. New York: Cooper Square Publishers, 1966.

COLLECTED EDITIONS

A new edition of the complete works of Stephen Crane is being prepared at the University of Virginia.

The Work of Stephen Crane, edited by Wilson Follett. 12 vols. New York: Knopf, 1925–27. (Reprinted in 6 vols., New York: Russell and Russell, 1963.)

Stephen Crane: An Omnibus, edited by R. W. Stallman. New York: Knopf, 1952.

Stephen Crane: Uncollected Writings, edited with

an introduction by Olov W. Fryckstedt. Uppsala: Almqvist and Wiksell, 1963.

LETTERS

Stephen Crane: Letters, edited by R. W. Stallman and Lillian Gilkes. New York: New York University Press, 1960.

BIBLIOGRAPHY

A new bibliography has been prepared by R. W. Stallman for Iowa State University Press. Since 1963 Syracuse University has issued an annual Crane bibliography in *Thoth*.

Williams, Ames W., and Vincent Starrett. *Stephen Crane: A Bibliography*. Glendale, Calif.: John Valentine, 1948.

BIOGRAPHIES

Beer, Thomas. *Stephen Crane*. New York: Knopf, 1923.

Berryman, John. *Stephen Crane*. New York: William Sloane Associates, 1950. (Reprinted in 1962 as a Meridian paperback with an additional preface.)

Gilkes, Lillian. *Cora Crane*. Bloomington: Indiana University Press, 1960. (Although centered on Cora, this contains much information on the life of the couple in England.)

Raymond, Thomas L. *Stephen Crane*. Newark, N.J.: Carteret Book Club, 1923.

Stallman, R. W. *Stephen Crane*. New York: Braziller, 1968.

CRITICAL STUDIES

Bassan, Maurice. "Crane, Townsend, and Realism of a Good Kind," *Proceedings of the New Jersey Historical Society*, 82:128–35 (April 1964).

Berryman, John. "The Red Badge of Courage," in *The American Novel*, edited by Wallace Stegner. New York: Basic Books, 1965.

Berthoff, Warner. *The Ferment of Realism: American Literature, 1884–1919*. New York: Fress Press, 1965.

Cady, Edwin H. *Stephen Crane*. New York: Twayne, 1962.

Cazemajou, Jean. *Stephen Crane, écrivain journaliste*. Paris: Didier, 1969.

Colvert, James B. "The Origins of Stephen Crane's Literary Creed," *University of Texas Studies in English*, 34:179–88 (1955).

Ellison, Ralph. Introduction to *The Red Badge of Courage*. New York: Dell, 1960. (Reprinted in *Shadow and Act*. New York: Random House, 1964).

Geismar, Maxwell. *Rebels and Ancestors*. Boston: Houghton Mifflin, 1953.

Gibson, Donald B. *The Fiction of Stephen Crane*. Carbondale: Southern Illinois University Press, 1968.

Gordan, John D. "*The Ghost* at Brede Place," *Bulletin of the New York Public Library*, 56:591–96 (December 1952).

Greenfield, Stanley B. "The Unmistakable Stephen Crane," *PMLA*, 73:562–72 (December 1958).

Gullason, Thomas. "Stephen Crane's Private War on Yellow Journalism," *Huntington Library Quarterly*, 22:200–08 (May 1959).

Hoffman, D. G. *The Poetry of Stephen Crane*. New York: Columbia University Press, 1957.

——. "Stephen Crane's Last Novel," *Bulletin of the New York Public Library*, 64:337–43 (June 1960).

Katz, Joseph. " 'The Blue Battalions' and the Uses of Experience," *Studia Neophilogica*, 38:107–16 (1966).

——., ed. *Stephen Crane Newsletter,* Fall 1966 to date.

Kazin, Alfred. "American Fin de Siècle," in *On Native Grounds*. New York: Reynal and Hitchcock, 1942.

La France, Marston. *A Reading of Stephen Crane*. London: Oxford University Press, 1971.

Lytle Andrew. " 'The Open Boat': A Pagan Tale," in *The Hero with the Private Parts*. Baton Rouge: Louisiana State University Press, 1966.

Martin, Jay. *Harvests of Change: American Literature, 1865–1914*. Englewood Cliffs, N.J.: Prentice-Hall, 1967.

Modern Fiction Studies, 5:199–291 (Autumn 1959). (Essays on Crane by Thomas A. Gullason, Robert F. Gleckner, Peter Buitenhuis, James B. Colvert, R. W. Stallman, Hugh Maclean, Eric Solomon, James T. Cox; also contains a good selective bibliography.)

Nelson, Harland S. "Stephen Crane's Achievement as a Poet," *University of Texas Studies in Literature and Language*, 4:564–82 (Winter 1963).

Ross, Lillian. *Picture*. London: Penguin Books, 1962. Reprinted from the *New Yorker*, May-June 1952. (An account of the filming of *The Red Badge of Courage* for MGM under the direction of John Huston.)

Schneider, Robert W. *Five Novelists of the Progressive Era*. New York: Columbia University Press, 1965.

Solomon, Eric. *Stephen Crane: From Parody to Realism*. Cambridge, Mass.: Harvard University Press, 1966.

Vasilievskaya, O. B. *The Work of Stephen Crane*. Moscow: Nayka Editions, 1967. (A critical study in Russian.)

Walcutt, Charles Child. *American Literary Naturalism, a Divided Stream*. Minneapolis: University of Minnesota Press, 1956.

Weisenberger, Bernard. "The Red Badge of Courage," in *Twelve Original Essays on Great American Novels,* edited by Charles Shapiro. Detroit: Wayne State University Press, 1958.

Weiss, Daniel. "The Red Badge of Courage," *Psychoanalytic Review*, 52:32–52 (Summer 1965), 52:130–54 (Fall 1965).

Westbrook, Max. "Stephen Crane's Poetry: Perspective and Arrogance," *Bucknell Review*, 11:23–34 (December 1963).

Ziff, Larzer. *The American 1890s*. New York: Viking Press, 1966.

—*JEAN CAZEMAJOU*

E. E. Cummings
1894-1962

OBEDIENT to the world spirit of change, in the early decades of the twentieth century a group of notable poets, by diverging from traditional practices, transformed American poetry. The most thorough "smasher of the logicalities" among them was a transcendentalist: one who views nature as a state of becoming rather than as a stasis and who believes that the imaginative faculty in man can perceive the natural world directly. He was also a troubadour who said: "enters give/whose lost is his found/leading love/whose heart is her mind." He was not only poet but novelist, playwright, and painter. In following his vision he roused hostility in academic critics and readers, apparently repelled by his idiosyncratic typographical and stylistic devices, but he was from the beginning admired by his fellow innovators, William Carlos Williams, Marianne Moore, Ezra Pound, and T. S. Eliot—and eventually he won the esteem of his critics.

"I am someone," remarked E. E. Cummings late in his career, "who proudly and humbly affirms that love is the mystery-of-mysteries . . . that 'an artist, a man, a failure' is . . . a naturally and miraculously whole human being . . . whose only happiness is to transcend himself, whose every agony is to grow." In a world oriented to dehumanized power, transcendentalism is a synonym for absurdity. Cummings recognized this early. In an address at his Harvard commencement in 1915, he had said, "we are concerned with the natural unfolding of sound tendencies. That the conclusion is, in a particular case, *absurdity,* does not in any way impair the value of the experiment, so long as we are dealing with sincere effort." The manifesto he issued then was that of one man to himself. He would experiment, and he would not fear being absurd; he would use the absurdity principle to the limit of its usefulness. As he worked at his trade of wordsmith, the implications of what he had said in 1915 were clarified in a remarkable stream of poems. From the start he used absurdity to leaven the commonplace, to startle readers into "listening" instead of merely hearing. In his later years he discovered a new significance in the concept: experimental living and the practice of his craft had redefined absurdity; it came to mean the truth of earthly living and a promise of eternity.

Edward Estlin Cummings, son of the Reverend Edward Cummings (lecturer at Harvard and Unitarian minister) and of Rebecca Haswell Clarke Cummings, was born at Cambridge, Massachusetts, on October 14, 1894.

His parents had been brought together by their mutual friend William James. Dr. Cummings was a woodsman, a photographer, an actor, a carpenter, an artist—and talented in all that he undertook. Mrs. Cummings was a shy woman who overcame conventional influences to respond joyously and effectively to life. The son was educated in public schools and at Harvard University where he received an A.B., *magna cum laude,* and an M.A. for English and classical studies.

While Cummings was in graduate school he helped to found the Harvard Poetry Society. He and some of his friends in the society put together *Eight Harvard Poets* (published in 1917). In it, by a printer's error, according to one story, Cummings' name and the "I's" as well were set in lowercase letters. He seized upon this as a device congenial to him and later had "e. e. cummings" legalized as the signature to his poems.

After Harvard, Cummings went to New York. In this city he held his first and only job, three months with P. F. Collier & Son, Inc., mail-order booksellers. He was twenty-one at the time. In mid-1917 he went to France to serve as a volunteer ambulance driver. There he was interned for a minor military offense—what happened was that he refused to say he hated Germans; instead, with typical Cummings care for precision, he repeated: "I like the French." From his experiences at La Ferté Macé (a detention camp) he accumulated material for his documentary "novel," *The Enormous Room* (1922), one of the best war books by an American.

Upon his release, he returned to the United States, but when the war ended he went back to Paris—this time to study art. He made the acquaintance of the poet Louis Aragon and of Picasso and their circle of poets and painters; he became friendly with many visiting writers such as Archibald MacLeish and Ezra Pound. On arriving back in New York in 1924 he found himself a celebrity—for his documentary novel and for *Tulips and Chimneys* (1923), his first book of poems. The next year he won the *Dial* Award for "distinguished service to American Letters." A roving assignment from *Vanity Fair* in 1926 permitted him to go abroad again, where he established a routine he was to follow most of his life: he painted in the afternoons and wrote at night.

From his experiences in the two cities he loved, New York and Paris, came the material for scintillating or extravagant essays on burlesque, the circus, modern art, and the foibles of the day, later collected into *A Miscellany* (1958) and *A Miscellany, Revised* (1965). He wrote forewords to books and brochures for art exhibits, and he sold sketches and paintings. Three volumes of poetry appeared in quick succession: *&* (*And*) and *XLI Poems* in 1925, *Is 5* in 1926. The play *Him,* a phantasmagoria in 21 scenes, which was a forerunner of what is now called the Theater of the Absurd, was published in 1927 and produced by the Provincetown Players in 1928 and was acclaimed by avant-garde critics. In 1931 he published a collection of drawings and paintings, *CIOPW,* which took its title from the initial letters of the materials used: charcoal, ink, oil, pencil, watercolor. In that same year came *W* (*ViVa*), a thick book of poems. A travel journal published in 1933, *Eimi* (I Am), recorded his revulsion against an even more "enormous room" than the military detention camp: the collectivized Soviet Union.

After 1930, although Cummings continued to travel abroad, he divided most of his time between a studio apartment in Greenwich Village, at 4 Patchin Place, and the family farm at Silver Lake, New Hampshire. This yearly contact with New England soil occasioned one of his finest poem-portraits: "rain or hail/sam done/the best he kin/till they digged his hole." A similar earthy wisdom is in a poem that may be a comment on himself: "my specialty is living said/a man(who could not earn his bread/because he would not sell his head)."

Because he had in common with T. S. Eliot not only a New England Unitarian background but also cosmopolitan traits, it is stimulating to observe the differences between them. Eliot became a British citizen. Cummings, responding to French art, always admiring the French civilization, nonetheless spent most of his life in the United States. He was a goldfinch needing a native tree to sing from. Through the years, from his perch, he continued to pour forth his songs: *No Thanks* (1935), *50 Poems* (1940), *1 x 1* (*One Times One*, 1944) *Xaipe* (1950). A *Collected Poems* appeared in 1938. The ballet *Tom* was published in 1935 and the plays *Anthropos* and *Santa Claus* were published in 1944 and 1946.

Honors and rewards came with frequency—now. In 1950, for "great achievement," he was given the Fellowship of the Academy of American Poets. In 1952 he was invited to give the Norton Lectures at Harvard (published as *I: Six Nonlectures* in 1953), an urbane but lively analysis of the Cummings quest to discover "Who as a writer am I?" These lectures could have been subtitled "And who as a person are you?" because—like Walt Whitman with his phrases addressed to future generations who would cross on Brooklyn Ferry—Cummings was always reaching out from the persona, the neutral "i," to the "you" out there. In 1955 he received a special citation from the National Book Awards for *Poems 1923–1954* (1954) and in 1957 he received both the Bollingen Prize for Poetry and the Boston Arts Festival Poetry Award. A year later the last of his poetry collections to appear during his lifetime

was published, *95 Poems*. Cummings the painter was also honored: he had one-man shows in 1944 and 1949 at the American-British Art Centre, and in 1945 and 1959 at the Rochester Memorial Gallery. His wide-ranging interest in the visual arts was reflected in *Adventures in Value* (1962), on which he collaborated with his third wife, photographer Marion Morehouse.

Cummings died on September 3, 1962, in New Hampshire. He left a manuscript of poetry published the following year as *73 Poems*.

"The artist's country is inside him," said Cummings. This was another way of saying that he would abide only by the laws of his own mind. His formalities—the literary devices he developed—were intended to show how the outer appearance reinforces the inner vision. His disordered syntax and typographical disarrangements were intended, not to bewilder, but to heighten the understanding. He described what he was trying to do in the 1926 Foreword to *Is 5*: "my theory of technique, if I have one, is very far from original; nor is it complicated. I can express it in fifteen words, by quoting The Eternal Question And Immortal Answer of burlesk, viz. 'Would you hit a woman with a child?—No, I'd hit her with a brick.' Like the burlesk comedian, I am abnormally fond of that precision which creates movement." One of his methods to achieve this was tmesis (the separation of parts of words by intervening words). It became almost like a signature for him. As Karl Shapiro put it in his *Essay on Rime*, Cummings was concerned with the "Integers of the word, the curve of 'e',/Rhythm of 'm', astonishment of 'o'/And their arranged derangement." By the analysis of words into their parts, both syllables and individual letters, and by considered use of space and punctuation marks, as well as by "arranged derangement," Cummings hoped to extend meaning beyond traditional limits.

Cummings used space in his typographical rhetoric to indicate tempo of reading: single words may have spaces within them to force the reader to weigh each syllable, as in "can dy lu/minous"; or words may be linked, as in "eddieandbill," to convey the act of boys running. A comma may be used where a period is expected, within a poem or at the end of it, to produce a pause for the reader to imagine what the next action might be. Or commas, colons, and semicolons may be used within a word to arouse new sensations and intuitions. In examining the poem beginning "as if as" (*No Thanks*) the reader disentangles from the typography the idea that it is a poem about sunrise. But it is not like other accounts of sunrise, nor, probably, does it reflect the reader's own experience. Toward the end of the poem the word "itself" is fractured into "it:s;elf." The "s" suggests the sun as well as the viewer. "Elf," relating to an earlier phrase, "moon's al-down," is a hint, in this instance, of the supernatural impact of dawn. The daily sun is no longer a habit but a miracle. In a later work (Number 48 in *73 Poems*), the word "thrushes" is divided into "t,h;r:u;s,h;e:s" so that the reader may perceive, with the poet, the individual sleepy birds gripping a branch at moonrise and, by implication, the transcendental relationship between all living things. Of the exclamation point beginning the first poem in *50 Poems*, "!blac," Cummings himself said that it might be called an emphatic "very"; the unpronounceable "?" and ")" are often similarly used. To focus the reader's attention a capital letter may be thrust into the middle of a word. In the opening poem of *No Thanks* capitals are used to imitate the roundness of the moon and to imply the eternity of the circle:

mOOn Over tOwns mOOn

whisper

less creature huge grO

pingness

In "i will be" (*And*) the word "SpRiN,k,LiNg" is manipulated to make a visual representation of sunlight filtering through wing feathers. In this poem, too, a parenthesis is used in the middle of the word "wheeling" to place simultaneously before the reader's mind the flutter of the pigeons and their effect on the sunlight:

whee(:are,SpRiN,k,LiNg   an   in-stant   with
    sunLight
t h e n)l -
ing . . .

Cummings made varied use of parentheses: for an interpolated comment or to split or combine words as a guide to his thought. Frequently they occur, in poem-parables, to clarify the relationship between two sentences that run simultaneously through the poem. In "go (perpe)go," published in *No Thanks,* we have a typical Cummings juxtaposition. The parenthetical sentence is a surrealist collection of "perpetual adventuring particles" describing the action of a disturbed ant heap and an anteater getting his dinner. The sentence outside the parenthesis, "go to the ant, thou anteater," is an allusion to Proverbs 6:6: "Go to the ant, thou sluggard." The poem is description and social comment, disguised as a joke. Critic Norman Friedman analyzed it succinctly: "Cummings is satirizing a certain kind of worldly and prudential wisdom. The ant's activity represents for Cummings merely busy work rather than a model of industry, and he who is advised to 'go to the ant' is the one creature who can possibly profit from such a visit—the anteater. In thus reducing the proverb to its simply 'realistic' aspects—by refusing to make the metaphorical transference intended—Cummings deflates the whole implied point of view."

Some of Cummings' poems utilize the "visual stanza" in which lines are arranged in reference, not to rhyme and meter, but to a shape reflecting the poet's thought. This kind of typographical design, with poems contrived in the form of roses, diamonds, and hourglass figures, was in fashion during the Elizabethan age and continued to be used in the seventeenth century. With changes in taste and technical practice in the last two centuries, this device fell into disuse, although it has been revived occasionally, as when Lewis Carroll used it for his mouse's "long and sad tale." More recently it appeared in the *Calligrammes* of Guillaume Apollinaire and in the "quaint" patterning of Dylan Thomas' poem "Vision and Prayer." However, the visual appearance of Cummings' poems can be largely accounted for by his interest in contemporary art forms, rather than by influence from other writers. From artists like Picasso who were bringing new vitality to painting, he learned the effectiveness of distorting lines and reshaping masses; and he juxtaposed words as they did the pigments (in John Peale Bishop's apt phrasing)—to bring perception of things into sharper focus. Cummings specifically disclaimed any stylistic influence from Apollinaire's mimetic typography, and as Gorham B. Munson observed very early, Cummings' typographical design, unlike that of the *Calligrammes,* reinforces the literary content of his poems. Some of Cummings' poems are designed to be read vertically; in others, stanzaic structures are balanced for mass, as are certain colors in painting. Effective examples of Cummings' use of the visual stanza are the poem "!blac" and the ironic dedication to *No Thanks,* which lists in the shape of a wineglass all the publishers who had rejected the manu-

script. In *XLI Poems* there is a poem, "little tree," that visually suggests a Christmas tree, and another that on the page resembles smoke puffing out of a locomotive:

> the
>   sky
>   was
> can dy lu
> minous

Another important device by which Cummings intended to enlarge the reader's comprehension was word coinage. He kept already existing root words, joining to them new affixes. In such compounded words the prefixes are familiar enough, but his use of the suffixes *-ly, -ish, -est, -ful* and adverbs (such as *less*) in unexpected combinations, a dimension natural to classical and romance languages, produces in English an intensifying of perception. Introduce one or two of these words— *riverly, nowly, downwardishly, birdfully, whichful, girlest, skylessness, onlying, laughtering,* etc.—into a verse of recognizable words and the reader has to explore possibilities in a creative way. In reading creatively a phrase like "on stiffening greenly air" he will cross the threshold of transcendence. Articles and particles were rearranged by Cummings for the same purpose—"some or if where." One part of speech may be used for another, as in the first line of a much-anthologized poem from *And,* "Spring is like a perhaps hand." The charm of this line is due in large part to the use of an adverb when an adjective is expected, to emphasize the tentative nature of springtime. This is reinforced by an image of the window dresser who moves things and changes things "without breaking anything," in contrast to the destruction of winter.

In all of these ways Cummings broke language from its conventionalized mold; it became a nourishing soil through which "faces called flowers float out of the ground" (*Xaipe*). Cummings' virtuosity was directed to capture in words what the painter gets on canvas and what children, violently alive in response to objects and seasons, display in their street games. His poems are alive on the page, as he told the printer when he instructed him not to interfere with the "arrangement." Any change would be an injury to living tissue. In discontinuous poems he tried to pin down the "illuminated moment," to ransom from oblivion the fleeting present, in words seasonal, contemporary, and timeless—like a writer of haiku. To get at the realities, Cummings smashed the logicalities, an idea in harmony with Oriental art and philosophy, with which he had acquaintance, as shown by a quotation from the Tao that appears near the end of *Eimi*: "he who knoweth the eternal is comprehensive . . . therefore just; just, therefore a king; a king, therefore celestial; celestial, therefore in Tao; in Tao, therefore enduring." Cummings' perpetual concern with transcendental ideas led to the shining leaps on the page that make his work unique.

One needs to remember, however, that this innovating poet was practiced in conventional Western literary tradition. The young Cummings learned from Elizabethan song and eighteenth-century satire, as well as from the Pindaric ode. He was rooted in the same soil as Thoreau, Emerson, and Emily Dickinson. Intermittently he read Aeschylus, Homer, and the French troubadours—as evidenced by his quotations in the *Six Nonlectures*. He cut his literary teeth on the strict rules of villanelle, roundel, and ballade royale. Nonetheless his genius led him to quite different patterns: a poem in *ViVa*, for example, records phonetically not only a conversation but a revelation of the hearts of lost men: "oil tel duh woil doi sez/dooyah unnurs tanmih essez pullih nizmus tash,oi/dough un giv uh shid oi sez. Tom."

The emphasis is deliberate and made with care.

Cummings said that Josiah Royce (who appears in one of the poem-portraits) directed his attention to Dante Gabriel Rossetti, especially to Rossetti's sonnets, and that made him a sonneteer. Certainly Cummings wrote some of the finest sonnets of our century: celebrating love, savagely ridiculing human stupidity, and recording his pilgrimage to the transcendental. From the somewhat conventional, Cummings' sonnets developed, as Theodore Spencer has said, to achieve "specific gravity." Yet the only discernible influence of the Pre-Raphaelite school is in the early lyrics and might as easily have been been picked up direct from a reading of the sonnets of Dante. There is internal evidence that Shakespeare was the dynamic influence in his sonnet-making: sensory details, the absence of hypocrisy, even the rhythm of the snap at the end, as in a couplet from "being to timelessness as it's to time" in *95 Poems*: "—do lovers love?Why then to heaven with hell./Whatever sages say and fools,all's well." In an interview with Harvey Breit in 1950 Cummings said: "Today so-called writers are completely unaware of the thing which makes art what it is. You can call it nobility or spirituality, but I should call it intensity. Sordid is the opposite. . . . Shakespeare is never sordid . . . because his poetry was the most intense."

Cummings' experimentation was clearly within Western literary tradition, as was Eliot's, but, finally, whatever he did resulted in poems that could not have been written by anyone else. He has had no sucessful imitators. And because of its nature Cummings' work cannot be held within the bounds of conventional literary analysis. The critic must stretch his own powers to find the significant new insights waiting to be revealed by this poet's language in action. What is required is "intelligence functioning at intuitional velocity"—Cummings used the phrase to characterize a work of the sculptor Lachaise but it admirably describes the approach a perceptive critic-reader must take to Cummings' writing.

For a study of Cummings' philosophy and of his devices to achieve art in motion and at a peak of excitement, the play *Him*, called by the critic Edmund Wilson "the outpouring of an intelligence, a sensibility, and an imagination of the very first dimension," is especially useful.

The action is divided between "exterior" and "interior" happenings that develop the love story of a man and the predicament of an artist. The satirical exterior scenes are presented before a garish curtain like that used in carnival shows. The deliberate lack of a third dimension is one of the poet's "absurdities"; it symbolizes the "unworld." The curtain and the parodies of circus and burlesque in the play's action reflect his interest in folk amusements. The interior scenes explore the psyche of the creative temperament. Connecting the two phases is the chorus: the three Fates, Atropos, Clotho, Lachesis. They are disguised as the Misses Weird and are nicknamed "Stop," "Look," and "Listen." They sit with their backs to the audience, rocking and knitting, as they swap a nonsensical version of backfence talk and advertising slogans. The stage directions integrate the themes and devices of the play.

In the complex design of *Him*, described by one commentator as "a play of lucid madness and adventurous gaiety," Cummings sets up a confrontation: man, a social being, versus the artist. In the *Six Nonlectures* he repeats: "Nobody else can be alive for you; nor can you be alive for anybody else. . . . There's the artist's responsibility. . . ." Yeats knew this human instinct to fulfill strenuous conditions for the

sake of an ideal: writing of the Irish playwright J. M. Synge, he said, ". . . to come out from under the shadow of other men's minds . . . to be utterly oneself: that is all the Muses care for." At first glance Yeats's statement seems callous but when it is illustrated in the creative life it leads to service for the community. In the poems beginning "i sing of Olaf glad and big" (*ViVa*) and "a man who had fallen among thieves" (*Is 5*), Cummings is urging awake the sleeping conscience of his fellows. And in *Him* Cummings develops a metaphor, found with varying emphasis in his poetry, that strikingly illustrates his view. The artist is likened to a circus performer who sits astride three chairs stacked one on top of the other and balanced on a high wire. He explains to his lover, "Me," that the three chairs are three facts: "I am an Artist, I am a Man, I am a Failure."

The label on the top chair, "Failure," is disconcerting but acceptable when the reader becomes familiar with the paradoxes of Cummings' vocabulary. To distinguish true accomplishment from the disappointing successes of the salesman-politician-warmongering world, he uses words that for him state the ultimate emptiness of the prizes the crowd pursues and often captures. Throughout Cummings' poems occur the words *failure, nothing, nobody, zero* and the prefixes *non-* and *un-*. They are also scattered through the prose of *The Enormous Room* and *Eimi*. By these negatives he separated his ideals from the pleasures of a conformist world and showed his condemnation of "mobs" and "gangs" and his concern for the individual. The phrase "you and i" dominates his response to relationships: lovers, mother and child, a man and a city, a man and a tree.

The other two "chairs" of *Him* have a subordinate but vital function in the metaphor. The experiences of the man are limited to the senses until they are fused with the perceptions of the artist. It is from the artist and his transcendental realizations that the reader or viewer learns to distinguish the genuine from the pinchbeck. The artist is also dependent on the report from his five senses to actualize his ideas. So Cummings found spiritualities in "facts" and celebrated them in his poems of love and compassion. The significance that Cummings assigned to "failure" is further evident in a sonnet from *Is 5*, "if i have made, my lady, intricate/imperfect various things . . ." And a study of the Foreword to *Is 5* will reveal affirmations of the themes of *Him*: that the poet knows he is "competing" with reality and therefore "failure" is predestined. What is increasingly noticeable in the play and in the volumes of poems that follow it is the changing concept of love and the frank presentation of the artist's self-doubt. He insists on finding out who he is before he can be either artist or lover. Cummings' belief that the artist's total attentiveness to an object or subject should result in simultaneity for his audience—which was also the aim of the Imagist movement in poetry and of Cubism in painting—was not completely realizable. He therefore began to think of art as a series of mirrors reflecting the "object" in various lights and not as the thing-in-itself. So, with a sense of the "awful responsibility" of the poet, he regarded his extraordinary successes in putting on the page a flying bird, a grasshopper, a falling leaf as "failures" and called himself a nonhero.

The falling leaf poem is the first of the *95 Poems*. It is not a complete sentence and there are only four words. The form has the narrowness of a needle. In a time when novels tell no story and music is not melodic—relatively speaking—this pictogram brings new insights, which have been perceptively set forth by Norman Friedman and Barry A. Marks in their critical studies of Cummings; their lead is followed here.

l(a

le

af

fa

ll

s)

one

l

iness

Each of the first four lines has but one consonant and one vowel: two *l*'s, three *a*'s, one *e*, and two *f*'s. This suggests the fluttering pattern of a falling leaf. The next line, treated as a stanza, is a double *l*, extending meaning as the reader waits for the necessary completion. The poem ends on a shifting note which accentuates the import of "alone," "one," and "oneliness" (defined as "own").

The mind of the reader seizes the two ideas: loneliness and the parenthetical interjection of the fall of a leaf. In splitting "loneliness" Cummings shows by variations on a word blurred by indiscriminate use that it is, as Marks noted, "quite a singular word." Cummings strips the sheath from the ordinary, and the extraordinary is revealed. The "le/af/fa/ll" involves both sound and visual values; the musical relation echoes the meaning emerging from "le" and "af."

The *l* in "leaf" repeats the first *l* in "loneliness" and helps the reader keep in mind simultaneously the material inside and outside the parentheses. His old typewriter played an important role here in Cummings' idea of form as it affects thought: in the first line *l* can be either the digit "one" or the letter "el." A parenthesis separating it from *a* suggests that while the idea of doubling up on "oneness" is attractive, it is not plausible. Following the trail of the parenthesis, the reader discovers a "verse" that reinforces the necessity that *l* be "el" in the fourth stanza. The word "one" and an apparent digit reflect back to the initial *l* and in their interplay the digit vanishes into the letter.

The reader is pleased with his success in working out the "puzzle"; casually he has participated in the dance of the poet's mind. Then he arrives at the last line, "iness." The isolation and the desolation of the individual, the I alone with the I, be it a leaf or a man, have been established. Forgotten are the secondary ideas of oneness with the universe or the intimations of autumn: the reader now knows he has misunderstood the form if he accepted it as a needle stitching together all created things. However, as Henry James asserted by implication in *The Wings of the Dove*, the tragic element is art and art is delight. Yet another idea is added to the possibles of interpretation: man's unhappy isolation comes from self-loving activities and trivial goals. Self-forgetfulness is the reward of the disciplined athlete and of the artist, with the result an unblemished performance. The ever-evolving devices of Cummings are a witness to his profoundly moral nature in conflict with an imperfect world, and to his vision that it *could* be perfected.

The "puzzle" of the following lines from *No Thanks* is similarly rewarding to the reader willing to work it out:

        r-p-o-p-h-e-s-s-a-g-r
                who
a)s w(e loo)k
upnowgath
        PPEGORHRASS
                eringint(o-

        aThe):l
            eA
                !p:
S   a

The poet, through spacings of word and letter and the unorthodox use of capitals, presents a grasshopper living in his muscles. At first he is invisible, coming from the grass to us only in the sounds reverberating from earth or pebbles. But as Lloyd Frankenberg pointed out in his study of modern poetry, *Pleasure Dome*: "These sounds—some soft, some loud, some intermittent—are rearrangements of his name; just as he rearranges himself to rub forewing and hind leg together. Then he 'leaps!' clear so that we see him, 'arriving to become, rearrangingly, grasshopper.' " The reader has been, briefly, the grasshopper and that has extended his capacity for being alive. Note that in this poem Cummings used a device resembling Cubistic painting: "r-p-o-p-h-e-s-s-a-g-r" and "PPEGORHRASS" and ".gRrEaPsPhOs" (which appears after the lines quoted above) record the "realization" of experiences that he wished to share with his readers.

In other poems which demonstrate his delight in the natural world, Cummings often used mimicry. Cummings had a talent like that of the Greek comic playwright Aristophanes, who in his oft-quoted line "Brekekekéx koáx koáx" sought to reproduce the sound of frogs. A similar mimicry is found in such unlikely Cummings poems as the colloquial "buncha hardboil guys from duh A.C. fulla" (*ViVa*) and "joggle i think will do it although the glad" (*Tulips and Chimneys*). In a punning poem, "applaws)" (*One Times One*), the "paw" is a kind of mimicry and a reminder that fundamentally we are animals.

Another aspect of the "creaturely" life that interested Cummings is to be found in his poems about horses, those animals now vanishing from sight, except in parades or circuses. In the lines below from a poem in *No Thanks* the scene is set by "crazily seething of this/ raving city screamingly street." What opens the windows to be "sharp holes in dark places" is the light from flowers. And what do the "whichs" and "small its," the half-alive, half-asleep people see?

what a proud dreamhorse pulling(smoothloom-
    ingly)through
(stepp)this(ing)crazily seething of this
raving city screamingly street wonderful

flowers And o the Light thrown by Them opens

sharp holes in dark places paints eyes touches
    hands with new-
ness and these startled whats are a(piercing
    clothes thoughts kiss
-ing wishes bodies)squirm-of-frightened shy
    are whichs small
its hungry for Is for Love Spring thirsty for
    happens
only and beautiful

Through the raucous sounds of a city street a horse is pulling a load of flowers. In that setting his movements have a grace such as is found in dreams. The horse establishes his reality as we watch him "stepp . . . ing"—the poet has plowed with horses his family's fields; he has watched milk wagons in the city. However, as Lloyd Frankenberg has suggested, the horse, "whose feet almost walk air," brings to mind Pegasus. That wingèd steed of the Muses is associated in legend with Hippocrene, the fountain of inspiration, which supposedly sprang from the earth at a blow from his forehoof. In one legend the Greek hero Bellerophon, with the aid of Pegasus, slew the Chimaera, a ravaging beast. Then he tried to fly to heaven, thereby offending the gods, and

fell to earth. A poet is often trying to fly and often he fails. So we come back to the name that Cummings gave himself, "nonhero."

In another city sonnet, from *And* ("my sonnet is A light goes on in"), we meet the dray horses that sleep upstairs in a tenement stable. "Ears win-/k funny stable. In the morning they go out in pairs." Implied in the poet's words is the ancient horse sacrifice to the sun, to encourage the sun to rise again. So the sonnet comes to a climax on a line of life and beauty: "They pull the morning out of the night." There is the same fidelity to sensory perception in poems that include references to rain: "the rain's/pearls singly-whispering" (from "the moon is hiding in," *Tulips and Chimneys*) and "i have found what you are like/the rain" (*And*).

The opening lines of an early poem, from *Tulips and Chimneys*, show both Cummings' delight in the natural world and his ability to respond freshly to it:

    stinging
    gold swarms
    upon the spires
    silver

        chants the litanies the
      great bells are ringing with rose
      the lewd fat bells

The poet avoided the obvious ideas that cluster around the subject of sunset: the timeworn meanings of silver and gold are freshened by the adroit combination of "stinging" and "swarms"; sound and image suggest the flight of a young queen and the creation of a new hive. "Spires" is echoed later in the poem in the phrase "a tall wind," and the poem concludes with an image of a dreamy sea. In an experiment Laura Riding and Robert Graves converted the pattern of this poem, the last part of which imitates a retreating wave, into conventional stanzas and concluded, rightly, that in the process the significance as well as the poetry was lost.

Informed critics, among them Barry A. Marks and the poet William Carlos Williams, have directed attention to "nonsun blob a" as probably the most difficult of Cummings' poems and yet as one containing very useful clues for the reader. It has a regularity of stanza, an Elizabethan tone, and a simplicity that might place it among the poet's charming verses for children. However, it offers a severe challenge to the mind: to put away old habits of associative thinking and to examine each stanza, line by line and word by word, for the relationships the poet has evoked. It also sums up Cummings' innovations and ideas to a remarkable degree. The emphasis Cummings himself placed upon it is evident in its position as the opening poem of the volume *One Times One*.

> nonsun blob a
> cold to
> skylessness
> sticking fire
>
> my are your
> are birds our all
> and one gone
> away the they
>
> leaf of ghosts some
> few creep there
> here or on
> unearth

Here the senses become elements of thought and the emotions are objectified to an extreme degree. The first stanza has neither verb nor expected sequences nor is it broken up to be reassembled, like an anagram. Each word compresses experiences from years of winter days; it is demanded of the reader that he be alert

at all points so he may follow the clues in this celebration of bare, daunting specifics of a northern winter. Look at a winter sky: sunlessness is its chief characteristic but there is a gray waver, a "blob," sending out an almost invisible shine. The closing line, "sticking fire" —in which some critics observe a sexual connotation—brings into focus a dumb fear of being lost in a glacial world and paradoxically suggests all the physical and moral efforts to bring life-giving warmth to man, from Prometheus to nuclear industrial activities.

As we move on to a consideration of the second stanza, an observation made by Marks in his *E. E. Cummings* is especially illuminating. He noted: "the words of the first two lines . . . form two mathematical equations. One says, 'my + your = our.' The other, based on the phonetic pun, 'our' and 'are,' says, 'my = your'; 'my + your = birds'; 'my + your + birds = all.'" Intimations of what concerned Cummings—that the nature of unity is love—occur in the merging of the possessive pronouns: "mine" into "yours" into "ours" into "all." This unity is felt on repeated readings of the poem. But a Cummings poem is always in motion; the second stanza ends with the unity destroyed, the bird flock scattered in quest of a vanished leader.

The "a" which ends the first line of the poem is significant for an understanding of the third stanza. In its isolation it is related to autumn leaves creeping like crippled birds on a cold earth as indifferent as the cold sky recorded in the third stanza. Unfriendliness deprives the earth of its nourishing function; therefore Cummings used the prefix *un-* to modify the word *earth*. What is to be made of a typical Cummings inversion: "leaf of ghosts"? A remnant of birds or leaves in the increasing cold is described in the first stanza; later, birds reduced to creeping are non-birds, and cold earth is heartless as cold sky; both environments when deprived of their function as givers and nourishers, and therefore of their reality, are also ghosts. What Henry James called "perception at the pitch of passion" is involved in this "circular" poem. The implication is that of Greek tragedy: the helplessness of the alive, be it leaf or bird or a man and a woman. Yet there is joy in the contemplation of the real: a sun so clouded it may have burned out centuries ago; the relationship between the afflicted birds, leaves, and lovers—and the reader of the poem. Cummings, keeping his agonies to himself, nearly always ends on a note of joy.

This poem in twelve lines anticipates the essence of the nine stanzas of a later poem, "rosetree,rosetree" (95 Poems). The last stanza of "rosetree,rosetree" tells us again what the poet believes and hopes for:

lovetree!least the
rose alive must three,must
four and(to quite become
nothing)five times,proclaim
fate isn't fatal
—a heart her each petal

The reader may wonder why this master of experimental form chose rhymed stanzas for this piece. It is another instance of Cummings' sensitivity to choice among the formalities—an Elizabethan song brimming with transcendental ideas although the rose is a literal rose in a sizzle of bees. Traditional form attracts simple ideas: tree-bird, mob-war, flower-death-love. In this poem it serves as a counterweight to the complex ideas of a mystic, the poet "dreaming-true." Norman Friedman in a reasoned study of 175 worksheets of "rosetree, rosetree," rescued by Marion Morehouse Cummings from the usual destruction of preliminary work, reveals Cummings as a craftsman perfecting his materials over a long period of time. Throughout the fifty-four lines of the poem—in the adjustment of negative to positive, the victory in the final stanza over darkness and fatality—the cerebral element is always in play.

A poem that relates to this one—by melodic form and a transformation of abstracts so that they are vivid images—is the remarkable "what if a much of a which of a wind" (One Times One). Its rhythm perhaps reflects the influence of a ballad (attributed to Thomas Campion) which begins with "What if a day or a month or a year." But there the similarity ends. In the Cummings poem we have a deeply felt comment on the plight of universal life—nature and man—communicated by pairs of opposites: "gives the truth to summer's lie"; "when skies are hanged and oceans drowned,/ the single secret will be man." In this "song" there are combinations that are reminiscent of Cummings' intriguing phrase "the square root of minus one" which he employed in at least three different contexts, notably in the Introduction to his Collected Poems where he wrote: "Mostpeople have less in common with ourselves than the squarerootofminusone." When he says, "Blow soon to never and never to twice/(blow life to isn't:blow death to was)/ —all nothing's only our hugest home," he has made eloquent poetry of his abstract idea.

William Troy has commented that certain pages of Cummings' Russian travel journal, Eimi, are as good as all but the best of his poetry. Certainly there is a relation between the prose and poetry in theme and technique.

In Eimi Cummings' words are positioned logistically to establish the impact of viewing Lenin's tomb. Others had written, according to their political bias, of that tomb. Cummings presented what his senses reported: the smells and sounds of the never-ending line of humanity descending into the bowels of the earth to get a glimpse of the corpse of a small man with a small face, their Messiah—as secret in death as he was in life. Cummings had gone to Russia to find out what the socialistic experiment was doing to help man toward being more alive. He found men and women with "a willingness not to live, if only they were allowed not to die," in John Peale Bishop's words. In some circumstances apathy is a means of survival, but for the poet this was too little—or so it seemed to the young man of Harvard and New Hampshire. Vivid, even gay, portraits of Russians lighten the record but the following passage—illustrative of his firming style, that "specialization of sensibility"—is what he understood at Lenin's tomb:

facefacefaceface
   hand-
        fin-
           claw
   foot-
      hoof
   (tovarich)
              es to number of numberlessness (un
-smiling)
   with dirt's dirt dirty dirtier with others' dirt
       of themselves
dirtiest waitstand dirtily never smile shuffle-
      budge dirty pausehalt
   Smilingless.

Francis Fergusson has referred to this passage as the beginning of "a sleepwalking death-rite." Cummings' deliberate abandonment of conventional syntax, which is based on an arrangement of thoughts and sensations already completed, makes the "instantaneous alone . . . his concern," as Troy put it, and he takes the reader into "an unworld of unmen lying in unsleep on an unbed of preternatural nullity."

Sensory awareness has been a dominant theme of Cummings' work discussed so far. A second primary theme in his work, both poetry and prose, is the integrity of the individual. The last lines of a sophisticated little poem about a Jewish tailor in Greenwich Village, "i say no world" (*50 Poems*), put his view succinctly: "unsellable not buyable alive/one i say human being)one/goldberger." Beginning with *The Enormous Room* and *Tulips and Chimneys*, Cummings celebrated individuals, perceiving the transcendental under the ephemeral disguise. Some of his poem-portraits focused on the famous: Buffalo Bill ("Buffalo Bill's/defunct," *Tulips and Chimneys*), the tragicomic dancer Jimmy Savo ("so little he is," in "New Poems" of *Collected Poems*), Picasso ("Picasso/you give us Things," *XLI Poems*). In others he turned a clear but sympathetic eye on burlesque queens, circus clowns, "niggers dancing," the Greenwich Village "Professor Seagull." He wrote too of bums —and caught the spirit of their search for a "self" even as they scoured the gutters for a cigarette butt.

It follows that anything threatening individuality would be the object of his hatred. War, for example:

   you know what i mean when
   the first guy drops you know
   everybody feels sick or
   when they throw in a few gas
   and the oh baby shrapnel
   or my feet getting dim freezing or
   up to your you know what in water or
   with the bugs crawling right all up
   all everywhere over you all . . .

In these lines from "lis/-ten" (*Is 5*) Cummings conveys—through the agonized, almost hysterical, words of a soldier who was there—his deep-felt indignation against the senseless destruction of individuals. And the poet's skill transforms the ephemeral statistic of a newspaper battle account into transcendental man.

The threats to the integrity of the individual

posed by a mechanized society are many and pervasive. "Progress is a comfortable disease," commented Cummings in "pity this busy monster, manunkind" (*One Times One*), but a disease nonetheless. The attempts of man to identify with his inventions—to become the turbines and computers he developed—stir Cummings to remark: "A world of made/is not a world of born." And so "when man determined to destroy/himself he picked the was/ of shall and finding only why/smashed it into because" ("when god decided to invent," *One Times One*).

In the morality *Santa Claus* Cummings speaks sharply against the blighting forces that keep a man from knowing his spontaneous self. "Knowledge has taken love out of the world/and all the world is empty empty empty . . . joyless joyless joyless." The Child in the morality, however, can "truly see," as in Hans Christian Andersen's story "The Emperor's New Clothes." And when the Woman calls for death and Santa dressed as Death enters, she sees through the disguise because she looks with the eyes of the heart. Ironies of belief and unbelief are frequent in *Santa Claus*; the interchange of mask and costume is reminiscent of Shakespeare, and even more of the melodramatics of tent shows that toured the hinterland of the United States, and these again are related to the commedia dell'arte which began as skits performed on a wooden cart pulled by a donkey—to amuse Italian peasants. Cummings, writing to Allen Tate in 1946, said that the whole aim of *Santa Claus* was to make man remove his death mask, thereby becoming what he truly is: a human being.

In his concern to remove the death mask Cummings often employed satire. The satirist, it has been said, needs both irreverence and moral conviction. Cummings had both. His satire is like that of Swift; it comes from con-

viction that something is awry, as when he declared that this world is all aleak and "i'd rather learn from one bird how to sing/than teach ten thousand stars how not to dance" ("New Poems," *Collected Poems*).

In the successful satires the penetration is trenchant, underlined by a cheerful ribaldry. At other times his intention is mislaid in a junk pile of name calling and irrelevant detail. Indignation sometimes results in an absence of poetic statement and a series of stereotypes. As Philip Horton has noted, Cummings is at times guilty of bad puns and satires that miss their mark ("a myth is as good as a smile" from "little joe gould"; "obey says toc,submit says tic,/Eternity's a Five Year Plan" from "Jehovah buried,Satan dead," both in *No Thanks*). However, in a notable example of the satiric, "A Foreword to Krazy" (1946; collected in *A Miscellany*), Cummings explained the symbolism of George Herriman's comic-strip characters and at the same time he defined his own position as a satirist. The cast is made up of Ignatz Mouse, a brick-throwing cynic, Offissa Pupp, a sentimental policeman-dog, and the heroine, "slightly resembling a child's drawing of a cat." On the political level Offissa Pupp represents the "will of socalled society" while Ignatz Mouse is the destructive element. The benevolent overdog and the malevolent undermouse, as Cummings saw it, misunderstood Krazy Kat. Not only is she a symbol of an ideal democracy but she is personal—she transforms the brick into a kiss; the senses aided by the spirit produce joy.

These ideas ran counter to those expressed in T. S. Eliot's essay "Tradition and the Individual Talent" which for so long after its publication made the personal in literature suspect. But the swing of the pendulum through the centuries from the formalized prosaic (classic) to the formalized romantic is always rectifying the errors of critics. Poets like John

Berryman and Robert Lowell have carried on experiments in the personal that Cummings would have found in his vein.

In two poems, "anyone lived in a pretty how town" and "my father moved through dooms of love" (both in *50 Poems*), Cummings very effectively worked the personal into a universal application. He used for one a contemplative narration of ideal lovers and for the other a portrait of the ideal man. The maturity of the poet's insights is displayed by his bold use of regular, rhymed stanzas to control a considered emotion and to weld it to his opinions, now sufficiently explored, of the social dilemma. The refrains are a charming blend of nursery rhyme ("sun moon stars rain" and "with up so floating many bells down") and sophisticated observation ("My father moved through theys of we").

Barry Marks has pointed out that as contemporary painters (like Juan Gris and Picasso) ambiguously employed a single curve for the neck of a vase and the edge of a guitar, so Cummings often deranged his syntax in order that a single word would both intensify a statement and question its validity; an example is the "how" in "anyone lived in a pretty how town." This word suggests, among other things, that the townspeople ask how and why about things from an emptiness of mind and an incapacity for simultaneity and the intuitive grasp. The direct vision of the painter-poet is similar to a child's delight in believing that a rain puddle is the ocean; it is a transcendental conception.

In the pretty how town "anyone" and "noone" are lovers; they live and love and die in a landscape of changing seasons, among children growing into adults and forgetting the realities and adults, "both little and small," without love or interest in life—from Cummings' penetrative view. The lively series of contrasts reinforces the ballad form; emotion

and thought are strictly held to the development of the charade: "anyone" versus "someones," the individual opposed to the anxious status-seekers who "sowed their isn't" and "reaped their same." Children guessed the goodness of love between anyone and noone, because children are close to the intuitive life, but living things grow by imitation, so the children forgot as they imitated their "someones."

In the last line of the third stanza, "that noone loved him more by more," the word "noone" is emphasizing the public indifference as well as providing the identification of the "she" in the next stanza:

> when by now and tree by leaf
> she laughed his joy she cried his grief
> bird by snow and stir by still
> anyone's any was all to her

A compression of meanings is achieved in "when by now," "bird by snow," "tree by leaf," and they in turn are manipulated by repetitions suggested by later rhyme and alliteration: "all by all and deep by deep/and more by more . . ." The climax of the ballad is in the line "and noone stooped to kiss his face." In the second to the last stanza the poet states the triumph of the individual way of life, as the lovers go hand in hand into eternity:

> noone and anyone earth by april
> wish by spirit and if by yes

Cumming's testament for his father, "my father moved through dooms of love," is a ballad only by stanza and innerly varied refrain; intertwined are seasonal references, as in "septembering arms of year extend," which gives individuality to the general term "harvest." It is heroic by virtue of lines that paraphrase the Prophets: "his anger was as right as rain/his pity was as green as grain." The poem is distinguished by some fine couplets:

"and should some why completely weep/my father's fingers brought her sleep," and "if every friend became his foe/he'd laugh and build a world with snow," which describes pretty accurately the poet himself. There is no narrative as such, but the poem is held together by the feeling of compassion toward humble or unfortunate people.

In contrast to the abstract quality of "my father moved through dooms of love," a sequence of colorful details characterizes an early poem for Cummings' mother, "if there are any heavens" *(ViVa)*. The opening lines establish clearly the heroic light in which Cumming's viewed this woman who said of herself after a remarkable recovery from an automobile accident, "I'm tough":

if there are any heavens my mother will(all by
    herself)have
one. It will not be a pansy heaven nor
a fragile heaven of lilies-of-the-valley but
it will be a heaven of blackred roses

Cummings' virtuosity in the management of his mechanics may especially be noted in several poems revealing his intense concern with the individual. In one, the free-form poem beginning "5/derbies-with-men-in-them" *(XLI Poems)*, the reader is presented with a charade. With the poet he has entered a café that, like the Englishman's pub, seems more a social club than a restaurant: the customers play games such as backgammon and read and discuss the news while drinking coffee. Identity of place is established in the fourth stanza when one of the customers buys the Bawstinamereekin from a paperboy. But Cummings builds up an un-Yankee atmosphere with carefully chosen details: the men smoke Helmar cigarettes, one of them uses the word "effendi" and "swears in persian," two speak in Turkish, an Armenian record is played on the phonograph. This is, then, a Near Eastern café in Boston. Far from the feuds of the Old Country, proprietor and customers are united by homesickness. The men are not named; instead Cummings identifies them by lowercase letters:

a has gold
teeth b pink
suspenders c
reads Atlantis

And x beats y at backgammon. This device permits Cummings both to control his flood of feeling for the men and to stress their brotherhood. When two of them—the man with the gold teeth and the winner at backgammon—leave, Cummings says "exeunt ax"; and the coupled "by" follow. Cummings' characteristic use of space and capitals to underscore meaning is also to be found in this poem: "the pho/nographisrunn/ingd o w, n" and then "stopS."

Capital letters (not meant to be pronounced) serve as an organizing and emphasizing device in "sonnet entitled how to run the world)" *(No Thanks)*, which begins:

A always don't there B being no such thing
for C can't casts no shadow D drink and

E eat of her voice in whose silence the music
    of spring
lives F feels opens but shuts understand
G gladly forget little having less

with every least most remembering
H highest fly only the flag that's furled

Here we have a commentary on the existence of "mostpeople." This satire on the "unworld" employs the comparatives "less" and "least" to emphasize the triviality and sterility of that world, while the clause "in whose silence the music of spring/lives" indicates what, for Cummings, is one of the symbols of the real world, the transcendental world. There is a flash of mocking humor in the repetition of the pedantic "entitled" in the ninth line of the poem, "(sestet entitled grass is flesh . . ." but even this line has a serious purpose: to reinforce the idea of a world where people merely exist. It is followed by a richly thought-provoking statement, "any dream/means more than sleep as more than know means guess)," which prepares the way for the masterly concluding line, "children building this rainman out of snow." In this poem Cummings uses for the most part simple words but combines them so that the repetitions and contrasts of sound add a fresh dimension to the theme and subtly contribute to the feeling of empathy evoked for the individuals trapped in the "unworld."

Where in these two poems Cummings used, variously, lowercase and capital letters as controlling devices, in "there are 6 doors" (*ViVa*), it is repetition of the phrase "next door" that governs the orderly sequence. "Next door(but four)" lives a whore with "a multitude of chins"; "next door/but three" a ghost "Who screams Faintly" is the tenant and "next/Door but two" a man and his wife who "throw silently things/Each at other." Then Cummings tells what happens to some men who have been jettisoned by society.

,next door but One
a on Dirty bed Mangy from person Porous
sits years its of self fee(bly
Perpetually coughing And thickly spi)tting

Finally, "next door nobody/seems to live at present . . . or,bedbugs." The reader is left to ponder several kinds of waste of human life. Emerson wrote in his essay "Self-Reliance," "This one fact the world hates, that the soul *becomes*"; Cummings recorded in poem after poem instances of the world preventing the action of the soul—but with the purpose of rousing the transcendental spirit latent in his readers.

The individuals pictured in "mortals)" (*50 Poems*) are very different from those in the

rooms "next door" and so are the technical devices used. Cummings here turns to highly skilled acrobats and puts them into motion on the page:

mortals)

climbi
    ng i
    nto eachness begi
    n
dizzily
      swingthings
of speeds of
trapeze gush somersaults
open ing
      hes shes
&meet&
    swoop
        fully is are ex
              quisite theys of re
turn
   a
   n
   d
fall which now drop who all dreamlike

(im

"Eachness" is a critical word in this poem: as George Haines IV has pointed out, the individuality of the performers is emphasized by the separation of "climbi" and "begi" from the end letters "ng" and "n"; the swinging of the trapeze is in the line repetition "of speeds of." The reader discovering a similar pattern in "&meet&" by this time is responding with a jump of his muscles, as occurs in watching ballet or circus. As the "fully" continues into "is are ex," movement has entered the area of the unknown; the symbol *x* ("ex") is equal to the mystery of the encounters of the "is" and "are," "the "hes" and "shes." The use of "a/n/d" permits visualization of the trapeze.

The fortunate climax of "who all dreamlike" brings together the specific skills and the hovering mystery of art, whose function is to redeem what otherwise would vanish from the earth like a dream. In another sense, the acrobats are a congruent image since even the most skilled is in peril at every performance (mortals, Cummings called them), yet they are completely and happily themselves in the exercise of their art. From the final line to the first one in this "circular" poem—"im" plus "mortal"—the poet justifies his contention that precision makes motion which makes life, and that the "dark beginnings are his luminous ends."

Why did Cummings choose the symbol of acrobats for a metaphysical statement? He may have been inspired, as was Rilke, by "Les Saltimbanques" of Picasso. More likely, his enjoyment of folk amusements dictated the vehicle for his fundamental belief: mortals, by devotion to a skill, an art, become immortal.

Before leaving this aspect of Cummings' work, we may appropriately turn back to his prose to find a revealing conjunction of theme and technique. In *The Enormous Room* Cummings had used a phrase of John Bunyan's, the "Delectable Mountains," to refer to certain individuals—physically mistreated, spiritually mutilated, and yet triumphantly overcoming their situations. Of one example, whom he christened The Zulu, he said, "His angular anatomy expended and collected itself with an effortless spontaneity. . . . But he was more. There are certain things in which one is unable to believe for the simple reason that he never ceases to feel them. Things of this sort—things which are always inside of us and in fact are us and which consequently will not be pushed off or away where we can begin thinking about them—are no longer things; they, and the us which they are, equals A Verb; an IS. The Zulu, then, I must perforce call an IS." Thus, using one of his typical devices, substitution

of one part of speech for another, Cummings converted one way of seeing and of thinking into another to emphasize a theme that would be meshed in all of his writings. Whenever *is*, the verb, is turned into a noun, it becomes even more of a verb; it is dramatized, it gains—as Lloyd Frankenberg put it—the force of the colloquial "He is somebody." In other words, the quality of being becomes an active principle, the individual becomes a whole person, responding to the totality of experience.

A third major theme in Cummings' work, already touched upon, is the revelation of what it means *truly* to love. In his experiments with the idea of love Cummings assigned to the word the multiple connotations inherent in it: sexual, romantic, platonic. The most intense love, paradoxically, must function with the greatest objectivity; subjective impressions must be corrected by intent observation of objects, human or otherwise. Dante could write of his ideal Lady; Cummings addressed to a platonic vision a bawdy valentine that is revelatory of his stance toward life and art ("on the Madam's best april the," *Is 5*).

In the era following World War I and acceleration of industrial growth, disregard of an earlier generation's restraints on sex became a means of protesting against the increased restrictions of the national life. In literature, Sherwood Anderson, Ernest Hemingway, Eugene O'Neill, and Henry Miller emphasized the necessity for sexual freedom. Cummings participated in this critique of the dehumanizing forces dominating the modern scene. Frankly rejoicing in sexuality as a nourishing element in an integrated life, a bond between man and the cosmos, or satirizing customs based on habit and fear of public opinion, he wrote "O sweet spontaneous" (*Tulips and Chimneys*) and "she being Brand" (*Is 5*) and "i will be/Moving in the Street of her" (*And*). A poem on Sally Rand, "out of a supermetamathical subpreincestures" (*No Thanks*), is not only a celebration of the fan dancer of the 1930's but also a transcendental view of the wonder of life. And it is a significant contrast to "raise the shade/will youse dearie?" (*And*), a realistic piece exposing the joylessness in the pursuit of "pleasure."

Cummings eventually went "beyond sex as a critique of society and . . . beyond self-indulgence to self-discipline based on a new understanding of love," as Barry Marks put it. Cummings believed that morality depends on whether there is genuine giving on both sides. Sexuality is an ingredient of any I-you relationship, in the impersonal way that there is a trace of sugar in all vegetable and animal tissues, even if they taste salty or bitter. He illustrated insights into giving in a philosophical poem, "(will you teach a/wretch to live/ straighter than a needle)," and in a comment on poverty that moves in nursery-rhyme couplets from realistic deprivations to a more desperate psychological dilemma, "if you can't eat you got to/smoke and we ain't got/nothing to smoke" (both in *50 Poems*). And a poem (from *No Thanks*) with neat stanzas to control his vehemence tells the reader from what a distance the poet has come, smiling in a wry wisdom:

> be of love(a little)
> More careful
> Than of everything
> guard her perhaps only
>
> . . . .
>
> (Dare until a flower,
> understanding sizelessly sunlight
> Open what thousandth why and
> discover laughing)

Lloyd Frankenberg, in his introduction to a London reprint of *One Times One*, said that, in effect, all of Cummings' poems were love poems. A neat summation, but then an "anatomy" of love is also necessary. Conventional behavior in love is related to conventional punctuation in prosody. And for a poet who lived on the tips of not only his nerves but also his mind, love covers all of existence: in one aspect it is involved with spit on the sidewalk and in another with moonlight on the thighs of his lady; the value of a thing or an experience is its revelation of an involvement with life. Finally, in *95 Poems* and *73 Poems*, Cummings came to a position whose simplicity may have surprised him: a filial relation to the Divine So this was what it meant, the witty comment he made on his own struggles in *Is 5*:

> since feeling is first
> who pays any attention
> to the syntax of things
> will never wholly kiss you;
>
> . . . .
>
> for life's not a paragraph
>
> And death i think is no parenthesis

In his critical studies T. S. Eliot repeated his view that the entire output of certain writers constitutes a single work similar to an epic (*The Divine Comedy* or Williams' *Paterson*) and that individual pieces are endowed with meaning by other pieces and by the whole context of the work. This view may assist to an understanding of Cummings: fragmentation dissolves in the continuity of recurrent themes; interrelated images and symbols by their organizing force reflect and echo each other with cumulative effect. Cummings would have said it more specifically: in the here and now we can be happy and immortal if we use our wits and our will. Even if evil and death are the co-kings of this world, love is my king, and in serving him is my joy.

It is a leap into faith when a man casts off the customary motives of humanity and ventures to trust himself as taskmaster; he will need courage and vision "that a simple purpose may be to him as strong as iron necessity is to others"—so Emerson thought. From *Tulips and Chimneys* to *Poems 1923–1954*—a constellation of refracted and repeated images—to the posthumous *73 Poems*, Cummings led a succession of readers to accept his declaration: "I have no sentimentality at all. If you haven't got that, you're not afraid to write of love and death."

The metaphysical cord on which Cummings' sonnets are threaded was in evidence in the early "a connotation of infinity/sharpens the temporal splendor of this night" (*Tulips and Chimneys*), in "put off your faces,Death:for day is over" (*ViVa*), and in "Love/coins His most gradual gesture,/and whittles life to eternity" ("it is so long since my heart has been with yours," *Is 5*). The efficacy of love in its multiple aspects pervades the notions of death until death becomes a gate to life. Dying is a verb as opposed to a deathly noun: "forgive us the sin of death." In another early poem, "somewhere i have never travelled,gladly beyond/any experience" (*ViVa*), the abstraction "spring" is personified and its essential mystery is presented through the adverbs *skilfully, mysteriously, suddenly*, used as in the later poetry are *miraculous, illimitable, immeasurable*: adjectival aspects of natural phenomena capable of being perceived but incapable of being truly labeled or measured.

The concern of Cummings, even in his Sitwellian phase, with juxtaposed improbables—locomotives with roses—was an effort to get at the quintessence of an apparently trivial subject. Its mystery could be reached successfully only by the evolution of devices he had scrupulously crafted. In his war against formal "thinking" he was not against study or ideas; it was an opposition to the conformity which the accumulation of "knowledge" is inclined to impose. To discover the true nature of the world—to know it; to act in it; for the artist, to depict it—is the Cummings metaphysic, his politics, and his aesthetic. The world of cyclical process is for him a timeless world. He does not deny either the past or the future; rather he denies that hope or regret should warp the living moment. In this way he is related to Coleridge and to Blake (related doubly to the latter by reason of his sensitive drawings, such as the celebrated sketch of Charlie Chaplin). His eyes are fixed on fulfillment, consenting to the perpetuation of life through death, as in "rosetree, rosetree." The individual rose dies that a hundred roses may be born; true lovers will be reborn into perfect love.

The antithesis between the false routine world and the true world is seen with icy clarity by a poet who feels mortality sitting on his shoulder. The result is a complexity of vision. That it should have cost so much to get there does not trouble the poet of transcendence; he is a compeer of all seekers, including a tramp on the highway. A poet's function is to embody in a poem the dynamics of nature (including his own response), which is primarily a mystery. Heightened awareness leads to a new dimension that leads into transcendentalism supported by specific detail: in "luminous tendril of celestial wish" (*Xaipe*), the cyclical moon is regarded as evidence of process leading to death and rebirth; the poet's humility is indicated by "teach disappearing also me the keen/illimitable secret of begin."

In *95 Poems* the poetic argument rises into an intense clarity. The affirmative transcending the negative as in "All lose,whole find" ("one's not half two," *One Times One*) and in "the most who die,the more we live" ("what if a much of a which of a wind," *One Times One*) has entered a final phase. The poet has now realized that the transcendental cannot abolish the "fact" of death but he proves the worth of the affirmative as the polarizing element of his philosophy. The former devices of making nouns into verbs and shifting the placement of antitheses are less in evidence; the reality of "appearances" is acknowledged: "now air is air and thing is thing:no bliss/of heavenly earth beguiles our spirits,whose/miraculously disenchanted eyes/live the magnificent honesty of space." This is a reminder of the early "let's live suddenly without thinking/under honest trees" (*And*). The poet, however, has come into the higher turn of the spiral of mystical development where the phenomenal world is transfigured and a tree is really understood.

In this volume Cummings has collected all of his phases: (1) look at what is happening around you; (2) the imagination is more real than reality; (3) the search for life and self brings you back to a transformed reality that is shared with a grasshopper on a flowering weed. As S. I. Hayakawa wrote in *Language in Thought and Action*, the only certainty and security is within the disciplined mind; so when Cummings says in "in time of daffodils(who know"

> and in a mystery to be
> (when time from time shall set us free)
> forgetting me,remember me

the troubadour is telling his lady to forget his life *in* time; to remember that his mortal love always looked toward lovers in immortality. Just so did his preoccupation with twilight reach beyond mist and the "dangerous first stars" to a world new to the senses.

Begin as you mean to go on. The English proverb may explain why the young Cummings was attracted to a statement of Keats: "I am certain of nothing but the holiness of the Heart's affections, and the truth of Imagination." The innovative devices that the young Cummings developed to implement this idea were a successful means of communication in the modern world. But the Cummings of *73 Poems* has traveled farther than that: into the realm of transcendence. The poet who said "—who'll solve the depths of horror to defend/a sunbeam's architecture with his life" ("no man, if men are gods," *One Times One*) has earned the right to explain time by timelessness. In total compassion he declares, in the last poem in *73 Poems*:

> (being forever born a foolishwise
> proudhumble citizen of ecstasies
> more steep than climb can time with all his
>   years)
>
> he's free into the beauty of the truth;
>
> and strolls the axis of the universe
> —love. Each believing world denies, whereas
> your lover(looking through both life and death)
> timelessly celebrates the merciful
>
> wonder no world deny may or believe.

Growing from poem to poem—shedding skin after skin—Cummings emerges as really himself, and therefore as everyone: that is the true definition of transcendence. The artist's formalities have become clear as a washed windowpane, or the purity of a flower upturned to receive a heavenly dew—the canticles of a mystic.

Selected Bibliography

WORKS OF E. E. CUMMINGS

For convenience of reference the capitalization of book titles in this essay follows conventional form rather than the typographical style of the title page in each book, which often reflected Cummings' own preference for lowercase letters.

Eight Harvard Poets: E. Estlin Cummings, S. Foster Damon, J. R. Dos Passos, Robert Hillyer, R. S. Mitchell, William A. Norris, Dudley Poore, Cuthbert Wright. New York: Laurence J. Gomme, 1917. (Contains eight poems by Cummings.)

The Enormous Room. New York: Boni and Liveright, 1922.

Tulips and Chimneys. New York: Seltzer, 1923.

& (And). New York: Privately printed, 1925.

XLI Poems. New York: Dial Press, 1925.

Is 5. New York: Boni and Liveright, 1926.

Him. New York: Boni and Liverright, 1927.

Christmas Tree. New York: American Book Bindery, 1928.

[No title] New York: Covici, Friede, 1930.

CIOPW. New York: Covici, Friede, 1931.

W (ViVa). New York: Horace Liveright, 1931.

Eimi. New York: Covici, Friede, 1933.

No Thanks. New York: Golden Eagle Press, 1935.

Tom. New York: Arrow Editions, 1935.

1/20 (One Over Twenty). London: Roger Roughton, 1936.

Collected Poems. New York: Harcourt, Brace, 1938.

50 Poems. New York: Duell, Sloan and Pearce, 1940.

1 x 1 (One Times One). New York: Henry Holt, 1944.

Anthropos: The Future of Art. Mount Vernon, N.Y.: Golden Eagle Press, 1944.

Santa Claus: A Morality. New York: Henry Holt, 1946.

Puella Mea. Mount Vernon, N.Y.: Golden Eagle Press, 1949.

Xaipe. New York: Oxford University Press, 1950.

I: Six Nonlectures. Cambridge, Mass.: Harvard University Press, 1953.

Poems 1923–1954. New York: Harcourt, Brace, 1954.

E. E. Cummings: A Miscellany, edited by George J. Firmage. New York: Argophile Press, 1958.

95 Poems. New York: Harcourt, Brace, 1958.

100 Selected Poems. New York: Grove Press, 1959.

Selected Poems 1923–1958. London: Faber and Faber, 1960.

Adventures in Value, with photographs by Marion Morehouse. New York: Harcourt, Brace and World, 1962:

73 Poems. New York: Harcourt, Brace and World, 1963.

E. E. Cummings: A Miscellany, Revised, edited by George J. Firmage. New York: October House, 1965.

LETTERS

Selected Letters of E. E. Cummings, edited by F. W. Dupee and George Stade. New York: Harcourt, Brace and World, 1969.

BIBLIOGRAPHIES

Firmage, George J. *E. E. Cummings: A Bibliography.* Middletown, Conn.: Wesleyan University Press, 1960.

Lauter, Paul. *E. E. Cummings: Index to First Lines and Bibliography of Works by and about the Poet.* Denver: Alan Swallow, 1955.

CRITICAL COMMENTS AND STUDIES

Abel, Lionel. "Clown or Comic Poet?" *Nation,* 140:749–50 (June 26, 1935).

Baum, S. V. "E. E. Cummings: The Technique of Immediacy," *South Atlantic Quarterly,* 53:70–88 (January 1954).

————, ed. *ΕΣΤΙ: E. E. Cummings and the Critics.* East Lansing: Michigan State University Press, 1962. (Good bibliography.)

Blackmur, R. P. "Notes on E. E. Cummings' Language," in *Language as Gesture.* New York Harcourt, Brace, 1952. Pp. 317–40.

Bode, Carl. "E. E. Cummings and Exploded Verse," in *The Great Experiment in American Literature.* New York: Praeger, 1961. Pp. 79–100.

Breit, Harvey. "The Case for the Modern Poet," *New York Times Magazine,* November 3, 1946, pp. 20, 58, 60–61.

————. "Talk with E. E. Cummings," *New York Times Book Review,* December 31, 1950, p. 10.

Davis, William V. "Cummings' all in green went my love riding," *Concerning Poetry,* 3:65–67 (Fall 1970).

————. "Cummings' next to of course god america i," *Concerning Poetry,* 3:14–15 (Spring 1970).

Deutsch, Babette. *Poetry in Our Time*. New York: Henry Holt, 1952. Pp. 111-18.

Dickey, James. "E. E. Cummings," in *Babel to Byzantium: Poets and Poetry Now*. New York: Farrar, Straus and Giroux, 1968. Pp. 100–06.

Fergusson, Francis. "When We Were Very Young," *Kenyon Review,* 12:701–05 (Autumn 1950).

Frankenberg, Lloyd. *Pleasure Dome: On Reading Modern Poetry*. Boston: Houghton Mifflin, 1949. Pp. 157–94.

Friedman, Norman. *E. E. Cummings: The Art of His Poetry*. Baltimore: Johns Hopkins Press, 1960.

––––––. *E. E. Cummings: The Growth of a Writer*. Carbondale: Southern Illinois University Press, 1964.

Gunter, Richard. "Sentence & Poem," *Style,* 5:26–36 (Winter 1971).

Haines, George, IV. "::2:1—The World and E. E. Cummings," *Sewanee Review,* 59:206–27 (Spring 1951).

Hart, J. "Champion of Freedom and the Individual," *National Review*, 21:864 (August 26, 1969).

Harvard Wake, No. 5 (Spring 1946). (A special Cummings number.)

Hollander, John. "Poetry Chronicle," *Partisan Review*, 26:142–43 (Winter 1959).

Honig, Edwin. " 'Proud of His Scientific Attitude,' " *Kenyon Review,* 17:484–90 (Summer 1955).

Horton, Philip, and Sherry Mangan. "Two Views of Cummings," *Partisan Review,* 4:58–63 (May 1938).

Marks, Barry A. *E. E. Cummings*. New York: Twayne, 1963.

Metcalf, Allan A. "Dante and E. E. Cummings," *Comparative Literature Studies,* 7:374–86 (September 1970).

Moore, Marianne. "People Stare Carefully," *Dial,* 80:49–52 (January 1926).

––––––. "One Times One," in *Predilections*. New York: Viking Press, 1955. Pp. 140–43.

Munson, Gorham B. "Syrinx," *Secession,* 5:2–11 (July 1923).

Norman, Charles. *E. E. Cummings: The Magic-Maker*. New York: Macmillan, 1958.

Riding, Laura, and Robert Graves. *A Survey of Modernist Poetry*. London: Heinemann, 1927. Pp. 9–34.

Shapiro, Karl. *Essay on Rime*. New York: Reynal and Hitchcock, 1945. Pp. 20–21.

Sitwell, Edith, *Aspects of Modern Poetry*. London: Duckworth, 1934. Pp. 251–57.

Spencer, Theodore. "Technique as Joy," *Harvard Wake,* 5:25–29. (Spring 1946).

Tate, Allen. "E. E. Cummings," in *Reactionary Essays on Poetry and Ideas*. New York: Scribners, 1936. Pp. 228–33.

Time, September 14, 1962. (A full-page obituary.)

Troy, William. "Cummings's Non-land of Un-," *Nation,* 136:413 (April 12, 1933).

Untermeyer, Louis. "Quirky Communications from an Exuberant Hero," *Saturday Review,* 52:25–26 (July 5, 1969).

Voisin, Laurence. "Quelques poètes américains," *Europe: Revue Mensuelle,* 37:36–37 (February–March 1959).

Von Abele, Rudolph. " 'Only to Grow': Change in the Poetry of E. E. Cummings," *PMLA,* 70:913–33 (December 1955).

Wegner, Robert E. *The Poetry and Prose of E. E. Cummings*. New York: Harcourt, Brace and World, 1965.

Williams, William Carlos. "E. E. Cummings' Paintings and Poems," *Arts Digest,* 29:7–8 (December 1, 1954).

Wilson, Edmund. *"Him," New Republic,* 70:293–94 (November 2, 1927).

—*EVE TRIEM*

Emily Dickinson
1830–1886

ONE IMAGE OF Emily Dickinson is found on T-shirts and coffee mugs and in the ever-growing number of studies of her life and work. She is seventeen, a student at a rigorous school for young women. No effort has been spared in standardizing her appearance. Her hair, which she described as brash like a chestnut burr, must have tended to wildness; in the school photograph, her hair lies obedient. She gazes unsmilingly at the camera, or if there is a smile, it is suppressed into one corner of her mouth.

No American poet—and no woman poet writing in English—has enjoyed wider circulation, greater popularity, or more secure canonicity than Dickinson. Critics have celebrated her body of short poems as if they encapsulate structures of the psyche that transcend time and place. Yet she wrote during a time of dramatic social change and national trauma. Sequestering herself in an upper-middle-class private life, Dickinson fended off historical forces, encoding events such as the Civil War with cryptic metaphysical symbols. She wrote for her own purposes, "publishing" her poems by copying them into personal correspondence. By avoiding the literary marketplace, she exercised strict control over who would read her poems and protected her sensibility from commercialism. Yet in the ways she organized and

stored her poems, and in their preoccupation with the vocation of the poet, Dickinson seems to have anticipated what would become of them after her death: they would be taken from their hiding place, published, read, loved, and immortalized.

"And once you begin, how to tell the story of a life that had no story?" Richard Sewall asked himself this question as he prepared a two-volume biography of Dickinson in the 1970s. Because of her reclusiveness and her refusal to publish, Dickinson's life and poems were continually reinvented long after her death. The posthumous publication of her poems and letters occurred in several phases, under different editorial hands, and spanned more than half a century. Her letters are nearly as enigmatic as her poems and do not provide clear windows onto her life. Firsthand reports of her life came from relatives and family friends who had their own secrets to hide. The story seemed to be one of genius, with little of what is usually called experience. She made trips to Philadelphia, Washington, D.C., and Boston, but otherwise spent most of her life in her father's house in Amherst, Massachusetts. Dickinson was a nearly blank screen receptive to projected myths.

Sewall recalled that when he first taught Dickinson's poetry to college classes in the 1930s, she was summed up in clichés: Frustrated Lover, Great Renunciation, Queen Recluse, New England Nun, Moth of Amherst. The myth of a mad, mystical, diminutive genius began to take shape in her lifetime. An often-cited account of her comes from Thomas Wentworth Higginson, a correspondent who met her in 1870. In a letter to his wife, he described Dickinson as a little, plain woman in a white dress whose puzzling chatter and childlike anxiety drained his nerves.

Because Dickinson did not write in order to publish, readers have been tempted to see in her poems an extreme honesty free from social repression. Yet many critics have found her to be a versatile poseur. Writing to Higginson, she strikes the pose of a giddy pupil, while in letters to the writer Helen Hunt Jackson she is a warm, respectful colleague. Jackson's fictionalized impressions of Dickinson in *Mercy Philbrick's Choice* (1876) fall just short of linking the truthful Dickinson to the poseur. The novel's heroine, modeled after Dickinson, suffers pangs of conscience about the lies one must tell for the sake of social decorum. It is a sin, she believes, to act in such a way that people "think you're glad to see them when you're not. . . . A lie's a lie, let whoever will call it fine names, and pass it off as a Christian duty." Mercy's conflicts leave her "morally bruised, and therefore abnormally sensitive to the least touch. She was in danger of becoming either a fanatic for truth, or indifferent to it."

Dickinson's poems, like her life, tend to be treated as reflections of the concerns and convictions of their readers. Grammatical distortions and startling word choices make variant readings equally plausible. "So much Summer" illustrates qualities common to much of her verse:

So much Summer
Me for showing
Illegitimate—
Would a Smile's minute bestowing
Too exorbitant

To the Lady
With the Guinea
Look—if She should know
Crumb of Mine
A Robin's Larder
Would suffice to stow—   (P 651)

(Selections from the poems of Emily Dickinson are taken from the 1955 edition edited by Thomas H. Johnson and are indicated in this essay by the letter P, followed by the number of the poem.) Like most of Dickinson's poems, "So much Summer" consists of altered ballad stanzas. Conventionally each stanza would have four lines, the first and third lines would have four beats, and the second and fourth would rhyme and have three beats. The poem begins with vastness ("So much Summer") and ends with something small ("A Robin's Larder"); the interplay of such natural extremes is frequent in Dickinson's imagery. The language is hyperbolic, dramatizing the voice of the speaker, who seems to be experiencing an inner struggle.

What is going on in this poem? It encrypts a recognizable experience. Someone has given the speaker a strange look that makes her feel out of place. She wonders if a tiny smile would have been too much to expect. If only that woman knew how little it took to satisfy me; she could have just tossed me a crumb. But what does the line "So much Summer" have to do with this situation? Suppose it's a busy summer in Amherst, the summer of 1862. Much is occurring that makes Dickinson feel how improper others consider her increasingly frequent retreats to her room. Someone gives her a look that reminds her of a gold coin or of a guinea fowl demanding to be fed: the woman wants something from her, perhaps a donation to a charitable cause, or a loaf of bread to sell at a church bazaar to raise funds for the Union cause. It's not that Dickinson would be satisfied with a crumb but that she has little to give, or nothing appropriate; she finds feeding birds more gratifying than submitting to community obligations. And who failed to smile, the other woman or Dickinson? Perhaps the speaker is not Dickinson at all but a knight out of an old romance wooing an elusive lady, with the summer stimulating his ardent desire. Or is the lady's suitor a woman? Maybe the speaker *is* the lady sequestered in an upper room, looking down at the suitor and wondering if it would cost her too much to smile.

CHILDHOOD AND EDUCATION

Emily Dickinson was born in Amherst, Massachusetts, on December 10, 1830. She was the middle child in a prominent family whose male members helped to establish and run the town and its institutions. Her ancestor Nathan Dickinson was among those who founded the town in 1745, and her grandfather, Samuel Fowler Dickinson, took part in the founding of Amherst Academy in 1814 and Amherst College in 1821. Emily's father, Edward Dickinson, a lawyer and treasurer of Amherst College, served in state public offices during her childhood and was elected to Congress in 1852. Her mother, Emily Norcross Dickinson, tended to charitable duties in the community as well as the care of the household. The Dickinson home, known as the Homestead, was a center of Amherst society. Emily's brother, William Austin Dickinson, born in 1829, married her close friend Susan Gilbert and built a house called the Evergreens next to the Homestead. He followed in his father's footsteps, becoming a lawyer and college treasurer and also serving on corporate and civic boards. Lavinia Dickinson, born in 1833, remained unmarried like her sister, and the two grew old together in the Homestead after their parents' deaths.

Nostalgic illustrations of old New England towns show tranquil places where church spires sanctify the wilderness and modest homes promise protection against rough weather. Dickinson's life did not fit neatly into such a simple, harmonious setting. Helen Hunt Jackson, born in Amherst the same year as Dickinson, found a virulent tedium at the heart of "the ordinary New England town." In *Mercy Philbrick's Choice* she wrote:

> The community is loosely held together by a few accidental points of contact or common interest. The individuality of individuals is, by a strange sort of paradox, at once respected and ignored. This is indifference rather than consideration, selfishness rather than generosity; it is an unsuspected root of much of our national failure, is responsible for much of our national disgrace. . . . Our people are living, on the whole, the dullest lives that are lived in the world, by the so-called civilized.

Jackson gives her heroine a passion for beauty and truth that makes her a misfit in this place. For pathos, Jackson portrays Mercy as an impoverished widow. Dickinson was never poor, but social and economic change did threaten her family's status. Edward Dickinson, like his father, was a town squire. He functioned as a justice of the peace but the title conveyed the social status of an English country gentleman. During the 1830s and 1840s Amherst and other New England towns became increasingly dependent on the wider industrialized economy. The rising class of merchants and manufacturers began to displace New England's old aristocracy at the top of local social hierarchies.

The fortunes of the Dickinson house illustrate the family's vulnerability to such change. The Homestead's alternate names, the Manor and the Mansion, signify the borrowing of status from English feudalism for an American setting. It was the first brick house built in Amherst. Its double parlors, high ceilings, large bedrooms, and extensive landscaping on Main Street bespoke money and success. Yet soon after Samuel Fowler Dickinson built it in 1813, he had to sell it to relatives, who leased it back to him. Edward Dickinson bought half of the house in 1830, and in 1833 David Mack, an industrialist, foreclosed on the half that Samuel Fowler Dickinson occupied. Having lavished his wealth on public projects, the house's builder moved to Ohio in a state of financial ruin. Edward Dickinson's family, with three small children and only two bedrooms, was crowded in their half of the house. By 1840 Edward's financial condition allowed him to sell his half to Mack and move the family to a nearby wood frame house spacious enough to accommodate social gatherings. It was not until 1855, when Emily was twenty-five, that the Dickinson family took possession of the entire Homestead.

In private letters Edward Dickinson wrote of his fears about "democratic mixing," the opening of civil-service jobs to lower-class workers, the prospect of losing property and falling in the social hierarchy. In 1835 he wrote anxiously to his wife about the need to make money. Soon afterward he entered politics. When other members of the Whig party defected to the antislavery Republican Party, Edward Dickinson stayed in the conservative ranks, resisting the fervor of abolitionism. His daughter, too, would resist the rising social impulses of democratization, protest, and reform.

Emily Dickinson's upbringing was divided between an exceptionally serious education and an induction into domestic duties. She began attending primary school before her fifth birthday and at nine entered Amherst Academy, where she earned a reputation as school wit. In letters written during her teens, she reports studying grammar, composition, and a wide range of subjects in the humanities and natural sciences. At age sixteen she entered Mount Holyoke Female Seminary in nearby South Hadley. Mount Holyoke offered the nearest thing to a college education that was then available to women. Its founder, Mary Lyon, directed instruction toward producing young women who would subordinate their personal desires to the social good. Such notions of a woman's role in society were much in the air during the decades before the Civil War. Seeking to raise women's status without challenging male dominance in public life, writers and educators articulated a philosophy that saw women's special mission as one of improving the nation by exerting a moral influence in the home and community.

Confining as this philosophy may seem today, it inspired many women to become writers, speakers, and activists for social reform. Dickinson, however, mocked efforts to mold her character. In a letter to her brother, Austin, she writes that she pondered whether she should present his letter to Lyon's assistant for approval before reading it herself:

> The result of my deliberation was a conclusion to open it with moderation, peruse it's contents with sobriety becoming my station, & if after a close investigation of it's contents I found nothing which savored of rebellion or an unsubdued will, I would lay it away in my folio & forget I had ever received it. (L 22)

(Selections from the letters of Emily Dickinson are taken from the 1958 edition edited by Thomas H. Johnson and Theodora Ward and are indicated in this essay by the letter L, followed by the number of the letter.)

Dickinson withdrew from Mount Holyoke after two terms and became immersed in domestic responsibilities. In a letter to her childhood friend Abiah Root, she described her duties with flippancy and exasperation:

> I am yet the Queen of the court, if regalia be dust, and dirt, have three loyal subjects, whom I'd rather releive from service. Mother is still an invalid tho' a partially restored one—Father and Austin still clamor for food, and I, like a martyr am feeding them. Would'nt you love to see me in these bonds of great despair, looking around my kitchen, and praying for kind deliverance. (L 36)

In Paula Bennett's 1990 study of female creativity, *My Life a Loaded Gun*, she argues that Dickinson believed her mother tried to coerce her into accepting a life of drudgery that would destroy her individuality. As Joanne Dobson has pointed out in *Dickinson and the Strategies of Reticence*, the sheer amount of domestic labor needed to sustain an entertainment schedule like the Dickinsons' would have been formidable. Servants did the heavy work, but Emily and Lavinia would have shopped, cooked, mended, and cleaned. Eventually Emily specialized in baking bread and creating extravagant desserts, which she gave to neighbors' children. (Local legend has it that at her most reclusive she lowered a cream puff from her window to a waiting child.)

That growing up was difficult for Dickinson is evident from the letters she wrote during her teens, particularly those to Abiah Root. Abiah formed part of an intimate circle Dickinson called "the five" and attended school with her until they were fifteen. The early letters to Abiah are full of news and questions about mutual friends. Quickly, though, Emily begins to sound fearful that Abiah no longer cares about her. From Mount Holyoke, where she was the only student who resisted the wave of Christian revivalism sweeping the region, she confessed to Abiah her regret that she did not "give up & become a Christian." Now, she thought, it was too late, and she could not honestly say that her only desire was to be good (L 23). In a letter written late in 1850, Emily contrasted herself with Abiah and another childhood friend. They were becoming women, engaging in good works and learning "control and firmness," but Emily loved "to be a child" and to let her imagination wander: "Oh I *love* the *danger*!" (L 39). Yet a letter Dickinson wrote to Susan Gilbert in 1852 suggests that she saw a greater danger in being a wife. "You have seen flowers at morning, *satisfied* with the dew," she writes. At noon those same flowers bow their heads "in anguish before the mighty sun." The sweet romance of youthful female friendships gives way to addiction to male power: "They will cry for sunlight, and pine for the burning noon, tho' it scorches them, scathes them; they have got through with peace—they know that the man of noon, is *mightier* than the morning, and their life is henceforth to him" (L 93).

In November 1855 the Dickinson family moved into the Homestead, an event that Emily jokingly called a "catastrophe." Her mother was ill again, so a great deal of the work of settling into the new home must have fallen on Emily. The following summer Austin and Susan married and moved into the Evergreens, an elegant Italianate-style house linked to the Homestead by a flower-lined path. Few records remain of Dickinson's life during this time, and although her earliest poem can be dated to around 1850, there is no evidence that she wrote poems between 1854 and 1858. By the end of the decade, however, she had begun her lifework as a poet.

THE POET AT WORK

In 1858 Dickinson started to make fascicles or manuscript books. R. W. Franklin, who edited a facsimile edition of these booklets in 1981, reconstructed her composition habits from the evidence provided by the manuscripts. She would draft a poem on any piece of paper that came to hand—a shopping sack, a used envelope, the back of a recipe. Later she would rework the poem, make a fair copy on a folded piece of stationery, and usually destroy the draft. She filled all four sides of the folded sheet with poems, attaching a partial sheet with a pin if a poem extended beyond the available space. She selected four or five sheets, stacked them rather than setting them inside one another, and bound them by stitching a cotton string along the left margin with a darning needle, then tying the ends in a bow.

At first she treated the bound poems as completed drafts. Starting around 1861, however, many of the fascicles include alternate wordings, some added long after she copied the poem. Franklin speculates that as she leafed through her poems, perhaps searching for just the right one to send to a friend, she would start composing again, turning a fair copy into a working draft that could be altered for different purposes or recipients. In 1862 she began leaving some copied poems unbound, and she stopped binding them altogether in 1864, having created forty fascicles containing over eight hundred poems. From 1867 on her practice of making fair copies became intermittent. During the last years of her life she left poems on the odd bits of paper on which she had first drafted them.

From 1858 to 1862 Dickinson's productivity increased. The fair copies of 366 poems have been dated to 1862 based on an analysis of the manuscripts. Whether she actually composed all these poems during this remarkable year or copied some of them from earlier drafts is not known since she did not date the poems herself. In any case, she must have devoted time each day to her poems, writing, revising, copying, and organizing them. The burst of productivity continued in 1863 (141 poems) and 1864 (174 poems), and in later years it leveled off to an average of 50 poems annually.

From her letters and poems it is evident that Dickinson attained a new sense of seriousness about her calling as a poet during these years. It was also during this time that a few of her poems appeared in print. Karen Dandurand has found ten Dickinson poems published during her lifetime, six of them reprinted one or more times, totaling twenty publications. The poems are " 'Sic transit gloria mundi' " (P 3), "Nobody knows this little Rose—" (P 35), "I taste a liquor never brewed—" (P 214), "Safe in their Alabaster Chambers—" (P 216), "Success is counted sweetest" (P 67), "These are the days when Birds come back—"

(P 130), "Flowers—Well—if anybody" (P 137), "Blazing in Gold and quenching in Purple" (P 228), "Some keep the Sabbath going to Church—" (P 324), and "A narrow Fellow in the Grass" (P 986). All were published anonymously with varying degrees of editing. They appeared in periodicals published in Springfield (a city near Amherst), Boston, New York, and Brooklyn, as well as in an anthology.

RESISTING PUBLICATION

The paucity of works published during her lifetime enhanced the fascination of readers who discovered her through the posthumously published books of poems. She seemed to have been a genius who was neglected or suppressed, either because she was a woman or because she was far ahead of her time. Recent studies, however, have shown that she had ample opportunity to publish but regarded the literary marketplace as an anxiety-provoking diversion from her purposes in writing. Friends tried to persuade her to send her work to publishers, and literary figures such as Samuel Bowles, editor of the *Springfield Republican*, repeatedly urged her to give them poems for publication. When Bowles did print "A narrow Fellow in the Grass" without her permission, Dickinson complained to Higginson on February 14, 1866, that it was robbed from her (L 316).

Resisting publication out of modesty was a conventional stance for women, and yet the nineteenth century saw unprecedented numbers of women making successful careers as writers. For much of the century they dominated the literary marketplace. From the 1830s on, women writers and editors built a flourishing female print culture, extending their belief in women's special mission to enter the field of public discourse. Some of these writers avoided controversy by concentrating on genteel subjects, while others tackled injustice. Helen Hunt Jackson, for example, documented the United States' breach of trust with Native Americans and distributed copies of her book *A Century of Dishonor* to every member of Congress. As Joanne Dobson has shown, although Dickinson had little interest in social issues, few of her poems would have been out of place in the literary culture of her time. The need to earn money was a commonly accepted justification for women publishing. Although she herself had no need to earn an income, Dickinson begrudgingly allows this exception in "Publication—is the Auction" (P 709): "Poverty—be justifying / For so foul a thing // Possibly." Comparing the literary marketplace to a slave auction, she declares, "Publication—is the Auction / Of the Mind of Man," generalizing the degradation regardless of gender. To publish was to reduce the human spirit to a price.

Dickinson's attitude toward publishing reflects fears that some mid-nineteenth-century critics expressed as American publishing grew into a thriving industry, namely, that literature would become just another trade—mechanical, commercial, and subject to the laws of supply and demand. Given her reservations about publishing, why Dickinson chose to send poems to Thomas Wentworth Higginson during her most productive year is a mystery. Higginson, then editor of the *Atlantic Monthly*, was a leading liberal who crusaded for women's rights and the abolition of slavery. Perhaps Dickinson wanted to test her estimate of her writing against that of an influential arbiter of taste, or perhaps she was testing her negative idea of the literary marketplace against Higginson's optimistic view. In an article entitled "Letter to a Young Contributor," published in the April 1862 issue of the *Atlantic*, Higginson promoted an idea of poetry as a craft of expressive language that Dickinson would have found compatible with her own practice. However, he also asserted his faith in the judgment of the literate public, suggesting that their expecting "the same dash and the same accuracy" from literature as they did from the providers of goods and services would benefit the craft of poetry.

Two weeks after the issue was published, Dickinson sent Higginson four poems with a note asking him "to say if my Verse is alive" (L 260). She did not ask him to consider publishing the poems, and he recommended that she learn to control the "spasmodic" movement of her lines before submitting poems for publication. Dickinson rejected his editorial advice and never accepted any instruction he tried to give her, but he became a trusted friend. She sent him a hundred poems over the course of their twenty-three-year correspondence, and they met twice. Perhaps combining an ironic pose with real gratitude, she signed her letters "Your pupil" and said he had saved her life.

Of the people who urged Dickinson to publish, none was more emphatic than Helen Hunt Jackson. Like Higginson, Jackson believed that placing a market value on the quality of a literary work did not detract from it but rather encouraged writers to develop their skill. The daughter of an Amherst professor, Jackson became acquainted with Dickinson in 1860. Jackson, herself a highly regarded poet, probably appreciated Dickinson's poetry more fully than did any other literary figure of the time. She copied Dickinson's poems in her notebooks and from them learned to pay close attention to the formal qualities of her own verse. One difference between Dickinson and Jackson's fictional heroine Mercy Philbrick is that Mercy publishes her poetry, attaining a saintlike status because of her ability to comfort readers through her poems. From 1876 on, Jackson repeatedly pressured Dickinson to publish, even offering strategies for protecting her anonymity.

At one point an exasperated Dickinson solicited Higginson's help in getting Jackson to stop pressuring her, but she did agree to allow "Success is counted sweetest" (P 67) to appear in *A Masque of Poets*, an anthology published by Roberts Brothers of Boston in 1878. The poem was well received, quoted in a review of the anthology, and was attributed by many readers to Emerson. With the title "Success," added by her editors, it would play a prominent role in the unfolding of Dickinson's works to a wider readership after her death; it was placed first in collections of her poems published between 1890 and 1937. The poem's aphoristic lines declare that victory is apprehended most fully by someone

> defeated—dying—
> On whose forbidden ear
> The distant strains of triumph
> Burst agonized and clear!

Read as an introduction to Dickinson's works, the poem seems to invite readers to join in vanquishing her unjust obscurity.

During the last year of her life, Jackson wrote to Dickinson from California, "What portfolios of verses you must have.—It is a cruel wrong to your 'day & generation' that you will not give them light." For Jackson publishing was a moral obligation: "I do not think we have a right to with hold from the world a word or a thought any more than a *deed*, which might help a single soul" (L 937a). Dickinson may have partly agreed with Jackson; she generously offered up her words to people known to her, but she firmly resisted releasing them to the wider public.

RECLUSIVENESS AND COMMUNITY

During her period of tremendous productivity, Dickinson began to withdraw from the social world. She no longer attended church, stopped visiting friends and relatives, and eventually refused to see people in her home. Reclusiveness is central to the legend of Emily Dickinson that developed when her poems were posthumously published, but even before her death it was rumored that she was eccentric, misanthropic, ill, mad, or lovelorn. Lavinia insisted that Emily was

not withdrawn; she was always glad when someone "rewarding" would come to the house, but she was very busy: "She had to think." In her obituary of Emily, Susan Dickinson also attributed Emily's retreat to that of a brilliant mind with a sense of mission.

Dickinson did maintain a sense of community through her abundant correspondence. She wrote many of her poems to send to friends on special occasions: to mourn the loss of a loved one or mark the anniversary of a death, to congratulate or sympathize, or to accompany gifts of dried flowers. Parts of the letters themselves have the same meter that she used in most of her poems. The letters that have been published—numbering well over a thousand—represent only a fraction of what she wrote. Several important groups of letters, such as those to Charles Wadsworth, a clergyman with whom she corresponded for at least twenty years, were destroyed. There are dozens of addressees for the surviving correspondence, some names appearing on one or two brief notes and others on letters that cover many years, giving evidence of strong, enduring attachments. There are letters addressed to her childhood schoolmates, close and distant relatives, friends and their relatives, associates of her father and grandfather, and people she met through other family members. Among her frequent correspondents were Samuel Bowles and his wife, Mary; Elizabeth Holland and her husband, Josiah, an associate of Bowles; Judge Otis Phillips Lord, with whom Dickinson formed a romantic attachment after he was widowed in 1877; and her younger cousins Louise and Frances Norcross.

Three letters found in draft form among Dickinson's papers have attracted much attention because of their apparent relevance to her reclusiveness. They are addressed to an unknown recipient whom Dickinson calls "Master." Their estimated dates are 1858, 1861, and 1862. The third letter sounds especially anguished:

Oh, did I offend it— ~~Did'nt it want me to tell it the truth~~ Daisy—Daisy—offend it—who bends her smaller life to his/it's meeker/lower every day—who only asks—a task— ~~who~~ something to do for love of it—some little way she cannot guess to make that master glad— (L 248)

The "Master" letters have fueled speculation that an unfulfilled love for someone inaccessible (probably married) caused an emotional crisis that prompted Dickinson's withdrawal and ignited her creativity. That Dickinson did experience a life-altering crisis is evident from the available documents. In her second letter to Higginson, for instance, she hints: "I had a terror—since September—I could tell to none" (L 261). Guesses as to the object of her injured love have included Higginson, Wadsworth, Bowles, Lord, Susan Dickinson, and Susan's friend Catherine Anthon. She clearly had strong feelings for all of these people, but there is no solid evidence as to who the Master was or even that the Master was a real person. In *My Emily Dickinson* the poet and critic Susan Howe reads the letters as literary exercises, noting that the fallen women in Elizabeth Barrett Browning's *Aurora Leigh* and Charles Dickens' *David Copperfield* are likely sources. Rather than reflecting emotional desperation, Howe argues, the letters show Dickinson experimenting with distorted language, "forcing, abbreviating, pushing, padding, subtracting, riddling, interrogating, re-writing—," in other words practicing the techniques of her craft.

FAMILY MATTERS

Dickinson's biographers have struggled with the apparent eventlessness of her life. Yet her family's intrigues could have inspired a work of modern fiction. The texture of the Dickinsons' family life was one of secrets not revealed but recycled, masked in conflicting reports. As the Dickinsons'

story unfolded long after the poet's death, Austin's marriage proved a bitter failure, with Susan perceived as a destructive influence who caused a rift in the family—grandiosely referred to as "The War between the Houses." Yet Susan may be a scapegoat in this account. Stories of her depravity were filtered through the prism of class prejudice and largely based on an aging Austin's complaints to his young lover, Mabel Loomis Todd—who would become the first editor of Emily's poems—about how unhappily married he was.

Smith, Bennett, and other critics have called attention to Dickinson's relationship with her sister-in-law, arguing that it was her most powerful bond and had the strongest influence on her writing. As different as they appeared, Susan was Emily's intellectual match and their lives complemented each other. In *Mercy Philbrick's Choice* Jackson predicted that the time would come when the dullness of New England towns "will have crystallized into a national apathy, which will perhaps cure itself, or have to be cured, as indurations in the body are, by sharp crises or by surgical operations." Both Susan and Emily conducted their lives on the fringes of Amherst's conventions, generating crises in the dullness and performing surgery on its rigidities.

Susan Gilbert's marriage to Austin Dickinson was a step up for her socially; she was the orphaned daughter of a tavern keeper. The Dickinson family approved of the match, but years later Susan's class origins became the favored explanation of family and friends for the unhappiness prevailing in the Dickinson households. Austin told Mabel Todd that he once believed that a vigorous, lower-class woman would strengthen the Dickinson line, but that Susan had disappointed him. He reported that his wife feared sex and childbearing and had had several abortions before giving birth to their first son.

Susan managed the household in a manner antithetical to the puritanism of the Dickinsons' forebears. Preceding her as the family hostess, Emily Norcross Dickinson, like many other women of her class, worked hard until she collapsed with vague but disabling illness. Susan, by contrast, spent money, exercised her good taste, and enchanted rooms of people with her presence. Accounts of gatherings at the Evergreens describe fine meals, luscious decor, and conversation ranging over limitless topics, often with such visiting luminaries as Ralph Waldo Emerson or Harriet Beecher Stowe in attendance. Austin, who paid the bills for these events, eventually found this way of life distasteful. He complained in his diary that his house was his wife's tavern, a place of riotous hedonism. Other Amherst citizens praised her brilliance and taste, albeit with a note of distrust, as if expecting her to veer into impropriety. As the austere ways of the old elite class passed into anachronism, however, Susan's gift for staging "sprees" (as Austin called them) revitalized the Dickinson family's social prominence.

Susan and Emily met in early adulthood as Emily's childhood friends were marrying and moving away from Amherst. Emily's letters display a sense of jealousy and grief over the loss of Susan to Austin during their courtship, but during their early years in the Evergreens Emily joined the couple for laughter-filled evenings. What became of the friendship in later years is uncertain because of contradictory reports. Mabel Todd claimed that when she arrived on the scene in 1881 the most notorious story in Amherst concerned Susan's turning against Lavinia and Emily. Lavinia's complaints against Susan were extreme; she asserted that her sister-in-law's cruelty shortened Emily's life by ten years. Yet the correspondence shows that Susan visited Emily often until 1883, the year that Austin and Todd began meeting secretly at the Homestead. If sheer quantity is an indicator of the value Dickinson placed on a reader of her poetry, then Susan must have been Emily's ideal audience. She sent Susan over four hundred pieces of correspondence—most including poems—during their thirty-five-year relationship. Emily expressed high regard for Susan's literary taste; she once wrote her that she had learned more from her than she had from anyone excepting Shakespeare.

From the beginning of their friendship, Emily's letters show that her love for Susan was passionate and intense. Intimate romantic friendships between women were common in the nineteenth century; it was not until the end of the century that these relationships were understood to have a sexual dimension and were stigmatized. Sometime after Dickinson's death, someone at the Evergreens—possibly Austin—went through her letters to family members and disguised expressions of praise or love for Susan. The poem "One Sister have I in our house" (P 14), for example, was cut into two pieces and blacked out, with the last line ("Sue—forevermore!") marked up especially heavily. The poem acknowledges that Susan is different from the rest of the family: "She did not sing as we did— / It was a different tune." But the speaker commits herself to this second sister with sensual, romantic images:

> I spilt the dew—
> But took the morn—
> I chose this single star
> From out the wide night's numbers—
> Sue—forevermore!

Edward Dickinson died in 1874. The following year Emily Norcross Dickinson was stricken with paralysis. Her daughters nursed her until her death in 1882. In 1884 Emily Dickinson made a now uncustomary trip along the path to the Evergreens to see her young nephew Gilbert, who was dying of typhoid. She had not been well since an attack of flu in 1882, and after Gilbert's death she became weaker, suffering bouts of unconsciousness—early symptoms of the progressive kidney disease of which she died on May 15, 1886. She left instructions for her correspondence to be destroyed. Lavinia was carrying out her instructions when she came across the locked wooden box in which Emily kept her poems. No one had known of this box, nor had she given anyone any idea how much she wrote.

EARLY EDITIONS OF THE POETRY

The task of introducing Emily Dickinson's poetry to the public fell to Mabel Loomis Todd and Thomas Wentworth Higginson. Just thirty when Dickinson died, Todd had begun her own literary career with the publication of several short stories; later she wrote books on her travels with her husband David, an astronomer. Although Todd visited the Homestead regularly after 1881 and exchanged poems and drawings with Dickinson, she never met the poet face to face. While Mabel and Lavinia visited in the parlor—with Mabel sometimes performing on the piano—Emily eavesdropped from the next room.

Dickinson's readers are often horrified to learn that Todd and Higginson altered her poems. Yet they were not meddling with the words of a famous and revered poet; they were preparing new material by an unknown author. If Dickinson was to be read, they needed to create a niche for her in the current marketplace, and they were pressed to believe their efforts would fail. The editors at Houghton Mifflin, the first publisher Higginson approached, ridiculed him for promoting Dickinson's work. Thomas Niles at Roberts Brothers expressed reluctance to "perpetuate" the poems; he thought them "quite as remarkable for defects as for beauties [and] generally devoid of true poetical qualities." When the poet Arlo Bates reviewed Todd and Higginson's first selection of Dickinson's poems, he disagreed with Niles but thought half of the poems needed careful editing. Together Todd and Higginson edited two volumes, with the poems arranged under such headings as "Life," "Love," "Nature," and "Time and Eternity." *Poems by Emily Dickinson* (1890) and *Poems by Emily Dickinson, Second Series* (1891) met with mixed reviews but unanticipated commercial success. Todd next spent several years collecting Dickinson's letters, from which she prepared a two-volume edition, which was published in 1894; later, without Higginson's help (he was seventy-one and unwell), she edited *Poems by Emily Dickinson, Third Series* (1896).

Todd's work on Dickinson's manuscripts ended with the "War between the Houses" embroiling her in a lawsuit. At Austin's insistence, Lavinia agreed that a strip of land owned by the Dickinsons would be deeded to Todd in partial payment for her work. In 1895 Austin died; the following year Lavinia signed the deed over to Todd, but while the Todds were away on an astronomical expedition, Lavinia changed her mind and filed suit to recover the property, alleging that she did not know the paper she had signed was a deed. Despite a weak case, Lavinia won the suit and the Todds lost an appeal. Mabel Todd returned the land but accused Lavinia of fraud and renounced their friendship.

Emily Dickinson's manuscripts were divided up between Todd and Lavinia. When Lavinia died in 1899, her portion went to Susan Dickinson, and when Susan died in 1913, it went to Susan's daughter, Martha. For over twenty years Martha Dickinson Bianchi controlled the release of her aunt's poems to the public. *The Single Hound* (1914) included poems Emily had sent to Susan and her family. These were collected with the first three volumes and published as *The Complete Poems of Emily Dickinson* (1924), supposedly exhausting the manuscripts. But Susan's portion of the divided manuscripts had yet to be published. Some appeared in *Further Poems of Emily Dickinson* (1929), incorporated in *The Poems of Emily Dickinson* (1930). Still more new poems appeared in *Unpublished Poems of Emily Dickinson* (1935), followed by another collected edition, *Poems of Emily Dickinson* (1937).

In their introductions, Bianchi and her collaborator, Alfred Leete Hampson, portrayed Dickinson as a modern mystic who renounced her love for a married man and became obsessed with death and immortality. They also defended the continuing arrangement of the poems by topic, as opposed to a more scholarly chronological arrangement, insisting that the poems could not be dated with certainty. When Bianchi died in 1943, all the poems that Lavinia had kept when the manuscripts were divided up had been published. In 1945 Mabel Todd's daughter, Millicent Todd Bingham, released *Bolts of Melody*, which included the previously unpublished poems from Todd's portion of the manuscripts. In her introduction Bingham indirectly denounces the "false legends" about the poet as a result of Bianchi's cultivation of the Dickinson mystique. She devotes most of her discussion to the manuscripts. Not denying the difficulty of the task, she concluded that the poems should be arranged chronologically.

Thomas H. Johnson, the first scholar to edit Dickinson's work, undertook the dating of Dickinson's manuscripts, beginning in 1950. In the three-volume variorum edition published in 1955, Johnson listed Dickinson's alternate wordings for each poem. For the reader's edition published in 1960, he made choices among alternative wordings but tried to base them on Dickinson's preferences. He replicated Dickinson's capitalization and punctuation, though Dickinson's intention frequently was far from obvious. The marks he usually transcribed as dashes, for instance, sit short or long, high or low, angled upward or downward on the manuscript pages. His editions contain 1,775 poems.

Johnson's chronological arrangement of the poems and restoration of Dickinson's stylistic eccentricities made it possible for readers to discover an unfolding story of rebellion against literary and social authority. For some readers the new editions exploded the myth that Bianchi had promoted. According to the poet and critic Louise Bogan ("A Mystical Poet"), Johnson's work made accessible an exceptionally full picture of a poet's development:

> We ourselves can discover, in the index to the three volumes, that her favorite subject was not death, as was long supposed; for life, love and the soul are also recurring subjects. But the greatest interest lies in her progress as a writer, and as a person. We see the young poet moving away, by gradual degrees, from her early slight addiction to graveyardism, to an Emersonian belief in the largeness and harmony of nature. Step by step, she advances into the terror and anguish of her destiny; she is frightened, but she holds fast and describes her fright. . . . Nature is no longer a friend, but often an inimical presence. Nature is a haunted house. And—a truth even more terrible—the inmost self can be haunted.

For the poet Adrienne Rich, the legend of Dickinson's life had been disturbing "because it seemed to whisper that a woman who undertook such explorations must pay with renunciation, isolation, and incorporeality." Johnson's collected edition of the poems, however, revealed a mind so powerful that, for Rich at least, the myth became unimportant.

THE CRITICAL RECEPTION

During the decades when Dickinson's poems were first published, the social factors shaping reading in the United States changed greatly, but they proved continually hospitable to her canonization. In the 1890s popular magazines and women's literary clubs largely determined American reading habits, but starting in the 1920s academic influences played an increasingly important role. The methods and goals of teaching literature in schools also changed. The old system was to have students study literary language in order to acquire refined habits of speech developed through oral performance. The new approach, which became known as New Criticism, emphasized the interpretation of texts. Poetic language was conceived of as something apart from educated Standard English, and authentic poetry was seen as complex—figurative, ironic, paradoxical. Strongly influenced by the modernist poet and critic T. S. Eliot, the New Critics concentrated on texts that supported these precepts.

In the 1930s and 1940s, the field of American studies took shape as critics began to formulate a literary canon. Seeking to transform a vast, heterogeneous cultural history into an academic discipline, scholars organized the new field around key myths, one of which concerned the centrality of the Puritans in the nation's intellectual life. The simultaneous development of New Criticism and American studies subjected literary works to conflicting standards. According to the former, a work should reward formal aesthetic readings disengaged from historical contexts; according to the latter, a work should contribute to an account of the nation's cultural history.

The influential critic Allen Tate succeeded in linking these two academic approaches in his praise of Emily Dickinson. Historically, according to Tate, Dickinson wrote at a time when a balance existed between the old and the new, a cultural context that produces "a special and perhaps the most distinguished kind of poet." The work of such a poet meets the aesthetic requirement of complexity because it reflects a mind held in "lucid tension." Indebted to Puritanism for her habit of internal discipline, Dickinson nevertheless overturned the Puritan code of absolute truth: "Her poetry is a magnificent personal confession, blasphemous and, in its self-revelation, its honesty, almost obscene. It comes out of an intellectual life towards which it feels no moral responsibility. Cotton Mather would have burnt her for a witch." Dickinson's ambiguous, difficult poems suited the methods of New Criticism, and her Puritan background appealed to the codifiers of the American literary canon. Nonacademic reading prac-

tices had laid the groundwork for her canonization, and the inclusion of her work in academic texts reflected and reinforced her canonicity.

In the early 1990s William Harmon used the ninth edition of a venerable reference work (*Granger's Index to Poetry*) to produce an anthology of the five hundred most frequently published poems in the English language. Harmon's project proved that Dickinson is by far the most established woman poet in the English language, but it also reveals that the Dickinson canon—the list of her most frequently read poems—had begun to take shape before the academy's cultural influence took hold. With the exception of "After great pain, a formal feeling comes" (P 341), all fourteen of the Dickinson poems in Harmon's collection first appeared in print either during her lifetime or in the 1890s. The two linked themes of isolation and death dominate these poems, portraying a Dickinson much like the heartbroken mystic whose legend Bianchi promoted. Only four of the poems depart from these topics: "A Bird came down the Walk" (P 328), "I like to see it lap the Miles" (P 585), "A narrow Fellow in the Grass" (P 986), and "I never saw a Moor" (P 1052).

In four poems isolation is associated with an individual's distinctiveness or superiority over the majority. "I taste a liquor never brewed" (P 214) represents the poet's distinctiveness with a parodic play on spiritual inebriation. When the bee is evicted for drunkenness and the butterfly takes a temperance oath, the speaker keeps drinking until even heaven is scandalized:

> Till Seraphs swing their snowy Hats—
> And Saints—to windows run—
> To see the little Tippler
> Leaning against the—Sun—

"The Soul selects her own Society" (P 303) presents isolation as a matter of choice, absenting oneself from the "divine Majority" and holding back feeling and attention to all but one. "Much

Madness is divinest Sense" (P 435) distinguishes the exceptional individual with a paranoid note:

'Tis the Majority
In this, as All, prevail—
Assent—and you are sane—
Demur—you're straightway dangerous—
And handled with a Chain—

"Success is counted sweetest" (P 67) links isolation to death, singling out the special awareness of a dying person who hears someone else's triumph being trumpeted in the distance.

Many critics consider Dickinson's poems about death and despair to be among her greatest works, modern in their resistance to sentimental consolation. A common comfort presented in nineteenth-century verse was the anticipation of meeting loved ones in heaven. Dickinson skeptically inverts this hope in "My life closed twice before its close—" (P 1732): whether death represents a loss as terrible as those she has experienced in life remains to be seen, but the experience of parting blurs the difference between heaven and hell. In "There's a certain Slant of light" (P 258), despair is projected onto outward images to describe a sense of inward disruption: " We can find no scar, / But internal difference, / Where the Meanings, are." The landscape and its shadows, rather than any human subject, notice the arrival of this terrible feeling, and when it leaves, " 'tis like the Distance / on the look of Death—." Death is a metaphorical frame for "After great pain, a formal feeling comes—" (P 341). Here, as in other poems, Dickinson does little more than exquisitely capture an instance of anguish. "The Nerves sit ceremonious, like Tombs—," the heart vaguely questions Christian precept, the feet become mechanical. The hour of the "formal feeling" is "Remembered, if outlived, / As Freezing persons, recollect the Snow— / First—chill—then Stupor—then the letting go—." In "I felt a Funeral, in my Brain" (P 280), as in many of Dickinson's poems about death, the voice speaks from beyond the grave. Sensational and Poe-like,

the poem ends with the speaker crashing through world after world, as if the very scaffolding of existence were collapsing. The posthumous voice speaks with irreverent humor in "I heard a Fly buzz—when I died—" (P 465). While mourners wait for God to appear in the death room, a fly "With Blue—uncertain stumbling Buzz—" occupies the last of the dying person's consciousness.

"BECAUSE I COULD NOT STOP FOR DEATH—"

For all these poems, the versions that circulated in anthologies and textbooks and inspired literary critics for several decades contained editorial changes that went beyond punctuation, changes made to appeal to the reader's taste and comprehension rather than according to scholarly standards. Three poems were drastically altered. The last stanza of "I felt a Funeral, in my Brain" was omitted, leaving the poem less extreme in its irrationality, and five lines of "I heard a Fly buzz—when I died—" were altered to smooth the rhythm and rhyme scheme.

The publication history of "Because I could not stop for Death—" (P 712), Dickinson's most anthologized poem, makes a revealing case study. For the 1890 edition of the poems the editors altered the wording of the third stanza from:

We passed the School, where Children strove
At Recess—in the Ring

to:

We passed the school, where children played
Their lessons scarcely done.

The change creates a rhyme for the stanza but eliminates the paradox that leisure involves effort. For the 1924 edition Bianchi and Hampson restored "strove" but rewrote the next line as "At wrestling in a ring," carrying through the sense of effort but still avoiding the paradox. In the fifth stanza Dickinson rhymes "Ground" with itself; the editors replaced "in the Ground" with "but a mound" to eliminate the repetition. Most drastically, in the 1890 edition Todd and Higginson eliminated the fourth stanza altogether, so that the poem read:

> Because I could not stop for Death,
> He kindly stopped for me;
> The carriage held but just ourselves
> And Immortality.
>
> We slowly drove, he knew no haste,
> And I had put away
> My labor, and my leisure too,
> For his civility.
>
> We passed the school where children played,
> Their lessons scarcely done;
> We passed the fields of gazing grain,
> We passed the setting sun.
>
> We paused before a house that seemed
> A swelling of the ground;
> The roof was scarcely visible,
> The cornice but a mound.
>
> Since then 'tis centuries; but each
> Feels shorter than the day
> I first surmised the horses' heads
> Were toward eternity.

The missing stanza, finally restored in Johnson's editions, blocks the motion of the poem while adding hints of carnality.

> Or rather—He passed us—
> The Dews drew quivering and chill—
> For only Gossamer, my Gown—
> My Tippet—only Tulle—

The carriage seems to stop as the sun passes, leaving the air damp and cold. Clad in gauzy fabrics, the speaker is ready for a wedding or a sexual encounter but not for the night air. The "Dews" take on characteristics of flesh passing into death.—

For fifty years the poem appeared in anthologies in the edited versions. The history of its selection for inclusion closely parallels reading trends in the United States throughout the twentieth century; it is as if at every stage the poem's canonicity were assured—as if, in fact, it helped to set the standards of canonicity rather than being subject to them. The first *Granger's Index of Poetry*, published in 1904, lists forty of Dickinson's poems as having been included in collections. "Because I could not stop for Death—" was chosen for two songbooks, reflecting the era's use of poetry in performance. By 1940 it was included in collections with titles reflecting the efforts of both the New Critics and the scholars of American studies to define their respective fields.

By 1973 nearly five hundred of Dickinson's poems—now in Johnson's transcriptions—were included in anthologies. The collections in which "Because I could not stop for Death—" appeared from the 1950s through the early 1970s further secured the poem's place in the fields of American, modern, and world literature. Two publication trends became especially prominent during this period: an explosion of inexpensive paperback anthologies, part of a broad effort to make literature accessible to readers from all economic classes; and the proliferation of school and college textbooks. From the end of the 1960s through the 1990s, poetry textbooks surpassed paperback anthologies and dominated the list of those works that included "Because I could not stop for Death." In his 1992 survey of American studies, *Redrawing the Boundaries*, Phillip Fisher commented: "No cultural fact is more decisive in the past fifty years than the wholesale movement of every component of our literary life, past, present, and future, into the universities." Dickinson's poems followed this trend, their audience becoming increasingly defined as students with reading assignments and academics with professional obligations to fulfill.

One reason for the prominence of "Because I could not stop for Death—" in the Dickinson canon may be that the situation it reenacts epitomizes the critic's engagement with the Dickinson mystique. In the textbook *Understanding Poetry,* by Cleanth Brooks and Robert Penn Warren, whose editions spanned the era of New Criticism, students were asked to ponder Tate's comments on "Because I could not stop for Death—." Despite its appearance in 1960 after the restored text of this poem was published, the third edition of *Understanding Poetry* retained the version that omitted the fourth stanza. Tate's comments also refer to the shortened version: "If the word great means anything in poetry, this poem is one of the greatest in the English language."

Tate discusses the technical proficiency of the rhythm, the synthesis of image and idea, and the restraint that prevents the poem from becoming "ludicrous." Death "is a gentleman taking a lady out for a drive," he remarks. He highlights "the subtly interfused erotic motive" and associates the pairing of love and death with Romanticism. Having invoked the story of a "genteel driver" who embodies the terror of death, Tate ignores the implied seduction scene and praises Dickinson for showing readers a juncture of immortality and physical dissolution without telling us what to think. Brooks and Warren also cite the critic Richard Chase, who restates the allegory that death "is apparently a successful citizen who has amorous but genteel intentions. He is also God."

Reviewing the criticism written during the decades of Dickinson's canonization in *Becoming Canonical in American Poetry,* Timothy Morris claims that male academic critics inserted themselves into the role of lover–God, certain that they would succeed in understanding Dickinson as Higginson did not. Morris argues that these critics heard Dickinson's voice "not as the distinctive idiom of a particular Victorian woman, but as the secret, unrepressed voice of Everywoman—a voice that was largely the creation of their own fantasies."

A disturbing fact surrounding Dickinson's canonization is that the works of other women writers disappeared from anthologies at the same time that her poems appeared; by midcentury she had become the token woman writer of nineteenth-century American literature. The 1950 *Oxford Book of American Verse,* edited by the influential scholar F. O. Matthiessen, is an important touchstone in this process. His selection of poets includes, together with forty-three men, the colonial poet Anne Bradstreet, Dickinson, and six modernist women poets. Black and working-class authors also disappeared from textbooks and reading lists during this period. White male academics homogenized the canon as they defined their role as defenders of cultural masterpieces rather than shapers and disseminators of literary culture (the role that Higginson, for example, had assumed). There were specific reasons for the elimination of women writers. Nineteenth-century women's literary culture was seen as promoting feminine values that could undermine the masculine toughness needed to fortify the culture of a modern world power.

Morris speculates that Dickinson posed no threat because she did not publish during her lifetime and was dead before her works entered the critical discourse. As early as 1896 critic Harry Lyman Koopman had celebrated Dickinson as a voice of feminine truth free of the "decorous support networks" of women's print culture. Dickinson seemed the exception to those nineteenth-century commonplaces that repelled these critics, from women's sexual unavailability to their prominence on the literary scene. Morris speculates that through her secret poems Dickinson seemed "to reach out to the virile male," who arrived in his carriage to rescue her from "immurement in the culture of ladylike gentility."

FEMINIST LITERARY CRITICISM

Welcome as Johnson's editions were among Dickinson's readers in the 1950s and 1960s, his transcriptions and arrangements of the poems stirred controversy. Critics debated the significance of Dickinson's odd capitalization and punctuation, some claiming that she capitalized important words to indicate that she intended them as archetypes and that the dashes were actually a system of elocution marks showing how the poems should be recited aloud. R. W. Franklin, however, pointed out in *The Editing of Emily Dickinson* that Dickinson's handwritten texts were typical of the casual writing of her time, and that the same irregularities appeared in her household notes. Some scholars have claimed that Johnson overused the dash and that Dickinson herself would have used other punctuation if she had prepared the manuscripts for publication—something we will never know.

Working closely with Dickinson's writing, Franklin discovered an apparent contradiction in the tenets of New Criticism. Paradoxically, what the author intended to say was treated as irrelevant to the poem's meaning, whereas the author's text was considered sacred; the textual scholar's goal was to reproduce the poem exactly as the poet meant it to appear. Franklin observed that a scholar editing Dickinson's work faces an unresolvable problem since she provided no authoritative version of hundreds of her poems.

In the last quarter of the twentieth century, two developments revolutionized the reading of Dickinson's work: the advent of feminist literary criticism in the 1970s and the publication in 1981 of Franklin's facsimile edition of *The Manuscript Books of Emily Dickinson*. Both represented powerful challenges to earlier approaches to Dickinson's poems. Feminist critics challenged the New Critical view that poems could be evaluated and understood apart from their social settings, while the publication of the fascicles called into question whether individual poems could be treated as separate entities.

In the 1970s Dickinson's poems began to appear in anthologies of women's poetry intended to revive the reputations of forgotten women authors and to present canonical works in a new light, calling attention to how the writers resisted sexist oppression. "Because I could not stop for Death—" was included in the first of these feminist anthologies, *Women Poets in English* (1972) edited by Ann Stanford, as well as in several subsequent collections. Read in this new context, the focus shifts toward the speaker's experience and away from the formal and metaphysical tensions that Tate stressed in his reading. Another study exercise for this poem in Brooks and Warren's *Understanding Poetry* asks students to consider this leading question: Has the lady died, or is the poem about awareness? The expected answer, of course, is the latter: students are meant to subordinate the speaker's experience to an abstract interpretation concerning a state of mind. If one rejects the "right" answer and asks what the encounter means in material terms, the poem becomes a protest against the limited options in women's lives. The carriage ride may represent marriage or rape, but both signify moral and spiritual death.

Read in a more theoretical light, the poem protests women's roles in a centuries-long poetic tradition. In 1845 Edgar Allan Poe declared, "The death of a beautiful woman is, undoubtedly, the most poetical of topics," thereby underscoring an assumption that stretches from classical poetics to the modern lyric. In the Renaissance sonnet cycle, for example, a male courtier might worship an idealized dead woman or pursue a living but unattainable feminine ideal. In the Romantic lyric female figures are often interchangeable with inanimate nature. In this tradition male figures seek, create, and articulate knowledge, transcending physicality through a tragic understanding of the limits of human rationality. Female figures, silent and passive, serve as the medium through which male transformation takes place.

Because Dickinson was one of very few women writers whose works had not been forgotten when feminists began to write literary criticism in the early 1970s, revisionary readings of her poetry contributed to the formation of methods and articulation of tenets of feminist criticism. Her texts were often read as being distinctly feminine—sometimes even feminist—and many critics treated her as the very type of the woman poet struggling against patriarchal oppression. The most influential feminist essay on Dickinson, "Vesuvius at Home" by Adrienne Rich, brought to the fore a poem (P 754) that until then, had been little discussed:

My Life had stood—a Loaded Gun—
In Corners—till a Day
The Owner passed—identified—
And carried Me away—

And now We roam in Sovereign Woods—
And now We hunt the Doe—
And every time I speak for Him—
The Mountains straight reply—

And do I smile, such cordial light
Upon the Valley glow—
It is as a Vesuvian face
Had let its pleasure through—

And when at Night—Our good Day done—
I guard My Master's Head—
'Tis better than the Eider-Duck's
Deep Pillow—to have shared—

To foe of His—I'm deadly foe—
None stir the second time—
On whom I lay a Yellow Eye—
Or an emphatic Thumb—

Though I than He—may longer live
He longer must—than I—
For I have but the power to kill,
Without—the power to die—

To Rich, writing in the 1970s, this poem seemed central to understanding not only Dickinson but also women of her own time and the condition of the female artist. "I think it is a poem about possession by the daemon," that is the

"Genius of Poetry," Rich wrote. The poet is split between "an active, willing being" and "an object, condemned to remain inactive until the hunter—the *owner*—takes possession of it." Rich suggests that the "female consciousness" in this poem "exists in the ambivalence toward power, which is extreme." In defying the role of passive object, the poet risks being defined as "unwomanly" and "potentially lethal."

In their groundbreaking 1979 study of nineteenth-century women writers, *The Madwoman in the Attic,* Sandra Gilbert and Susan Gubar amplified Rich's view: they assert that Dickinson enacted anger at female subordination not only in her poetry but also in her reclusive life, through which she recovered a powerful, creative, autonomous self. As scholars read the works of forgotten nineteenth-century women writers, however, it became clear that Dickinson could not be treated as an exemplary case of resistance to sexist oppression. In *Dickinson and the Strategies of Reticence,* Joanne Dobson shows that nineteenth-century women writers had a multitude of strategies available to them in opposing conventional gender roles and that many took great risks in their lives and in their writing. In contrast, Dickinson's life appears almost fanatically conventional. In *Emily Dickinson: Woman Poet* Paula Bennett takes a different view of Dickinson's apparent conformity to gender norms, seeing it as a parodic shield for her strong challenge to "phallocentrism," the cultural centrality of male desire. Emphasizing the homoeroticism in Dickinson's poetry, Bennett rejects the supposition that her roles as a woman and a poet were in conflict.

Reading Dickinson's works in the context of class history also undermines the exemplary position early feminist critics accorded her. The pursuit of an autonomous self is common to Romantic poetry and is most accessible to writers like Dickinson, who had no need to earn money. Betsy Erkkila in "Emily Dickinson and Class" has argued that Dickinson's very resistance to patriarchy was grounded in class privilege. Her methods reinforced her elite status. In stitching together her manuscripts, she engaged in "a precapitalist mode of manuscript production" similar to those modes practiced in royal courts during earlier eras. "Publishing" her poems in letters to friends was also an aristocratic form of circulation. For Erkkila, Dickinson's resistance to the values of the marketplace had an ironic effect: "She, like other Romantic poets, ended by enforcing the separation of art and society and the corresponding feminization, trivialization, and marginalization of art."

THE CONTEXT OF THE FAST CIRCLES

In contrast to Erkkila, Martha Nell Smith views Dickinson's resistance to the marketplace positively, stating that her self-made "books"—her fascicles and correspondence—present a "radical alternative" to commercial publishing. Smith advocates reading Dickinson's poems in their contexts in the letters and fascicles. Franklin did not see any deliberate order to the poems within a fascicle, but Smith and other scholars have shown that reading a familiar poem within its fascicle can undermine long-held assumptions about its meaning. For example, Sharon Cameron, in her 1992 study of Dickinson's fascicles, *Choosing Not Choosing,* discovered that other poems in the fascicle that contains "Because I could not stop for Death—" raise questions about who has died; it may not be the speaker—as nearly every critic has assumed—but her lover.

Susan Howe, an early advocate of reading the poetry within the context of the manuscripts, provides a start in contextualizing "My Life had stood—a Loaded Gun—" in *My Emily Dickinson* (1985). Like Rich, she reads it as a poem about gender and power, but her reading sets the poem within the context of history and literary texts. She interlaces Renaissance and colonial history and narratives of the frontier and the Civil War with citations from Dickinson's favorite authors: Shakespeare, Emily Brontë, Robert Browning, and Elizabeth Barrett Browning. She also links the poem to Dickinson's "Master" letters and other correspondence, as well as to poems within and beyond the fascicle that holds it.

To read "My Life had stood—a loaded Gun—" within its fascicle (numbered 34 by Franklin) places it in contiguity with poems from which it had been separated throughout its publication history. The eighteen poems comprising the fascicle first appeared dispersed among seven books that were published between 1890 and 1945. Johnson, too, separated them; their numbers in his editions range from 478 to 993. Franklin found that three sheets of the fascicle had long been kept with a group of poems with which they did not belong. "My Life had stood—a loaded Gun—" falls in the middle of the restored fascicle.

Martha Nell Smith argues that what binds the poems in a fascicle together is not formal unity, thematic progression, or an underlying story. She proposes that by responding to the movement of images and themes throughout the fascicle, the reader becomes aware of an overall texture of resonance and meaning. Read as Smith suggests, fascicle 34 is remarkably coherent. Scenes and tones shift, but the whole works as a poem cycle exploring connections between death and aesthetic value. Sharon Cameron points out that the first and last poems of this fascicle both concern death, but the subject in the first one ("Bereavement in their death to feel" [P 645]) finds no compensation, while that of the last one ("Essential Oils—are wrung" [P 675]) does. Furthermore, the first poem describes the situation of a reader (Howe associates this poem with Dickinson's reading of Emily Brontë), while the last poem explores the craft of the poet. For William Shurr this fascicle is one of several whose subjects include Dickinson's status as a poet and the presence-through-absence of a beloved. These are central themes in the tradition of the love lyric, particularly the sonnet cycle: the poet exercises his skill by laboring to transcend his frustrated desire for a dead or unattainable lady. Fascicle 34 blurs the gendered roles of the male-authored lyric tradition: it abounds in dead women, but the gender of the speaker—whether the voice of Dickinson herself or of a female or male persona—is never made clear.

The poems following "Bereavement in their death to feel" begin to explore various ways of transcending the problem that the "vital kinsmanship" one feels with "immortal friends" concerns mortality. The speaker posits opposite modes of imagining, one vast and the other small ("I think to live—May be a Bliss" [P 646] and "A little Road—not made of Man—" [P 647]) and dismisses both as inaccessible means of transcendence. The next poem ("Her Sweet turn to leave the Homestead" [P 649]) imagines a journey that, like "Because I could not stop for Death—," conflates a wedding and a funeral. This poem becomes a romance about a princess whose suitors must pursue quests through impossible landscapes if they wish to win her:

Of Her Father—Whoso ask Her—
He shall seek as high
As the Palm—that serve the Desert—
To obtain the Sky—

Distance—be Her only Motion—
If 'tis Nay—or Yes—
Acquiescence—or Demurral—
Whosoever guess—

He—must pass the Crystal Angle
That obscure Her face—
He—must have achieved in person
Equal Paradise—

The lady may be dead, accessible only to those who die, or the "Crystal Angle" may represent an upper window obscuring her face. By giving the lady's home the same name as her own Dickinson suggests self-referentiality implying the inaccessibility of her own hermetic verse.

"Pain—has an Element of Blank—" (P 650) describes the ground zero of trauma: there is no transcendence other than insight into the nature of pain. "So much Summer" (P 651) fits into both the fairy-tale and love-lyric traditions if it is read as an interaction between a suitor and an inaccessible lady. A feeling of illegitimacy is associated with the vast mode, while the small mode represents sufficiency. "Promise This—When You be Dying—" (P 648) casts the theme of unattainable love as a first-person plea without specifying the gender of either the speaker or the beloved. The speaker pleads to possess the beloved's body after his or her death. The following stanza takes up the common theme of sonneteers, namely, that poetry will immortalize the beloved by creating her likeness:

Poured like this—My Whole Libation—
Just that You should see
Bliss of Death—Life's Bliss extol thro'
Imitating You—

The lover imagines not that the beloved's soul will go to heaven, as in popular mourning verse, but that the lover will have the power to manipulate natural events surrounding the beloved's corpse—a selfish, possessive wish:

Mine—to guard Your Narrow Precinct—
To seduce the Sun
Longest on Your South, to linger,
Largest Dews of Morn

To demand, in Your low favor
Lest the Jealous Grass
Greener lean—Or fonder cluster
Round some other face—

In the next poem the speaker claims, "I had no time to Hate—" (P 478), adding,

Nor had I time to Love—
But since
Some Industry must be—
The little Toil of Love—
I thought—
Be large enough for Me—

This might be the frustrated lover of the previous poem explaining his or her morbid labors, but its humility reflects ironically on the inflation of those toils.

In "My Life had stood—a Loaded Gun—" (P 754), which follows, the dialectical tension of hate and love unabated in the previous poem is sustained as ammunition. Utilizing the metaphor of a gun and a hunter, Dickinson seems to solve problems that remained unresolved in the first half of the fascicle. The Owner who appears in the poem provides transport into the previously inaccessible scenery of the sublime, where the speaker's agency surpasses that imagined by the lover pleading to tend the beloved's corpse. Gone are the smallness, illegitimacy, and contortion associated with self-expression in "So much Summer"; the speaker's smile itself is sublime, drawing a vast response from the landscape. The "Toil of love" is hunting the doe and killing the foe, causing death rather than tending to the dead. The sexual consummation missed by failed suitors is dismissed as inferior to protecting the Owner. The speaker delights in the mastery achieved through evasions of the gendered polarity of male subject and female object. The hunted doe or foe would represent the elusive ladylove in an Elizabethan sonnet, but here the speaker joins the "master" on the hunt, as if he were the courtly poet and the speaker, if human, a devoted page, crossgendered like a disguised Shakespearean heroine, if female. Speaking as a metaphorical weapon that acts only through the master's agency, Dickinson speaks as the voice of craft itself.

The last stanza presents another twist on the theme of art's immortality and human mortality:

Though I than He—may longer live
He longer must—than I—
For I have but the power to kill,
Without—the power to die—

No poet boasts of his ability to immortalize the beloved. The instrument must preserve its user if it is to be of use, but nature and the feminine are merely the means for this dyad's (gun and hunter) interdependent, destructive action.

Viewed within the context of the fascicle, "My Life had stood—a Loaded Gun—" looks transitional—perhaps a pivotal but not a final statement. Dickinson goes on to reinvent the vast and the small, exploring both from the point of view of experience rather than inaccessibility. Feminine nature returns as an agent of reconciliation rather than a scene of destruction, joining an unspecified pair through domestic "Toils of love" administered on a cosmic scale ("The Sunrise runs for Both—" [P 710]). The small world is not complete in itself and suffers from the loss of the sublime, a loss compensated for by brave singing ("No Bobolink—reverse His Singing" [P 755]). "One Blessing had I than the rest" (P 756) describes an experience of the sublime. The "good Day" in "My Life had stood—a Loaded Gun—" resonates in this experience, which is so fulfilling that it resembles its opposite, despair or pain. It stupefies the speaker, who claims it stifled her questioning:

Why Bliss so scantily disburse—
Why Paradise defer—
Why Floods be served to Us—in Bowls—
I speculate no more—

But the questioning immediately resumes ("Victory comes late—" [P 690]). As in "No Bobolink—reverse His Singing," it is small creatures who suffer in the meeting of large and small: "Cherries—suit Robins— / The Eagle's Golden Breakfast strangles—Them—." The last two lines link this poem to the theme of unfulfilled love and give a plaintive edge to the dutiful voice in "I had no time to Hate—": "God keep His Oath to Sparrows— / Who of little Love—know how to starve—." The fascicle turns again to the vast in a poem that transforms the master–gun scene into a harmonious landscape ("The Mountains—grow unnoticed—" [P 757]), where the mountains, needing no audience, reflect the sun's colors back to him when he seeks "fellowship—at night—."

Dickinson next returns to the problem of death and compensation, first separating the death of a woman from the masculine lyric tradition and then experimenting with compensations related to the sublime. "These—saw Visions—" (P 758) cryptically imitates popular funeral verse, closing with a reference to paradise, as if Dickinson discarded the imaginary elements of the earlier poems of death to fashion a simple memorial. The poem avoids idealizing the dead girl, highlighting her agency in life (she saw visions, spoke, and ran) and a very material "Toil of Love," the traditionally female task of preparing a corpse for burial. The speaker in "Strong Draughts of Their Refreshing Minds" (P 711) is again a reader (like the speaker in the fascicle's first poem) who comments on the power of texts, figured as a liquor distilled from "an Hermetic Mind—," to sustain one through vast landscapes, the settings of sublime agency. "We miss Her, not because We see—" (P 993) links the loss of a woman to the theme of union through the sublime by scrambling a common sentiment of the funeral-verse tradition: Our missing her is mitigated by the knowledge that she watches us from her place among heavenly beings:

We miss Her, not because We see—
The Absence of an Eye—
Except its Mind accompany
Abridge Society

As slightly as the Routes of Stars—
Ourselves—asleep below—
We know that their superior Eyes
Include Us—as they go—

"Essential Oils—are wrung—" (P 675) returns to the theme of art's immortality, much altered since it first appears in "Promise this—when you be dying" and "My Life had stood—a Loaded Gun—." The "Sealed Wine" extracted from the "Hermetic Mind" reappears here as the perfume extracted from a rose. The sublime alone is insufficient:

The Attar from the Rose
Be not expressed by Suns—alone—
It is the gift of Screws—

A tool is needed to extract essence. As instruments, the screws are kindred to the gun, but their destructive work is feminized. They create a sachet reproducing the vast ("Summer") in an enclosed feminine space ("Lady's Drawer"). Dickinson separates the rose, a standard lyric symbol for the beloved, from the lady whose body lies in rosemary, an herb symbolizing remembrance. The closing lines suggest collaboration between the two scents (rose and rosemary) in keeping the dead woman's memory alive.

Beyond reading the poems within their fascicles, Martha Nell Smith recommends that the correspondence also be read within context for the poems. To pursue the threads of fascicle 34, following Smith's guidelines, one should note that Dickinson sent "Victory—comes late" to Bowles and "We miss Her, not because we see" and "Essential Oils—are wrung—" to Susan Dickinson. Susan's version of "Essential Oils—are wrung—" separates the craft of poetry from the lyric object, the beautiful dead woman. It ends with the lady lying in "spiceless Sepulchre," implicitly decaying. No essence assists in keeping her memory alive; the art of extracting essence condenses the dialectic of the vast and the small, but it does not memorialize. The compensation for death in this conclusion comes not from artfully preserving the memory of the dead but from the inner workings of a made object, its reproduction of the sublime in an enclosed, private space.

"READING" DICKINSON

A new variorum edition of Dickinson's poetry, with typographical reproductions of the manuscripts edited by R. W. Franklin, was scheduled to appear in 1998. Yet in some scholarly circles this long-awaited project was already considered obsolete. Jerome McGann has asserted that typography fundamentally misrepresents Dickinson's work. He points out that Dickinson treated her "textual medium." as an end in itself, "as part of the aesthetic field of writing."

> In an age of print publication, manuscripts of writers tend to stand in medias res, for they anticipate a final translation into that "better world" conceived as the printed word. In Dickinson's case, however, the genres that determine the aspirations of her work are scriptural rather than bibliographical: commonplace book writing, on one hand, and letter writing on the other.

McGann argues that in order to edit Dickinson's work adequately "one needs to integrate the mechanisms of critical editing into a facsimile edition." Such a project is under way. Headed by Martha Nell Smith, the Emily Dickinson Editorial Collective is preparing a CD-ROM edition that not only reproduces the visual qualities of Dickinson's pages but also allows the reader to explore the many linkages between Dickinson's poems and letters.

If, indeed, Dickinson's individual works should each be treated as contextually interconnected, then hypertext would seem her perfect medium. One is tempted to theorize that if she had owned a computer, she would not have needed to stitch fascicles; interlinked electronic files would have been far superior for her purposes. But will the hypertext edition give readers a more authentic experience of Dickinson? Her "intentions" for the posthumous publication of her work—if she had any such intentions—remain as obscure today as ever. Hypertext will not provide access to the

lady beyond the Homestead's "Crystal Angle." The movement way from typeset books into hypertexted facsimiles does, however, once again indicate her poetry's resistance to any single standardized form of presentation and its adaptability to new ways of reading.

What is suggested about the reader if the "right" way to read Dickinson's work is in an intricate contextual web? Each experience of reading her, whether as a specialist or an amateur, becomes an editorial performance. When the facsimile edition was published, Susan Howe noted: "The Franklin edition is huge, Dickinson's handwriting is often difficult to decipher, and the book is extremely expensive. Few readers will have a chance to use it for reference, which is a pity, because it is necessary for a clearer understanding of her writing process." If this was the right way to read the poems, it was inaccessible to most readers, and a CD-ROM will be even less accessible than a printed edition of her collected works in a paperback selection.

For readers without access to Dickinson's "context," Rich's reading of "My Life had stood—a Loaded Gun—" remains exemplary. She does not claim to have arrived at the ultimate meaning; instead, through the poem she gains insight into her own situation. Rich writes: "More than any other poet, Emily Dickinson seemed to tell me that the intense inner event, the personal and psychological, was inseparable from the universal; that there was a range for psychological poetry beyond mere self-expression." For Rich, writing in the 1970s, this unprecedented validation had a political dimension: she was creating art within a movement whose theme was that power relations pervade the personal sphere, where middle-class women spent most of their lives. In 1891 Mabel Todd saw a different manifestation of the "intense inner event" in readers' sensitivity to Dickinson's poetry. Despite the shallowness of their era, Todd noted, they responded to fundamental themes.

Perhaps one key to the fascination of Dickinson's writing is that it may not represent a structure of intended connections at all but rather something informal that has been preserved. Suppose that the formal and conceptual experimentation in her verse represents not an open rebellion against public cultural forms but a private casualness, a determined amateurism—or suppose that private casualness *is* the rebellion. The little poems would then be crafted correlates to our everyday thoughts, few of which we speak or act upon. The passion with which Dickinson's readers have carried her poems away for over a century like lovers rescuing them from the narrow privacy of the Homestead, may be a disguised desire to have our own haunted, hermetic inner lives transported and their significance validated— even (improbably) canonized. To consider this possibility is to enter into a cyberspace where the vast and the small morph into one another, and virtual love and virtual death travel together toward virtual immortality.

Selected Bibliography

WORKS OF EMILY DICKINSON

POETRY

Poems by Emily Dickinson. Edited by Mabel Loomis Todd and T. W. Higginson. Boston: Roberts Brothers, 1890. Reprinted, Boston: Little, Brown, 1922.

Poems by Emily Dickinson, Second Series. Edited by Mabel Loomis Todd and T. W. Higginson. Boston: Roberts Brothers, 1891.

Poems by Emily Dickinson, Third Series. Edited by Mabel Loomis Todd. Boston: Roberts Brothers, 1896.

The Single Hound: Poems of a Lifetime. Edited by Martha Dickinson Bianchi. Boston: Little, Brown, 1914.

The Complete Poems of Emily Dickinson. Edited by Martha Dickinson Bianchi and Alfred Leete Hampson. Boston: Little, Brown, 1924.

Further Poems of Emily Dickinson. Edited by Martha Dickinson Bianchi and Alfred Leete Hampson. Boston: Little, Brown, 1929.

The Poems of Emily Dickinson. Edited by Martha Dickinson Bianchi and Alfred Leete Hampson. Boston: Little, Brown, 1930.

Unpublished Poems of Emily Dickinson. Edited by Martha Dickinson Bianchi and Alfred Leete Hampson. Boston: Little, Brown, 1935.

The Poems of Emily Dickinson. Edited by Martha Dickinson Bianchi and Alfred Leete Hampson. Boston: Little, Brown, 1937.

Bolts of Melody: New Poems of Emily Dickinson. Edited by Mabel Loomis Todd and Millicent Todd Bingham. New York: Harper, 1945.

The Poems of Emily Dickinson. Edited by Thomas H. Johnson. 3 vols. Cambridge, Mass.: Belknap Press of Harvard University Press, 1955.

The Complete Poems of Emily Dickinson. Edited by Thomas H. Johnson. Boston: Little, Brown, 1960.

The Manuscript Books of Emily Dickinson. Edited by R. W. Franklin. 2 vols. Cambridge: Belknap Press of Harvard University Press, 1981.

CORRESPONDENCE

The Letters of Emily Dickinson. Edited by Mabel Loomis Todd. 2 vols. Boston: Roberts Brothers, 1894.

The Life and Letters of Emily Dickinson. Edited by Martha Dickinson Bianchi. Boston: Houghton Mifflin, 1924.

Letters of Emily Dickinson. Edited by Mabel Loomis Todd. New York: Harper, 1931.

Emily Dickinson Face to Face: Unpublished Letters, with Notes and Reminiscences. Edited by Martha Dickinson Bianchi. Boston: Houghton Mifflin, 1932.

Emily Dickinson's Letters to Dr. and Mrs. Josiah Gilbert Holland. Edited by Theodora Van Wagenen Ward. Cambridge, Mass.: Harvard University Press, 1951.

The Letters of Emily Dickinson. Edited by Thomas H. Johnson and Theodora Ward. 3 vols. Cambridge, Mass: Harvard University Press, 1958.

The Years and Hours of Emily Dickinson. Edited by Jay Leyda. 2 vols. New Haven, Conn.: Yale University Press, 1960.

Emily Dickinson: Selected Letters. Edited by Thomas H. Johnson. Cambridge, Mass.: Belknap Press of Harvard University Press, 1986.

MANUSCRIPT PAPERS

The Dickinson Papers manuscript collection is housed in the Houghton Library of Harvard University, Cambridge, Mass.

CRITICAL AND BIOGRAPHICAL STUDIES

Bennett, Paula. *Emily Dickinson: Woman Poet*. New York: Harvester Wheatsheaf, 1990.
———. *My Life, a Loaded Gun: Dickinson, Plath, Rich, and Female Creativity*. Urbana: University of Illinois Press, 1990.
Bingham, Millicent Todd. *Emily Dickinson: A Revelation*. New York: Harper, 1954.
Bogan, Louise. "A Mystical Poet." In *Emily Dickinson: Three Views* by Archibald MacLeish, Louise Bogan, and Richard Wilbur. Amherst, Mass.: Amherst College Press, 1960. Pp. 27–34.
Cameron, Sharon. *Lyric Time: Dickinson and the Limits of Genre*. Baltimore, Md.: Johns Hopkins University Press, 1979.
———. *Choosing Not Choosing: Dickinson's Fascicles*. Chicago: University of Chicago Press, 1992.
Capps, Jack L. *Emily Dickinson's Reading, 1836–1886*. Cambridge, Mass.: Harvard University Press, 1966.
Chase, Richard. *Emily Dickinson*. New York: William Sloane Associates, 1951.
Dandurand, Karen. "New Dickinson Civil War Publications." *American Literature* 56: 17–27 (March 1984).
———. *Dickinson Scholarship: An Annotated Bibliography, 1969–1985*. New York: Garland, 1988.
Diehl, Joanne Feit. *Dickinson and the Romantic Imagination*. Princeton, N.J.: Princeton University Press, 1981.
Dobson, Joanne. *Dickinson and the Strategies of Reticence: The Woman Writer in Nineteenth-Century America*. Bloomington: Indiana University Press, 1989.
Emily Dickinson Journal, vols. 1–5. Niwot: University of Colorado Press, 1992–1997.

Erkkila, Betsy. "Emily Dickinson and Class." In *The American Literary History Reader*. Edited by Gordon Hutner. New York: Oxford University Press, 1995. Pp. 291–317.
Farr, Judith. *The Passion of Emily Dickinson*. Cambridge, Mass.: Harvard University Press, 1992.
Fisher, Phillip. "American Literature and Cultural Studies since the Civil War." In *Redrawing the Boundaries*. Edited by Stephen Greenblatt and Giles Gunn, eds. New York: Modern Language Association, 1992. Pp. 232–250.
Franklin, R. W. *The Editing of Emily Dickinson: A Reconsideration*. Madison: University of Wisconsin Press, 1967.
Gilbert, Sandra M., and Susan Gubar. *The Madwoman in the Attic: The Woman Writer and the Nineteenth-Century Literary Imagination*. New Haven, Conn.: Yale University Press, 1979.
Holland, Jeanne. "Scraps, Stamps, and Cutouts: Emily Dickinson's Domestic Technologies of Publication." In *Cultural Artifacts and the Production of Meaning: The Page, the Image, and the Body*, edited by Margaret J. M. Ezell and Katherine O'Brien O'Keeffe. Princeton, N.J.: Princeton University Press, 1993. Pp. 139–181.
Homans, Margaret. *Women Writers and Poetic Identity: Dorothy Wordsworth, Emily Brontë, and Emily Dickinson*. Princeton, N.J.: Princeton University Press, 1980.
Howe, Susan. *My Emily Dickinson*. Berkeley, Calif.: North Atlantic Books, 1985.
———. "These Flames and Generosities of the Heart: Emily Dickinson and the Illogic of Sumptuary Values." *Sulfur* 28: 134–155 (Spring 1991).
Loeffelholz, Mary. *Dickinson and the Boundaries of Feminist Theory*. Urbana: University of Illinois Press, 1991.
McGann, Jerome. "The Rationale of Hypertext." Institute for Advanced Technology in the Humanities, University of Virginia. http://jefferson.village.virginia.edu/public/jjmzf/rationale.htm/
Morris, Timothy. "Dickinson: Reading the 'Supposed Person.'" In his *Becoming Canonical in American Poetry*. Urbana: University of Illinois Press, 1995. Pp. 54–80.
Oberhaus, Dorothy Huff. *Emily Dickinson's Fascicles: Method and Meaning*. University Park: Pennsylvania State University Press, 1995.

Reynolds, David S. "The American Women's Renaissance and Emily Dickinson." In his *Beneath the American Renaissance: The Subversive Imagination in the Age of Emerson and Melville*. Cambridge, Mass.: Harvard University Press, 1988. Pp. 387–437.

Rich, Adrienne. "Vesuvius at Home: The Power of Emily Dickinson." In her *On Lies, Secrets, and Silence: Selected Prose, 1966–1978*. New York: Norton, 1979. Pp. 157–183.

Sewall, Richard B. *The Life of Emily Dickinson*. 2 vols. New York: Farrar, Straus and Giroux, 1974.

Sewall, Richard B., ed. *Emily Dickinson: A Collection of Critical Essays*. Englewood Cliffs, N.J.: Prentice-Hall, 1963.

Shurr, William H. *The Marriage of Emily Dickinson: A Study of the Fascicles*. Lexington: University of Kentucky Press, 1983.

Smith, Martha Nell. *Rowing on Eden: Rereading Emily Dickinson*. Austin: University of Texas Press, 1992.

Smith, Robert McClure. *The Seductions of Emily Dickinson*. Tuscaloosa: University of Alabama Press, 1996.

Tate, Allen. *On the Limits of Poetry*. New York: Swallow Press, 1948.

Wilson, R. Jackson. *Figures of Speech: American Writers and the Literary Marketplace, from Benjamin Franklin to Emily Dickinson*. New York: Knopf, 1989.

Wolff, Cynthia Griffin. *Emily Dickinson*. New York: Knopf, 1986. Reprinted, Reading, Mass.: Addison-Wesley, 1988.

—*JANET GRAY*

John Dos Passos

1896-1970

OVER a period of forty years, in some thirty published volumes, John Dos Passos carried on a romantic, constantly disappointed love affair with the United States. His books, crowded with personal experiences and historic events, are at once celebrations, indictments, and pleas for reform. Yet though his passionate complaints seem always to be set in political terms, his own political attitudes swung in a large arc from left to right. Obviously something profounder than politics was at work.

Dos Passos was not the first to try to encompass in fiction the whole history of his time. In France Alfred de Musset, writing after the glory and defeat of Napoleon, discovered postwar generations—especially "lost" ones—as literary material. Balzac, conceiving a social generation as "a drama with five or six thousand leading characters," thought that the novelist, "by making a selection from the chief social events of the time and composing types made up of traits taken from several homogeneous characters," could go deeper into social reality than historians had. Emile Zola took the next step by treating social institutions —the church, the army, department stores, farms, and mines—as superhuman beings with lives of their own.

If what Balzac said is true, that a novelist is simply a secretary who writes down what society dictates to him, then much still depends on the secretary's training and temperament. For the ambitious task Dos Passos set himself, his background seems ideal.

His paternal grandfather was a Portuguese immigrant from Madeira who married a Quaker of early Colonial stock. Their son, John Randolph Dos Passos, fought in the Civil War when he was not much younger than his son would be in 1917. He was fifty-two in 1896 when this son was born; thus, by the time John Dos Passos produced *Midcentury*, his own and his parents' experience had spread over more than 110 years of American history.

Time was not the only spectacular span. The father rose from poverty to the highest levels of law, big business, and finance. After he had educated himself in Philadelphia, he became a criminal lawyer in New York, defending notorious murderers, including the one who killed Jim Fisk. Then he moved on to corporation law, and for organizing the American Sugar Refining Company received the largest fee ever paid a lawyer up to that time. He knew several Presidents while he was lobbying in Washington, and in the year of his son's birth was campaigning for his friend William McKinley.

John Randolph Dos Passos was even an author. Most of his books were legal or business texts, but one—*The Anglo-Saxon Century*

—was an appeal to the American people, with perspectives as bold as those beginning his son's *U.S.A.* The Boer War and the Spanish-American War, he said, marked the end of an era. By intervening in Cuba and the Philippines our country had become committed on a world scale. We would be the dominant power of the next hundred years if we worked closely with the British. From England we had received our language, our religion, the blood of our founding fathers, and—even more precious—our common-law tradition, respect for life, liberty, and property, and a government with sharply restricted powers. It was to preach exactly these principles that his son was to write *Midcentury* sixty years later.

This was clearly no coincidence. But the younger Dos Passos was not just an admiring disciple of his father. Theirs was a complex relationship, as any reader can see from the novels. The fathers are usually remote, often repellent figures, their strengths and weaknesses mingled in such a way as to make life very troubled for the sons. Toward the end of his own life, in the autobiography, *The Best Times (1966),* Dos Passos gave a rather different impression. There the father, so affectionate toward his son and so adventurously interested in everything—food, fox hunts, yachts, the English gentry, financial speculation, politics, Greek, singing, legal reform—is a fascinating, appealing figure.

To Dos Passos the problem of identity was more than a popular literary theme. Because his own family circumstances were like those described in *Chosen Country*, he and his mother lived apart from his father, often in Europe, and he himself was not publicly acknowledged as a son until 1916. His mother was forty-eight when he was born, and after this Caesarean birth she was frail and dependent like the typical mother in his novels. His years with her on the Continent gave him vivid memories

of places—his books are rich with them—but he always felt homeless, different from other boys, especially when he went to school in England. His return to America, repeating in a sense his grandfather's immigration, is reflected in the beginning of *Manhattan Transfer*, where Jimmy Herf is first seen as a boy debarking with his mother from an ocean liner in New York on the Fourth of July.

After Choate School, Dos Passos entered Harvard in 1912, a year of great cultural stir in America. *Poetry* was only one of the periodicals springing up to welcome new artistic impulses from Europe and to rediscover native folk strains at home. The Imagist movement, started in England by T. E. Hulme and Ezra Pound, was rapidly being Americanized by Amy Lowell, sister of the president of Harvard. Pound began referring to it as "Amygism." For the Harvard *Advocate* Dos Passos reviewed Edgar Lee Masters, T. S. Eliot, and Pound. Some of his own college verse was later collected in *Eight Harvard Poets* (1917) along with the poetry of Robert Hillyer and E. E. Cummings, his fellow ambulance drivers in France.

This early exposure to imagism and aestheticism kept out of his work the drabness that sometimes goes with naturalism. He would never write like Theodore Dreiser or James T. Farrell. In *Manhattan Transfer* passengers pour out of the ferry house "like apples fed down a chute into a press"; a newborn baby squirms "in the cottonwool feebly like a knot of earthworms." Sometimes he is too literally colorful, as if the names of pigments could actually create an impressionistic painting on the printed page.

Harvard gave Dos Passos more than aestheticism. He began reading Thorstein Veblen as well as James Joyce. Much of his fiction, with its language borrowed from *A Portrait of the Artist as a Young Man* and *Ulysses*, is an extended illustration of *The Theory of the Leisure Class* and *The Engineers and the Price System*. To a mind absorbing Veblen's ironic analyses of American capitalism, the news in the papers had a sharpened impact. It was the time of the textile workers' strike in Lawrence, Massachusetts, with the poet Giovannitti as its leader, and of another in Paterson, New Jersey, for which John Reed helped stage a pageant in Madison Square Garden.

Dos Passos reviewed Reed's *Insurgent Mexico* and heard him lecture at Harvard. Reed was a great romantic, an impressionist poet, who could throw himself passionately into social struggles. Then, too, there was the contemporary Belgian poet Verhaeren, an impassioned traveler, who described his intense inner life in images drawn from his fascination with factories, railroads, stock markets, and the "tentacular" industrial cities of Europe.

After he graduated from Harvard in 1916, Dos Passos was eager to join the Norton-Harjes volunteer ambulance service, not because he approved of the war but because he loved adventure and wanted to help his fellow men. Afraid that he would be killed, his father offered him a year of architectural study in Spain instead. Dos Passos yielded, but when his father died suddenly the next spring, he volunteered, serving in Italy as well as France.

Out of this war experience came his first brief novel, *One Man's Initiation—1917* (published in England in 1920). In it he seems perhaps less the man of action than the aesthete, the sensitive spectator. It is dedicated to "those with whom I saw rockets in the sky a certain evening at sunset on the road from Erize-la-Petite to Erize-la-Grande."

Like most of his later books it begins with a man traveling, this time to France. Snatches of war songs set the mood, and a pretty girl offers to chloroform all surviving Germans. It ends with a long discussion between the young hero, Martin Howe, and a group of French soldiers. He asks, as John Reed might have, whether they can carry through the social revolution they feel coming. They say No, they are only intellectuals. The ones who have the power and nerve are "the stupid average working-people." The intellectuals can only try to fight falsehood.

In "Hugh Selwyn Mauberley" Ezra Pound tells of young men dying for old men's lies, and in *A Farewell to Arms* Ernest Hemingway describes how soldiers at the front felt when they had to listen once again to the words "sacred, glorious and sacrifice and the expression in vain." Only the names of places retained their dignity. Martin Howe says of the propaganda that takes away our humanity, "We are slaves of bought intellect, willing slaves."

The writing in *One Man's Initiation* is young and self-conscious, still in the aesthetic mode of Walter Pater and the early Joyce. Unlike Hemingway, whose youthful work was blue-penciled by Ezra Pound and Gertrude Stein, Dos Passos had no master hand to cut out his excessive description and the parts of his dialogue that did not ring true. He never learned to "listen completely" when people talked, to discover the revealing phrase and then play on it wittily, as Hemingway and F. Scott Fitzgerald at their best could do. Even after Martin Howe reaches the front to take up ambulance duty, passages from Shelley and Blake run through his head, and he spends his off-hours contemplating a ruined abbey and dreaming of the Middle Ages. But when this poetic impressionism is used to describe the chaos of war in the French countryside, the results are brilliant.

The book is purely episodic, made up of unconnected scenes, but they take separate and satisfying shape as vignettes or short stories. There is not just one initiation but a whole series of them—encounters with death, fear,

Paris, women, theft, corruption, anarchism, Catholicism. In both style and construction the novel is clearly indebted to *The Red Badge of Courage* by Stephen Crane.

One Man's Initiation was a kind of preparatory exercise to the far maturer novel, *Three Soldiers*, written the following year, mostly in Spain, while Dos Passos was free-lancing as a journalist and essayist. The most vivid direct account of army life among our common soldiers during World War I, *Three Soldiers* helped create an antimilitaristic mood in readers of the twenties and thirties, and even left its mark on major novels written after World War II. *The Naked and the Dead* and *From Here to Eternity*, for instance, have leading characters chosen much as Dos Passos had chosen his. Mailer and Jones follow his pattern, too, in stressing the intensity of the conflicts within the army itself.

Dos Passos gives his three soldier parts to Andrews, a Harvard-educated pianist-composer from New York and Virginia; Fuselli, an optical worker from San Francisco eager to make good in the army; Chrisfield, a home-sick farm boy from Indiana obsessed with hatred for a sergeant whom he finally kills with a hand grenade in the confusion after a battle.

All three men are broken by the army. Fuselli contracts a serious venereal disease. Chrisfield deserts and leads a precarious underground existence in Paris. Andrews, studying at the Sorbonne while still in the army, gets into trouble with some M.P.'s who dislike his manner, is beaten up and sent to a labor battalion. He escapes by plunging into the Seine, helped by a working-class soldier who drowns while trying to rescue him. Saved then by an anarchist bargeman, Andrews finds his way, after many adventures, to the French girl he loves. She lets him down badly when she learns of the trouble he is in. He is rearrested, with a long federal prison term ahead of him. The

music he has been working on, inspired by his reading of Flaubert, blows symbolically away.

Certainly Dos Passos was stacking the cards by having all three soldiers end badly, but this was the mood of the best postwar writers. Robert Graves called his war reminiscences *Goodbye to All That*. The hero of Hemingway's *Farewell to Arms* makes a "separate peace" by plunging into the Arno. *The Enormous Room* by E. E. Cummings is an account of his experiences in a French military prison after being arrested for something he wrote in a letter home. Dos Passos himself was threatened with disciplinary action because of his views.

Antagonism is evident enough in the titles he uses for the divisions of the book, "Making the Mould," "The Metal Cools," "Machines," "Rust," "The World Outside," and "Under the Wheels." In *Three Soldiers* there is no discussion of military tactics, the strategy of trying to defeat Germany, or even international politics. Compared with the French, its American characters have little interest in ideas, radical or otherwise. Andrews is an exception, but his mood is one of total rejection of the "system." And after his experience in the labor battalion, he says something to the French girl that suggests the persistent fear of organized society of any kind which underlies Dos Passos' frequent shifts in political position.

Andrews lands in prison because he has refused to give himself up passively to dehumanized power. But at times he fears that society will always be anti-individualist: "organizations growing and stifling individuals, and individuals revolting hopelessly against them, and at last forming new societies to crush the old societies and becoming slaves again in their turn. . . ."

Many readers were shocked by the spade-calling realism of *Three Soldiers*. Despite this and its attitude toward the army, it was enthusiastically received. Heywood Broun called it a book "with not an atom of pose," representing "deep convictions . . . eloquently expressed." Critics were amazed that in a book describing free souls crushed and deadened by an institution there could be "a sense of beauty on every page." Dos Passos was bitterly critical of army life, but he had a young and romantic appreciation of new experience of every kind. Both created intensity: at the same time they sufficiently balanced each other so that *Three Soldiers* remains one of the best novels of World War I as well as one of the most objective accounts of what war service in France was like.

Between the two major books of his early period, *Three Soldiers* (1921) and *Manhattan Transfer* (1925), Dos Passos not only wrote a play, *The Garbage Man*, and many articles for magazines, but published his volume of poems, *A Pushcart at the Curb*; his collection of essays on Spain called *Rosinante to the Road Again*; and a novel, *Streets of Night*. Much of this is apprentice work, but very revealing of the man who made himself secretary to American Society in *U.S.A.*, *District of Columbia*, and *Midcentury*.

Before Hemingway visited Spain to study death in the bull ring, Dos Passos, a friend of Hemingway, already had chosen it as the best place in which to get a clear perspective on his own values and those of his native country. He liked Spain and sympathized with Spanish reasons for being distrustful of America.

Rosinante to the Road Again (1922) describes this experiment. Essays on Spain and Spanish writers alternate with the dialogue of two travelers who represent different aspects of the author, or perhaps represent the author as he was and as he would have liked to be. Telemachus is thoughtful, inhibited, questing; his friend Lyaeus is relaxed, spontaneous, daring, enjoying life in a mildly Dionysian way.

It is remarkable that *Rosinante* was published in the same year as Joyce's *Ulysses*, in which Stephen Dedalus is Telemachus. But Dos Passos had stronger personal reasons than Joyce —or Thomas Wolfe, who also used the name —to identify himself with a classic hero whose whole youth was spent separated from his wandering warrior father. Moreover, in exploring Iberian life Dos Passos was returning to the sources of the immigrant strain which figures so largely in his sense of himself.

He read the Spanish social novelists, especially Pío Baroja, a kind of Spanish Gorki, who believed that everything of value in a country comes from the despised and neglected masses. "A profound sense of the evil of existing institutions," Dos Passos said, "lies behind every page he has written." Dos Passos spoke of Baroja as believing that a writer of the middle classes can serve the revolution only through his negations, his nay-saying, but found such negation perfectly compatible in Baroja with an intense feeling for immediate reality. His characters are "men of the day, people in love with the passing moment." Like Dos Passos, Baroja was fantastically productive. Among his scores of novels were three social trilogies. He changed his political position even more extremely than did Dos Passos. In 1937 he came out for fascism as the lesser of two evils. After exile in France during World War II, he returned to become a highly honored writer in Franco's Spain. Yet his individualism and skepticism about institutions persisted.

Many of the poems in *A Pushcart at the Curb* are set in Spain or Portugal. Though the poet and social critic in Dos Passos collaborate brilliantly in the novels, the poet, when alone, writes in a soft and outmoded vein. With none of the tough wit of Eliot or the later Yeats, these poems are mere traveler's sketches, imitating with words the brightly pigmented street scenes of a Pissarro or Sisley.

In one important respect, these poems are closer to *One Man's Initiation* than to the later fiction. Martin Howe's romanticism is still expressed by frequent references to medieval and ancient history, to Isis, Pan, spice cargoes entering Venice, nightingales strangled for Nero's supper, and a Bacchic rout of "ruddy boys with vineleaves in their hair." Praising *Ulysses* in 1925, T. S. Eliot proclaimed that the future of the novel depended on its moving toward myth. But this was just the time when the legendary and mythical elements vanished from Dos Passos' writings, never to return. If he had kept and nurtured them, perhaps his characters would not have been so completely the creatures of their social roles, and his criticism of American culture itself would have had more depth.

His play *The Garbage Man*—first produced at Harvard in 1925 under the title *The Moon Is a Gong*—is poetically far more vigorous than *A Pushcart at the Curb*. Like John Howard Lawson's *Processional* and Elmer Rice's *The Adding Machine*, it derives from the German Expressionist theater of Georg Kaiser and Ernst Toller.

Kaiser's play *Gas* dramatizes the dangers of uncontrollable industrial power; his *From Morn to Midnight* is about money madness. Toller wrote *Masses and Man* when he was in prison for his part in the Bavarian Communist *Putsch* of 1919. He shows how the common people and the capitalists are alike dehumanized by industrialization. It is Man who counts, and he can be saved only by love and individual responsibility. The themes are boldly stated, with striking mass effects and much use of rhythm and recurrence. Stockbrokers dance a foxtrot to the clink of coins, and chant higher and higher bids in musical crescendo as war reports pour in.

Tom, the musical-comedy-type hero of *The Garbage Man*, says: "We'd pick up raindrops for quarters. We'd skim greenbacks off the rollers out at sea. There's a lot of gold in your hair Jane." Jane is more realistic, and knows that money has to come from somebody's hard work. "Tom listen to the engine in the powerplant; that's all people. The engines are made out of people pounded into steel. The power's stretched on the muscles of people, the light's sucked out of people's eyes."

Jane seems to approach success, but it is in the false world of publicity and the theater. She wants "act, not dream" from Tom. After roaming romantically through the far places of the world, Tom actually does climb up to the moon, whereas Jane is in danger of being carried off by the mysterious figure of the garbage man. At the final curtain, Tom and Jane fly off up into space together.

Though romantically confused in its "message," *The Garbage Man* makes lively reading, offering train wrecks, jewel robberies, prosperity parades, and patriotic oratory. A Negro servant breaks out into an eloquent sermon. The telescope man sees the city in the same sort of total vision that *Manhattan Transfer* will create: "In all the offices . . . typewriters clucking an' chirruping like canarybirds . . . an' tickers roll out fours an' eights an' dollar signs an' ciphers, reeling out millions that don't exist. In all the houses, in apartments like shoeboxes, women in sacques and old pink kimonos . . . ."

Streets of Night (1923), begun while Dos Passos was still an undergraduate, is very immature but it shows how personal relations looked to him before he began treating them socially and mixing them up with public events.

The "three soldiers" of *Streets of Night* are Fanshaw, an art instructor at Harvard, Wendell, a graduate student in anthropology, and Nancibel, a bachelor girl studying music. Fanshaw, very much a mother's boy, had been unable to make love to a chorus girl on an outing at Norumbega Park. He daydreams of marrying Nancibel, but realizes that he is "much too fond of Wenny, his dark skin, his extraordinary bright eyes." Nancibel is also drawn to Wendell, but is afraid of commitment and the act of sex. Tantalized by Nancibel's hesitations, Wendell picks up a prostitute, but flees when she confronts him naked. Convinced that his clergyman father has made life impossible for him, he shoots himself on a bridge parapet and drops into the Charles River. "Now in me," he thinks, "my father'll be dead." In Faulkner's *The Sound and the Fury*, Quentin Compson, another father-doomed Harvard man, dies in very much the same way.

Though *Streets of Night* is entirely non-political, the lower classes, especially the recent immigrants, are romantically endowed with superior freedom and vitality. Before his suicide Wenny has a long envious talk with a hungry vagabond. He dreams of being like him, "walking down roads, hopping freights: Tallahassee and South Bend and Havana and Paris and Helsingfors and Khiva and Budapest and Khorasan." After Wenny's death, Fanshaw gazes at the muscles of workers repairing tracks. "Wenny would have wanted to be one of them, redfaced spitting men with skillful ugly hands."

Finally in Italy, with the war over (only a page is devoted to it), Fanshaw gets drunk with an offensive Frenchman and goes with him—purely out of curiosity, he thinks—to a house of assignation, where he wakes up in a strange room beside a sleeping girl. It is not clear from Fanshaw's speedy retreat whether he is any surer of his sexual orientation than before.

The wasted lives in *Three Soldiers* are attributed to the crushing effects of the military machine. The characters in *Streets of Night* are under no such pressure, but end badly too.

They blame their parents and their parents' values. Dos Passos may have had an unusual personal reason for his sense of alienation and his inability to participate spontaneously in "real" life. But it was one that drove him to use even more intensely the theme that was popular with writers as varied as Van Wyck Brooks, Edwin Arlington Robinson, Sherwood Anderson, and Edgar Lee Masters. In Joyce's *Dubliners* the key word is "paralysis."

Though *Orient Express* did not appear until 1927, it describes a trip which Dos Passos had taken for the Near East Relief before he returned to New York to write *Manhattan Transfer*. Far more brilliant and evocative than his later travel books, it deserves to rank with the best in this genre by Graham Greene or Evelyn Waugh.

When only four years old he had gone aboard a fully equipped Trans-Siberian train in a dark shed at the Paris Exposition of 1900. Lighted scenes of exotic places rolled past the windows. "I've often wondered about the others who had tickets taken for them on that immovable train of the Trans-Siberian in the first year of the century," he wrote in *Orient Express*, "whose childhood was full of *Twenty Thousand Leagues* and Jules Verne's *sportsmen* and *globetrottairs* (if only the ice holds on Lake Baikal), and Chinese Gordon stuttering his last words over the telegraph at Khartoum, and Carlotta come back mad from Mexico setting fire to a palace at Terveuren. . . ."

Dos Passos goes where his romantic heroes had dreamed of going—to Trebizond, Ararat, Baghdad—but as an official trying to deal with famine, disease, revolution. He sees ways of life, unchanged since the time of Mahomet or Moses, about to be destroyed by Americanism, or at least by some of its exportable industrial techniques. "Henry Ford's gospel of multiple production and interchangeable parts will win hearts that stood firm against Thales and Democritus, against Galileo and Faraday. There is no god strong enough to withstand the Universal Suburb."

The exciting urban novel *Manhattan Transfer* was written by a man now mature, who had come back after seven years to look critically at his own country in a time of boom and changing mores. Though this is a long novel, it is as crowded as *The Garbage Man* with short, swift scenes full of crime, violence, and destruction, especially by fire. The book has the same conventional sort of heroine and hero, too. Ellen Thatcher, an actress, had grown up with a doting father who found her more fascinating than his sick, complaining wife. Jimmy Herf's early years were spent alone with his mother in Europe. Like Wenny and Fanshaw in *Streets of Night*, he looks wistfully at workingmen and wonders how it would feel "to be dirty and handle coal all day and have grease in your hair and up to your armpits." Later as a reporter he becomes the friend of a dark-skinned curly-haired former cook's helper from a French liner, who is dangerously and profitably involved in bootlegging.

Sex is no longer a fearful wonder. Jimmy and Ellen marry and have a baby, but the marriage does not last. Restless, unsure of herself, not really enjoying the life of the body, Ellen plunges into a series of love affairs. In the last pages of the novel, she marries an aging politician, chiefly because she needs security. Life in New York seemed full of possibilities, but because of her inner emptiness they come to nothing. It is the same mood that Sister Carrie reached in the end. And although Jimmy Herf, just turned thirty, is too young to be a Hurstwood, we see him penniless in the last scene, trudging out of the city past acres of smoldering dumps. When a truckdriver asks him how far he is going, he says, "I dunno. . . . Pretty far."

The life of the city is refracted through the minds of a dozen people nearly as important as Jimmy and Ellen: politicians, laborers, swindlers, chorus girls, housewives, down-and-outers, prissy vulgarians, high-class drunks. Many are mere types—Dos Passos always has this problem—but what they see and remember is vividly particular. With unfailing resourcefulness Dos Passos can create what seems like spontaneous memories appropriate to literally hundreds of variegated characters. And though the scenes often flash past two or three to the page, they have such consequence for the human beings in them—a girl going to an abortionist, a man discovering arson—that they never blur or seem perfunctory. Public moods are recalled with equal intensity. While Ellen Thatcher's father waits at the hospital for her birth, he reads about the legislation that is full of promise for the new century in New York.

Dos Passos sharpens even more the sense of moment and movement—to which the whole turbulent life of the city contributes—by shifting rapidly back and forth from one group of characters to another. A business, political, amatory, or criminal affair is treated for a few pages as if it were the center of the world—which it would be, of course, in real life, for the people concerned—and then cut off abruptly, to be picked up again without explanation, twenty or thirty pages later.

The division of chapters into as many as fifteen separate sections recalls the "Wandering Rocks" chapter of *Ulysses*, which describes eighteen incidents occurring in various parts of Dublin between three and four o'clock on one afternoon. Dos Passos was also influenced by the montage experiments of the film directors David Wark Griffith and Sergei Eisenstein. Griffith's fantastically ambitious *Intolerance* tries to tell four stories at once: the fall of Babylon, the crucifixion, the St. Bartholomew's Day massacre, and the suppression of a strike in a modern mill town. As the narratives approach a climax, the scenes become briefer, with quicker changes from story to story. Even more complex shifts without transition make Eliot's *The Waste Land* and Pound's *Cantos* such difficult reading.

Manhattan Transfer is clearly selective, as *Three Soldiers* had been. While responding imaginatively to the vigor and beauty of a great city, it concentrates on those characters most easily led astray by its temptations or least able to bear its pressures. It has very little more directly political implication than Dreiser's *Sister Carrie*, which had treated the same theme twenty-five years earlier.

What New York in the 1920's meant to Dos Passos is vividly described in the autobiography, *The Best Times*. It was the speakeasy period, a period of cynicism and disenchantment, but also of gaiety and wit. "Conversation in the early twenties had to be one wisecrack after another." Dos Passos knew intimately some of the most brilliant writers and talkers of his generation, E. E. Cummings, the Scott Fitzgeralds, Robert Benchley, Edmund Wilson, John Howard Lawson, Edna St. Vincent Millay. Too, there was romance at "a time in a man's life when every evening is a prelude. Toward five o'clock the air begins to tingle. It's tonight if you drink enough, talk enough, walk far enough, that the train of magical events will begin. Every part of town had its own peculiar glow."

What had happened to Dos Passos' political convictions since his Near East trip shows more clearly in the play *Airways, Inc.*, written in 1928. This was the year he visited Russia, the year after Lindbergh's flight and the execution of Sacco and Vanzetti. A drunken aviator, prototype of Charley Anderson in *U.S.A.*, breaks his back in a crash when he is sent to scatter leaflets over a strikers' meeting. The characters are crushed by a variety of disasters,

all blamed on the social roles they choose or are forced to play.

Edmund Wilson reviewed the play admiringly, feeling that Dos Passos was superior to Hemingway, Fitzgerald, and Thornton Wilder in his ability to view society as a whole. But he doubted that American life then, or human life almost anywhere, was as unattractive as Dos Passos made it. Those on the right side suffer and are snuffed out; those on the wrong side are unattractive even when young, even in their pleasures. "We begin to guess some stubborn sentimentalism at the bottom of the whole thing . . . of which misapplied resentments represent the aggressive side. And from the moment we suspect the processes by which he has arrived at his political ideas, the ideas themselves become suspect."

These ideas were tested in action while Dos Passos was writing his great trilogy, *U.S.A.* The first volume, *The 42nd Parallel,* was published in 1930, the year after the stock market crash. In 1931, Dos Passos was indicted for criminal syndicalism when he and Theodore Dreiser tried to help the striking miners in Harlan County, Kentucky. The second volume, *1919*, came out in 1932, the year its author publicly supported the Communist candidate for President. Dos Passos was then treasurer of the National Committee for the Defense of Political Prisoners. But by 1936, when *The Big Money* concluded the trilogy, Dos Passos had attacked the Communists and backed Roosevelt's bid for a second term.

Though Dos Passos was never a Marxist he shared the belief current among intellectuals that history was heading toward some sort of final conflict. No writer could stand aloof. Whatever he said would add its thrust to one of the forces—progressive or destructive—that were coming into collision. The sense of social change, of released energy, which had given power to *Manhattan Transfer*, was expressed on a far vaster scale in *U.S.A.*

Like *Manhattan Transfer*, *U.S.A.* begins around 1900, at the time of the fighting in Cuba and the Philippines. The oratorical prophecies in the first Newsreel recall his father's expectations in *The Anglo-Saxon Century*. The trilogy is intended to be a total history of public moods and social changes through some twenty-five years, as experienced by twelve very different Americans. Public events are far more important than in *Manhattan Transfer*; the political analysis is more explicit and revolutionary. To cope with such tremendous matters, Dos Passos makes daring experiments in form. Never afterward did he use these techniques so fully.

In *U.S.A.* four distinctive modes of presentation have crystallized: the Newsreel; the Camera Eye; biographical sketches; and extended fictional narratives.

Dos Passos had always enlivened his narratives with newspaper quotations, political oratory, and popular songs. Now, in the Newsreels, he brings this material together as in a collage, juxtaposing verbal fragments in an artful pattern that has its own rhythms and recurrences. Not only does he evoke the events and moods of past years, but by mixing the trite and trivial ironically with the crucial he shows how fatuous and inconsistent America's public image of itself can be.

The Camera Eye sections are brief, impressionistic prose poems capturing poignant or decisive moments in the narrator's life. They are brilliantly done, and remind us that *U.S.A.* does not give us social reality as such, but social reality viewed by a particular man with a particular past—"I, John Dos Passos" succeeds the "I, Walt Whitman" of an equally formidable try at embracing the whole American experience of the century before.

The biographical portraits, vivid and compressed, describe as poetically but in expressionist style the lives of prominent Americans of the period. The inventor Steinmetz, for instance, "jotted a formula on his cuff and next morning a thousand new powerplants had sprung up and the dynamos sang dollars." For John Reed he uses a refrain, "Reed was a westerner and words meant what they said."

The choice of public figures in *U.S.A.* reflects the author's political mood and the limitations of his interests. In the first volume are two radical labor leaders, Eugene Debs and Bill Haywood; two defeated politicians, William Jennings Bryan and Robert La Follette; two capitalists, Andrew Carnegie and Minor C. Keith; and three experimenters, Thomas Edison, Luther Burbank, and Charles Proteus Steinmetz. The range is about the same in the second volume, but in *The Big Money* Isadora Duncan, Frank Lloyd Wright, Rudolph Valentino, and Thorstein Veblen provide more diversity. Only Veblen is strictly a man of ideas, and in all of *U.S.A.* there are no medical men, athletes, philosophers, creative writers, pure scientists, or religious leaders.

Most of *U.S.A.* lavishly reproduces the immediately felt experiences of its twelve chapters, in diction and rhythms and ways of thought appropriate to them. Dos Passos learned this mode from Joyce, but he uses it here with great authority and flexibility, especially when he enters the minds of women and children. The characters who dominate the trilogy toward the end are types already familiar from *Manhattan Transfer*—nervously ill wives and mothers, unmarried career women and dabblers in the arts, men of power corrupted by success, unsuccessful men who become mere drifters. Everybody is on the move, socially and geographically. Even more than *Manhattan Transfer, U.S.A.* dramatizes American mobility. Sex as a driving force, a nervous release, adds to the general restlessness. But profound and sustained love, like profound religious or creative excitement, is totally absent.

The individual lives tend to start and finish badly. We are introduced to Eleanor Stoddard by these sentences: "When she was small she hated everything. She hated her father, a stout redhaired man smelling of whiskers and stale pipetobacco." True to the odorous tradition of naturalism, the house where Fainy McCreary was born "was choking all day with the smell of whale-oil soap."

The ends are bad in more spectacular ways. Charley Anderson and Daughter die in plane and motor accidents, Eleanor Stoddard by suicide. Even more significant is the inner defeat, the degradation unsuccessfully narcotized by drunkenness. This is a society in which success—the success of power or money—is really failure. There are no sustaining values, except in rebellion. No one takes satisfaction in building or creating, whether it be a house, a family, an institution, a work of art.

Two leftists, Ben Compton and Mary French, are shown at the end still devoting their lives to unselfish purposes, but Ben has been thrown out of the Communist party for opposing its betrayal of the striking miners, and Mary has been deserted by the Communist functionary she has loved.

Even so, *U.S.A.* creates a positive effect because of the richness of the felt experience, the importance of the events, and the boldness of its challenge. And though the four separate modes of presentation might seem a confession of disunity, they are skillfully employed to bring diverse materials together according to certain dominant themes.

Toward the end of *The 42nd Parallel*, for instance, Eleanor Stoddard's frequent meetings with J. Ward Moorehouse cause his wife to threaten divorce. This is serious; Mrs. Moorehouse controls the fortune that can save him from bankruptcy. But then America declares war on Germany, and the resulting sudden shift in the business situation seems certain to benefit him. He is put on the President's Public Information Committee. He and Eleanor face his wife and persuade her that nothing is wrong. With everyone in a patriotic, excited mood, his personal crisis passes.

As Eleanor and Moorehouse cross Times Square "suddenly a grindorgan began to play *The Marseillaise* and it was too beautiful; she burst into tears and they talked about Sacrifice and Dedication and J.W. held her arm tight through the fur coat and gave the organ-grinder man a dollar." On the way to Long Island the drive over the Queensboro Bridge "was like flying above lights and blocks of houses and the purple bulk of Blackwell's Island and the steamboats and the tall chimneys and the blue light of powerplants." At the confrontation, Mrs. Moorehouse's "salmon-colored teagown stood out against the black. His light hair was ashgray in the light from the crystal chandelier against the tall ivorygray walls of the room." Eleanor finds the whole scene "like a play, like a Whistler, like Sarah Bernhardt." She decides to join the Red Cross and go to France.

The Newsreel immediately following echoes these themes in its snatches of the war song "Over There," its scraps of patriotic oratory, and its references to war profiteering.

The next Camera Eye describes the narrator's journey at this time to France on a ship containing Red Cross officials. He lands in Bordeaux to find profiteering there too: "up north they were dying in the mud and the trenches but business was good in Bordeaux and the winegrowers and the shipping agents and the munitionsmakers crowded into the Chapon Fin and ate ortolans and mushrooms and truffles. . . ." Some of the prose in this Camera Eye suggests Hemingway's "In Another Country." On the voyage, "the barman was brave and the stewards were brave they'd all been wounded and they were very glad that they were not in the trenches and the pastry was magnificent."

Then comes a sketch of Fighting Bob La Follette which also dramatizes the politics of the declaration of war. Dos Passos says that "we will remember" how in March 1917 La Follette, trying to block the drive toward war, held the vast governmental machine at deadlock for three days, though the "press pumped hatred into its readers" against him and "they burned him in effigy in Illinois." He died "an orator haranguing from the capitol of a lost republic."

All this is covered in just eighteen pages of the nearly fifteen hundred in the trilogy. The brief accounts of Joe Williams' many voyages as seaman and of Charley Anderson's financial involvements are equally packed. Dos Passos devotes ten pages to experiences which Henry James or Joseph Conrad would have analyzed in three hundred. Obviously he cannot equal them in depth of character or dramatic implication, but the narrative is more than mere synopsis. The authentic details seem remembered rather than invented. The result is to give history the grounding which Balzac thought only a novelist could give it, in the day-to-day lives of the people of a nation or a generation.

The history Dos Passos sees, though, is rather limited. He has not used what he knows of the world outside the United States to help us understand the unique character of the American experience. Even when he devoted himself after 1940 to an intensive study of the founding fathers, the books that came from it—such as the composite account of Hamilton and Jefferson, *The Men Who Made the Nation* (1957)—focus so sharply on the immediate events that the larger issues are blurred.

Even in so massive an undertaking as *Mr. Wilson's War* (1962) his "Notes on Sources" shows how novelistic and personal his approach as a historian remained. "My method was to try to relate the experience of the assorted personalities and their assorted justifications to my own recollections of childhood and youth during those years; and to seek out, wherever possible, the private letter, the unguarded entry in the diary, the newsreport made on the spur of the moment." In his youth, under his father's direction, Dos Passos had been given a sound classical education, including the study of Greek, but with very little effect on his later thinking. It never seemed to occur to him to judge the American republic with Plato's *Republic* in mind, or Roosevelt's New Deal in reference to Machiavelli or Tacitus.

No one in *U.S.A.* thinks of the centuries before. It is as if history began with the sinking of the battleship *Maine* in Havana Harbor. In his sketch of La Follette, Dos Passos applies the term "lost" not only to his own generation but to the republic as well. Here again he speaks in the accents of his period, when the most talented writers, in exile and at home, tended to blame all that they disliked about America on the war of 1917–18, with the profiteering, propaganda, intolerance, and xenophobia that accompanied or followed it. But many charges Dos Passo makes in *U.S.A.* could as well have been made at the time of the suppression of the Philippine rebellion, or during the Reconstruction period after the Civil War, or even during the 1830's. Indeed, they were made, and just as emphatically, by Mark Twain, Whitman, and Emerson.

As a second-act curtain to the trilogy as a whole, *1919* concludes with a portrait of the unknown soldier—the most terrifying expression Dos Passos ever gave of his emotions about World War I and the men who made it. The bewildered lost soldier, hit by a chance shell as he tries to find his way back to his outfit, is a composite of all Dos Passos' heroes, with the working-class vagabond to the fore. There is an echo of Whitman's "Carol of Occupations" in the list of the soldier's jobs: "busboy harveststiff hogcaller boyscout champeen cornshucker of Western Kansas bellhop at the United States Hotel at Saratoga Springs office boy callboy fruiter telephone lineman longshoreman lumberjack plumber's helper." Yet he is a unique living being with all his stored experience blasted into nullity in an instant of time. "For twentyodd years intensely the nerves of the eyes the ears the palate the tongue the fingers the toes the armpits, the nerves warmfeeling under the skin charged the coiled brain with hurt sweet warm cold mine must dont saying print headlines."

What remains after the trench rats and bluebottle flies have done their work is taken to God's Country on a battleship and buried under the folds of Old Glory. For his montage Dos Passos makes a selection that contrasts with devastating irony the soldier's real life and the cynical, sentimental oratory of the official ceremonies led by President Harding.

The climax of the third volume, *The Big Money,* is a Camera Eye section on the electrocution of the anarchists Sacco and Vanzetti, found guilty six years earlier of murder during a payroll robbery. They had been arrested on the basis of rather questionable evidence during the wave of hysterical antiradicalism and fear of foreigners which was a direct consequence of the war and its propaganda. The fact that the passionate united effort of thousands of liberals had failed to save Sacco and Vanzetti convinced Dos Passos that reaction ruled the country. "All right we are two nations," the narrator concludes. "They"

have won; "we" are defeated. "They" control the politicians, newspaper editors, judges, college presidents. "America our nation has been beaten by strangers who have turned our language inside out who have taken the clean words our fathers spoke and made them slimy and foul."

In its context—coming after scenes outside the Charlestown jail in which the fictional characters Mary French and Don Stevens are beaten by the police—this Camera Eye is deeply moving. Of all Dos Passos ever wrote, it is the most eloquent statement of a militant personal commitment to a specific cause. In the light of the earlier works, we can see why the Sacco-Vanzetti case had such appeal. These were immigrants, anarchists, individualists crushed, like John Andrews, by an official juggernaut impervious to reason.

As objective political analysis, however, this Camera Eye is very confusing, especially in the terms it uses. It speaks of "the old words of the immigrants" that are "being renewed in blood and agony tonight," and of "the immigrant haters of oppression" who lie quiet in black suits in an undertaking parlor in the North End of Boston. The earlier immigrants were "our fathers," haters of oppression, creators of democracy and a language in which "words meant what they said." But at some point "our nation" was beaten by mysterious strangers who "cut down the woods for pulp and turned our pleasant cities into slums and sweated the wealth out of our people."

In the final Camera Eye, describing the visit of a delegation to terror-haunted mine country, he speaks in even more extreme language about being made to feel like a foreigner in his own country. "They" are a conquering army which has "filtered into the country unnoticed they have taken the hilltops by stealth." "They" have the "strut of the power of submachineguns sawed-offshotguns teargas and vomitinggas the power that can feed you or leave you to starve . . . we have only words against."

This conquest of the country by an identified "they," by strangers, is imaginatively exciting, but has a paranoiac quality, and is not a very precise picture of social fact. President A. Lawrence Lowell of Harvard, one of those most condemned by intellectuals for his part in the Sacco-Vanzetti case, came of an old and cultivated American family, as did Supreme Court Justice Oliver Wendell Holmes, whose refusal of a stay of execution is announced in one of the Newsreels. President Lowell, along with his sister Amy, derived his fortune from the exploitation of labor in the mills of Lawrence and Lowell, but these had sprung up before the Civil War. The great power of the House of Morgan, blamed in *1919* for the way America went to war and the way it made peace, grew from family speculations in Hartford, Connecticut, in the 1830's.

It is hard to say what Dos Passos means by "strangers." Most of his capitalists and wielders of power, both actual and fictional, have thoroughly American backgrounds. America and American standards of success have shaped them, as *U.S.A.* itself makes amply clear. The trilogy gives no adequate explanation of what went wrong and how it can be corrected, or which of the opposed elements in the American tradition are responsible for the good "we" and the bad "they." Things are amiss in the nation because the wrong "they" have taken over, and only a few brave individuals are trying to do something about it. This is why the later novels can continue to accuse in the same tone, whether the villains are capitalists, Communists, labor leaders, or New Dealers.

Dos Passos wrote social novels without sociology, without social institutions. He could show powerful individuals making secret deals, but not the corporate determination of policy within churches, universities, magazines, the Senate, or even the Communist party. Because of this inadequacy, when Dos Passos wrote introductory and concluding sketches for the 1937 one-volume *U.S.A.* he could not find a symbol that would really suggest either the country or his own vast and important work of imagination. At the beginning he lists a jumble of things or qualities, and then decides that "mostly U.S.A. is the speech of the people."

This is not borne out by the trilogy itself. Like other writers as different as Ezra Pound and Sherwood Anderson, Dos Passos speaks of the way language is being corrupted by the false commercial and political uses to which it is put. But reproducing the direct speech of common Americans is what he does least well. He gives it a very mechanical "dese-dem-dose" character with none of the delightful comedy discovered in it during the same period by Ring Lardner, Sinclair Lewis, and James Thurber, not to mention Hemingway and Fitzgerald, who could themselves be extremely witty.

The 1937 edition's final summarizing sketch, entitled "Vag," repeats exactly the situation at the end of *Manhattan Transfer.* A young man with no prospects stands at the side of a concrete road beckoning with his thumb as cars hiss past. Wants "crawl over his skin like ants." Romanticized in the earlier novels, now the vag travels hopelessly, uselessly, from nowhere to nowhere, hectored by bullying cops, his belly knotted with hunger. Overhead flies a silver transcontinental plane, occupied by men with bank accounts, thinking of "contracts, profits, vacationtrips." One of them, airsick, vomits into his carton container the steak and mushrooms he ate in New York. America is represented by two individuals with queasy stomachs. In between there is nothing but air and the names of places the plane has flown over, the vast geography of the continent.

Dos Passos expresses his most personal and nostalgic identification with the country in some of the early Camera Eye pieces. One of them poignantly re-creates the experience of hearing *The Man without a Country* read aloud. The young listener identifies the voices of the judge and naval officers with the voice of Mr. Garfield, who is reading, and feels that he himself is Philip Nolan. Tears come into his eyes when he finds himself rejected by his country and condemned to endless travel abroad. He doesn't remember whether after he dies he is brought home or buried at sea, but anyway, "I was wrapped in Old Glory." Here, in a mingling of alienation and patriotism, are the basic emotions of all Dos Passos' writing.

Though *Adventures of a Young Man* (1939) is politically symptomatic, it is a great letdown after *U.S.A.* Dos Passos had gone to Spain with Hemingway and Joris Ivens to help make a documentary film about the Civil War. His sympathies were as deeply engaged as theirs, but he withdrew because of Communist interference. Party functionaries directed by Russians had taken over in Spain, liquidating those they could not dominate. When he heard that a Spanish doctor friend had been killed by one of their firing squads, Dos Passos began to write his novel.

Only the last twenty pages of *Adventures of a Young Man* are devoted to Spain. Where Andrews in *Three Soldiers* was beaten up and imprisoned by military authority, Glenn Spotswood is shot. In both cases an isolated individual is destroyed by a machine, but in the second case the circumstances are more explicitly political. The killing is done by Communists.

Glenn Spotswood is a typical young American radical of the thirties who risks his life for striking miners and reacts violently when the Communists cold-bloodedly sacrifice the miners to other party interests. Here Dos Passos draws again on his experience in Harlan County, Kentucky, but the political arguments which were the breath of life to American intellectuals in the late thirties are treated in a very perfunctory fashion. Never much interested in leftist theory, Dos Passos is now too completely alienated to be able to re-create the highly involved quasi-theological debates that went on endlessly among and within the various factions of the left. But without these debates, in which the debaters thought they spoke for History itself, the intellectual fascination of Marxism cannot be understood.

Much of the novel, in a kind of reversion to *Streets of Night*, recounts Glenn's immature love affairs. As a student boarder he has awkward, rather amusing romances with two young married women, one Communist, one left-liberal. No matter how many love affairs Dos Passos describes—and there must be well over a hundred in his novels—the circumstances are always new, and the emotional perturbations convincing. But the *Adventures of a Young Man* holds little of the romantic joy in experience for its own sake that had countered the social negativism in *U.S.A.* Experimental techniques have been abandoned completely.

The elder Spotswood, a weak man who burdens Glenn and his older brother, Tyler, with moralistic advice, recalls in his inadequacy the father figures of earlier novels. And the talks Glenn has in Spain with anarchists are like the youthful discussion at the end of *One Man's Initiation*.

In his later book, *The Theme Is Freedom*, Dos Passos blames the defeat of the Spanish republic on a combination of communism and American neutralism. Since Russia was the only country supplying arms to the Loyalists, it could dictate policy, and it did so in an entirely divisive and self-interested way. Hemingway and George Orwell describe this death struggle directly; Dos Passos, in *Adventures of a Young Man,* devotes himself to the narrower topic of Communist factionalism in American labor defense cases. The subject had already been introduced in *The Big Money,* but as one strand in a richly woven fabric. Here it is the only social theme, and it is treated in the narrowly didactic fashion that makes us feel, in much of Dos Passos' later fiction, that we are not confronting life itself but incidents invented to illustrate a lecture.

Number One (1943), based on the career of Huey Long, is more forceful politically. Tyler Spotswood has the same relation to Chuck Crawford that Jack Burden has to Willie Stark in *All the King's Men* by Robert Penn Warren. Though Tyler is less philosophical and eloquent than Jack Burden, the vigor, unscrupulousness, and political agility of the Huey Long figure keep the action lively. But the end is disappointingly sentimental. After he has been trapped and ruined by corrupt politicians, as Glenn had been by the Communists, Tyler receives a letter which Glenn wrote before he was executed. It warns Americans not to let "them sell out too much of the for the people and by the people part of the oldtime United States way." Tyler, very drunk, has patriotic visions like those of the small boy in *U.S.A.*—"the little dome above the big dome and the clouds around and Old Glory nailed to the top of the mast . . ." He becomes obsessed with Custer's Last Stand. Custer had made a military mistake and he bravely took the consequences. Glenn made a political mistake and died bravely too. Tyler has made a moral mistake, and now he decides to take the consequences, take them on his own, beholden to nobody. In the last sentence

he walks alone "with fast strides up the windy avenue."

The Grand Design (1949) followed *Adventures of a Young Man* and *Number One* to complete a rather loose trilogy called *District of Columbia.* Though the books of *U.S.A.* had been bound together by techniques, themes, and characters, there is little of that unity here. Actually *The Grand Design* resembles the earlier trilogy more than it does its two companion novels, and can be read most satisfactorily as a separate work.

Dos Passos was clearly moved to try, as he had in writing *1919,* to capture the mood of a war in fiction. He had plenty of material from his wide travels at home and at the front during the forties. And since his two books of war reportage—*Tour of Duty* and *State of the Nation*—consisted chiefly of letting ordinary Americans speak for themselves, he had learned to listen. This improved the dialogue in *The Grand Design.* Its narrative moves swiftly, too, but the style is perfunctory, with little of the sensuous vividness of *U.S.A.*

Imperfect as the book is in execution, it has actually a rather grand design. It is one of the few novels bold enough to describe the later New Deal years in Washington. Henry Wallace, Felix Frankfurter, and other leaders appear in very transparent disguises, though in the formal disclaimer Dos Passos goes even further than is customary, declaring that each character is invented "through and through."

The novel is frankly didactic, showing the psychological and political dangers of giving great power to administrators and makers of opinion. (Glenn Spotswood's father, rather incredibly, has become a famous radio commentator.) The Communists successfully exploit this situation. Opposing them are the self-sacrificing officials Paul Graves and Millard Carroll. They try to protect local initiative, aid small farms and businesses, preserve popular control over the national administration, and, after the war breaks out, prevent aid to the U.S.S.R. from serving the Soviet drive toward world conquest. They fail, and have to leave government service.

Franklin Roosevelt in *The Grand Design* is strikingly like Woodrow Wilson in *U.S.A.* Both men are increasingly shut off from the people in their self-righteous use of the colossal power the people have handed over to them. "Wilson became the state (war is the health of the state), Washington his Versailles." Roosevelt, aging, ill, a cripple, "could play on a man like a violin. . . . We danced to his tune. Third Term. Fourth Term. Indispensable. War is a time of Caesars." In *The Theme Is Freedom* (1956) Dos Passos says, "The political act I have most regretted in my life was voting for Franklin D. Roosevelt for a third term."

In *1919*, three old men, Wilson, Clemenceau, and Lloyd George, sitting alone together, dealt out the destiny of peoples as they might have dealt out cards. Wilson was outplayed by the other two. At Teheran once again a triumvirate of old men—Roosevelt, Stalin, and Churchill—without consulting their peoples, "divided up the bloody globe and left the freedoms out. And the American People were supposed to say thank you for the century of the Common Man turned over for relocation behind barbed wire so help him God."

The endings of the three novels in *District of Columbia* show isolated individuals being bowled over by different kinds of political combinations. Their resistance to the abuse of power is a principled one, of the good old American sort, but deeply imbued with Dos Passos' sense of alienation. They are a remnant, fighting those who have taken over, seized control. There is no suggestion that they are, or could be, a saving remnant. The trilogy is quite undialectical politically. We are given no objective picture of the mixture of elements

in the New Deal, the genuinely American character of the compromises it often made, and the renewal of spirit it brought to so many individuals on so many levels of society. Nowhere in this trilogy or the one which preceded it does Dos Passos offer dramatic evidence of the continuing sources of democratic strength which enabled him to feel—as his war reporting revealed—so much better about America in the Pacific in 1944 than he had in France in 1918.

To see what literary difference a fascination with religion can make—even when it is skeptical or ironic—one need only compare this purely political and moral treatment with Thomas Mann's rich mythologizing of the New Deal in the Joseph series. Dos Passos always showed remarkably little interest in theological or metaphysical questions. When he edited a selection of Tom Paine's writings, he omitted the notorious attack on Biblical Christianity in Paine's *Appeal to Reason*. He left it out not because he disagreed with Paine but because he did not feel that this was a live or relevant issue.

For the three novels published between *The Grand Design* and *Midcentury,* Dos Passos drew on autobiographical materials he had used before. Of the three, *Chosen Country* (1951) has most substance. In his parents, his war experience, his travels in the Middle East, his involvement in something like the Sacco-Vanzetti case, Jay Pignatelli is a composite of the earlier autobiographical heroes. When stirred by patriotic emotion, he is like Tyler Spotswood, or the small boy in *U.S.A.*: "the yearning of a man who might have been a man without a country (Damn the United States: I never want to hear her name again) for the country of his choice that made him feel so proud and humble when he saw the striped flag fly." The end is even more sentimental. This time no one walks off alone down a concrete road. Jay is honeymooning in a cottage by the sea. "The waves breathed in the cove. 'Husband,' she said. 'Wife,' he said. The words made them bashful. They clung together against their bashfulness. 'Today we begin,' he said, 'to make . . .' 'This wilderness our home,' she said. The risen sun over the ocean shone in their faces." The best parts of the novel, which have the same evocative magic as the high points of *U.S.A.*, are five biographies of Americans of an earlier generation.

During the writing of *Chosen Country*, Dos Passos had remarried and was living on a portion of the old family farm in Virginia. His daughter Lucy, his only child, was born in 1951. His first wife had been killed in 1947 in an automobile accident in which Dos Passos was badly injured.

In contrast to *Chosen Country, The Great Days* (1958) is thoroughly negative and bitter. Once again a book starts with its hero at the top of a gangway, but now he is a man of fifty-nine, in a belted raincoat like a Graham Greene adventurer, going to meet a much younger woman for a holiday in Cuba. A once-famous journalist, he is sick of seeing himself in print. "Every time he publishes anything the critics tear down his poor old name." All he believed important about America he had put into *Blueprint for the Future,* a title suggesting *The Prospect before Us*, in which Dos Passos had made his proposals for the future. "Nobody read it. What's the use of writing things nobody reads?"

The journalist's romance is a failure and he is robbed of three thousand dollars, his total resources. While life deteriorates in Havana, he thinks back over his past, his wife's death, his troubles with his sons, his long relationship with a government leader who—especially in the way he dies—suggests Secretary of the Navy James Forrestal. The journalist has worked with him as Tyler Spotswood had worked with Chuck Crawford, but this official is an unselfish man who fears that the country will be outmaneuvered and destroyed by the Soviet Union. When he cannot convince others of the danger, he kills himself.

The journalist's reminiscences of the war and its aftermath are copied almost verbatim from the author's own previously published reportage. This is only one indication of Dos Passos' refusal to distance himself artistically from his material. In his uncomfortably personal tone, his emphasis on the hero's age and distinction and on the world's lack of appreciation, Dos Passos matches Hemingway's self-exposure in *Across the River and into the Trees*. He spares us one major embarrassment, though, in his realistic treatment of the love affair.

The preceding novel, *Most Likely to Succeed* (1954), is even less engaging. Many reviewers said it meant the final exhaustion of Dos Passos' talents. Its hero, a crude fellow named Jed Morris, has returned from adventures in Morocco to write proletarian dramas for the Craftsman's Theatre. After leftist politics and other troubles destroy the enterprise, the survivors move on from New York to fortune and power in Hollywood.

In both places Jed's dealings with the Communists are as confused and emotional as George F. Babbitt's with his fellow Rotarians. Though he is almost feeble-minded politically, Jed is chosen for important work by the Russian agent who directs the local party operations. When the Communists stop him in an act of human sympathy, he tries to resist, but his old comrades threaten to destroy him. He yields (lacking the courage of General Custer or Glenn Spotswood) in a scene of melodramatic humiliation.

The role of Communists in political and cultural affairs on the West Coast during this period has real historical interest because of the accusations made in later congressional inquiries. But Dos Passos is too impatient, just as he was in *Adventures of a Young Man,* to re-create the situation as it looked to some of the idealistic and extremely intelligent people involved in it. Once again, the love affairs are more convincing than the politics. Even the once popular television serial *I Led Three Lives* was a more serious study of Communist operations.

After these two minor novels, the scope and technique of *Midcentury* (1961) came as a surprise.

In style, selection, and explicitness, the biographical sketches are very like those in *U.S.A.* Labor leaders are most numerous, and Dos Passos shows his changed attitude toward military responsibility, if not toward war, by including two generals. There had been none in *1919.* The twenty-five Documentaries are soberer than the Newsreels of *U.S.A.,* with longer excerpts and more attention to science.

In the portraits, Dos Passos repeats what he had said in *District of Columbia* and *The Theme Is Freedom*: that America conducted the war and made the peace in a way that chiefly benefited the Communists. "People in America discovered that the war had been won," he writes, telling the story of Robert Oppenheimer, "not by their kind of democracy (where everybody tells everybody else what to do) but by 'people's democracy' where everybody does as he's told . . . can that be what the dogooding professors wanted?"

Robert La Follette, Jr., understood this while it was happening. "When secret agreements at Teheran, Yalta, Potsdam portended the loss of the peace young Bob tried to remind the Senate and the American people of the tragic results of the Peace of Versailles twenty-five years before." But he spoke to deaf ears, and ended his life a suicide.

Reporting the war in the Pacific, Dos Passos had felt a great life of spirit from living and talking with ordinary Americans who were tackling difficult jobs under strange circumstances and doing them well. He missed "the feeling of crazy adventure of the first world war," but he reports in *The Theme Is Freedom* that he came back with deep respect for the professionals of the army, navy, and marine corps.

His mood darkened as he reported the Nuremburg Trials. Though he spoke of the Nazi atrocities in *The Theme Is Freedom*, he gave more coverage to American misdeeds, the mass air bombings of civilians, the postwar mistreatment of the Germans, and our failure to check Russia's subjugation of many small nations formerly friendly to us. Dos Passos always had curiously little to say about naziism, perhaps because he feared communism so much more. During the war, when the Communists were busy entrenching themselves, "American liberals were too busy hating Hitler to see anything amiss." This bias makes him say in *Midcentury* that Senator Joseph McCarthy was "hounded to his grave by the same strange alliance, the same 'storm of smearing vilification and misrepresentation' that had caused the last La Follette to lose his seat in the Senate."

His mood darkened still further during the Korean war. In his *Midcentury* portrait of General Dean, the heroic prisoner, he is bitter about the younger Americans who surrendered in such numbers and behaved so shamefully while imprisoned. They were "the kids who'd been soaked in wartime prosperity while their elder brothers manned the amphibious landings and the desperate beachheads and the floating bases and the great air-strikes of World War II; raised on the gibblegabble of the radio between the family car and the corner drugstore and the Five and Ten. Nobody had ever told them anything except to get more and do less."

The very youngest generation comes off even worse. The last portrait, called "The Sinister Adolescents," sketches the short resentful life of James Dean and the commercially exploited cult his death started among teen-agers. "Kicks are big business: the sallow hucksters needle the nerves." In the final fiction narrative the disillusioned young nephew of a business leader, sounding like Holden Caulfield of *Catcher in the Rye,* tells how he started out on a spending spree with his uncle's credit card. Its title, "Tomorrow the Moon," recalls the fantastic flight which ended *The Garbage Man.*

Principally *Midcentury* is an attack on the kind of leadership given to labor unions by Harry Bridges, Dave Beck, Jimmy Hoffa, John L. Lewis, and even the Reuther brothers. Many of the incidents could have been drawn from evidence produced before Senator McClellan's Select Committee on Improper Activities in the Labor and Management Field.

Organized labor, with tough, shrewd, imperially ambitious leaders, gained power phenomenally in the favorable atmosphere of the New Deal and the war. At first, while business also prospered, no one seemed to care how this was done. Then complaints increased, and the Senate committee discovered "denial of the working man's most elementary rights, the underworld's encroachment on the world of daily bread, sluggings, shootings, embezzlement, thievery, gangups between employers and business agents, the shakedown, the syndicate, oppression, sabotage, terror." Seven sections of "Investigator's Notes" in *Midcentury* show such evidence being gathered, often from victims afraid to talk.

The longer stories are of men defeated while bucking the interests. Terry Bryant is forced out of union organizing because he won't let racketeers and politicians betray the workers. Col. Jasper Milliron is forced out of a huge milling company because he fights for a scientifically improved product. Terry Bryant finally gets his head bashed in, working for Jasper Milliron's son-in-law who is trying to save an independent taxicab company against an alliance of union gangsters, politicians, and financiers. Though the company has put up a glorious fight, it seems likely to slip into the hands of the same hissing Judge Lewin who was a party to Milliron's ouster. Lewin, who compares himself to Spinoza and Einstein, says that when his skills win him control of a corporation, "I have to consider it a problem in pure finance. I can't be bothered with what it takes or what it sells. I can't be distracted by worrying about administration, who gets fired from what job, all the grubby little lives involved. . . . I leave that sort of thing to my public relations men."

Quite separate is the life of Blackie Bowman told from a bed in a veterans' hospital. Blackie has been a Wobbly, a reader of Kropotkin, an admirer of Eugene Debs, a fighter in some of the great labor battles early in the century. By evoking Joe Hill, Centralia, and the McNamara case, Dos Passos recaptures the spirit of the Fainy McCreary and Ben Compton sequences in *U.S.A.* But the unnatural sentences in which Blackie tells his story make a far less flexible medium than the indirect discourse of *U.S.A.*

Presenting Blackie so sympathetically, Dos Passos means to show how consistent his own underlying principles have been. "It's mass organization that turns man into a louse," Blackie declares, echoing the sentiments which

John Andrews expressed at the end of *Three Soldiers*. The unions "opened up the Promised Land to dues paying members only, and then only so long as you keep your trap shut." The Communists took the hopes of mankind and shut them up in a concentration camp.

In *The Theme Is Freedom,* Dos Passos wrote that "If some of us who had seen the Abominable Snowmen, pointed out that the Communist Party was a greater danger to individual liberty than all the old power mad bankers and industrialists from hell to breakfast, we were promptly written down in the bad books as reactionaries." Radicals and liberals froze in their attitudes, and refused to see that the causes which had cost them so much could become vested interests too. The standards learned "trying to defend Sacco and Vanzetti and the Harlan miners, the Spanish republicans and a hundred other less publicized victims of oppression" must be applied impartially against threats to freedom from any quarter. The power of the bureaucrats and social engineers was far greater than that of J. P. Morgan, and equally liable to abuse.

Strangely mixing didacticism and despair, *Midcentury* attacks financiers and labor leaders with equal bitterness. Sounding at first like an illustrated editorial intended to provoke effective action against specific abuses, it shades off into old-fashioned pessimistic naturalism. Right-thinking individuals stand up for their principles, and without exception are defeated or destroyed. They have done the best they could, and the author—though he speaks out freely enough on all subjects including psychoanalysis—does not suggest how other people, perhaps working together, can do better. In the grimmest of postscripts he makes the situation seem hopeless.

Once more at the last a man trudges along a highway, though this time, his comfortable house nearby, he is walking a dog. He "drags beaten strides, drained of every thought but hatred." He declares his loathing for those who have risen to power by exploiting hatred, but his own disgust, which he permits to overwhelm all thought, goes unexamined.

The quarrel with others makes rhetoric, Yeats said; the quarrel with oneself makes art. The sole formal device which Dos Passos never revived after *U.S.A.* was the Camera Eye, with a uniquely sensitive and developing personality—his own—behind it. At the end of *Midcentury* he denounces men of power as passionately as he had cried out against the executors of Sacco and Vanzetti thirty years earlier. But there is no longer the positive passion for experience which once enabled him to live out so fully the lives of all his characters, good and bad. In *U.S.A.* he had understood the self-doomed, like Dick Savage and Charley Anderson, as well as those doomed from outside. With the weakening of this savoring of experience for its own sake came a deadening of his prose.

In his later work Dos Passos mentions good and evil frequently, and even speaks of God, but without the kind of thought which Berdiyaev and Niebuhr, Camus and Sartre, devoted during these same years to the problem of moral man in an immoral society. Dos Passos studied American history, but the character of the country eluded him because he had stopped trying to define himself as well.

Abuse of power and disrespect for the individual are not peculiar to America. The year after the war Dos Passos quoted in agreement this indignant statement from an army captain in Berlin: "With all our faults we have invented a social system by which the majority of men for the first time in human history get a break, and instead of being cocky about it we apologize."

The democratic strengths which made the captain proud are never dramatized in Dos

Passos' novels. His imagination seizes almost exclusively on lost causes, beaten men, sensitivity helpless before power. Clearly it is not America he is writing about, but the human condition. In the historical America, good as well as evil sometimes triumphs; civil liberties and democratic self-government somehow survive and grow.

Dos Passos as Quixote or Telemachus sets out on a search that could have no terminus in space. This is why his novels—thematically unresolved—so often conclude with the image of a man striding he knows not where. The inner needs of Dos Passos were mixed up with politics and patriotism in ways he never attempted fully to understand or to express. He kept blaming America for the fickleness of Dulcinea, for the many years Odysseus had to wander.

So long as his quest preserved its romantic spirit, the infusion of nostalgia and hope into politics made art possible. When romance faded, only bitter partisanship remained.

American writers have always been romantic, absorbed in experience, unwilling to master a difficult traditional wisdom. Growing old is a desperate business for them, and in the latter half of their careers they fail to find new sources of power and depth. This was notably true of the novelists of the twenties and thirties: Hemingway, Lewis, Fitzgerald, Wolfe, Anderson, Steinbeck, and O'Hara.

Dos Passos had been particularly at the mercy of changing historical moods, since he was at once their product, their chronicler, and their judge. When his own sense of alienation and historic commitment coincided—as during the writing of *U.S.A.*—with the profoundest feelings of the best minds of his generation, the result was one of the greatest works of the rich period between the wars.

Despite the weaknesses of the later novels, he gave us altogether—even more in what he implied than in what he stated—a challenging commentary on the quality of American experience. The idealism which made Dos Passos so critical of his nation is itself very American. So is the stubborn individualism and distrust of authority which led him to regard each new institutional development as a final threat to popular government. And yet the lost republic is always there to be lost again, and the leaders he attacks so bitterly are as traditionally American as his complaints against them. In ways that Dos Passos himself did not recognize, his fiction as a whole drew its strength from its subject, his chosen country.

Selected Bibliography

WORKS OF JOHN DOS PASSOS

One Man's Initiation—1917. London: Allen and Unwin, 1920.
Three Sodliers. New York: Doran, 1921.
A Pushcart at the Curb. New York: Doran, 1922.
Rosinante to the Road Again. New York: Doran, 1922.
Streets of Night. New York: Doran, 1923.
Manhattan Transfer. New York: Harper, 1925.
The Garbage Man. New York: Harper, 1926.
Orient Express. New York: Harper, 1927.
Facing the Chair: Story of the Americanization of Two Foreignborn Workmen. Boston: Sacco Vanzetti Defense Committee, 1927.
Airways, Inc. New York: Macaulay, 1928.
The 42nd Parallel. New York: Harper, 1930.
1919. New York: Harcourt, Brace, 1932.
In All Countries. New York: Harcourt, Brace, 1934.
Three Plays. New York: Harcourt, Brace, 1934. (Contains *The Garbage Man, Airways, Inc.,* and *Fortune Heights.*)
The Big Money. New York: Harcourt, Brace, 1936.

U.S.A. New York: Harcourt, Brace, 1937. (Comprises *The 42nd Parallel, 1919,* and *The Big Money,* together with the prologue "U.S.A." and the epilogue "Vag.")

Journeys between Wars. New York: Harcourt, Brace, 1938.

Adventures of a Young Man. New York: Harcourt, Brace, 1939.

The Living Thoughts of Tom Paine: Presented by John Dos Passos. New York: Longmans, Green, 1940.

The Ground We Stand On. New York: Harcourt, Brace, 1941.

Number One. Boston: Houghton Mifflin, 1943.

State of the Nation. Boston: Houghton Mifflin, 1944.

First Encounter. New York: Philosophical Library, 1945. (Reprint of *One Man's Initiation —1917,* with a new introduction by the author.)

Tour of Duty. Boston: Houghton Mifflin, 1946.

The Grand Design. Boston: Houghton Mifflin, 1949.

Life's Picture History of World War II. New York: Time, Inc., 1950.

The Prospect before Us. Boston: Houghton Mifflin, 1950.

Chosen Country. Boston: Houghton Mifflin, 1951.

District of Columbia. Boston: Houghton Mifflin, 1952. (Comprises *Adventures of a Young Man, Number One,* and *The Grand Design.*)

The Head and Heart of Thomas Jefferson. New York: Doubleday, 1954.

Most Likely to Succeed. Englewood Cliffs, N.J.: Prentice-Hall, 1954.

The Theme Is Freedom. New York: Dodd, Mead, 1956.

The Men Who Made the Nation. New York: Doubleday, 1957.

The Great Days. New York: Sagamore Press, 1958.

Prospects of a Golden Age. Englewood Cliffs, N.J.: Prentice-Hall, 1959.

Midcentury. Boston: Houghton Mifflin, 1961.

Mr. Wilson's War. New York: Doubleday, 1962.

Brazil on the Move. New York: Doubleday, 1963.

Occasions and Protests. New York: Regnery, 1964.

World in a Glass: A View of Our Century Selected from the Novels of John Dos Passos, with an introduction by Kenneth Lynn. Boston: Houghton Mifflin, 1966.

The Best Times: An Informal Memoir. New York: New American Library, 1966.

The Shackles of Power: Three Jeffersonian Decades. New York: Doubleday, 1966.

The Portugal Story. New York: Doubleday, 1969.

Easter Island. New York: Doubleday, 1971.

BIBLIOGRAPHY

Potter, Jack, *A Bibliography of John Dos Passos.* Chicago: Normandie House, 1950.

CRITICAL AND BIOGRAPHICAL STUDIES

Astre, Georges-Albert. *Thèmes et Structures dans l'oeuvre de John Dos Passos.* 2 vols. Paris: Lettres Modernes, 1956.

Belkind, Alan, ed. *Dos Passos, the Critics and the Writer's Intention.* Carbondale, Ill.: Southern Illinois University Press, 1972.

Brantley, J. D. *The Fiction of Dos Passos,* New York: Humanities Press, 1968.

Eastman, Max, and others. *John Dos Passos, An Appreciation.* New York: Prentice-Hall, 1954.

Gelfant, Blanche H. *The American City Novel.* Norman: University of Oklahoma Press, 1954. Pp. 133-74.

———. "The Search for Identity in the Novels of John Dos Passos," *PMLA,* 76:133–49 (March 1961).

Kazin, Alfred. *On Native Grounds.* New York: Reynal and Hitchcock, 1942. Pp. 341–59.

Sartre, Jean-Paul. "John Dos Passos and '1919,'" in *Literary and Philosophical Essays.* London: Rider, 1955. Pp. 88–96.

Wrenn, John H. *John Dos Passos.* New York: Twayne, 1961.

—ROBERT GORHAM DAVIS

T. S. Eliot
1888–1965

*I*N THE 1920s, T. S. Eliot's densely allusive style gained him an international reputation on the order of Albert Einstein's, but his fondness for European models and subjects prompted some of his compatriots to regard him as a turncoat to his country and to the artistic tradition of the new it had come to represent. Yet Eliot's allusiveness recalls a distinctively native tradition of self-consciousness that precedes the idea of America his critics invoked. Perhaps the most useful way to characterize Eliot, in fact, is as a New England writer burdened by religious questioning and riven by conflicts about internal and external authority. That he managed to transform this struggle into the mark of a modern sensibility says something both about the power of his writing and about the complexities of what we mean when we talk about modernist literature.

The first and probably the definitive questioning of Eliot's American qualities took place in the 1910s and 1920s and involved a dialogue between William Carlos Williams and Ezra Pound. Williams, a passionate admirer of Thoreau's concentration on the local and the here and now, was particularly offended by *The Waste Land* and the poems that preceded it, and lamented in his *Autobiography* that the publication of *The Waste Land* "wiped out our world. . . . Eliot returned us to the classroom just at the moment when I felt that we were on the point of an escape to matters much closer to the essence of a new art form" rooted in "locality. . . . To me especially it struck like a sardonic bullet. I felt at once that it had set me back twenty years."

But Williams' notion of American poetry did not go unchallenged even then. Ezra Pound replied to an earlier expression of Williams's sentiments in no uncertain terms:

> BALLS! My dear William. At what date did you join the ranks of the old ladies? . . . You can idealize [America] all you like but . . . . you have the advantage of arriving in the milieu with a fresh flood of Europe in your veins, Spanish, French, English, Danish. You had not the thin milk of New York and New England from the pap, and you can therefore keep the environment outside you, and decently objective.

AN AMERICAN POET

Pound's perception was acute. Whether we regard Eliot's literary self-consciousness, still unsettling, as the expression of an empowering tradition or a debilitating disease, it remains the distinctive trace of a New England sensibility, not a departure from it. Eliot himself recognized as much early on and caricatured himself in self-portraits in which he appears as a New Englander more comfortable in literature than in life—in his memorable phrase, a "Burbank with a Baedeker" on a permanent grand tour.

At the end of the twentieth century, Eliot's relationship with the past looked much more remarkable than his self-caricature or Pound's defense, and uncannily like that of Williams' principal American predecessor, Walt Whitman. Writing on contemporary poetry in July 1919 in the *Egoist*, for example, Eliot spoke of the way poetry affected him in erotic and occult terms that unmistakably recall the following from one of Whitman's "Calamus" poems, "Whoever You Are Holding Me Now in Hand":

Whoever you are holding me now in hand,
Without one thing all will be useless,
I give you fair warning before you attempt me
    further,
I am not what you supposed, but far different.

Who is he that would become my follower?
Who would sign himself a candidate for my
    affections?

The way is suspicious, the result uncertain, perhaps
    destructive,
You would have to give up all else, I alone would
    expect to be your sole and exclusive standard

"There is a close analogy," Eliot writes in the *Egoist*, "between the sort of experience which develops a man and the sort of experience that develops a writer." To write is to be touched by a relation

of profound kinship, or rather of a peculiar personal intimacy, with another, probably a dead author. It may overcome us suddenly, on first or after long acquaintance; it is certainly a crisis; and when a young writer is seized with his first passion of this sort he may be changed, metamorphosed almost, within a few weeks even, from a bundle of second-hand sentiments into a person. The imperative inti-

macy arouses for the first time a real, an unshakable confidence. That you possess this secret knowledge, this intimacy, with the dead man, that after few or many years or centuries you should have appeared, with this indubitable claim to distinction; who can penetrate at once the thick and dusty circumlocutions about his reputation, can call yourself alone his friend: it is something more than *encouragement* to you. It is a cause of development, like personal relations in life. Like personal intimacies in life, it may and probably will pass, but it will be ineffaceable. . . . The usefulness of such a passion . . . [is] various. For one thing it secures us against forced admiration. . . . We may not be great lovers; but if we had a genuine affair with a real poet of any degree we have acquired a monitor to avert us when we are not in love. . . . [For another] our friendship gives us an introduction to the society in which our friend moved; we learn its origins and its endings; we are broadened. We do not imitate, we are changed, and our work is the work of the changed man; we have not borrowed, we have been quickened, and we become bearers of a tradition.

It is as if, finally, "dead voices speak through the living voice"—a real "incarnation."

Eliot's account suggests something fundamental about the way his poetry compounds exquisite sensitivity to verbal nuance with uncommonly direct access to unconscious power. This was what Randall Jarrell had in mind in an essay entitled "Fifty Years of American Poetry" when he wrote that, far from being an over-intellectualized poet, Eliot managed to convey raw unconscious power. "From a psychoanalytic point of view," he suggested, Eliot was "far and away the most interesting poet of [the] century" and perhaps "one of the most subjective and daemonic poets who ever lived, the victim and helpless beneficiary of his own inexorable compulsions [and] obsessions."

Nor is the psychological power that Jarrell describes the only quality that safeguards Eliot's allusiveness from the whiff of the classroom Williams ascribed. If Eliot's verse (especially his early verse) is saturated with earlier poetry, it is also instinctively and programmatically suspicious of the claims of the writing it invokes. In part this is because from the time he was very young Eliot temperamentally questioned everything about himself. Indeed his truest sense of himself, like that of Lord Claverton, his alter ego in his 1959 play, *The Elder Statesman*, seems to have included the feeling that

> Some dissatisfaction
> With myself, I suspect, very deep within myself
> Has impelled me all my life to find justification
> Not so much to the world—first of all to myself.
> What is this self inside us, this silent observer,
> Severe and speechless critic, who can terrorise us
> And urge us on to futile activity,
> And in the end, judge us still more severely
> For the errors into which his own reproaches
>   drove us?

This self-distrust forms Eliot's literary style, generating a characteristic self-reflexive irony that his philosophical studies deepened into a principled and radical resistance to positives of many kinds—propositional, stylistic, and emotional. Early in the century the force of this irony helped define writing in English and, more generally, the sensibility of the modern mind. For it is related to fundamental twentieth-century paradigms of thought. (As in the work of Ludwig Wittgenstein, for instance, for whom, as Richard Shusterman reminds us, "doctrines of the radical indeterminacy of aesthetic concepts and the logical plurality and essential historicity of aesthetic judgment . . . work to undermine the charm and credibility of both deductive and inductive models of critical reasoning.") Eliot's irony conditions not only his characteristic tone but also the structural procedures of his narrative verse, producing the jumps and fragmentation that caused so many of his first readers to associate his work with jazz.

Eliot himself articulated his intellectual skepticism in specifically American terms. Reviewing Henry Adams' autobiography, *The Education of Henry Adams*, in the 1919 *Athenaeum*, he spoke of "the Boston doubt: a scepticism which is difficult to explain to those who are not born to it"—"a product, or a cause, or a concomitant, of Unitarianism" that "is not destructive, but it is dissolvent." And in examining Eliot's early life and writing, recent commentators (particularly Eric Sigg and Manju Jain) have pointed to peculiarly American contexts of his skepticism and of its poetic and intellectual products. Eliot's ironic attitudes were early associated with his membership in an American social elite in decline, and with the disdain of that elite for the forces of immigration and tolerance that were transforming the nation. From another perspective, both Eliot's religious leanings and his tendency to reformulate them in poetic terms derive, as his remarks about "the Boston doubt" suggest, from his family's Unitarian roots, and from the Unitarians' struggle to universalize traditional authority.

And yet Unitarian universalism, from the perspective of traditional New England Calvinism, seems inadequate, and behind Eliot's questioning of Unitarian universalism stands a substantial literary history that includes the critiques of Ralph Waldo Emerson in the fiction of Nathaniel Hawthorne and Henry James. Some if not all these issues played themselves out in the development of pragmatist philosophy at Harvard in what has been called the golden age of American philosophy, and as a graduate student in the discipline trained there at that moment, Eliot honed his skepticism in a climate that both encouraged radical thinking and disapproved of it when it overstepped the bounds of humanitarian meliorism.

BACKGROUND AND YOUTH

But such matters are better considered in relation to the particulars of Eliot's life. Thomas Stearns Eliot was born in Saint Louis, Missouri, the youngest member of a family that took pains to impress on him the importance of its history and achievement. His paternal grandfather, William Greenleaf Eliot, was distantly related to Henry Wadsworth Longfellow, John Greenleaf Whittier, and Herman Melville, and had been a protégé of William Ellery Channing, the dean of American Unitarianism. William Eliot graduated from Harvard Divinity School, then moved toward the frontier. He founded the Unitarian church in Saint Louis and soon became a pillar of the midwestern city's religious and civic life. He helped start the Academy of Science and Washington University (where he taught metaphysics) as well as Smith Academy for boys and the Mary Institute for girls. Because of William's ties to these schools, the Eliot family chose to remain in their urban Locust Street home long after the area had run down and their peers had moved to suburbs.

William Greenleaf Eliot dearly wanted his son to enter the clergy, but Henry Ware Eliot resisted. In 1865 (after his father had alienated a substantial part of his congregation by his Unionist loyalties), Henry arranged for a commission as lieutenant in the Union army, but the war ended before his commission arrived. He thereafter made a life in business, starting in wholesale grocery and going bankrupt manufacturing acetic acid. By the time Thomas Eliot was born, however, Henry was the prosperous president of the Hydraulic-Press Brick Company. Eliot's mother, Charlotte Champe Stearns Eliot, was a former teacher, an energetic social work volunteer at the Humanity Club of Saint Louis, and an amateur poet with a taste for Emerson. She augmented her husband's sense of duty and industry with an idealism and humanitarianism that T. S. Eliot resisted all his life.

Eliot was by far the youngest of seven children, born when his parents were secure in their mid-forties and his siblings were half grown. Afflicted with a congenital double hernia, he was in the constant eye of his mother and five older sisters, when he was not left in the care of an Irish nurse, Annie Dunne. Dunne sometimes took him with her to Catholic mass. In his youth, Eliot passed through the city's muddy streets and its exclusive drawing rooms. He attended Smith Academy until he was sixteen. The year he graduated he visited the 1904 Saint Louis World's Fair and was so taken with the display of native villages from around the world that he wrote short stories about primitive life for the Smith Academy Record. In 1905 he departed for a preparatory year at Milton Academy outside of Boston, prior to following his older brother, Henry, to Harvard.

Eliot's attending Harvard seems to have been a foregone conclusion. His father and mother, jealously guarding their connection to Boston's Unitarian establishment, brought the family back to Boston's North Shore every summer and in 1896 built a substantial house at Eastern Point in Gloucester. As a boy, Eliot foraged for crabs and became an accomplished sailor, trading the Mississippi in the warm months for the rocky shoals of Cape Ann. This seasonal migration deprived him of regional identity and reinforced his social alienation. Looking back in 1928, he wrote his friend, the English critic Herbert Read, that he had always wanted to write

an essay about the point of view of an American who wasn't an American, because he was born in the South and went to school in New England as a small boy with a nigger drawl, but who wasn't a southerner in the South because his people were northerners in a border state and looked down on all southerners and Virginians, and who so was never anything anywhere and who therefore felt himself to be more a Frenchman than an American and more an Englishman than a Frenchman and yet felt that the U.S.A. up to a hundred years ago was a family extension.

Beginning Harvard in the fall of 1906, Eliot impressed many classmates with his archness and his cosmopolitan social ease. Like his brother Henry before him, Eliot lived freshman year in a fashionable private dormitory in a posh neighborhood around Mt. Auburn Street known as the "gold coast." He joined a number of clubs, including the literary Signet. And he began a romantic attachment to Emily Hale, a refined Bostonian who once played Mrs. Elton opposite his Mr. Woodhouse in an amateur production of Jane Austen's *Emma.* Among his teachers, Eliot was drawn to the forceful moralizing of the scholar of world literature Irving Babbitt and the stylish skepticism of the philosopher and critic George Santayana, both of whom reinforced his distaste for the reform-minded, progressive university shaped by his cousin, Charles William Eliot, who was then in the final years of his long, distinguished presidency. His attitudes, however, did not prevent him from taking advantage of the elective system that President Eliot had introduced. As a freshman, his courses were so eclectic he soon wound up on academic probation. He recovered his academic standing and persisted in his studies, attaining a B.A. in an elective program best described as comparative literature in three years, and an M.A. in English literature in the fourth.

In December 1908 a book that Eliot found in the Harvard Union library changed his life: Arthur Symons' *The Symbolist Movement in Literature* introduced him to the poetry of Jules Laforgue. Laforgue's combination of ironic elegance and psychological nuance effected the literary communion with the dead Eliot describes above, convincing Eliot that he was a poet and giving him a voice. By 1909–1910 his vocation had been confirmed: he joined the board and was briefly secretary of Harvard's literary magazine, the *Advocate,* and he could recommend to his classmate William Tinckom-Fernandez the last word in French sophistication—the *vers libre* of Paul Fort and Francis Jammes. (Tinckom-Fernandez returned the favor by introducing Eliot to Francis Thompson's "Hound of Heaven" and John Davidson's "Thirty Bob a Week," poems Eliot took to heart, and to the verse of Ezra Pound, which Eliot had no time for.) At the *Advocate,* Eliot started a lifelong friendship with Conrad Aiken.

In May 1910 a suspected case of scarlet fever almost prevented Eliot's graduation. By that fall, though, he was well enough to undertake a postgraduate year in Paris, where he felt as if he was alive for the first time. (Lyndall Gordon, in *Eliot's Early Years,* notes that his handwriting even changed its shape.) He lived at 151 bis rue St. Jacques, close to the Sorbonne, and struck up a warm friendship with a fellow lodger, Jean Verdenal, the medical student who died in the battle of the Dardanelles and to whom Eliot dedicated "The Love Song of J. Alfred Prufrock." With Verdenal he entered the intellectual life of France, which Eliot later recalled, was then swirling around the figures of Émile Durkheim, Pierre Janet, Rémy de Gourmont, Pablo Picasso, and Henri Bergson. Eliot attended Bergson's lectures at the College de France and was temporarily converted to Bergson's philosophical interest in the progressive evolution of consciousness. Characteristic of a lifetime of conflicting attitudes, though, Eliot also gravitated toward the politically conservative (indeed monarchistic), neoclassical, and Catholic writing of Charles Maurras. Warring opposites, these enthusiasms worked together to foster a professional interest in philosophy and propelled Eliot back to a doctoral program at Harvard the next year.

INVENTIONS OF THE MARCH HARE

In 1910 and 1911 Eliot copied into a leather notebook he entitled "Inventions of the March Hare" the poems that would establish his reputation: "The Love Song of J. Alfred Prufrock," "Portrait of a Lady," "Preludes," and "Rhapsody on a Windy Night." Combining some of the robustness of Robert Browning's monologues with the incantatory elegance of symbolist verse, and compacting Laforgue's poetry of alienation with the moral earnestness of the "Boston doubt," these poems explore the subtleties of the unconscious with a caustic wit. Above all they express Henry James's lament that Americans living in the confines of their gentility and idealism never seem to live at all. Eliot's expression of this lament can be found in "The Love Song of J. Alfred Prufrock":

There will be time, there will be time
To prepare a face to meet the faces that you meet;
There will be time to murder and create,
And time for all the works and days of hands
That lift and drop a question on your plate;
Time for you and time for me,
And time yet for a hundred indecisions,
And for a hundred visions and revisions,
Before the taking of a toast and tea.

What universalizes the upper-class angst of these poems is Eliot's ability (as in the following extract from "Portrait of a Lady") to translate social claustrophobia into images of life and death, vitality and asphyxiation, and most interestingly into a verbal struggle for existence between fleeting moments of authentic expression and a conventional and suffocating rhetoric.

And I must borrow every changing shape
To find expression . . . dance, dance
Like a dancing bear,
Cry like a parrot, chatter like an ape.
Let us take the air, in a tobacco trance—

The combined effect of Eliot's early poems was unique and compelling and their assurance staggered contemporaries who were privileged to read them in manuscript. Conrad Aiken marvelled at "how sharp and complete and *sui generis* the whole thing was, from the outset. The *wholeness* is there, from the very beginning."

Eliot's youthful notebook, including some poems he never published, has recently been edited and annotated by Christopher Ricks. Ricks's annotations confirm Eliot's scattered remarks about his debt not only to Laforgue and Charles Baudelaire but also to the British poets of the 1890s who first began to explore the French symbolists—the group of writers including Stéphane Mallarmé, Paul Verlaine, and Arthur Rimbaud. To Ricks's account one must add Eliot's most interesting assessment of the situation in English letters at the time of his first composition. Writing in French in *La Nouvelle revue française* in May 1922, Eliot confessed that his generation of American poets owed its opportunity to an accident of literary history. The British poets of the 1890s, who had just succeeded in emancipating themselves from the worst insularities of Victorian poetry, died before they could fully exploit their French inheritance. Symbolism, with its appeal to the suggestive rather than to the explicit, its appeal to the unconscious, and its daring manipulation of syntax in the service of hermeticism was an untapped resource.

His own generation, he said, owed a special debt to Oscar Wilde, the most talented writer of that generation. For not only had Wilde showed them the way and then died, but the disgrace of his trial and subsequent imprisonment for homosexual offenses eliminated any influence his British friends had on English culture, and required their successors to disguise affiliations with aestheticism the public would probably never have accepted. Wilde's criticism, as collected in his book called *Intentions*, Eliot said, was the focus of a new movement, and the source of a genuine moral value—the indifference to worldly consequences—that might have revolutionized British literature in the 1890s, and would revolutionize it in the next generation. With Wilde's fall, the link of Eliot's generation to the tradition of fine writing in English represented by Ben Jonson, John Dryden, Samuel Johnson, Matthew Arnold, John Ruskin, and Walter Pater had been effaced, and remained to be reestablished by three literatures isolated by the break and rendered "provincial"— British, American, and Irish.

Though Eliot's notebook poems suggest only in part his involvement with British aestheticism, they do reveal crucial interests associated with the decadents (the group of late-nineteenth-century French and English writers) to which Eliot was unable himself to give poetic form in 1910–1911, but that would condition the poetic and intellectual preoccupations of the next part of his life. Among these was a fascination with insanity and unmoored perspective, like that in a suppressed section of "Prufrock" called "Prufrock's Perivigilium" (not published with the original edition of the poem but included in Ricks's edition):

> And when the dawn at length had realized itself
> And turned with a sense of nausea, to see what it
>   had stirred:
> The eyes and feet of men—
> I fumbled to the window to experience the world
> And to hear my Madness singing, sitting on the
>   kerbstone
> [A blind old drunken man who sings and mutters,
> With broken boot heels stained in many gutters]
> And as he sang the world began to fall apart . . .

GRADUATE STUDIES

In the fall of 1911 Eliot returned from France, and as part of his graduate studies in philosophy at Harvard began to examine border states of consciousness of many kinds, from insanity in Janet's studies of hysteria, to the "primitive mind" as it had been adumbrated by Durkheim and Lucien Lévy-Bruhl, to the literature of mystic vision, both Western and Eastern. (He took almost as many courses in Sanskrit and Hindu thought as he did in philosophy. He had, as Cleo McNelly Kearns points out, inherited this interest from Emerson, but he pursued it with a scholarly rigor that far surpassed the American poets of the previous century.)

Working in a faculty that included Santayana, William James, the visiting Bertrand Russell, and Josiah Royce, Eliot eventually undertook a dissertation on Bergson's neo-idealist critic F. H. Bradley and produced a searching philosophical critique of consciousness. Acute especially about the way interpretation constitutes and constructs mental objects and discourses, Eliot's philosophical work was highly critical of the platitudes of the nascent disciplines of pyschology and the social sciences. Using Bradley's skepticism to question vast areas of the contemporary intellectual landscape, he finally turned it even against its source, attacking especially Bradley's suggestion of the possibility of a synthesis or harmony of momentary perspectives.

It is hardly surprising, therefore, that much of his poetry from these years has to do with madness and disconnection. In a letter to Conrad Aiken in September 1914 he speaks of three years of worry and nothing good written since "Prufrock," but also shares this uncertainly hopeful thought: "It's interesting to cut yourself to pieces once in a while, and wait to see if the fragments will sprout." This is what he tried to do in a long fragmentary work ("the 'Descent from the Cross' or whatever I may call it"), part of which he sent to Aiken. This work was intended to include the sado-masochistic "Love Song of St. Sebastian":

> You would love me because I should have stran-
>   gled you
> And because of my infamy.
> And I should love you the more because I had
>   mangled you
> And because you were no longer beautiful
> To anyone but me.

"Then," he wrote Aiken, "there will be an Insane Section, and another love song (of a happier sort) and a recurring piece quite in the French style. . . . Then a mystical section—and a Fool-House section beginning

> Let us go to the masquerade and dance!
> I am going as St. John among the Rocks
> Attired in my underwear and socks . . ."

But Eliot was "disappointed" in the verses and wondered whether he "had better knock it off for a while." The stuff, he wrote Aiken in November 1914, seemed to him "strained and intellectual." "I know," he said, "the kind of verse I want, and I know that this isn't it, and I know why."

As John Mayer has pointed out in his 1989 work *T. S. Eliot's Silent Voices*, "The Descent from the Cross" with its associated poems (some of which were published in *Inventions of the March Hare* and some in *"The Waste Land": A Facsimile and Transcript*) represented an early staging of the great poems of the 1920s. Eliot's "descent" was a parody of the New Testament's, and the sequence described what Mayer calls "a parody hero engaged in a parody quest, his movement no longer physical and outward . . . but inward and psychic into the self and its nightmare world." For Eliot and for modern poetry, though, the important issue was not the subject but the treatment, with outrageous parody allowing Eliot to produce camp juxtapositions of wildly different tonalities. This was "cut[ting] yourself to pieces . . . and wait[ing] to see if the fragments will sprout" with a vengeance, but in 1914 it was, as Eliot said, still strained and intellectual. It lacked the disciplined representation of dramatic vignettes and ventriloquized voices that Eliot was soon to master. And beyond that it lacked a feeling for how to register and organize vision and voice as if extensions of a single sensibility.

ELIOT SETTLES IN ENGLAND

By 1914, when Eliot left on a traveling fellowship to Europe, he had persuaded a number of Harvard's philosophers to regard him as a potential colleague. However, as Manju Jain argues in *T. S. Eliot and American Philosophy*, his willingness to turn radical skepticism against the highminded humanitarianism of his colleagues alienated the department and would have cost him a position in it had he wanted one. Eliot spent the early summer

of 1914 at a seminar in Marburg, Germany, with plans to study in the fall at Merton College, Oxford, with Harold Joachim, F. H. Bradley's colleague and successor. The outbreak of war quickened his departure from Germany. In August he was in London with Conrad Aiken, and by September Aiken had shown Eliot's manuscript poems to Ezra Pound, who, not easily impressed, was won over. Pound called on Eliot in late September and wrote to Harriet Monroe, the editor of the Chicago-based *Poetry* magazine, that Eliot had "actually trained himself *and* modernized himself *on his own.*" Eliot and Pound initiated a collaboration that would change Anglo-American poetry, but not before Eliot put down deep English roots.

In early spring 1915 Eliot's old Milton Academy and Harvard friend Scofield Thayer (later editor of the *Dial),* also at Oxford (where Eliot had been since October 1914), introduced Eliot to Vivienne (also Vivien) Haigh-Wood, a dancer and a friend of Thayer's sister. Eliot was drawn instantly to Vivienne's exceptional frankness and charmed by her family's Hampstead polish. Abandoning twenty-five years of social tentativeness, on June 26, 1915, he married Vivienne on impulse at the Hampstead Register's Office. His parents were shocked, and then, when they learned of Vivienne's history of emotional and physical problems (and her associated history of taking opiates), profoundly disturbed. The marriage nearly caused a family break, but it also indelibly marked the beginning of Eliot's English life. Vivienne refused to cross the Atlantic in wartime, and Eliot took his place in literary London.

Eliot and his wife at first turned to Bertrand Russell, who shared with them both his London flat and his considerable social resources. Russell and Vivienne, however, became briefly involved, and the arrangement soured. Meanwhile Eliot tried desperately to support himself by secondary school teaching and with a heavy load of reviewing and extension lecturing. To placate his worried parents, he labored on with his Ph.D. thesis, "Experience and the Objects of Knowledge in the Philosophy of F. H. Bradley." (Eliot finished it in April 1916, but did not receive his degree because he was reluctant to undertake the trip to Massachusetts required for a thesis defense.) As yet one more stimulating but taxing activity, he became literary editor of the avant-garde magazine the *Egoist.* Then in spring 1917 he found steady employment; his knowledge of several languages qualified him for a job in the foreign section of Lloyds Bank, where he evaluated a broad range of continental documents. The job gave him the financial security he needed to turn back to poetry, and in 1917 he received an enormous boost from the publication of his first book, *Prufrock and Other Observations*, printed by the *Egoist* with the silent financial support of Ezra and Dorothy Pound.

For a struggling young American, Eliot soon acquired extraordinary access into British intellectual life. With Russell's help he was invited to country house weekends where visitors ranged from political figures like Herbert Henry Asquith to a constellation of writers, artists, and philosophers from the influential Bloomsbury group that included such figures as Virginia Woolf, Lytton Strachey, and E. M. Forster. At the same time Pound facilitated Eliot's entry into the international avant-garde, where Eliot mixed with the aging Irish poet William Butler Yeats, the English painter and novelist Wyndham Lewis, and the Italian futurist writer Tommaso Marinetti. More accomplished than Pound in the manners of the drawing-room, Eliot gained a reputation in the world of belles lettres as an observer who could shrewdly judge both accepted and experimental art from a platform of apparently enormous learning. It did not hurt that he calculated his interventions carefully, publishing only what was of first quality among his work and creating around himself an

aura of mystery. In 1920 he collected a second slim volume of verse (*Poems*) and a volume of criticism (*The Sacred Wood*). Both displayed a winning combination of erudition and jazzy bravura, and both built upon the understated discipline of a decade of philosophical seriousness. Eliot was meanwhile proofreading the *Egoist's* serial publication of Joyce's *Ulysses* and, with Pound's urging, starting to think of himself as part of an international movement in experimental art and literature.

Especially in *The Sacred Wood*, Eliot took care to cover over his roots. The volume was originally conceived as a mixture of criticism and poetry under the title of "The Art of Poetry" and was intended as the expression of an American poet-critic aimed at an American audience. Eliot wrote in a July 1919 letter to the lawyer and patron John Quinn, who was attempting to place the book in New York, that he believed it "appropriate" to showcase the review of Henry Adams' *Education* and another article on American literature he had written for the *Athenaeum,* and offered that Adams was "a type that I *ought* to know better than any other." But the volume was rejected first by Knopf and then by Boni and Liveright and John Lane. In revising it for a British press Eliot chose to emphasize abstract literary categories like "The Perfect Critic" rather than the cultural and moral categories that had characterized his recent articles on Adams, Henry James, and Nathaniel Hawthorne. He also strategically placed himself in a context of European artistic endeavor. In "Tradition and the Individual Talent," for example, he famously admonishes the aspiring writer to develop a "historical sense" that will compel him to write "not merely with his own generation in his bones, but with a feeling that the whole of the literature of Europe from Homer and within it the whole of the literature of his own country has a simultaneous existence and composes a simultaneous order." The original, intended venue of Eliot's first collection of criticism would in contrast have sharply outlined his own social and intellectual setting and would have gone a long way toward clarifying the American background of his poetry from "Prufrock" to *The Waste Land* (1922).

Yet if Eliot was about to persuade the London literary world of his cosmopolitanism with the publication of *The Sacred Wood*, circumstances contrived to drive him inward and back as well. Eliot's father died in January 1919, producing a paroxysm of guilt in the son who had hoped he would have time to heal the bad feelings caused by his marriage and emigration. At the same time Vivienne's emotional and physical health deteriorated, and the financial and emotional strain of her condition took its toll. After an extended visit in the summer of 1921 from his mother and his sister Marion, Eliot suffered a nervous collapse and, on his physician's advice, took a three month's rest cure, first on the British seacoast at Margate and then at a sanatorium at Lausanne recommended by Bertrand Russell's friend Ottoline Morrell.

THE WASTE LAND

Whether because of the breakdown or the long-needed rest it imposed, Eliot broke through the limitations he had felt since 1911 and completed the long poem that he had envisioned in 1914 and had begun in earnest in 1919. Assembled out of dramatic vignettes based on Eliot's London life, *The Waste Land*'s extraordinary intensity stems from a sudden fusing of diverse materials into a rhythmic whole of great skill and daring. Though from the 1930s onward it would be forced into the mold of an academic set-piece on the order of Milton's "Lycidas," *The Waste Land* was at first correctly perceived as a work of jazz-like syncopation. His friend Conrad Aiken insisted that Eliot's "allusive matter" was important primarily

for its private "emotional value" and described the whole as "a powerful, melancholy tone-poem"— a work like 1920s jazz that was essentially iconoclastic and provocative.

Aiken's intuition is confirmed by the opening of *The Waste Land*'s third section, "The Fire Sermon," which demonstrates how inappropriate it is to call Eliot's allusiveness imitative. Here it is clear that for Eliot literary borrowings represent sites at which eruptions of identification from below the level of one's own voice struggle for authenticity with the clichéd rhetoric of the quotidian self. In *The Waste Land*, Eliot's composite narrator is intensely aware of the literariness, the rhetorical quality, of his every utterance. Much of the poem's characteristic irony and punch comes from this self-consciousness. As in not only Eliot's own experience but also the fictional lives of Prufrock, Gerontion, and his other dramatic figures, one of the terrors of the narrator of *The Waste Land* is that he has forfeited life to books, and is trapped in ways of thinking and feeling acquired through convention. To use the bitter phrases of Eliot's essays contemporary with *The Waste Land*, his emotional life is a terminal victim of "the pathology of rhetoric" and the "pastness of the past." And so in the opening of "The Fire Sermon," the horrors of Eliot's vision are compounded by a self-consciousness that shadows every attempted escape from solipsism into the imaginative richness of poetry.

In the following passage, every allusion is set off by implied quotation marks and so renders a self-consciousness on the part of the speaker that poetry is only literature and that to quote poetry is less to express genuine feeling than to sink deeper into solipsism:

The river's tent is broken: the last fingers of leaf
Clutch and sink into the wet bank. The wind
Crosses the brown land, unheard. The nymphs are
    departed.
Sweet Thames, run softly, till I end my song.
The river bears no empty bottles, sandwich papers,

Silk handkerchiefs, cardboard boxes, cigarette ends
Or other testimony of summer nights. The nymphs
   are departed.
And their friends, the loitering heirs of city
   directors;
Departed, have left no addresses.
By the waters of Leman I sat down and wept . . .
Sweet Thames, run softly till I end my song,
Sweet Thames, run softly, for I speak not loud or
   long.
But at my back in a cold blast I hear
The rattle of the bones, and chuckle spread from
   ear to ear.
A rat crept softly through the vegetation
Dragging its slimy belly on the bank
While I was fishing in the dull canal
On a winter evening round behind the gashouse
Musing upon the king my brother's wreck
And on the king my father's death before him.
White bodies naked on the low damp ground
And bones cast in a little low dry garret,
Rattled by the rat's foot only, year to year.
But at my back from time to time I hear
The sound of horns and motors, which shall bring
Sweeney to Mrs. Porter in the spring.
O the moon shone bright on Mrs. Porter
And on her daughter
They wash their feet in soda water
Et O ces voix d'enfants, chantant dans la coupole!

These lines take their dominant tone from a series of surrealistic images in which subconscious
anxiety, as in a bad dream or a psychotic delusion,
is projected onto human and nonhuman objects.
In them, emotional fantasies, sometimes of self-
loathing, extend through a series of unconnected
images in a medium where ego integration seems
to be nonexistent. In synecdochic progression, a
river, falling leaves, the brown land, bones, a rat,
Ferdinand, his brother and his father (ll. 19–20
above, alluding to *The Tempest*), Mrs. Porter and
her daughter all become extensions of a whole
(but not continuous) state of anxiety. Eliot's narrator projects his feelings of isolation, vanished
protection, and loss first onto the river, whose tent
of leaves is "broken" (the inappropriately violent
adjective emphasizes the feeling of grief behind

the loss), and then onto the falling leaves, which
animistically have fingers that "clutch" for support as they sink into decomposition and oblivion.
Then defenselessness becomes a shrinking from
attack as the leaves fade into the brown land,
"crossed" by the wind. (Ten lines hence the
crossing wind will become a "cold blast" rattling
sensitive bones, and, metamorphosed, the insubstantial malevolence of a "chuckle spread from
ear to ear.") Still later, after an interlude of deep-
seated loss, isolation turns into self-disgust as the
narrator projects himself onto a rat whose belly
creeps softly and loathsomely through the vegetation. (Both rat and vegetation are extensions of
the decomposing leaves.) The rat's living body
merges with a corpse's, and the narrator appre-
hends himself first as rotting and sodden flesh,
feeling "naked on the low damp ground," and then
as dry bones, rattled by the rat's foot as he was rattled before by the cold wind.

But the opening of "The Fire Sermon" is not
simply an English version of the kind of French
symbolist poetry that uses images to express the
ambivalence of the subconscious mind. Eliot's
poetry is self-dramatizing. In the way it echoes
literature of the past and in its self-conscious use
of elevated or colloquial language, it dramatizes
a Prufrockian sensibility with a power and subtlety
unavailable to the Eliot of 1911. In the passage
we are considering, this sensibility is caught between two double binds: a yearning for the vitality of common life combined with a revulsion
from its vulgarity, and an inclination toward
poetry combined with a horror of literature. This
vacillation, superimposed over the poetry's *progression d'effets*, brings the world of unconscious
impulse into contact with the humanized world of
language. In "The Fire Sermon," this drama begins
as the literary word "nymphs" emerges from a series of more or less pure images. As it unfolds, the
phrase "the nymphs are departed" suggests Eliot's
desire to recuperate his lost sense of fullness in a
world of pastoral poetry, and for a moment Eliot

appropriates Edmund Spenser's voice: "Sweet Thames, run softly, till I end my song."

The immediate result is a disgust with modern life. Hence the following three lines, where that disgust can be heard in a series of jolting colloquialisms. But both Eliot's poetic nostalgia and his disgust with the quotidian soften in the ninth line: there is real sorrow in the speaker's statement that the "nymphs" and their vulgar friends have deserted him—a sorrow sounded in the repetition of "departed" twice in two lines. When the speaker reassumes the linguistic personae of the past in the glissando of the next three lines, therefore, it strikes us as a gesture taken faute de mieux. That is, we sense by this point that Eliot's speaker has some awareness that the great phrases of the past are as unreal as they are beautiful. As his reminiscence of Spenser's "Prothalamion" sounds, we detect a note of self-consciousness in the nostalgia, as if the voice inhabiting the lines were feeling its own inauthenticity. When yet a third quotation is added, to the Psalms and again to Spenser, this discomfort explodes in mid-flight. "But at my back," the speaker begins, and we expect to hear the rest of Andrew Marvell's immortal lines: "But at my back I always hear / Time's wingéd chariot hurrying near." Instead, the feeling of desolation that had called up the line swells out into bitterness: even the cherished texts of the past cannot charm away the bleak realities of life. This realization shatters Eliot's poetic continuity, and causes him to interrupt Marvell's lines with a sardonic assertion of the primacy of the here and now ("the rattle of the bones, and chuckle spread from ear to ear"). This tune, like Mrs. Porter's, is not Spenserian and its leering swell only mocks. At which point the last line, from Paul Verlaine, combines the highest reaches of eloquence with an icy rejection of eloquence itself.

If Williams is right and this is poetry of the classroom, it must also be said that the classroom belongs in the kind of American school in which student back talk abounds. No less than Emerson

in *The American Scholar* or Thoreau in the opening of *Walden*, Eliot here seems only able to respect that part of the past that genuinely comes alive in the present. And when it does, as for example in passages in which Dante seems to speak through Eliot's voice ("I had not thought death had undone so many"), one feels an uncanny power that has more to do with relations with the dead than with imitations of previous masters.

AMERICAN RESONANCES

Moreover, the situations of *The Waste Land* are no less American than Eliot's characteristic attitudes and procedures. The poem presents a number of circumstances in which an Emerson-like consciousness, savoring its own transcendental insight, blunders into the web of human relations and is then shocked awake by the evil produced by withdrawing from a relationship it had entered half aware. This situation Eliot once described (in an essay on Thomas Middleton's *Changeling*) as "the tragedy of the not naturally bad but . . . undeveloped nature . . . suddenly trapped in the inexorable toils of morality . . . and forced to take the consequences of an act which it had planned light-heartedly."

From "Portrait of a Lady" to the stage play *The Family Reunion* (1939) and beyond, Eliot makes such situations his subject. As his youthful letters to Conrad Aiken suggest, he considered himself aloof, a cold observer of others, but a man who by that very condition understood the secret heart of humanity. His stance in *Prufrock and Other Observations* recalls Hawthorne's comment early in his career (in "Sights from a Steeple") that "the most desirable mode of existence might be that of a spiritualized Paul Pry, hovering invisible round man and woman, witnessing their deeds, searching into their hearts, borrowing brightness from their felicity and shade from their sorrow, and retaining no emotion peculiar to himself." And the self-disgust that pervades Eliot's observer's voice—most striking perhaps in "La Figlia che Piange"—resonates with Hawthorne's own ambivalent identifications with Chillingworth in *The Scarlet Letter* or Holgrave in *The House of the Seven Gables* or Coverdale in *The Blithedale Romance* or Kenyon in *The Marble Faun*.

But Eliot's most important affinities with Hawthorne emerge in *The Waste Land*, where his representations of criminal-clairvoyant and observer-alien converge. The poem illustrates what Eliot meant when he said in a 1918 essay called "The Hawthorne Aspect [of Henry James]" that in Hawthorne character is always "the relation of two or more persons to each other." In the poem's different voices, we hear not solitaries but people striving for life's feast of relation, only to fall instead into ghoulish patterns of victim and victimizer. And the central observer, personified as Ovid's Tiresias, presents us with the archetype of these failed relations—a figure implicated in the situations he perceives and menaced by the truths they threaten to impart.

For the most part oblivious to the American resonances of these themes, postwar Britain claimed *The Waste Land* as its own. Pound, who helped pare and sharpen the poem when Eliot stopped in Paris on his way to and from Lausanne, praised it with a godparent's fervor not as an American but as a modern achievement. It did not hurt that 1922 also saw the long-heralded publication of *Ulysses*, or that Eliot in 1923 linked himself and Joyce with Einstein in the public mind in an essay entitled "*Ulysses*, Order and Myth." Meteorically, Eliot, Joyce, and to a lesser extent Pound were joined in a single glow—each nearly as notorious as Picasso.

CLASSICIST, ROYALIST, ANGLO-CATHOLIC

The masterstroke of Eliot's career was to parlay the international success of *The Waste Land* by means of an equally ambitious (and equally inter-nationalist) publication of a different kind. With Jacques Rivière's *La Nouvelle revue française* in mind, in 1922 Eliot jumped at an offer from Lady Mary Rothermere, wife of the publisher of the *Daily Mail*, to edit a high-profile literary journal. The first number of the *Criterion* appeared in October 1922. Like *The Waste Land*, it took the whole of European culture in its sights. As the *Criterion*'s editorial voice Eliot was placed at the center of first the London and then the Continental literary scene.

In 1923 Eliot, however, was too consumed by domestic anxiety to appreciate his success. In 1923 Vivienne nearly died, and Eliot, in despair, came close to a second breakdown. The following two years were almost as bad, and Eliot, disabled by his desperation was prevented from further exploration of his psychological situation, writing his friend, the English poet and critic Richard Aldington, that "*The Waste Land* . . . is a thing of the past . . . and I am now feeling toward a new form and style." One result was "The Hollow Men" (1925), concerned, as Eliot said about Dante, with "the salvation of the soul" rather than for human beings "as 'personalities' ":

> Those who have crossed
> With direct eyes, to death's other Kingdom
> Remember us—if at all—not as lost
> Violent souls, but only
> As the hollow men
> The stuffed men.

In 1925, Eliot's material situation was relieved by a lucky chance that enabled him to at least escape from the demands of his job at the bank. Geoffrey Faber, of the new publishing firm of Faber and Gwyer (later Faber and Faber), saw the advantages of Eliot's dual expertise in business and letters and recruited him as literary editor.

At about the same time, Eliot reached out for religious support. Having long found his family's Unitarianism unsatisfying, he turned to the Anglican church. The seeds of his faith might have already been obvious in "The Hollow Men," but the poem was read as a sequel to *The Waste Land*'s philosophical despair when it first appeared in *Poems, 1909–1925* (1925). Thus few followers were prepared for Eliot's baptism into the Church of England in June 1927. And so, within five years of his avant-garde success, Eliot provoked a second storm. The furor grew in November 1927 when Eliot took British citizenship and again in 1928 when he collected a group of politically conservative essays under the title of *For Lancelot Andrewes* and prefaced them with a declaration that he considered himself "classicist in literature, royalist in politics, and Anglo-Catholic in religion."

Eliot's poetry now addressed explicitly religious situations. In the late 1920s he published a series of shorter poems in the Faber "Ariel" series— short pieces issued in pamphlet form within striking modern covers. These included "Journey of the Magi" (1927), "A Song for Simeon" (1928), "Animula" (1929), "Marina" (1930), and "Triumphal March" (1931). Steeped in Eliot's study of Dante and the late Shakespeare, all these meditate on spiritual growth and anticipate the longer and more celebrated *Ash-Wednesday* (1930), a dialogue of self and soul:

> Because I do not hope to turn again
> Because I do not hope
> Because I do not hope to turn
> Desiring this man's gift and that man's scope
> I no longer strive to strive towards such things
> (Why should the agèd eagle stretch its wings?)
> Why should I mourn
> The vanished power of the usual reign?

"Journey of the Magi" and "A Song for Simeon," Browningesque dramatic monologues, speak to Eliot's desire, pronounced since 1922, to exchange the symbolist fluidity of the psychological lyric for a more traditional dramatic form:

> 'A cold coming we had of it,
> Just the worst time of the year
> For a journey, and such a long journey:
> The ways deep and the weather sharp,
> The very dead of winter.'
> And the camels galled, sore-footed, refractory,
> Lying down in the melting snow.
>
> ("Journey of the Magi")

KINDS OF DRAMA

Eliot spent much of the last half of his career attempting one kind of drama or another, with an idea of reaching (and bringing together) a large and varied audience. As early as 1923 he had written parts of an experimental and striking jazz play, *Sweeney Agonistes*, never finished but published in fragments in 1932 and performed by actors in masks by London's Group Theatre in 1934. The play contains some of Eliot's most striking lines, and perhaps his most explicit statement of the recurrent situations of *The Waste Land*:

> I knew a man once did a girl in
> Any man might do a girl in
> Any man has to, needs to, wants to
> Once in a lifetime, do a girl in
> . . . .
> He didn't know if he was alive
>   and the girl was dead
> He didn't know if the girl was alive
>   and he was dead
> He didn't know if they both were alive
>   or both were dead
> If he was alive then the milkman wasn't
>   and the rent-collector wasn't
> And if they were alive then he was dead.
> . . . .
> When you're alone like he was alone
> You're either or neither
> I tell you again it don't apply
> Death or life or life or death.

Some critics consider Eliot's decision to pursue West End drama rather than to follow up the jazz idiom of *Sweeney Agonistes* the biggest mistake of his career. To Eliot, however, the development was a natural and inevitable part of the public duties of his new spiritual life. In early 1934 he composed a church pageant with accompanying choruses entitled *The Rock*, performed in May and June 1934 at Sadler's Wells. Almost immediately following, Bishop Bell commissioned a church drama having to do with Canterbury Cathedral. The play, entitled *Murder in the Cathedral*, was performed in the Chapter House at Canterbury in June 1935 and was moved to the Mercury Theatre at Notting Hill Gate in November and eventually to the Old Vic. At its best, the dramatic poetry of *Murder in the Cathedral* incorporates the fraught tensions of self-examination in the rhythms of public speech:

> You know and do not know, what it is to act or
>   suffer.
> You know and do not know, that acting is suffer-
>   ing,
> And suffering action. Neither does the actor suffer
> Nor the patient act. But both are fixed
> In an eternal action, an eternal patience

In the plays that he wrote starting in the late 1930s, Eliot attempted to conflate a drama of spiritual crisis with a Noel Coward-inspired treatment of social manners. Though Eliot based *The Family Reunion* on the plot of Aeschylus' *Eumenides*, he designed it to tell a story of Christian redemption. The play opened in the West End in March 1939 and closed to mixed reviews five weeks later. Eliot was disheartened, but after World War II he fashioned more popular (though less powerful) combinations of the same elements to much greater success. *The Cocktail Party*, with a cast that included Alec Guinness, opened to a warm critical reception at the Edinburgh Festival in August 1949 and enjoyed a popular success starting on Broadway in January 1950. Eliot's last two plays were more labored and fared less well. *The Confidential Clerk* had a respectable run at the Lyric Theatre in London in September 1953, and *The Elder Statesman* premiered at the Edinburgh Festival in August 1958 and closed after a luke-warm run in London in the fall.

FOUR QUARTETS

Eliot's reputation as a poet and man of letters, increasing incrementally from the mid 1920s, advanced and far outstripped his theatrical success. As early as 1926 he had delivered the prestigious Clark Lectures at Cambridge University (published posthumously in 1993 as *The Varieties of Metaphysical Poetry*), followed in 1932–1933 by the Norton Lectures at Harvard (published in 1933 as *The Use of Poetry and the Use of Criticism*). Thereafter he won just about every honor the academy or the literary world had to offer. In 1948 Eliot received the Nobel Prize for literature during a fellowship stay at the Princeton Institute for Advanced Study. By 1950, his authority had reached a level that seemed comparable in English writing to figures like Samuel Johnson or Samuel Taylor Coleridge.

The lasting achievement of the second half of Eliot's career—a poetry of introspective self-accusation—contrasted, however with his swelling celebrity. After 1925 Eliot's marriage steadily deteriorated, making his public success hollow. During his Norton year at Harvard he separated from Vivienne, but would not consider divorce because of his Anglican beliefs. For most of the 1930s he secluded himself from Vivienne's often histrionic attempts to embarrass him into a reconciliation and made an anguished attempt to order his life upon his editorial duties at Faber and the *Criterion* and around work at his Kensington church. He also reestablished communication with Emily Hale, especially after 1934, when she began summering with relatives in the Cotswolds.

Out of an experience that inspired feelings of 'what might have been' associated with their visit to an abandoned great house, Eliot composed "Burnt Norton," which was published as the last poem in his *Collected Poems, 1909–1935*. With its combination of symbolist indirection and meditative gravity, "Burnt Norton" gave Eliot the model for another decade of major verse. In its first movement, the poem questioned the familiar through riddling negations and reaching for (and finally attaining) a hold on a mysterious reality by a semantic, syntactic, and prosodic mastery Eliot would never thereafter surpass:

> What might have been is an abstraction
> Remaining a perpetual possibility
> Only in a world of speculation.
> What might have been and what has been
> Point to one end, which is always present.
> Footfalls echo in the memory
> Down the passage which we did not take
> Towards the door we never opened
> Into the rose-garden. My words echo
> Thus, in your mind.

In 1938 Vivienne Eliot was committed to Northumberland House, a mental hospital north of London. In 1939, with World War II impending, the *Criterion*, which had occupied itself with the deepening political crisis of Europe, ceased publication. During the blitz Eliot served as an air raid warden, but spent long weekends as a guest with friends in the country near Guildford. In these circumstances he wrote three more poems, each more somber than the last, patterned on the voice and five-part structure of "Burnt Norton." "East Coker" was published at Easter 1940 and took its title from the village that Eliot's ancestor Andrew Eliot had departed from for America in the seventeenth century. (Eliot had visited East Coker in 1937.) "The Dry Salvages," published in 1941, reverted to Eliot's experience as a boy sailing on the Mississippi and on the Massachusetts coast. Its

title refers to a set of dangerously hidden rocks near Cape Ann. "Little Gidding" was published in 1942 and had a less private subject suitable to its larger ambitions. Little Gidding, near Cambridge, had been the site of an Anglican religious community that maintained a perilous existence for the first part of the English civil war. Paired with Eliot's experience walking the blazing streets of London during World War II, the community of Little Gidding inspired an extended meditation on the subject of the individual's duties in a world of human suffering. Its centerpiece was a sustained homage to Dante written in a form of terza rima dramatizing Eliot's meeting with a "familiar compound ghost" he associates with Yeats and with Swift.

Its effect is stunning, mesmerizing, and, unobserved by its first readers, it represents a culminating instance of the experience Eliot alludes to in the passage from the *Egoist* from more than twenty years previous, in which writing poetry approximates a submission of body and soul to the restless spirits of the dead:

> So I assumed a double part, and cried
> And heard another's voice cry: 'What! are *you* here?'.
> Although we were not. I was still the same,
> Knowing myself yet being someone other—
> And he a face still forming; yet the words sufficed
> To compel the recognition they preceded.
> And so, compliant to the common wind,
> Too strange to each other for misunderstanding,
> In concord at this intersection time
> Of meeting nowhere, no before and after,
> We trod the pavement in a dead patrol.

Four Quartets (1943), as the suite of four poems was entitled, for a period displaced *The Waste Land* as Eliot's most celebrated work. The British public especially responded to the topical references in the wartime poems and to the tone of Eliot's public meditation on a common disaster. Eliot's longtime readers, however, were more reticent. Some, notably F. R. Leavis, praised the philosophical suppleness of Eliot's syntax, but distrusted his swerve from a rigorously private voice.

A SUMMING UP

Eliot wrote no more major poetry after the war, turning entirely to his plays and to literary essays, the most important of which revisited the French symbolists and the development of language in twentieth-century poetry. After Vivienne died in January 1947, Eliot led a protected life as a flatmate of the critic John Hayward. In January 1957 he married his secretary Valerie Fletcher and attained a degree of contentedness that had eluded him all his life. He died on January 4, 1965, and, following his instructions, his ashes were interred in the Church of Saint Michael in East Coker. A commemorative plaque on the church wall bears his chosen epitaph—lines chosen from *Four Quartets*: "In my beginning is my end." "In my end is my beginning."

At century's end, Eliot's reputation stood lower than at any time since 1922. Frequently criticized (as he himself—perhaps just as unfairly—had criticized Milton) for a deadening neoclassicism, Eliot in the eyes of post-structuralist critics is guilty of far worse. Suspicious of his conservative religious and political convictions, readers have reacted with increasing impatience to his assertions of authority—obvious in *Four Quartets* and implicit in the earlier poetry. The result, amplified by the intermittent rediscovery of Eliot's occasional anti-Semitic rhetoric, has been a progressive downward revision of his once towering reputation and an attack on his sophisticated irony from the position of a supposedly more sophisticated postmodernism. Thus Paul de Man (whose own wartime anti-Semitism, discovered after his criticism of Eliot, complicated the issue) in *Blindness and Insight* reduced Eliot's subject to a "nostalgia for

immediate revelation." De Man's comments, reinforced by the influential judgments of Harold Bloom ("anyone adopting the profession of teaching literature in the early 1950s entered a discipline virtually enslaved . . . by the entire span of [Eliot's] preferences and prejudices") and of Terry Eagleton (who in *Criticism and Ideology* calls Eliot's modernist fragmentation simply a disguise for "totalising mythological forms"), have become staples of postmodernist criticism, and Eliot has acquired the status of a "bad eminence" (Bloom's term) on the contemporary scene.

However, multivarious tributes from practicing poets of many schools during the Eliot centenary year of 1988 indicate that at least some of the prevailing negative reaction has to do with the continuing intimidation of Eliot's poetic voice. In a period less engaged with politics and ideology than the 1980s and 1990s, the lasting strengths of his poetic technique will likely reassert themselves. Already the strong affinities of Eliot's post-symbolist style with such influential poets as Wallace Stevens (Eliot's contemporary at Harvard and a fellow student of George Santayana) have been reassessed, as has the tough philosophical skepticism of his prose. A master of poetic dissonance and poetic syntax, a poet who shuddered to repeat himself, a dramatist of the terrors of the inner life (and of the evasions of conscience), Eliot remains one of the twentieth century's major poets. And, as he himself affirmed at the end of his life, in a 1960 address entitled "The Influence of Landscape upon the Poet," his success cannot be dissociated from his New England origins. Acknowledging the Emerson-Thoreau Award and membership in the American Academy of Arts and Letters, Eliot said he had been forced to "as[k] myself whether I had any title to be a New England poet—as is my elder contemporary Robert Frost, and as is my junior contemporary Robert Lowell." And disarmingly—but firmly—he replied: "I think I have."

Selected Bibliography

WORKS OF T. S. ELIOT

POETRY AND PLAYS

Prufrock and Other Observations. London: The Egoist Ltd., 1917.

Ara Vos Prec. London: The Ovid Press, 1920; *Poems*. New York: Knopf, 1920.

The Waste Land. New York: Boni and Liveright, 1922; Richmond, Surrey: The Hogarth Press, 1923.

Poems, 1909–1925. London: Faber & Gwyer, 1925; New York: Harcourt, Brace, 1932. (Includes the first book publication of "The Hollow Men.")

Journey of the Magi. London: Faber & Gwyer, 1927; New York: William Edwin Rudge, 1927.

A Song for Simeon. London: Faber & Gwyer, 1928.

Animula. London: Faber & Faber, 1929.

Ash-Wednesday. London: Faber & Faber, 1930; New York: The Fountain Press, 1930.

Anabasis: A Poem by St.-J. Perse with a Translation into English by T. S. Eliot. London: Faber & Faber, 1930. (Eliot's free translation, supervised by Perse.)

Marina. London: Faber & Faber, 1930.

Triumphal March. London: Faber & Faber, 1931.

Sweeney Agonistes: Fragments of an Aristophanic Melodrama. London: Faber & Faber, 1932.

The Rock: A Pageant Play. London: Faber & Faber, 1934.

Murder in the Cathedral. London: Faber & Faber, 1935; New York: Harcourt, Brace, 1935.

Collected Poems, 1909–1935. London: Faber & Faber, 1936; New York: Harcourt Brace, 1936. (Includes the first publication of "Burnt Norton.")

The Family Reunion. London: Faber & Faber, 1939; New York: Harcourt, Brace, 1939.

Old Possum's Book of Practical Cats. London: Faber & Faber, 1939; New York: Harcourt Brace, 1939.

East Coker. London: Faber & Faber, 1940.

The Dry Salvages. London: Faber & Faber, 1941.

Little Gidding. London: Faber & Faber, 1942.

Four Quartets. New York: Harcourt, Brace, 1943; London: Faber & Faber, 1944.

The Cocktail Party: A Comedy. London: Faber & Faber, 1950; New York: Harcourt Brace, 1950.

The Confidential Clerk. London: Faber & Faber, 1954; New York: Harcourt, Brace, 1954.

The Elder Statesman. London: Faber & Faber, 1959; New York: Farrar, Straus and Cudahy, 1959.

The Complete Poems and Plays, 1909–1950. New York: Harcourt Brace, 1952. Reprint, 1971.

Poems Written in Early Youth. London: Faber & Faber, 1967; New York: Farrar, Straus and Giroux, 1967.

Complete Plays. New York: Harcourt, Brace, 1967; also published as *Collected Plays*. London: Faber & Faber, 1962.

The Waste Land: A Facsimile and Transcript of the Original Drafts Including the Annotations of Ezra Pound. Edited by Valerie Eliot. London: Faber & Faber, 1971; New York: Harcourt, Brace, Jovanovich, 1971.

Inventions of the March Hare: Poems, 1909–1917. Edited by Christopher Ricks. London: Faber & Faber, 1996; New York: Harcourt, Brace, Jovanovich, 1997. (Eliot's first poetic notebook and some early typescripts. Lavishly annotated.)

CRITICISM AND OTHER PROSE

"In Memory of Henry James." *Egoist* 5(1):1–2 (January 1918).

"The Hawthorne Aspect [of Henry James]." *Little Review* 5(4):47–53 (August 1918).

"A Sceptical Patrician." [Review of Henry Adams, *The Education of Henry Adams*] *Athenaeum* 4647:361–362 (May 23, 1919).

"Reflections on Contemporary Poetry, IV." *Egoist* 6(3):39–40 (July 1919).

The Sacred Wood: Essays on Poetry and Criticism (London: Methuen, 1920; New York: Knopf, 1921).

"Lettre D'Angleterre." *La Nouvelle Revue Française* 9(104):617–624 (May 1922).

Homage to John Dryden: Three Essays on Poetry of the Seventeenth Century. London: Hogarth Press, 1924.

For Lancelot Andrewes. London: Faber & Gwyer, 1928; New York: Doubleday, 1929.

Dante. London: Faber & Faber, 1929.

Selected Essays, 1917–1932. London: Faber & Faber, 1932; New York: Harcourt, Brace, 1932. Revised and amplified as *Selected Essays*. New York: Harcourt, Brace, 1950; London: Faber & Faber, 1951.

The Use of Poetry and the Use of Criticism: Studies in the Relation of Criticism to Poetry in England. London: Faber & Faber, 1933; Cambridge: Harvard University Press, 1933. (The Harvard Charles Eliot Norton Lectures for 1932–1933.)

After Strange Gods: A Primer of Modern Heresy. London: Faber & Faber, 1934; New York: Harcourt, Brace, 1934. (The Page-Barbour Lectures at the University of Virginia, 1933.)

Elizabethan Essays. London: Faber & Faber, 1934; reprinted as *Essays on Elizabethan Drama*. New York: Harcourt, Brace, 1956. (The London volume includes the first book publication of "John Marston.")

Essays Ancient and Modern. London: Faber & Faber, 1936; New York: Harcourt, Brace, 1936. (Revision of *For Lancelot Andrewes*.)

The Idea of a Christian Society. London: Faber & Faber, 1939; New York: Harcourt, Brace, 1940.

A Sermon Preached in Magdalene College Chapel. Cambridge: Cambridge University Press, 1948.

Notes Towards the Definition of Culture. London: Faber & Faber, 1948; New York: Harcourt, Brace, 1949.

American Literature and the American Language. Saint Louis, Mo.: Washington University, 1953. (An address delivered at Washington University, with an appendix on the Eliot Family and Saint Louis.)

Of Poetry and Poets. London: Faber & Faber, 1957; New York: Farrar, Straus, and Cudahy, 1957.

"The Influence of Landscape upon the Poet." *Daedalus* 89(2):420–422 (Spring 1960).

George Herbert. London: Longmans, 1962.

Knowledge and Experience in the Philosophy of F. H. Bradley. London: Faber & Faber, 1964; New York: Farrar, Straus, 1964. (Eliot's 1916 Harvard Ph.D. dissertation in philosophy.)

To Criticize the Critic and Other Writings. London: Faber & Faber, 1965; New York: Farrar, Straus & Giroux, 1965.

The Varieties of Metaphysical Poetry. Edited by Ronald Schuchard. London: Faber & Faber, 1993; New York: Harcourt, Brace, 1994. (Eliot's 1926 Cambridge University Clark Lectures and 1933 Johns Hopkins University Turnbull Lectures, extensively annotated.)

CORRESPONDENCE

The Letters of T. S. Eliot: Volume I, 1898–1922. Edited by Valerie Eliot. London: Faber & Faber, 1988; New York: Harcourt, Brace, 1988. (The first of a projected four-volume edition.)

INTERVIEWS

Hall, Donald. "The Art of Poetry, I: T. S. Eliot." *Paris Review* 21: 47–70 (Spring/Summer 1959). Reprinted in *Writers at Work: Interviews from "Paris Review."* Edited by Dick Kay. London: Penguin, 1972.

Lehmann, John. "T. S. Eliot Talks about Himself and the Drive to Create." *New York Times Book Review*, 20 November 1953.

Shahani, Ranjee. "T. S. Eliot Answers Questions." *John O'London's Weekly* 63(1369):497–498 (19 August 1949). Reprinted in *T. S. Eliot: Homage from India*. Edited by P. Lal. Calcutta: Writers Workshop, 1965. Pp. 120–34.

"T. S. Eliot: An Interview." *Granite Review*, 24(3): 16–20 (1962).

"T. S. Eliot Gives a Unique Photo-Interview." *Daily Express*, 20 September 1957.

MANUSCRIPT PAPERS

The most important collections of Eliot's manuscripts can be found at the Houghton Library, Harvard University, at the New York Public Library, and at the libraries of King's and Magdalene College, Cambridge. Smaller collections exist at the Bienecke Library, Yale, the Bodleian Library, Oxford, and (largely correspondence) the Humanities Research Center, Austin, Texas, the Huntington Library, San Marino, California, and the library of Princeton University, among others.

BIBLIOGRAPHY

Gallup, Donald. *T. S. Eliot: A Bibliography. Revised edition*. New York: Harcourt, Brace, 1969.

BIOGRAPHICAL AND CRITICAL STUDIES

Ackroyd, Peter, *T. S. Eliot: A Life*. New York: Simon and Schuster, 1984.

Aiken, Conrad. "An Anatomy of Melancholy." *New Republic*, 7 February 1923. Reproduced in *T. S. Eliot: The Waste Land: A Casebook*. Edited by C. B. Cox and Arnold Hinchliffe. London: Macmillan, 1969. Pp. 93–99.

Bloom, Harold. "Reflections on T. S. Eliot." *Raritan* 8(2): 70–87 (1988).

Browne, Martin. *The Making of T. S. Eliot's Plays.* Cambridge: Cambridge University Press, 1969.

Bush, Ronald. *T. S. Eliot: A Study in Character and Style.* New York: Oxford University Press, 1984.

———. *T. S. Eliot: The Modernist in History.* Cambridge: Cambridge University Press, 1991.

Cooper, John Xiros. *T. S. Eliot and the Ideology of "Four Quartets."* New York: Cambridge University Press, 1995.

Cox, C. B., and Arnold Hinchliffe, eds. *T. S. Eliot: The Waste Land: A Casebook.* London: Macmillan, 1969.

Crawford, Robert. *The Savage and the City in the Work of T. S. Eliot.* New York: Oxford University Press, 1987.

Davidson, Harriet. *T. S. Eliot and Hermeneutics: Absence and Interpretation in "The Waste Land."* Baton Rouge: Louisiana State University Press, 1985.

Eagleton, Terry. *Criticism and Ideology:* 1976. Reprint, London: Verso, 1985.

Ellis, Steve. *The English Eliot: Design, Language and Landscape in "Four Quartets."* New York: Routledge, 1991.

Gardner, Helen. *The Art of T. S. Eliot.* 1950. Reprint, New York: Dutton, 1959.

———. *The Composition of "Four Quartets."* London: Faber & Faber, 1978.

Gordon, Lyndall. *Eliot's Early Years.* New York: Oxford University Press, 1977.

———. *Eliot's New Life.* New York: Oxford University Press, 1988.

Grant, Michael, ed. *T. S. Eliot: The Critical Heritage.* 2 vols. London: Routledge & Kegan Paul, 1982.

Gray, Piers. *T. S. Eliot's Intellectual and Poetic Development, 1909–1922.* Brighton, Sussex: Harvester Press, 1982.

The Harvard Advocate. 125(3) (December 1938). (Special T. S. Eliot issue; contains an important memoir by W. G. Tinckom-Fernandez and essays by Conrad Aiken, Robert Lowell, Wallace Stevens, Robert Penn Warren, among others.)

Howarth, Herbert. *Notes on Some Figures behind T. S. Eliot.* London: Chatto and Windus, 1965.

Jain, Manju. *T. S. Eliot and American Philosophy: The Harvard Years.* Cambridge: Cambridge University Press, 1992.

Jarrell, Randall. *The Third Book of Criticism.* New York: Farrar, Straus & Giroux, 1969.

Julius, Anthony. *T. S. Eliot, Anti-Semitism, and Literary Form.* New York: Cambridge University Press, 1995.

Kearns, Cleo McNelly. *T. S. Eliot and Indic Traditions: A Study in Poetry and Belief.* New York: Cambridge University Press, 1987.

Kenner, Hugh. *The Invisible Poet: T. S. Eliot.* New York: McDowell, Obolensky, 1959.

———, ed. *T. S. Eliot: A Collection of Critical Essays.* Englewood Cliffs, N.J.: Prentice-Hall, 1962.

Kojecky, Roger. *T. S. Eliot's Social Criticism.* New York: Farrar, Straus & Giroux, 1971.

Leavis, F. R. *New Bearings in English Poetry.* London: Chatto and Windus, 1938.

———. *The Living Principle: English as a Discipline of Thought.* New York: Oxford University Press, 1975.

Litz, A. Walton, ed. *Eliot in His Time.* Princeton, N.J.: Princeton University Press, 1973.

Lobb, Edward, ed. *Words in Time: New Essays on Eliot's "Four Quartets."* London: Athlone, 1993.

Longenbach, James. *Modernist Poetics of History: Pound, Eliot, and the Sense of the Past.* Princeton, N.J.: Princeton University Press, 1987.

Menand, Louis. *Discovering Modernism: T. S. Eliot and His Context.* New York: Oxford University Press, 1987.

Matthiessen, F. O. *The Achievement of T. S. Eliot.* New York: Oxford University Press, 1935.

Mayer, John. *T. S. Eliot's Silent Voices.* New York: Oxford University Press, 1989.

Moody, A. D. *Thomas Stearns Eliot, Poet.* Cambridge: Cambridge University Press, 1979.

———, ed. *The Cambridge Companion to T. S. Eliot.* Cambridge: Cambridge University Press, 1994.

Olney, James, ed. *T. S. Eliot: Essays from the Southern Review.* New York: Oxford University Press, 1988. (Includes an important unpublished essay of Eliot's and valuable memoir material.)

Read, Herbert. "T.S.E.: A Memoir." In *T. S. Eliot: The Man and His Work.* Edited by Allen Tate. London: Chatto and Windus, 1967.

Ricks, Christopher. *T. S. Eliot and Prejudice.* London: Faber & Faber, 1988.

Sencourt, Robert. *T. S. Eliot: A Memoir.* New York: Dodd, Mead, 1971.

Shusterman, Richard. *T. S. Eliot and the Philosophy of Criticism.* London: Duckworth, 1988.

Sigg, Eric. *The American T. S. Eliot: A Study of the Early Writings*. New York: Cambridge University Press, 1989.

Skaff, William. *The Philosophy of T. S. Eliot: From Skepticism to a Surrealist Poetic, 1909–1927*. Philadelphia: University of Pennsylvania Press, 1986.

Smith, Carol H. *T. S. Eliot's Dramatic Theory and Practice*. Princeton, N.J.: Princeton University Press, 1963.

Smith, Grover. *T. S. Eliot's Poetry and Plays: A Study in Sources and Meaning*. Chicago: Chicago University Press, 1950. Enlarged ed., 1960.

———. *"The Waste Land."* London: Allen & Unwin, 1983.

Soldo, John. *The Tempering of T. S. Eliot*. Ann Arbor, Mich.: UMI Research Press, 1983.

Southam, B. C. *A Student's Guide to the Selected Poems of T. S. Eliot*. 1968. Revised ed., New York: Harcourt, Brace, 1996.

Tate, Allen, ed. *T. S. Eliot: The Man and His Work*. London: Chatto and Windus, 1967.

Williams, William Carlos. *Autobiography*. New York: New Directions, 1951.

Witemeyer, Hugh, ed. *Pound/Williams: Selected Letters of Ezra Pound and William Carlos Williams*. New York: New Directions, 1996.

—RONALD BUSH

Ralph Ellison

1914 –

One of the "enduring functions of the American novel," Ralph Ellison has written, "is that of defining the national type as it evolves in the turbulence of change, and of giving the American experience, as it unfolds in its diverse parts and regions, imaginative integration and moral continuity. Thus it is bound up with our problem of nationhood." In *Invisible Man* (1952), one of the most significant American novels since World War II, Ellison gives us a terrifying and yet vibrant national metaphor: we are invisible men.

In Ellison's created world, as in American society, the quick pace of change, the caprice, the arrogance alongside the innocence, the newness and the general instability of institutions, and, above all, the impulse to recoil from the awful demands of American democracy—all keep Americans from seeing each other or even themselves. The complexity and diversity of American life, along with the development of the novel as form, has brought forth novels like *Invisible Man:* "picaresque, many-leveled . . . swarming with characters and with varied types and levels of experience." Ellison's novel is more than a "slice of life": it is an attempt at no less than a new definition of the national character, a modern national epic.

Accordingly, the vision in Ellison's novel, and indeed throughout his fiction, is ultimately af-

firmative. Virtually all of his fiction—ten stories before the novel, eleven after—features a young black man stretching toward adulthood. We see in this work the evolution of a central theme: the more conscious a person is of his individual, cultural, and national history, the freer he becomes. As a young writer, Ellison quickly became dissatisfied with the typical naturalistic scenarios in which characters struggling to survive the merciless American environment are eventually overcome by impersonal forces. To Ellison, this documentary fiction was dull—and failed to capture the richness and variety of black life as he knew it. Influenced by a broad range of writers, including Richard Wright, André Malraux, and Ernest Hemingway, Ellison began to focus on the person who, by force of character and will, manages to endure.

Ralph Waldo Ellison was born in Oklahoma City, Oklahoma, on March 1, 1914. Aggressiveness and optimism about life seem to have run in his family. His grandfather, Alfred Ellison, was an illiterate ex-slave who had nonetheless served during Reconstruction as constable, marshal, and magistrate in the Ellison clan's hometown, Abbeville, South Carolina. In the tense and violent post-Reconstruction days, Alfred Ellison lost his political titles and returned to driving a dray and chopping cotton, while his wife, Harriet, worked as a washer-woman. Still, he retained his defiant willingness to assert his rights. Once, after a friend had been lynched, he walked through Abbeville with his hands clasped behind his back, announcing to the whites on the street, "If you're going to kill me, you'll have to kill me right here because I'm not leaving. This is where I have my family, my farm, my friends; and I don't plan to leave." Another time Alfred Ellison talked a white mob out of lynching one of his friends. The old man, said Ralph Ellison many years later, must have talked to the whites in an "unknown tongue."

At four Ralph and his younger brother, Herbert, were taken to South Carolina to see Grandfather Alfred and his brother, the boys' Uncle Jim. A half-century later Ellison still remembered the scene: Uncle Jim in his horse and buggy, the bridge to the homestead, the pecan trees planted by the boys' father, the reaping and gathering of vegetables, the old church that was used as a chicken house, the immense fireplaces inside which he could stand and see light flickering down. In Ellison's words, "it was very important for me to go to South Carolina and to visit and see the old house, to see those fireplaces, to see the forms, to see how fertile things were, to see what my relatives did."

If South Carolina evokes for Ellison sacred memories of places and persons, Oklahoma, his birthplace, does even more so. "I dream constantly of Oklahoma City," he told an interviewer in 1975. "My childhood is there." His parents, Lewis Alfred Ellison and Ida Millsap Ellison, left the Deep South for Oklahoma in 1911, only four years after the territory was granted statehood. At least Oklahoma (a word coined by the Reverend Allen Wright, a Choctaw-speaking Indian, to mean "red man") had no firm tradition of slavery. As it turned out, segregation laws were imported from neighbor-ing Texas and Arkansas; but even so, the blacks who had trekked west in wagon trains to escape southern oppression fought hard for their political rights. The blues lyric "I'm going to the Territory, baby / I'm going to the nation" meant, for blacks heading west during this hopeful period, "I'm going to be free." This determination for freedom, the fighting spirit of the people, and the sense of possibility suggested by the vast expanses of undeveloped land gave Oklahoma a frontierlike aspect. All the same, Oklahoma City was an established place. The capital city, recalls Ellison, "seemed fully articulated with its streetcars and its tall buildings. It appeared to be in the same class with say Kansas City or St. Louis or Chicago—only it was much smaller and very much better."

Especially after the death in 1917 of Lewis Ellison (who had worked as a construction foreman and then as an independent businessman, selling ice and coal), the Ellisons were poor—at times extremely poor. Still, Ralph and Herbert were made to feel that the worlds of the rich and the white were approachable. This confidence had been their father's; Lewis Ellison, an avid reader, named his son after Emerson. It was reinforced by Ida Ellison, a woman of enormous determination, faith, and purpose. A stewardess at the Avery Chapel Afro-Methodist Episcopal Church, who valued action in *this* world, she brought home records, magazines, and books discarded in white homes where she worked as a maid. And she saw to it that her sons had electrical and chemistry sets, a rolltop desk and chair, and a toy typewriter. Her activism extended to politics. "If you young Negroes don't do something about things," she would tell her sons, "I don't know what's going to happen to this race." An ardent supporter of Eugene Debs's Socialist party, she canvased for the party's gubernatorial candidate in 1914. In 1934, after Ralph had gone off to Tuskegee Institute, she was jailed for attempting to rent buildings that Jim Crow laws had declared off limits to blacks.

Usually the family lived in a three-room shot-gun house. "We ate poor food," Ellison remembers, "which was generally well-prepared, sometimes not, because my brother and I were taught to take care of ourselves when my mother went out and worked." The Ellisons became so close to their neighbors, the Randolphs, that Ralph considered the families to be extensions of one another. Taylor Randolph recalls that his family would assist Ida Ellison, whom his parents called "Brownie," during this trying period: "I remember one day when it was so cold and snowy that we didn't dream Brownie could have gone out to work. But our mother thought she had better go over and check anyway. And when she got there, she found that Brownie *had* gone out to work. And, sure enough, the fire had gone out, and Ralph and Herbert were huddled up, freezing. My mother took them right back to our house and kept them there until Brownie came home from work. This was a time when there was a great togetherness among families, and when there was a great sympathy for people who had to struggle to bring up their children."

Despite hard times, breaks in the pattern of segregation contributed to the relatively free atmosphere. Indians and blacks had lived side by side in Oklahoma for generations. "There were Negroes who were part Indian," observes Ellison, "and who lived on reservations, and Indians who had children who lived in town as Negroes." The Ellisons had many white friends, and black-white cultural integration, at least, was relatively widespread. Downtown theaters were not segregated until the 1920's. And after blacks were barred from the white theaters, black actors like Richard B. Harrison (who later played De Lawd in Marc Connelly's *The Green Pastures*) continued to perform regularly on "Deep Second" (the blacks' nickname for Second Street, the main strip in Oklahoma City's black neighborhood); Harrison included Shakespearean soliloquies in his repertory. Miss Clark, the maid of the English actress Emma Bunting, used to stay with the Ellisons when Bunting's repertory company came to Oklahoma City, and she brought stories of the professional theater and of England into the Ellison household.

As teen-agers Ellison and his comrades dreamed of being latter-day Renaissance men; they snatched desired symbols along with attitudes and values from blacks, Indians, and whites alike. Ellison wanted to read everything he could at the Paul Laurence Dunbar Library: fairy tales, James Fenimore Cooper, Bernard Shaw, and even a translation of Freud's *Interpretation of Dreams,* which he thought to be a fanciful version of the dream books used by certain "scientific" players of the numbers game. He wanted to play expert "sheenee" (a kind of street hockey played with sticks and tin cans) and varsity football, to imitate the styles of certain "vague and constantly shifting figures"— from his community, from lore and literature, from the movies—figures "sometimes comic but always versatile, picaresque, and self-effacingly heroic." He identified with people he met on odd jobs around town: in private clubs where he waited tables, at buildings where he ran the elevator, on downtown streets where he shined shoes and hawked newspapers. He identified too with the tellers as well as the heroes of the tales that he heard in J. L. Randolph's pharmacy, where he also worked. On rainy or snowy days, local men would pack the store and trade yarns, some of which had been told best, he was informed, years before by his father. J. L. Randolph recalls that Ellison "was always delving into things. He asked about the drugs we sold, and asked about what it felt like to be a druggist. By fifteen or sixteen Ralph was quite a talker. He would sit at the fountain and talk about doing things in a big way. His concern back then was how to get started."

Not all of Ellison's early job experiences were uplifting. The battle-royal scene in *Invisible Man* was suggested not only by similar scenes that he had read about but also by those he had witnessed as a waiter at private clubs. The specific event that ignited his imagination occurred while he was job hunting as a youngster:

One summer when I was still in high school I was looking for a job (and it gets to be 105 to 110 in the shade in Oklahoma City; it used to, anyway). I met a friend and he said, "If you go up to Broadway between Ninth and Tenth there is a car lot there and the man wants someone to help him around the car lot." He said, "I couldn't take it because I got another job, but you better hurry up there." So I turned on the fan, as they say; and by the time I arrived, I was pretty moist. There was this white man sitting out under a tree; and I said, "Sir, I understand you need someone to work here"; and he said, "Yes, sit over here on this box." (He had a crate with a cushion on it.) He said, "Sit over here and tell me about yourself." He began to ask me about my grades, about my parents, and so on; and I began to feel that I was getting this job. And then, at the moment when I was most certain that the job was mine, I felt a charge of electricity in my tail; and I went up in the air and I came down. . . .The whole thing, again, was a ritual of initiation—a practical joke—wherein a Ford coil, a coil from an old Model T Ford, has been hooked up to a battery. . . . Of course, there was no job.

In the music-centered Oklahoma City of the 1920's Ellison heard church performers, marching bands, tent showmen, silent movie accompanists, and those who amused themselves by improvising on ukuleles, kazoos, and C-melody saxophones. With musicians as the heroes most revered, it is small wonder that from age eight through his middle twenties, he wanted to be a musician. Ellison himself wanted to be able to read music as well as to improvise. Thanks to Zelia N. Breaux, supervisor of the music program for the Negro schools in Oklahoma City, Ellison learned music theory at Douglass High School and soon picked up a working knowledge of the soprano saxophone and several brass instruments. As first-chair trumpeter in the Douglass school band, and then as the group's student conductor, Ellison played light classics and marches at church recitals, graduation exercises, football games, lodge and fraternity social functions, and for special productions at the Aldridge Theater, of which Mrs. Breaux was co-owner. Meanwhile, Ludwig Hebestreit, conductor of the Oklahoma City orchestra, taught Ellison privately and invited him to the Little Symphony concerts for children. Ellison recalls being "the only brother of color" permitted to attend these concerts at that time. In return for these favors, young Ellison cut the conductor's lawn.

Ellison admired the elegance, artistic discipline, and seemingly infinite capacity for self-expression that were the hallmarks of jazz musicians. These men and women, some of whom played by ear, some of whom were conservatory-trained, were the heroes of Deep Second. At the Aldridge Theater and at Slaughter's Hall (the public dance hall), Ellison heard Ma Rainey, Ida Cox, and King Oliver as well as the Old Blue Devils band (the nucleus of which became the Count Basie band), with Walter Paige, Oran ("Hot Lips") Page, Eddie Durham, and Jimmy Rushing. As a high school student, Ellison played occasional dance jobs in pickup groups, sat in on rehearsals of the Blue

Devils, and learned the jazz idiom at jam sessions. In Halley Richardson's shoeshine parlor, for instance, Ellison heard Lester Young playing with and against other tenor-sax men, sitting in the shoeshine chair, "his head thrown back, his horn even then outthrust, his feet working on the footrests."

In 1933 Ellison left Oklahoma for Tuskegee Institute, to which he had been accepted as a scholarship student. He wanted to write a symphony encompassing his varied experiences: as a poor black boy who never felt inferior to anyone because of race or class, as a frontier boy with a certain city slickness, and as a classically trained musician steeped in blues and jazz who wanted to capture their rocking power in classical forms.

Tuskegee was a trade and teachers' school, and its founder, Booker T. Washington, was an apostle of intellectual conservatism; still, Ellison developed there as a musician. The dean of the music school was William L. Dawson, best known as a skillful arranger of spirituals and as the composer of the *Negro Folk Symphony*. In the face of deeply entrenched segregation law and custom, Dawson had built Tuskegee into one of the major music centers of the South, with department heads like the pianist Hazel Harrison, who had been one of Ferruccio Busoni's prize pupils in Berlin. As in high school, Ellison played first trumpet in the school orchestra and, on occasion, served as the band's student director.

He also delved into other arts at Tuskegee. He played a leading role in a campus play and in his third year began to test his powers in painting and photography; between school classes he attended an art class to learn watercolor. The instructor, Eva Hamilton, encouraged Ellison to try sculpture. Another favorite teacher, Morteza Drexel Sprague, guided much of his wide reading. But on his own Ellison dis-

covered T. S. Eliot's "The Waste Land," and the poem deeply engaged him: "I was intrigued by its power to move me while eluding my understanding. . . .There was nothing to do but look up the references in the footnotes to the poem." So began Ellison's conscious study of literature. In 1935, as a "reflex" of his reading, Ellison tried his hand at writing poetry. It was at first "an amusing investigation of what seemed at best a secondary talent . . . like dabbling in sculpture."

Because of a mix-up about his scholarship, at the end of his third year Ellison found that he had neither the forty-dollar tuition fee for the coming term nor any money to live on. He decided to venture to New York City, where he thought he could make and save money for the fall more easily than in Alabama. Though she knew that music was his first love, Eva Hamilton was enthusiastic about Ellison's prospects as a sculptor and gave him a letter of introduction to Augusta Savage, a black sculptor in Harlem. Fully intending to return to school, Ellison headed north to New York.

Apart from the winter of 1937, which he spent in Dayton, Ohio, the war years in the merchant marine, and two years (1955–1957) in Rome as a guest of the American Academy of Arts and Letters, Ellison has lived in New York City since his arrival there in 1936. Although he journeyed north specifically to study sculpture and to earn money as a musician, he was also drawn to New York by its glamour and promise of greater freedom. "New York," he has said, "was one of the great cities prominent in the Negro American myth of freedom, a myth which goes back very far into Negro American experience. In our spirituals it was the North Star and places in the North which symbolized Freedom and to that extent I expected certain things from New York." He expected, in fact, a dazzling fulfillment of "an irrepressible belief in some Mecca of equality." Harlem he supposed to be "a glamorous place, a place where wonderful music existed and where there was a great tradition of Negro American style and elegance."

In *Invisible Man,* the protagonist informs the outspoken veteran of the Golden Day brothel that he is on his way to New York, and the vet responds excitedly:

"New York! . . . That's not a place, it's a dream. When I was your age it was Chicago. Now all the little black boys run away to New York. Out of the fire into the melting pot. I can see you after you've lived in Harlem for three months. Your speech will change, you'll talk a lot about 'college,' you'll attend lectures at the Men's House . . . you might even meet a few white folks. And listen," he said, leaning close to whisper, "you might even dance with a white girl!"

The vet recites portions of the southern black myth of New York and tells some of its history to his medical attendant: " . . . think of what this means for the young fellow. He's going free, in the broad daylight and alone. I can remember when young fellows like him had first to commit a crime, or be accused of one, before they tried such a thing. Instead of leaving in the light of morning, they went in the dark of night. And no bus was fast enough. . . ." In fact the Invisible Man has himself been accused by the college president, Bledsoe, of a crime against the "beautiful college": he has allowed a rich, white "friend of the school" to see the nearby black slum and to be hit in the face. Although Ellison had had no climactic run-in himself with the Tuskegee administration, when he headed north he too looked forward to breaking away from southern Jim Crow practices as well as from a certain provincialism that he had confronted at Tuskegee.

Harlem was not exactly the promised land heralded by the folklore. Twelve years after coming north, Ellison wrote: "To live in Harlem is to dwell in the very bowels of the city . . . a ruin . . . overcrowded and exploited politically and economically." Black Manhattan he found the "scene and symbol of the Negro's perpetual alienation in the land of his birth." For when the black southerner moves north, he surrenders vital cultural supports:

He leaves a relatively static social order in which . . . he has developed those techniques of survival to which Faulkner refers as "endurance," and an ease of movement within explosive situations which makes Hemingway's definition of courage, "grace under pressure," appear mere swagger. He surrenders the protection of his peasant cynicism—his refusal to hope for the fulfillment of hopeless hopes—and his sense of being "at home in the world" gained from confronting and accepting (for day-to-day living, at least) the obscene absurdity of his predicament. Further, he leaves a still authoritative religion . . . family . . . and a body of folklore—tested in life-and-death terms against his daily experience with nature and the Southern white man—that serves him as a guide to action.

More than one newcomer has found Harlem and New York City to be a battleground of wills, chaos continually erupting within the orderly pattern of streets and traffic lights. Many of the so-called surreal city scenes in Ellison's fiction derive from his attempt to bring into focus the contradictions and confusions actually observed in Harlem:

. . . the most surreal fantasies are acted out upon the streets of Harlem; a man ducks in and out of traffic shouting and throwing imaginary grenades that actually exploded during World War I; a boy participates in the rape-robbery of his mother; a man beating his wife in a park uses boxing "science" and observes Marquess of Queensberry rules (no rabbit punching, no blows beneath the belt); two men hold a third while a lesbian slashes him to death with a razor blade; boy gangsters wielding homemade pistols (which in the South of their origin are but toy symbols of adolescent yearning for manhood) shoot down their young rivals. Life becomes a masquerade, exotic costumes are worn every day. Those who cannot afford to hire a horse wear riding habits; others who could not afford a hunting trip or who seldom attend sporting events carry shooting sticks.

Yet, if many blacks have been bent and broken by Harlem, if one sees "white-haired adults crawl in the feudal darkness of their childhood," if Harlem "is the scene of the folk-Negro's death agony, it is also the setting of his transcendence." In Harlem "you see the transformation of the Southern idiom into a Northern idiom . . . Harlem is a place where our folklore is preserved and transformed. It is the place where the body of our Negro myth and legend thrives. It is a place where our styles, musical styles, the many styles of Negro life, find continuity and metamorphosis." Like Ellison, millions of blacks have brought their institutions and optimism to the cities of the North; and the emerging northern black culture did provide some sense of continuity for them. In the midst of Harlem's fantasticality and turmoil, opportunities for personal and artistic growth abounded. In 1966 Ellison observed that "Harlem was and still *is* a place where a Southern Negro who has a little luck, and who has a little talent, can actually make himself into the man or woman of his dreams."

In *Invisible Man,* the factory hospital is a metaphor for the modern industrialized city that fractures black folk-consciousness. There the white doctors, with shrieks and electric shocks, endeavor to force the young fellow to learn his place, to forget his history and identity, and to yield to the power of the cold, steely machine. Their intention backfires, however, and the Invisible Man is only purged of his fear of the North and of whites. Emerging from the hospital, he feels transformed and realizes dimly that he is still on the twisting road to freedom.

In 1936, well before World War II (when the police began to warn whites away from that vast black neighborhood) Harlem was evolving into what James Weldon Johnson called the black American cultural capital, beckoning to artists and intellectuals, black and white. In the 1930's and 1940's Ellison could be found browsing at the Schomburg Library and at Lewis Michaux's bookstore, then located on Seventh Avenue at 125th Street. Ellison would save his nickles and dimes to go to the Savoy Ballroom once or twice a week. "The Savoy was thriving and people were coming to Harlem from all over the world. The great European and American composers were coming there to listen to jazz—Igor Stravinsky, Francis Poulenc. The great jazz bands were there. Great dancers were being created there." Twice a week, often with Langston Hughes, Ellison went to Harlem's Apollo Theater. By 1940 Ellison was going to after-hours hangouts where musicians jammed: to Sidney Bechet's place, where Teddy Wilson or Art Tatum held down the house piano, to the Rhythm Club, to Clark Monroe's Uptown House, or to a place where the waiters sang as they served drinks. "Jazz was part of a total culture, at least among Afro-Americans," said Ellison. And as in Oklahoma City, jazzmen were heroes.

During the heyday of the jazz club Minton's, Ellison was among those "who shared, night after night, the mysterious spell created by the talk, the laughter, grease paint, powder, perfume, sweat, alcohol and food—all blended and simmering, like a stew on the restaurant range, and brought to a sustained moment of elusive meaning by the timbres and accents of musical instruments locked in passionate recitative." There Ellison would listen to musicians he had first heard in Oklahoma City: Charles Christian, Lester Young, "Hot Lips" Page, Ben Webster. Also at Minton's he heard the creators of the "bop" idiom: Charlie Parker, Thelonious Monk, Dizzy Gillespie, Bud Powell, and Charles Mingus.

Because he lacked the money for a musicians' union license, and because there was such an abundance of talent in New York, Ellison did not find steady work as a trumpeter. In fact, he performed only once in public, his last engagement as a professional musician, playing the trumpet for a dance recital by Anna Sokolow. But he still wanted to write symphonies and studied for about a year with Wallingford Riegger. In 1936 a friend took him to the Edgecombe Avenue apartment of Duke Ellington, who remembered seeing Ellison at Tuskegee. The bandleader invited the young man to the following day's rehearsal but then had to cancel the invitation. Not wanting to press the point, Ellison said no more about the matter, and it was dropped. By the late 1930's, when he became immersed in writing fiction, Ellison laid down his trumpet forever, refusing even to attend concerts for fear of being diverted.

During the Great Depression finding work of any kind was not easy. At first, still hoping to return to Tuskegee, he worked for almost a year behind the food bar of the Harlem YMCA, where he had a room. Many odd jobs followed, one of the most interesting of which was as substitute receptionist and file clerk for the psychoanalyst Harry Stack Sullivan. That job lasted only a few months, but the experience proved instructive: as he was filing, Ellison would glance through patients' case histories, and what he read spurred him to reconsider the importance of dreams. When he began writing

fiction and reading authors who employed dreams in their fiction—especially Dostoevsky, who, as Ellison has said, "taught the novelist how to use the dream"—the young writer realized how much his stint with Sullivan had shown him.

In 1936 and 1937 Ellison also worked in factories around New York. Later he worked as a free-lance photographer and builder of record players and radios. During one series of weeks without work, he slept on the daybed in a friend's living room and on benches in St. Nicholas Park.

The sculptor Augusta Savage explained that her duties on a WPA arts project made it impossible for her to instruct Ellison. Alain Locke and Langston Hughes, impressed with Ellison's sculpture, suggested that he work with another Harlem artist, Richmond Barthé, and Ellison studied with him for about a year before abandoning sculpture.

Ellison's contact with the literary world was already made. He had met Hughes quite by chance on his second day in New York. Through Hughes he met Richard Wright, whose poems "I Have Seen Black Hands" and "Between the World and Me" Ellison considered the best ever written by a black writer; and their friendship blossomed. Although Wright was six years older and on the verge of his first major literary success (*Uncle Tom's Children* in 1938), the two were in basically the same predicament: they were radically inclined black intellectuals with southern backgrounds, trying to survive in New York and struggling to make art in the midst of the Great Depression. They talked endlessly about politics and art, drank, and exchanged jokes and stories.

Wright said candidly that Ellison had started too late to develop into a serious writer, but he was impressed with his friend's ability to discuss literature and urged him to write a short story for *New Challenge,* a leftist literary magazine of which Wright was an editor. Ellison begged off. He was at that time still a musician and lacked writing experience. Wright forced his hand by asking instead for a short review of Waters Edward Turpin's novel *These Low Grounds.* With this review, entitled "Creative and Cultural Lag" (Fall 1937), Ellison took the decisive step toward becoming a writer.

When Wright again asked Ellison to write a short story, for the Winter 1937 issue of *New Challenge,* Ellison agreed. Drawing on his experience of bumming on trains, he wrote "Hymie's Bull," his first short story. Although heavily derivative of Hemingway, it impressed Wright and got as far as galley proofs. But in the end some new poems by Margaret Walker and others superseded "Hymie's Bull" and the story was dropped—as was the Communist party's moral support. Problems between the other editors, Dorothy West and Marion Minus, led to the magazine's suspension and the Winter 1937 number went unpublished.

In February 1937 Ellison's mother died in Dayton, Ohio. In a haunting memoir, "February" (1955), he recalls her death and the awesome Dayton winter during the recession of 1937:

February is a brook, birds, an apple tree—a day spent alone in the country. Unemployed, tired of reading, and weary of grieving the loss of my mother, I'd gone into the woods to forget. So that now all Februarys have the aura of that early morning coldness, the ghost of quail tracks on the snow-powdered brook which I brushed aside as I broke the brook to drink; and how the little quail tracks went up the ice, precise and delicate, into the darker places of the bank-ledge undisturbed.

Ida Ellison's death proved a painful initiation into manhood for her son: ". . . I was in my early twenties then, and I had lived through my mother's death in that strange city, had sur-

vived three months off the fields and woods by my gun; through ice and snow and homelessness. And now in this windless February instant I had crossed over into a new phase of living. Shall I say it was in those February snows that I first became a man?"

Ellison's statement that he survived by his gun through ice, snow, and homelessness is no mere figure of speech. He and his brother both arrived in Dayton almost completely out of money. At night, when the temperature skidded toward zero, they slept in a car parked in a garage open at both ends. They supported themselves by hunting quail, which they either ate or sold to local General Motors executives. Although the Ellison brothers had hunted since childhood, never had it been such a serious enterprise. By reading Hemingway's descriptions of "leading" a bird in flight, Ellison became an excellent hunter during those lean months. Years later he said of Hemingway: "When he describes something in print, believe him . . . he's been there." Ellison returned to New York weary and distraught, but one issue was settled: all of his creative energies would be channeled into becoming a good writer.

In Ohio, Ellison had begun writing in earnest. After hunting all day, he wrote at night and studied Joyce, Dostoevsky, Gertrude Stein, and Hemingway—"especially Hemingway," he recalls. "I read him to learn his sentence structure and how to organize a story." Ellison began to arrange his life so that writing would be his main focus, "to stake my energy against the possibility of failing." Out of money but determined to continue writing, in 1938 Ellison was hired by the Federal Writers' Project.

Ellison's four-year experience on the project provided $103.50 monthly, enough money to live on, and a good deal more. Besides rescuing him from unemployment, the work stocked him with "information and insights about [his] country during a highly formative period of

[his] literary life." It also made Ellison aware of being part of a community of writers, black and white, fledgling and established, all trying to perfect their craft. And it was on the project that Ellison began to find his voice in fiction. He grappled with questions that were to provide the dominant themes in his writing: Who is the American? Who is the black American? How is a man's past related to his identity? What role does folk art play?

Ellison pursued his project assignments with diligence. One of the first, a study of "Famous New York Trials," gave him the opportunity to learn something of the history of New York's political and legal systems. The aspiring writer spent many days at the New York Court of General Sessions, reading crime reports and court transcripts. Even when the research was tedious, the drama and ritual of the courtroom suggested forms to consider as possible material for fiction.

Along with about twenty other black employees of the writers' project, Ellison spent months in the Schomburg Library doing research for a projected book of social history, *The Negro in New York*. As a member of that research team, Ellison wrote a series of short memorandums, several hundred words in length, on prominent black New Yorkers and historical incidents involving the black community. From June 9, 1938, to June 29, 1942—almost his entire tenure on the project—Ellison submitted such papers as "Negro Instructors in New York Institutions of Higher Learning," "Jupiter Hammond," and "Great Riots of New York; Complete Account of the Four Days of the Draft Riot of 1863." These essays were interpretive as well as expository and often prefigured the balance and grandeur of Ellison's later prose, although many of them lacked his characteristic precision and zest.

From 1938 to 1940 Ellison worked also under the supervision of Nicholas Wirth of the New York "Living Lore Unit." This group of twenty-seven writers sought to recount the history of New York City in the words of its inhabitants. The resulting unpublished collection of "urban and industrial folklore," assembled under the working title "Chase the White Horse," testified to their conviction that a vital part of American history lies in the tales, toasts, songs, and boasts of folklore. In this research group, Ellison collected children's game-rhymes, chants, and taunts, some of which turned up later in his fiction. Part of the song "Buckeye the Rabbit," which Ellison heard recited by five Harlem girls while playing, appears in *Invisible Man*:

> I'm riding through Kentucky
> I'm riding through the sea,
> And all I catch behind me
> Is a buckle on my knee.
> Buckeye the Rabbit,
> Shake it
> Shake it
> Shake it
> With a buckle on my knee.
> I swing to the bottom
> I swing to the sea
> And all I catch behind me
> Is a buckle on my knee
> So Buckeye the Rabbit
> Shake it
> Shake it
> With a buckle on my knee

Ellison sometimes recognized a remnant of a saying or rhyme he had heard in the South, reduced to a mumble or nonsense phrase in Harlem. Out of the rural context in which the story or rhyme had originated, the meanings of the folk art changed—and at times appeared to dissolve entirely. Even reduced to mumbles, however, the folklore often retained ritual meanings and signified a tradition, a bridge to the South and to the past. "That's what the people have to work out of," Ellison has said. "This tradition goes way back to the South, and some of it goes back to Africa."

Ellison also visited hundreds of Harlem apartments and public places, where he collected stories from adults. This process of interviewing and transcribing sharpened his ear for idiosyncrasies of language and his mind for getting particular patterns of speech onto paper. He was often able to get a story on paper "by using a kind of Hemingway typography, by using the repetitions . . . I could get some of the patterns and get an idea of what it was like."

On May 10, 1939, Ellison talked to a man in Eddie's Bar in Harlem, described as a modernistic room with green walls, marine designs, red imitation leather upholstery, mirrors, and a nickel phonograph—"all of this in good taste." The unnamed man, who brings to mind Langston Hughes's character Jesse B. Simple, told Ellison:

Ahm in New York, but New York aint in me. You understand? Ahm in New York but New York aint in me. Who do I mean? Listen. Im from Jacksonville, Florida. Been in New York twenty-five years. Im a New Yorker! But Im in New York an New York aint in me. Yuh understand? Naw, naw, yuh dont get me. What do they do; take Lenox Avenue. Take Seventh Avenue; take Sugar Hill! Pimps. Numbers. Cheating these poor people outa whut they got. Shooting, cutting, backbiting, all them things. Yuh see? Yuh see whut Ah mean? *I'M* in New York, but *New York aint* in me! Dont laugh, dont laugh. Ahm laughing but Ah dont mean it; it aint funny. Yuh see. Im on Sugar Hill, but Sugar Hill aint on me.

The man ended his song of himself with a eulogy to "spirits": "Whut did the saint say? He said a little spirits is good for the stomach, good to warm the spirit. Now where did that come from? Yuh dont know, yuh too young. Yuh

young Negroes dont know the Bible. Dont laugh, dont laugh. Look here Ahll tell you somethin: Some folks drinks to cut the fool but some folks drinks to think. Ah drinks to think."

Ellison submitted one especially vivid report on June 14, 1938. Standing on 135th Street and Lenox Avenue, Leo Gurley told Ellison about "Sweet-the-monkey." Gurley began his story with what folklorists term a "signature": "I hope to God to kill me if this aint the truth. All you got to do is go down to Florence, South Carolina and ask most anybody you meet and they'll tell you its the truth."

Gurley's "Sweet-the-monkey" in some respects resembles the narrator of *Invisible Man:*

It was this way: Sweet could make hisself invisible. You don't believe it? Well here's how he done it. Sweet-the-monkey cut open a black cat and took out its heart. Climbed a tree backwards and cursed God. After that he could do anything. The white folks would wake up in the morning and find their stuff gone. He cleaned out the stores. He cleaned up the houses. Hell, he even cleaned out the dam bank! He was the the boldest *black* sonofabitch ever been down that way. And couldn't nobody do nothing to him. *Because* they couldn't never see im when he done it. He didn't need the money. Fact is, most of the time he broke into places he wouldn't take nothing. Lots a times he just did it to show 'em he could. Hell, he had everybody in that lil old town scaird as hell; black folks and white folks. . . .He wont let himself be seen.

Many of the verses, jokes, and peculiarities of speech that enrich Ellison's fiction were drawn from his experience in Oklahoma and Alabama; other are based on notes made in Harlem for the Federal Writers' Project. There he refined his sense of the folkloric context: the occasions in which persons were likely to use the stylized speech of folklore. Thus in his fiction, the lore is more than mere "local color"; it is ritualistic and reflective of a whole cultural style. For example, in *Invisible Man* the protagonist tells a black man on the street to "take it easy" and the man replies with an ebullient boast, here serving an initiatory function:

"Oh, I'll do that. All it takes to get along in this here man's town is a little shit, grit, and mother-wit. And man, I was bawn with all three. In fact, I'maseventhsonofaseventhsonbawnwitha cauloverbotheyesandraisedonblackcatbones highjohntheconquerorandgreasygreens . . . I'll verse you but I won't curse you—My name is Peter Wheatstraw, I'm the Devil's only son-in-law, so roll 'em! . . . My name's Blue and I'm coming at you with a pitchfork. Fe Fi Fo Fum. Who wants to shoot the Devil one, Lord God Stingeroy! . . . Look me up sometimes, I'm a piano player and a rounder, a whiskey drinker and a pavement pounder. I'll teach you some good bad habits. You'll need 'em."

On the Federal Writers' Project, writers studied folklore and exercised their literary craft transposing the lore into written literature. Ellison collected lore and studied history by day, but wrote his own fiction by night. The project inspired some writers' rediscovery of the American vernacular in the 1930's, and in those years Ellison applied his new awareness of language and folklore to the past and to human identity. "The character of a people," he has said, "is revealed in their speech." The project's structured examination of language and folklore helped his writing grow beyond the limits of literary realism. If Harlem proved a somewhat tarnished "Mecca of equality," it did offer young Ellison opportunities for artistic growth.

Ellison's increasing maturity as a writer coincided with a gradual shift in his political perspective. During the late 1930's he was an enthusiastic supporter of many Communist party tenets, but by the mid-1940's he was publicly denouncing the party. He was first drawn to left-wing politics by his mother's involvement with the Socialist party in Oklahoma; by his own experience of poverty, segregation, and hard times; and by the impact of such events as the Scottsboro and Herndon cases and the Civil War in Spain. André Malraux's political, critical, and fiction writings also affected Ellison profoundly and further stirred in him the prospect of participating in a concerted effort by—in Malraux's word—"conscious" revolutionary artists, intellectuals and the people to redeem an immoral world torn by war and depression. Ellison recalls that the "swell of events which I plunged into . . . the stimulus that existed in New York during the thirties was by no means limited to art; it was also connected with politics; it was part of the *esprit de corps* developed in the country after we had endured the Depression for a few years. It had to do with my discovering New York and the unfamiliar areas of society newly available to me."

Ellison's friends influenced his leftward progress. Wright was an active member of the Communist party when they met. Having been secretary of the John Reed Club in Chicago, he was considered a party spokesman. Hughes was a charter member of the radical American Writers' Congress and had been writing leftist articles, fiction, and poetry for almost ten years. In 1937 Hughes traveled to the Soviet Union, which he described in reports for the *Chicago Defender* as a haven of interracial cooperation. Though never a member of the Communist party, Hughes often wrote and spoke in behalf of party causes.

Fron 1937 to 1944 Ellison wrote over twenty book reviews for such radical periodicals as *New Challenge, Direction,* and the *Negro Quarterly;* in 1940 the *New Masses* printed at least one piece of his every month.

In the 1930's Ellison joined the chorus of critics calling for realism as the literary mode appropriate for the radical writer. Mirroring the Communist party position of the day, Ellison's criticism often described black Americans as members of a state or nation (like a Russian soviet) within the United States. The literature of black Americans (the subject of about half of his reviews of the 1930's and 1940's) was, he believed, an emerging national literature that should serve to heighten the revolutionary consciousness of black people. The black writer should instill in his audience not merely "race consciousness" but awareness of class. Ideally, the revolutionary black writer should inspire black working people to unite with workers of other "nationalities" against the bourgeoisie, white and black.

While the Great Depression years brought tremendous difficulties, they were also, in Ellison's words, "great times for literature," times for "the conscious writer" to study his society's laws and to examine its citizens' emotions "stripped naked." Furthermore, the writer could perceive the great American themes of tomorrow shining "beyond the present chaos." The black writer's particular duty was to overcome the handicap of living in racist, capitalist America and to teach his readers to do likewise. His greatest responsibility, said Ellison, echoing Joyce's phrase, was "to create the consciousness of his oppressed nation."

Toward this nation-building effort, Ellison's first published writing, his review of *These Low Grounds* (1937), called for a greater awareness of literary technique and tradition among what he called "realistic" black writers. He also steadfastly maintained, then and in years to come, that black folklore is one of the richest sources for the black writer.

In 1940 and 1941, Ellison published "Stormy Weather" and "Recent Negro Fiction," his

longest and most searching critical essays up to that time. They were pioneering works in establishing the creative use of folklore as a touchstone for evaluating black literature. While reviewing one of Langston Hughes's autobiographies, *The Big Sea,* Ellison proclaims that of the "New Negro movement" in American letters in the 1920's, only Hughes, much of whose poetry had been based on black speech and the blues, transcended the "bourgeois," white-imitating wave of black writing and survived the shattering impact of the Great Crash. Most black writers of the 1920's wrote as if blind to the technical experiments of Hemingway, Gertrude Stein, and Joyce; furthermore, they had ignored what Ellison termed "the folk source of all vital Negro art." Hughes, however, "castigates the Negro bourgeoisie. . . .Declining its ideological world, he gained his artistic soul. . . .Hughes's vision carried him down into the black masses to seek his literary roots. The crystallized folk experience of the blues, spirituals, and folk tales became the stuff of his poetry."

Obviously there is a nationalistic—perhaps a proletarian—note struck here. There is also a point about diction and rhetoric. Ellison explains that the black writer of the 1930's, discovering the path mapped out by Hughes, began to sense that black workers spoke a "language of protest," a black urban idiom, and that "the speech patterns of this new language had long been present in Negro life, recorded in the crystallized protest of American Negro folklore." Hughes's fiction reflected the transformation of rural folk expression into urban folk expression, which, by the 1930's, was fast becoming "the basis of a new proletarian literature." His radical perspective and power as a spokesman for the people derived from Hughes's having followed "the logical development of the national folk sources of his art." In other words, Hughes used the language, tone, and structure of the blues and spirituals in his work; writing from the perspective of the folk, his radicalism glowed with the energy and irony of "the dozens," the boast, the deadpan tale.

The Big Sea, however, is not explicit enough for Ellison in its realism or radicalism. Its use of understatement as a narrative pose was "charming in its simplicity" but risked the possibility of being misunderstood:

Many *New Masses* readers will question whether [understatement] is a style suitable for the autobiography of a Negro writer of Hughes's importance; the national and class position of the writer should guide his selection of techniques and method, should influence his style. In the style of *The Big Sea* too much attention is apt to be given to the esthetic aspects of experience at the expense of its deeper meanings. Nor—this being a world in which few assumptions can be taken for granted—can the writer who depends upon understatement to convey these meanings be certain that they do not escape the reader. To be effective the Negro writer must be explicit; thus realistic; thus dramatic.

Ellison has remained somewhat suspicious of understatement in fiction. In a review in 1946 he attacked his literary hero Hemingway for using understatement as a deceptive mask; beneath his clipped prose, writes Ellison, Hemingway takes reactionary positions. As late as 1953, upon accepting the National Book Award, Ellison explained that he chose not to take the narrative stance of the "'hard-boiled' novel, with its dedication to physical violence, social cynicism, and understatement. Understatement depends, after all, upon commonly held assumptions and my minority status rendered all such assumptions questionable."

Ellison also criticized Hughes's self-portrayal as a picaresque figure rather than a tough-minded hero whose self-awareness deepens with experience. Using Malraux's terminology, Ellison observed that by rendering himself as picaresque, "Hughes avoids analysis and comment, and, in some instances, emotion." Hence "a deeper unity is lost. This is the unity which is formed by the mind's brooding over experience and transforming it into conscious thought. Negro writing needs this unity, through which the writer clarifies the experiences of the reader and allows him to recreate himself." In a proper autobiography, writes Ellison, the black writer is responsible for revealing the process whereby he has gained his artistic consciousness in a world in which "most of the odds are against his doing so." In the South "the attainment of such a consciousness is in itself a revolutionary act." The black writer's duty is to recognize that "the spread of this consciousness, added to the passion and sensitivity of the Negro people . . . will help create a new way of life in the United States."

The desire for a "conscious hero" in American literature has remained a theme of Ellison's. In 1942, reviewing William Attaway's *Blood on the Forge* for the *Negro Quarterly,* Ellison commended the author's presentation of southern "folk" blacks as harried and confused in the concrete mazes of the urban North. He pointed out that the artistic vision is incomplete, however, without the presence of a character whose consciousness is reborn in the North:

Conceptually, Attaway grasped the destruction of the folk, but missed its rebirth on a higher level. The writer did not see that while the folk individual was being liquidated in the crucible of steel, he was also undergoing fusion with new elements. Nor did Attaway see that the individual which emerged, blended of old and new, was better fitted for the problems of the industrial environment. As a result the author is so struck by the despair in his material that he fails to see any ground for hope in his characters. Yet hope is there....

A few years later, in "Flying Home" (1944), "King of the Bingo Game" (1944), and *Invisible Man* (1952), Ellison would present his own black protagonists threatened with liquidation in modern industrial society. His heroes' resiliency, folk memories, and luck, however, help them to "fuse" with "new elements" in their environment; they are "reborn" better able to deal with the churning world of airplanes and factories. In 1948 Ellison described the bemused protagonist of *Invisible Man,* which he was then writing, as "a character who possesses both the eloquence and the insight into the interconnections between his own personality and the world about him to make a judgment about our culture." Ellison's early desire for conscious heroes in American writing foreshadowed his eventual break with many of his literary and political friends, including Wright.

But in his literary essays of the early 1940's Ellison champions Wright as living testimony to the shining possibilities within the black community. Against all odds, Wright had made himself into a highly conscious activist and writer. For Ellison, Wright's early novellas, published as *Uncle Tom's Children* (1938), constituted his best fiction; their protest and existential themes emerged not from overt Marxist or Kierkegaardian theorizing but from the fiction itself, rich in folklore. And in the review "Recent Negro Fiction" (1941), Ellison held up *Native Son* (1940) as "the first philosophical novel by an American Negro. This work possesses an artistry, penetration of thought, and sheer emotional power that places it in the front rank of American fiction." Wright's autobiography, *Black Boy* (1945), prompted Ellison to compare it with works by Joyce and Dostoevsky, and with the blues. Wright's eloquent "song" of trouble and trial is filled "with blues-

tempered echoes of railroad trains, the names of Southern towns and cities, estrangements, fights and flights, deaths and disappointments, charged with physical and spiritual hungers and pain. And like a blues sung by such an artist as Bessie Smith, its lyric prose evokes the paradoxical, almost surreal image of a black boy singing lustily as he probes his own grievous wound."

Despite Ellison's admiration for his mentor, and despite Wright's encouragement (he inscribed a copy of *Uncle Tom's Children* "To Ralph, who I hope will someday write a better book than this"), by 1940 a degree of "anxiety of influence" afflicted the friendship. Ellison's early fiction style so resembled Wright's that Wright protested. Upon seeing one short-story manuscript, Wright exclaimed, "Hey, that's my stuff!" Ellison deliberately left the piece unpublished, like most of his exercises of the period, and afterward he never showed Wright any work in progress. "You might say," Ellison later commented, that in this awkward scene Wright "influenced me *not* to be influenced by him."

That Ellison was finding his own direction in writing is clear from his fiction of the 1940's. And in critical essays of the 1960's he explains his early dissatisfaction with *Native Son* and *Black Boy.* Recognizing that Bigger Thomas in *Native Son* represents black humanity smoldering under the ashes of despair and white oppression, Ellison nevertheless cannot accept Bigger as an adequate portrait of the Afro-American. To him this character is little more than an ideological formulation, a sociological mortar shell fired at the guilty conscience of white America. Blacks themselves know that life in the ghetto is not as dimensionless and dull as Wright paints it. *Native Son* is too deterministic and anchored in Marxist ideology:

In *Native Son* Wright began with the ideological proposition that what whites think of the

Negro's reality is more important than what Negroes themselves know it to be. Hence Bigger Thomas was presented as a near-subhuman indictment of white oppression. He was designed to shock whites out of their apathy and end the circumstances out of which Wright insisted Bigger emerged. Here environment is all—and interestingly enough, environment conceived solely in terms of the physical, the non-conscious. Well, cut off my legs and call me Shorty! Kill my parents and throw me on the mercy of the court as an orphan! Wright could imagine Bigger, but Bigger could not possibly imagine Richard Wright. Wright saw to that.

Black Boy fared little better in Ellison's later criticism. Here again the portrait of black life is too raw and hopeless in Ellison's view. When Wright decided to employ determinist ideology and to dwell upon the crushing power of environment, instead of the individual's ability to overcome it, that, wrote Ellison, was doubtless "the beginning of Wright's exile."

In 1944, when Ellison's disagreement with radical American leftists was already strong, the war policies of the American Communist party impelled Ellison and many other blacks to leave the organized Left entirely. When the party lent what Ellison called its "shamefaced support" to segregation in the armed forces, many blacks became bitterly disillusioned with the radicals' vaunted good will toward minorities.

The party blundered in ignoring the fact that "little Hitlers" (white racists and racist policies) plagued blacks at home; for blacks the war against fascism had to continue on the home front as well as overseas. When the party attacked this position as "narrowly nationalistic," it seemed to Ellison that Soviet foreign policy moved the American Communist party more than did the plight of its local black members. In an interview years later, Ellison said of the Communist party:

They fostered the myth that Communism was twentieth-century Americanism, but to be a twentieth-century American meant, in their thinking, that you had to be more Russian than American and less Negro than either. That's how they lost the Negroes. The Communists recognized no plurality of interests and were really responding to the necessities of Soviet foreign policy, and when the war came, Negroes got caught and were made expedient in the shifting of policy. Just as Negroes today who fool around will get caught in the next turn of the screw.

However radical their politics, American Communist party leaders often suffered from what Gunnar Myrdal called "the American dilemma." In Ellison's words:

the Party had inherited the moral problem centering upon the Negro.... For in our culture the problem of the irrational, that blind spot in our knowledge of society where Marx cries out for Freud and Freud for Marx, but where approaching, both grow wary and shout insults lest they actually meet, has taken the form of the Negro problem.

In *Invisible Man,* the protagonist's decision to renounce his wholehearted support for the Brotherhood is based on his discovery that the radical group is racist. The Brotherhood sacrifices Harlem's interests for the sake of "international" goals and tries to mold the Invisible Man into their conception of the Good Negro: one passively willing to use his energy and his art (which is his oratory) exactly as the Party commands. In the novel the Brotherhood stands, to a large extent, for the American Communist party. But Ellison also wanted the Brotherhood to be seen in a larger context: the party was not the only group of white American political activists to betray their black countrymen for narrow political ends.

In 1942 Ellison quit the Federal Writers'

Project to become managing editor of the *Negro Quarterly* and worked on its staff for one year, leaving just before the journal closed. Angelo Herndon, who was just then breaking away from the Communists, was the editor of this radical "Review of Negro Life and Culture," which featured leftist artists and scholars, black and white. Sterling A. Brown, Herbert Aptheker, Richard Wright, Norman McLeod, J. Saunders Redding, E. Franklin Frazier, Owen Dodson, and Stanley Edgar Hyman all contributed to the *Negro Quarterly* during its brief existence (only four issues were published). Besides his review of William Attaway's *Blood on the Forge,* Ellison wrote an unsigned editorial that obliquely criticized the Communist party and urged black leaders to concentrate more on the interests and needs of blacks.

Calling for black unity and self-determination, without mentioning the Communists, he warned that when black leadership is provided from outside the black community,

Negro people [are] exploited by others: either for the good ends of democratic groups or for the bad ends of Fascist groups. And they have the Civil War to teach them that no revolutionary situation in the United States will be carried any farther toward fulfilling the needs of Negroes than Negroes themselves are able, through a strategic application of their own power, to make it go. As long as Negroes fail to centralize their power, they will always play the role of sacrificial goat, they will always be "expendable." Freedom, after all, cannot be imported or acquired through an act of philanthropy, it must be won.

In this comment, as in several of Ellison's early political writings, the artist inadvertently upstages the political analyst. Black leaders, he argues, must realize that the hope of consolidating black power rests on their ability to analyze and use the lore and language of black

Americans. Without understanding Afro-American myths and symbols, no black leader can succeed, regardless of his program's merits:

Much in Negro life remains a mystery; perhaps the zoot suit conceals profound political meaning; perhaps the symmetrical frenzy of the Lindyhop conceals clues to great potential power—if only Negro leaders would solve this riddle. On this knowledge depends the effectiveness of any slogan or tactic.... [American war aims] will be accepted by the Negro masses only to the extent that they are helped to see the bright star of their own hopes through the fog of their daily experiences. The problem is psychological; it will be solved only by a Negro leadership that is aware of the psychological attitudes and incipient forms of action which the black masses reveal in their emotion-charged myths, symbols and wartime folklore.

Ellison calls here for a more efficient propaganda effort by black leaders and for their increased identification with the political interests of the black masses. He also seems to call on the black artist and the student of black culture to express the true values and forms of black life. But it was Ellison himself who went on to explore the mysterious relation of folklore, art, and politics most daringly in his own early stories.

The years 1939 to 1944 were years of apprenticeship for Ellison who, in a *New York Post* feature story of 1943, was identified as "a short story writer." He published eight stories during this period, and his writing grew in eloquence and complexity from one work to the next. He wrote many more stories than he tried to publish, looking upon some as exercises.

As we might expect, his first short stories, "Slick Gonna Learn" (1939) and "The Birthmark" (1940) were in the realistic mode and highlighted the jagged edges of the black-American environment. These stories offer explicitly political resolutions. But as early as 1940, as Ellison began to draw upon his Oklahoma City background, his vision was not so much that of a political realist as of a regionalist: his first Buster and Riley stories, "Afternoon" (1940), "Mister Toussan" (1941), and "That I Had the Wings" (1943), explored the language, folklore, and unique features of a southwestern town as seen by two curious and daring black boys. "It Is a Strange Country" (1944) is a transitional wartime story, important because of its heightened technical complexity. Here too an Ellison protagonist first declares his ineradicable Americanness as well as his blackness.

The final two stories of the early 1940's, "Flying Home" and "King of the Bingo Game," are more than mere apprentice pieces. In these works the young fiction writer discovers his own surrealistic voice and manages to integrate folklore, ritual, politics, history, and an absurdist vision of American experience in a way that may be termed "Ellisonian." These important early stories center on the individual's struggle to cope with a world that has become machine-mad; in both works a black protagonist struggles to confront the question, Who am I?

In 1943 Ellison joined the merchant marine, in part because he had belonged to the National Maritime Union since 1936, when he picketed for them, but mainly because he "wanted to contribute to the war, but didn't want to be in a Jim Crow army." While still in the service, Ellison was awarded a Rosenwald Fellowship to write a novel. In fact, he already had one outlined: a wartime story in which a black pilot is shot down, captured by the Nazis, and placed in a detention camp where he is the highest-ranking officer, and pitted by his Nazi guards against the white prisoners. Ellison continued working on this novel even after he began *Invisible Man* in 1945. But it never achieved

enough unity to satisfy its maker, and only one section, "Flying Home," was published.

Constructed as a story within a story, "Flying Home" deals with two thwarted flights: that of the black pilot Todd, whose plane collides with a buzzard and crashes in a field in Macon County; and that of Jefferson, who comes to Todd's rescue and who in his "tale told for true" sails from heaven back to the hell of Alabama. Jefferson's uproarious folktale, cataloged by collectors as early as 1919, eases the pain of Todd's injured ankle and his wait for a doctor's help. It also serves an initiatory function for this starry-eyed greenhorn, who, like Jefferson's heavenly flier, must eventually confront the evils of Jim Crow Alabama, however high he has flown. In this brilliantly layered story (which nods cordially to the swing instrumental of the same name and period) a variety of other folk motifs directs the young pilot on his looping homeward flight.

The critic Walter Blair has written that comic folklore aids the American's attempts to adjust to "totally new ways of living" as well as to "amazing differences between himself and his neighbors." In a lecture on American humor, Ellison himself has pointed out that funny tales provide not only escape and entertainment but also instruction. "Americans began," he says, "to tell stories which emphasize the uncertain nature of existence in the new world and as we did so, we allowed ourselves some relief from the pain of discovering that our bright hopes were going to be frustrated." Thus we have tall tales about the flintiness of farmland bursting with mile-high cornstalks, corroded buried treasure, and the brutality and sorcery of the Indians. Thus in the land of the free and the brave, we have humorous tales about the hatred and the casual violence of surly white men toward men black and red.

Jefferson's tale, listed by the folklorist Richard Dorson as "Colored Man in Heaven," provides Todd with a perspective for viewing his plight as a black trainee flier whose plane has been knocked down by a buzzard (called a "jimcrow bird" locally) onto the land of a racist white man named Graves. The folkloric lesson also needles the segregated air force of World War II, during which the question was raised of whether black fliers could be trusted in combat. Implied, too, is the more general question of how to face a segregated society that is patrolled by violence—or yet more generally, how to confront a manmade world full of sorrow and death. From Jefferson's tale Todd learns to laugh at the fact that his brightest and loftiest hopes may at last be grounded by jimcrow birds.

Like many Afro-American humorous tales, the "Colored Man in Heaven" joke momentarily accepts as true certain black stereotypes. As Jefferson tells it, the moment he got to heaven he raised such a ruckus by speeding that he scared the white angels and "knocked the tips offa some stars." Some of the heavenly "boys" even claim that Jefferson, flying with just one wing, stirred up a storm in Alabama and caused some lynchings. "Like colored folks will do," he forgets a warning from St. Peter, who finally loses patience with the "flying fool" and sends him back to Alabama. But Jefferson has the last word. "Well," he says, "you done took my wings. And you puttin' me out. You got charge of things so's I can't do nothin' about it. But you got to admit just this: while I was up here I was the flyingest sonofabitch what ever hit heaven!" Far from expressing self-hatred, this tale turns the black stereotype of the unmanageable, forgetful, smart-mouthing black man inside out. As a black in-joke, "Colored Man in Heaven" takes the teeth from racist charges by accepting them as true and then laughing at their foolishness. If he does "act up" in heaven, at least while there Jefferson is the "flyingest" of the heavenly fliers.

This tale also gives historical perspective to the dilemma of living in Jim Crow America. Jefferson finds that black angels do not fly, because they are required to wear heavy harnesses. He himself refuses to be encumbered and discovers that, "smooth as a bird," he can "loop-the-loop," even on one wing. But all this earns him a dressing-down by St. Peter in front of smirking white angels. Jefferson is finally thrown back into segregated Alabama. Similarly, not only were blacks in the "heaven" of America burdened with the harness of slavery, but at the abrupt end of Reconstruction the political freedoms tentatively held out were snatched back. Blacks again found themselves in a society filled with restrictions based on race. By the 1940's black men were trained to fly planes at the Tuskegee airfield, but for a long time black air force pilots (like Todd) were barred from combat duty. Knocked back by "jimcrows," Todd must learn the old survival technique of laughing at—or otherwise distancing himself from—an oppression with deep historical roots.

This tale is also part of a greenhorn's initiation into a complex and violent society. Todd's greenness is reflected in his undue optimism about being allowed to fly in combat. Why does he want to fly? "It's as good a way to fight and die as I know," he tells Jefferson. Asked if he has ever been hindered by whites who don't want blacks to be pilots, Todd tightens up and says, "No one has ever bothered us." To this the older man says, "Well, they'd like to." In Jefferson's tale even St. Peter and God himself seem involved in the conspiracy to keep blacks harnessed. The whole story angers Todd at first, but he relaxes as he sees that symbolically he too has been knocked down from the heaven of his aspiration. In the end he is freer of illusions; he is more shrewd and wary. Like the Invisible Man, Todd has crossed over into the fallen realm of adulthood. As he is carried from the field by Jefferson and Jefferson's son it is "as though he had been lifted out of his isolation, back into the world of men. A new current of communication flowed between the man and boy and himself."

The last story Ellison published before he began to work full-time on *Invisible Man* was "King of the Bingo Game." This compelling story, the first in which he felt he had discovered his own fictive voice, synthesizes much that he had learned as an apprentice and foreshadows certain of the most memorable forms and themes of *Invisible Man.* As in "Slick Gonna Learn," the protagonist is an unemployed young black man whose wife's need for medical care has made him desperate for money. Here again, as in all his previous stories, a young black man fights for freedom in a land tightly gripped by authority figures. In this surrealistic story, however, with its dreamlike shifts of time and levels of consciousness, the struggle is seen in its most abstracted form. In an epiphany the unnamed hero realizes that his battle for freedom and identity must be waged not against individuals or even groups but against no less than history and fate.

The King is Ellison's first character to sense the frightening absurdity of everyday American life. He has seen a woman walking into the bright street with a bedbug on her neck. He dozes in a theater and imagines himself a boy in the South, chased by a train that has jumped the track to pursue him, "and all the white people laughing as he ran screaming." He sees himself as "a long thin black wire that was being stretched and wound upon the bingo wheel." His nose begins to bleed, and he feels "as though the rush of blood to his head would burst out in baseball seams of small red droplets, like a head beaten by police clubs." It is in this wildly imagistic realm, where past and present, dreaming and waking converge, that the King, like the Invisible Man, sees the visions that may spell salvation.

In Ellison's earliest stories, Buster and Riley find that southern folk culture—despite its sudden violence—provides clear and stable definitions of black manhood. Up north, however, the King discovers that the values he had learned in Rocky Mount, North Carolina, do not apply. He is hungry and thirsty but knows better than to ask strangers in a movie theater for food and drink. "Up here it was different. Ask somebody for something, and they'd think you were crazy." When the King stands perplexed on the bingo stage, not only does the white master of ceremonies laugh at him ("So you decided to come down off that mountain to the U.S."), so do the blacks. "Ole Jack thinks he done found the end of the rainbow," someone shouts. As his emotions mount, the audience claps and shouts in mockery:

> Shoot the liquor to him, Jim, boy!
> Clap-clap-clap
> Well a-calla the cop
> He's blowing his top!
> Shoot the liquor to him, Jim, boy!

With no encouraging spiritual or anthem, with no guide like Jefferson to remind him of the way home, this hero must make his way alone. "He felt alone, but that was somehow right." Finding his southern folk consciousness shattered and half-forgotten in the North, the King must rely on his creativity and resilience to win his freedom and identity.

His fate seems to have been irreversibly determined long before his birth. Standing before the bingo wheel, he feels that he has "moved into the spell of some strange mysterious" being and that he is blinded by the wheel's lights and awestruck by its power: "He felt vaguely that his whole life was determined by the bingo wheel; not only that which would happen now . . . but all that had gone before, since his birth, and his mother's birth and the birth of his father. It had always been there, even though he had not been aware of it, handing out the unlucky cards and numbers of his days." Here the King echoes a question posed by the Invisible Man: What if history is a gambler?

If it is, the King feels he must do more than hope his lucky number comes up: he must subvert the process that has left him and his generations luckless. His refusal to stop turning the bingo wheel symbolizes this forthright subversion. By refusing to play a game that he has been fated to lose, he discovers who he is. First he realizes that he has lost the old identity: "somehow he had forgotten his own name. It was a sad, lost feeling to lose your name, and a crazy thing to do... 'Who am I?' he screamed." Then "he was reborn. For as long as he pressed the button he was The-man-who-pressed-the-button-who-held-the-prize-who-was-the-King-of-Bingo." Like the Invisible Man, the King frees himself when he discovers that he has been a sleepwalker, a fool, naive enough to accept unquestioningly the judgments handed down by an indifferent bingo wheel of fate, of circumstance, of history. Like the Invisible Man, he sees the cruelty of the culture and society that have shaped his personality; the vision frees him of his illusions. The instant before he is hit by the descending stage curtain, he is in full control of his fate. Moreover, he is symbolically reborn, better able to deal with life's absurd and dreadful turns. Before the curtain is rung down, the King hears the taunts and laughter in the theater but, foreshadowing the steely determination of Jim Trueblood in *Invisible Man,* he says, "Well, let 'em laugh. I'll do what I gotta do."

In 1945, exhausted by hard work and by a grueling merchant marine voyage, and hopeless over the unfinished war novel, Ellison went to recuperate at a friend's farm in Wakesfield, Vermont. Certain ideas seemed to come into focus there. He had been reading Lord Raglan's *The Hero,* a study of historical and mythic heroes, and had been thinking about leadership in the Afro-American community. Why, he wondered, did black leaders so often seem uncommitted to their black constituents? Why did they so often seem dependent not on the will of blacks but on the largesse of white patrons? Along with these questions, Ellison was pondering a number of others—and overall, the persistent problem of finding a literary form flexible enough to contain his vision of the wild and shifting American hodge-podge of cultures and characters. He determined to write a novel about black identity, heroism, and history, and to write it in a style "unburdened by ... narrow naturalism."

One morning in 1945, still in Vermont, Ellison scribbled the words, "I am an invisible man"—his novel's first sentence. He recalls that he played with the idea and "started to reject it, but it intrigued me, and I began to put other things with it. And pretty soon I had a novel going, and I began to work out of a conceptual outline on it. And as fast as I could work out the concepts, the incidents started flowing in on me." Back in New York, Ellison continued work on the novel in his apartment on St. Nicholas Avenue, but he also went downtown every morning to work like any businessman. Using a friend's Fifth Avenue office, he put in at least eight hours a day writing before returning to his home.

The project was blessed with the support of Ellison's present wife, Fanny McConnell, of whom he has written "my beloved wife ... has shown, again and again, through her sacrifices, encouragement and love, more faith in the writer and his talent than the writer has shown in himself."

He worked on *Invisible Man* for five years, taking one year off to work on another novel. *Invisible Man* was published in 1952. To many critics the novel seemed like a miraculous first work. But Ellison's first published fiction, "Slick Gonna Learn," had been conceived as part of a novel. By the 1940's, with "Flying Home" and "King of the Bingo Game" he had discovered a voice and a set of questions and concerns that were timeless but were his own. By the mid-1940's he had absorbed the lessons of Mark Twain, Hemingway, Richard Wright, and the social realists; and he had experimented with the narrative devices of many writers, especially Henry James, Faulkner, Dostoevsky, and Joyce. The sentence "I am an invisible man" started him on a work into which he could pour all he had learned as an apprentice perfecting his craft.

With the publication of *Invisible Man,* Ellison moved suddenly into the front ranks of American writers. His novel evokes visions and tensions peculiar to American life as Afro-Americans know it: Ellison's brown-skinned, nameless seeker suffers and scoots, forth and back through a thicket of briars well-known to American blacks. Yet *Invisible Man* is a modern masterpiece that, as Wright Morris has written, "belongs on the shelf with the classical efforts man has made to chart the river Lethe from its mouth to its sources." Expressing richly the meaning of life in Harlem (and the southern background of that life), Ellison manages to describe what he says he finds in the work of the painter Romare Bearden: "the harlemness of the human condition." *Invisible Man* is a deeply comic novel, with moments of terror and tragedy; it is a *Bildungsroman* in which a young man awakens to consciousness by piecing together fragments and symbols from history, myth, folklore, and literature, as well as his own painful experience.

Set in the approximate period 1930–1950, *Invisible Man* is the story of the development of an ambitious black, a young man from the provinces of the South, who goes to college and then to New York in search of advancement. This greenhorn at first wants no more than to walk in the footsteps of Booker T. Washington, whose words he quotes at his high school graduation and at a smoker for the town's leading white citizens. At the smoker he is given a new briefcase and a scholarship, but is first required to fight blindfolded in a "battle royal" with other black youths. That night he dreams that his grandfather tells him to open the briefcase, which contains a document reading: "To Whom It May Concern, Keep This Nigger-Boy Running." But the youngster remains naive. He goes off to college but is expelled when he makes the fatal mistake of taking a visiting white trustee to a section of the local black community (and, metaphorically, to a level of black reality) never included in the college-town tour. Bledsoe, the college president, sends the hero packing to New York, first giving him a set of private letters of introduction that, he finally discovers, also courteously request that he be kept running—and jobless.

Eventually he does find work in New York, first in a paint factory, where he is discharged after being seriously hurt in an explosion—one that ultimately jars him into a new self-awareness and courage. He gives a moving speech at the eviction of an elderly Harlem couple and is hired by a predominantly white radical political organization called the Brotherhood. The group seems to confirm his childhood wish by telling him he will be made the "new Booker T. Washington . . . even greater than he." But the Brotherhood also sets him running. Despite his success in Harlem, the downtown "brothers" withdraw support for his program. A race riot erupts, and, still carrying his briefcase, which now contains, besides his diploma, several other mementoes of his adventures, he falls down a manhole into an abandoned, bricked-up cellar. There he closely examines the papers in his briefcase and realizes how fully he has been betrayed by those who had professed to help him. And yet he discovers too that not only "could you travel upward toward success but you could travel downwards as well." He will remain down there, bathed in stolen light from the power company, and in blues music; he will compose his memoirs in his hole at the edge of Harlem, in hibernation. "Please, a definition: A hibernation is a covert preparation for a more overt action." If others cannot or will not see him, he at least will see himself. His narrative, full of irony, insight, and fury, shows that he has attained full self-awareness—even a certain wisdom—and that he has been able to act, to write this stunning book.

The shape and style of *Invisible Man* bespeak its determination to step toward the universal through "the narrow door of the particular." The novel resounds with black folklore, in which, says Ellison, "we tell what Negro experience really is. We back away from the chaos of experience and from ourselves, and we depict the humor as well as the horror of our living. We project Negro life in a metaphysical perspective, and we have seen it with a complexity of vision that seldom gets into our writing." Blues, spirituals, sermons, tales, boasts, and other black American folk forms influence the characters, plot, and figurative language in this teeming novel. The striving young man is drawn toward the freedom of consciousness and conscience by the magic horns and voices of the folk. Nonetheless, he himself is never so much a blues hero or Bre'r Rabbit as he is like Bre'r Bear, outmaneuvered until the end by Bre'rs Fox and Dog—in his case Bledsoe; Brockway, the factory supervisor; and One-Eyed Jack, who recruits him for the Brotherhood. Like the befuddled butt of many a folktale, this young man seems determined to be somebody's greenhorn, somebody's fool.

The novel is built not only upon the foundation of black lore but also of black literature. It is a benchmark black novel that seems aware of the entire tradition of Afro-American letters. In it one overhears the black and white tricksters (slaves and slaveholders) of slave narrative locked in combat. One senses again the slaves'

desperate yearning for education, mobility, and individual and communal freedom. There are particularly strong echoes of works by W. E. B. Du Bois, James Weldon Johnson, Zora Neale Hurston, and Richard Wright, all of whom wrote fictional portraits of tragicomic characters, "articulate heroes" in search of broader freedom.

But the power of *Invisible Man* is more than that of a repository of black influences. As if in defiance of the single-minded critic, Ellison adapted symbolism and rhetorical strategy from any and every source he felt would enrich the texture and meaning of his work: Sophocles, Homer, Dostoevsky, Malraux, Joyce, and Freud all figure in *Invisible Man*. Some allusions and symbol clusters fade out like wistful jazz riffs; others recur and provide the novel with structure. But no single critical "method" can explain this capacious novel, which owes as much to the symbolist tradition of Melville and Hawthorne as it does to the vernacular tradition of Mark Twain and Hemingway. This is not a "realistic" novel or an understated "hard-boiled" novel, or a symbolist romance (it is not, in any case, to be *only* so categorized); instead, it is an epic novel of many voices, an experimental narrative constructed upon the author's mastery of American language: as he describes it, a

rich babel . . . a language full of imagery and gesture and rhetorical canniness . . . an alive language swirling with over three hundred years of American living, a mixture of the folk, the Biblical, the scientific, and the political. Slangy in one instance, academic in another, loaded poetically with imagery at one moment, mathematically bare of imagery in the next.

The Invisible Man embodies this confluence of traditions. He is a modern Odysseus, a latter-day Candide, a "black boy" comparable to Wright, a black and obscure Jude, a Yankee yokel, a minstrel endman. Of the several secondary characters who also embody a rich mixture of allusions, two stand out: Trueblood and Rinehart. Both are significant influences on the protagonist's growing awareness.

It is Trueblood, the sharecropper, whom the hero encounters when giving Mr. Norton, the white trustee, a tour of the college environs. "Half-consciously" the student drives over a hill into a section of the black community built during slavery and, at Norton's "excited command," stops in front of Trueblood's shack. Trueblood had, in earlier days, been invited to entertain white guests of the school, but no more: he has brought disgrace to the black community by impregnating his own daughter. "You have looked upon chaos and are not destroyed!" says Norton. "No suh! I feels all right," says Trueblood. Not just willingly but "with a kind of satisfaction and no trace of hesitancy or shame," Trueblood recites the exuberant tale of his forbidden act; it is a private performance for the student and Norton, whose face, at story's end, "had drained of color." Shaking, the white man gives the farmer a hundred-dollar banknote: "Please take this and buy the children some toys for me," the northern philanthropist says.

Rinehart enters the narrative late in the novel. To escape two followers of Ras, a black nationalist whose organization rivals the Brotherhood, the Invisible Man puts on glasses with lenses so dark that they appear black; he is immediately mistaken for Rinehart. "But . . . where's your new hat I bought you?" a young woman asks. To complete his disguise he buys the widest white hat in stock at a local store and is mistaken for Rinehart all evening: Bliss Rinehart, gambler and pimp; Rine the lover and cool "daddy-o"; Rine the briber and "confidencing sonofabitch"; Rine the numbers runner; Reverend B. P. Rinehart, "Spiritual Technologist . . . No Problem Too Hard For God."

The Invisible Man is stunned by Rinehart: "Could he himself be both rind and heart? What is real anyway? . . . The world in which we lived was without boundaries. A vast seething, hot world of fluidity, and Rine the rascal was at home."

Trueblood and Rinehart make their homes in quite different worlds. Trueblood has remained in the South, in a log-cabin homestead dusty with slave history. By contrast, while Rinehart may once have preached in Virginia, he has become a master manipulator of a chaos that is distinctively northern in scope. Indeed, what these black men have most in common is that both have stood before teeming chaos and have survived. Rinehart has embraced chaos. Trueblood has faced his crime of incest—the sin associated with confusion, degeneracy, and death, from Sophocles' *Oedipus Rex* to Freud's *Totem and Taboo*.

Both characters bring to mind the Afro-American musical form, the blues. Trueblood has done wrong (but didn't mean to) and is bashed in the head by his wife, who leaves him for a time and spreads the tale of his wrongdoing until even the preacher calls him "the most wicked man" he has ever seen. Yet Trueblood tells his story until it achieves a certain cadence, and it ends with song. "Finally, one night, way early in the mornin', I looks up and sees the stars and I starts singin'. I don't mean to, I didn't think 'bout it, just start singin'. I don't know what it was, some kinda church song, I guess. All I know is I *ends up* singin' the blues. I sings me some blues that might ain't never been sang before, and while I'm singin' them blues I makes up my mind that I ain't nobody but myself and ain't nothin' I can do but let whatever is gonna happen, happen. I made up my mind that I was goin' back home. . . ." Trueblood is what Albert Murray has called a "blues hero": a resilient improviser who confronts the low-down dirtiness of life, the "changes" and the "breaks," and who manages with style and grace to keep on keeping on.

Rinehart is no blues man in this broadly heroic sense. "Rinehart, Rinehart," thinks the Invisible Man, "what kind of man is Rinehart?" His name is a name from a blues song: "Rinehart, Rinehart, / It's so lonesome up here / On Beacon Hill. . . ." But instead of evoking terror or pity, instead of putting confusion into perspective, as does Trueblood, Rinehart personifies confusion. He is the no-good "sweet-back," the evil mistreater that the blues bemoan. Trueblood sings the blues as a cathartic statement to assuage a tragic predicament, but Rinehart dispenses the blues to others: he distributes travail and thrives off it.

Trueblood's classical ancestors include Oedipus the King, but Rinehart's forebears are shape-changers and tricksters. His middle name, Ellison has written, is Proteus.

Yet both characters capture the note and trick of Afro-American life and function in quite specific ways. Trueblood's tale is a lesson and a graphic warning, from which the Invisible Man learns that "there's always an element of crime in freedom." Trueblood's breaking of the incest taboo (even if, as he insists, he was asleep while doing so) suggests that the Invisible Man can also break the law and so extend the definition of what it means to be black and what it means to be human. Rinehart's lesson is that the world is much more ambiguous—and, again, full of possibility—than any narrow-minded, strict, schematic thinkers like the Brotherhood can know. "Underground" in Harlem there are operators undreamed of by One-Eyed Jack and his "brothers." Some, like the unscrupulous Rinehart, prosper in the dark maze. Others, like the "hip" young men the narrator sees in the subway station, have also been ignored by the Brotherhood. "Men out of time, who would soon be gone and forgotten. . . . But who knew but that they were

the saviors, the true leaders, the bearers of something precious? . . . What if history was a gambler, instead of a force in a laboratory experiment, and the boys his ace in the hole?" Rinehart the trickster is a figure of escape and of possibility whose presence suggests that beneath the surface of the American commonplace there burns a bright and raging world.

Invisible Man is a complex, ironic novel in which the hero discovers a great deal about American history and culture. In the end he sees that he has been a fool, that, like Trueblood and Rinehart, he must confront chaos or it will engulf him. When he plunges underground, he vows to stop running the course that Bledsoe and others had set for him and can say with Trueblood: "I ain't nobody but myself . . . I made up my mind that I was goin' back home."

Ellison's only book since *Invisible Man* has been the excellent collection of essays, *Shadow and Act* (1964). Its initial appeal seemed to be that in it the "invisible" author would at last emerge from underground: here, as one reviewer proclaimed, was Ralph Ellison's real autobiography." And *Shadow and Act* does contain autobiographical essays, notably its introduction and "Hidden Name and Complex Fate"; while in the reviews and interviews here collected the author also draws extensively upon his own experience. Because the essays (none retouched) were written over a twenty-two-year period, they reveal certain aspects of his development from the twenty-eight-year-old, Marxist-oriented WPA worker of "The Way It Is" (1942) to the seasoned writer of 1964: by the latter date he is not "primarily concerned with injustice, but with art."

In his introduction Ellison offers a sort of apologia, explaining that the essays "represent, in all their modesty, some of the necessary effort which a writer of my background must make in order to possess the meaning of his experience." When the first essay appeared, he tells us, he regarded himself "in my most secret heart at least [as] a musician," not a writer. "One might say that with these thin essays for wings," he notes, "I was launched full flight into the dark." Thus, "their basic significance, whatever their value as information or speculation, is autobiographical." Nonetheless, the book contains thematic unities that are even more compelling. A good deal of the cumulative power of *Shadow and Act* derives from its contrasting black American life as seen through the lenses of politics, sociology, and popular culture and as observed and lived by one sensitive, questioning man.

Shadow and Act has enduring validity as a unified work of art because of its author's single-minded intention to define Afro-American life. Ellison sometimes gently punctures, sometimes wields an ax against inadequate definitions of black experience. In place of what he detects as false prophecy, usually uttered by social scientists, he chooses as broad a frame of reference as possible to interpret black experience in richly optimistic terms. "Who wills to be a Negro?" he asks, rhetorically. "I do!"

Once Ellison had released the galley proofs for *Invisible Man,* he felt emotionally and artistically spent. But he had begun jotting down ideas for a new novel even before *Invisible Man* was published, so that if it failed he would be too busy to worry. In 1952 he said he had a new novel "on the bench." In 1953, shortly after the National Book Award ceremonies honoring *Invisible Man,* he suggested that his new novel might be an elaboration of the first. "I don't feel that I have exhausted the theme of invisibility," he said. Indeed he felt that he could salvage some material edited out of the several drafts of the novel. "Out of the Hospital and Under the Bar" (1953), an early version of a chapter in *Invisible Man,* works well as a short story, not as a mere clipping from the larger work; "Did You Ever Dream Lucky?" (1954) concerns

Mary Rambo, the novel's Harlem landlady. As early as 1953, however, Ellison had begun laying the structural framework for a totally new novel that he felt sure would be much better and more complex than *Invisible Man.* Since then Ellison has been stoking the fires of this new novel. Its eight published sections, along with sections read on public television and on college campuses, have made the wait for the finished volume—or volumes, as Ellison has tantalizingly suggested—something of a vigil.

In 1965 Ellison told an interviewer that he wanted to publish a book "in the coming year," adding, "so the pressure's on." Where is this long-promised novel? When he is at all willing to discuss its progress, Ellison recites the history of a wayward work, tedious in the initial construction and reconstruction; destroyed, in part, by fire; bedeviling in the re-reconstruction. In 1970 James McPherson noted that tales concerning the awaited novel were plentiful: "One man has heard that he has pulled it back from his publisher again for more revisions; another says that Ellison worries about its being dated; a third man says that Ellison cannot finish it." One explanation was heard from the writer's wife. "She says she heard him in his study at night turning pages and laughing to himself. He enjoys the book so much that he isn't in a hurry to share it with the public." Richard Kostelanetz reports that an old friend of Ellison's has said: "Ralph is insanely ambitious. He actually writes quickly but won't release this book until he is sure it is the greatest American novel ever written." Ellison refuses to publish more selections from the novel's current manuscript not only because he is "not so strapped for money that I have to publish those pieces" but also because he wants "the impact of the total book . . . rather than the published pieces." "Can you say when it will be finished?" an interviewer inquired in 1978. "No," responded Ellison, "I've done that too many times and been wrong."

The writing slowed to a baffled halt, for a time, after the hail of assassinations in the 1960's—President John F. Kennedy, Martin Luther King, Robert Kennedy. With the assassination of a major political figure as the novel's central incident, the eruption of real killings "chilled" Ellison, for "suddenly life was stepping in and imposing himself upon my fiction." Ellison's conviction that his new novel must somehow deal with these real assassinations kept the book in blueprint:

Much of the mood of this book was conceived as comic. Not that the assassination was treated comically, but there is humor involved.... Anyway, I managed to keep going with it ... I know that it led me to try to give the book a richer structuring, so that the tragic elements could contain the comic and the comic the tragic, without violating our national pieties— if there are any left.

That Ellison was far out of step with the most vocal black ideologists of the 1960's also slowed his writing. When Haki Madhubuti (Don L. Lee), Amiri Baraka (LeRoi Jones), and other black writers and social critics were asserting the national identity and the Africanness of black Americans, Ellison stiffly dissented: "I'm not a separatist. The imagination is integrative. That's how you make the new—by putting something else with what you've got. And I'm unashamedly an American integrationist." At Oberlin in April 1969 Ellison was given a brittle reception by black students, one of whom complained: "His speech was about how American black culture had blended into American white culture." Ellison had noted, for example, that the Afro hairstyle had become "a part of American popular culture" and warned the black students not to be surprised if whites began to adopt it. "The students went out screaming," a young woman recalled. "Who is he to insult what we wear? No honky could wear an Afro.

They're stealing what is ours." At a meeting after the speech, the black students said, "You don't have anything to tell us." One student said of *Invisible Man:* "Your book doesn't mean anything, because in it you're shooting down Ras the Destroyer, a rebel leader of black people." Ellison said that the book was written a long time ago but that he would not apologize for it, to which the student answered, "That just proves you're an Uncle Tom."

At Harvard in December 1973 Ellison spoke about the philosopher Alain Locke as a champion of American pluralism. By then the mood on campus had changed. There were awkward silences when Ellison told the gathering that blacks are not an African people but an American one; yet the final applause was enthusiastic. At that point Ellison appeared to have weathered the radical tempest. By 1980 he could look back on those difficult days with irony, defensive pride, and some anger. Of those who contributed strident attacks to a special Ellison issue of *Black World,* a defunct black journal, Ellison has said.

Safe behind the fence provided by a black capitalist, they had one big "barking-at-the-big-gate" go at me. They even managed to convince a few students that I was the worst disaster that had ever hit Afro-American writing. But for all their attacks I'm still here trying—while if I'm asked where is *Black World* today my answer is: Gone with the snows of yester-year / down the pissoir—Da-Daa, Da-Daaa—and good riddance!

In Richard Kostelanetz's words, "One reason Ellison has not been able to complete his second novel is that all these distractions demand so much of his attention, as much to flush the ideological junk out of his own head as to speak about corruption in the social world." Black writers, Kostelanetz comments, seem to have a harder role to play than do white writers because blacks are cornered into commenting on sociopolitical issues that white writers can avoid.

As if these deflections were not enough, in the late 1960's Ellison's summer home in Massachusetts was destroyed by fire, as were 365 pages of the new novel, an entire year's revisions. "I assure you, that's a most traumatic experience," he recalled, "one of the most traumatic of my life!" The writer Jervis Anderson has noted:

Perhaps nothing more painful occurred in the working life of a well-known writer since Thomas Carlyle lost the manuscript of the first volume of his history of the French Revolution, a servant in the home of John Stuart Mill having used it to help get a fire going. Carlyle is said to have sat down, with astonishing calmness, and reproduced what he had lost. Ellison found it difficult to begin the task of restructuring, rewriting, and recapturing the fluid composition and insights of the first draft. The subtleties and rhythms of a first inspiration are almost impossible to reclaim. But if it is at all possible to overcome these problems, then Ellison, with his belief that difficult circumstances can almost always be made to yield benefits and victories, is the sort of writer to do it.

Like most of his earlier fiction, the new work is experimental: now familiar, focused, compelling; now ill-lit, uncertain, frightening. "The new book's form," explains Ellison, is "a realism extended beyond realism." This is "a crazy book, and I won't pretend to understand what it's about. I do think," he adds, "there are some funny passages in it." The mixture of allusions is characteristic; images and narrative strategies echo Joyce and Faulkner especially, as well as classical and religious myth. And as in *Invisible Man,* popular American sources also energize the narrative: "I use anything from movies to comic strips," he says. "Anything: radio, sermons, practical jokes. In fact anything that suggests new ideas for handling narrative; even jazz riffs." Startling shifts in point of view change the shape of events in sometimes surprising ways: everything depends on whether we view the action through the Reverend Hickman (black blues musician turned evangelist, whose voice and eloquence have earned him the nickname "God's Trombone"); Bliss (Hickman's adopted son, a boy preacher who abandons his calling, disappears, passes for white, and emerges as Senator Sunraider, the venomously antiblack representative from Massachusetts); McIntyre (naive but sincere white reporter); Lee Willie Minifees (jazz musician who, enraged at Sunraider's racism, burns his gleaming Cadillac on the senator's lawn); or Cliofus (stuttering man-child with a terrifyingly clear memory and a way with words). Thrust into the realm of such tales as "And Hickman Arrives," "Night-Talk," "Juneteenth," "Cadillac Flambé," "Backwacking," "The Roof, the Steeple and the People," "It Always Breaks Out," "A Song of Innocence"—stories told as letters, fuzzy musings, tirades, sermons, or lies—the reader is forced to confront questions that Ellison says issue from the heart of America's condition as a nation still unformed. Where, what, who am I? What is illusion, what is real? What is black, what is white, what is American?

This is fiction scored for many voices. In the 1920's, working the southern revival circuit, the Reverend Hickman and the Reverend Bliss deliver the dialogue sermon published as "Juneteenth." Blending with his mentor's trombone voice, Bliss's voice is a clear piccolo. The two trade phrases about the losses sustained by blacks during slavery, and the tragic recital swerves at comedy's edge as Bliss says:

. . . Amen, Daddy Hickman! Abused and without shoes, pounded down and ground like grains

of sand on the shores of the sea ...
... Amen [Hickman answers] And God—
Count it, Rev. Bliss ...
... Left eyeless [Bliss responds] earless, nose-
less, throatless, teethless, tongueless, handless,
feetless, armless, wrongless, rightless, ... motherless, fatherless, sisterless, brotherless, plow-
less, muleless, foodless, mindless—and Godless,
Rev. Hickman, did you say Godless?

Even so, laments Hickman. But in this sermon of redemption, blacks are shown stripped
of African culture—but are reborn as Afro-
Americans, tempered for struggle in this land
of trouble and sacrifice. The trombone enters
Hickman's voice as he says:

Ah, but though divided and scattered, ground
down and battered into the earth like a spike
being pounded by a ten-pound sledge, we were
on the ground and in the earth and the earth
was red and black like the earth of Africa. And
as we moldered underground we were mixed
with this land. We liked it. It fitted us fine. It
was in us and we're in it. And then—praise
God—deep in the ground, deep in the womb of
this land, we began to stir!

Between sermons, Bliss chats with his friend
Body, who swears he has sat in a dark room and
watched white men and "hosses" and an entire
railroad train shine out of a black box and move
around on a glistening screen. The little
preacher, who has never seen a movie, shakes
his head and warns Body about the sin of false
witness; but Body, speaking a broad vernacular,
stings Bliss with a warning of his own:

... dont come preaching me no sermon. Cause
you know I can kick your butt. I dont have to
take no stuff off you. This here aint no Sunday,
no how. Can't nobody make me go to church on
no Friday, cause on a Friday I'm liable to boot
a preacher's behind until his nose bleeds....

That's the truth, Rev, and you know the truth
is what the Lord loves.

In Ellison's new fiction, antagonists include
elementary-school principal Dr. Peter Osgood
Eliot, "who usually looked no more human than
a granite general astride a concrete horse," and
school disciplinarian the Reverend Blue Goose
Samson, "with his well-stropped head," who,
informed of trouble, comes to class "dragging
half a tree limb behind him" to whip the of-
fender along with "all the boys in the first five
rows." The teacher is Miss Mabel Kindly.
"What's the difference," she quizzes her scholars,"between a multplier and a multiplicand?"
On a field trip to view the remains of a whale,
she is ultraproper in manners and enunciation:
"The whale, chill-dreen, is an ani-mule." Small
wonder Cliofus dislikes school and prefers the
easing music and language of distant, highball-
ing trains:

Miss Janey's right, though [he reflects]; those
trains ease me.—Eeeeease me! What I mean is,
they ease my aching mind. When I watch those
engines and boxcars and gondolas I start to
moving up and down in my body's joy and when
I see those drivers start to roll, all those words
go jumping out to them like the swine in the
Bible that leaped off the cliff into the sea—only
they hop on the Katy, the Rock Island and the
Santa Fe.... Space, time and distance, like
they say, I'm a yearning man who has to sit still.
Maybe those trains need those words to help
them find their way across this here wide land
in the dark, I don't know. But for me it's like
casting bread on the water because not only am
I eased in my restless mind, but once in a while,
deep in the night, when everything is quiet and
all those voices and words are resting and all
those things that I've been tumbling and running and bouncing through my mind all day
have got quiet as a ship in a bottle on a shelf,
then I can hear those train whistles talking to

me, just to me, and in those times I know I have all in this world I'll ever need mama and papa and jellyroll. . . .

It is a similarly innocent boy, Severen, who by the 1950's has grown up to stand in the gallery of the Senate and to gun down Sunraider. Bliss/Sunraider is also from the South—his white-black, sacred-secular, revival-sideshow, city-country, downside-up boyhood eventually driving him to insulate himself behind the alabaster walls of jingoism and white-is-rightness. The novelist Leon Forrest has said that Bliss/Sunraider emerges as "something of a brutalized metaphor himself of what happened to the baby democracy, tossed from hand to hand and born out of wedlock (*à la* Fielding's Tom Jones, to say nothing of some of the leading people in the U.S.)." In Ellison's vision, America is a 200-year-old child, a strangely wrinkled baby, a Bliss destined to choose among heritages.

Some of Ellison's detractors charge that he dotes on the complexity of American experience in order to avoid speaking out against simple injustice; that he hides behind the grand banner of high art rather than "telling it like it is." He believes that the American melting pot has in fact melted and that blacks are as American—in some ways more so—as any Johnny Appleseed. This conviction, some critics say, obscures the fact that black Americans constitute a distinctive group with particular strengths as well as special troubles. As for Ellison's "complexity," it is part and parcel of his discipline as a writer. It is the novelist in him that insists on asking such bothersome questions as, "What, by the way, is one to make of a white youngster who, with a transistor radio, screaming a Stevie Wonder tune, glued to his ear, shouts racial epithets at black youngsters trying to swim at a public beach—and this in the name of the ethnic sanctity of what has been declared a neighborhood turf?" Ellison told a Harvard gather-

ing in 1973: "All of us are part white, and all of y'all are part colored." The novelist also insists on the cruel and tragic aspects of American comedy, on the blues side of black religion, on the upper-class elegance of the black poor, on the universality of what Ellison still calls "Negro" experience, and on the "harlemness" of the human condition.

Many of Ellison's critics do not know that he was a left-wing critic and author for the *New Masses* and an advocate of black nationalism who has done his share of political stumping. Even now, Ellison maintains that writing novels is bound up with the process of nation-building: rediscovering, redefining, revitalizing America. The critic Kimberly W. Benston has observed that although their conclusions are often at odds, Ellison and Baraka have much more in common than is usually noticed. Both are concerned with various, crisscrossing lines of tradition that inform peculiarly Afro-American "responses to life"; both have looked upon an American scene marbled with ambiguity and contradiction and have sought "strategies for saving and improving the best aspects of the black self." Both see clearly that in the melting pot are ingredients unmistakably and magnificently black.

In fact, with Baraka and Richard Wright, Ellison has been the most eloquent and influential spokesman for what, "on the lower frequencies" (Ellison's phrase), it means to be black and American. In Ellison's work one finds penetrating and yet lyrical descriptions of black life, insider's rare perceptions of the contour and meaning of a peculiarly American experience. Greater than these other writers is Ellison's sense of America's confusion and of the bleakly tragic barriers (underrated by most conservatives, liberals, and revolutionaries alike) against which we all struggle. Greater, too, is his faith in America's possibility of redemption and his awareness of the difficulty of securing true redemption from that most American sin, vanity. "Remember," he told a graduating class in 1974, "that the antidote to *hubris,* to overweening pride, is irony, that capacity to discover and systematize ideas. Or, as Emerson insisted, the development of consciousness, consciousness, *Consciousness.* And with consciousness, a more refined conscientiousness, and most of all, that tolerance which takes the form of humor." With his unfailing humor and tragic awareness, Ralph Ellison is an important voice in American fiction, a "man of good hope" whose work bespeaks his dedication to artistic craft and to the idea that writers are among America's most vital nation-builders.

Selected Bibliography

WORKS OF RALPH ELLISON

BOOKS
Invisible Man. New York: Random House, 1952.
Shadow and Act. New York: Random House, 1964.

SHORT FICTION
"Slick Gonna Learn." *Direction,* 2:10–11, 14, 16 (September 1939).
"The Birthmark." *New Masses,* 36:16–17 (July 2, 1940).
"Afternoon." In *American Writing,* edited by Hans Otto Storm et al. Prairie City, Ill.: J. A. Decker, 1940. Pp. 28–37.
"Mister Toussan." *New Masses,* 41:19–20 (November 4, 1941).
"That I Had the Wings." *Common Ground,* 3:30–37 (Summer 1943).
"In a Strange Country." *Tomorrow,* 3:41–44 (July 1944).
"King of the Bingo Game." *Tomorrow,* 4:29–33 (November 1944).

"Flying Home." In *Cross Section,* edited by Edwin Seaver. New York: L. B. Fischer, 1944. Pp. 469–485.
"Did You Ever Dream Lucky?" *New World Writing,* 5:134–145 (April 1954).
"February." *Saturday Review,* 38:25 (January 1, 1955).
"A Coupla Scalped Indians." *New World Writing,* 9:225–236 (1956).
"And Hickman Arrives." *Noble Savage,* 1:5–49 (1960).
"The Roof, the Steeple and the People." *Quarterly Review of Literature,* 10:115–128 (1960).
"Out of the Hospital and Under the Bar." In *Soon, One Morning,* edited by Herbert Hill. New York: Knopf, 1963. Pp. 242–290.
"It Always Breaks Out." *Partisan Review,* 30:13–28 (Spring 1963).
"Juneteenth." *Quarterly Review of Literature,* 13:262–276 (1965).
"Night-Talk." *Quarterly Review of Literature,* 16:317–329 (1969).
"A Song of Innocence." *Iowa Review,* 1:30–40 (Spring 1970).
"Cadillac Flambé." *American Review,* 16:249–269 (February 1973).
"Backwacking, a Plea to the Senator." *Massachusetts Review,* 18:411–416 (Autumn 1977).

SELECTED ESSAYS AND REVIEWS
"Creative and Cultural Lag." *New Challenge,* 2:90–91 (Fall 1937).
"Stormy Weather." *New Masses,* 37:20–21 (September 24, 1940).
"Recent Negro Fiction." *New Masses,* 40:22–26 (August 5, 1941).
"Collaborator with His Own Enemy." *New York Times Book Review,* February 19, 1950, p. 4.
"Society, Morality, and the Novel." In *The Living Novel: A Symposium,* edited by Granville Hicks. New York: Macmillan, 1957. Pp. 58–91.
"What These Children Are Like." In Seminar on Education for Culturally Different Youth, *Education of the Deprived and Segregated.* New York: Bank Street College of Education, 1965.
"Tell It Like It Is, Baby." *Nation,* 201: 129–136 (September 20, 1965).
"The Novel as a Function of American Democracy." *Wilson Library Bulletin,* 41:1022–1027 (June 1967).

"What America Would Be Like Without Blacks." *Time*, 95:54–55 (April 6, 1970).

"The Little Man at Chehaw Station." *American Scholar*, 47:25–48 (Winter 1977–1978).

BIOGRAPHICAL AND CRITICAL STUDIES

Anderson, Jervis. "Going to the Territory." *New Yorker*, 52:55–108 (November 22, 1976).

Baker, Houston. *Long Black Song: Essays in Black American Literature and Culture.* Charlottesville: University Press of Virginia, 1972.

Benston, Kimberly W. "Ellison, Baraka, and the Faces of Tradition." *boundary 2*, 6:333–354 (Winter 1978).

Blake, Susan L. "Ritual and Rationalization: Black Folklore in the Works of Ralph Ellison." *PMLA*, 94:121–136 (January 1979).

Callahan, John F. "The Historical Frequencies of Ralph Waldo Ellison." In *Chant of Saints*, edited by Michael S. Harper and Robert B. Stepto. Urbana: University of Illinois Press, 1979. Pp. 33–52.

College Language Association. *CLA Journal*, 13 (March 1970); special Ellison issue.

Covo, Jacqueline. *The Blinking Eye: Ralph Waldo Ellison and His American, French, German and Italian Critics, 1952–1971.* Metuchen, N. J.: Scarecrow Press, 1974.

Davis, Arthur P. *From the Dark Tower.* Washington, D. C.: Howard University Press, 1974.

Gibson, Donald B., ed. *Five Black Writers: Essays on Wright, Ellison, Baldwin, Hughes, and LeRoi Jones.* New York: New York University Press, 1970.

Hersey, John, ed. *Ralph Ellison, a Collection of Critical Essays.* Englewood Cliffs, N. J.: Prentice-Hall, 1974.

Kazin, Alfred. *Bright Book of Life.* New York: Dell, 1971.

Kent, George. *Blackness and the Adventure of American Culture.* Chicago: Third World, 1972.

Kist, E. M. "A Laingian Analysis of Blackness in Ralph Ellison's *Invisible Man.*" *Studies in Black Literature*, 7:19–23 (Spring 1976).

Kostelanetz, Richard. "Ralph Ellison: Novelist as Brown Skinned Aristocrat." *Shenandoah*, 20, no. 4: 56–77 (Summer 1969).

Murray, Albert. *The Omni-Americans.* New York: Outerbridge and Dienstfrey, 1970.

Nash, Russell W. "Stereotypes and Social Types in Ellison's *Invisible Man.*" *Sociological Quarterly*, 6:349–360 (Autumn 1965).

O'Meally, Robert G. *The Craft of Ralph Ellison.* Cambridge, Mass.: Harvard University Press, 1980.

Reilly, John M., ed. *Twentieth Century Interpretations of Invisible Man: A Collection of Essays.* Englewood Cliffs, N. J.: Prentice-Hall, 1970.

Scott, Nathan A., Jr. "Black Literature." In *Harvard Guide to Contemporary American Writing*, edited by Daniel Hoffman. Cambridge, Mass.: Harvard University Press, 1979. Pp. 287–341.

Stepto, Robert B. *From Behind the Veil: A Study of Afro-American Narrative.* Urbana: University of Illinois Press, 1979.

Tischler, Nancy M. "Negro Literature and Classic Form." *Contemporary Literature*, 10:352–365 (Summer 1969).

—ROBERT O'MEALLY

Ralph Waldo Emerson

1803-1882

FROM wise men the world inherits a literature of wisdom, characterized less by its programmatic informativeness than by its strength and brevity of statement. *Proverb, aphorism, maxim* are terms for the succinct wise sayings which we have from every language, from Moses and Jesus, from Confucius, Buddha, and Mohammed, from Heraclitus, Martial, and Marcus Aurelius, from Montaigne and Bacon, down the traditions of time to America's man of wisdom, Ralph Waldo Emerson.

To understand Emerson's writing we had best try to follow what he has to say in the way that he says it. First, in three maturely characteristic books, let us look at his setting forth of ideas. Then, in all his writing from youthful speculation to aging reminiscence, let us trace his suiting of thought to event. Finally, let us try to specify, by a closer look at his traits of style, some of the particular individuality of our wisdom-writer in his tradition.

One of his most solidly organized and directly speaking books is *The Conduct of Life,* published along with *Representative Men* and *English Traits* in Emerson's mature years and representing the fullness of his achievement. Before these three, he had made many beginnings in journals, sermons, lectures, poems, and such widely discussed volumes as *Nature*

of 1836 and the two *Essays* series. And in the later years, he continued his writing and lecturing, with special emphasis on the Civil War and the new science. To both beginnings and conclusions, *The Conduct of Life, Representative Men,* and *English Traits* were central. If we look at them first, for Emerson's chief ideas as they concern us, we may then turn to a more historical and a more literary view for further understanding of his purposes and effects.

The Conduct of Life begins with one main question: How shall I live? Not, What is the theory of the age, or What is the spirit of the times, or What can we do to reform men? The question is not *What,* but *How;* the questioner not *we,* but *I;* the problem, *to live.* These characteristics of active and personal process establish the tone and the construction of Emerson's whole book, and of his whole work.

Say that you, as reader, have this book in hand, a gracefully compact volume of two hundred pages, how will you most easily follow its thought? By following Emerson's belief that the parts of an idea are given meaning by the whole, as they in their turn give substance to the whole. The parts in *The Conduct of Life* are nine chapters, derived from nine lectures which Emerson had given in sequence to an audience of Boston townspeople gathered together in the 1850's to hear him because of his great reputation for saying well what they needed to hear. What audiences in the 1970's might hear on the theme "How Shall I Live?" would depend, probably, on the speaker's specialization; they might get a businessman's or a churchman's answer, a scientist's answer, a psychologist's or an artist's answer, an "academic" or a "journalistic" answer. For each specialty, there would be a series of informative topics, say, "Automation," or "Renaissance Humanism," or "Zen." In contrast, how surprising in their speculative generality are Emerson's nine: "Fate," "Power," "Wealth," "Culture," "Behavior," "Worship," "Considerations by the Way," "Beauty," and "Illusions." How, the reader may wonder, can he make a whole of these? And where is the information in them? Our modern habit of information-seeking will probably lead to doubts about such a list of contents. Emerson's own hearers probably felt a different doubt. Bred to churchgoing and sermon-listening, they may have wondered at the nonreligiousness of such titles, their lack of Biblical texts and canons. So this list has a kind of daring to it, for either century, moral yet secular as it is. Few writers except wisdom-writers have the power to span the years by the endurance of their generalities in combination with the immediacy of their references to daily life.

How shall I live? With fate; that is, with the limitations of my inheritance and the natural world. With power, my abilities and energies. With wealth, my gains or losses. With culture, my widest sympathies and affinities. With behavior, my manner of life. With worship, my belief. With considerations, the positive centers for my action. With beauty, the underlying likenesses of the beautiful. And with illusions, the games and masks of my self-deception.

The sequence of answers begins with fate, impersonally and negatively; grows more and more strongly personal through the center in worship; then adds in conclusion a triad of impersonal and negative warnings on the dissonances and consonances of the process of composing a living and a life. The last essay ends as the first ends, with the axiom, the accepted, undemonstrated, intuitive assertion that there is no chance, no anomaly, in the universe; that all is system and gradation; and that the young mortal, the pure in heart, survives with the true, beautiful, and moral gods.

To see more clearly how Emerson established this coherent universe, it is useful to look closely at the form of the first essay, "Fate"; then, to gain a sense of the complementary solidity of individual choice and action, to look at "Wealth"—to relate, that is, life to the living of it. Note the difference from the Christian incarnation, which Emerson had studied to preach and had resigned from preaching. Incarnation draws mind and spirit downward into body, into the crucifixion and redemption of body. For Emerson, the motion is upward, cyclical, opposing and circling into spiral, through the power of every individual soul as it participates in the unifying force of the one soul, the over-soul, which composes all. The positive energy is earthly as well as heavenly.

The essay "Fate" proceeds through a half-dozen steps of four or five pages each. The first step is to make use of the limitations, negations, brute facts, tyrannies of life. The second, in both individual and national inheritance, is to accept the force of such restrictive circumstance. "Nature is, what you may do. There is much you may not. . . . Once we thought, positive power was all. Now we learn, that negative power, or circumstance, is half. Nature is the tyrannous circumstance, the thick skull, the sheathed snake, the ponderous, rock-like jaw; necessitated activity; violent direction; the conditions of a tool, like the locomotive, strong enough on its track, but which can do nothing but mischief off of it; or skates, which are wings on the ice, but fetters on the ground. The book of Nature is the book of Fate." But the third step is to recognize the power of thought in man—"On one side, elemental order, sandstone and granite, rockledges, peat-bog, forest, sea and shore; and, on the other part, thought, the spirit which composes and decomposes nature,—here they are, side by side, god and devil, mind and matter, king and conspirator, belt and spasm, riding peacefully together in the eye and brain of every man." The fourth is to see that man's thought not only counters but uses fate, by design, by dream, by will, by moral purpose. "Fate, then, is a name for facts not yet passed under the fire of thought;—for causes which are unpenetrated." The fifth is to see that their inter-relations, fate's and thought's, are manifold. The sixth is to think about the spirit of the age as the interworking of event and person, the advance out of fate into freedom, and their rebalancing. The soul "contains the event that shall befall it, for the event is only the actualization of its thoughts; and what we pray to ourselves for is always granted." So finally, the peroration of the pulpit and lecture hall: "Let us build altars to the Beautiful Necessity" which rudely or softly educates man to the perception that there are no contingencies.

The following essay, "Power," stresses again the potential force of man, especially the strength that comes with concentration and habituation of his abilities, and uses the analogy of the energy and husbandry of a machine, which is constructed by man to exclude follies and hindrances, broken threads and rotten hours, from his production.

Coming then to the essay on production, called "Wealth," we may stop to take note of another of Emerson's characteristics as essayist, his sermonlike use of a verse text not

scriptural but his own. We note key lines from the poem that stands at the head of this essay:

And well the primal pioneer
Knew the strong task to it assigned
Patient through Heaven's enormous year
To build in matter home for mind.

The whole poem is a treatise, a history, a four-beat, irregularly rhyming re-creation of past wealth, of wheat, metal ores, coal, and then the binding threads of city and trade, the ties of nature and of law which hold even in the most youthful being.

In the essay itself, the theme is set early: "How does that man get his living? . . . He fails to make his place good in the world, unless he not only pays his debt, but also adds something to the common wealth." "Wealth," says Emerson, "has its source in applications of the mind to nature, from the rudest strokes of spade and axe, up to the last secrets of art." It is "the greatest possible extension to our powers, as if it added feet, and hands, and eyes, and blood, length to the day, and knowledge, and good-will."

By a law of nature, man feeds himself, fills his own needs. "He is the richest man who knows how to draw a benefit from the labors of the greatest number of men, of men in distant countries, and in past times." Economy is moral when it makes for profound, not trivial, independences. No man, in whatever time, is as rich as he ought to be. Property is an intellectual production; commerce, a game of skill; money, the delicate measure of civil, social, and moral changes. "A dollar in a university, is worth more than a dollar in a jail . . . the value of a dollar is social, as it is created by society." Economy has its own inner balances.

In the essay, Emerson makes four main points about economy, that is, about means related to ends: that each man's expense should proceed from his character; that each man should proceed by system; that each should follow the custom of the country; that each will reap what he sows, for "the counting-room maxims liberally expounded are laws of the Universe." Investment is the final significance: from wealth, to money, to value, to expenditure; from bread, to strength, to thought, to courage, invested toward higher goods. Like "Fate," then, "Wealth" is organized by a handful of sections, one moving into the next, with an initial question answered early and then finally raised to a higher power.

The idea of culture tempers the ideas of power and wealth by moderating and expanding them. Books, travels, cities, solitude, with all their difficulties, carry man from focused energy to widening thought, from quadruped to human. Superficially, but no less significantly, the *how* of men's life is the *how* of "Manners." Manners are the best ways of doing things, the gentlest laws and bonds. Their basis lies in self-reliance, in thoughtful choice; their grammar of gesture is clearer than English grammar, a part of both nature and character.

"Worship," in turning back from spirit in body to body in spirit, takes note of criticisms made by hearers of the earlier lectures in this series: that there is too much of body in the lectures; that they grant too much power either to animal man or to negative man. But Emerson says he will persist, against all sanctified airs, in recognizing both, the one for praise, the other for blame. Religious worship is a flowering from bodily stems: it needs the vigor of nature. Vigorless worship, institutionalized, dogmatized, sectarian, as in many of the churches of his day, is weak and wrong; where it exists new forms are needed, new channels for spirit to move in. "In our large cities, the population is godless, materialized,—no bond, no fellow-feeling, no enthusiasm. These are not men, but hungers, thirsts, fevers, and appetites walking. How is it people manage to live on,— so aimless as they are? After their peppercorn aims are gained, it seems as if the lime in their bones alone held them together, and not any worthy purpose." We need not fear, on the other hand, if creeds and sects decline. "The public and the private element, like north and south, like inside and outside, like centrifugal and centripetal, adhere to every soul, and cannot be subdued, except the soul is dissipated. God builds his temple in the heart on the ruins of churches and religions."

Vividly in this climactic chapter, Emerson makes clear the bent of his philosophy. It is not methodology, not logic, not systematic analysis or inquiry that concerns him; it is the creation of a pattern of thought and observation in reasonable harmony with certain accepted axioms of intuited belief. First, "We are born believing. A man bears beliefs, as a tree bears apples." Second, morality and intellect are related in growth. "Every man takes care that his neighbor shall not cheat him. But a day comes when he begins to care that he does not cheat his neighbor. Then all goes well. He has changed his market-cart into a chariot of the sun. What a day dawns, when we have taken to heart the doctrine of faith! to prefer, as a better investment, being to doing . . . the life to the year. . . ." The word *investment*, echoing from the essay on wealth, carries the sense of treasure used, of active commitment, in faith, to present and future. After a number of examples, for those faint in heart, comes the peroration of "Worship," which we may take for as strongly and briefly phrased a conclusion as Emerson ever came to. "And so I think that the last lesson of life, the choral song which rises from all elements and all angels, is, a voluntary obedience, a necessitated freedom. Man is made of the same atoms as the world is, he shares the same impressions, predispositions, and destiny. When his mind is illuminated, when his heart is kind, he throws himself joyfully into the sublime order, and does, with knowledge, what the stones do by structure."

To this larger theme of detail in the sublime order, the last three essays in *The Conduct of Life* devote themselves.

"Considerations" deals with true and false bonds, true and false allegiances and centers, for groups and for individuals. "Our chief want in life, is, somebody who shall make us do what we can. This is the service of a friend." This is the service, too, of a good minority in a government, and of any heroic, obligable nucleus—to loose false ties, to give us the courage to serve and to be what we are.

"Beauty" also stresses such relations of harmony. Like science, beauty extends and deepens us, takes us from surfaces to the foundations of things. That which is beautiful is simple, has no superfluous parts, serves its end, stands related to all things, is the mean of many extremes. Each of these qualities Emerson illustrates further; the structure of this essay is a series of exemplifications moving toward the highest power of beauty—to relate.

He concludes with an essay on deceptive relations, "Illusions," to remind us what we are so conscious of today—false fronts, masks. He will not allow us to rest easy; we must ride a beast of ever-changing form. With the young mortal and the gods together in the realm of pure truth, Emerson ends his advices on the conduct of life, catching up in his last sentences what he had set forth in his first: "If we must accept Fate, we are not less compelled to affirm liberty, the significance of the individual, the grandeur of duty, the power of character." He has harped on each string, as he has said, through nine essays, in order to harmonize them. His compositions have been played on these few main themes. Do we grant

him his premises, his intuitive beliefs? Whether or no, at least we can grant him his questions and therefore follow where he leads in his ever-varying range of effort to answer.

The Conduct of Life was Emerson's last, most coherent, and for many his most admirable book. We may take it as the mature effort of his thought in his fifties, tried out in journal entries and on lecture platforms, and finally published forth in 1860. Even more than the *Conduct,* the other two books of his maturity, *Representative Men* (1850), and *English Traits* (1856), harped on certain strings. The lifelong personal question of *Conduct*—How shall I live?—they asked more historically and descriptively: How do great men and nations live?

We know that one of the much-read books of Emerson's youth was Plutarch's *Lives*—lives of soldiers and statesmen, of men of political action in Greece and Rome. We know that he admired Carlyle's kind of hero, as Divinity, Prophet, Poet, Priest, Man of Letters, King. He might be expected, then, to give us in *Representative Men* American leaders and prophets, like George Washington, Benjamin Franklin, Thomas Jefferson, or one of the men he most admired in his own day, like Daniel Webster. But we perhaps have learned enough from *The Conduct of Life* to know that Emerson's men will not be such models. He believes in aspiring men, of negative as well as positive quality. To be representative, they may be villains as well as heroes. So we find the six of them: Plato the philosopher, Swedenborg the mystic, Montaigne the skeptic, Shakespeare the poet, Napoleon the man of the world, Goethe the writer—no one a hero or even a heroic type, but each representative of a complex of traits of thought in human kind. Note the introductory essay, "Uses of Great Men." *Uses,* indeed! How shall they live? *For us.*

To begin once more with the assumption

of belief: "It is natural to believe in great men. . . . Nature seems to exist for the excellent. The world is upheld by the veracity of good men: they make the earth wholesome. . . . The search after the great man is the dream of youth, and the most serious occupation of manhood." But now when he asks how such men aid us, we see Emerson's surprising yet clearly characteristic point: "Each man seeks those of different quality from his own, and such as are good of their kind; that is, he seeks other men, and the *otherest*." Their service therefore is indirect, not by gift, but by representation, each "connected with some district of nature, whose agent and interpreter he is; as Linnæus, of plants; Huber, of bees . . . Euclid, of lines; Newton, of fluxions." "Every ship that comes to America got its chart from Columbus. Every novel is a debtor to Homer."

One danger is that these men become too much our masters. But change carries them and their kind along. "In some other and quite different field the next man will appear; not Jefferson, not Franklin, but now a great salesman; then a road-contractor; then a student of fishes; then a buffalo-hunting explorer; or a semi-savage western general. . . . With each new mind, a new secret of nature transpires; nor can the Bible be closed until the last great man is born." Nature protects each from every other in his variety; from what varieties can we learn?

From "Plato": "He represents the privilege of the intellect, the power, namely, of carrying up every fact to successive platforms, and so disclosing, in every fact, a germ of expansion." From "Montaigne": "Who shall forbid a wise skepticism, seeing that there is no practical question on which any thing more than an approximate solution can be had?" From "Shakespeare": "The greatest genius is the most indebted man. A poet is . . . a heart in unison with his time and country." From "Napoleon": "He had a directness of action never before combined with so much comprehension."

English Traits, the third in his trio of mature volumes, asks How shall I live? by asking it of a country, and, note, a country to which America was only recently opposed, yet from which it was descended. Oppose Goethe, oppose Montaigne, oppose England: and learn from these oppositions. Why is England England?—this is the way Emerson puts the question now. His steps of inquiry proceed via "Land" to "Race," to "Ability," to "Manners," to "Truth," to "Character," to "Cockayne" (Humor), to "Wealth," to "Aristocracy," to "Universities," to "Religion," to "Literature," to "Result." Each general concern is given its specific English location and form: the land locates the race; aristocracy, the wealth; and humor, the character.

Each section has its theme: "England is a garden." "The English composite character betrays a mixed origin. Everything English is a fusion of distant and antagonistic elements." "The Norman has come popularly to represent in England the aristocratic, and the Saxon the democratic principle." "I find the Englishman to be him of all men who stands firmest in his shoes." "The Teutonic tribes have a national singleness of heart, which contrasts with the Latin races." "The English race are reputed morose." "The English are a nation of humorists." "There is no country in which so absolute a homage is paid to wealth." "The feudal character of the English state, now that it is getting obsolete, glares a little, in contrast with the democratic tendencies." "The logical English train a scholar as they train an engineer. Oxford is a Greek factory, as Wilton mills weave carpet and Sheffield grinds steel." "The religion of England is part of good-breeding." "England is the best of actual nations. . . . Broad-fronted, broad-bottomed Teutons, they stand in solid phalanx foursquare to the points of compass; they constitute the modern world, they have earned their vantage ground and held it through ages of adverse possession. . . . They cannot readily see beyond England."

These brief statements of idea, one for almost each section, let us know how much we can learn, in specific documentation, analysis, anecdote, and in the personal experience of the twice-visitor. Together they let us know about the English, that they have gained by opposing, and that we will gain by opposing them.

Emerson has carried his sense of moral unity from person to object, to representative man, to nation and type, and through all of these the active and creating power of inner divinity, of intuition, gives shape to the natural forces of heredity, geography, history. English traits are English fate; within them move man's powers. His study of England puts Emerson's theories to a strong test; to see what Nietzsche and Spengler have since done with them, would, as Philip Nicoloff suggests, put them to a still stronger test. But it is not one Emerson would avoid. Form, change, purpose were organic for him in the classic sense, a part of a pattern, as he said, not a romantic caprice. So England could not but add strength to his beliefs; as his beliefs could not but inform that Saxon substance.

These three main volumes in the decade of his maturity were built upon works already established in the heart of New England readers through the two series of *Essays* and the *Poems* of the 1840's. Together these six collections of his thoughts give us Emerson's most formal and formulated wisdom. The startling assertions of such essays as "Self-Reliance" and "The Over-Soul," the contained force of "Woodnotes" and "Threnody," find their stability of focus in the various forms of the question How shall I live? It may now be helpful to consider what in Emerson's earlier world and purpose had helped bring the several forms of this question into being.

The events of Emerson's life in brief summary provide a context for his thought—the *why* of his beliefs. He was born on May 25, 1803, in Boston, in a family of merchants and ministers. His father, the Reverend William Emerson, Unitarian minister and chaplain of the state senate, died in 1811, and his mother turned to boardinghouse keeping to support the children. He attended Boston Latin School from 1812 to 1817 and Harvard College from 1817 to 1821, where he kept journals of his reading and thought, and won prizes for his essays. Encouraged by his Aunt Mary Moody, Emerson early began to write poetry, on the victories of 1812, for example. He taught at his brother William's school for young ladies, studied for the ministry at Harvard, went south to Florida to cure a long-threatening tuberculosis, came back to more preaching, and in 1829 was ordained pastor of the Second Church in Boston, in the same year he was married to the young and fragile Ellen Tucker. She died in 1831, and in 1832 Emerson resigned his pastorate, preached a farewell sermon, and went to England to try to recover strength and purpose.

Though he visited the literary men he most admired, Coleridge, Wordsworth, Carlyle, remarkably it was the botanical world of France's Jardin des Plantes which most gave him what he sought. He returned then to begin in Concord in 1834 his years of leadership in thought and expression. He married Lydia Jackson, and of their four children three survived to later life, the while he lost his eldest, his brothers, and later his mother. He met in the next years new friends, Margaret Fuller, Bronson Alcott, Horace Greeley, the elder Henry James, Hawthorne, Thoreau, Whitman. He began to turn his early practice in sermon making to lecture making on the new lecture circuits which were to illuminate the cities, villages, and frontiers of America for the rest of the century. He turned from much-argued-about lectures, like the early "The American Scholar," to much-argued-about publications: *Nature* in 1836, the writings for the *Dial* in 1840–44, the *Essays* of 1841 and 1844, the *Poems* of 1846. He took a number of further trips west and abroad, gave the first of many speeches on problems of slavery, the war, and the nation's leadership, and in the fifties published his three most thematically integrated books—*Representative Men*, *English Traits*, and *The Conduct of Life*—which took their place alongside the other great volumes of that era, Thoreau's *Walden* and Whitman's *Leaves of Grass*. The sixties brought the Civil War, the death of Lincoln, of Thoreau, of Hawthorne, and a gradual slowing for Emerson: the effort to meet honors at Harvard with new explorations of science and intellect, trips as far as California as guest of his son-in-law, loss of his home by fire, final journeyings abroad, final collecting, despite failing memory, of loved work, like *Parnassus*, and death on April 27, 1882, at Concord.

As a boy, Emerson had looked to his family and town and school for his ideas. What wisdom did he seek in these busy and hard-pressed years? Records of reading in his *Journals* and, more indirectly, in the lists of withdrawals he and his mother made from the Boston Library Society, show his early concern with seeking out belief. His step-grandfather, Ezra Ripley, who lived in the Old Manse in Concord, which was later to be Hawthorne's, and his Aunt Mary Moody, devoted spurrer-on of his thought, both helped lead him in the direction of theology and of moral meditation, so that his readings through his twenties ran as fol-

lows: the novels of Sir Walter Scott, Mrs. Inchbald, and Mrs. Edgeworth; Thomas Campbell's long poem *The Pleasures of Hope* and Vicesimus Knox's *Elegant Extracts* in prose and verse; works of Benjamin Franklin, Cicero, Shakespeare, the English essayists like Bacon and Addison, and historians like Robertson; translations of Cervantes, Dante, Euripides, Montaigne, Pascal, Plutarch, Rousseau, *Arabian Nights' Entertainments*, and *Selections from the Popular Poetry of the Hindus*. Scott furnished his world of fictive landscape and romance, Cicero his world of oratorical meditation, Plato his world of speculation about what is true; English prose writers gave a solid professional background, and Eastern lore added a spice to the whole. His first poem, *The History of Fortus*, begun when he was ten, was a romance.

His college studies were standard; among them, first year, Greek Livy, Latin Horace, geometry, and Lowth's *Grammar*; second year, Cicero, history, geometry, Blair's *Rhetoric*, Locke's *Human Understanding*; third year, Homer, Juvenal, Hebrew, astronomy, Stewart's *Human Mind*; fourth year, chemistry, political economy, Butler's *Analogy*, and *The Federalist*. The members of his college literary club wrote essays and read them aloud.

There are qualities which can be called Emersonian even in his earliest works, in his two Bowdoin prize essays of 1820 and 1821, when he was not yet twenty, in his first printed essay, his first sermon, his first lecture. Consider his first Bowdoin essay, on the assigned topic "The Character of Socrates." It begins, as his essays were long to do, as his favorite Scott had done, with a poetic epigraph; and note the references: to Plato's academic walk, the Lyceum, which was to be the name for the great American lecture circuit established a decade later; reference also to *pure* and *stream*, terms to be especially characteristic of Emerson's writing; and reference to the needs of his own country:

Guide my way
Through fair Lyceum's walk, the green retreats
Of Academus, and the thymy vale
Where, oft enchanted with Socratic sounds,
Ilissus pure devolved his tuneful stream
In gentler murmurs. From the blooming store
Of these auspicious fields, may I unblamed
Transplant some living blossoms to adorn
My native clime.

Then this on his main topic: "Socrates taught that every soul was an eternal, immutable form of beauty in the divine mind, and that the most beautiful mortals approached nearest to that celestial mould; that it was the honor and delight of human intellect to contemplate this *beau ideal*, and that this was better done through the medium of earthly perfection." How much discussion of Emerson's mysticism would be tempered if it took into account this approbation of idea's form and substance!

How much too the stress on his individualism would be tempered by a reading of his senior essay of 1821. In it he traces "The Present State of Ethical Philosophy" from the limits of moral science set by the Greeks to the church's "obstinacy of ignorance," to Cudworth's and Burke's corrections of Hobbes, and the valuable common sense of the modern philosophers Clark, Price, Butler, Reid, Paley, Smith, and Stewart. Then he makes the important approving distinction that "The moderns have made their ethical writings of a more practical character than the sages of antiquity. . . . The ancients balanced the comparative excellence of two virtues or the badness of two vices; they determined the question whether solitude or society were the better condition for virtue. The moderns have substituted in-

quiries of deep interest for those of only speculative importance. We would ask in passing, what discussion of Aristotle or Socrates can compare, in this respect, with the train of reasoning by which Dr. Price arrives at the conclusion that every wrong act is a step to all that is tremendous in the universe." Democratically, too, modern moral philosophy shows "that a series of humble efforts is more meritorious than solitary miracles of virtue. . . . The plague spot of slavery must be purged thoroughly out. . . . The faith of treaties must be kept inviolate. . . ."

Earlier than most he expressed concern for his country. When he was nineteen, only a decade past the battles of 1812, in which as a boy he had served, reinforcing the barricades on Boston's lines to the sea, he feared the settling down of the national spirit. "In this merry time," he wrote to a classmate, "and with real substantial happiness above any known nation, I think we Yankees have marched on since the Revolution to strength, to honor, and at last to *ennui*. It is most true that the people (of the city, at least) are actually tired of hearing Aristides called the Just, and it demonstrates a sad caprice when they hesitate about putting on their vote such names as Daniel Webster and Sullivan and Prescott, and only distinguish them by a small majority over bad and doubtful men. . . . Will it not be dreadful to discover that this experiment, made by America to ascertain if men can govern themselves, does not succeed; that too much knowledge and too much liberty make them mad?"

In his notes for his first sermon, "Pray without Ceasing," he wrote, "Take care, take care, that your sermon is not a recitation; that it is a sermon to Mr. A. and Mr. B. and Mr. C." The idea for this he, a Unitarian, got not only from Thessalonians but from a Methodist farm laborer, who said to him that men are always praying. "I meditated much on this saying and wrote my first sermon therefrom, of which the divisions were: (1) Men are always praying; (2) All their prayers are granted; (3) We must beware, then, what we ask." Between this first sermon in Waltham in 1826, and his ordination at Boston's Second Church in 1829, he preached two hundred sermons, learning to dread the demands of Sunday, learning to use one sermon in different places and different ways, yet becoming so habituated that long after he had left the pulpit he still continued to make notes on sermon topics.

In the first Sunday of his Boston ministry, speaking of styles of preaching, he said that preaching should apply itself to the good and evil in men. "Men imagine that the end and use of preaching is to expound a text, and forget that Christianity is an infinite and universal law; that it is the revelation of a Deity whose being the soul cannot reject without denying itself, a rule of action which penetrates into every moment and into the smallest duty. If any one hereafter should object to the want of sanctity of my style and the want of solemnity in my illustrations, I shall remind him that the language and the images of Scripture derive all their dignity from their association with divine truth, and that our Lord condescended to explain himself by allusions to every homely fact, and, if he addressed himself to the men of this age, would appeal to those arts and objects by which we are surrounded; to the printing-press and the loom, to the phenomena of steam and of gas, to free institutions and a petulant and vain nation." In sermon after sermon, "The Christian Minister," "Summer," "The Individual and the State," "Trust Yourself," "Hymn Books," "The Genuine Man," he carries out this active relation. The active verbs of his talks are indicative of his manner.

During the three years of his ministry at Boston's Second Church, the old church of Increase and Cotton Mather in its Puritan tradition, Emerson's reading moved toward the specific wisdoms needed to support him against what his journals had referred to as his own "sluggishness," "silliness," "flippancy," even "frigid fear," along with his lack of unction at "funerals, weddings, and ritual ceremonies," his unwilling absorption in sick calls, in swelling of the poor fund, and in other managements. Here he became more philosophically focused. He borrowed from the library again and again in 1830 de Gérando's *Histoire comparée des systèmes de philosophie* (1804), which provided brief views of the pre-Platonists, pointed to their distinguishing of the ideal from the material, and, especially, emphasized God as unity, first cause, harmony, the law of order by abstraction, repulsion, relation. Then Plato abridged by Dacier, a Harvard text, then Thomas Taylor's editions of Plato's *Cratylus*, *Phaedo*, *Parmenides*, and *Timæus*, which he borrowed many times from 1830 to 1845 and finally bought, for their treasurable emphasis on the soul, its motion, being, and becoming. Then work on Neo-Platonism, possibly Cudworth's *The True Intellectual System of the Universe*, with its concept that nature "doth reconcile the contrarieties and enmities of particular things, and bring them into one general harmony in the whole." Then the English philosopher Berkeley, as against his predecessor Hobbes, on the laws of nature as they discipline us, and on "our delight in every exertion of active moral power." And then at last, along with Boehme and Swedenborg, his own contemporary, Coleridge, in whose *Aids to Reflection*, *Friend*, and *Biographia*, he found the distinctions between Reason and Understanding, Imagination and Fancy, which Coleridge had adapted from Kant and the Germans and which amounted to the nineteenth century's scientific "reasonable" renaming of the old pair Faith and Reason—that Faith which seems an inward Reason, a powerful and compelling intuition of validity, of the sort which finally enabled Emerson to write in his journal in 1831 the lines of "Gnothi Seauton," "Know Thyself," and to reason himself after his wife's death into a withdrawal from his career, into a year's journey away from America and his own youth.

When in 1832 he resigned his ministry, spoke against church dogma and the communion ceremony, left behind the sorrows of his wife's death and his family's illnesses, Emerson seemed to be seeking in Europe the strong sources of his bookish admirations, in Coleridge, Wordsworth, Carlyle, and others. But what he discovered was the Jardin des Plantes—in the Old World, its new world of biological and geological science. Finding his men of letters, except for Carlyle, self-centered, withdrawn, or garrulous, he found in zoological gardens and institutes of science the invigoration he sought. When he came back to America his ideas, perhaps under the pressures of a long hard sea voyage, combined youthful literary and religious studies with newly strengthened views of science. In a letter of 1834 he wrote, "Is it not a good symptom for society, this decided and growing taste for natural science which has appeared though yet in its first gropings? . . . I have been writing three lectures on Natural History and of course reading as much geology, chemistry, and physics as I could find." As the editors of his *Early Lectures* say, "The science which Emerson studied and professed was pre-Darwinian and concerned itself more with the classification than with the evolution of natural phenomena. Largely deductive in its theoretical base, it could serve as illustration of divine law and at the same time offer opportunities for observation and experimentation."

Emerson's first lecture to laymen in 1833 began, "It seems to have been designed, if anything was, that men should be students of Natural History." That Lyceum of which his junior essay had spoken was off to its great success. "The beauty of the world is a perpetual invitation to the study of the world." Emerson went on: "While I stand there [in the Jardin] I am impressed with a singular conviction that not a form so grotesque, so savage, or so beautiful, but is an expression of something in man the observer. . . . I am moved by strange sympathies. I say I will listen to this invitation. I will be a naturalist." The advantages of the study: health and useful knowledge, and delight, and improvement of character, and explanation of man to himself. "Nothing is indifferent to the wise. If a man should study the economy of a spire of grass—how it sucks up sap, how it imbibes light, how it resists cold, how it repels excess of moisture, it would show him a design in the form, in the color, in the smell, in the very posture of the blade as it bends before the wind. . . . the whole of Nature is a metaphor or image of the human Mind. The laws of moral nature answer to those of matter as face to face in a glass."

Such scientific titles as "On the Relation of Man to the Globe," "Water," and "The Naturalist" alternated throughout his lecturing career, in Boston, New York, Philadelphia, the Midwest, with those of a more historical and biographical order. The lectures of 1835 lauded Michelangelo, Chaucer, Shakespeare, Bacon, Milton, Jeremy Taylor for their earthiness, and Jonson, Herrick, Herbert for their strong and simple sentences and objects. The 1836 series in Boston on "Philosophy of History," and the later series on "Human Culture," "Human Life," "The Present Age," "The Times," stressed the common interests of men, saying of Michelangelo, as of Martin Luther, "so true was he to the laws of the human mind that his character and his works like Isaac Newton's seem rather a part of Nature than arbitrary productions of the human will."

In publication, Emerson's career began from Concord in 1836, when he was just over thirty years old, with a small, not popular, pamphlet called *Nature*, which stated succinctly in its third sentence: "But if a man would be alone, let him look at the stars." This early individual man of Emerson's is a man alone, apart from his friends and even from his own studies and pursuits, an unmediated part of the universe. By "nature," Emerson says, he means "the integrity of impression made by manifold natural objects. It is this which distinguishes the stick of timber of the wood-cutter from the tree of the poet." A good local example: "Miller owns this field, Locke that, and Manning the woodland beyond. But none of them owns the landscape."

The main parts of his essay rest upon these distinctions. The causes of the world he calls "Commodity," how things are served and used; "Beauty," how their harmony is perceived, in outline, color, motion, grouping; "Language," how they are signified and symbolized; "Discipline," how they are ordered and distinguished—these are his own versions of Aristotle's classical causes, material, effective, formal, and final. Then in three final sections, Emerson treats man's view of "Idealism," "Spirit," and "Prospects": his perspective through intuitive ideas stronger than that through sense or argument; his power, in incarnation, of worship; and his power to speculate, to guess about relations, *whence* and *whereto*. He draws upon *The Tempest*, the Bible's Proverbs, *Comus*, and George Herbert's "Man" to voice his guesses. Both learned and innocent men, he warns, limit their powers and fail to speculate. "The invariable mark of wisdom is to see the miraculous in the common," that is, idea in material, beauty and spirit in commodity and discipline. "What is a day? What is a year? What is summer? What is woman? What is a child? What is sleep? . . . Whilst the abstract question occupies your intellect, nature brings it in the concrete to be solved by your hands. . . . Every spirit builds itself a house, and beyond its house a world, and beyond its world a heaven. . . . Adam called his house, heaven and earth; Cæsar called his house, Rome; you perhaps call yours, a cobbler's trade; a hundred acres of ploughed land; or a scholar's garret. . . . Build, therefore, your own world. As fast as you conform your life to the pure idea in your mind, that will unfold its great proportions. A correspondent revolution in things will attend the influx of the spirit. So fast will disagreeable appearances, swine, spiders, snakes, pests, madhouses, prisons, enemies, vanish; they are temporary and shall no more be seen. . . . so shall the advancing spirit . . . draw beautiful faces, warm hearts, wise discourse, and heroic acts, around its way, until evil is no more seen."

Here in its peroration, the essay "Nature" makes the proposals of Emerson's whole lifetime on the simple questions of life, the range and scope of spirit, the fit of historical past and possible future, the nature of evil, the values of fact and of spirit. Emerson's future style, too, is proposed and exemplified here: the broad speculative generalizations followed by the simplest questions and instances; the speaking to *you*; the quick strides of survey covering miles and centuries; the parallels and dismissals; the earnest recommendations for the life of the universe as for the life of every day.

The poems and the two volumes of essays which follow in the 1840's, as well as some of his most moving lectures, such as "The American Scholar" and the "Divinity School Address," set the fame of Emerson moving into its channels. These accepted works we, too, may accept, to read them all, rather than to explore them here. The *Essays* followed patterns with which we have already learned to be familiar: from time in "History" to more than time in "Art," from art in "Poet" to religion in "Reformers," ending, as in his more loosely collected essays of the sixties and seventies, with transcendences of age and death. The poems, too, move toward "Terminus," "Farewell," and "In Memoriam."

But two fates, laws of his life, carried Emerson's work to less predictable intensities: one, the force of the slavery question and the Civil War; the other, the force of his concern with the "natural history of intellect" in poetry as in prose. In these we see not seasonal pattern and temporal decline, but the late maturing demanded by event and drawn from the aging seer after his chief works, his solidest books, were done. "Emancipation in the British West Indies" (1844), "The Fugitive Slave Law" (1851 and 1854), "John Brown" (1859), "The Emancipation Proclamation" (1862), "Abraham Lincoln" (1865), all carry the weight of a pressing issue.

Thoreau is said to have rung the bell for the public meeting at the Concord Court House in 1844, at which many citizens opposed Emerson's attitudes on emancipation. Emerson began: "Friends and Fellow Citizens: We are met to exchange congratulations on the anniversary of an event singular in the history of civilization; a day of reason; of the clear light; of that which makes us better than a flock of birds and beasts; a day which gave the immense fortification of a fact, of gross history, to ethical abstractions."

How he delights in the fact of the West Indies' final emancipation, in the fact of "the steady gain of truth and right," in the intelligent self-interest despite the voluptuousness of power. So in America in the fifties, the Whig *must*'s, the Liberal *may*'s, need to combine. So we need, like John Brown, to see the facts behind the forms. So, "this heavy load lifted off the national heart, we shall not fear henceforward to show our faces among mankind." And Providence makes its own instruments, "creates the man for the time." In verse, the Concord "Ode," read July 4, 1857:

> United States! the ages plead,—
>   Present and Past in under-song,—
> Go put your creed into your deed,
>   Nor speak with double tongue.

And the "Boston Hymn," read January 1, 1863, in Boston, when the President's Emancipation Proclamation went into effect:

> God said, I am tired of kings,
> I suffer them no more;
> Up to my ear the morning brings
> The outrage of the poor. . . .
>
> To-day unbind the captive,
> So only are ye unbound;
> Lift up a people from the dust,
> Trump of their rescue, sound!
>
> Pay ransom to the owner
> And fill the bag to the brim.
> Who is the owner? The slave is owner.
> And ever was. Pay him.

Emerson has said, "I compared notes with one of my friends who expects everything of the universe and is disappointed when anything is less than the best, and I found that I begin at the other extreme, expecting nothing, and am always full of thanks for moderate goods." Yet his intuition that God need not be so modest could find expression in God's own voice in this hymn and thus raise the responsive shouts of a Boston audience.

The work of his last active years, of the postwar sixties, was the work again of the "natural history of intellect." This theme he still wanted to clarify. "His noun had to wait for its verb or its adjective until he was ready; then his speech would come down upon the word he wanted . . ." as his biographer James Cabot commented. He never spoke impromptu; indeed, in his last years, he sought so long for the right word that he hesitated to appear in public. Part of his reticence was that, as he wrote in his journal of 1859, he wanted no disciples, he spoke to bring men not to him but to themselves. Harvard Phi Beta Kappa speaker in 1867, as in 1837, he took up again for Harvard in 1870 the series which he had projected thirty years before and had given in 1848 and later, in London, Boston, and New York, again in 1858 as a course on the "Natural Method of Mental Philosophy," and again in 1866 as "Philosophy for People." Now for a group of thirty students in 1870 and 1871 he would try to bring together what he had to say. He still was not satisfied. Nevertheless: "If one can say so without arrogance, I might suggest that he who contents himself with dotting only a fragmentary curve, recording only what facts he has observed, without attempting to arrange them within one outline, follows a system also, a system as grand as any other, though he does not interfere with its vast curves by prematurely forcing them into a circle or ellipse, but only draws that arc which he clearly sees, and waits for new opportunity, well assured that these observed arcs consist with each other."

This is the way his speaking seemed to a contemporary, W. C. Brownell: "The public was small, attentive, even reverential. The room was as austere as the chapel of a New England Unitarian church would normally be in those days. The Unitarians were the intellectual sect of those days and, as such, suspect. Even the Unitarians, though, who were the aristocratic as well as the intellectual people of the place,

found the chapel benches rather hard, I fancy, before the lecture was over, and I recall much stirring. There was, too, a decided sprinkling of scoffers among the audience, whose sentiments were disclosed during the decorous exit. Incomprehensibility, at that epoch generally, was the great offence; it was a sort of universal charge against anything uncomprehended, made in complete innocence of any obligation to comprehend. Nevertheless the small audience was manifestly more or less spellbound. Even the dissenters—as in the circumstances the orthodox of the day may be called—were impressed. It might be all over their heads, as they contemptuously acknowledged, or vague, as they charged, or disintegrating, as they—vaguely—felt. But there was before them, placidly, even benignly, uttering incendiarism, an extraordinarily interesting personality. It was evening and the reflection of two little kerosene lamps, one on either side of his lectern, illuminated softly the serenest of conceivable countenances—nobility in its every lineament and a sort of irradiating detachment about the whole presence. . . ."

To think about Emerson not only for himself in his own time and for us in ours, but in the larger context of tradition, we need to think of the qualities which relate him to others, as an author to other authors, as a writer of prose wisdom to other such writers. What place does Emerson hold in the tradition, of his own English literature and of the larger world of wisdom? This question cannot be answered by considering his ideas as if they were separable from his presentation of them. Rather, his presentation of them gives them their special identifiable character. We need to discover the special traits and traditions of this essayist of ours, how he differed from any other we may know—from Cicero and Seneca on old age, from Montaigne on life and friendship, from the Elizabethan essayists whom he read with such pleasure as a boy, from the sermons he heard, from the eighteenth- and nineteenth-century philosophic and journalistic prose which he kept reading in the English reviews, from Carlyle, whom he admired so directly, from his own American contemporaries, from the wisdom-literature of China, Persia, India, from his own Bible.

If we read the beginning of his perhaps most famous essay, "Self-Reliance," which followed "History" in introducing his popular series of *Essays* in the 1840's, we may catch his way of expression. In the atmosphere of three quotations to the effect that "man is his own star," Emerson begins: "I read the other day some verses written by an eminent painter which were original and not conventional. The soul always hears an admonition in such lines, let the subject be what it may. The sentiment they instil is of more value than any thought they may contain. To believe your own thought, to believe that what is true for you in your private heart is true for all men—that is genius. Speak your latent conviction, and it shall be the universal sense; for the inmost in due time becomes the outmost, and our first thought is rendered back to us by the trumpets of the Last Judgment. Familiar as the voice of the mind is to each, the highest merit we ascribe to Moses, Plato and Milton is that they set at naught books and traditions, and spoke not what men, but what *they* thought. A man should learn to detect and watch that gleam of light which flashes across his mind from within, more than the lustre of the firmament of bards and sages."

The tone of this whole beginning is at once particular and personal: "I read . . . your own"; general and confident: "the soul always hears"; evocative: "the trumpets of the Last Judgment"; wide-reaching: "Moses, Plato and Milton"; recommendatory: "speak . . . learn"; figurative: "that gleam of light . . . more than the lustre of the firmament."

In this combination of qualities, Emerson's style is more focused and condensed than Cicero's, say, or Seneca's, or Montaigne's, setting its generalities in specific actions and analogies. It is not what we traditionally call a classic style either in Latin or in English, because it does not carry the tone of a full and logical unfolding of the thought, but rather moves as if by flashes of illumination. This is not to say that it is unlogical, merely that it does not give the effect of explicit stress on logical connections. Nor does it stress the literal qualifications, descriptions, with which classical prose is concerned. Both adjectives and connectives are relatively subordinated to direct active verbs. This is to say that Emerson characteristically in this paragraph and throughout this essay, as still in "Illusions" twenty years later, writes a very active, predicative style, one in which the structure is basically simple statement, for which both modification and connective addition are only minimally necessary, and the sentences are relatively short, the central statements relatively unqualified.

There is scarcely another essayist like this among the famed of English prose. Closest to Emerson are sermon-makers like the pre-Elizabethan Latimer, or Tyndale in his translation of Paul to the Romans, or narrative writers, the Bunyan of *Pilgrim's Progress*, the Joyce of Molly Bloom's soliloquy; and these are styles we do not probably think of as Emersonian. Yet even less so are the styles of classic arguers in the tradition of Hooker, Bacon, and Locke, or of the soaring describers he loved: Sir Thomas Browne, for example, or his own contemporaries like Carlyle, or what he himself called the "mock-turtle nutriment as in Macaulay."

But there is one writer in the tradition with whom he is closely allied, one whose works in prose and poetry were Emerson's own favorite youthful reading: Ben Jonson. Jonson was as singular in his own time as Emerson in his: their sense of the English language as best used in active concise statements, making connections by implication, was a sense shared in its extreme by few others, and therefore especially lively both in its singularity and in its function as bond between them. Even their use of specific connectives and the proportion of relative clauses to causal clauses and locational phrases are striking. Not Plutarch, not Montaigne, not Bacon, but specifically the aphoristic Jonson of *Timber* is Emerson's direct model.

Emerson's critics, and he himself, have often complained of the sentences which seemed to repel rather than to attract one another. But lack of connectives does not necessarily mean lack of connections. The thought moves from general to particular, and from key word to key word. Such thought is logical, even syllogistic: the general, all men are mortal; the particular, a man; the conclusion, a man is mortal; you and I participate in this truth. But the *and*'s and *therefore*'s have been omitted, or have been used with relative infrequency. In other words, the logical relation of all to one is present, but not the explicit links in the steps of relation. Further, Emerson might begin with what we would call an untenable premise: "All men are immortal." He would feel this intuitively, "the blazing evidence of immortality," the "gleam of light which flashes across his mind from within," and so he would base upon it his logical argument for any one man and for us. And still further, he would treat key words like *man* in a special way, including in them all their degrees of evaluative

reference from lowest to highest; so that "man" would mean man in his limitless degree of spirit, as well as in his limiting degree of body, thus supporting by definition, implicit or explicit, the relation between *man* and *immortal* which the syllogism makes. It is as if Emerson were essentially satisfied to say, "All men are men (with all men's limitations and potentialities); a man acts like a man." The connective *therefore*'s and adjectival *immortal*'s are minimal; the subject-predicate *Men are, a man is,* is central.

In the early sermons, according to Kenneth Cameron's index-concordance, key terms are *God, Jesus, man, memory, mind, nature, self, soul, truth.* These suggest three centers, religious, psychological, scientific. Then in *Nature,* key terms are *action, beauty, God, man, mind, nature, poet, soul, spirit, thought, truth, world.* The changes make clear Emerson's motion away from religion in the shape of person toward religion in the sense of creation of beauty, whereby *action, thought,* and *world* are taken up into the forms and purposes of *spirit,* and thus made beautiful by their harmony.

Index terms tend to be nouns; but if we look more closely at the recurrent language of specific prose texts, early and late, we will see how strong and traditional are Emerson's verbs, especially those of feeling, knowing, thinking, how evaluative and discriminating his adjectives, as for example in "Self-Reliance," *divine, good, great, new, own, other, same, strong, such, true,* and in the later "Fate" and "Illusions," *fine, find,* and *hold.* The nouns of those essays also parallel the concordance listings for the whole work: the early *action, being, character, fact, friend, truth, virtue;* the later *circumstance, element, form, fate;* and the shared *God, law, life, man, mind, nature, nothing, power, thought, time, world.* The shift in emphasis from early *action* and *character* to later *circumstance* and *fate* is represented in the structure of the prose, as of the poetry also: an unusually high proportion of verbs and low proportion of connectives in the early work and "Self-Reliance" establishing later a proportion of about ten verbs and fewer adjectives to twenty nouns, achieving the precarious and shifting balance between action and circumstance which he argues for.

Poetry and prose for Emerson are not far apart. In syntax, in vocabulary, in idea, their likenesses are greater than their differences. The main differences are the larger proportion of sensory terms in the poetry, and the framing by meter and rhyme. His first poems appeared not in the volume called *Poems* but as epigraphs for essays. He saw poems as epigraphs, like Biblical verses, texts for sermons. Therefore his poetic allegiances were divided —on the one hand to the succinctness of a Jonson, as in prose, yet on the other to the materials and moods of his own day, which were freer, more natural, more exploratory.

His was a sensorily active and receptive vocabulary like that of the English eighteenth and American nineteenth centuries, its especial impact being in its direct joining of man and nature, a nature *wise* and *good*, an *air, sky, sea, star* related to *joy, form, beauty*. This stylistic joining of human and natural realms as both natural, though differently, is like the metaphysical joining, as in Cowper's "church-going bell," which Wordsworth with his more literal connecting processes disapproved; it made condensations of Emerson's widest extensions.

To this outreaching vocabulary he did at least consider suiting a freer form. Like Carlyle, he wearied of the "Specimens" of English verse he had read. Carlyle had written him in the 1830's, ". . . my view is that now at last we have lived to see all manner of Poetics and Rhetorics and Sermonics . . . as good as broken and abolished . . . and so one leaves the pasteboard coulisses, and three unities, and Blair's

Lectures quite behind; and feels only that there is *nothing sacred*, then, but the *Speech of Man* to believing Men! [which] will one day doubtless anew environ itself with fit modes, with solemnities that are *not* mummeries." Emerson's own *Journals* of this time (1839) expressed his interest not only in Pope's couplets and Scott's quatrains but in freer measures like those characteristic of Wordsworth's "Immortaliy Ode"—"not tinkling rhyme, but grand Pindaric strokes, as firm as the tread of a horse," suggesting not a restraint, "but the wildest freedom." Later he wrote to Herman Grimm concerning his *Life of Michelangelo*, "I hate circular sentences, or echoing sentences, where the last half cunningly repeats the first half,—but you step from stone to stone, and advance ever." And he expressed to Grimm his corollary lack of taste for drama: "Certainly it requires great health and wealth of power to ventriloquize (shall I say?) through so many bodies. . . ." Rather, "The maker of a sentence . . . launches out into the infinite and builds a road into Chaos and old Night, and is followed by those who hear him with something of wild, creative delight." And: "Who can blame men for seeking excitement? They are polar, and would you have them sleep in a dull eternity of equilibrium? Religion, love, ambition, money, war, brandy,—some fierce antagonism must break the round of perfect circulation or no spark, no joy, no event can be."

He is aware, too, of freedom in natural forms. In 1841: "I told Henry Thoreau that his freedom is in the form, but he does not disclose new matter. . . . But now of poetry I would say, that when I go out into the fields in a still sultry day, in a still sultry humor, I do perceive that the finest rhythms and cadences of poetry are yet unfound, and that in that purer state which glimmers before us, rhythms of a faery and dream-like music hall enchant us, compared with which the finest measures of English poetry are psalm-tunes. I think now that the very finest and sweetest closes and falls are not in our metres, but in the measures of eloquence, which have greater variety and richness than verse. . . ." Such freedom he aimed for in his prose and poetry of the sea, and such sense of freedom enabled him in 1855 to hail Whitman's new scope and form.

Yet there is a stronger controlling force for him, his youthful note-taking interest in pithy statements. As far back as 1820 we see his mood: "Have been of late reading patches of Barrow and Ben Jonson; and what the object —not curiosity? no—nor expectation of edification intellectual or moral—but merely because they are authors where vigorous phrases and quaint, peculiar words and expressions may be sought and found, the better 'to rattle out the battle of my thoughts.' " And in 1840, he stated his philosophical reasons for condensation: "yet does the world reproduce itself in miniature in every event that transpires, so that all the laws of nature may be read in the smallest fact."

Then in 1842 he expressed recognition of the power of concentration within scope and range: "This feeling I have respecting Homer and Greek, that in this great, empty continent of ours, stretching enormous almost from pole to pole, with thousands of long rivers and thousands of ranges of mountains, the rare scholar, who, under a farmhouse roof, reads Homer and the Tragedies, adorns the land. He begins to fill it with wit, to counter-balance the enormous disproportion of the unquickened earth."

While his chief substance, then, comes from the protestant naturalism of Sylvester and the eighteenth century, in *air, sea, sky, land, cloud, star*, and its American specifications in *beautiful river, music, morning, snow, rose*, like Whitman's *grass*, the counter, wry, limiting, and constructing tradition was his aphoristic one,

the *good and wise thought, nature, fate, form, time* of the Elizabethans. When, later in life, Emerson published his collection, *Parnassus*, of the poems he had liked best, the most space went to Shakespeare, the next to Jonson and Herrick, Wordsworth and Tennyson. While the nineteenth-century poets gave him his guide to beauty of reference, the seventeenth century, in poetry as in prose, gave him his form. The Jonson he called master of song he represented by lines which sound like his own:

Come on, come on, and where you go
So interweave the curious knot
As even the Observer scarce may know
Which lines are pleasures, and which not . . .
Admire the wisdom of your feet:
For dancing is an exercise
Not only shows the mover's wit,
But maketh the beholder wise,
As he hath power to rise to it.

So Emerson "studied thy motion, took thy form," giving to cosmos the active limitations of man's rhymes and meters in the shape of aphorism and epigraph, combining, from his favorite readings, the gnomic force of translations from the Anglo-Saxon and Persian with the pith of segments from Jonsonian "Old Plays" used as epigraphs in Scott's novels.

In "Permanent Traits of the English National Genius," for example, Emerson quotes and admires the strength of the Anglo-Saxon verse line:

O in how gloomy
And how bottomless
A well laboreth
The darkened mind
When it the strong
Storms beat
Of the world's business. . . .

This is much like Emerson's own "Gnothi Seauton":

He is in thy world,
But thy world knows him not.
He is the mighty Heart
From which life's varied pulses part.
Clouded and shrouded there doth sit.
The Infinite . . .

Such concision he found also when in 1842 he edited the prose and verse of the Persian Saadi's *Gulistan* ("Rose Garden"), a representative collection of wise maxims As he later explained, "The dense writer has yet ample room and choice of phrase and even a gamesome mood often between his valid words."

Emerson's cryptic and summary comment on more extended thought gave it the close form of meter and rhyme which he was concerned with as a part of the structure of the universe—its recurrent tide in season and in man. For him this form was not "organic" in the sense that we sometimes use the term, as Coleridge used the term, in the individual and spontaneous unfoldment of self as a flower. This Emerson called romantic and capricious. Rather, for him "organic" meant structural, necessary, recurrent in a context of use, in material, formal, and direct cause, that is, as he said, classic.

A close look at the form of his poetry in relation to his prose tells us much of the form of the world for him. Its lines, its regular or varied stresses, its coupled or varied rhymes, are part of the body, the law, of nature. With and against them the poet's free spirit works. Similarly, names are part of the categorizing force of nature. With and against them, through metaphor, the seeing of likeness in difference and difference in likeness, the seeing poet's vision of image and symbol, of individual entity, works. Similarly, sentence, generalizations, are part of the law of nature, and with and against them the vital instance works. In structure, in reference, in sound, his poetry gives

us, even more closely than his prose, and with the focus in which he believed, the presence of all in one, the interplay of likeness and difference in every entity of art.

Among Emerson's best-liked poems, "Each and All," "Uriel," "Good-Bye," "Woodnotes," "Merlin," "Concord Hymn," "Boston Hymn," "Brahma," "Days," "Terminus," as among his longer descriptions and shorter fragments, condensations and variations appear in all sorts of degrees, from the strictness of "Concord Hymn" to the obliquities of "Merlin." Even some of his choppiest addenda are likable— "Limits," for example, or "The Bohemian Hymn," or "Water" from "Fragments," or "Nature and Life," or

Roomy Eternity
Casts her schemes rarely,
And an æon allows
For each quality and part
Of the multitudinous
And many-chambered heart.

Or, from "The Poet,"

That book is good
Which puts me in a working mood.
    Unless to thought is added Will,
    Apollo is an imbecile.
What parts, what gems, what colors shine,—
Ah, but I miss the grand design.

This was Emerson's steadiest complaint about his style: that he dealt in parts and fragments and could not achieve the whole, which he himself bespoke. Yet his very worry about this achievement, as about his friendship and love, is indicative of their importance to him, their religious center for him. We must not take at face value his fears of coldheartedness, of infinitely repellent particles; these were the recalcitrances of substance in which his spirit worked. "It is very unhappy, but too late to be helped, the discovery we have made that we exist. That discovery is called the Fall of Man." Yet, "we are sure, that, though we know not how, necessity does comport with liberty," and, "a part of Fate is the freedom of man." These are the principles of his life; they are guides, too, to the form of his art. In the speculative turns of "Merlin," as in the steady pace of "Brahma" and "Days," is the strength of freedom joined with measure.

The essay "The Poet" makes specific application of these beliefs. Ideally, the poet is the sayer, the teller of news, utterer of the necessary and causal. "For the Universe has three children, born at one time, which reappear under different names in every system of thought, whether they be called cause, operation and effect; or, more poetically, Jove, Pluto, Neptune; or, theologically, the Father, the Spirit and the Son; but which we will call here the Knower, the Doer and the Sayer. These stand respectively for the love of truth, for the love of good, and for the love of beauty. These three are equal. Each is that which he is, essentially, so that he cannot be surmounted or analyzed, and each of these three has the power of the others latent in him and his own, patent."

The poet, by saying, makes new relations, heals dislocations and detachments, shows defects as exuberances, as in Vulcan's lameness, Cupid's blindness. "Every new relation is a new word." The world is thus "put under the mind for verb and noun" with an explicit connective. It is important to realize what this sense of saying means to Emerson's own poetry. It means that as a poet he is not an imagist, not a symbolist, but specifically a figurist. That is, he accepts image and symbol as vital, from the natural world; and then his contribution as poet is to show them in new relation. "He knows why the plain or meadow of space was strown with these flowers we call suns and moons and stars. . . ." There is the metaphoric way of speaking. He names now by appearances, now by essences, delighting in the intellect's sense of boundaries, and then in the ascension of things to higher kinds, that is, in both being and becoming, the inebriation of thought moving to fact—even in algebra and definitions, the freedom of trope. Emerson blames mystics, as he would blame modern ritualistic symbolizers, for too many fixities. "The history of hierarchies seems to show that all religious error consisted in making the symbol too stark and solid." "Let us have a little algebra"—a little relation and proportion! "I look in vain for the poet whom I describe. We do not with sufficient plainness or sufficient profoundness address ourselves to life, nor dare we chaunt our own times and social circumstance."

Is Emerson a philosopher? Yes, if we agree with William James (as John Dewey quotes him in a *Southern Review* article of 1937): "Philosophic study means the habit of always seeing an alternative, of not taking the usual for granted, of making conventionalities fluid again, of imagining foreign states of mind." In this way Emerson prepares for James, for Dewey, for Charles Peirce, the great American pragmatists. In this way, too, he prepares metaphysically for Nietzsche's Dionysus. But Emerson was not systematic and Germanic. Critics like René Wellek, writing on Emerson's philosophy, Andrew Schiller on his "gnomic structure," Kathryn McEuen on his rhymes, Frank Thompson on his theories of poetry, Walter Blair and Clarence Faust on his method, Nelson Adkins on his bardic tradition, J. D. Yohannan on his Persian translations, Percy Brown on his aesthetics, Vivian Hopkins and Stephen Whicher on his sense of form, and Frederic Carpenter on his use of Oriental materials, all suggest variations on the theme of his fragmentary illuminations. So did his elder critics like Carlyle, Arnold, Santayana.

So did he. When in 1870 he began his final series "On the excellence of Intellect, its identity with nature, its formations in Instinct and Inspiration, and relation to the existing religion and civility of the present," he warned his hearers that this series would consist of "anecdotes of the intellect; a sort of Farmer's Almanac of mental moods," and even defended this method, as we have noted before, in his metaphor of the dotted line. He had reasons for not filling in the lines, for not always writing a smoothly qualified prose, poetry, or philosophy. "I think that philosophy is still rude and elementary. It will one day be taught by poets. The poet is in the natural attitude; he is believing; the philosopher, after some struggle, having only reasons for believing." "I confess to a little distrust of that completeness of system which metaphysicians are apt to affect. 'Tis the gnat grasping the world."

But in his sense of metaphysics as useful, for daily use, he had a great deal of work to do in the world. To feed the hunger of the young for ideas; to think what simple pattern of being could include man's sense of joy in being as well as his fear and falsification of it; to draw the world as newly understood by scientific thought into the world of common intuition; to combine his feeling that "the beauty of the world is a perpetual invitation to the study of the world" with his explanation of such combination, as to his brother Edward in 1834, that visionary reason and toiling understanding work together, "by mutual reaction of thought and life, to make thought solid and life wise."

A man who has been called monist, dualist, pantheist, transcendentalist, puritan, optimist, pragmatist, mystic may well feel dubious about the validity of labels, of adjectives. His style shows us how all of these terms fit him and how they work together, and over and over he tells us that it is degree he believes in; in degree, the one and the many may work together, god, man, nature may work together; all varieties of difference, from dissimilar to contrasting, will share degrees of likeness. His common term *polarity* referred not to modern positive and negative poles merely, and not to modern negative correlations or annihilations, but to "action and interaction," to differences or counterparts which are unified by a common direction, a North Star, a magnetic field, a spirit in the laws and limits of body, a drawing of body along in the direction of spirit —a golden mean with a lodestar.

Emerson's plan for the *Essays*, early set down in his *Journals*, well summarizes his steadiest concerns:

There is one soul.
It is related to the world.
Art is its action thereon.
Science finds its methods.
Literature is its record.
Religion is the emotion of reverence that it inspires.
Ethics is the soul illustrated in human life.
Society is the finding of this soul by individuals in each other.
Trades are the learning of the soul in nature by labor.
Politics is the activity of the soul illustrated in power.
Manners are silent and mediate expressions of soul.

His plan, his tables of contents, his major vocabulary, his syntax, are all of a piece, seeking and finding, in what he sees to be the major activities of man, that unifying vitality of good, that one essential likeness, which he calls *soul*. He could say, "Within and Above are synonyms"—a metaphor crucial to belief in our day—so that "transcendental" could easily mean "a little beyond"; and he was able to say in another town or on a weekday what he had not felt able to say at home and on Sunday. For as one of his small-town congregations said, "We are very simple people here, and don't understand anybody but Mr. Emerson." And as their Emerson said, "What but thought deepens life, and makes us better than cow or cat?"

It was fortunate that there was enough of an artist in this wise man of America's nineteenth century, that he tried not only to advise but to preserve, not only to tell but to make and give; that the artistic power of Renaissance poets and prose writers gave him a means to hold and shape the fluent continuities of a liberal eighteenth- and nineteenth-century romanticism; that sermon structure, like rhyme and meter, gave him ways of holding fast the free Aeolian strains of sky and sea in their relevance to thought and fate and form.

There is no permanent wise man, Emerson says. Yet, "How does Memory praise? By holding fast the best." This is the work for a wise art, a laborious but joyful understanding.

Selected Bibliography

WORKS OF RALPH WALDO EMERSON

The standard collected edition is *The Complete Works of Ralph Waldo Emerson,* the Centenary Edition, edited by Edward Waldo Emerson and published in 12 volumes by Houghton Mifflin in 1903–04. It has been supplemented by the collections listed at the end of this section.

Nature. Boston: James Munroe, 1836.
Essays [First Series]. Boston: James Munroe, 1841.
Essays: Second Series. Boston: James Munroe, 1844.
Poems. Boston: James Munroe, 1847 [1846].
Nature, Addresses, and Lectures. Boston: James Munroe, 1849.
Representative Men. Boston: Phillips, Sampson, 1850.
English Traits. Boston: Phillips, Sampson, 1856.
The Conduct of Life. Boston: Ticknor and Fields, 1860.
May-Day and Other Pieces. Boston: Ticknor and Fields, 1867.
Society and Solitude. Boston: Fields, Osgood, 1870.
Parnassus, edited by Ralph Waldo Emerson. Boston: Osgood, 1875.
Letters and Social Aims. Boston: Osgood, 1876.
Selected Poems. Boston: Osgood, 1876.
Poems. Boston: Houghton, Osgood, 1876.
Miscellanies. Boston: Houghton Mifflin, 1884.
Lectures and Biographical Sketches. Boston: Houghton Mifflin, 1884.
Natural History of Intellect and Other Papers. Boston: Houghton Mifflin, 1893.
Two Unpublished Essays: The Character of Socrates; The Present State of Ethical Philosophy. Boston: Lamson, Wolffe, 1896.
Uncollected Writings: Essays, Addresses, Poems, Reviews and Letters by Ralph Waldo Emerson, edited by Charles C. Bigelow. New York: Lamb, 1912. (Includes especially work from the *Dial.*)
The Journals of Ralph Waldo Emerson, edited by Edward Waldo Emerson and Waldo Emerson Forbes. 10 vols. Boston: Houghton Mifflin, 1909–14. (Not all-inclusive.)
Young Emerson Speaks: Unpublished Discourses on Many Subjects, edited by Arthur C. McGiffert, Jr. Boston: Houghton Mifflin, 1938.
The Letters of Ralph Waldo Emerson, edited by Ralph L. Rusk. 6 vols. New York: Columbia University Press, 1939. (There are other major collections of letters to Thomas Carlyle, Arthur Clough, William Furness, Herman Grimm, John Sterling, Henry David Thoreau, and Samuel Ward.)
The Early Lectures of Ralph Waldo Emerson. Cambridge, Mass.: Harvard University Press, 1959.
The Journals and Miscellaneous Notebooks, edited by William H. Gilman and others. 8 vols.

Cambridge, Mass.: Harvard University Press, 1960–70.

BIBLIOGRAPHIES

The *Emerson Society Quarterly* (1955 to date), edited by Kenneth W. Cameron, provides bibliographical information on a continuing basis.

Carpenter, Frederic I. *Emerson Handbook.* New York: Hendricks House, 1953. (Invaluable for rich biographical and critical material also.)

Ferguson, Alfred Riggs. *Checklist of Ralph Waldo Emerson.* Columbus, Ohio: Merrill, 1970.

Hubbell, G. S. *A Concordance to the Poems of Ralph Waldo Emerson.* New York: H. W. Wilson, 1932.

Stovall, Floyd, ed. "Emerson," in *Eight American Authors: A Review of Research and Criticism.* New York: Modern Language Association, 1956.

BIOGRAPHIES

Cabot, James. *A Memoir of Ralph Waldo Emerson.* 2 vols. Boston: Houghton Mifflin, 1887.

Cameron, Kenneth. *Emerson the Essayist.* 2 vols. Raleigh, N.C.: Thistle Press, 1945.

Emerson, Edward Waldo. *Emerson in Concord: A Memoir.* Boston: Houghton Mifflin, 1889.

Firkins, Oscar W. *Ralph Waldo Emerson.* Boston: Houghton Mifflin, 1915.

Hoeltje, Hubert. *Sheltering Tree.* Durham, N.C.: Duke University Press, 1943.

Perry, Bliss. *Emerson Today.* Princeton, N.J.: Princeton University Press, 1931.

Rusk, Ralph L. *The Life of Ralph Waldo Emerson.* New York: Scribners, 1949.

Sanborn, F. B., ed. *The Genius and Character of Emerson.* Boston: Osgood, 1885. (Selected early views.)

Woodbury, Charles J. *Talks with Emerson.* New York: Horizon Press, 1970.

CRITICAL STUDIES

Adkins, Nelson F. "Emerson and the Bardic Tradition," *PMLA,* 63:662–77 (June 1948).

Berry, Edmund G. *Emerson's Plutarch.* Cambridge, Mass.: Harvard University Press, 1961.

Blair, Walter, and Clarence Faust. "Emerson's Literary Method," *Modern Philology,* 42:79–95 (November 1944).

Brown, Percy W. "Emerson's Philosophy of Aesthetics," *Journal of Aesthetics and Art Criticism,* 15:350–54 (March 1957).

Carpenter, Frederic I. *Emerson and Asia.* Cambridge, Mass.: Harvard University Press, 1930.

Cowan, Michael H. *City of the West: Emerson, America, and Urban Metaphor.* New Haven, Conn.: Yale University Press, 1967.

Harding, Walter. *Emerson's Library.* Charlottesville: University Press of Virginia, 1967.

Hopkins, Vivian C. *Spires of Form: A Study of Emerson's Aesthetic Theory.* Cambridge, Mass.: Harvard University Press, 1951.

Konvitz, Milton, and Stephen Whicher, eds. *Emerson, A Collection of Critical Essays.* Englewood Cliffs, N.J.: Prentice-Hall, 1962. (Reprints articles by Daniel Aaron, Newton Arvin, John Dewey, Charles Feidelson, Jr., Norman Foerster, Robert Frost, William James, F. O. Matthiessen, Perry Miller, Henry B. Parkes, Sherman Paul, George Santayana, Henry Nash Smith, and Stephen Whicher.)

McEuen, Kathryn A. "Emerson's Rhymes," *American Literature,* 20:31–42 (March 1948).

Nicoloff, Philip L. *Emerson on Race and History: An Examination of English Traits.* New York: Columbia University Press, 1961.

Paul, Sherman. *Emerson's Angle of Vision: Man and Nature in American Experience.* Cambridge, Mass.: Harvard University Press, 1952.

Schiller, Andrew. "Gnomic Structure in Emerson's Poetry," in *Papers of the Michigan Academy of Science, Arts and Letters*, Vol. 40. Ann Arbor: University of Michigan Press, 1955. Pp. 313–20.

Sealts, Merton M., Jr., and Alfred R. Ferguson, eds. *Emerson's "Nature": Origin, Growth, Meaning.* New York: Dodd, Mead, 1969.

Silver, Mildred. "Emerson and the Idea of Progress," *American Literature,* 12:1–19 (March 1940).

Smith, Henry Nash. "Emerson's Problem of Vocation: A Note on 'The American Scholar,'" *New England Quarterly,* 12:52–67 (March 1939).

Thompson, Frank T. "Emerson's Theory and Practice of Poetry," *PMLA,* 43:1170–84 (December 1928).

Wellek, René. "Emerson and German Philosophy," *New England Quarterly,* 16:41–62 (March 1943).

Whicher, Stephen. *Freedom and Fate: An Inner Life of Ralph Waldo Emerson.* Philadelphia: University of Pennsylvania Press, 1953.

Yohannan, J. D. "Emerson's Translations of Persian Poetry from German Sources," *American Literature,* 14:407–20 (January 1943).

Young, Charles L. *Emerson's Montaigne.* New York: Macmillan, 1941.

—*JOSEPHINE MILES*

Louise Erdrich

1954–

LOUISE ERDRICH FEELS compelled to tell the stories of Native Americans; she gives witness to the endurance of Chippewa people. The sheer chance of being a survivor herself, considering the millions who were here in the beginning and the very, very few who survived into the 1920s, drives her storytelling. As we listen to the many storytellers in Erdrich's North Dakota cycle of novels that have come to us since the publication of *Love Medicine* (1984), we try to reconcile the tangled polyphony of speakers. She interconnects the lives of Chippewa families—Kashpaws, Pillagers, Lazarres, Lamartines, Morrisseys, Tooses, and Nanapushes—and their immigrant-descendant, off-reservation neighbors—Adares, Jameses, and Kozkas.

The story of the families begins with *Tracks* (1988), which covers the years 1912 to 1924; continues with *Love Medicine* (1984), which extends the story from 1934 to 1984; and brings the details of the Chippewa families up to what we presume to be the present time in *The Bingo Palace* (1994). This last novel in the originally proposed quartet has no dates designated for the chapters, as her three previous novels do. Approximating the span of *Love Medicine, The Beet Queen* (1988) chronicles the lives of mixed bloods and whites in the town of Argus during the years 1932 to 1972. Although she has no particular recommendation for the reader concerning the order in which to read the four novels, the story lines begin in *Tracks,* which, she declared in an interview with Nancy Feyl Chavkin and Allan Chavkin, ''was the first manuscript I finished, the form of all else, still a tangle.''

One of her four novels, *Love Medicine,* was revised and expanded in 1993 to clarify events and relationships, in the process making more defined links to *Tracks* and the later *The Bingo Palace,* which, Erdrich declares, ''just intervened, proposed itself, took over.'' Together, these three narratives move events forward over three generations, beginning with Nanapush, survivor of the consumption epidemic of 1912, and ending with Lipsha Morrissey, his descendant through Nanapush's named granddaughter Lulu Lamartine, leaning into the future, an unknown path opening before him. In *Love Medicine,* there is also an indication of a fourth generation with Howard Kashpaw, son of Lynette and King. Thus, instead of the promised quartet of novels, there is actually a trilogy plus a fourth book, *The Beet Queen.* However, Erdrich says she does not know ''when these books will begin and end,'' thus leaving the story lines open for continuance. She also has published two volumes of poetry, *Jacklight* (1984) and *Baptism of Desire* (1989).

Numerous short stories have become chapters in the novels, there have been occasional essays, and the first full-length work of nonfiction, *The*

Blue Jay's Dance: A Birth Year, appeared in 1995. With her husband, Michael Dorris, a collaborator in all her work, Erdrich wrote *Crown of Columbus* (1991) and *Route Two* (1991). Earlier, Erdrich and Dorris had published several short stories under the name Milou North.

When asked the themes of her last narrative, *The Bingo Palace,* Erdrich responded by noting what she considers the usual: ''anxiety, money, chance, obsessed love, age, small griefs, failed friendship, self-denial, repressed sexual ardor.'' To a great extent, all her novels deal with these irritations of life. However, the deeper underlying issues of origin, place, connections to others, adaptability, and vision are the ones that continue to impress themselves on the reader's consciousness. They provoke a desire to interpret events in the lives of tribal people and become involved in their meaning. Like the oral storyteller's audience, readers become cocreators of the text, invited to that role by the many voices, each telling his or her own version of the story. One of the major themes in Erdrich's fiction concerns personal identity within family and tribal structures. Memory, language, trickster energy, and humor contribute to survival of her characters, who testify to the continuance of Chippewa people. To convey the realities of shifting and dwindling communities within and outside tribal culture, Erdrich invents narrative strategies that involve narrators and readers in interpretive dialogue, resulting in new understandings of the effects of the loss of community among both Indians and whites. Slim chances of survival and fragile threads of human endurance continue to amaze the reader of Erdrich's fiction.

Louise Erdrich declares Chippewa, French, Scottish, and German ancestry. An enrolled member of the Turtle Mountain Band, she connects to the people and the place of her beginnings: the Turtle Mountain Reservation, which is located in north-central North Dakota near the Canadian border. This reservation becomes the epicenter of the three novels that chronicle Chippewa family sagas, and it also figures, to a lesser extent, in *The Beet Queen.* Born on June 7, 1954, in Little Falls, Minnesota, Erdrich grew up in a family of nine—mother, Rita Joanne Gourneau, father, Ralph Louis Erdrich, and seven children—in Wahpeton, North Dakota, in a house that belonged to the government. Her parents were employees of the Bureau of Indian Affairs at the Wahpeton Indian School, where her grandfather had been educated. Erdrich's mother and grandparents, Patrick and Mary Gourneau, are from the Turtle Mountain Reservation. The Turtle Mountains cover about four hundred square miles on both sides of the border between the United States and Canada. The land that is not hilly is covered with water. There are at least thirty lakes of various sizes on the thirty-four thousand acres of reservation land, and many marshes. It is, therefore, not surprising that sloughs figure importantly in the terrain of Erdrich's novels. Water imagery predominates in *Love Medicine.*

Although she has never lived on the reservation, Erdrich has visited there often, and she has chosen to identify with her Chippewa origin. She uses the term ''Chippewa'' to refer to her people; however, the original woodland people were known as Anishinaabeg. In the nineteenth century these tribal people were often referred to as Ojibwa or Ojibway. Gerald Vizenor points out that the designations ''Chippewa'' and ''Ojibwa'' are colonial names for the original people.

Erdrich is also a member of the white community by blood and education. In 1972 she was one of the first female students admitted to Dartmouth College, which was then developing its Native American Program. Her husband, Michael Dorris, was a faculty member there and later became the founder and director of the Native American Studies Program. Erdrich graduated from Dartmouth in 1976 with a degree in English and creative writing, and obtained a master's degree in creative writing from Johns Hopkins University in 1979. She and Dorris were married on October 10, 1981.

Erdrich notes the dual citizenship of the individual who lives in the Anglo culture and at the same time remains connected to Indian identity. In an interview with Joseph Bruchac, she commented on the quest for background that is so much a part of her experience: "One of the characteristics of being a mixed-blood is searching. You look back and say, 'Who am I from?' You must question. You must make certain choices. You're able to. And it's a blessing and a curse. All of our searches involve trying to discover where we are from." Erdrich brings her mixed background into her characters' lives, creating the most significant narratives from the basic need to know who and where they came from.

In *Love Medicine,* the heart of the family sagas, understanding one's origin becomes problematic. Lipsha Morrissey has been told his mother tried to drown him in the slough, and his efforts to deal with the uncertainty of his beginnings obscure his ability to find a place for himself in life. Marie Kashpaw, who has raised Lipsha and whom he calls Grandma, says she saved him from his mother's attempts to drown him, but she doesn't identify Lipsha's mother. It remains for his other grandmother, Lulu Lamartine, to reveal that Lipsha is the son of June Kashpaw and Lulu's son, Gerry Nanapush, and to soothe Lipsha's worry about his mother's intent: "June was just real upset about the whole thing. Your Grandma Kashpaw took you on because the truth is she had a fond spot for June, just like she's got one for you." When Lipsha asks Lulu if his mother tried to drown him, she tries to divert his attention to the important information about his parentage. Lulu attributes Lipsha's oddness to his confusion about where he came from: "You never knew who you were. That's one reason why I told you. I thought it was a knowl-

edge that could make or break you." Knowing who you are and where you come from persists as a major theme in Erdrich's novels.

In *The Bingo Palace,* Lipsha tries to hold on to the belief that he was given to Grandma Kashpaw by "a mother who was beautiful but too wild to have raised a boy on her own." But Marie's daughter Zelda, who was brought up with June, makes sure Lipsha knows all the terrible details, how she saw June "slinging a little bundle into the slough." She describes how she made three or four dives before she finally located the gunnysack and her subsequent discovery that it contained Lipsha: "I opened that sack once I was out of the woods. I cried when I saw it was a baby! When you saw me you blinked your eyes wide and then you smiled." Worse than anything else, Lipsha can't dismiss Zelda's account as inventive. The hurt of his mother's action haunts him. Despite the whisky that Zelda has consumed at the bar where he works, Lipsha suspects that Zelda's version of his past is not embroidered, and he fights to forgive June. Lipsha persists in unraveling his family's secrets to satisfy himself and to prove his identity for the bureaucracy. He needs to obtain a band card, "proof-positive self-identification, a complicated thing in Indian Country." Lipsha observes that the dominant culture's bureaucratic requirements work against Indian self-actualization. Lipsha only knows his identity through his grandmothers, Marie and Lulu. Without government acceptance of his identity, his enrollment, and consequently his entitlements, elude him. The security of knowing a mother's love eludes him, too. His romantic pursuit of Shawnee Ray Toose in *The Bingo Palace* is in part a search for a mother. Without a full and clear understanding of origin, Erdrich's characters seem condemned to search; and in that sense, wholeness eludes Lipsha, as it does so many of the characters in her work.

One character who does know where he came

from is Nanapush, who shares the storytelling with Pauline Puyat in *Tracks*. He presents his legacy in his father's words: " 'Nanapush. That's what you'll be called. Because it's got to do with trickery and living in the bush. Because it's got to do with something a girl can't resist. The first Nanapush stole fire. You will steal hearts.' " For white readers, his name takes on mythic proportions in its identification with Prometheus, the fire stealer from Greek mythology. For Indian readers, and especially for the Chippewa audience, the reference to trickery signifies that Nanapush is a descendant of Naanabozho, who, Gerald Vizenor tells us (in *Interior Landscapes,* ''Measuring My Blood''), was "the first tribal trickster on the earth. He was comic, a part of the natural world, a spiritual balance in a comic drama, and so he must continue in his stories." Encoded in Nanapush's name is his identity as energy source and stabilizing agent in the lives he touches. He passes his name on to Fleur's child, Lulu, in the ritual of baptism, and in doing so, he ensures the continuance of his own name and adds more ambiguity to Lulu's paternal origin. The uncertainty of the gang rape that Pauline reported when she came back from Argus and the equal uncertainty of Eli as father of Fleur's child fade with the emergence of the name Nanapush. There is no doubt that Fleur was raped, according to Pauline's report, but the account is clouded by Pauline's unreliability as a witness.

In *Tracks,* Fleur, who has survived the consumption epidemic with Nanapush, knows her origin, but according to Nanapush, she and her cousin Moses, the only remaining Pillagers, have suffered the loss of family to the point where it is not clear whether they are in the land of the living or "the other place, boundless, where the dead sit talking, see too much, and regard the living as fools." Fleur's understanding of her origin is obscured by the spirits of her dead family: "She was too young and had no stories or

depth of life to rely upon. All she had was raw power, and the names of the dead that filled her. . . . Ogimaakwe, Boss Woman, his wife. Asasaweminikwesens, Chokecherry Girl. Bineshii, Small Bird, also known as Josette. And the last, the boy Ombaashi, He Is Lifted By Wind.'' The names of dead relatives alone cannot sustain Fleur; yet, like Nanapush, Fleur is a survivor. She is linked to him because he saved her from death by starvation when her family died from the illness called consumption, the dreaded tuberculosis, as deadly as the smallpox that preceded it. The historical reality of the tremendous loss of Indian lives by epidemics takes on human proportions in *Tracks.*

Like Nanapush, Fleur is linked to the traditional tribal ways, but she turns her knowledge into an occult power that Nanapush considers dangerous. She identifies with the animal and spirit world and the land around Lake Matchimanito, but when her power is threatened, she retreats further into the region surrounding the lake where, Nanapush tells Eli Kashpaw, ''The leaves speak a cold language that overfills your brain. You want to lie down. You want to never get up.'' Nanapush connects Fleur to the wildness and witchery of Lake Matchimanito. Fleur's power enchants Eli, who begs Nanapush for sexual knowledge so that he can be a pleasing lover to Fleur. Fleur's sexuality, unrepressed and lavish as the vegetation surrounding the lake, is reported to be linked to Misshepeshu, the water monster, the devil who wants strong and daring young girls.

Tracks' second narrator, Pauline Puyat, denied her origin by asking her father to send her to Argus, where she hoped to erase her identity as a mixed blood: ''I wanted to be like my mother, who showed her half-white. I wanted to be like my grandfather, pure Canadian.'' Wanting to learn the lacemaking trade from the nuns, Pauline begs her father to send her to his sister Regina, whose husband works in a butcher shop,

Kozka's Meats. Instead of learning "to thread the bobbins and spools," she sweeps the floors of the butcher shop and cares for Regina's son Russell as she watches Fleur, who also has come to Argus and has been hired at the butcher shop. Fleur's strength and power to attract men provoke Pauline's understanding of her own thin body and impoverished sexuality. Pauline's repressed sexuality stands in contrast to Fleur's extravagant supply.

Pauline's identity is compromised by her disconnection from her people, but even her rejection of her identity as a mixed blood is somewhat ambiguous, for she learns that her family moved away from the reservation while she worked in Argus. There is an implication that she has been left behind, a castaway, and so she becomes an apprentice to Bernadette Morrissey, helping prepare bodies of the dead, "death's bony whore." In a delusion, Pauline hears Christ asking her to bring more souls, and she responds in a frenzy of zeal. She gives up her baby, conceived in the raw union with Napoleon Morrissey, Bernadette's brother, and enters the convent: "I have no family, . . . I am alone and have no land. Where else would I go but to the nuns?" Pauline will become a handmaiden of God, having strangled the devil with rosary beads: "Eventually, it took on the physical form of Napoleon Morrissey." In a final act of defilement, Pauline desecrates herself physically and spiritually, allowing the blame for Napoleon's death to be assigned to Fleur.

In *Love Medicine*, Marie Lazarre, bastard child of Pauline, rejects her origin, too, but she is able to choose another option besides the church. In this case, sheer ambition counts enough to override the evil she came from and the evil of the convent. Marie confronts the crazed nun, Sister Leopolda, who is actually her own mother. (Sister Leopolda is the name Pauline took when she entered the convent.) Brought up by the Lazares, Marie despises her foster mother, who is a drunk,

and her foster father. She selects Nector Kashpaw as her route to identity, although he considers her "a skinny white girl from a family so low you cannot even think they are in the same class as Kashpaws." Marie's will and her humanity link her to the family she creates with Nector as well as to Lucille, her sister in the foster family of Lazares, whom she rejects. Her feeling for Lucille influences Marie to take Lucille's daughter June into her own family and to raise her as one of her own children; later she takes June's son Lipsha when June rejects him. Marie is strongly identified as a mother-woman by her actions within the family, and she is strongly connected to other females of the tribe. In the expanded version of *Love Medicine*, Marie is coached through the difficult birth of her last child by Rushes Bear (Margaret Kashpaw) and Fleur Pillager. Marie's use of the old Cree language to express her need to be taken by labor contractions (*babaumawaebigowin*) as a boat would be borne by waves identifies her as a traditional Indian woman.

Origin becomes a source of sadness for Lyman Lamartine, one of Lulu's nine offspring by different fathers. He is ambivalent about knowing that he is the son of Nector Kashpaw. "I don't really want to know," he tells Lulu. Part of Lyman's identity went with his brother Henry Jr., a severely traumatized Vietnam veteran, when he drove their red Oldsmobile convertible into the Red River and drowned.

In her revision of *Love Medicine*, Erdrich makes clear the importance of the relationship between origin and identity, particularly with regard to Lyman. The addition of the chapter "The Tomahawk Factory" provides important insights into Lyman's character, especially the inheriting of Nector's business sense, and it also paves the way for Lyman's role as developer of gaming enterprises in *The Bingo Palace*. Lyman's origin and his connection to the tribe are trivialized in his discovery of identity through a U.S. Department of the Treasury 1099 form, which jolts him out of his alcohol- and drug-induced stupor into existence. Filing his income tax return brings him his identity: "I was becoming legitimate, rising from the heap." Heightening the irony of becoming a person by filling out a form is Lyman's discovery that his box number had been mistakenly typed on a form that belonged to someone else. Lyman quickly joins the bureaucracy of the Bureau of Indian Affairs, and in this role must deal with his mother, Lulu, and Marie as they battle over authority and territory in the souvenir factory. In an outburst of anger, Marie identifies Nector as Lyman's father before the assembled workers, prompting bedlam on the assembly line; insults and beads fly through the air, and eventually Anishinabe Enterprises is destroyed. The additional chapter "Lyman's Luck" paves the way for Lyman's future, based on greed and luck —a gambling casino—in *The Bingo Palace*. Still, Lyman hurts when he remembers that Nector had never acknowledged him as a son. When Lyman thinks about it, there is nagging irritation in Lipsha's being given Nector's ceremonial pipe. Eventually Lyman makes a commodity of the sacred piece by buying it from Lipsha.

Albertine Johnson's knowledge of her origin comes through the uncommitted motherhood of her mother, Zelda, and through photos of her soldier father displayed in her mother's house: "All I knew of him was pictures, blond, bleak, and doomed to wander, perhaps as much by Mama's rage at her downfall as by the uniform." Her name is a feminine version of Albert, a link to her mother's "repressed history," for Albertine bears the name of Xavier Albert Toose, the boyfriend Zelda resisted but never relinquished. Albertine's father is dismissed as a mistake by Zelda: "Never marry a Swedish is my rule." In *The Bingo Palace,* Albertine seeks her identity in a ceremony conducted, ironically, by Xavier Toose. She takes the traditional name of Four Soul, a woman "sunk deep in the scattered records of the Pil-

lagers, into the slim and strange substance of the times and names." Albertine must search for an origin from the listing of names of those Chippewa who "in that first decade when people, squeezed westward, starving, came to the reservation to receive rations and then allotted land." Four Soul is the ancestor of Fleur; Albertine's traditional naming connects the lines of Kashpaws and Pillagers in a new tangle. With this naming, Erdrich resurrects the anguish of Chippewa people pushed out of their original land in the forced migration of the tribe.

In *The Beet Queen,* Mary Adare disconnects from her origin by willing herself to forget the loss of her mother, Adelaide, and her brothers: "I'd lost trust in the past. They were part of a fading pattern that was beyond understanding, and brought me no comfort." The mother's abandonment of her family causes Mary to develop an oddness that she recognizes in herself: "I said things too suddenly. I was pigheaded, bitter, moody, and had fits of unreasonable anger." Mary understands that her mother's flight from the Minneapolis Fairgrounds, the loss of her baby brother to a stranger, and the separation from Karl when the boxcar stops in Argus had affected her, creating a compulsion to clutch people to her, particularly Celestine James and her daughter, Dot Adare. Mary is condemned by her past to be a misfit.

Wallace Pfef, Celestine's neighbor, who helps to deliver Dot, connects his origin to a vegetable, the "raw white beet," that grew in the great Ruhr Valley from which his people came. The restlessness of the immigrant resonates in Wallace Pfef's family: "In America, we moved often, complaining that something was not quite right." Pfef finally settles down in Argus to belong to the "Chamber of Commerce, Sugar Beet Promoters, Optimists, Knights of Columbus, park board, and other organizations too numerous to mention." Wallace substitutes fraternal groups for family connections, and, for public consumption, he substitutes a picture of a woman bought at a Minnesota farm auction for a relationship with another human being. The picture serves to satisfy the curiosity of Argus residents who might wonder about his lack of interest in women. Wallace's identity as a homosexual would have placed him on the fringe of midwestern society in the 1930s; his identity as agriculture promoter would place him in the solid center. Sexually repressed, Wallace channels his energy into helping to parent Dot, another outlet to compensate for Karl Adare's sexual rejection of him. The fields of beets lead to the agribusiness of sugar refineries, and the North Dakota landscape of flowering beets fills Wallace Pfef's vision of the prairie.

For Erdrich the prairie with its vast space of land and sky is a homeplace that is imaged in her writing. The endless North Dakota fields of corn, wheat, soybeans, and flax viewed from her childhood home in Wahpeton are always in her mind's eye, directing her attention to the space above, as she noted in "Where I Ought to Be": "I often see this edge of town—the sky and its towering and shifting formations of clouds, that beautiful lighted emptiness—when I am writing."

Ten years later, in her home in the hills of New Hampshire, Erdrich's intense longing for the space of sky had not lessened. She wrote in *The Blue Jay's Dance:* "I want the clean line, the simple line, the clouds marching over it in feathered masses. I suffer from horizon sickness." The great nostalgia for open space, which she considers "both romantically German and pragmatically Ojibwa," informs Erdrich's writing. In the years between 1985, the date of her observation about the longing for place, and *The Blue Jay's Dance* in 1995, there has been no lessening of her identification with the Great Plains as home. Adapting to New England has meant substituting trees for sky; she says she has grown accustomed to the roaring of "thousands and millions of leaves brushing and touching one

another," making do with a new landscape, finding a new way to be at home, far from the open space of North Dakota.

Space in Erdrich's novels can be liberating or threatening, and sometimes both at once. In *Love Medicine,* the vast space of the prairie means death for June Kashpaw. She moves across open fields, headed for home after the empty encounter with the mud engineer, Andy. Turning away from the dull orange glow of the oil town of Williston, North Dakota, June keeps going although, as her niece Albertine Johnson says later, "the heaviness in the air, the smell in the clouds," would have told her that a snowstorm was coming. June's death from exposure to cold on the prairie could represent a deliberate decision to end a life that was marked early on by abuse. Lucille Lazarre, in her alcoholic stupor, inflicts physical abuse, and her boyfriend, Leonard, rapes June.

The ambiguity surrounding June's decision to head for home in a snowstorm despite having a bus ticket, which remains throughout *Love Medicine,* suddenly comes clear in the chapter "June's Luck" in *The Bingo Palace.* The impossibility of escaping from the past erupts in June's flight into a space where she can escape from pain that rang everywhere:

> Then she was so small she was just a burning dot, a flung star moving, speeding through the blackness, the air, faster and faster and with no letup until she finally escaped into a part of her mind, where she made one promise before she went out. *Nobody ever hold me again.*

June's entire life turns on that promise. She cannot be held, as her husband, Gordie, knows, nor can she hold anyone else, as her son Lipsha struggles to understand. Lipsha learns that we hurt others as we have been hurt, that his mother's attempts to drown him represent a circular pattern: "I know that she did the same that was done to her—a young girl left out to live on the woods and survive on pine sap and leaves and buried roots.'' The reader, knowing the truth of June's past—that she was raped by her mother's boyfriend—can fill in the space of Lipsha's incomplete understanding. The reasons for June's inability to connect to others are fully understood by the reader but only partially understood by Lipsha.

In *Love Medicine,* June's turning toward home suggests flight from the oppression that has followed her unrelentingly, but it also allows for the possibility of renewal. The Easter season and the egg imagery contribute to the understanding of her transformation. Though she perishes in the cold of a prairie storm that left more snow than it had in forty years, ''June walked over it like water and came home.'' In a transcendence of body, June's spirit comes home to the reservation.

In another flight into space, Adelaide Adare in *The Beet Queen* turns away from her family, scattering her children—Mary, Karl, and a new baby, whom she had refused to name—in all directions. Wandering into the Orphans' Picnic, having had to leave their home when the man who supported them died in a grain-loading accident, the family comes to the grandstand where the Great Omar offers rides to those who want to take a chance, and Adelaide chooses to be one of them. Mary, who has been left to care for her brothers, cannot watch the plane's maneuvers but is alerted to catastrophe by the ever decreasing sound of the plane's engine: ''By the time I dared look into the sky, The Great Omar was flying steadily away from the fairgrounds with my mother.'' In an image reminiscent of June's self-reducing to a burning dot, the orphaned children's pain is represented by the airplane as a white dot, blending into the pale blue sky and vanishing. In retribution, Mary constructs a scene in which Omar, with fuel supply dwindling, must lighten the load of his plane and pushes Adelaide overboard to save himself. In Mary's fantasy,

Adelaide falls through the awful cold, but Mary is unrelenting: ''I had no love for her. That is why, by morning, I allowed her to hit the earth.''

In another leap through space, Karl Adare jumps from the boxcar after his encounter with Giles St. Ambrose and is released into a life of passive helplessness. Rescued by Fleur and nursed back to health, he is brought to the reservation and then to the convent, where the nuns take charge of him; they send him to Minneapolis, to the orphanage on the grounds of which he had been left by his mother. Karl's flight brings him back full circle. He is sent to the seminary, but his days as a priest are marked by rendezvous with ''thin hard hoboes who had slept in the bushes.'' Karl is a bisexual, and his relationship with Celestine James produces Dot, but he can never accept the role of father. Ungrounded so many times in his life, Karl is perpetually traveling in his car, living the life of a salesman always on the road.

In *The Bingo Palace,* Redford, Shawnee Ray Toose's son, experiences the sky threatening him with a frightening premonition of disaster. It comes in the form of a ''large thing made of metal with many barbed hooks, points, and drag chains on it, something like Grandma Zelda's potato peeler, only a giant one that rolled out of the sky, scraping clouds down with it and jabbing or crushing everyone that lay in its path on the ground.'' Left by his mother with his aunts, Mary Fred and Tammy Toose, Redford had been shocked awake by the terrible dream, which is translated into reality by the arrival of Zelda with a tribal police officer and a social worker, with papers to take Redford from his mother's sisters. Mary Fred delivers a blow with a butterfly buckle to Officer Pukwan's chin; in turn, she is knocked out by the butt of Pukwan's gun as she leaps into the air, then falls as if she had been running into the earth.

Flight to doom is countered by a flight that heightens self-knowledge in Dot Adare's ascent into the sky over the Argus fairgrounds. Her flight into space in the crop duster's plane begins as an impulsive escape from the smothering attention of would-be parents and her election as queen of the Beet Festival, contrived by Wallace Pfef. Outraged by his engineering her crowning as the queen of Argus' Beet Queen Festival, Dot soars into space in the crop duster's plane, where she becomes sick from the motion and shock of the dizzying distance from earth, and begs to be returned to land. When the pilot lands, Dot is surprised to find that no one has remained to find out what has become of her except her mother, Celestine, whom she sees as if for the first time: "Her skin is rough. Her whole face seems magnetized, like ore. Her deep brown eyes are circled with dark skin, but full of eagerness. In her eyes I see the force of her love." In returning to her mother, who waits for her on the ground, Dot sees the constancy of her mother's love amid the wreckage of her turbulent adolescence.

Despite tragic occurrences, Erdrich's novels are not tragedies. Somewhere between the edge of tragic events and annihilation there is a thin margin of survival where comedy erupts. In an interview with Bill Moyers, Erdrich notes that the one universal thing about Native Americans, tribe to tribe, may be survival humor. She explains that Indians have developed a humor that allows them to live with the most difficult events in their lives: "You have to be able to poke fun at people who are dominating your life and your family." In the underseam of life, sometimes reduced to a narrow space of existence, Indians must poke fun at themselves, too: "If we took ourselves too seriously in any way, I feel we would be overwhelmed." Twisting and turning on the borderline between two cultures, Indians choose humor as a way to endure.

In *Love Medicine*, the humor of language and situation that is rooted in human vanity seems to overflow in Nector Kashpaw, son of Margaret, husband of Marie, and lover of Lulu. Signed up for a movie right out of school in Flandreau, the Indian boarding school where he first met Lulu, he is to play the part of an Indian who falls off a horse and dies. His experience reinforces the popular conception of Indians initiated by General Custer and generally adopted by whites: the only good Indian is a dead Indian. Although he ultimately rejects that role, Nector says the offers keep coming to him. He is selected to model for a rich old woman who persuades him to forget his dignity: "I was paid by this woman a round two hundred dollars for standing stock still in a diaper." The resulting painting, *The Plunge of the Brave*, hanging in the State Capitol in Bismarck, officially expresses the dominant culture's view of Indians. It shows Nector "jumping off a cliff, naked of course, down into a rocky river. Certain death." Either way, movies or painting, Nector represents dead Indians. The painting becomes a kind of symbol for Indians as well. Lulu purchases a copy of the painting for her new apartment at the Senior Citizens, noting that everyone owned it, "whether they liked Kashpaw and wanted to venerate his youth, or did not like him and therefore made fun of his naked leap." The painting evokes widely varying attitudes, and comes to symbolize both white and Indian ambivalence.

Nector's offers ultimately teach him something. Out of humiliation comes the determination to survive. Nector vows to fool that pitiful old woman who painted his death in the plunge down to the rock-strewn stream: "I'd hold my breath when I hit and let the current pull me toward the surface, around jagged rocks. I wouldn't fight it, and in that way I'd get to shore," he imagines. Nector survives by letting the current take him where it will. He can handle only one thing at a time. He wants to sit against a tree and watch the cows, but he is drawn into tribal politics without his intention: "I had to speed where I was took." There is both humor and pathos in Nector's situation, split as he is between Lulu and Marie.

There is tender humor with an ironic turn in Nector's first encounter with Marie. In the comedy of a chance meeting, Nector loses his way, weakened by her "tight plush acceptance, graceful movements, little jabs that lead me underneath her skirt where she is slick, warm, silk." On his way to the convent, where he hopes to sell the two geese he and Eli have shot, Nector dreams of Lulu and his plans for meeting her that night. When Marie comes down the hill straight from her duel with Leopolda, her fork-stabbed hand wrapped in a pillowcase emblazoned with the initials SHC, and into Nector's path, he challenges her. His hasty observation of Marie leads him to think she must have stolen the sisters' linen, and he wonders, ironically, what else she may have hidden beneath her skirt. His calculations are way off. He misreads the signs of Marie's flight from the convent. Trapped by his desire to earn a possible reward from the nuns for returning stolen goods, perhaps a chalice, from Marie Lazarre, "the youngest daughter of horse-thieving drunks," Nector is caught by Marie, whose wounded hand he cannot let go. In their sexual encounter on the hill, in full view of the convent, Nector is bound to Marie. His plans to buy the French-style wedding band for Lulu are thwarted.

There is human comedy as well in Nector's midlife crisis. He contemplates the passing of time, the accumulation of babies that he and Marie have produced and taken in: "Seventeen Years of married life and come-and-go children." Suddenly aware of a diminishing self, Nector begins to think of Lulu. Enlisting her help to deliver commodity butter on the reservation, Nector is outmaneuvered once again by a woman. Lulu drives him up to the lookout in her Nash Ambassador Custom automobile, complete with air conditioning, where they resume a relationship broken off years before by Nector's marriage to Marie. Nector, "middle-aged butter mover," has somehow been transformed into "the young hard-muscled man who thrilled and sparked her so long ago," and not entirely by his own intent.

The love medicine of the Chippewa provides another humorous instance of human vanity in the hands of Lipsha Morrissey. In an interview with Jan George, Erdrich says that humor is a tribal trademark: "The Chippewa have the best sense of humor of any group of people I've ever known." In the depiction of Lipsha as the wise fool, Erdrich creates the would-be trickster, the trickster gone off the trickster's tangent, an even more ridiculous version of the mythical trickster.

Lipsha, like the original trickster from Chippewa myth, Naanabozho, who was cared for by his grandmother, Nokomis, is raised by his foster grandmother, Marie. As the son of Gerry Nanapush, he inherits the tricky heart that keeps him out of military service, but as modern version of trickster, Lipsha loses the touch. Many times he tries to use the gifts that he believes have come down to him but fails to carry out his healing power. In his practice of love medicine, he tries to bring Marie and Nector back together with the frozen heart of a turkey bought from the Red Owl grocery store and blessed by himself at the holy water font at the convent. When Nector chokes on the cooked heart and Marie collapses from the shock of Nector's death, Lipsha begins to gain an understanding of love, and comforts his grandmother by reassuring her that Nector loved her "over time and distance," but he died so quickly he never got the chance to tell her. Though his grandmother doesn't believe his explanation, she does believe in Lipsha. In that way Lipsha regains some belief in himself.

In *The Bingo Palace,* joining with Lyman Lamartine, Lipsha participates in a secularized version of the vision quest that parodies the sacred. His visions consist of Big Macs and the retreat of the Chippewa to their beginnings: "In my mind's eye I see us Chippewa jumping back into the Big Shell that spawned us." He dreams of eluding Lyman, he and Shawnee Ray and Redford sailing off in the shell, leaving Lyman, contender for Shawnee's affection and also Redford's father, to watch until they disappear into space. Alternating between bouts of loneliness and movie scenes replayed in his head, Lipsha ends his vision quest visited by a skunk that shuts down his senses and sends Xavier Toose, his instructor in the quest, into attacks of laughter.

Trickster prevails in all cultures. In the myths of the Chippewa, Manobozho is the chief trickster. His name has many variants—Naanabozho, Nanapush, Nanabush, and Wenebojo, to name a few. There are literally hundreds of stories about him. He is a complex being who was the youngest son of the union of Epingishmook, the West, and a virgin mother named Winonah. Left an orphan, he was brought up by his grandmother, Nokomis. According to Basil Johnston, Nanapush could be both foolish and wise; he was a teacher who instructed in the art of healing, and he possessed the greatest of human virtues: kindness. Although known as a peacemaker, he also has an evil side, being capable of deceit, trickery, and lewdness. Trickster can change shape, cross existing borders, and subvert existing systems. Erdrich incorporates the idea of trickster in several of her characters, Nanapush in *Tracks* being the most obvious. Gerry Nanapush, his grandson through Lulu, and Lulu herself qualify for trickster status as well.

According to Lulu, Gerry's delicate energy and capacity to change his shape testify that he is a Nanapush man, the son of trickster—whom she identifies as Old Man Pillager, her mother's cousin Moses—although he bears the name of Nanapush, self-appointed grandfather to Lulu, to whom he gave his name in baptism. As trickster, master subverter of systems, Gerry will not be contained in a white man's jail. Over and over again he breaks out of prison. According to Albertine, "He boasted that no steel or concrete shit-barn could hold a Chippewa, and he had eellike

properties in spite of his enormous size." Myth springs up around Gerry. Once he had squirmed into a six-foot-thick prison wall and vanished. In true trickster fashion, Gerry rubs his belly for luck and escapes, appearing at Dot Adare's door, giving her a less than lucky assignment: "Hiding a six-foot-plus, two-hundred-and-fifty-pound Indian in the middle of a town that doesn't like Indians in the first place isn't easy." In another escape, he folds himself into the trunk of the Firebird bought by King with June's life-insurance money, and is rescued by Lipsha as his breath is about to give out.

Trickster's appetite is notoriously voracious. Gerry follows the pattern as he consumes "stacks of pork chops, whole fryers, thick steaks," tossing the bones out the window, heedless of the neighbors, who eventually complain and bring the law to his door. In her daydreams, Albertine pictures Dot and Gerry in Dot's trailer house, both hungry: "Heads swaying, clasped hands swinging between them like hooded trunks, they moved through the kitchen feeding casually from boxes and bags on the counters, like ponderous animals alone in the forest."

Possessing trickster's sexual prowess, Gerry manages to have sexual relations with Dot in a far corner of a state prison visiting room, away from the closed-circuit television camera's lens: "Through a hole ripped in her pantyhose and a hole ripped in Gerry's jeans they somehow managed to join and, miraculously, to conceive." Albertine imagines the two of them in the trailer settling themselves on Dot's king-size bed: "They rubbed together, locking and unlocking their parts. They set the trailer rocking on its cement-block-and-plywood foundation and the tremors spread, causing cups to fall, plates to shatter in the china hutches of their more established neighbors." The baby that comes of their union feeds voraciously, too, nursing for hours, refusing to be satisfied with pacifiers.

Like trickster, Gerry has a penchant for getting

into trouble. When he is caught on the Pine Ridge Reservation, he resists arrest, shooting and killing a state trooper. He is sent to the control unit of the federal prison in Marion, Illinois, "where no touching is allowed, where the voice is carried by phone, glances meet through sheets of Plexiglas, and no children will ever be engendered." Still, Gerry always manages to escape, usually when he is being transferred to another institution.

Constantly defying social order, in *The Bingo Palace* Gerry finds the trickster's luck again when, with some weighty assistance from Lulu's influence on the tribe, he is transferred from Illinois to a maximum-security prison in Minnesota. He survives a plane crash during a snowstorm, and even sends a call for assistance to his son, Lipsha, who steals a getaway car with him. In the chase over the snow, reminiscent of the snowstorm in which June had perished, Gerry, following a vision of June in her blue Firebird, leaves the road. Lipsha watches his father go to June: "It isn't that he doesn't care for me, I know that, it's just that his own want is too deep to resist." In this case, trickster escapes myth and enters the realm of human need.

Gerry's mother, Lulu, as female trickster and strong woman, possesses personal power and transcends conventional expectations. In the traditional dance and trill that she exhibits for the news cameras, Lulu demonstrates that she knows how to subvert the system. She leads the federal marshals first one way and then another as they question her about where her son has gone. Having taken him over the Canadian border, Lulu feigns confusion and memory loss, even fainting, proving more than a match for the investigators, who "spent a long time questioning a fish in the river, they spent a longer time talking to a turtle in its shell, they tried to intimidate a female badger guarding the mouth of its den and then, to fool an old lady coyote who trotted wide of the marks her pups had left." In true trickster fashion, Lulu leads first one way and then another, finally triumphing in gained time that allows Gerry to make his escape and in her victorious show of ceremony in a grand exit in full Chippewa regalia.

Lulu's independence of mind and body resonates in a poem from *Jacklight*, "The Lady in the Pink Mustang." Like the lady in the pink Mustang, Lulu has established a place for herself where she can move in either direction:

> She is always at that place, seen from behind,
> motionless, torn forward, living in a zone
> all her own. It is like she has burned right through time,
> the brand, the mark, owning the woman who bears it.

Lulu owns herself in her relationships with assorted husbands and lovers. Lulu explains in *Love Medicine* that she "was in love with the whole world and all that lived in its rainy arms."

Lulu is as audacious as the blue jay, in *The Blue Jay's Dance*, that defies the attacking hawk, continuing to dance, "hopping forward, hornpiping up and down with tiny leaps, all of its feathers on end to increase its size." Fierce and shrieking, the jay amazes and confuses the hawk into a puzzled retreat. In a similar outrage, in *Love Medicine*, Lulu confronts the tribe as business interests move to take her land. She threatens to name all the fathers of her children unless she is granted her home and the land it stands on. When the house is burned, Lulu and her boys camp out on the land until the tribe builds a government crackerbox house for them on a "strip of land rightfully repurchased from a white farmer." In their common defiance, Lulu, the blue jay, and the Chippewa face the enemy and endure. In refusing to move from her land, Lulu reminds the reader of the U.S. government policy that sent Chippewas from east of the Great Lakes westward to the prairie in the 1800s.

* * *

Erdrich's women are powerful. Some, like Marie Kashpaw, turn experience into helping and healing—themselves and others; others, like her daughter Zelda, resist experience and defer healing. There is transforming energy in Marie's raising a family of five children, molding Nector into tribal chairman, and proving to the world that she has risen above the "dirty" Lazarres from whom she came. Marie knows evil, for she has faced it in the drunken lives of her mother and father and in the fraud of Sister Leopolda. She meets evil in what happened to her sister's child, June, who came to her hardly able to stand up, "starved bones, a shank of black strings," a creature of the woods who "had sucked on pine sap and grazed grass and nipped buds like a deer."

In *Love Medicine,* Marie's ambition takes her first to the convent, where she intends to be worshiped by the nuns: "I'd be carved in pure gold. With ruby lips. And my toenails would be little pink ocean shells, which they would have to stoop down off their high horse to kiss." Escaping from Leopolda with a burned back and a pierced hand, Marie uses that experience to mold Nector into tribal chairman. Peeling potatoes, scrubbing floors, and churning butter, Marie plots Nector's future, relying on her own strength: "I don't pray. When I was young, I vowed I never would be caught begging God. If I want something I get it for myself." In claiming a respected role for herself in the community, Marie has transformed herself from a "dirty" Lazarre into a proud mother and the wife of a tribal official. In the process of self-transformation, she has learned to empathize. Even though she has barely enough to feed her children, she takes in June, just as she would later take in June's son, Lipsha. She can feel pity for Leopolda although it is mixed with a need to prove that she has not been condemned to the life of raising Indian brats that Leopolda had predicted.

As Marie helps others to survive, she too gets past the hurt of being left by Nector for Lulu. When Zelda brings her the note Nector left under the sugar jar, telling her he loves Lulu, Marie feels powerless, not even recognizing her own response, which is so far beyond anger. She describes a feeling of transcendence, of not being in her own body. Then she regains herself by falling back on potato peeling—"enough . . . to feed every man, woman, child of the Chippewas"—and floor waxing. Marie steps away from the sting, overcoming the hurt of being abandoned. In her vision of herself she is still Marie, Star of the Sea. She would be there intact when they stripped the wax off her floor! Returning the note to the table, this time placing it under the salt, Marie lets Nector wonder about her reaction to his announcement of love for Lulu. Did she get the note? Does she know? Marie never tells. She uses what she learned from her experience with Leopolda: "I put my hand through what scared him. I held it out there for him. And when he took it with all the strength of his arms, I pulled him in."

In *The Bingo Palace,* although Marie's daughter Zelda has inherited her mother's energy, it is without transforming power. Lipsha dreads the single-minded control that he feels surrounding him in Zelda's presence: "When women age into their power, no wind can upset them, no hand turn aside their knowledge; no fact can deflect their point of view. It is like that with the woman I was raised to think of as sister and call aunt in respect." Zelda, who needs outlets for her enormous supply of energy, turns her talents to engineering the marriage of Lyman Lamartine and Shawnee Ray Toose. She insinuates herself into their lives by caring for their son, Redford. Lipsha knows that he figures in Zelda's calculations as a device to get the wedding date moved up. He is to be the designated third element—a catalyst that will bring about the union of Shawnee Ray and Lyman. Any excess energy Zelda has, she expends caring for Redford, making sure he does not go back to Shawnee's sisters, whom she considers unfit to raise children.

Zelda has cultivated a history of goodness that begins with giving up Xavier Toose, whom she had resisted despite loving him ''with a secret unkilled feeling stronger than acids, unquenched, a coal fire set inside of her and running through each vein with a steady heat.'' Lighting candles to the saints to help her overcome her passion for Xavier Toose, Zelda refused him regularly in order to save herself for a white man who would take her away from the reservation to the city. She diverted the energy containing her passion to marry Swede Johnson, from off reservation. Their child Albertine arrived prematurely, and Swede went AWOL from the army, never to be seen again. Repressing her sexuality, Zelda subsequently channeled her energy into good works to build a public reputation. She intended never to be subject to love.

Remembering the fire that her father, Nector, started at Lulu's house, Zelda vows to exist without love ''in the dark cell of her body.'' Reminiscent of the crazed self-mortification of Pauline in *Tracks,* she becomes ''capable of denying herself everything tender, unspoken, sweet, generous, and desperate.'' And after thirty years' abstinence from feeling, Zelda feels desire rock her body, desire that drives her to Xavier Toose.

Albertine, child of Zelda's loveless marriage, bears the scars of her mother's life. She understands that she will need enormous support from a husband or lover because she has been emotionally deprived. Restlessly ambitious, Albertine finds power in learning to heal in the way that she herself needs healing. Deciding to become a doctor has enabled Albertine to gain perspective on her own experience. She remembers crawling under the quilts of her mother's bed but never daring to ''grab her tight.'' Once, running away from home to the city, Albertine lay in bed with a man she hated; later she comes to realize ''that the desperation with which she gave in to

his touch has been no more than a child's wish to crawl closer to the side of her mother.'' Albertine uses her knowledge of her own need to point out the needs of others. She reminds her mother of Shawnee's right to arrange her life as she wishes—to go back to school and take Redford with her. She lets Lipsha know that he must straighten out his own life before he involves Shawnee in it.

Mothering is an important issue in Erdrich's life and her art. She and Michael Dorris have three daughters and they have adopted three children as well, according to her ''Dedication and Household Map'' in *The Blue Jay's Dance.* Erdrich is very concerned with what it means to be a parent, and this book is intended to add to her daughters' memories. She considers mothering ''a subtle art whose rhythm we collect and learn, as much from one another as from instinct.'' Mothers collectively form a sacred alliance—a group that identifies the struggle common to all mothers. Outwardly they look secure in their knowledge of mothering, but as she talks with other mothers, Erdrich comes to recognize her own daily task of hanging on ''to the tiger tail of children's, husband's, parents', and siblings' lives while at the same time saving a little core of self in our own, just enough to live by.''

One measure of women's power in Erdrich's novels is expressed in the capacity to mother. Denied or misdirected sexual energy results in unsuccessful mothering. For example, Zelda's passionless life draws out Albertine's need. Pauline Puyat's loveless union with Napoleon Morrissey brings forth Marie, a daughter whom she finds repulsive and whom she gives to someone else to raise.

In *The Bingo Palace,* June could not be a mother to him, Lipsha reasons, because her own pain was too deep. As he contemplates how he was saved from drowning, he reaches back to the darkness in the bottom of the slough, where he feels his mother's touch and connects with the truth of her action in releasing him to the water.

> Pain comes to us from deep back, from where it grew in the human body. Pain sucks more pain into it, we don't know why. It lives, and we harbor its weight. When the worst comes, we will not act the opposite. We will do what we were taught, we who learnt our lessons in the dead light. We pass them on. We hurt, and hurt others, in a circular motion.

June, denied love by her own mother, has refused Marie's mother love; she chooses instead to live with Eli, who could chew the pine sap, as she had done. She cannot give emotionally to her husband, Gordie, or to her sons, Lipsha and King. The hurt is passed on.

Fleur's mothering loses strength when she fears her personal power has dried up. She sends Lulu away to boarding school, an act that alienates daughter from mother. Lulu laments her loss of a mother: ''I never grew from the curve of my mother's arms. I still wanted to anchor myself against her. But she had tore herself away from the run of my life like a riverbank. She had vanished, a great surrounding shore, leaving me to spill out alone.'' As she becomes more like Fleur, her need for her grows, especially when Nector begins to look at her. In the search for a mother, Lulu goes to Moses Pillager, Fleur's cousin, from whom she learns both the bitterness and the sweetness of love. Still, the rift between Lulu and Fleur never heals, the price of leaving a child retold to Lulu by Nanapush in *Tracks*.

Despite not being mothered, both Marie and Lulu know how to be mothers. Brought into the world by cooking spoons and quickly given over to Bernadette Morrissey, who turns her over to the Lazarres, Marie raises her own children, laments the ones that die, and takes in Lipsha and June. She becomes the solid rock, the matriarch of an expanding family. Although Lulu's boys are not the center of her life, she keeps them together on her plot of land, watches them grow up, and is proud of them.

In *The Beet Queen* mothering is foregrounded in the contrast between a woman who has been mothered successfully and one who has been abandoned by her mother. Celestine James speaks of her mother's dying early and being cared for by her older sister Isabel, who supports Celestine and her brother Russell until she ''married into a Sioux family and moved down to South Dakota.'' Celestine is able to raise Dot, devoting time and energy to her care despite the trying circumstance of dealing with Mary Adare, a motherless woman who wants to intervene in Dot's upbringing.

In Erdrich's novels, women become mothers to other women through the common experience of birthing. The power they hold over life establishes a strong kinship among women. Margaret Kashpaw's offices at Lulu's birth secure a bond with Fleur, whose delivery of Lulu is precipitated by the sudden appearance of a bear. The suggestion is that Margaret earned her traditional name, Rushes Bear, by confronting the bear face-to-face, thereby linking her to the power of the natural world. In the expanded version of *Love Medicine*, female connections empower and comfort Marie as she gives birth to her last child assisted by Margaret and Fleur, whose knowledge of the old medicines is needed to help direct Marie's difficult labor. Women adapt to each other's need in Erdrich's novels.

Adapting successfully means finding a new way to live without giving up the self, but it can also mean giving up the self. In *Tracks*, Nanapush survives disease and starvation by talking, by telling a story. When he was the last one of his family left during the year of the sickness, he kept talking: ''Death could not get a word in edgewise, grew discouraged, and traveled on.'' So he joins with Fleur and Margaret, putting together a family from the remnants of families. He thinks like animals; he can track deer back to where they were born. He coaches Eli in the hunt for deer and in the pursuit of Fleur. He survives the invasion of the land around Lake Matchimanito because he accepts the fact that the land will be sold. He understands the transience of power:

> Power dies, power goes under and gutters out, ungraspable. It is momentary, quick of flight and liable to deceive. As soon as you rely on the possession it is gone. Forget that it ever existed, and it returns. I never made the mistake of thinking that I owned my own strength, that was my secret. And so I never was alone in my failures. I was never to blame entirely when all was lost, when my desperate cures had no effect on the suffering of those I loved.

Like Nanapush, whom she calls Uncle, Lulu survives because she has the same transcending power. In *Love Medicine,* she admits to crying the only tears that she would ever cry in her life on the school bus that took her away from the reservation. Lulu understands the encumbrances of the body: "How come we've got these bodies? They are frail supports for what we feel. There are times I get so hemmed in by my arms and legs I look forward to getting past them. As though death will set me free like a traveling cloud." Lulu is able to transcend the past in her relationship with Marie. She discovers the way another woman feels for the first time. In bathing Lulu's eyes with drops, Marie puts the tears back. They mourn Nector together.

Critical appraisal of Erdrich's work has ranged from open acceptance of its innovative form and testament to the Chippewa tribal people to guarded concern about narrative method and suspicion regarding the further marginalization of Native Americans. With its multiple-narrator format, *Love Medicine* is considered by many reviewers to be strongly connected to the oral tradition of storytelling. The multivoiced structure and the involvement of the reader in reconciling the often competing versions of the stories have stimulated considerable critical response. In its departure from the pattern of other contem-porary Native American novels, *Love Medicine* has been noted for its concentration on community gossip instead of on the oral tradition and ritual associated with novels like N. Scott Momaday's *House Made of Dawn* and Leslie Marmon Silko's *Ceremony.* Instability of family, a dominant theme in both *Love Medicine* and *The Beet Queen,* begins in *Tracks.* The fluctuation of the term "family" is considered by Linda Ainsworth to be an apt metaphor for *Love Medicine,* and it is perpetuated in the novels that follow.

There are both speaking and nonspeaking voices in Erdrich's novels. Named narrators alternate with unidentified third-person narrators, and, in the case of *The Bingo Palace,* a community chorus. Stories change as tellers change. There are no narrators privileged to tell an authentic version of the story. Time is not always chronological; events loop around and fall back on themselves in unpredictable patterns. The novels speak to each other; the reader must play a role in the connecting of story lines. In the expanded version of *Love Medicine,* Erdrich forges the links that align events and develop character to bring the novels to the status of epic.

Tracks employs a dual narrator structure and a linear chronology. Nanapush and Pauline challenge one another's authority, leaving the reader to piece the story together. They agree only on what they have seen of the crazed behavior of creatures driven to the edge of life. Nanapush describes the buffalo dwindling, feeding on each other's flesh, and Pauline reports the same behavior in human beings crowding the new road of death, their numbers dwindling from influenza and consumption. They agree on the decimation of the tribe.

Love Medicine in its first version has seven named narrators: Marie, Nector, Albertine, Lulu, Lyman, Lipsha, and Howard Kashpaw. An unnamed teller recounts the story of June's death in the opening chapter. Another objective narrator tells the story of Lulu's eight sons. The middle chapter, "A Bridge," relates Albertine and Henry Lamartine's meetings in Fargo, and in the chapter "Crown of Thorns," another third-person narrator chronicles Gordie Kashpaw's hallucinations about his wife, June. All the narrators contribute some information about June, but Marie Kashpaw, Gordie, Albertine, and Lipsha are the most concerned about the meaning of her life and her place in the family.

In the revision of *Love Medicine* (1993), Erdrich clarified the chain of events that occurred when Nector met Marie on her way down the hill from the convent. She did not intend that their sexual encounter be interpreted as a rape, as some readers had done. When Marie tells Nector that she has had better, Nector's words indicate that no force has been used: "I know that isn't true because we haven't done anything yet. She just doesn't know what comes next."

There are four new chapters in the expanded version, each of which helps to make needed connections among the novels. "The Island," narrated by Lulu, gives her reaction to Marie's marriage to Nector, and her return to the reservation from boarding school. In a section added to "The Beads," Marie becomes connected to Rushes Bear when she assists at the birth of Marie's last child. Marie's role as mother is further developed in "Resurrection," in which she deals with Gordie's advanced alcoholic hallucinating. This chapter also provides a sense of the futility of Gordie and June's marriage. The chapters "The Tomahawk Factory" and "Lyman's Luck" give more dimension to Lyman's character, especially with regard to his devastation at his brother's death, and also set up his role as gambling entrepreneur in *The Bingo Palace*.

There is a more definite pattern to the narrative structure in *The Beet Queen,* in that the chapters are narrated by the main characters in the first person and their narrations are followed by a neutral consciousness that has gained entry into the consciousness of each character. The novel begins with a third-person account of Mary and Karl's separation on a cold spring morning in 1932, followed by Mary's full first-person account of how the family was left by Adelaide. Establishing the pattern of narration, the third part of the 1932 chapter is related by an impersonal third-person narrator who tells what happened to Karl when he was cut loose from the family. In this way a community of voices speak as one and as individuals.

In a departure from the alternating narrator pattern, *The Bingo Palace* contains ten chapters narrated by Lipsha Morrissey. There is a community chorus that speaks in the first person plural, and there is an account of the fortunes of Lyman, Fleur, June, Gerry, Albertine, Shawnee, Zelda, and Redford, as well as Lulu, rendered by an omniscient narrator. The novel begins and ends with the community voices, undesignated in time.

Louise Erdrich resists being labeled a Native American writer although she declares in an interview with Hertha Wong that it is very important to her "to be known as having been from the Turtle Mountain Chippewa and from North Dakota." Whether she writes about Indians or their white neighbors, Erdrich strives to depict human transcendence in all four novels as well as in her nonfiction. She is concerned about showing that tribal culture endures in new forms even as Indians are pushed to the margins of society by the dominant culture. Community voices join to tell the remembered stories. The loss of tribal land chronicled in *Tracks* has not diminished personal identity and human connections. That human beings endure despite holocaust is the overriding message in all of Erdrich's work.

Trickster goes on defying social order just as he did in Ojibwa myth. Mothers succeed and fail as they have always done. For every June and Adelaide, there is a Marie and Celestine. The absurdity of existence spills over in the trials of

Lipsha, the wise fool. Through it all, Indians have not been annihilated—that is Erdrich's message of hope.

Selected Bibliography

WORKS OF LOUISE ERDRICH

FICTION

Love Medicine. New York: Holt, Rinehart and Winston, 1984. New and exp. ed. New York: Henry Holt, 1993.

The Beet Queen. New York: Henry Holt, 1986.

Tracks. New York: Henry Holt, 1988.

The Crown of Columbus. New York: HarperCollins, 1991. Written with Michael Dorris.

Route Two. Northridge, Cal.: Lord John Press, 1991. Written with Michael Dorris.

The Bingo Palace. New York: HarperCollins, 1994.

NONFICTION

Imagination. Westerville, Ohio: Charles E. Merrill, 1981.

"Where I Ought to Be: A Writer's Sense of Place." *New York Times Book Review,* July 28, 1985, pp. 1, 23–24.

The Blue Jay's Dance: A Birth Year. New York: HarperCollins, 1995.

POETRY

Jacklight. New York: Holt, Rinehart and Winston, 1984.

Baptism of Desire. New York: Harper & Row, 1989.

CRITICAL STUDIES

REVIEWS

Ainsworth, Linda. Review of *Love Medicine. Studies in American Indian Literatures,* 9:24–29 (Winter 1985).

Banks, Russell. "Border Country." Review of *The Beet Queen. Nation,* November 1, 1986, pp. 460–463.

Bennett, Sarah. Review of *The Bingo Palace. Studies in American Indian Literatures,* 6:83–88 (Fall 1994).

———. Review of *Love Medicine: New and Expanded Version. Studies in American Indian Literatures,* 7:112–118 (Spring 1995).

Bruckner, D. J. R. Review of *Love Medicine. New York Times,* December 20, 1984, C21.

Jahner, Elaine. Review of *Love Medicine. Parabola: The Magazine of Myth and Tradition,* 10:96, 98, 100 (Summer 1985).

———. Review of *Jacklight. Studies In American Indian Literatures,* 9:29–34 (Winter 1985).

Kinney, Jeanne. Review of *Love Medicine. Best Sellers,* 44:324–325 (December 1984).

Lewis, Robert W. Review of *Love Medicine. American Indian Culture and Research Journal,* 9, no. 4:113–116 (1985).

Messud, Claire. "Redeeming the Tribe." A Review of *The Bingo Palace. Times Literary Supplement,* June 17, 1994, p. 23.

Nelson, John S. "*Beat Queen* Traces Delicate Web of Family Ties." *Wichita* (Kansas) *Eagle Beacon,* October 5, 1986, p. WE6.

Owens, Louis. "Acts of Recovery: The American Indian Novel in the 80s." Essay review of *The Beet Queen. Western American Literature,* 22:53–57 (May 1987).

Portles, Marco. "People with Holes in Their Lives." Review of *Love Medicine. New York Times Book Review,* December 23, 1984, p. 6.

Sands, Kathleen M. Review of *Love Medicine. Studies in American Indian Literatures,* 9:12–24 (Winter 1985).

Silko, Leslie Marmon. "Here's an Odd Artifact for the Fairy-Tale Shelf." Review of *The Beet Queen. Impact/Albuquerque Journal Magazine,* October 7, 1986, pp. 10–11. Reprinted in *Studies in American Indian Literatures,* 10:178–184 (Fall 1986).

Simon, Linda. "Small Gestures: Large Patterns." Review of *The Beet Queen. Commonweal,* October 24, 1986, pp. 565–566.

Strouse, Jean. Review of *Tracks. New York Times Book Review,* October 2, 1988, pp. 40–42.

Tyler, Anne. "After *Love Medicine,* a Still Better Novel from Erdrich." Review of *The Beet Queen.* (Raleigh, N.C.) *News and Observer,* August 31, 1986, p. 4D.

Vecsey, Christopher. "Revenge of the Chippewa

Witch." Review of *Tracks. Commonweal,* November 4, 1988, pp. 596–98.

CRITICISM

Bevis, William. "Native American Novels: Homing In." In *Recovering the Word: Essays on Native American Literature.* Edited by Brian Swann and Arnold Krupat. Berkeley: University of California Press, 1987. Pp. 580–620.

Castillo, Susan Pérez. "Postmodernism, Native American Literature and the Real: The Silko–Erdrich Controversy." *Massachusetts Review,* 32:285–294 (Summer 1991).

Flavin, Louise. "Louise Erdrich's *Love Medicine:* Loving over Time and Distance." *Critique* 31:55–64 (Fall 1989).

———. "Gender Construction Amid Family Dissolution in Louise Erdrich's *The Beet Queen.*" *Studies in American Indian Literatures,* 7:17–24 (Summer 1995).

Gleason, William. " 'Her Laugh an Ace': The Function of Humor in Louise Erdrich's *Love Medicine.*" *American Indian Culture and Research Journal,* 11, no. 3:51–73 (1987).

Harris, Patricia, and David Lyon. "The Fine Art of Collaboration." *Boston Globe Magazine,* November 15, 1987, pp. 58–62.

Lincoln, Kenneth. " 'Bring Her Home': Louise Erdrich." In his *Indi'n Humor: Bicultural Play in Native America.* New York: Oxford University Press, 1993. Pp. 205–253.

Magalaner, Marvin. "Louise Erdrich: Of Cars, Time, and the River." In *American Women Writing Fiction: Memory, Identity, Family, Space.* Edited by Mickey Pearlman. Lexington: University Press of Kentucky, 1989. Pp. 95–112.

McKenzie, James. "Lipsha's Good Road Home: The Revival of Chippewa Culture in *Love Medicine.*" *American Indian Culture and Research Journal,* 10, no. 3:53–63 (1986).

Peterson, Nancy. "History, Postmodernism, and Louise Erdrich's *Tracks.*" *Publications of the Modern Language Association,* 109:982–994 (October 1994).

Rainwater, Catherine. "Reading between Worlds: Narrativity in the Fiction of Louise Erdrich." *American Literature,* 62:405–420 (September 1990).

Silberman, Robert. "Opening the Text: *Love Medicine* and the Return of the Native American Woman." In *Narrative Chance: Postmodern Discourse on Native American Literatures.* Edited by Gerald Vizenor. Albuquerque: University of New Mexico Press, 1989. Pp. 101–120.

Slack, John S. "The Comic Savior: The Dominance of the Trickster in Louise Erdrich's *Love Medicine.*" *North Dakota Quarterly,* 61:118–129 (Summer 1993).

Woodward, Pauline G. *New Tribal Forms: Community in Louise Erdrich's Fiction.* Ph.D. dissertation, Tufts University, 1991. Ann Arbor, Mich.: Copyright, 1991. Order number 9126146.

———. "Chance in *The Beet Queen:* New Ways to Find a Family." *ARIEL: A Review of International English Literature,* 26, no. 2:109–127 (April 1995).

STUDIES OF THE CHIPPEWA

Camp, Gregory S. "Working Out Their Own Salvation: The Allotment of Land in Severalty and the Turtle Mountain Chippewa Band, 1870–1920," *American Indian Culture and Research Journal,* 14, no. 2:19–38 (1990).

Densmore, Frances. *Chippewa Customs.* Washington D.C.: U.S. Government Printing Office, 1929. New York: Johnson Reprint, 1970.

Helbig, Alethea K. *Nanabozhoo: Giver of Life.* Brighton, Mich.: Green Oak, 1987.

Johnston, Basil. *Ojibway Ceremonies.* Lincoln: University of Nebraska Press, 1982.

Schneider, Mary Jane. *North Dakota Indians: An Introduction.* Dubuque, Iowa: Kendall, Hunt, 1986.

Vizenor, Gerald. *The Everlasting Sky: New Voices from the People Named the Chippewa.* New York: Crowell-Collier, 1972.

———. *Interior Landscapes: Autobiographies, Myths, and Metaphors.* Minneapolis: University of Minnesota Press, 1990.

INTERVIEWS

Bonetti, Kay. *Interview with Louise Erdrich.* American Prose Library, 1986. Audiotape, fifty minutes.

Bruchac, Joseph. "Whatever Is Really Yours: An Interview with Louise Erdrich." In his *Survival This Way: Interviews with American Indian Poets.* Tucson: Sun Tracks/University of Arizona Press, 1987. Pp. 73–86.

Chavkin, Nancy Feyl, and Allan Chavkin. "An Interview with Louise Erdrich." In *Conversations with Louise Erdrich & Michael Dorris.* Edited by Allan Chavkin and Nancy Feyl Chavkin. Jackson: University Press of Mississippi, 1994. Pp. 220–253.

Coltelli, Laura. "Louise Erdrich and Michael Dorris." In her *Winged Words: Native American Writers Speak.* Lincoln: University of Nebraska Press, 1990. Pp. 41–52.

George, Jan. "Interview with Louise Erdrich." *North Dakota Quarterly,* 53:240–246 (Spring 1985).

Moyers, Bill. "Louise Erdrich and Michael Dorris." In *Bill Moyers' World of Ideas.* Audiotape transcript. New York: Journal Graphics, November 14, 1988.

Pearlman, Mickey. "Louise Erdrich." In *Inter/View: Talks With America's Writing Women.* Edited by Mickey Pearlman and Katharine Usher Henderson. Lexington: University Press of Kentucky, 1990. Pp. 143–148.

Wong, Hertha D. "An Interview with Louise Erdrich and Michael Dorris." *North Dakota Quarterly,* 55:196–218 (Winter 1987).

—PAULINE GROETZ WOODWARD